The Intellectual Life of Edmund Burke

The Intellectual Life of Edmund Burke

From the Sublime and Beautiful to American Independence

DAVID BROMWICH

The Belknap Press of Harvard University Press
CAMBRIDGE, MASSACHUSETTS
LONDON, ENGLAND
2014

Book design by Dean Bornstein

Library of Congress Cataloging-in-Publication Data

Bromwich, David, 1951–
  The intellectual life of Edmund Burke : from the sublime and beautiful to
American independence / David Bromwich.
    pages cm
  Includes bibliographical references and index.
  ISBN 978-0-674-72970-4 (hardcover : alk. paper)
  1. Burke, Edmund, 1729–1797.   2. Great Britain—Politics and government—
18th century.   3. Statesmen—Great Britain—Biography.   4. Political
scientists—Great Britain—Biography.   I. Title.
  DA506.B9B69 2014
  941.073092—dc23
  [B]   2013037807

To Georgann Witte

Preface

The title of this book conveys its purpose. I have tried to answer the question, What did it mean to think like Edmund Burke? To a great extent, Burke's was a life of ideas, yet he chose a career in politics. This is therefore in some measure the biography of a politician. But on matters such as Burke's relationships with his family, his series of residences, his financial arrangements, his lineage starting a generation or two before him, and the experiences that he had or is likely to have had as a child, the pages that follow cannot pretend to be a useful guide. The same can be said for most (though not all) of his particular dealings within his party and with other politicians. Readers interested in those indispensable parts of the history will profit, as I have, from the full-length biographies by F. P. Lock, Conor Cruise O'Brien, and Carl B. Cone and the recent shorter biographies by Stanley Ayling and Jesse Norman. I begin with a brief summary of Burke's career, in order to provide the largest of signposts, but the life that this book traces is a life conducted mostly in writings, speeches, and letters.

Interpretation must impose a degree of unity on its subject. But apart from the necessary convenience of a narrative—things happened in a certain order—I seek to understand the originality and the continuities of Burke's thinking and not the rise and fall of his fortunes. The chapters here are organized by episode: Burke's view of the emotions that govern human nature and his non-rational conception of habit and power, in his early books on natural society and the sublime and beautiful (Chapters 1 and 2); the credo he wrote for his party and his defense of an idea of party at a time of civil disorder (Chapter 3); his vindication of constitutional liberty and his protest against the violence of British policies during the American war (Chapters 4 and 5); his arguments on representative government and religious toleration, and his accompanying attempt to limit the power of the crown, during the domestic crisis of the late 1770s and early 1780s (Chapters 6 and 7). Here and there, episodes overlap, and one chapter ends later than the next one begins. Notice is given when that happens, and overall the movement of the book is straightforward.

Most of my primary sources are easily available in the eight published volumes of the projected nine-volume Oxford edition of Burke's *Writings and Speeches,* supervised by Paul Langford, and the ten volumes of Burke's *Correspondence,* supervised by Thomas Copeland. The second of these sources has been especially valuable at every stage of my thinking. The procedure here is to quote as much of Burke as possible and to comment adequately on what has been quoted. The paraphrases and shorter quotations are too many to number, or for me to be entirely conscious of, but I supply endnotes for the location of passages longer than two sentences. Readers who know Burke only from *Reflections on the Revolution in France,* and the smaller number who know some of his major speeches, have not yet been introduced to the scope and depth of his genius. This book attempts to characterize his achievement with the firsthand evidence of his writings.

Burke's speeches themselves are often writings, but they come to us in several forms, including drafts, manuscript notes, newspaper accounts, reports from the parliamentary history, and the pamphlets whose publication he oversaw. I treat the speeches as writings and have italicized their titles throughout, while allowing the condition of a given text to impose limits on interpretation: a deciphered scrap cannot overturn the inference from a full-length utterance published with the author's approval. Eighteenth-century spelling and punctuation were less regular than ours, and I have not purged any idiosyncrasies except in cases where the anomaly would force on the reader an inordinately long and distracting pause. I prefer not to crowd the text with inserted references and names of consulted sources but have taken care to register my strong reliance on a particular source where it occurs, as, for example, with Arthur Cash on the career of Wilkes and Herbert Butterfield on the insurrectionary threat of the years 1779–1780. A second volume will take up the rest of the story: from Burke's attempt to reform the government of British India to his pamphlets against the French Revolution. Burke's tract on the popery laws, chronologically appropriate here but digressive, has been deferred for consideration in the relevant context in the sequel.

As for the claim of my subject on a reader today, I cannot do better than the advertisement by French Laurence and Walker King in their 1803 edition of Burke's *Works* (Vol. 1, pp. xx–xxi): "The period during which he flourished was one of the most memorable of our annals. It compre-hended the acquisition of one empire in the east, the loss of another in the west, and the total subversion of the ancient system of Europe by the French Revolution; with all which events the history of his life is necessarily and intimately connected; as indeed it also is, much more than is generally known, with the state of literature and the elegant arts." Laurence and King added a warning, which I hope I have taken to heart: "Such a sub-ject of biography cannot be dismissed with a slight and rapid touch; nor can it be treated in a manner worthy of it, from the information, however authentick and extensive, which the industry of any one man may have accumulated."

A seminar on Burke that I taught occasionally at Yale University has influenced my approach, and I owe much to perceptions that could only have sprung from that collaborative setting. I was fortunate to have the opportunity to test some elements of the argument in 1995 at the Gauss Seminars in Criticism at Princeton University. The staffs of the Beinecke Library at Yale, the Walpole Library in Farmington, Connecticut, the British Library, the Sheffield Archives, the Libraries of the University of Massachusetts at Amherst, and the Houghton Collection at Harvard University were resourceful in locating materials that added to the interest of the book. For support of various kinds, I thank Winifred Amaturo, Akeel Bilgrami, Sir David Cannadine, Judith Hawley, Philip Horne, David Quint, Carol Rovane, Alexander Welsh, and Ruth Yeazell. Conver-sations with George Kateb over many years played a considerable part in defining my emphasis. For informal comments that deepened my under-standing of Burke, I am indebted to Ross Borden, Richard Bourke, Linda Colley, Ian Crowe, John Dunn, Harvey Mansfield, Uday Mehta, Jennifer Pitts, and Jeffrey Stout. Conor Cruise O'Brien offered a warm response to a lecture on *Reflections on the Revolution in France* and *King Lear*, which prompted further work on similar lines. I discussed the plan of the book in its early stages with a teacher, colleague, and friend, Martin Price, and now regret that I will not be able to put a copy in his hands.

Among scholars of the eighteenth century, my largest debt is to John Faulkner. He provided a constant fund of observations and recommended readings, and in going over all the chapters he has detected inaccuracies, secured the modification of several wrongheaded judgments, and contributed a number of clarifying phrases and sentences that I have adopted. A late draft was read by P. J. Marshall, and the book has benefited substantially from his criticism. I am also grateful to Professor Marshall for allowing me to read and quote from his edited texts of Burke's parliamentary speeches, 1774–1790, which will appear as Volume 4 of the Oxford edition of the *Writings and Speeches*. Comments by an anonymous reader for Harvard University Press were indispensable in pointing out the need for explanatory matter on Burke's stances and usage. At a difficult moment, Georges Borchardt gave encouragement I could not have spared; and John Kulka has been the most generous and attentive of editors. Between them, they made the result possible in its present form. I dedicate this book to the friend who has listened to my thoughts about Burke for two decades and who more than anyone else has made me know what to listen for.

Contents

Power, in whatever hands,
is rarely guilty of too strict limitations on itself.
—*A Letter to the Sheriffs of Bristol*

Introduction

WRITING and speaking can be a form of action. Never was the possibility more bravely tested than in the career of Edmund Burke.

He was born in 1730, in Arran Quay, Dublin, and educated at the Quaker school in Ballitore and Trinity College Dublin. Obedient to his father's wish, he embarked on the formal study of law in the Middle Temple at the Inns of Court in London: a curriculum of professional training he would never complete. He published two early books, *A Vindication of Natural Society* in 1756 and *A Philosophical Enquiry into the Origin of Our Ideas of the Sublime and Beautiful* in 1757, which caught the eye of David Hume, Samuel Johnson, and other illustrious contemporaries and established him as an author. Burke had already shown an interest in politics, informed by copious knowledge; and in 1758 he contracted with the bookseller Dodsley to produce the *Annual Register* and wrote the political history of the year for its first volume in 1759. The same year saw his appointment as private secretary to a member of Parliament, William Gerard Hamilton. In 1761, Hamilton was named chief secretary for Ireland, and Burke accompanied him to Dublin. A disagreement over the freedom that Burke was to be allowed for his own projects led in early 1765 to a falling-out with Hamilton; but a few months later, Burke found a new patron, the Marquess of Rockingham, the leader of a group of Whigs then pressing the House of Commons to assert its independence from the king. Rockingham made Burke his private secretary (a position he would hold for seventeen years), and through affiliation with the Rockingham party, Burke was returned as a member of Parliament for the pocket borough of Wendover. In January 1766, he gave his maiden speech, presenting a petition from Manchester merchants against restrictions on American trade. He went on to distinguish himself as a strategist for the Rockingham administration of 1765–1766 and assisted in its major achievement, the repeal of the stamp tax on the American colonies.

In 1769, Burke joined the parliamentary resistance to an effort by King George III and his parliamentary allies to prevent John Wilkes from taking his seat in the House of Commons. While the legal argument simmered, the Rockingham party began to concert a policy to check the increasing power of the king. Burke's view of the constitution at this crisis emerged in 1770, in his first political book, *Thoughts on the Cause of the Present Discontents*. This was a practical manifesto for the Rockingham Whigs and also a theoretical defense of the idea of a political party. An organized opposition, Burke argued, was a necessary bulwark of liberty; and to warrant the formation of such a party, one reason would always suffice: "When bad men combine, the good must associate; else they will fall, one by one, an unpitied sacrifice in a contemptible struggle." Whatever might alter in his subsequent stance, Burke would continue to speak for the good of "association" as a limit on the privilege and aggrandizement of court favorites.

Burke believed that the practice of politics could never be isolated from the ordinary work of moral judgment. Accordingly, he was skeptical of a priori theories of the social contract that codified the definitions of citizenship and state power. In the 1770s and 1780s, most of his energy was given to enlarging the liberty of the people by strengthening the protections against monarchical abuse of power. Yet he was never a believer in popular government: statesmanship always carried, for him, a sense of the dignity and ceremony that should accompany high enterprises, and the capacity to take long views without concern for popular support or mandates. Burke's exalted idea of political duty could not be fulfilled by a monarch. Its embodiment was the leader in a responsible assembly who, drawing on the skill and talents of others, labors to mold the sentiments of the people and to justify the policies and laws of a nation.

In 1774, Burke gained a chance to play such a part. A set of Whigs who admired his views on American affairs invited him to stand for Parliament in Bristol. This was a contested election (rare then), in the second city of the kingdom, and Burke's victory gave him a platform from which he could directly engage the public issues of the time. In the parliamentary sessions of 1774 and 1775, he pleaded for a sympathetic reception of the American protests against taxation. His *Speech on Conciliation with America*, delivered in March 1775, urged a policy of concession to the point of disowning any further intention to tax. The three-hour speech, with its history of trade with the colonies, its bold sketch of American manners and morals, and its genealogy of the descent of British liberty, has been considered from that day to this among the greatest orations in the language. "An Englishman," Burke told his listeners, "is the unfittest person on earth to argue another Englishman into slavery." The right use of the Americans, he concluded, was to take them as equal partners in trade and as allies in time of war. "Magnanimity in politics is not seldom the truest wisdom; and a great empire and little minds go ill together."

During his Bristol years, from 1774 to 1780, Burke stood out as a defender of free trade with Ireland, of liberalization of the laws controlling imprisonment for debt, and of repeal of the legal disabilities of Catholics—all unpopular positions in a Protestant and mercantile city. When threatened with loss of his constituency in 1780, he gave an unswerving defense of his actions in his *Speech at the Guildhall Previous to the Election*. Looking back on six years of service, Burke said to the voters of Bristol: "I did not obey your instructions: No. I conformed to the instructions of truth and nature, and maintained your interest, against your opinions, with a constancy that became me."

With Britain still fighting the American war, Burke at this moment began to follow the trail of abuse of power from the western to the eastern empire. A powerful interest linking British policy in those two regions was the East India Company. By the time he re-entered the House of Commons in 1781 as representative for Malton, Burke had found the cause that would occupy the remainder of his parliamentary career: to expose the injustices of the Company in India, where its actions had the corrupt and despotic character of "a state in the disguise of a merchant"; and when the investigation pointed finally to a responsible party, to impeach the highest resident officer of the Company, the governor-general of Bengal, Warren Hastings.

In March 1782, Burke was appointed paymaster of forces in the second Rockingham ministry—a subcabinet position that was the highest he would ever hold—but the administration ended in July with the death of Lord Rockingham. In the running of the party, Burke nevertheless continued to be a central figure, now as an adviser to Charles Fox. Twenty years Burke's junior, a popular leader and exuberant speaker with a genius for politics, Fox had begun his career as a Tory before acquiring a more generous understanding of constitutional liberty. As leader of the remnant of the Rockingham Whigs, he forged an improbable but politic alliance with Lord North, the minister who had presided over the American war; and from Burke and Fox together, in 1783 there issued a carefully drafted proposal on the governance of India. To rally support for the measure, Burke delivered his *Speech on Fox's East India Bill,* which recounted in unsparing terms the history of British India and urged a systematic reform of the empire. Fox's bill would have placed officers of the Company under parliamentary control; rejection of the plan by the House of Commons precipitated the fall of the Fox–North coalition. Burke's response was to speak more pressingly for the impeachment of Hastings. He took his party with him—Fox, Sheridan, and others—and having secured the partial support of the prime minister, William Pitt, the House of Commons launched the trial of Hastings before the tribunal of the House of Lords. Meeting on the days Parliament could spare from other business, the process stretched from 1788 to 1795 and ended with the acquittal, on all counts, of Warren Hastings by the House of Lords. Burke would look back on this attempt at full-scale reform as his proudest achievement—"my monument."

A surer fame in his lifetime came from his pamphlets of the 1790s against the French Revolution. The first and most influential of these was *Reflections on the Revolution in France.* Published in November 1790, it would provoke, by the end of the decade, more than a hundred replies. Burke warned against a great change in the spirit of society from aristocratic to democratic manners, and from the authority of an ancient landed nobility to that of a mobile commercial class. He spoke as a believer in precedent and prescription and as a defender of natural feelings such as reverence for an established church and a hereditary nobility. Against the promise of a society based on contract, he offered his vision of a society rooted in trust—"a partnership not only between those who are living, but between those who are living, those who are dead, and those who are to be born." Burke believed that the advent of democracy would destroy the very idea of a human partnership spread out over generations. He gave reasons to support his fear that democracy could never correct the errors that "the people" given unchecked power would commit on a new and terrifying scale. With its broad exposition of political principles and its dramatic narrative of crisis, the *Reflections* did more than any other book to create the French Revolution as a world-historical event for the mind of Europe.

Burke's attack on the revolutionists in France was also an attack on their allies in England. It split the Whig Party; and in 1791, after a bitter exchange with Fox in the House of Commons, Burke crossed the floor to the administration side. In 1794, he was awarded a pension by Pitt and George III, and retired to his estate in Beaconsfield. Two pamphlets of Burke's final years exhibit the continuity and the ambivalence of his political views. In 1792, *A Letter to Sir Hercules Langrishe* made an impassioned plea for the rights of Catholics in Ireland. The *Letters on a Regicide Peace*, in 1796, sought to justify and instigate a counterrevolutionary war against France. He died in 1797, ending as he began, in isolation.

The complexity of Burke's greatness stems from the double nature of his work. He was a thinker and a politician—a thinker above all and by vocation; a politician accidentally, though the accident could seem his essence. He was a man of imagination. Yet he chose to perform in an arena where his work would submit to a practical test. He was a student of society, which he called a "dense medium": the never entirely penetrable atmosphere of the real-life relations of men and women. The particulars that interest Burke are stubborn, intractable, not easy to bring under the rule of an ordering principle. "I must see with my own eyes," he wrote. "I must, in a manner, touch with my own hands, not only the fixed, but the momentary circumstances, before I could venture to suggest any political project whatsoever. I must know the power and disposition to accept, to execute, to persevere. I must see all the aids, and all the obstacles. I must see the means of correcting the plan, where correctives would be wanted. I must see the things; I must see the men."[1] To insist on deliberation and public care, to desire an almost physical grasp of the objects of policy, is only an annoyance to the problem solvers in politics. Burke was willing to disappoint them; a sort of piety was involved in his patience. The resistance that habit and instinct offer against all speculative plans for reform seemed to him a necessary feature of political life.

Coercion and cruelty never had a fiercer enemy than Burke. Yet throughout his career, he was a defender of hierarchy, the tacit principle of subordination that cements an aristocratic society. His resistance to uniformity, innovation, and violence made him an acute critic of democracy and empire at the moment of their ascent in modern history. We now accept with little challenge the arrangements of a commercial democracy and an empire at once commercial and military. Burke is a historian of their human cost. No other writer has seen so comprehensively what was gained and what was sacrificed with the coming of political modernity: the rise of the bureaucratic state and, balancing and partly counteracting it, the mystique of the race or the nation; the triumph of a democratic deference to majority rule and, balancing and partly counteracting it, the institution of a powerful and expansive system of trade. The complex interactions of all these tendencies were apparent to Burke at the end of the eighteenth century.

What exactly were his politics? The resources for an answer are to be found in the totality of his published works. They also emerge from his *Correspondence*, and from drafts of speeches and manuscript notes. These writings and archival documents together make a coherent impression. They reveal Burke as a man of his time—a man of talent destined for the "middle station" in life—whose imaginings went far beyond his time. In a sentimental age, he stood for the integrity of ideas. In a class distinguished by its faith in reason, he stood for the inseparable value of feeling. The impact of his thoughts went deeper than Burke's day-to-day understanding of events. A similar reach can be claimed for few of his contemporaries, though one clear candidate is Rousseau—a less circumstantial thinker than Burke but comparable in the urgency with which he brings conscience to bear on politics. Burke came to detest the disciples of Rousseau, yet he recognized early the depth of Rousseau's originality.[2]

A fairer comparison may be Shakespeare. One finds in Burke the same sympathy with wayward impulse and self-assertion and the same wariness of that sympathy. There is a shade of pity in the frankness with which Burke registers the suavity and strut of men of power. Such people use others as means to an end, whereas Burke asks us to regard human beings as ends. Ambition and greed, the will to dominate and the indifference it sows against feeling and nature, these things were to him the curse of life, beside which its other evils fade into secondary effects. And yet, accompanying his intensity of suspicion, Burke can show a power of admiration as instinctive as Shakespeare's—admiration, above all, for acts of unbidden self-sacrifice, like that of Kent who follows Lear from first to last. Such triumphs of feeling over calculation are at once ordinary and miraculous, and Burke aims to impart a reverence for this unbetrayable impulse as it appears in history and experience. "A common soldier, a child, a girl at the door of an inn, have changed the face of fortune, and almost of Nature."

Like Shakespeare, Burke knew the glamour and influence of the Machiavellian morality, in politics and in smaller-scale human wheeling and dealing. He was a consistent anti-Machiavellian but not a complacent one; he often conveys a sense of being bound in spite of himself to a world in motion. Again, like Shakespeare he holds a greater respect for the contradictions and hesitations of thought than for the single-mindedness of action. Shakespeare can awaken new thoughts by the force and patience of words; and Burke is the writer of English prose who suggests a similar intuition and command. Read him for an hour or two, and try to disagree. It is harder than it should be. And the next author whom you read seems to be playing an inferior instrument. It must be added that the initial difficulties of reading Burke are sometimes as great as the initial difficulties of reading Shakespeare. The job of a commentator is to respect the difficulties and not to make them both shallower and more cumbersome by placing the author wholly at the mercy of context. Knowledge of the eighteenth-century politics of empire is a necessity for understanding Burke—or rather for understanding what he says. To determine what he means is a more intricate task. What was partly known in the eighteenth century and has now come to be much better known may be a help in mastering the implications of his writing; but the dialogue works both ways. To learn what Burke meant in his time may also deepen one's sense of why he matters today.

❀

A curious fact about Burke's fame in his own lifetime is how quickly he came to be regarded as a great man. One finds evidence of such an estimate in the mid-1760s, when he had little to show besides his book on the sublime and beautiful and his first speeches on the floor of the House of Commons. His career would perform what it promised, and yet—a problem that confronts us again and again—the genre of the performance is hard to define. He was seen as transferring (perhaps illicitly) the power of genius from literature to politics; he was thought to be someone who, "born for the universe, narrowed his mind, / And to party gave up what was meant for mankind." The lines from Oliver Goldsmith's good-natured satire "Retaliation" are a telling stroke, but they also reveal the grandeur of the early hopes associated with Burke. That an eloquent voice should be raised for civil liberty (in the Wilkes controversy) and for the rights of Englishmen penalized by the empire (in the American war) was a distinction that took an added luster from his already acknowledged stature. The dismay, among his early friends and allies, at his decision to oppose the French Revolution derived from the spectacle of a generous thinker siding now with established power. Yet Burke had a way of shifting his emphasis without fundamentally changing his ground.

Nineteenth-century admirers of Burke, such as Wordsworth, Tocqueville, and Matthew Arnold, praised him for his unique gift of imagining society. "He brings thought to bear on politics," as Arnold memorably said, "he saturates politics with thought."[3] By the Whig historians of the nineteenth century, he was prized as a pattern of statesmanship. "The nucleus of the Liberal party" in the nineteenth century, remarked G. O. Trevelyan, was created by the rise of the Rockingham Whigs "between the fall of Pitt in 1761 and the fall of Grenville in 1765."[4] But in the twentieth century and especially in the United States, Burke came to be esteemed for a separate accomplishment: his insight as a prophet of totalitarianism. To what extent was that reputation justified?

Burke wrote about the French Revolution as if it were the Russian Revolution, about the terror of 1793–1794 as if it were the terror of Stalin's purges of the 1930s. Such power of accurate foresight by means of allegorical heightening is not altogether to his credit as a historian. If, in the 1950s, the effect was to give his anti-revolutionary writings a timely purchase, this did not improve the intelligence with which he was understood. A prophet is generally supposed to see with an insight beyond the limits of worldly knowledge. But to exempt Burke from the human liability to error means to forget the virtue in his humility, in the determination to see with his own eyes, to touch with his own hands. He was indeed prophetic, and one of the things he foresaw, and feared, was a society rigged for total control of its members. But the image of Burke the anti-communist, Burke the anti-totalitarian, Burke the scourge of domestic subversion, always contained a large ration of mummery and journalism. "Every honest man," wrote Blake, "is a Prophet. He utters his opinion both of private & public matters. Thus: if you go on so the result is so. He never says such a thing shall happen let you do what you will. A Prophet is a Seer not an Arbitrary Dictator."[5] Burke, let us say, was a prophet in Blake's sense. He was not a prognosticator. He gave honest advice to statesmen because he was a curious and fearless inquirer into the causes of political discontents.

Had he written nothing but his tracts on the state of the nation, had he delivered none but his speeches on domestic reform, Burke would have come down to us as the ablest pamphleteer of the age and the most observant of social critics. But it is his writings on the American colonies, on the reform of British India, and on the French Revolution that give him a special claim on thoughtful readers today. He was the first internationalist among British political writers. His very distance from America, India, and France—the unfamiliarity of a separate history, a strange religion, a different world of manners—gave scope to his moral imagination. As a commentator on English politics, by contrast, Burke often defended the existing order by the mere force of "untaught feelings." Even so, he was prepared to meet the demands of an emergency: the exclusion of Wilkes from Parliament, the suspension of habeas corpus during the American war, the attempt by the Gordon mob to force Parliament to legalize the persecution of Catholics.

He had a way of staying calm when others were heated by passion and of becoming ferocious while others basked in the comfort of prosperity. In

England in the 1780s, the geographical remoteness of India served to excuse a self-protective detachment. The difficulty, as Burke pointed out, even of pronouncing Indian names confirmed the indifference of a public that had ceded control of India to a trading monopoly. Reflection on the method of British rule could be avoided by treating the question as a narrowly commercial matter, a business arrangement in which subordinates would do what employers asked. A similar inertia prevailed in early discussions of the French Revolution. England had spent half the eighteenth century at war, and many of the wars were with France. The revolution could be understood as one more episode of sparring against a rival empire. Not to welcome the revolution but to trust that things would work out and leave England anyway better off than in the age of Louis XIV—this was the predictable response of a moderate Whig in 1789. Yet Burke looked with astonishment at the impotence of the French king and the savagery of the Paris crowd. From the first, he regarded the change with a suspicion poised at the brink of fear.

A unity may be discerned between his stance as a reformer in India and as a skeptic of the revolution in France. Where acceptance or detachment was possible, Burke's impulse was not to let matters rest. He asked instead: if France remains our enemy, but now with "armed doctrine" on its side, ought we not to oppose the revolution decisively? Of India he asked: suppose the vast subcontinent has come into our hands by providential design, does that absolve Britain of responsibilities toward the people whom it governs? The East India Company acted as if it had not even the obligations of an honest merchant toward employees and customers. Burke began to challenge this selfish premise in the committee reports he wrote in the 1780s, and the burden of all his proceedings on India can be reduced to a sentence. *Commerce is not government.* Nor does commerce bring with it a stable social order. The interests of the British constitution might be not only distinct from but at variance with the interests of the East India Company.

Burke's anxiety regarding the empire in the East was heightened by the loss of the empire in the West. In the mid-1770s, George III, Parliament, and the East India Company all believed that England had a right to tax the American colonists and that a policy of taxation was therefore justified. Burke asked them to look to the purpose of their policy. Did

they want to enforce their will as governors? Or was their aim to profit
decently by the connection with North America? He warned that England
faced not a rebellion that could be conveniently muffled but the loss of its
most vital trading partner and ally. In assessing the mood of the colonists
themselves, he may have underrated the violence of their hostility. His
strategy of concession (it has been argued) could no longer have appeased
the American anger in 1775. But to be satisfied with that answer is to neglect
the visionary quality of Burke's belief in a generous empire that should
bind together the diverse elements of human nature. This ideal meant more
to him than may seem compatible with the character of a practical thinker
averse to speculation.

But the portrait of Burke as an anti-theoretical critic of modern politics,
a "pragmatic" adapter to local needs, has always been overdrawn. The truth
is that he cherished certain abstract ideals unconditionally. He drew support from his faith in human nature more than from any religious faith.
What does that mean? The defense of human nature is a secular ideal untouched by fanaticism. Human nature, for Burke, is defined by feelings that
are customary, reasonless, and unselfish. He says that such feelings will
endure as long as we recognize the quality and the limits of our constitution
as moral beings. We have duties to family and neighbors, to fellow citizens,
and to persons farther off, merely on account of their humanity. Burke admits that the social affections work from the inside out: "to love the little
platoon we belong to in society is the first principle (the germ as it were) of
public affections. It is the first link in the series by which we proceed towards a love to our country and to mankind." These sentences have been
thought to establish Burke as the first modern philosopher of community.
Yet, by "the little platoon" he may have meant a political party, or the members of a class, order, or profession. His stress anyway falls on the expansive
end of the series and not its first "germ." We move from sympathy with our
neighbors or clan or tribe to a feeling about mankind at large.

This pattern governs men and women in their social relations. But
what of man in a presocial state, in the "state of nature," as Hobbes, Locke,
and Rousseau variously imagined it? Burke refused in principle to reflect
on such a state. He seems to have thought that nothing of value could
come of the exercise. Still, he does find a motive of action separate from

society and prior to sociability. "The first and the simplest emotion which we discover in the human mind, is Curiosity." That is the opening sentence of *A Philosophical Enquiry into the Origin of Our Ideas of the Sublime and Beautiful*. It is significant that the emotion Burke calls the first and the simplest in human nature is neither good nor evil.

Burke will praise curiosity where it leads to improvement. He knows, however, that it may likewise inspire acts of cruelty. Almost as elementary as curiosity is the feeling he calls sympathy: the faculty of imagining the feelings of others as if in the place of others, which is assisted by "sensibility." Here again, Burke's description stays as close as possible to the physical texture of experience, for by sensibility he means nothing but an aliveness of the senses. This is not a gift bestowed by culture, and its opposite is not coarseness but insensibility. All these words belong to an idiom of psychological explanation that is startling and persuasive; and it is inseparable from the interest of Burke's political writings. An accident of classification has made scholars look for one story about Burke from literary critics, based on the *Sublime and Beautiful,* and another from political theorists, based on the American speeches and the *Reflections*. Burke acknowledged no such division in his thinking.

The desire to create works of art, to ameliorate the conditions of life through science, to diffuse the benefits of peace and liberty—these widely separate human drives can hardly be thought about, Burke argues, without our concluding that they have a common source. For the wish to discover and impose an order on the world is natural to "that wonderful structure, Man; whose prerogative it is, to be in a great degree a creature of his own making." We are wrong to suppose that people adopt one set of perceptions for reality and another for imagination. The various spheres of exertion are all one to the race of beings whom Burke describes. People are driven to political activity (however dangerous) and to aesthetic activity (never as innocent as it looks) by the same unreasoning and irreducible energy.

❧

How far did Burke's political bearings shift when the French Revolution became his central concern? He watched, in 1788 and 1789, uneasily at first and with growing apprehension as the old order collapsed. By the beginning of 1790, he had decided to write a book about the change he was seeing. Yet the book kept expanding and its aim altered as its subject matter broadened, until, in the course of the writing, Burke found himself gripped by an apocalyptic theme. His arresting and unusual phrase, "the revolution in France," calls attention to a general crisis. A revolution is sweeping the world. We see it now in France. Soon it may erupt elsewhere. Burke conveys this intuition in many ways—saying, for example, that the French Revolution is the "most astonishing" change that the world has ever witnessed; saying, again, that the revolutionists are "at war with heaven itself." The last phrase brings to mind the fable of *Paradise Lost:* a tactic that Burke's parliamentary follower William Windham took a step further when he called the revolution "the worst, the second fall of Man."

Now and then, Burke's language is religious. Yet his deepest meaning is not that this revolution is ungodly but that it is inhuman. Modern freedom is possible only under a regime of self-restraint, which we inherit from the chivalry of the Middle Ages. And that ancient "system of opinion and sentiment" had been shaken once before: the radical reinvention of conscience by Protestants in the sixteenth and seventeenth centuries gave a shock to the traditional assurance that docility and obedience were written on our hearts by God. Once that confidence was gone, a range of innovations became imaginable; and yet a radical revolution in morality did not occur in the seventeenth century, according to Burke. Because of the Protestant revolution, "fear of man" took over the work of moral discipline that was no longer performed by the fear of God. But this new revolution is different. Its pursuit of the idea that man is susceptible of infinite improvement, just as a machine may be improved, and that society itself can be turned into an instrument for operation of the machine—this monstrous hope the revolutionists of France were reducing to a practice. The design of the revolution signified for Burke a surrender of the idea of human nature.

What therefore confronted Europe was a moral as well as a political revolution, a full-scale experiment of the human creature upon itself. Burke had long suspected such an attempt was coming—it was in the nature of human will and curiosity—yet he felt astonishment (this is always his word) to see it arrive first in France. He did what he could to assure that it would be debated first in England. His own position as a commentator on the revolution is above all dramatic. "As to us here," he writes to an Irish friend in August 1789, "our thoughts of every thing at home are suspended, by our astonishment at the wonderful Spectacle which is exhibited in a Neighbouring and rival Country—what Spectators, and what actors! England gazing with astonishment at a French struggle for Liberty and not knowing whether to blame or to applaud!" Not knowing whether to blame or to applaud, because the French, after all, have learned about liberty from the English. "The old Parisian ferocity," Burke continues, "has broken out in a shocking manner. It is true, that this may be no more than a sudden explosion. . . . But if it should be character rather than accident, then that people are not fit for Liberty."[6] He followed with disgust and horror the events of October 6, when the king and queen were forcibly taken by a mob and "led in triumph" from Versailles to Paris.

Loss of the fear of God can be borne, but not loss of the fear of man. Once people come to understand that they are innovators in society and experimenters on themselves, they will feel that any means are justified in the creation of an unlimited good. The people, in France, had become indistinguishable from the mob: so Burke thought already by the end of 1789. The people were shameless now and therefore fearless. For it is fear—fear, even, of what we ourselves may do—that makes people conservative. It may be fairer to say that it makes us conservationist toward human things. All of Burke's later writings are directed to readers who have kept contact with this intimate fear—so closely linked to memory, loyalty, and affection. To be instructed by the fear of man is to admit that the moral order is real, that it hangs together as if by its own power and yet (under the pressure of violence) it could be destroyed. We cannot change or upgrade with impunity the feelings that attach us to ourselves, and to our neighbors, and to mankind at large. We cannot repair and revise at pleasure. The order of our feelings, once lost, cannot be regained. When we have torn to pieces the whole "contexture" of our sympathies—the sense of reverence and the sense of abomination—we will have made ourselves into something monstrous: laboratory creations about whose character no previous experiment affords a clue.

Thus Burke seems to gravitate to an ideal of "natural piety" (though he seldom used that phrase). His thinking has much in common, too, with the motives of a more conventional religious piety. Yet the character of the belief is different when, as is the case with Burke, the defense of human nature has to find its final justification in life on earth.

☙

If *Reflections on the Revolution in France* is Burke's greatest book, the reason is that it leaves the deepest impression of the crisis of human nature to which all his writings testify. It seems to me his most revealing work, the one that, in a single frame, offers the most comprehensive statement of his politics while drawing on all the reserves of his insight. Yet *Reflections* was not intended as a summing-up. Burke probably wrote it as a manual for statesmen, or perhaps for a single statesman who could move Whig opinion against the revolution. Such was the conscious purpose he declared to private correspondents. He ended up doing less and more than that. He confused his party and wrote a new chapter in the history of human feeling. The least rewarding approach to the *Reflections* is to treat it as a diagnosis of a problem: the problem of culture or the problem of ideology or the nature and destiny of Europe.

As his speeches and writings on America show, Burke believed that secularization had increased, was increasing, and could not be reversed. He devoted none of his energy to programmatic efforts to reverse the process. He supposed that enlightenment, properly understood, was a name for the development by which we move from fear of God to fear of man. This change (of which Burke's own career in politics and letters was an inseparable product) entails a displacement of religious by moral authority and the accompanying intuition that the idea of the good is prior to the idea of God. Replying once to a question about his religious beliefs, Burke said he was a Christian "much from conviction; more from affection." The remark is open to various readings. I take it to imply that for him, ordinary feelings such as trust, though they have a Christian correlative, themselves supply a sufficient groundwork of moral conduct. This is possible if we take the claim of certain feelings and the requirement of certain actions to be unconditional. When understood as commandments, the secular virtues carry a trace of the religious piety in which they originate.

Depending on the source one consults, one may find *Reflections on the Revolution in France* classified as a work of eighteenth-century literature, of political theory, of sociology, or of economic history. Its author has been called a conservative, a Whig, a liberal, and a Tory radical. I write about Burke as a moral psychologist. If a psychologist addresses the workings of the individual mind, a moral psychologist is concerned at once with the individual and society. He interprets actions and motives that contain an element of coerciveness that is absent in relationships of smaller groups. Errors or missteps in the larger society may have consequences on a scale that defies calculation, yet they spring from the same unconscious or involuntary causes at work in all human action. Burke's effort is not to tame or reduce but to understand this complex object of inquiry. He starts from two irreducible principles. First, human beings are strongly drawn to imitation. And second, they love to be excited—to be roused by new or strong sensations. The sensations need not be wholly agreeable, so long as they are striking. The instinct of imitation and the love of excitement are originally as non-social and non-moral as the emotion of curiosity.

Yet Burke is also interested in a particular natural drive that becomes the foundation of prudence, namely, the tendency to turn from a state of arousal and restore a previous state of equilibrium. This is a bodily necessity, but it brings with it a habit of mind; and in that habit lies the vital principle of a society based on mutual respect and self-restraint. Burke often writes in defense of the force of custom and habit that guides cooperative enterprises; but when he speaks for such accommodation, he is always aware of the claim of the presocial and premoral instincts. The love of imitation and excitement gives an animating impulse to all life, whereas custom and habit give form only to a life that already exists.

This double emphasis is typical of Burke. He can write stirringly of the French aristocracy and their devotion to the queen: "I thought ten thousand swords must have leaped from their scabbards to avenge even a look that threatened her with insult." Yet he also deliberately praises the inertia of English custom, the virtue of "a dull sluggish race, rendered passive by finding our situation tolerable." Both of these appeals, which may seem contradictory from an emotional standpoint, are consistent with Burke's insight as a moral psychologist. His early aphorism, "custom reconciles us to every thing," and his late aphorism, "art is man's nature," are meant to be taken together. Energy must find its appropriate restraint in a society capable of improvement.

❀

Intellectual biography is a familiar genre, yet it remains easy to confuse with criticism or biography. A life of Burke must connect a narrative of a life and an interpretation of ideas; and in dealing with an author so prolific and miscellaneous, the task is unusually complicated.[7] Three of his major works are unfinished: *An Essay towards an Abridgment of the English History, Fragments of a Tract Relative to Laws against Popery in Ireland,* and *Letters on a Regicide Peace.* Even his first book, *A Vindication of Natural Society,* is marked by a peculiar ambiguity of intention: a satire on utopian thought, it was taken by many as a work of radical criticism and enjoyed a questionable influence in that capacity. From this enigmatic start, his career never lends a decisive clue to biography by clarifying itself. Most of Burke's writings of short or medium length are parliamentary speeches that survive in the form of drafts, fragments, reports by newspapers or freelance auditors, or reconstructions by Burke himself and his assistants. But the parliamentary reporters, efficient as they are and deft at memorization, frequently throw up their hands and admit that Burke is too fast to follow. Their reports often stop midway in his speeches, with a tactful compliment to the speaker's "wealth and variety of illustration." The descent from quotation of Burke to loose paraphrase is a common experience for a reader of the *Parliamentary History.*

In this two-volume study, I single out a few finished performances to epitomize Burke's thought: on the function of party and representative government, *Thoughts on the Cause of the Present Discontents* (1770) and the *Appeal from the New to the Old Whigs* (1791); on the American crisis and its threat to the British Empire, the *Speech on Conciliation with America* (1775); on the French Revolution, the *Reflections* (1790) and the *Letters on a Regicide Peace* (1796). Out of the possible archive on reform of the empire in India—two thousand pages of committee reports, parliamentary speeches, the charges against Warren Hastings, and three full-length speeches at the trial (covering four days in 1788, four days in 1789, and nine days in 1794)—the central statement seems to me Burke's piercing inauguration of his enterprise in the *Speech on Fox's East India Bill* (1783).

Only by quoting him at length can one show how he "winds into a subject like a serpent"—a characterization of his manner by Dr. Goldsmith that is impossible to improve on. Yet this is a critical biography, and I have felt obliged, when quoting, to suggest why Burke would have wanted to say a given thing at a given time. This does not mean that I consider his style a quality somehow separate from his thought or that I would want readers to admire him as a "literary writer," even if one could know what that meant. Burke is a thinker. He thinks in writing. His speeches, as Hazlitt said, are also writings; and to see how they carry conviction, one must listen closely.

Admiration for a thinker is compatible with a refusal to trust him as the judge in his own cause. Burke's engagements did not always allow him to speak with the disinterestedness, the freedom from self-protective anxiety and mere sectarian feeling, which he valued as the highest quality in a statesman. His warmest partisans confess that Burke could never admit he was wrong. Nor is he the soundest judge of why his reasoning ought to be credited. His entanglements stretch too far, his relations are too intricate for his mind to be always at liberty. There is no escaping the fact that from 1765 to 1794, Burke held a political position and had a certain side to represent. He is apt to overrate the abilities of his patrons and disciples, to subject the motives of his antagonists to unearned contempt, and to exaggerate rumors of the forces arrayed against him. An eloquent witness to the power of accident in history, he must sometimes be quoted against himself.

When Burke in 1767 politely deflected a hint that might have given him a place in the Chatham-Grafton ministry, his decision showed his strength of character and a high-minded belief in the virtue of his party; yet this act of principle was also a gamble on Lord Rockingham's re-emergence as prime minister, which was expected after a shorter pause than the fifteen years it took. Again, in 1772, Burke turned down an invitation to serve as head of a commission to be sent to India to investigate the abuses of the East India Company. Had he taken the opportunity, the office of governor-general might have been offered to him and not to Warren Hastings. Luckily, Burke stayed out of the Chatham administration and kept away from the East India Company; and his later estimates of both entities show the frank intelligence of an outsider. His triumphs as much as his defeats were made possible by the play of accident.

Burke's admirers have a tendency to acquit him of all charges of expedience or caprice. His detractors resolve most puzzles about his conduct by the imputation of a low motive. I see Burke's career as an imperfect attempt to organize an honorable life in the dense medium he knew politics to be. One must read him suspiciously, and this means quarreling sometimes with Burke's dramatic view of his life. His allusion to "that hunt of obloquy, which ever has pursued me with a full cry" refers to actual enemies, but an extreme wariness also blunted his discernment. Can his achievement nevertheless stand up to an impartial test?

I give credence to three sorts of contemporary witnesses: first, public opponents of some weight—a group that includes Richard Price, Josiah Tucker, Mary Wollstonecraft, Thomas Paine, and Joseph Priestley. A second set of persons, more apt to be charitable to Burke, are the working associates he trusted in later years, such as Gilbert Elliot, William Windham, French Laurence, and Walker King. These were younger men (Fox had been the first), and frequent consultations with them were obligatory. When Richard Burke Jr. remarks to his father in a passing comment in a letter of 1792, "Walker is a sad dog not to write," the reproach typifies an expectation of "keeping up" that was impressed on members of the circle. Still another sort of testimony is afforded by friends or familiar observers who, by their station and competence, appear well qualified to judge Burke's claims. The Irish peer Lord Charlemont, Horace Walpole, Sir Joshua Reynolds—these were not docile pupils or malleable followers. Where the suffrage of all three categories points in one direction, I have supposed that their judgments are accurate.

No serious historian today would repeat the commonplace that Burke was the father of modern conservatism.[8] To be a Tory in the eighteenth century meant believing in the sovereignty of the crown, affirming a social order ruled by a landed aristocracy, and refusing to extend the practical meaning of the liberty of "the people." People, populace, and mob are synonymous to the Tory mind. "A vile Whig" was the proper description of Burke in politics, according to his friend Samuel Johnson; and a Whig, for Dr. Johnson, was a supporter of the revolution settlement of 1689, a believer in the authority of Parliament as superior to the king, a person who saw frequent causes for alarm at encroachment by the king on parliamentary sovereignty. These make a fair summary of Burke's commitments from 1766 to 1790. How large a residue survived the coming of the French Revolution is a matter open to dispute, but one may guess from Burke's last writings about India, about Ireland, and about himself that much of his earlier belief in progress and his passion for reform did survive.

A test of the consistency of his thought is the steadiness of the point of view extractable from his *Correspondence.* The letters reveal a character much in keeping with the *Works,* and they assist an understanding of Burke's thoughts and actions without much call for deciphering. From the letters, more than the published writings, one can piece together an understanding of Burke's view of the desirable relationship of politics to religion. He believed that man is a symbol-making animal and that religious faith is the leading expression of an instinct by which people exalt a more-than-human power above themselves. This feeling, says Burke (mostly to private correspondents), ought never to be discouraged so long as it does not take a political form. Yet concerning the place of religion in politics, Burke is a doubter through and through. He believes in the instrumental good of an established church because it contributes to social stability. He distrusts any encroachment of state on church or of church on state: "politics and the pulpit are terms that have little agreement." The human creature in society must not be allowed to grow used to exorbitant excitements, whether the intoxicant is religion or ideology.

About the ways in which historical circumstance shaped Burke's language and ideas, I have been instructed by W. E. H. Lecky, G. O. Trevelyan, Herbert Butterfield, Richard Pares, Ian Christie, John Brewer, Linda Colley, J. C. D. Clark, and many others. On both the details and the larger bearings of Burke's career, I have learned most from the writings of P. J. Marshall. All of these historians frequently convey a lack of coherence between events and the intentions of political actors in the eighteenth century. The reminder is welcome in the face of an opposite impression Burke himself often conveys: that the reform of society is a drama whose outcome is decided by heroes. "When bad men combine, the good must associate." This aphorism of 1770 is grand, but it savors of a party leader's assurance: he knows who the good men are, even before the association is formed. Burke had a mind retentive of facts, but vehement passion sometimes draws his history writing into the precincts of legend. It is easy to take his word prematurely about an interpretation that his language implies is a fact—regarding (say) the degree of tranquility that the repeal of the Stamp Act brought to England's relations with the American colonies or the supposed tendency of Dr. Price's discourse *On the Love of Our Country* to excuse the violence of the revolutionary mob at Versailles.

The study of the British eighteenth century was dominated in the mid-twentieth century by historians who minimized the influence of ideas. From this, it was a short step to supposing that the ideas of a politician as unusual as Burke were fanciful and unreal. The latter-day conservative Lewis Namier and the latter-day Whig J. H. Plumb alike depreciated his writings and mocked his pretense of high-mindedness. Yet a perfect distrust of ideas may harbor its own dogmatism, while the most uncompromising idealism is sometimes vindicated in practice. L. T. Hobhouse in *Liberalism* summed up Gladstone's view of the statesman as "a man charged with maintaining not only the material interests but the honour of his country. He is a citizen of the world in that he represents his nation, which is a member of the community of the world." This has a familiar sound, to readers of Burke, and the summary goes on in a manner still more evocative: "There is no line drawn beyond which human obligations cease. There is no gulf across which the voice of human suffering cannot be heard, beyond which massacre and torture cease to be execrable."[9] Realists may object that such ideas, whether spun out by Gladstone or Burke, always end up being the rationalizations of a party; and that such lofty phrases are dear to the very "men of theory" whose pretensions Burke so distrusted. To the charge that he was a thinker after all, Burke must plead guilty. He was indeed a man of ideas. If he was not, no politician ever was.[10]

Yet his was an age of ideology, as well as an age of overseas investment and local place-hunting and patronage. Nor is it always true that force and interest are a reliable guide to human motives. Their infallible dictates are occasionally disobeyed. Scores of well-drilled realists failed to predict the fall of communism. They had a theory of society under totalitarian regimes which ruled out that eventuality. Up-to-date believers have picked, as the law for the twenty-first century, the rational good of the global market. It is possible that their predictions, too, will be upset. The practical-minded often fail to reckon with the strength of apparently groundless beliefs and the weakness of apparently solid beliefs. I may want to act selfishly yet be unable to get a grip on the self I would like to serve. Nations are prone to this error as much as individuals: if people acted only for selfish ends, the world would be a more restful place. This truth Burke teaches unremittingly, and in doing so, he calls into question the research methods of the "oeconomists, sophisters, and calculaters" of every subsequent generation.

The most fantastic projects have been nursed, the most repellent schemes reduced to a practice by state advisers from Burke's time to our own. They do it because they are certain that they know what people need or what people must be given. Here we come to a central insight of Burke's, namely the importance of wrong ideas. They are important not only in getting people to go to war or trade their liberty for a promise of safety but in recruiting support for vacuous remedies. Wrong ideas act through the medium of plausible beliefs. They may teach people to believe that they are acting for the common good when they are acting to enrich themselves. Not to recognize this ever-operative power of delusion as a major cause in history is to remain an innocent where ideas and action are concerned.

But not all ideas are equally delusive. There are some, demonstrably the product of a given time and place, which break free of their original limits. Such was the idea of a generous commonwealth that Burke bequeathed to the nineteenth century, a commonwealth founded on "the natural equality of mankind at large." Though he was not a democrat, he remains for this reason a thinker whom democrats must learn from. The party he served is long dead, and no successor can claim him, but every party has been the better for what it learned from Burke. Thoughts of permanent value, universal in their application, appear in his writings to arise from the ground of mere legislative business. He is, by temper, the reverse of those tacticians who would confine political discourse to piecemeal engineering. He refers political decisions to the same tribunal at which we reflect on the most exacting of moral choices.

When action is required, each person asks himself: "What shall I do?" The answer, for Burke, must pass through another question. What would I feel as a member of an audience, if I saw a certain action performed at this moment? So one looks at oneself just as a spectator looks at an actor. "The minds of those who do not feel thus," he said of someone who did not share his pity at the fall of the queen of France, "are not even Dramatically right."[11] Burke offers himself as a mind sensitive to the results of such an inquest. Here (he says) is what I must feel when I see such things.

Why has the individuality of Burke's appeal to "natural feelings" been so little emphasized? Mostly, the failure has come from a wrong understanding of his occasional shows of hostility toward individual judgment. There is a tradition in political thought which denies public legitimacy to all private judgments. Hobbes in *Leviathan* defined "conscience" satirically as the convergence of two opinions and warned that to allow the disputation of rival creeds would be to usher into politics the greatest destroyer of politics; for such freedom gives a perpetual warrant to enthusiasm; and enthusiasm, without restraint, is fanaticism. Burke may seem to write from a similar wariness when he remarks of the Protestant rigor of the Reverend Dr. Richard Price, "His zeal is of a curious character. It is not for the propagation of his own opinions, but of any opinions. It is not for the diffusion of truth, but for the spreading of contradiction."

Yet Burke denies an exemption to private judgment only to place civic conscience at the heart of politics. He speaks for a habit of feeling at once British and cosmopolitan, pious toward the customs it knows well, yet answerable to a standard of right and wrong that is not circumscribed by the nation. His indictment of Warren Hastings in the *Speech Opening the Impeachment* builds to a climax of three clauses: "I impeach him in the name of the Commons of Great Britain," "I impeach him in the name of the people of India," "I impeach him in the name of human nature itself." The last authority is the highest because the judgments of conscience are universal. This explains his affirmation that "the principles of true politicks are those of morality enlarged, and I neither now do nor ever will admit of any other."[12] Burke's greatest fear was that the rule of modern society by considerations of sheer utility would eradicate conscience from the mind of man.

Two forces combined to make this possible: the adoption of the index of common usefulness as the final measure of social good; and the rise of modern commercial and military power to an ascendancy that could dominate subject nations more completely than the ancient empires ever did. In response to those developments, Burke supported his belief in civic conscience with a desire for an impartial authority to stand above the interests of a single nation or people. He thought the House of Commons might become such a tribunal for deliberation on the crises of the age.

The later eighteenth century was in truth a period of continuous crisis: the Seven Years War (1756–1763); the prosecution of Wilkes for a libel on the king (1763); the Stamp Act crisis (1765–1766); the refusal by Parliament to abide by the results of the election of Wilkes (1768–1769); the first exchange of hostilities with the American colonists (1775) and the declaration of independence by the colonists (1776); the uprising of the Irish Volunteers (1779–1780); the loss of America (1782); the disclosure of a system of bribery and extortion in the management of the East India Company (1783); the publication of the charges of impeachment of the governor-general of Bengal (1786); the onset of the madness of George III (1788) and the "Regency crisis" concerning the location of monarchical authority while his madness persisted (1788–1789); the revolution in France (1789); the declaration of war by the French republic against England (1793).

Throughout this series of both foreseen and unforeseeable events, Burke insisted that politics was, among other things, a dramatic art, and that the theater was "a school of moral sentiments." Here a necessary figure for comparison is Cicero, a precursor occasionally noticed by Burke's contemporaries. It is Burke who seems to me the subtler thinker of the two. He is more consistent in his reasoning and more varied in his eloquence; yet from Cicero he inherited a conception of the nature and scope of the work of a representative. Cicero also was Burke's tactical model, to an imposing degree, in the impeachment of Warren Hastings, which followed the pattern of the prosecution of the Roman governor Verres. From the bias of his rhetorical training, Burke always gave a minute attention to words, sentiments, and gestures hallowed by custom and memory. Over three decades he evolved an idea of the statesman as a kind of performer—

one who explains public affairs with clarity and passion to his listeners and leads them from deliberation to action.

Burke's idea of the function of statesmanship emerges in his praise of the contemporaries whom he could regard as his equals. Thus in 1792, in a letter to his son, he comments on a speech of February 18 by Henry Grattan on the rights of Irish Catholics. "A noble performance," Burke calls it, "eloquent in conception and in Language, and when that is the Case, being on the Right side is of some importance to the perfection of what is done. It is of great consequence to a Country to have men of Talents and Courage in it, though they have no power."[13] Articulate energy matters greatly, whether or not its bearer holds high office. Burke always believed this, and he acted on the belief, as not all gifted politicians do; but persuasion (as he saw it) was only part of the work of a statesman. Just as important is the work of thought by which one draws the audience to reflect on the course of action one recommends. A great political speaker or writer makes people think. The aim is to bring their actions into line with their beliefs about what they are and what they hope to become.

We learn most about the nature of a society when its order is threatened by destruction. We are then "alarmed into reflection"—reflection on the extent to which society is bound by common sentiments and the way its unity is materially confirmed in the presence of disaster; reflection on the manner in which the good and evil of certain acts seem printed on the face of things. *Fear of a general loss of trust* is Burke's constant subject. The commonest exchanges between persons—hospitality, consent, justification—all require a steady confidence that people will act properly and that, without elaborate construal or inquiry, they will do what they are entrusted with doing. Liberty and restraint support each other in a society bound by trust. Together they make for an order whose dependence on force is offset by a chastened understanding of the limits of the good that force can accomplish.

Burke's fame has long been international. It is going to become more so. At the start of the age of modern empire, he asked his listeners to avoid the peril of a great empire governed by little minds. His political imagination is unyielding in its demand for credence, and yet, to profit from his discoveries, we must never wholly comply with his demands. Without this excess to the point of exorbitance, Burke would lack the confidence that makes for his power. But it is remarkable, when one considers the length of his career, that in that span of service hardly a credible word is uttered against his probity. We seldom hear the suggestion that he let one person think one thing while giving another to understand the opposite; that he promised what he did not perform; that he changed his view on a critical question without offering a solid reason. There have been periods when the word *principle* seemed close to cant, but principle is the word that comes to mind when one thinks of Burke.

Something about the man will always remain beyond our grasp. We feel it clearly when he writes to a young friend, Mary Palmer, about his prosecution of the East India Company: "I have no party in this business, my dear Miss Palmer, but among a set of people, who have none of your lilies and roses in their faces, but who are images of the great Pattern as well as you or I. I know what I am doing; whether the white people like it or not."[14] For so personal a writer, he possessed, to an astonishing degree, the ability to stand outside himself. There is a passion in him that is finally mysterious, a passion almost outside the reach of words; and it was this that gave his words their power to invigorate and unsettle.

❧ I ❧

Early Ambition and the Theory of Society

Edmund Burke made no pretense of humble beginnings. His father, Richard Burke, was a successful lawyer, and the family was free of money worries. Once, when a newspaper story drawn from his friend Richard Shackleton conveyed a wrong impression of his father's social standing, Burke sent an immediate reproof to Shackleton denying that his father had been "an hedge Country Attorney of little practice." There was, wrote Burke, a distinction between the upper and lower parts of the profession, and "the fact is, that my father never did practice in the Country, but always in the superior Courts; that he was for many years not only in the first *Rank*, but the very first *man* of his profession in point of practice and Credit." Burke took the time to correct this error, he added, because "poverty is the greatest Imputation (very unjustly I think) that is ever laid on that profession."[1] The genius of Burke was unique—not something he owed to a party or sect—but his lot was cast with the professional classes: a truth he neither concealed nor embellished. Probably he would have done well in any career he embraced. He seems to have entered the world confident of his talents and secure in the belief that nothing could stop him for long.

Yet we are speaking of Ireland, so a complication must be added. Burke's was the Ireland of the Protestant ascendancy: the system of privations and exclusions, stemming from Cromwell's invasion in the seventeenth century, which had made Protestants into a superior caste. An Irish Catholic in 1730 could not bear arms, could not inherit property from a Catholic, was excluded from the professions and from public life, and, by an act of 1728, was forbidden to vote.[2] Distrust of the Protestant ascendancy seems to have left its mark on Burke; yet his experience would seldom have exposed him to the worst subjections. For the Burke clan, the system was an unpleasant extrinsic fact rather than a galling irritant.

Nominally, they were Protestants; but Richard's wife, Mary Nagle, remained an observing Catholic; and the family looked back on a member of the Nagle line who had been speaker of the Irish House of Commons in the reign of James II. As was common in such marriages, the daughter, Juliana, was brought up Catholic, while the sons, Garrett, Edmund, and Richard, were guided into the established Church of Ireland.

Richard Burke may have conformed to the established church as late as 1722 and under a semblance of coercion, since the Penal Laws forbade Catholics from the practice of law.[3] If the Richard Burke who appears on the Convert Rolls is Edmund's father, we may count the early humiliations of compelled conformity among the motives of Edmund's later dedication to political reform. Yet his passion for reform had sufficient cause in the broader abuses that he witnessed in Ireland; and his appeal for Catholic rights—privately in the 1760s, publicly in the 1790s—was not an appeal for national liberation; it was a protest against a human injustice. Burke's "real impulse," H. N. Brailsford accurately observed, "was hatred of cruelty."[4]

From his sixth to his tenth year, Edmund was raised by his mother's relatives in Ballyduff, in County Cork; and one recent biographer, Conor Cruise O'Brien, has speculated that he attended a "hedge school" (so called because Catholic schools were prohibited and classes met in the open to allow for quick dispersal).[5] What is known is that his school in Ballyduff was on the Blackwater River, within sight of the Nagle Mountains, and Edmund's time there fostered affections that would accompany his onward life like an underground stream. These were familiar and local attachments, about which Burke himself never made the romantic claims that commentators have been drawn to.[6] He did not suppose that men's ideas can be traced to their native soil and environment. His characterization of an ideal House of Commons as "the express *image of the feelings* of the nation" (emphasis added) points to an element of artifice in every national identity or affiliation.[7] Whatever loyalties Burke may have cherished, his actual returns to Ireland after the age of twenty were sparse and dutiful;[8] and though, in a long career, he was to pay many compliments to public men, love of their country is seldom made to appear the highest of their virtues. Patriotism, Burke seems to have thought, is a good thing, in measure. It does not compete with such qualities as acting honorably, thinking rigorously, speaking candidly, or being ready to sacrifice one's popularity in the cause of justice.

❀

This is a history of the life of a mind, and the sort of testimony that differentiates Burke does not begin in his earliest days. Still, a few circumstances may be counted as formative. To have been sent at the age of six to live with his maternal uncle, Patrick Nagle, in Ballyduff, must have equipped Edmund early to understand home and family in an enlarged and non-parochial sense. Life in the country and in the city would be alike familiar to his thinking ever after; and he would be rare among thinkers of the eighteenth century in understanding the virtues of both and idealizing neither. At the age of eleven, he was sent to Abraham Shackleton's school at Ballitore, in the county of Kildare. There the Quaker schoolmaster's son Richard became his closest friend. To the elder Shackleton, the most important of his mentors, Edmund felt something of the filial attachment that seems to have been missing in his relationship with his father. The loyalty was mutual, and it held fast. Invited to Burke's estate many years later, Shackleton was so overwhelmed at first by the family coach Burke had sent to fetch him from London that he declined the use of it, saying that he preferred to ride on horseback.[9] The venerable schoolmaster would die a year after that visit; and Burke spoke of him as "a man of singular piety, rectitude and virtue" with "a native elegance of manners which nothing but genuine good-nature and unaffected simplicity of heart can give." Under Shackleton's instruction, Burke advanced so far in Greek and Latin that, by the time he went on to college, he read the classical authors to satisfy his curiosity and not mainly to fill a regimen of formal study.

Of the religious education imparted by Abraham Shackleton, we have a revealing hint in Burke's speech on toleration in 1780, delivered in the wake of the anti-Catholic Gordon Riots. "Mr. Burke" (the *Parliamentary History* tells us) remarked that he "had been educated as a Protestant of the Church of England—by a dissenter, who was an honour to his sect, though that sect was considered one of the purest. Under his eye he had read the Bible morning, noon and night, and had ever since been the better man for such reading."[10] When Burke spoke that eulogy, he knew his

29

audience would be aware of his Catholic affiliations. The assertion that he had been educated *in* the established church *by* a dissenter from the established church was to be taken as an homage to the spirit of toleration.

Trinity College

Burke entered Trinity College Dublin at the age of fourteen. Poetry and history were his favorite studies, but he found the time to start a debating club and to contribute essays to a magazine, *The Reformer,* whose usual subjects were the theater, taste, and morality. The first words of *The Reformer* declare an intention of taking up the satirical calling of Pope's *Dunciad* (a work congenial to the iconoclastic mood of the young Burke and his circle):[11]

> There is a certain Period when *Dulness* being arrived to its full Growth, and spreading over a Nation becomes so insolent, that it forces Men of *Genius* and *Spirit* to rise up, in Spite of their natural Modesty, and work that Destruction it is ripe for. If we may judge of the Empire of *Dulness* by other great ones, whose Unwieldiness brought on their Ruin, this is certainly its Time; for the Depravation of Taste is as great as that of Morals, and tho' the correcting the latter may seem a more laudable Design, and more consistent with *public-Spirit;* yet there is so strong a Connection between them, and the Morals of a Nation have so great Dependence on their Taste and Writings, that the fixing the latter, seems the first and surest Method of establishing the former.[12]

The close connection between taste and morals would be a preoccupation of Burke's writings from this first editorial through the essay on "the manners of Jacobinism" in the last of his published works, the *Letters on a Regicide Peace.*

Of the remaining numbers of *The Reformer,* the third suggests a more particular thought that Burke would make his own. (The essays are signed in code, but on internal evidence I suspect that Burke wrote this one.) The young critic argues that it is wrong to portray vices on the stage that would be disapproved of or discountenanced in actual life. The notion of aesthetic distance—that we may somehow admire the artistic qualities of a work that gives a pleasant picture of unseemly manners or supports obnoxious views—has crossed his mind, but he firmly rejects it. There never can be such a distance between the emotions created by a work of art and the feelings of actual life. We may think ourselves free to indulge the most wayward passions in fiction simply because we admit that the source of our pleasure is fictional. But the *Reformer* critic judges it false that, by such a conscious understanding, we can render ourselves immune to the poison of ugly imaginings or wicked ideas. He suspects, on the contrary, that people enjoy seeing acted what they would wish to see done. We are drawn to witness actions on the stage that we might perform if we could be separated from our responsible selves.

"So far" (argues *Reformer* No. 3) "from being disgusted at seeing any thing immoral represented, we are seldom better pleas'd."[13] The illicit pleasure of drama therefore can be sapped of its poison only by vigilant countermeasures. We ought to judge the actions of a play as we would judge corresponding actions in life. Speaking of "the Practice of Kissing" on stage, Burke cites a precept of French criticism: "nothing should be done" in a play "which was not allowable in a genteel private Company"; and to enforce such a policy of restraint, "every Person who goes to a Play, should endeavour to persuade himself, he sees some real Action."[14] You will not go wrong in judging a play, Burke says again in *Reflections on the Revolution in France*, if you treat the fiction as you would treat the reality; for taste and morals have a steady and reciprocal influence. The *Reformer* essay stops short of offering a design for censorship; and yet, to judge by its argument, Burke shared a central perception of Plato, Rousseau, and other republican writers who do advocate censorship. When we permit a practice on the stage, we give encouragement to that practice in life (if only because we allow our feelings to grow accustomed to it). A critic who supposes works of art can be cleared of practical influence has been taken in by a false psychology that divides the mind into separate chambers. In reality, all thoughts and feelings are permeable by other thoughts and feelings.

At Trinity College, "Burke appears to have found," observed W. E. H. Lecky, "an amount of intellectual activity considerably greater than that which Gibbon a few years later found at Oxford." We may take as partial corroboration the pursuits of the debating club founded by Burke and his friends. This was the germ, Marianne Elliott has noted, of the College Historical Society—"the first college debating society in the British Isles" and in later years (with allotted rooms) a cherished institution of Trinity, which supplied "the training ground for almost all the leading political figures in the age of Grattan's Parliament."[15]

One may consider a typical entry in the minutes of the club: "Friday, June 5, 1747, Mr. Burke being ordered to speak the speech of Moloch"—the speech occurs in the debate in Hell, in Book 2 of *Paradise Lost,* where the fallen angels hammer out a strategy for a second assault on heaven. The question before the gathered rebels is whether they should conciliate the wrath of God, provide for themselves by building in hell, or avenge the loss of heaven by perverting the latest of God's creations, Man. The last plan eventually prevailed, according to Milton, but not before Moloch had pressed for a bolder policy: "My sentence is for open war." In the autumn of 1796, Burke would speak this sentiment against France, having written a year earlier that the Jacobins were "sprung from Night and Hell." According to the club minutes of 1747, he *receives applause for the delivery, it being in character.*[16]

Among the formal topics set for debate was the proper punishment of the Stuart rebels of 1745. Here, the minutes tell us, Burke "accused" and "corrected" a speech by another member which tended to excuse the rebels on the ground that their motives were honorable. Justice, not mercy, said Burke, should be observed in punishing those who break the public peace and expose their country to the worst of all political evils, civil war.[17]

A letter written from college brings out again his temperamental leaning toward satire. He boasts to Richard Shackleton that he could (if he pleased) "shew how excellent I was in the Thersitical way."[18] Thersites is the one-man chorus of Shakespeare's *Troilus and Cressida* who impartially denounces everyone he meets. A revealing choice of a model: Burke throughout his life would excel in the "Thersitical way." The most dire jokes in his later writings are sometimes issued in code, as when he advises Dr. Richard Price (a Christian moralist well versed in economics who praised the French Revolution in 1789) to calculate the compound interest on thirty pieces of silver over 1790 years. There is the same reckless freedom in many of Burke's muttered asides. Hearing how Lord Malmesbury found that the wet roads in France slowed the progress of his mission to negotiate peace in 1796, Burke would comment: "No wonder, as he went the whole way on his knees."

Of his early correspondents, Richard Shackleton draws the warmest interest from Burke and receives the best letters. A letter of November 12, 1745, concludes: "Pray let me have a place in your affection, You are never out of mine."[19] To Shackleton, once more, he writes from Trinity College to advertise his composition of "a moral treatise forsooth": "Almighty Self-flove and her Power I sing / Of all we do first mover and first Spring." The opening lines suggest the libertine skepticism of Lord Rochester, more than the polished irony of Pope, and Burke's comment in prose adds to the impression. Once, he says, he wrote a panegyric on John Damer (a wealthy moneylender and client of his father's), but "I utterly detest all sort of Flattery" and he now regrets having ever dedicated verses to such a person: "Were he a Peer or one who posessd any eminent employment in the State I would think no crime in giving him a little spice of that flattery, but as he is a private Gentleman had he a million a year I should scorn for the sake of the finest presents he could possibly make me to send him a mean Scroll of Lying Verse."[20] One notes here the contrast, typical of the period and its manners, between a public man of "eminent employment" and a mere private gentleman.

By his seventeenth year, Burke had delved further in the vein of criticism and ridicule, and he began to show an affinity for satire in the manner of the apocalyptic ending of the *Dunciad:* "Thy hand, great Anarch, lets the curtain fall, / And universal darkness buries all." World-despising resignation was an attractive posture among his friends at Trinity—disenchanted witnesses (as they supposed) of a dying culture inundated by literary cant and political rant. The saving remnant would consist of a few choice spirits entrusted with the conservator's task of selecting items for preservation from the ruin. Thus Burke plumed himself on the heady distinction of one who has seen the worst. "Believe me Dear Dick," he writes to Shackleton, "we are just on the verge of Darkness and one push drives us in—we shall all live if we live long to see the prophesy of the *Dunciad* fulfilled and

the age of ignorance come round once more."[21] About this time, he reports to Shackleton an interesting purchase: "I could not get e'er a Second
hand Longinus but rather than you should want it I bought a new one."[22]
The future author of *A Philosophical Enquiry into the Origin of Our Ideas of
the Sublime and Beautiful* was eager for his friend to read the ancient treatise *On the Sublime*.

A friend of another sort was William Burke (no relation but often
called Burke's kinsman or "cousin"). Always a loyal associate of Edmund's, William Burke was a loose liver and an adventurer who became
a dangerous speculator in India stocks. Edmund addresses to him an
exuberant verse meditation on a theme familiar from Pope's moral essays: the "ruling passion" that penetrates every recess of human character. It is the nature of a ruling passion to refine and limit the possible
forms of success; if allowed to operate unchecked, the passion will assist
every instinct of self-destruction. Burke associates ruling passions with
habits that can never be shaken. And passion more broadly conceived—
whether directed toward domination or sheer excitement—is the subject
of this poem:

> The strong and weak consume in the same fire,
> The force unequal, equal the Desire.
> What Whips! What Stings! What furies drive us on?
> Why all this Mighty rage to be undone?
> Why still persist when ruin and Disgrace,
> When want and Shame present their hideous face?
> When scornful Silence loudly cries, Abstain,
> Our friends advise, our parents preach in vain.
> Well sage Astrologers, I yield at Last,
> I own the folly of my Wisdom past.

The Burke who writes these lines is a man of strong self-will, yet capable
of regret. His questions show it. But once he has acknowledged his faults,
which way he ought to turn seems a matter of stunning arbitrariness:

> Whate'er the stars determine at our Birth,
> Whether to conquer, or to Plough the Earth;

> Whether to wear the Ribband, or the Rope,
> Whether to be, or whether burn a Pope.

Pause at that last line. One might imagine the author to be a thorough-bred nihilist, possibly six months from joining a terrorist band or taking his own life.

To Burke at the time he wrote these verses, the vocation of authorship afforded the likeliest answer to his questions. But whatever he ends up doing, he suspects that he can only

> preach to others in the same distress,
> Dissuade with Words, and then dissuade no less
> By sad Example of my own success.

There appears to be only one cure for the malady. The natural corrective to the ceaseless demand of our appetites is friendship:

> Can we, my friend, with any Conscience bear
> To shew our minds sheer naked as they are,
> Remove each veil of Custom, pride or Art,
> Nor stretch a hand to hide one Shamefull part?
> An equal Share of Scorn and Danger find,
> A Naked body, and an open mind
> Both sights unusual, sights which never fail
> To make the Witty laugh, and pious Rail,
> The Children fly for fear, the women scream
> And Sages cry the World has Lost its Shame.
> And ev'n some friends (that sacred Name) we have
> Whom so to keep, 'tis proper to deceive—
> Who Lofty Notions build on Plato's plan—
> And grow quite angry when they find you *man;*
> Who can be friends, and yet be Judges too?
> Few can be such, then Let me keep those few.[23]

Such friendship is the best consolation Burke can imagine (as it was for Pope in his epistles to Martha Blount and Dr. Arbuthnot); yet it offers at most a partial remedy. He speaks throughout the ambitious verse-letter in a voice reminiscent of Hamlet, antic and unsettled; the Hamlet who sees the skull beneath the skin and declares that nothing can denote him truly—"I know not *seems*."

These early verses by Burke are strongly written and exhibit some permanent traits of character. The appeal against prejudice, against custom, against art, is advanced here on grounds consistent with his later defense of prejudice, custom, and art. Habits and artificial ties narrow the scope of personal freedom, but they are also, Burke realizes, the cement of social life. What he defends is an ideal of restrained energy, yet this does not imply a defense of moderation: "The space betwixt is but a mangled Scene, / Here the Extreams are Golden not the mean." Judgment informed by passion is the unshakable good that comes from friendship, and the trust it creates is a bulwark against insanity—above all, the insanity of attempting to serve as the judge in one's own cause. Indeed, the danger of the ever-present wish to act as the judge of oneself will become a central lesson of Burke's political writings. All his genius and all his art will be given to finding checks against that relentless motive of domination.

The Missing Years

The eight years between Edmund Burke's graduation from Trinity College in January 1749 and his public emergence in London starting in 1757 were called by Dixon Wecter "the missing years." Suppositions about this interval have gone under darker names. What is certain is that we know very little about Burke's life during this long and hidden apprenticeship. He said intriguingly of some months he spent with William Burke in Monmouth, in 1751, that their adventures "almost compose a novel."[24] The years 1752–1757 comprise the most obscure period: a single letter survives, torn and incomplete; we have a hint, in 1757, of a plan to immigrate to America, and that is all.

Recent and well-founded surmises by two scholars, Ian Crowe and Richard Bourke, have helped to fill out this picture. In *Patriotism and Public Spirit*, Crowe traces Burke's apprenticeship in political thought and writing to a specific milieu: Robert Dodsley's bookshop, Tully's Head, in Pall Mall. From strong evidence as well as inference, Crowe has been able to reconstruct an image of the young Burke in the early 1750s as someone well equipped to throw doubt on analogies between religion and politics, analogies of just the sort Pope and other legatees of Bolingbroke had taken on trust. In this view of his early career, the controversy over theatrical manners at Trinity College and a campaign of protest against the demagogy of the Dublin politician Charles Lucas combined to harden the weapons Burke would deploy in his earliest rhetorical battles. In a complementary finding, Richard Bourke has recovered, from a notebook containing draft materials by Burke, an unpublished essay that makes explicit, as early as 1757, Burke's defense of party. Already here, we see his definition of a political party as a group of men superior to the rewards of well-fed dependency and secret gifts; men associated in a public cause that is a natural outgrowth of long-standing divisions of public sentiment.[25]

For all the maturity of Burke's interest in politics in his twenties, it is known that he intended to practice law, as his father meant that he should. Yet by 1757, he had decided against that plan, giving up at once the pursuit of the law as a calling and any idea of returning to Ireland. The evidence suggests that his father felt the disappointment keenly and that, for many years after, they were hardly on speaking terms. Burke's own dissatisfactions with his abortive choice of a profession are reflected in an eloquent passage of his *Fragment on the Laws of England* (composed about 1757):

> The Law has been confined and drawn up into a narrow and inglorious study. And that, which should be the leading science in every well-ordered commonwealth, remained in all the barbarism of the rudest times, whilst every other advanced by rapid steps to the highest improvement, both in solidity and elegance; insomuch that the study of our jurisprudence presented to liberal and well-educated minds, even in the best Authors, hardly any thing but barbarous terms, ill explained; a coarse but not a plain expression; an indigested method; and a species of reasoning, the very refuse of the schools; which deduced the spirit of the Law, not from original justice or legal conformity, but from causes foreign to it, and altogether whimsical. Young men were sent away with an incurable, and if we regard the manner of handling rather than the substance, a very well-founded disgust.[26]

Though Burke is describing the study of law a century earlier, these sentences bristle with a resentment closer to home. In a letter to Joseph Emin, in August 1757, he called himself "a man of the Gown," but when he first met Emin by chance in St. James's Park, after hearing his story Burke had announced jauntily: "Sir, my name is Edmund Burke, at your service. I am a runaway son from a father, as you are."[27]

To become a man of letters was now his chief pursuit in life, and it marked his bearing in every company. Horace Walpole would describe Burke a few years later as someone "who has not worn off his authorism yet—and thinks there is nothing so charming as writers and to be one—he will know better one of these days."[28] He probably wrote a good deal anonymously, but he was careful to cover his tracks.

In April 1758, Burke contracted with Dodsley to produce the *Annual Register of the Year's Events*.[29] This was to be a historical and literary review that anthologized specimens of broad interest to an enlightened public. Two of its features, of particular importance to Burke, were the "historical article" on the previous year's political events (the size of a small book itself) and the book reviews (a few paragraphs of description followed by quotation at length). It is not certain for which volumes Burke wrote the historical article, but in the first five years of the *Annual Register*, he had the time as well as the interest and competence to do so; and his hand would certainly be present after 1765, when this section became a valuable instrument for conveying the Rockingham party's view of events. It is generally agreed that Burke wrote several book reviews in the first years of the *Register*. From internal as well as circumstantial evidence,[30] a few traits of Burke's editorial conduct may be inferred. His selection of books was discriminating, he sometimes used his platform to advance the literary fortunes of his friends, and his judgments were candid and perceptive.

Burke reviewed Samuel Johnson's *Rasselas, Prince of Abissinia* with a sympathetic understanding of its peculiar strengths:

the tale is not near so full of incidents, nor so diverting in itself, as the ingenious author, if he had not had higher views, might easily have made it; neither is the distinction of characters sufficiently attended to: but with these defects, perhaps no book ever inculcated a purer and sounder morality; no book ever made a more just estimate of human life, its pursuits, and its enjoyments. . . . The stile, which is peculiar and characteristical of the author, is lively, correct, and harmonious. It has however in a few places an air too exact and studied.

Johnson, in this novel, put into the mouth of the man of learning Imlac a good many aphorisms in his own style, pithy and yet balanced with a conscious sententiousness: "Human life is every where a state in which much is to be endured, and little to be enjoyed"; "If you are pleased with prognosticks of good, you will be terrified likewise with tokens of evil." This was a manner that Burke could also command but would never adopt as a method; prose, for him, should imitate the irregularity and exuberance of nature and not the uniformity of nature's laws.

In a review of Rousseau's *Letter to D'Alembert Concerning the Effects of Theatrical Entertainments*, Burke observes that an attack on the morals of theater comes as an anticlimax from an author who has already written against art and learning and against the very idea of society. Oddly and revealingly, Burke refers to Rousseau's *Discourse on the Sciences and Arts* and his *Discourse on Inequality* as "satires." Yet he places Rousseau at the head of the present generation in learning and talents, while noting, as a characteristic fault, "a tendency to paradox" along with "a splenetic disposition carried to misanthropy, and an austere virtue pursued to an unsociable fierceness." He calls the *Letter to D'Alembert* (the estimate is generous but accurate) "by far the most ingenious, spirited, and philosophical performance that ever appeared on theatrical entertainments"—adding by the way that "more good pieces have been written against the stage than in its favour."

Burke's praise is cooler, though his approval is firmer, when he comes to review Adam Smith's *Theory of Moral Sentiments*. "This author has struck out a new, and at the same time a perfectly natural road of speculation on this subject." He would tell Smith in a private letter that the *Moral Sentiments* savored too much of the study: it works up distinctions that are not in human nature. This was another way of saying that regular passions such as social sympathy and approval, rather than irregular passions such as love and hatred, formed the basis of Smith's understanding of morals. His theory is true, therefore, to the extent that such regular passions govern our loves and hates. To the extent they do not, the theory is inadequate. "The author seeks for the foundation of the just, the fit, the proper, the decent, in our most common and most allowed passions; and making approbation and disapprobation the tests of virtue and vice, and shewing that those are founded on sympathy, he raises from this simple truth, one of the most beautiful fabrics of moral theory, that has perhaps ever appeared." For Burke, the choice of the adjective *beautiful* to describe a philosophical argument must have meant to insinuate a polite question. Was Smith's theory perhaps more beautiful than true?

About the poetry of Ossian—the supposed translation by James Macpherson of a Celtic epic, already suspected of being a forgery—Burke writes as an admirer but with a major reservation. The impressiveness of the work, he thinks, does depend on its authenticity. The reality of the imagined objects in this case is a necessary proof of the feelings they evoke. If, he adds, the epic "should prove, after all, a modern composition; then would its faults admit of little extenuation, its beauties sink in that peculiar value which they derive from primitive simplicity; and the poem, however well imagined, and happily executed, and with all the merit of a fine original, be nevertheless esteemed but as a grand imposture." What is remarkable in this judgment is the romantic and historicist assumption that the quality of a performance depends on the associations which individual readers bring to it. We ourselves may vouch for the reality of our feelings; yet it matters to Burke that the associations be true.

He turned again to Rousseau in a review of *Emile*. This book has not, says Burke, the insipidness of most treatises on education. It is not commonplace: "To know what the received notions are upon any subject, is to know with certainty what those of Rousseau are not." Admitting that there are "very considerable parts that are impracticable, others that are chimerical; and not a few highly blameable, and dangerous both to piety and morals"—does he have in mind the profession of faith cleansed of miracle by the Savoyard Vicar?—Burke nonetheless admires *Emile* for its "thousand noble hints," which reflect "a profound knowledge of the human mind, and the order of its operations." The leading qualities of Rousseau's mind are "vivid imagination," "an animated, glowing, exuberant style," and "infinite spirit." Like all of Rousseau's writings, however, *Emile* suffers from one considerable fault: "He never knows where to stop."

A Vindication of Natural Society

Henry St. John, Lord Bolingbroke, was the intellectual leader of a set of dissident politicians and thinkers, at once aristocratic and libertarian, who first embodied in a coherent literature a reaction against the settlement of 1689. The junction of the Bolingbroke circle with established power was a finite episode in the reign of Queen Anne, but it might easily have lasted longer. In 1714, Bolingbroke engineered the fall of Robert Harley, Earl of Oxford, with whom he had served as secretary of state; and had the queen not died, he probably would have succeeded Oxford as head of the ministry. Bolingbroke was, in fact, a vehemently anti-Christian Deist who in office catered to Tory extremists; but the ascendancy of Robert Walpole, during much of the reigns of George I and George II, witnessed the decline of his group into standard-bearers of an honorific and ideal opposition. Yet these men defined an important aspect of what came to be called "the country party": an opposition whose line of descent reached back to the republican writings of James Harrington.[31] When Bolingbroke's reputation prospered, in his earlier years, Pope was the great man of the circle, and yet Bolingbroke himself was something just as consequential: their cherished and never-to-be-anointed statesman. Remote from power in the latter part of his career—in 1715 he had followed the Pretender in his flight to France—Bolingbroke went on refining, to an inside audience, his stratagems for the attainment of a politics beyond party. He carried out the task in a petulant-polished manner that was congenial to the vanity of an excluded elite. His commonest trick of argument was to appeal from the miscellaneous data of history and practical experience to the irrefutable edicts of theory. Rational theory, which had its religious correlative in deism, was shown to make the relevant deductions about society and morality from the transparent knowledge of a universal Nature. When David Mallet in 1754 printed Bolingbroke's unpublished philosophical essays, their undermining attacks on orthodox Christianity and on organized religion generally revived his fame as a center of public controversy.[32] Dr. Johnson, prompted by Boswell, said of Bolingbroke, "Sir, he was a scoundrel, and a coward: a scoundrel, for charging a blunderbuss against religion and morality; a coward, because he had not the resolution to fire it off himself, but left half a crown to a beggarly Scotchman, to draw the trigger after his death." Before pronouncing, Johnson did not take the trouble to look into the new writings, the "wild and pernicious ravings" as Boswell called them, which "gave great offense to all well-principled men." Sound opinion had settled its score with Bolingbroke long ago.

Yet, for Burke, coming of age in the late 1740s and early 1750s, Bolingbroke's public character was hedged about with a good deal of implicit awe. We are apt to forget this under the influence of Burke's own mocking question in *Reflections on the Revolution in France*, "Who now reads Bolingbroke?" In the years after 1754, many people did, as they had read him a generation earlier. Montesquieu was influenced by his anti-parochial ideas of civility and prudence, and Montesquieu was the writer on politics whom Burke admired above all others. Burke, too, read Bolingbroke. He was still taking him seriously in 1770 when he published his own book about the duties of political opposition, *Thoughts on the Cause of the Present Discontents*. That manifesto of the Rockingham Whigs, Harvey Mansfield has suggested,[33] began as a reply to Bolingbroke's *Dissertation upon Parties*. Where Bolingbroke had run together the neutral term *party* and the pejorative *faction* and denounced both in the name of rational consensus, Burke would offer a defense of party itself as a cure for selfish ambition and the mania of political idealism. Party in Burke's view, as we shall see, came to appear the remedy best adapted to the diseases of political activity. By deriving a coherent policy from agreement within a representative group, a party becomes the pattern of a fidelity to *principle* that includes the defense of *interests*. The most elemental difference between Burke and Bolingbroke will prove to be that, for Burke, principle and interest need not denote opposite things.

In 1756, Burke published anonymously *A Vindication of Natural Society:* an all-out parody of Bolingbroke. It is a curious performance in several respects. The thesis is that society, as it exists at present, corrupts human life and deters us from the guidance of nature and reason that is sufficient for the attainment of general prosperity and harmony. Natural society thus presents itself as the ideal opposite of the forms of artificial society that have flourished and decayed in Greece, Rome, and Christian Europe. The screen of anonymity allowed Burke to insinuate, by the manner of the writing, that the narrator of his pamphlet was a complacent optimist a good deal like Bolingbroke. The narrator asks his readers to deplore the past ages in which Man has been the creature of artificial society and invites them to embrace a future that will restore our "natural" state.[34] This is Bolingbroke raised to the second power.

The device of rigging a public exposure by having the contents of a satire spoken by the person satirized had been used by Swift, among others. Like Swift's *Modest Proposal* and like his *Argument against Abolishing Christianity,* Burke's *Vindication of Natural Society* is a utopian hoax—a mock proposal by a mad projector, which explodes the doctrine of natural society by displaying an excess of credulity toward the favorite topics and commonplaces of that system. Yet there is something strange in the mixture. The *Vindication* offered so finished an imitation of Bolingbroke's style—the cartoon of the master's vices was drawn out by such insensible gradations—that it could be mistaken for a lately recovered work by Lord Bolingbroke himself. There is a tradition that Mallet, the executor of Bolingbroke's literary estate, "went to Dodsley's, when filled with literati, purposely to disavow" the book.[35] Burke (unlike Swift and Pope in a similar situation) did not try to prolong the joke; and he certainly did intend the *Vindication* as a parody. Yet parody is an ambiguous genre. By 1761, Burke was known to Horace Walpole as "a young Mr Burk, who wrote a book in the style of Bolingbroke."[36] Disciple, imitator, or mocker? Walpole may not have been sure which. Even a reader familiar with the range of Burke's styles cannot shake the suspicion that he was here involved in an experiment with his own views as much as Bolingbroke's.

The book has a charmless sangfroid. Why, one wonders, does it push to such convincing lengths its thesis that Nature provides the standard against which society must be condemned? Why ridicule a doctrine you have taken the trouble almost to persuade your readers of? It is true that this way of appealing to nature and reason was in the air—Rousseau's *Discourse on Inequality* had appeared two years before, and it is possible that Burke's target in the *Vindication* was Rousseau as much as Bolingbroke. Even supposing that to be so, a doubt remains whether the speculations Burke satirized, on the uses of nature as a standard for society, are not speculations that he in part espoused. Is the *Vindication* the anatomy of an error, or the exposure of a truth made wrong by fanaticism?

Burke goes far to undermine his own belief in nature by making the appeal in Bolingbroke's accent and by caricaturing the bland self-assurance of his delivery. The pamphlet, in this sense, is an act of literary as well as moral criticism: it shows how Bolingbroke would have spoiled the argument. Yet the cover of anonymity seems to have encouraged Burke to find the wisdom in a paradox to which he was receptive in some degree. It may be fairest to consider the result, as originally published, a "test" whose effects Burke did not mean to answer for. Read without irony, the book was a major influence on William Godwin, the radical theorist of the 1790s who traced his doctrine of rational reform to the *Vindication* (along with two other works that Godwin read straight, Plato's *Republic* and Book 4 of *Gulliver's Travels*). To judge by the evidence of echo and paraphrase, Burke's argument also influenced Thomas Paine. It could hardly have had the effects it did a generation later if such readers did not feel that the author was half in earnest.

The *Vindication* proposes as self-evident truths a number of axioms to which Burke might provisionally have assented. For example: the reasons we give for an action are related to our inward nature, to the way we are constituted as finite beings. Or again: a moral agent in a given situation can strip away the adventitious layers of circumstance, plot the relations between possible causes and the most desired consequences, and determine the right course of action. Up to a point, these dicta merely express a truth of common sense; and utilitarian philosophers have credited a version of them ever since Hartley and Helvetius traced the workings of the mind to the laws of association. The *Vindication*, however, makes the case for moral action on more purely rational grounds; and this is where the opportunities for ridicule open up. The anonymous narrator simply asserts that there is an unchanging natural law, that this law regulates moral conduct, and that human beings have immediate access to it through introspection.

Summarized thus, the premises of the *Vindication* seem a travesty of science. Yet, in the book itself, the hum of a conciliating style wraps the doctrine in a wadding of affability and good sense: "Many Things have been said, and very well undoubtedly, on the Subjection in which we should preserve our Bodies to the Government of our Understanding; but enough has not been said upon the Restraint which our bodily Necessities ought to lay on the extravagant Sublimities, and excentrick Rovings of our Minds. The Body, or as some love to call it, our inferior Nature, is wiser in its own plain Way, and attends its own Business more directly than the Mind with all its boasted Subtilty."[37] The narrator goes on to assert that moral virtue is innate, that it comes from an absolute knowledge of what is right, and that it can therefore have no relation to custom, experience, or training in ordinary life. Bigots and enthusiasts may

> argue against a fair Discussion of popular Prejudices, because, say they, tho' they would be found without any reasonable Support, yet the Discovery might be productive of the most dangerous Consequences. Absurd and blasphemous Notion! As if all Happiness was not connected with the Practice of Virtue, which necessarily depends upon the Knowledge of Truth; that is, upon the Knowledge of those unalterable Relations which Providence has ordained that every thing should bear to every other. These Relations, which are Truth itself, the Foundation of Virtue, and consequently, the only Measures of Happiness, should be likewise the only Measures by which we should direct our Reasoning. To these we should conform in good Earnest; and not think to force Nature, and the whole Order of her System, by a Compliance with our Pride, and Folly, to conform to our artificial Regulations.[38]

Two axioms that the passages above take for granted—the unqualified authority of reason and its ability to discover truth from perspicuous evidence of the mind and body—are all the narrator needs to clinch his defense of natural society.

The trouble is that his defense of natural morality entails an attack on all education, all acquired virtue and wisdom, and the experience by which practical wisdom is arrived at. If it were true that our ideas occur in simple conformity to physical stimuli, then what we learn artificially could only distort what we know immediately through Nature. Again, if the "unalterable Relations of Things" render futile every human effort to change or reform those relations, it must follow that intuition is superior to educated judgment. What we may call history or reality or the conditions of life— all this becomes a distorting medium that only obscures the truth of Reason. In the argument from Bolingbroke that Burke here ventriloquizes, history and experience are an obstacle that stands in the way of nature.

Nothing could be more remote from the habits of mind of the later Burke. For him, "art is man's nature." He thinks of nature as a tendency always modified by human adaptation; "artificial," in his usage, can never be assumed to be a pejorative epithet. Indeed, society is artificial, not natural, once it has adapted itself to changing mores and once morality is understood as a structure of greater complexity than a chain of answers to questions put by reason. This much Burke expects his readers to see for themselves. By forcing us to recover the common defense of artificial society that the *Vindication* suppresses, his satire may sharpen our awareness of the characteristic weaknesses of theories based on natural rights and on utility. Both sorts of theory promise a transparency in the grounds of moral reasoning that artificial society can never supply.

Yet Burke in the *Vindication* has still another target: "natural religion." The enlightened faith of natural religion holds that the uniformities underlying various codes of ethics point to a truth shared by all religions once they are cleared of revelation. His aim, Burke would say in a preface to the second edition of the *Vindication*, was to demonstrate that the very arguments by which natural religion had been proved superior to institutional religion could also be taken to show that natural society is superior to artificial society. And more: "The same Engines which were employed for the Destruction of Religion, might be employed with equal Success for the Subversion of Government."[39] One thing only Burke must assume if his satire and incidental observations are to convince: namely, that his readers admit the good of religion and society, and are wary of any idealism that would cancel the adequate embodiments of religion and society in the world.

The *Vindication* accordingly has the shape of an *a fortiori* argument. If its satire holds true of projectors about religion, it will be so much the truer of projectors about society. Burke would have recognized a strong anticipation of his strategy here in Swift's *Abolishing Christianity*. The Christianity of the Gospels, Swift pretended to believe, was too difficult a model for human conduct, but the case for abolishing Christianity on grounds of convenience had been overdrawn.[40] Total abolition would be attended by greater inconveniences than preservation of the religion on the terms allowed by an enlightened age. Swift's was an oblique proof of the hazards of judging the good of religion by criteria relating to mere expedience or utility. So, too, with Burke on natural religion and natural society: if you suppose it wrong for religious projectors to tamper with the fear of God, how much worse the offense when political speculators undermine the fear of man.

Success in such an indirect argument, of course, presumes a high degree of stability in the society the author addresses. Yet stability is an ideal notion: we may suppose that social cohesion is always crystallized gradually, but as J. H. Plumb remarked, it may appear to solidify in a society from one moment to the next, as water at a certain temperature turns to ice. The consensus Burke was counting on did not feel like thin ice in the 1750s. Things looked different by the 1770s and 1780s; and this may account for the enthusiastic misreading of his pamphlet by radicals of the later period. If they had read Burke in line with his intentions, his satire against natural society and natural religion would have seemed merely complacent. Burke's moral criticism also came to appear ambiguous because, a generation later, natural religion was a harmless orthodoxy. In the writings of Diderot and Condorcet, and of Catharine Macaulay and Joseph Priestley, the idea of "natural society" by then had also lost its air of paradox. Though Burke could not have secured his intended meaning against changes of this magnitude, the puzzle remains. With what levity he tempts his reader to try the effects of an inadvisable experiment!

This lightness or archness is produced in part by a style of eloquent certainty—a style of which Burke was sometimes a dangerous master (whether using his own voice or imitating someone else's). But the stylistic traits of Bolingbroke are scarcely separable from his rationalist assumptions; and the pressure Burke puts on that discovery enables him to slide over narrative stretches composed almost entirely of topical cant. The primary assumption that he associates with Bolingbroke is that facts do not matter. Reason can show how any historical narrative would have run if the characters operated as they ought to. For "every man's reason is every man's oracle," wrote Bolingbroke, and he added: "this oracle is best consulted in the silence of retirement"[41]—not, that is, under the scrutiny of public debate. Retirement also meant in this context a fastidious unconcern with facts.

Here is Burke's parody of the historian Bolingbroke consulting his rational oracle:

> It is a cheap Calculation to say, that the *Persian* Empire in its Wars, against the *Greeks,* and *Scythians,* threw away at least four Millions of its Subjects, to say nothing of its other Wars, and the Losses sustained in them. These were their Losses abroad; but the War was brought home to them, first by *Agesilaus,* and afterwards, by *Alexander.* I have not, in this Retreat, the Books necessary to make very exact Calculations; nor is it necessary to give more than Hints to one of your Lordship's Erudition. You will recollect his uninterrupted Series of Success. You will run over his Battles. You will call to mind the Carnage which was made. You will give a Glance of the Whole, and you will agree with me; that to form this Hero no less than twelve hundred thousand Lives must have been sacrificed.[42]

"Nor is it necessary," "to say nothing of," "you will agree with me," "at least," "must have been"—the phrases are all aglow with the confidence of a mind governed by words and indifferent to things.

A second assumption of Bolingbroke's which Burke takes pains to discredit is that history is nothing but philosophy teaching by example. "It is right, no doubt," D. G. James has commented on this element of Bolingbroke's stance, "to want to be 'philosophical'; but you are no more a philosopher for denying that historians have a right to exist."[43] Bolingbroke granted himself a free hand with facts, in accordance with the discretion of reason, and the soothing flow of his narrative manner was a natural consequence. So Burke's parody has Bolingbroke say of Judea that, though the nation may seem "a very inconsiderable Spot of the Earth in itself," yet

> this Spot happened, it matters not here by what means, to become at several times extremely populous, and to supply Men for Slaughters scarcely credible, if other well-known and well-attested ones had not given them a Colour. The first settling of the *Jews* here, was attended by an almost entire Extirpation of all the former Inhabitants. Their own civil Wars, and those with their petty Neighbours, consumed vast Multitudes almost every Year for several Centuries; and the Irruptions of the Kings of *Babylon* and *Assyria* made immense Ravages. Yet we have their History but partially, in an indistinct confused manner; so that I shall only throw the strong Point of Light upon that Part which coincides with *Roman* History, and of that Part only on the Point of Time when they received the great and final Stroke which made them no more a Nation; a Stroke which is allowed to have cut off little less than two Millions of that People. I say nothing of the Loppings made from that Stock whilst it stood; nor from the Suckers that grew out of the old Root ever since.[44]

"It matters not here by what means," "It is a cheap Calculation"—in phrases like these, Bolingbroke's trust in the priority of reason is seen to work hand in hand with his belief in the hollowness of facts. Symptoms of his drawling suavity ("Loppings," "Suckers," "the old Root") are shown by Burke to be exactly on a par with the false precision of his estimates. The effect is to display the refinement and carelessness that together form the essence of Bolingbroke's literary manner.

Enough has been shown of Burke's parody to warrant some extracts from Bolingbroke himself. *Letters on the Study and Use of History* is a probable source, as F. P. Lock has argued;[45] but we may begin with his *Dissertation upon Parties,* a treatise Burke is likely to have known (*Thoughts on the Cause of the Present Discontents* seems designed to refute it). Speaking of the complaints against party feeling among those who fomented the Monmouth rebellion, the actual Bolingbroke quoted a passage from Algernon Sidney and commented: "I could easily multiply proofs of this kind; but I think I need not take any pains to show that there was such a faction formed at this time."[46] He spares his reader the tedium of printed accounts to support his assertion that the parties of the 1680s were masks for selfish interests, with "whigs very often under the tory standard, tories very often under the whig standard." Instead, the burden of proof is transferred to common knowledge and the author's probity: "This general representation, which I have made of the state of parties at the revolution, is, I am verily persuaded, exactly just; and it might be supported by many particular proofs, which I chose rather to suggest than to mention."[47] One can see the justice of the comment on Bolingbroke by Leslie Stephen: "Pedantic in his style, he has yet an indiscriminating hatred for that laborious investigation of facts by which pedants have laid a sound foundation for more scientific methods."[48] Modern readers may bear this warning in mind when they hear Burke dismissed as an "irrationalist." Burke was in fact a defender of reason so sure of its value that he hated to see it counterfeited.

Yet, some way under the surface, we may be struck by an affinity between Burke and Bolingbroke. Both believe that governments exist for the sake of the public good, and that the public good is to be reckoned by a standard of common utility. Bolingbroke's *Idea of a Patriot King,* which Burke would have disdained for its spurious attack on the divisiveness of parties, argues for the utility of monarchy on the very grounds of precedent and convenience that Burke would later make his own. The *Patriot King* also derives a proper loyalty to governors (again in a way that anticipates Burke) from our duty to obey two laws: the universal law of reason and the particular constitution of laws by which a given community elects to be governed. The manners and practices of a community, says Bolingbroke, supervene upon and modify the law of reason; so that the acknowledgment of Divine Right, for example, is always interpreted through the laws of the community and its beliefs about governing well. Here again the later Burke would have agreed. Custom, says Bolingbroke, gives sufficient support to the reverence owed to majesty, for "Majesty is not an inherent, but a reflected light." It follows that hereditary and elective monarchies "are sacred alike, and this attitude is to be ascribed, or not ascribed, to them, as they answer, or do not answer, the ends of their institution."[49] One may thus reasonably prefer a monarchy to a republic because its very simplicity renders monarchy the more susceptible to reform.

"When monarchy is the essential form," Bolingbroke concludes, "it may be more easily and more usefully tempered with aristocracy, or democracy, or both, than either of them, when they are the essential forms, can be tempered with monarchy." Burke mentions this passage appreciatively in the second half of the *Reflections,* where his subject is the inutility of democracy as the *basis* of a mixed constitution; and Bolingbroke continues the thought in a manner suggesting that Burke was right to suppose him a useful ally: "very considerable aristocratical and democratical powers may be grafted on a monarchical stock, without diminishing the lustre, or restraining the power and authority of the prince, enough to alter in any degree the essential form."[50] If anything separates Bolingbroke from Burke on this point of constitutional prudence, it is the amount of credulity Bolingbroke packs into a phrase like "essential form." Yet echoes of Bolingbroke in the later Burke show that the satirical edge of the *Vindication* is not an adequate index of Burke's thinking. An awkward fact thus presents itself to an interpreter of this enigmatic book. Burke's ventriloquized attack on artificial society (for all its extravagance) carries conviction: a kind of conviction superior to Bolingbroke's but not incompatible with his doctrine of natural society. Actual sympathy cuts through the pretense of ironic detachment when Burke allows the narrator of the *Vindication* to plead for compassion toward the poor. Even here, it might be argued, Burke is throwing his voice; yet the voice we hear is in some sense his own; and the plea is not ludicrous. It seems a truth of rhetoric that there are certain jokes that cannot be told in jest—or rather, truths whose telling in a comic frame only the callous will interpret jokingly.

What are we to make of the passage near the end of the *Vindication* where Burke describes the sufferings of those whom artificial society has made wretched?

A Constitution of Things this, strange and ridiculous beyond Expression. We scarce believe a thing when we are told it, which we actually see before our Eyes every Day without being in the least surprised. I suppose that there are in *Great-Britain* upwards of an hundred thousand People employed in Lead, Tin, Iron, Copper, and Coal Mines; these unhappy Wretches scarce ever see the Light of the Sun; they are buried in the Bowels of the Earth; there they work at a severe and dismal Task, without the least Prospect of being delivered from it; they subsist upon the coarsest and worst sort of Fare; they have their Health miserably impaired, and their Lives cut short, by being perpetually confined in the close Vapour of these malignant Minerals. An hundred thousand more at least are tortured without Remission by the suffocating Smoak, intense Fires, and constant Drudgery necessary in refining and managing the Products of those Mines. . . . But this Number, considerable as it is, and the Slavery, with all its Baseness and Horror, which we have at home, is nothing to what the rest of the World affords of the same Nature.[51]

The narrator (we may admit) is the fictional carrier of a hoax. Still, what could it mean to deny that these are conditions that cry out for remedy? Burke's parody has become a medium in which every resonant saying of the narrator is discredited in advance. Yet by these words we are moved. The passage confronts the reader with a dilemma that will become familiar in the writings of Burke, often when he writes as a satirist and occasionally when he writes in earnest. Through his own exertions, we find our feelings turned in a direction he has taught us to distrust.[52]

Suppose someone you believe to be a scoundrel breaks his usual demeanor and imparts a touching confidence, which he begs you to use with delicacy. It is like that with Burke's narrator. The serial litanies of barefaced assertion and empty hypothesis have inoculated us against anything he could possibly say. Then comes the reversal: a picture of men suffocating in the coal mines with nothing to alleviate their lot. Our emotions are at a standoff, and the narrator is no help. Such a literary exercise might be taken as a sort of therapy against false feeling, a limit case that shows the difficulty of not being wrongly moved. But this pedagogic solution explains away the problem. The truth is that Burke has recruited for the project of reform, which he aims to discredit, some part of our moral self-respect, our esteem of ourselves as sympathetic persons. The project belongs to the ventriloquized narrator and not to Edmund Burke, or so we had thought. Yet it is as if the projector of A Modest Proposal had listed among the motives for his enterprise the piteous spectacle of impoverished women living in vagrancy; and as if he did so, not as Swift did, at the start of the pamphlet but rather at its climax and with irresistible eloquence. What would we say in that case about his detailed suggestion that the cooking of infants makes "a most delicious, nourishing, and wholesome food, whether stewed, roasted, baked, or boiled, and I make no doubt that it will equally serve in a fricassee or a ragout"? In the altered proportions of such a work, Swift's extravagant satire would cease to be intelligible as satire.

I do not mean to suggest that Burke's parody, which leans so perilously both ways, ends by tipping over and adopting the point of view it has satirized. But it comes close. For more than moments, havoc is played with the relaxed rhythm of attention by which we were reassured. The ironic frame seems to have been forgotten and the rogue elements of the story are free to pasture. We will confront this phenomenon in other writings by Burke that are neither framed nor intended as parodies.

So one may look back on certain passages of the *Vindication* with a hilarity tinged by doubt. For example: to raise sympathy for someone (says the narrator), you should speak of him not as a person who is French or English but as "a *Foreigner,* an Accident to which all are liable. You would represent him as a *Man;* one partaking with us of the same common Nature, and subject to the same Law. There is something so averse from our Nature in these artificial political Distinctions, that we need no other Trumpet to kindle us to War, and Destruction. But there is something so benign and healing in the general Voice of Humanity, that maugre all our Regulations to prevent it, the simple Name of Man applied properly, never fails to work a salutary Effect."[53] The observation is too pleased with itself to give much pleasure, and the sentiment it conveys was already hackneyed in Pope's *Essay on Man.* Yet, for readers prepared to assent to the idea of a common nature—as many would in Burke's time, and many would today—human dignity appears admirably vindicated by the narrator's advice.

Burke's preface (added the year after the first edition) tries to prevent a wrong interpretation by referring to "an Under-plot, of more Consequence than the apparent Design." His intent had been, he says, by drawing out the reader's natural credulity to show the seductiveness and absurdity of a certain idiom of speculation. The apparent design of the book, its affirmation of one unchanging human nature and reason, will, Burke hopes, be refuted by every reader's experience of the mind of another person or another culture, "whenever we examine the Result of a Reason which is not our own." He thus implies that reason varies as society varies: neither can be supposed to have a substantial nature apart from its costume. Yet the trick may have worked too well. The idea that elementary relations of nature, available to the understanding, can dictate a plan of action by "naked and moderate calculation" carries an appeal that is almost impervious to mockery.

Probably Burke had hoped to control his ambiguities beyond the reach of doubt. To explode a fallacy by giving a bad speaker good arguments or a good speaker bad arguments, and yet to remain a secure guide to the listener's response—Burke in some moods thought this was possible, and the fact shows how deep was his own faith in reason. But the *Vindication* for its part suggests how uncertain a guardian reason may become when the feelings of the audience are startled into impassioned response. Consider a last illustration: "The Monarchic, Aristocratical, and Popular Partizans have been jointly laying their Axes to the Root of all Government, and have in their Turns proved each other absurd and inconvenient. In vain you tell me that Artificial Government is good, but that I fall out only with the Abuse. The Thing! the Thing itself is the Abuse!"[54] What must have been Burke's emotion thirty-five years later when he cast his eye on the page of *Rights of Man* in which the author asks whether the violence of the mob that stormed the Bastille was really the fault of the mob. Paine there took up the cry of *A Vindication of Natural Society:* "From whom do they learn these dreadful vices? They learn them from their governments. Lay then the axe to the root, and teach governments humanity." Other unexpected voices would return to echo the *Vindication* as time went on. William Cobbett, whose youth coincided with the old age of Burke, would nickname the English social establishment "The Thing."

One may feel after several readings that the *Vindication* is a medicine that must be judged chiefly by its effects. Burke, in this early book, was attempting to work out to their full extent certain doubts about the present ordering of society, which he partly shared; the first corroborating evidence, in his own voice, would be the unpublished *Fragments of a Tract*

Relative to the Laws against Popery in Ireland, which he drafted in 1762. One comes to see there and elsewhere that Burke, like the narrator of the *Vindication,* held the Enlightenment belief that right and wrong are not a matter of "geographical morality," with different moral laws according to place and preference. So this shallow narrator teaches over his head; and his wisdom often enough resembles Burke's. Like many eighteenth-century works whose genre evades description—*The Beggar's Opera, A Sentimental Journey, A Tale of a Tub*—Burke's *Vindication of Natural Society* is an experiment in honest observation and ridicule. Taken as a *reductio ad absurdum* of rationalist social theory, it does not quite come off. Parody of this kind is "a dangerous weapon," remarked Stephen, "which is apt to go off at both ends." As for those of his listeners who were lured into the game only to be rebuked for having mistaken its rules, at what point do they cease to be spectators and become partisans? And (the equivocal text of the *Vindication* obliges us to ask): partisans of what cause?

Jane Nugent

About the time Burke was seeing the *Vindication* through press, he was courting the daughter of Dr. Christopher Nugent, an amiable and respected physician in Bath; and on March 12, 1757, he married Jane Mary Nugent. The Burke household in London—before the purchase in 1768 of Gregories, a 600-acre estate near Beaconsfield—was graciously run and accommodated with ease the comings and goings of friends and members of both families. Dr. Nugent lived there for a time. So did Burke's friend Will and Jane's brother Jack, as well as Burke's own brother Richard, who came over from Ireland.

Early in their time together, Edmund made this portrait in prose of Jane:[55]

> She is handsome, but it is a Beauty not arising from features, from Complexion and Shape; She has all these in an high degree, but whoever looks at her never perceives them, nor makes them the Topic of his Praise. 'tis all the Sweetness of Temper, Benevolence, Innocence and Sensibility, which a face can express, that forms her beauty—

She has a face, that just raises your attention at first sight; it grows on you every moment, & you wonder it did no more than raise your Attention at first.—

Her Eyes have a mild light, but they awe you when she pleases; they command like a good man out of office, not by Authority but by virtue—

Her features are not perfectly regular; this Sort of Exactness is more to be praised than loved, it is never animated—

Her Stature is not tall she is not to be the admiration of every body, but the happiness of one.

She has all the Delicacy that does not Exclude firmness—

She has all the softness that does not imply weakness.

There is often more of the Coquet shewn in an Affected plainness, than a Tawdry finery; she is always clean without preciseness or affectation—

Her Gravity is a gentle thoughtfulness that Softens the features without discomposing them, she is usually grave—

Her Smiles are———inexpressible—

Her Voice is a low, Soft musick; not form'd to rule in publick Assemblies, but to charm those who can distinguish a Company from a Croud. It has this advantage you must come Close to hear it.

To describe her body, describe her mind, one is the Transcript of the other.

Her understanding is not Shewn in the Variety of matters it exerts itself on, but the goodness of the Choice she makes.

She does not Shew it so much in doing or Saying striking things, as in avoiding such as she ought not to say or do—

She discovers the right from the wrong in things not by reasoning but Sagacity—

Most women and many good ones have a Closeness & something Selfish in their Disposition, she has a true generosity of Temper; the most extravagant cannot be more willing to give; the most Covetous, not more Cautious to whom they give.

No person of so few years can know the world better; no person was ever less corrupted by that knowledge.—

Her politeness seems to flow rather from a natural disposition to oblige, than from any rules on that subject, and therefore never fails to Strike those who understand good breeding, and those who do not—

> She does not run with a Girlish eagerness into new friendships; which
> as they have no foundation in reason, only tend to multiply and imbitter
> disputes; 'tis long before she chuses, but then it is fix'd for ever.[56]

The delicacy of the portrait speaks for itself. One may compare Burke's
with other sketches of the kind—on the eighteenth-century stage they are
a property as common as fans—but no other rises above conventional sentiment quite as this does. The sketch, like its model (one feels), is unusual
in its reserve. It is also remarkable that this portrait refuses to draw a line
between friendship and love. The feminine qualities of Jane Nugent are
caught and admired, yet little is made of the customary distinction between virtue in a man and virtue in a woman. To say that her integrity
resembles "a good man out of office" plays against expectation in a way
that is disarming as well as minutely revealing: only Burke would have
said it like that. Reason and intuition are joined in the woman he describes, but the quality we are shown unforgettably is her power to inspire
affection, a devotion that has no wish to harness her beauty or virtue for
some useful purpose. As for her judgment, it is plain that her experience
has only deepened a principle that was already unshakable.

The real-life model of Burke's portrait compels a respect that he turns
to deference. "Her voice was ever gentle, soft and low, an excellent thing
in woman"—Lear's words about Cordelia receive a distant echo here, to
remind us of the world of chivalry and Kent's mysterious pledge: "You
have that in your countenance which I would fain call master." This is a
truth of her character felt by the refined and the rude, by "those who understand good breeding" and those who, from her example, may begin to
understand it. Burke thinks and feels already as a defender of the chivalric
ethic of courage tamed by beauty. Indeed, the words of the portrait hold a
large clue to the Romantic element in his political thought: his belief in
the force of untaught feelings, of "wisdom without reflection." Jane Nugent
in this portrait owns such feelings herself and conveys the knowledge of
them to others. Yet she differs from her predecessors in chivalric literature. The woman portrayed here by Burke stands level with the observer.
It is not a portrait of a lady but a woman drawn from ordinary life. You
must come close to hear her voice.

Burke would always have the capacity to speak and feel in a calmer register than the grand style permitted; and it is the alternation of such separate modes of feeling that best captures the depth and energy of his mind. He can say of the queen of France in 1790 (in the gravest of ceremonial tones) that she bears "the whole weight of her accumulated wrongs, with a serene patience, in a manner suited to her rank and race." Yet he can reflect, in the midst of the public calamity of the Gordon Riots, when he talks to people in the streets: "I think the far greater part of those, whom I saw, were rather dissolute and unruly, than very ill-disposed. I even found friends and well wishers amongst the blue cockades." How to explain the confidence with which he passes between responses so different in kind? "The characters of nature," Burke would write in his preface to the second edition of the *Sublime and Beautiful,* "are legible it is true; but they are not plain enough to enable those who run, to read them." His thoughts were always fast paced, and yet he makes us aware of the necessary pauses to read "the characters of nature." In his first great book, he will present himself as a master psychologist of art and manners, an interpreter qualified by training and sensibility to render those characters legible.

❧ II ❧

The Sublime and Beautiful

CRITICISM in the mid-eighteenth century was deeply interested in the influence of taste on morals: a delicate taste was felt to imply a high average of personal conduct. The French word *moeurs* suggests this relationship better than any English word, and the connection between politeness and policy offers another clue. Underlying such parallels is a concern with *proportion* as the guide of action. Proportion, in the ethical realm, is prudence. Yet the laws of proportion, which answer to neoclassical ideas of regularity and decorum, had been challenged as far back as Joseph Addison's *Spectator* No. 412: "Our imagination loves to be filled with an object, or to grasp at anything that is too big for its capacity."[1] Addison's leading example is a dome, but the context shows that he has in mind any object too large to be held by the retina, or any object partly hidden from view so that an aspect of the image must be supplied by imagination. Hume in his *Dissertation of the Passions* took a step further in characterizing the mind's fascination with things half shown and half implied: "Nothing more powerfully excites any affection than to conceal some part of its objects, by throwing it into a kind of shade, which, at the same time, that it shows enough to prepossess us in favour of the object, leaves still some work for the imagination. Besides, that obscurity is always attended with a kind of uncertainty; the effort, which the fancy makes to compleat the idea, rouzes the spirits, and gives an additional force to the passion."[2] To trace the implications of such a remark is to recognize an emerging conflict in the mid-eighteenth century between aesthetics and morality. Taste, like morality, aims to methodize and regulate. But if, as Hume says, the mind is always stretching to feel what it does not comprehend and is naturally charmed by things that evade the understanding, it is not clear that much can be done to save the idea of informed admiration. It appears on the contrary that the instinct that informs our fascination with certain people or sensations or works of art finally resists analysis.

The radical challenge posed by art to human understanding was ignored by a long line of distinguished writers on taste. Montesquieu and Voltaire, Lord Kames and Adam Smith, all took their turns at the subject and all associated the rule of taste with civility, progress, and refinement. Alexander Gerard's *Essay on Taste,* which contains the most thorough and sensitive discussion Burke is likely to have come across, had described sublimity as an expansion of the mind along a predictable path toward a limit determined by the size of the object. Aesthetic admiration, for Gerard, merges with a "noble pride" that is assimilable to such worldly feelings as ambition. In a typical refinement of his theory, Gerard asserts that the moral sense "claims a *joint authority* with the other principles of Taste" and then adds conscientiously: "Nay our moral sense claims authority *superior* to all the rest."[3] The premise of his analysis is that taste is "of a progressive nature." So, the fascination of sublime objects is linked to moral education: "The mind acquires a habit of enlarging itself to recieve the sentiment of sublimity, by being accustomed to expand its faculties to the dimensions of a large object."[4] A pedagogic purpose can be felt in the turn given to the words *enlarging* and *large:* largeness of mind, magnanimity, the ability to take long views, all are thought to derive from the habit of looking at large objects. A correct taste may thus resemble polished manners: it leads to the prizing of objects at their true value, which is their conventional value. And the result of enforcing this understanding is a pattern of conduct and judgment beneficial to society. "Vice is often promoted by taste ill formed or wrong applied," says Gerard. "Let taste be rendered correct and just, vice will be almost extinguished." When we cast our eye on the crimes or abuses of common life, we see that "most wrong passions may be traced up to some perversion of taste."[5]

The originality of Burke on the sublime was to reject utterly the connections between sublimity, good taste, probity, and sanity. His originality was so marked that many of his contemporaries, as well as commentators in later periods, have chosen to misunderstand his argument rather than confront his radical surmise about the emotions associated with art and their possibly tenuous connection to morals.

There is, however, one earlier writer on the arts who anticipates Burke's skepticism. The Abbé Du Bos began his *Réflexions Critiques sur la Poésie et sur la Peinture* with the remark that all didactic justification of the arts is defeated by the nature of our interest in particular works of art: "One notices every day that poems and pictures cause a sensible pleasure, but it is difficult to explain in what that pleasure consists, which often resembles pain, and whose symptoms are sometimes identical with those of the deepest suffering. The art of poetry and the art of painting are never more applauded than when they cause us pain."[6] So the motives that lead us to admire works of art also drive us away from regulating the passions that a theorist like Gerard had supposed would obey a well-formed taste. As Du Bos puts it: "the pleasing charm of emotion cancels the first principles of humanity in the most polite and most tender-hearted nations; and obliterates, in people of the greatest christianity spirit, the most evident maxims of their religion."[7] Human beings have an irreducible love of sensation that may cancel morality, and "the greater the need, the sharper is the pleasure of satisfying it."[8] Du Bos asserts the prevalence of an instinct that prompts exposure to objects and feelings which bring no benefit to ourselves. This hunger for the sharpest stimulus—a love of sensations for their own sake—may occupy an outer edge of conscious experience, but it is known to everyone. The arts, Du Bos suspects, more than any other domain of human experience, exist to satisfy that hunger. Whether the power of art can be characterized as moral has become to him a matter of some doubt.[9]

Here, perhaps, lies the largest separable motive for the argument Burke eventually made in *A Philosophical Enquiry into the Origin of Our Ideas of the Sublime and Beautiful*. Du Bos went a long way on a negative path; and Burke must have been glad of the company. Yet Burke will go much further than Du Bos to associate the interest of works of art with the stance of a spectator: the person who comes to a performance not in order to watch the triumph of virtue but simply to watch. The *Enquiry* affords the ground note, more broadly, of all Burke's subsequent writings by examining our affections and susceptibilities according to a universal standard of humanity. But his thinking starts from the human creature as nature and society show it to be. What we have made of ourselves—by habit and by consciousness—Burke takes to be relevant evidence of what we are. That is why works of art may be instructive for the science of human nature. As Adam Ferguson observed at the start of his *Essay on the History of Civil Society:* "We speak of art as distinguished from nature; but art itself is natural to man. He is in some measure the artificer of his own frame, as well as his fortune, and is destined, from the first age of his being, to invent and contrive." Human beings are animals capable of reflection. We can go some way to form and reform ourselves, but we are susceptible to jarring changes of feeling when roused by sensations that excite and disturb. To qualify the optimism of the doctrine of art as "second nature" (evident in Ferguson's emphasis on salutary invention and contrivance), Burke will say that we are creatures of a self-correcting but also perhaps a self-destructive species. Morals are useless if they cooperate with the mere desire of the mind to be aroused; yet art itself cooperates with that desire, to the extent that it strives for impressive effects. How far our interest in art is compatible with our interest in right and wrong is a question that Burke's *Enquiry* recognizes but does not attempt to answer. Rather, it sets in motion a train of thought in which that question must recur.

The Sublime

First published in 1757, revised and expanded in 1759, the *Enquiry into the Origin of Our Ideas of the Sublime and Beautiful* looks at the whole field of art or representation. Man, says Burke, is naturally a spectator, a maker and watcher of representations. We may find it difficult to justify this activity, it is so idle. Yet any trait that is apparently useless and inimical to social habits must, Burke thinks, be adapted to our nature in some hidden way: that is the promise that sets him on the track of "the origin of our ideas of the sublime and beautiful." Trace the human creature as far back as you can, and as widely as possible in different societies, and you find that the trail of art never grows thin. It is as if the existence of works of art and the feelings of the sublime and beautiful which those works can make us recognize were an inseparable condition of life. But if that is true, it is true for none of the reasons normally cited—not because art is instructive or edifying with regard to a customary way of life, or even necessarily pleasing. Burke assumes that works of art are nonetheless the inseparable offspring of human nature. To satisfy our instinct for looking at a spectacle that holds our interest, we build what we can out of what we are.

The *Enquiry* is composed in a deliberately dry scientific idiom. Unlike the *Vindication of Natural Society*, it has generally not been considered a hoax; yet the degree of its commitment to "science" remains in doubt, and one piece of testimony deserves to be considered. An *Encyclopedia Britannica* article on James Barry (the young painter whose patron Burke became in the 1760s) relates the following anecdote: "During their early acquaintance, having fallen into a dispute on the subject of taste, Barry quoted a passage in support of his opinion from the *Essay on the Sublime and Beautiful*, which had just then been published anonymously, and which Barry, in his youthful admiration of it, had, it seems, transcribed entire. Burke affected to treat this work as a theoretical romance, of no authority whatever, which threw Barry into such a rage in its defense, that Mr. Burke thought it necessary to appease him by owning himself to be the author."[10] The writer who conveys the anecdote is William Hazlitt, a reliable witness and a critic on friendly terms with many painters of Barry's generation. Assuming the veracity of his report, it may suggest second thoughts or anyway a second perspective on Burke's aesthetic research. The phrase "theoretical romance" is tantalizing but inconclusive. Burke dismissed "these theorists" of natural rights in his writings on France in the 1790s; but one has to be wary of shading his early speculations with his later doubts. He never disdained the attempt to derive limited general truths from experience. "A theory," he says in the 1759 preface to the *Enquiry*, "founded on experiment and not assumed, is always good for so much as it explains. Our inability to push it indefinitely is no argument at all against it."[11]

What is Burke's theory of the sublime? He narrates the book in an impartial style which recalls that of Hobbes; and this itself is a clue. The book speaks of the power of bodies to affect other bodies—taking *body* to refer to objects both animate and inanimate. The sublime overwhelms us, and makes us fear alike the power it reveals and the power it conceals. The word *impression*, which Burke might have drawn from Hume to signify an experience forcibly impressed on the mind and leaving a residue, may seem essential to his purpose but is seldom used, perhaps because of its apparent imprecision. All is clinical here: bodies carry powers into minds that have feelings or passions. That is the extent of the technical language Burke requires. An idea, in most of his argument, will denote an image in the mind; and in this sense, the word *ideas* in the title is a cunning evasion, for Burke's finding will be that the sublime actually fails to produce a clear image. The same is true of the beautiful when it touches us most deeply. The task of the theorist, therefore, is to show how the affective powers of the sublime and beautiful can be causes of mental activity without relying on clear and distinct ideas or images. A fair account of the process, for Burke, must turn to the connection of sublimity with words: the most immaterial and symbolic of ideal objects. Words, which bear no resemblance to things and which at the height of their influence on the passions leave no trace behind, are at once the most artificial and the most natural source of our sympathy with the sublime and beautiful. But this is to look ahead in an argument that is as much concerned with nature as it is with rhetoric.

Like all ideas, those of sublimity and beauty must have their origin in the senses; and all sensations, says Burke, are of pleasure and pain, both of them simple kinds. Pleasure reduced is not a kind of pain, and pain reduced or removed is not a kind of pleasure. (Even so, the sense of a diminution or cessation of pain is important in art, and we need a word for it. Burke calls it *delight*.) Pleasure and pain, then, exist independently, they are not relations, and (Burke adds) they come with vastly different associations. Ideas of pain turn on self-preservation; ideas of pleasure turn on society. Compare them and you see that pain predominates over pleasure. This is true not just at moments when both are present but over the course of a life: "I am in great doubt whether any man could be found who would earn a life of the most perfect satisfaction, at the price of ending it in the torments, which justice inflicted in a few hours on the late unfortunate regicide in France."[12] All pain, Burke suspects, must be associated with the fear of death: "What generally makes pain itself, if I may say so, more painful, is that it is considered as an emissary of this king of terrors." But the total experience of the passions is in large measure painful. Why then do we allow such experience to continue unmodified? Unless our exposure to pain served some interest of the human constitution, it would surely have been uprooted in the progress of society toward greater organization and security. There is in fact, Burke suggests, a danger from apathy greater than any we incur from pain: a danger lest we merely "acquiesce in life and health." This suggestion is made briefly, at several points in the book, rather than emphatically in one place; but on a close reading its force becomes inescapable. We must not acquiesce in life and health—an existence sunk in mere habit and routine—no matter how pleasant it may be. The imagination, by acting as it does on pleasure and pain and affording the mind obstacles or occasions to grapple with, prevents us from declining into that indolence, which would be our constant state if we were subject to nothing but the milder sensations.

Pleasures and pains tend to be channeled, according to Burke, into three capital motives of action—sympathy, imitation, and ambition—and it is clear that of the three, sympathy holds the largest fascination for him. Granted, without imitation little could ever be learned; most learning is by imitation and not by precept; yet as a motive, imitation has nothing to do with the passions that inform energetic action: it relates only indirectly to objects of the will. By contrast, ambition is a spur to action. It has been planted in us lest we "remain as the brutes do, the same at the end . . . that they were at the beginning of the world." Ambition makes us want to raise ourselves in our own opinion, so that "without danger we are conversant with terrible objects; the mind always claiming to itself some part of the dignity and importance of the things which it contemplates." Here Burke's description comes close to the accents of the sublime; and if there were such a thing as a "political sublime," its mainspring would be ambition. Yet ambition is a late-coming and reflective motive, like imitation, since it associates an idea of the self with preexisting objects.

Sympathy is a more primitive feeling: an entry to a sensation that belongs to someone else, which may include the delight of imagining a pain that is not one's own. And sympathy implies a spectator. It "must," says Burke, "be considered as a sort of substitution" of one person for another. It does not refer to general objects or to objects at a distance; the feeling approaches and wants to touch specific objects. Here Burke's perception goes against the common view that sympathy requires an assured distance from its objects—a sense aptly conveyed in Samuel Johnson's *Preface to Shakespeare:* "The delight of tragedy proceeds from our consciousness of fiction; if we thought murders and treasons real they would please no more."[13] Burke maintains on the contrary that sympathy always comes as close as possible to a scene of pain.

He offers this intuitive proof:

> Chuse a day on which to represent the most sublime and affecting tragedy we have; appoint the most favourite actors; spare no cost upon the scenes and decorations; unite the greatest efforts of poetry, painting, and music; and when you have collected your audience, just at the moment when their minds are erect with expectation, let it be reported that a state criminal of high rank is on the point of being executed in the adjoining square; in a moment the emptiness of the theatre would demonstrate the comparative weakness of the imitative arts, and proclaim the triumph of the real sympathy. I believe that this notion of our having a simple pain in the reality, yet a delight in the representation, arises from hence, that we do not sufficiently distinguish what we should by no means chuse to do, from what we should be eager enough to see if it was once done. We delight in seeing things, which so far from doing, our heartiest wishes would be to see redressed. This noble capital, the pride of England and of Europe, I believe no man is so strangely wicked as to desire to see destroyed by a conflagration or an earthquake, though he should be removed himself to the greatest distance from the danger. But suppose such a fatal accident to have happened, what numbers from all parts would croud to behold the ruins, and amongst them many who would have been content never to have seen London in its glory?[14]

Of course, the choice between the theatrical spectacle and the execution can seldom occur in quite this way. Burke's proof is speculative—but not less empirical for that. He appeals to what every reader can know from experience, assisted by introspection and analogy.

In this brilliant and carefully built-up example, a verbal detail that stands out is "the real sympathy." The ambiguity may have been unintended: "sympathy with the real event" is Burke's primary sense. Yet the word *real* seems to modify *sympathy,* as if our feeling in response to the tragedy of real life became more real because of its practical consequences. On the distinction between real and fictive sympathy, which Burke has here confused, a further important discrimination depends, namely the difference between our critical interest in the imitative arts and the non-critical interest Burke associates with the sublime. For the experience of the sublime induces astonishment, or "that state of the soul, in which all its motions are suspended." Should we say that here, once again, feeling becomes so vivid that all distinctions lose their force? Certainly the *Enquiry* evinces a notable coolness toward the idea of judging objects with a serene concern for nothing but artistic merit. Burke does not care for that job, even if somebody has to do it. Maybe we are judges of an art (properly understood) only when addressing the accuracy and decorum of a particular work. Still, in cases where a strong emotion was called forth by an object of no artistic mark, merit, or originality, or by an actual event that was never intended to be taken as art, if we consult our feelings we shall find (says Burke) that we were drawn by the real sympathy and not by the quality of the performance. Ordinary experience confirms his view. This is why the works of art that we loved in childhood continue to exert a power over our memory and feelings, which few of the greatest works can claim.

At the end of the preceding passage, Burke speaks of distinguishing between "what we should by no means chuse to do" and what we "should be eager enough to see if it was once done." The part of our moral training that makes us choose not to *do* the forbidden thing is powerless to prevent our curiosity to *see* it. In the next sentence, he retrenches a little: "We delight in seeing things, which, so far from doing, our heartiest wishes would be to see redressed." What is at stake is not conscious inclination so much as unconscious attraction. And yet a touch of scandal remains in the Burkean hypothesis. The "ghouls" or "rubbernecks" who pass slowly by the scene of a traffic accident to be sure of catching a glimpse of the carnage will serve as a modern correlative of the spectators of London in ruins. Such gazers include many who would have been content never to look at the mangled vehicles when they were new, and who would be shocked to suppose that their friends are among the dead or injured. This way of turning a scene of suffering into a site of spectatorship Burke believes to be a condition of all sympathy with pain. The resulting emotion is simple but strange, and it bears out the assumption he has stated in his opening sentence: "The first and the simplest emotion which we discover in the human mind, is Curiosity."

The motive for looking at a work of art (a tragedy above all) is the same as the motive for witnessing and acting to relieve suffering. In life, witnessing and acting may be insensibly confused. Yet to watch is, itself, a source of delight, even where we cannot assist. It is quite wrong, Burke believes, to trace this elemental fascination to the onlooker's supposed immunity to the danger, or to his consciousness of good fortune compared with the sufferer. The interest we take in the spectacle is a given fact of human nature. The paragraph of the *Enquiry* in which Burke says so— Part I, Section XIV—would become the most controversial passage on aesthetics in the eighteenth century:

> I am convinced that we have a degree of delight, and that no small one, in the real misfortunes and pains of others; for let the affection be what it will in appearance, if it does not make us shun such objects, if on the contrary it induces us to approach them, if it makes us dwell upon them, in this case I conceive that we must have a delight or pleasure of some species or other in contemplating objects of this kind. . . . Terror is a passion which always produces delight when it does not press too close, and pity is a passion accompanied with pleasure, because it arises from love and social affection. Whenever we are formed by nature to any active purpose, the passion which animates us, is attended with delight, or a pleasure of some kind, let the subject matter be what it will; and as our Creator has designed we should be united by the bond of sympathy, he has strengthened that bond by a proportionable delight; and there most where our sympathy is most wanted. If this passion was simply painful, we would shun with the greatest care all persons and places that could excite such a passion; as, some who are so far gone in indolence as not to endure any strong impression actually do. But the case is widely different with the greater part of mankind; there is no spectacle we so eagerly pursue, as that of some uncommon or grievous calamity. . . . The delight we have in such things, hinders us from shunning scenes of misery; and the pain we feel, prompts us to relieve ourselves in relieving those who suffer; and

all this antecedent to any reasoning, by an instinct that works us to its own purposes, without our concurrence.[15]

It is a disturbing analysis. We are driven to sympathize with scenes of actual or fictive suffering by a delight in pain that does not "press too close" upon us. Placed at the right distance, we bestow our attention first merely as spectators, without any thought of the pangs of the sufferers.

The passage implies that we desire a stimulus as keen as we can get, and will take it where we can, in any spectacle that implicates human life and fortunes.[16] The instinct that compels our attention "works us to its own purposes": it may contain undetermined proportions of cruelty (toward others and perhaps toward ourselves) and pity (for others and implicitly for ourselves). But to moralize the instinct further would take us outside the neutral language that deliberately constrains Burke's argument. His reference to an instinct that works us to its own purposes is nothing more than a reminder that we belong to the human species. Providential design comes into the argument only later, and at just one point, where Burke confesses his suspicion that without this interest in dwelling on the pain of others, the disagreeableness of suffering would make us avoid such experiences of sympathy altogether. Morally ambiguous tears would then become impossible, but so would the act of nursing and giving medical care to the wounded. Burke's scrupulous formulation is cast here as a double negative: the instinct *hinders* us from *shunning* such scenes. There is an opposite instinct, of resistance to any exposure to misery, discernible in those "so far gone in indolence" that they will not "endure any strong impression." It is only to the extent that we do endure a lively impression of pain that we unite ourselves to "the greater part of mankind." In this way, the attention of the spectator helps to perpetuate human nature itself. Works of art multiply the occasions for such attention, and in this rather strange sense, they humanize.

It does not follow that works of art tend to edify or improve the person who comes to know them. We may judge Burke's unsentimental impartiality here by comparing a familiar eighteenth-century argument on sympathy that tied aesthetic judgment to the moral sense. "People are hurry'd," Francis Hutcheson had written, "by a *natural, kind Instinct*, to see objects of Compassion." The word *kind* need only denote belonging to the same species, and Hutcheson's view thus far seems compatible with Burke's. Yet Hutcheson, an admired moralist of the previous generation, uses the word *kind* also for certain ameliorative overtones. Spectators, he says, would not "be pleas'd, barely to see fictitious Scenes of Misery, if they were kept strangers to the *moral Qualitys* of the Sufferers."[17] This piety is utterly absent from Burke's picture of an audience "erect with expectation" at the execution of a state criminal. But the very refusal by Burke of such a moral emphasis raises the question how far his theory allows for a distinct sphere of activity belonging to art. Burke seems to have drawn real and artificial suffering too close together to permit such a distinction; indeed, he writes of the practical effect of a violent stimulus: "The nearer it approaches the reality, and the further it removes us from all idea of fiction, the more perfect is its power."[18] This specification would draw the ridicule of Richard Payne Knight—one of the more resourceful polemicists against the *Sublime and Beautiful*—who pointed out how easy it was to imagine events in the street that would make Burke's audience gladly return to the theater.[19] A comment of greater interest here, because it goes beyond ingenuity, occurs in Diderot's *Salon* of 1767.

Diderot begins his analysis with a text from La Rochefoucauld: "Dans l'adversité de nos meilleurs amis nous trouvons quelque chose, qui ne nous déplaît pas" (In the misfortune of our best friends, we find something that does not displease us).[20] Do we not recognize, says Diderot, in this very saying the compound of cruelty and pity that Burke had identified with the spectator? "We are less frank with ourselves about this matter than a certain surgeon who said to his friend: 'I wish your leg were broken, then you'd see what I'm capable of.'"[21] So far, Burke would have agreed. Yet Diderot insists that there must be a conventional distance, plainly signaled, in order for us to take delight in a spectacle of suffering: "the orchestra of the theatre is full while the places marked by real misery are empty." Why should that be so? Our attendance at a given spectacle, he observes, is decided by our attraction to the surprising over the customary and not by a preference of the real over the fictive sympathy.[22] "It is pretended that the actual object is more striking than its imitation; one would rush out from Cato dying on stage to witness Lally's execution. A matter of curiosity. If Lally were beheaded every day, you would stick with Cato. The theatre is the Tarpeian Rock, and the orchestra the quay Le Pelletier of respectable people."[23] The mention of "respectable people" does a good deal of work in Diderot's analysis; it points, in fact, to an understanding of art more aristocratic than Burke's; while the clause that follows—"But *the people* never tire of public executions"—makes what Burke would have thought a false distinction and a false inference. Burke, in this connection, wrote a sentence that we will have occasion to look at again: "It is thus with the vulgar, *and all men are as the vulgar in what they do not understand*" (emphasis added). Diderot's fear, which his objection to Burke lays open to view, is that in the absence of taste the refined gentleman may suddenly descend to the level of the people. His argument reflects a characteristic anxiety of the period, and it throws unexpected light on Burke's indifference to that anxiety in the 1750s.

A modern reader is apt to have a vague idea of what sublimity means, and to suppose that the thing itself is probably vague. Burke's theory offers a startling rebuke to that assumption; and when one reads his book today, one can share the sensations of its first readers: excitement, then consternation, then wonder at his quickness of mind. It was this quality, as much as the inventiveness of Burke's division of the subject, that made the *Enquiry* dominate the literature of the arts from its publication until the appearance of a strong alternative view three decades later, in Kant's *Critique of Judgment*.

The headings under which Burke outlines the "causes" of sublimity give a practical sense to his idea of sublimity itself. Among the causes are *privation, suddenness, successiveness* (when irregular), and *obscurity*. The last may seem especially provocative; Burke makes it more so with an epigram: "A clear idea is therefore another name for a little idea." This stricture means neither to praise nor to blame; it merely says that sublimity cannot coexist with clarity: the virtues of one exclude the virtues of the other. Burke elaborates: clearness is "an enemy to all enthusiasms whatever." He has in mind the principle by which a sublime idea, say of a hallowed person or power, may be rendered more majestic by shrouding the relevant object from public view—a principle well understood by Milton in *Paradise Lost,* and put into practice by despotic governments when they conceal the person of heads of state.

All the attributes of sublimity come into play in Burke's use of quotations. It is the most inventive such use in the history of criticism, after Longinus. Yet Burke, unlike Longinus, stays clear of political oratory or persuasive discourse of any kind. His first quotation is among his most revealing; it comes from Pope's translation of the *Iliad,* and plucks a metaphor out of context:

> As when a wretch, who conscious of his crime,
> Pursued for murder from his native clime,
> Just gains some frontier, breathless, pale, amaz'd;
> All gaze, all wonder.

Burke quotes these lines as an instance of the cessation or removal of pain that he calls *delight;* and the context makes his nomenclature even odder than it already seemed. The astonished gaze belongs to Achilles as he looks at Priam, the king of Troy, bowed before him in an attitude of pleading and submission. Priam is about to ask Achilles to return the corpse of Hector out of pity for a father's suffering. So much for the dramatic posture and the sublime emotions of the scene; but the choice of the passage reflects a broader propensity of Burke's. A surprising number of his quotations turn out to be associated with a hero pausing in flight, or passing over a boundary, or being glimpsed as he grows conscious of the effects of an act he does not own or acknowledge. The hero is seen doing something he would by no means have chosen to do, and we are made to feel a strange delight at the hero's bewilderment.

So, too, with another quotation: "In thoughts from the visions of the night, when deep sleep falleth upon men, fear came upon me and trembling, which made all my bones to shake." Thematically and psychologically, this moment from the book of Job is close to the passage from Homer, but the terror at being searched and known has passed here into the mind of one person. The witness is no longer an enemy ruler but God.

How is the spectator involved in scenes like these? The two examples have in common an escape from the consequences of a crime or transgression or an affliction whose cause is unseen. Far from being rendered certain of our own detachment by immunity or aesthetic distance, we are brought closer to the source of a self-division we share with the hero. We would by no means choose to do or suffer what we are eager enough to see. The function of art, I think Burke is saying, is to deliver at this boundary a constant admonition as our constant reward. It is the furthest thing imaginable from a justification of art on the ground that it offers a guide to virtuous conduct. Burke appears by implication skeptical of the promise of fiction to heal and edify; a mood of doubt that recalls Lichtenberg's question whether fantasy ever allows an escape from ourselves: "A punishment in a dream is still a punishment." In works of art, as in dreams, we are allowed temporarily to disown an act that is ours, at the price of taking no credit for its power. So, to adapt Burke's words about the ambivalence of the spectator: by agreeing to witness the forbidden thing that "we should by no means chuse to do," we oblige conscience to exact something in return for delight. We acknowledge that "our heartiest wishes would be to see redressed" an occurrence which we find enthralling. Our primitive fascination with the scene unsettles us.

The Idea of Power

The most remarkable speculation in the *Enquiry* is the paragraph five pages long which Burke devotes to "power." Remarking that, in contrast with power, "pleasure must be stolen, and not forced upon us," he observes that when we think of anything under the aspect of *use,* we consider it as subservient to our will. This holds true for objects of satisfaction, perhaps even for objects of love, since love "approaches much nearer to contempt than is commonly imagined." When we look at a powerful creature, our first thought does not concern its use but rather the possibility that the creature may overwhelm us:

> Look at a man, or any other animal of prodigious strength, and what is your idea before reflection. Is it that this strength will be subservient to you, to your ease, to your pleasure, to your interest in any sense? No; the emotion you feel is, lest this enormous strength should be employed to the purposes of rapine and destruction. . . . Let us look at another strong animal in the two distinct lights in which we may

consider him. The horse in the light of an useful beast, fit for the plough, the road, the draft, in every social useful light the horse has nothing of the sublime; but is it thus that we are affected with him, *whose neck is cloathed with thunder, the glory of whose nostrils is terrible, who swalloweth the ground with fierceness and rage, neither believeth that it is the sound of the trumpet?* In this description the useful character of the horse entirely disappears, and the terrible and sublime blaze out together.[24]

This illustration from Job, like Burke's other illustrations of power, evokes the presence of a body we might suppose amenable to our will—a body which proves, however, to have a will of its own and tremendous power. It thereby sheds all associations of utility, and passes beyond the control of human purposes.

It is of the essence of sublimity to be experienced as an idea—an idea that can never be brought under the survey of reason. Burke's final example in his section on power is the idea of divinity. The Godhead, considered at a distance of refined abstraction, may be sufficiently an object of reverence; yet follow this moral train of thought from its cause to "the effect by which we are led to know it," and you will be impressed by an alien power. The discipline of fear which we derive from a sense of God's power has seldom been explained so disturbingly as this; indeed, a perplexity of Burke's argument is that it raises doubts about the efficacy of the Christian belief in a God of love. He quotes from Statius the maxim *primos in orbe deos fecit timor* (fear made the first god on earth) and comments:

This maxim may be, as I believe it is, false with regard to the origin of religion. The maker of the maxim saw how inseparable these ideas were, without considering that the notion of some great power must be always precedent to our dread of it. But this dread must necessarily follow the idea of such a power, when it is once excited in the mind. It is on this principle that true religion has, and must have, so large a mixture of salutary fear; and that false religions have generally nothing else but fear to support them. Before the christian religion had, as it were, humanized the idea of the divinity, and brought it somewhat nearer to us, there was very little said of the love of God. The followers of Plato have something of it, and only something. The other writers of pagan antiquity, whether poets or philosophers, nothing at all. And they who consider with what infinite attention, by what a disregard of every perishable object, through what long habits of piety and contemplation it is, any man is able to attain an entire love and devotion to the Deity, will easily perceive, that it is not the first, the most natural, and the most striking effect which proceeds from that idea. Thus we have traced power through its several gradations unto the highest of all, where our imagination is finally lost; and we find terror quite throughout the progress, its inseparable companion, and growing along with it, as far as we can possibly trace them.[25]

The God of Christianity presents an outermost possibility as an object of religious belief: the sublime idea of divinity passes thereafter into something more human, more worthy of reverence, and less pronounced in its quality of menace. To say so is doubtless to commend the resourcefulness of the faith. Yet Burke is also saying that Christianity goes as far as any religion can to humanize God without losing the fear that prompts all belief from the start.

This genealogy of religion, which traces its power over the mind to an elemental fear, is consistent with Burke's understanding that human customs develop by a process like that of natural selection. In this sense, he thinks, religion is one more adaptation—one of those ideas naturally suited to the appetites and frailties of human nature. To what extent does the triumph of Christianity mark an exception to the principle that ideas of pain always predominate over those of pleasure? Burke may not have thought it an exception at all; yet his explanation carries a hint that Christianity, of all the systems of belief, performs the softening work of manners that is characteristic of the beautiful; and that in bringing the idea of God "somewhat nearer" to us, it lightens the sense of fearful domination that had been part of the sublime idea of omnipotence. This passage lays the groundwork for the view of chivalry Burke will offer in *Reflections on the Revolution in France*—a view according to which a morality dedicated to the beautiful may take on something of a sublime dignity. But the same difficulty complicates both the early passage on the God of love, in the *Sublime and Beautiful,* and the more famous passage in the *Reflections* on the queen of France "glittering like the morning-star, full of life, and splendor, and joy." It would seem that only one who stands outside religion could consider the humanizing loveliness of Christian belief as merely a possible motive of faith, taking the question abstractly—so much utility assigned to the God of love, so much to the God of fear. In the same way, Burke's emphasis on the social benefit of honorable manners, rather than the intrinsic good of honor itself, will later present a puzzle to readers of his writings on France. There is, in his genealogy of religion, a strange apparent indifference to revealed truth, and there is a comparable indifference to intrinsic virtue in his judgment that among the nobility of ancien régime, "vice lost half its evil, by losing all its grossness." Or does Burke in both works simply despair of an audience that can be appealed to by revelation and an idea of intrinsic virtue? At any rate, Christianity, its morality softened by pity, earns his defense in the *Enquiry* because it modulates fear into love by a delicate human shading; just as aristocratic society draws his loyalty in the *Reflections* because it ameliorates vice by a protective demonstration of sensibility. This is an adventurous style of analysis, and Burke makes the style his own. His viewpoint may be called naturalistic, yet his understanding of nature also includes artifice, and his account of the rightness of beliefs is inseparable from a sense of their adaptation to human nature. This complex stance will become a source of Burke's irony in writings of the 1770s and 1780s, where the most unyielding convictions are arrived at through an understanding of the need for accommodation. It is the motive for his return to a favorite metaphor—the image of clothes which, when well adapted to a body, come to be felt as part of the body.

The passage above on Christian morality is not typical of the *Sublime and Beautiful*. The predominant mood of the book is aesthetic—a word that needs justifying in this context, since it had not entered English usage at the time Burke wrote. Let us take the aesthetic idea of experience to imply an absorbing concern with sensations and impressions. These are prized for what we can make of them without regard to their utilitarian or social value. In his narrow or intensive focus, Burke, like other aesthetic critics, was concerned with the mind and its objects in the world; and he took as a subject for aesthetic analysis (in a peculiarly abstract form) the love of power: the tendency of human beings to engross themselves in more-than-human effects. Burke is everywhere a natural historian of the mind that seeks in outward things some image of itself. Such a primitive interest in sensations need not entail a rejection of moral sentiments conventionally understood. It does mean, on Burke's analysis of art, that the aesthetic motive is prior to the moral. And "aesthetic" here must be taken to encompass the most various stimuli: those drawn from works of art, or personalities, or the natural world—everything that has the power to surprise and take us out of ourselves.

I have tried to avoid giving an excessively idealist undertone to this exposition of Burke on the sublime. Burke does not believe, as his successor Kant would do, that there is a promise of "the kingdom of ends" implicit in our treatment of works of art as ends in themselves. Burke, it is true, like Kant rejects all utilitarian justifications of art, but unlike Kant he denies that our interest in art is separate from our ordinary fears, hopes, and desires. And this last difference brings out a larger ambiguity in his relationship to Enlightenment rationalism. Kant would aim to liberate taste from its bondage to the senses, and yet the point (for Kant) of art's contact with a non-empirical ideal was to detach art itself from the base inclinations of the artist, just as duty frees morality from the base inclinations of the moral agent. (In a related deduction of the *Critique of Judgment*, Kant observes that the virtuous man fears God without being afraid.) By contrast, Burke's understanding of religion, virtue, and fear renders unintelligible any distinction between the fear of God and other sorts of fear. For him, reverence, respect, and fear exist on a single continuum.

The same contrast emerges when one compares Kant and Burke on the sublime. Kant speaks of our rational satisfaction in the sublime, and says that the reason can "find a superiority to nature even in its immensity," since our own idea of nature must be immense to recognize an external greatness there. The Kantian pattern of affirmation—by which, as we are overwhelmed in an attitude of awe, we discover also a source of awe in our attitude—suggests that the power outside us is matched by a power within.

Kant signaled that discovery with his metaphor "the stars in the heavens, the moral law in our hearts"—a metaphor that is stirring but also consoling, because it makes us part of whatever greatness we find. This moralized sense of the sublime is not to be found in Burke; yet it is so attractive that it has influenced many commentaries on the *Sublime and Beautiful*. Kant, in fact, was drawing on Burke for his distinctions and classifications to propound an utterly different theory.

How would Kant have answered the thesis that the sublime is the result of a hunger for sensation which finds itself overwhelmed by fear and understands nothing? We do not have to guess his response, because we have it in the *Critique of Judgment*. "Without development of moral ideas, that which we, prepared by culture, call sublime, presents itself to the uneducated man merely as terrible." To Burke's flat assertion that the sublime is that which we do not understand, Kant replies that reflection exalts our ignorance of causes into a higher sense of human majesty. One cannot escape the fact that for Burke, the fascination of power, or the love of powerful sensations, is a motive of the sublime that covers all the relevant phenomena. For Kant, this conclusion is unsatisfactory because it leaves human beings in the situation of non-rational creatures, hunters of things in the world that serve our appetites.

The tendency of Burke's argument, at once abstract and intuitive, emerges vividly in his treatment of a passage from Shakespeare. He quotes it as an example of "magnificence," and mentions that it comes from *Henry IV*, but otherwise says only that it is a description of a king's army.

> All furnished, all in arms,
> All plumed like ostriches that with the wind
> Baited like eagles having lately bathed:
> As full of spirit as the month of May,
> And gorgeous as the sun in Midsummer,
> Wanton as youthful goats, wild as young bulls.
> I saw young Harry with his beaver on
> Rise from the ground like featherd Mercury;
> And vaulted with such ease into his seat
> As if an angel dropped down from the clouds
> To turn and wind a fiery Pegasus.

Try to see this as a picture of a king's army and you will be disappointed by the sparseness of tractable detail. It is one of those descriptions (to borrow a phrase of Burke's) that "owe their sublimity to a richness and profusion of images, in which the mind is so dazzled as to make it impossible to attend to that exact coherence and agreement of the allusions, which we should require on every other occasion." Look further into the context, however, and the description turns out to be a speech. It is said by Vernon and is calculated to raise Hotspur to fighting pitch: the words imagine his enemy and show what he is up against. Burke, incidentally, allows in the passage a line of uncomplicated embellishment—"And gorgeous as the sun in Midsummer"—and elects to drop the last line of the speech, "And witch the world with noble horsemanship." He also omits the reply of Hotspur: "No more, no more! Worse than the sun in March, / This praise doth nourish agues. Let them come." With those additions in view, one can see that the full context gave the words some utilitarian value after all. The passage is intent on dazzling a particular person who will act with a purpose.

Why did Burke omit the part of the speech that explains its function? Because, I suspect, he was seeking to preserve a truth about the sublime. To the extent that a passage is woven into a context and becomes accessible to narrative understanding, to that extent it loses its sublimity. Narrative and probability are the enemies of enthusiasm. The nature of the sublime is to smash context—both the awareness of context and the memory of it—in order to create an impression of tremendous and irresistible energy. That is why it is hard to credit the efforts of recent commentators to expose a political underplot in the *Sublime and Beautiful*.[26] Burke's criterion of sublimity—*Does it make you feel afraid?*—need not exclude politics, but it does not eminently include politics. The sublime, to repeat, is associated with fear. Ultimately it is associated with death. A *stench* may be sublime, Burke says, quoting Virgil for proof: "the poisonous exhalation of Acheron" is terrible by association with a hellish place. There may be something sublime about riots and revolutions, if we suppose that such upheavals render human nature a monstrous emanation of itself. Yet Burke's usage is non-social in its bearings, and intends to be descriptive rather than honorific.

Beauty and Sociability

What of the beautiful? Over long stretches of his argument, Burke seems to have forgotten the second half of his announced subject. He began by saying that the passions associated with the idea of beauty turn on society, whereas those of sublimity turn on self-preservation. It might seem that the beautiful therefore would be the more ordinary and indeed the normative idea. Probably this was Burke's original intention. According to his plan, he should have had more to say about the beautiful than about the sublime, but the little he does say turns out to be contradictory, and the more he tells us about the beautiful, the more it sounds like the sublime.[27] Beauty is "a social quality," his discussion begins, with conscientious blandness, "for where women and men, and not only they, but when other animals give us a sense of joy and pleasure in beholding them, (and there are many that do so) they inspire us with sentiments of tenderness and affection towards their persons; we like to have them near us." This easy intimacy grows troubled in "the society of the sex" (the company of women), where inevitably men's feelings include a passion that has some "mixture of lust." On the other hand, "the *general society*," says Burke, "which we have with men and with other animals," is served by a similar affection, which, because it is free of lust, may offer a finer registration of beauty. The force of these discriminations would seem to exclude from the beautiful, or to keep there on sufferance, all the passions that relate to sexual desire.

Burke thinks beauty is anything but a utilitarian good, and this negative emphasis is in line with his polemic against decorum, regularity, and proportion, the neoclassical ideas that helped assimilate all art to the practical arts. To retain what is worth having of "proportion," Burke suggests that we substitute the idea of a common form. But what positive quality, in such a form, will make us judge it beautiful? Here we seem at a standstill. For Burke's several definitions are mostly negative, and they do not add up. Beauty must have been purged of "an energy of mind, that hurries us on to the possession of certain objects"—because without such purification it would still carry a taint of lust. Nor can beauty be the result of observing laws of proportion: such laws relate "almost wholly to convenience," that is, to usefulness, which has nothing to do with beauty. Again, beauty "is no idea belonging to mensuration," since—a wonderful and characteristic phrase—"it is not measure, but manner, that creates all the beauty which belongs to shape." What are we left with, after so many exclusions and qualifications? The closest Burke comes to a general formulation is that beauty is a result of gradual variation, itself gradually varied. This is suggestive but not satisfying.

In Part IV of the *Enquiry* (which could have been entitled "the beautiful and the sublime compared"), Burke tries a last time to enforce a distinctive formal contrast between the two ideas. This indeed is what his entire book has seemed to promise. Yet from the definitions listed above, one can see how nearly for Burke the beautiful has come to resemble the sublime. We were told that the sublime has no relation to utility; nor does the beautiful. The sublime cannot be brought under the rule of habit or will; and the beautiful is "so far from belonging to the idea of custom, that in reality what affects us in that manner is extremely rare and uncommon. The beautiful strikes us as much by its novelty as the deformed itself." The last sentence could have been written by William Blake,[28] and it indicates that Burke has tacitly at stake an idea of character—an idea centered on the energy of mind and temperament peculiar to an individual.

In fact, he has in mind an idea of *original* character, such as a poet might show in words; and perhaps of *innovative* or *unconforming* character, such as a statesman might show by deeds. We depend on custom, says Burke, to assign value to conventional objects, but different objects and different affections hold us in the presence of beauty. "If we suppose proportion in natural things to be relative to custom and use, the nature of use and custom will shew, that beauty, which is a *positive* and powerful quality, cannot result from it. We are so wonderfully formed, that whilst we are creatures vehemently desirous of novelty, we are as strongly attached to habit and custom. But it is the nature of things which hold us by custom to affect us very little whilst we are in possession of them, but strongly when they are absent."[29] Custom binds us to the past, to things we may have been hardly aware of while they were passing. By contrast, the beautiful and the sublime belong to the present moment and dominate by their presence. Custom therefore is linked by Burke to utility: it assists our survival by connecting past with present. The sublime and beautiful sever that link. The better we know things, and the better we know our reasons for possessing them, the less sublime and beautiful their effect will be. Thus our ideas of the sublime and beautiful pull away from any positive knowledge of art, and away from connoisseurship.

Burke says of the sublime (in an aphorism so impartial it may escape notice on a first reading): "It is our ignorance of things that causes all our admiration, and chiefly excites our passions. Knowledge and acquaintance make the most striking causes affect but little. It is thus with the vulgar, and all men are as the vulgar in what they do not understand."[30] This remark will reverberate through all his writings. For it points to a reason why custom and habit can never satisfy the imagination. Our craving for excitement is such that we re-create for ourselves that ignorance which lies at the source of our admiration. And the learned as much as the vulgar is at a loss in accounting for this process. Knowledge and acquaintance, which improve our judgment, dull the possibility of excitement; and if familiarity is useful because it "at last takes off the painful effect of many things," the truth is that "it reduces the pleasurable effect of others in the same manner, and brings both to a sort of mediocrity and indifference. Very justly is use called a second nature; and our natural and common state is one of absolute indifference, equally prepared for pain and pleasure."[31] Prescription, the knowledge of how things have been and ought to be (so vital in Burke's understanding of political morality), is by this sentence excluded as a possible guide to art, or to any area of feeling connected with the sublime and beautiful. The words *natural* and *common*, normally used in the eighteenth century with the intent to praise the just equilibrium of taste or things as they are—those very words are here deployed ironically to describe a state of apathy that resembles a waking sleep.

If the beautiful as much as the sublime is associated with the striking and irregular, and if, as much as the sublime, it resists all measure or uniformity, a question arises whether either quality can assist much in the formal characterization of a work of art. Burke seems to think not. He takes his definition of art a good deal on trust, but he certainly disclaims all attempts at formal definition. This is the aspect of his argument that most deserves the compliment a later generation paid by calling it Romantic. I do not think that Burke fully understood his own radicalism. Yet he says explicitly, in a curious reserve clause, that though proportion and fitness may have a place in works of imitation, "works of art are the proper sphere of their power; and here it is that they have their full effect." The tone of this is surely concessive and lowering. For when Burke speaks of the strong feelings we may have toward beauty, he adopts a very different tone. Passing from the "unmixed" quality of emotion we feel regarding man and the animals to the mixed quality that appears in sexual passion, he notes that the step down in purity is also a step toward the cherished good of friendship and love: "Whenever the wisdom of our Creator intended that we should be affected with any thing, he did not confide the execution of his design to the languid and precarious operation of our reason; but he endued it with powers and properties that prevent the understanding, and even the will, which seizing upon the senses and imagination, captivate the soul before the understanding is ready either to join with them or to oppose them."[32] From this prevention or anticipation of the understanding—this operation by "powers and properties" not reducible to rules—one can infer the revolutionary aesthetic maxim that Burke would enunciate in a famous chapter heading: "Perfection Not the Cause of Beauty."[33]

Not to want things perfect: again his bias appears distinctly non-moral. For in the sphere of moral conduct, we do seek perfection, even if we know that the best we can hope for is improvement from worse to better. Yet Burke has said that our faculty of admiration is satisfied in the sublime and beautiful by something other than regularity. Now he concedes that the beautiful is the imperfect and that we have no wish to see it improved. The aesthetic and the moral are finally, in Burke's treatment, driven further apart than they had been by any earlier writer. A century later, the aphorisms of Baudelaire and Oscar Wilde will digest in a coherent doctrine the suspicion that all beautiful things are useless, and that moral-minded supervision renders things merely useful, uniform, and ugly. Yet the first and longest step on this path was taken by Burke.[34] One of his closest readers, Mary Wollstonecraft, looking back in the early 1790s, had no doubt that the *Sublime and Beautiful* had left its mark on *Reflections on the Revolution in France*. Only a dandy, far gone in the love of sensations for their own sake, could have produced the rhapsodic description of the "unbought grace of life" that issued from Burke's memory of the queen of France in her youth. The prophecy of his early essay in aesthetics was thus borne out: the sublime is indifferent to morality. Under the ancien régime, Burke will say in 1790—under that "mixed system of opinion and sentiment" which placed aristocratic beauty at its pinnacle—"vice lost half its evil, by losing all its grossness."

Words and Things

We come now to a larger puzzle about the fame of Burke's *Sublime and Beautiful*. Its least important section has been the most discussed, and its most original train of thought has largely escaped notice. Part IV of the book, which discovers in sensations the efficient causes of our aesthetic ideas, was quickly and almost universally taken to embody Burke's central contribution to aesthetic theory. This fine-tuned annex of the argument is not where the author's interest lies, yet the clean and memorable outlines of his descriptions of *pain, fear, terror, unity, succession, darkness, the infinite,* as well as of *smoothness, sweetness, smallness,* and *variation,* mark out a distinct emphasis which even the casual reader can hardly miss, and they almost invite the classification of Burke as a "physiological" theorist or an "impressionist" critic. It is, in fact, Part IV, along with the introduction on taste, that has determined the account of the book in most commentaries, including that of Croce in his *History of Aesthetics*. It is easy to see why. This part, more than the rest of the *Sublime and Beautiful,* belongs to an anatomical mode of criticism that had been imprinted on the public mind by William Hogarth's *Analysis of Beauty,* with its identification of the all-important "serpentine line."[35] Yet Burke's empirical excursus on shapes, textures, and other sensory stimuli retracts the promise of a cookbook of artistic methods in a single ironic sentence: "Custom reconciles us to every thing." If custom can habituate us to everything, it follows that by adapting ourselves to a stimulus we began by finding disagreeable, we can modify the range of phenomena from which we derive aesthetic pleasure. There is no such thing as a necessary cause of beauty, and no such thing as an object that might not, by custom and association, come to be recognized as beautiful. The matching of our ideas to their origins in the senses turns out to be a project as delusive as the design of the *Vindication of Natural Society* to infer the truth about man in society from the authority of reason.

By contrast, Part V of the *Enquiry* has received far less attention from scholars. Yet it is anything but an afterthought: once one has recognized that Burke cares for the sublime as an idea and not as an image, this concluding stretch of his argument may be understood to generate all the rest.[36] Here, too, Burke at last connects his enquiry into our ideas with a vivid application to the arts. But why should a discussion of the motives of *imagination* have led him finally to *words*? Because, says Burke, words are an abstracting medium and so lend themselves to the production of sublimity. The very quality that makes words, if relied on for the truth about things, uncertain and ambiguous markers, renders them favorable to the creation of obscure ideas and the raising of enthusiasms. The sounds of words over time "utterly lose their connection with the particular occasions that gave rise to them." This fact is not lamented by Burke. He believes that the abstracting power of language is the reason why we use words and why we grant them the right to use us. Admittedly, there is a risk in the sublimity of words, akin to the risk of morbid fascination that Burke describes in connection with hopeless love. The sublime idea may so engross us "as to shut out by degrees almost every other, and to break down every partition of the mind which would confine it." Yet the principle is the same that we observe at work in commonplace tricks of language.

Burke illustrates the process by composing a sample passage, a fluent period of topographical prose about the course of a river, which incorporates buried metaphors of mouth and heart, along with such images as "moist and mountainous soil," "winding to and fro," and "a vast flood augmented by" tributaries. Mischievously he asks whether, while all these images were passing, his reader has *pictured* anything. We have not; but why should we want a picture? We can take in the total meaning without such help, and this, Burke concludes, is our usual way with words. "It is impracticable to jump from sense to thought, from particulars to generals, from things to words, in such a manner as to answer the purposes of life; nor is it necessary that we should." Meaning is conveyed by a sequence of recognitions that are neither abstract nor concrete but follow a train of thought. The mind fills in the lacunae or gaps of meaning in the same way when dealing with sublimity or bathos, eloquence or bombast, epigram or cliché. What makes writing great (and genuine rather than spurious) cannot be explained by reference to a mental process or technique.

The final part of the *Enquiry*, on words, plays another trick on the reader that has a still more disorienting effect. A section headed "General Words before Ideas" begins by asserting that words about virtue and vice are normally taught to us before we know the things they describe. Burke here associates himself with a conventional authority, John Locke; but while Locke agreed that general words come before the things they point to, he also believed that ideas come before words. Burke sets against Locke's belief in the secondariness of words an extreme nominalism of his own, which he tests by printing a string of words that looks on the page like a line of verse:

> It is hard to repeat certain sets of words, though owned by themselves unoperative, without being in some degree affected, especially if a warm and affecting tone of voice accompanies them, as suppose,
>
> *Wise, valiant, generous, good and great.*
>
> These words, by having no application, ought to be unoperative; but when words commonly sacred to great occasions are used, we are affected by them even without the occasions.[37]

The italicized words, uttered in a vacuum, automatically call up warm ideas and feelings, even though they connect with nothing and hang in a senseless limbo. To acknowledge the power of words to this extent is to concede the prevalence of credulity—a hunger for belief, or a susceptibility to excitement no matter what its source, by which even empty beliefs can attract us with a dependable magnetism. It is as if Burke said to the reader: "Let me speak these words and see how they move you. Notice that you were moved. But here is something odd: the words meant nothing. And they describe nothing. I can assure you that this is so, because it is I who spoke them and I had nothing in mind. I strung together a conventional chain of attributes that I knew would make you twitch. And by the way: I could do the same with lots of other strings of words." His experiment, so coolly planned and executed, may provoke us to try it in reverse. What if the occasion were tremendous but the words inadequate? We would feel little and we would not be prompted to act.

It is words that chiefly create our emotions. We are trained by words (*virtue, liberty, honor*) to respond in a certain manner, but the training always precedes the event; just as, in Burke's argument in Part I, our readiness to be moved by a spectacle assists in moving us whether the spectacle is real or fictional. Burke uses this fact to explain how people who love virtue and detest vice may nevertheless "act ill and wickedly in particulars without the least remorse." That happens, he says, "because these particular occasions never came into view, when the passions on the side of virtue were so warmly affected by certain words heated originally by the breath of others." It is not clear whether the word *others* refers to other persons or other words. Either way, it is words that are said to affect conduct, words rather than any immediate perception of right and wrong. These words have been heated by "the breath of others," and they breathe life into an energetic speaker. Without the motive that they supply, the speaker would be silent. Under their power, he may become an automaton. But what species of morality can come from words that hold priority over things, words that are supposed to supply a warmth that people themselves may lack? It seems that an immense burden—the responsibility for touching the springs of moral action—rests with the discoverer or user of persuasive words.

This is the same insight that was carried into practical criticism in the earlier parts of the *Sublime and Beautiful*. Words can evoke feelings without being linked to any substantial object, and they can prompt ideas, sufficient for a complex train of thought, without ever producing a distinct image. These, to repeat, are truths about ordinary language, but they are truths Burke believes to apply with the same force in the greatest literature. Between the elaborate mock-up sentence about the river and Milton's picture of the fallen Satan—

> His form had not yet lost
> All her original brightness, nor appeared
> Less than archangel ruin'd, and th'excess

> Of glory obscured: as when the sun new ris'n
> Looks through the horizontal misty air
> Shorn of his beams; or from behind the moon
> In dim eclipse disastrous twilight sheds
> On half the nations; and with fear of change
> Perplexes monarchs

—the relevant difference seems to be that Milton holds out the possibility of jumping from sense to thought (from the mixed images of light and darkness to the political fear of change), yet the complex quality of his metaphor defeats the attempt; whereas no one but a rhetorician would think of performing such an experiment with ordinary descriptive prose. The inference from Burke's question, "Did you really *see* anything?" can only be that words are not by nature tied to sense. The sublime, in the greatest poetry, is thus a heightening and bringing to awareness of a state of disjunction or derangement that is a normal condition of language.[38]

In the presence of the sublime, says Burke, "we yield to sympathy what we refuse to description." This insight lies at the heart of his analysis and is a clue to much else in Burke's writings. The last of his many quotations from Milton shows how a literal catalogue may evade the reach of imaginable description and so become sublime:

> Rocks, caves, lakes, fens, bogs, dens, and shades of death,
> A universe of Death.

Images of natural formations, in Milton's portrayal of the underworld, crowd each other until the picture is too dense and confused for coherence. The particulars are then given imaginative force by a governing idea ("a universe of Death") which cuts every link to sensory images. The abstract phrase "and shades of death" marks the pivot between the real and the unrealizable; and even that phrase is ambiguous between physical shadows and allegorical ghosts. In view of his discovery, Burke can say without exaggeration, in the final sentence of his book, that words "were able to affect us often as strongly as the things they represent, and sometimes much more strongly."

Domestication of the Idea

Two considerable stretches of the *Sublime and Beautiful* were added for the second edition in 1759. The section on "Power"—whose remarks concerning the relation between fear and divinity we have already touched on—was one of these. The other was an introduction on taste. These additions press Burke's argument in almost contradictory directions. The essay on taste removes the arts a certain distance from the brute fear of "astonishment"; the section on power turns back to fear itself as a source of religion and morality. It is possible that Burke never recognized this tension within his argument. In his 1759 preface, he confirms what will become the common view—readily extractable from his table of contents—namely, that he sets great store by the antithesis of the sublime and the beautiful. The sublime, he hopes to have demonstrated, is associated with self-preservation and irresistible masculine power, the beautiful with society and irresistible feminine suasion. I have argued that this is not what the book actually shows. So clear-cut a division is not established by the argument and does not emerge as either its strongest or its final emphasis. A deeper preoccupation throughout the *Enquiry* appears to be the human imagining of catastrophe—the mind's fascination with all that overbears its capacity and makes it lose control of understanding.

The appeal of both the sublime and the beautiful draws on this fascination. But the merely imitative aspect of the beautiful holds little interest for Burke, compared with the kind of pleasure that must be "stolen." And the conventional topics of the sublime—dragon, demon, famine, slaughter—do not begin to suggest the craving he has described, which springs from an irreducible sympathy with power. Indeed, in dispensing with all guidelines for the sublime and the beautiful, Burke's aesthetic treatise offers not so much a survey of its subject as a psychological analysis of the priority of feeling to thought. That is one reason why it remains a shocking book—a work discontinuous with most earlier writing on the arts, as it is with much of Burke's later writing (which has positive things to say about moderation, regularity, and proportion). Its final message for aesthetics is: *No more art talk*. We may still find intelligent ways to speak of the effects of art; and Samuel Johnson did so in a manner that showed the influence of Burke when he said of *Paradise Lost:* "The characteristic quality of [Milton's] poem is sublimity. . . . He can please when pleasure is required; but it is his peculiar power to astonish." The sharpness of the contrast here between pleasure and greatness—familiar to the reader of Burke's *Enquiry*—was not a feature of Johnson's earlier critical writings.

According to Burke, criticism that adequately describes the non-moral bearings of literature will always be mainly a discussion of effects—effects that by their nature are often painful or somehow verge on pain. We cannot bring the energy of the mind under a rule of the mind. As for the social interpretation of art, applied to the greatest works it would seem to be a delusion, as much so as a social interpretation of dreams would be. The truth is that Burke's idea of the sublime cannot be incorporated with society in any way. Society depends on custom and habit, but a custom or habit of the sublime, if one could conceive of such a thing, would mean an end of the self or an end of society.

Yet art must serve some human interest. It must prove itself to be not the enemy of life, even if it is not "a friend to man." Burke leaves us with the hypothesis that art assists human beings in a kind of adaptation that is fundamentally non-social; and it is here that he breaks drastically from the prevalent understanding of the work of taste. The modern language of taste was spoken first by Lord Shaftesbury, who in *Characteristics* (1711) asked himself why he could not perform a noxious act, and gave the witty reply, "Because I have a nose"—thus appealing from virtue to a *moral sense* and making that sense almost identical with taste. This was the premise that Francis Hutcheson and succeeding moralists would adopt in speculations that added to Shaftesbury's quasi-physiology a semblance of mathematical rigor. Even before he wrote the first page of the *Sublime and Beautiful,* Burke stood outside this way of thinking.[39]

Yet in his second edition, in 1759, he chose to lead off the book with an introduction on taste, written in apparent conformity to the very doctrine he had rejected. He offers a somewhat pared-down version of the hope that, through education and the diffusion of taste, we can be assured that the judgments of different people will at last be rendered uniform. He suggests that we rely on a residuum of unchanging cognition, which makes sugar sweet and vinegar sour for everyone; but this conceit is hedged by a doubt whether such regularities can really offset the variability of our judgments. Burke here was joining a dispute that would continue through the century. On one side were those who asserted a natural standard of taste. They tended to believe such a standard was a precise index of morals and that ultimately it governed the uses we could make of art. (Addison spoke for this position with complacent authority.) On the other side were those, like Hume and Montesquieu, who argued that even if a natural standard does exist, it cannot be what determines judgment, which is an artificial function mediated by the accidents of education and manners. Burke in the five parts of the *Enquiry* had aligned himself implicitly with Hume and Montesquieu, with their sense of the priority of manners to morals and of the affections to rational judgment. Yet, until the careful revision embodied by his introduction on taste, he seems to have looked on all this controversy as a pastime of doctors and dilettanti. What prompted his change of tactics?

The author of the introduction on taste of 1759 is careful to sound conventional. He allows that taste "is a matter curious in itself; and it leads naturally enough to the principal inquiry"—a meek exordium by Burke's standard. The most notable shift of emphasis lies in his discovery of a basis in the senses for the verdicts of reason and taste: this basis must be "the same in all human creatures," since if it were variable we would lack the instruments "to maintain the ordinary correspondence of life." The new speculation is compatible with the rest of the book, yet it avoids the question whether the sublime and beautiful are not a thing apart from such "ordinary correspondence." Burke had seemed to say before that we require reason and even regularity in most of life, but not in our ideas of the sublime and beautiful, whose purpose is to rouse us from inertia and apathy. I suspect that a particular circumstance accounts for his delayed discovery of the interest of ordinary life.

Hume published his essay "Of the Standard of Taste" in 1757, the same year as Burke's first edition, and the essay must have piqued Burke's interest.[40] For Hume argued from the efficacy of habit (an emphasis agreeable to Burke: "custom reconciles us to every thing") to the acceptance of a standard of taste. What is taste but the repetition and the application to new contexts of certain well-defended habits of judgment? The wonder of Hume's argument lay in the deftness with which it passed from the premise that beauty is not a quality of things themselves to the conclusion that, nevertheless, conformity of judgment is not only theoretically possible but visibly in effect in any organized society. The solution emerges from the relation Hume establishes between custom and the uses of probability.[41] In his *Treatise of Human Nature*, he had observed that judgments are "the effect of custom on the imagination," not the effect of objects themselves: no object itself implies the existence of another object, yet a judgment always does imply other judgments. As a recent commentator summarizes his position: "Causal reasoning, for Hume, is reasoning which projects past uniformities into the future, whereas probability estimation projects past frequencies into the future."[42] Taste would seem to afford occasions only of "frequencies"; but that is acceptable since, in art as in human action, we expect and require no better guide than probability. Hume's essay "Of the Standard of Taste" goes on to suggest that, by serving common utility, a standard settled by mere convention may pass for a "natural" standard.

Burke was generally sympathetic to Hume's search for patterns derivable by observation of human nature. And the idea that habit becomes our second nature, on which Hume's argument on taste depends, had already appeared in Part III of the *Sublime and Beautiful*. Its force, however, was blunted there by the warning that usefulness has no commerce with sublimity. But the idea of habit and custom as second nature, and of art as man's nature, would appeal to Burke increasingly as his political thinking advanced. This language gave him a cover under which the stirrings of American liberty could be answered with an argument for conciliation: the British and Americans shared a common heritage of liberty, the colonists were being faithful to that tradition in stretching their loyalty to a point of political rupture, but the memory of a shared and glorious inheritance should allow both sides to continue as partners in trade, each pursuing its version of English liberty. The appeal to habit as second nature also gave Burke an enormously flexible critical weapon for asserting that the revolution in France, starting in June 1789, was nothing but the revolt of perverted ambition against all custom and prescription. Thus the analyst of the sublime as an abrupt transition of the soul would become the advocate of reform as a gradual transition of society. One can call the result a change of emphasis or a change of subject.

The question for Burke was not whether art belonged to human nature—how could it not?—but whether its terms of naturalization could be as steadily influenced by utility and convention as Hume made them out to be. On this point, the text of 1757 had been firmly negative. But what must it have been for the young Burke to read the new exposition of the problem by the master analyst of human nature? Hume's essay, with its triumphant meliorism, its atmosphere of Addison and *Don Quixote* rather than Milton and Job, was almost the antithesis of his own discussion; it assured the refined that the sensations of art are moderate on the whole and that all disputes about taste are subject to adjudication by rational men who perceive aspects of a single truth.[43] This testimony, from a philosopher so little liable to underrate the strength of the passions, must have made Burke feel himself much further out on a limb than he had realized. Hume's temperateness on the subject would have brought to mind a pragmatic consideration as well. "Of the Standard of Taste" grants the existence of disputes about taste, and provides for their settlement by a qualified judge. No such figure appears anywhere in the text of Burke's *Sublime and Beautiful*. Yet to whom else was a theorist to appeal when asked (for example) what authority supports his quotation of certain passages as having particular value? A more personal consideration may have helped in Burke's unpredictable conversion to the language of taste. By 1759, he knew Hume well enough to ask for Adam Smith's address in order to write a complimentary letter to the author of the *Theory of Moral Sentiments*.[44] When, in 1765, the French translation appeared of *A Philosophical Enquiry into the Origin of Our Ideas of the Sublime and Beautiful* (*Recherches philosophiques sur l'origine des idées que nous avons du beau et du sublime, précédées d'une dissertation sur le goût*), it was dedicated to Lord Hertford, the British ambassador in Paris. Lord Hertford's secretary was David Hume. The editor of Burke's early letters, Thomas Copeland—a great scholar, apt to err if at all by understatement—writes that Hume "very likely took some part in the enterprise."

The surmise I offer about Hume's tactical influence on Burke is nothing but informed conjecture. It is possible that none of this sequence indicates cause and effect, that the resemblances between Hume's essay and Burke's 1759 introduction on taste are accidental. Still, one can imagine Hume saying to Burke: "You have just written a book of great originality and discernment, but your refusal to deal with taste and judgment, and with the ordinary productions of art, makes it more anomalous than you can possibly intend or wish. It is the sort of book the French will like, and they will like it none the worse for being told that they are the most polished and perfect of nations but there is something, an I-don't-know-what, which they inexplicably lack. But look: when the French talk about these matters, they do it in essays on taste. Why not write them an essay on taste? Show how the idea of taste in nature, far from constituting an exception to all you say, only confirms the necessity of understanding the sublime and beautiful in the customary medium of the affections. This little elaboration will reassure them and will do no injustice to your views." An essay on taste was as advisable a prefatory measure for a book of criticism in the mid-eighteenth century as an essay on culture is for a book of criticism today.

So we find Burke in his introduction of 1759 writing for the first time as if sensibility (a natural endowment whose opposite is insensibility) were no more important than judgment (an artificial acquisition which can be taught) and tracing a moderate and Humean progression from sensations (which are universal) to manners (which are variable but capable of refinement). And so the customary phrases are slotted in—"as the arts advance towards their perfection, the science of criticism advances with equal pace." There was some canniness, some craft, some desire to please at home and pass in translation, doubtless assisting in the change, but it was not all a matter of making a career and getting readers by writing in code. Burke had balanced his argument delicately in 1757, and this would be a natural source of anxiety when he came to revise. For he had said that the passions involved in the most affecting works of art do not enter fluently into the intercourse of society. The *Enquiry* does make a case for the human necessity of art, but at a certain cost to our opinion of human nature: we attend the hanging as we would attend the theatrical performance, and our fascination is supposed in neither case to be especially generous-hearted. We do not have the authority of Burke's treatment of the sublime and beautiful if we want to say that the arts advance toward perfection. They advance, in each individual mind, only as they are admired; and "it is our ignorance of things that causes all our admiration. . . . It is thus with the vulgar, and all men are as the vulgar in what they do not understand." The sublime and beautiful are by definition that which we can never understand.

The introduction on taste does much to remedy these doubts by proceeding as if the author had not read the book he was introducing. But the book remains more impressive without it. Leave out this softening of the foreground and the essay gives a stark anticipation of Burke's mature writings on politics—a foreshadowing more potent if less obvious than the satire of *A Vindication of Natural Society*. It has been usual for literary scholars to project a high degree of continuity between the *Enquiry* and the later writings of Burke that treat revolution or imperial conquest as an admonitory kind of sublime spectacle.[45] By contrast, it has been usual for historians and biographers to gloss over the book as part of an apprenticeship that Burke chose not to build upon.[46] The perception of continuity is truer than the assumption that Burke's career divides into a short experiment in literature and a long fulfillment in politics. But how shall we describe the connection between the *Enquiry* and all that follows?

At its deepest layer, this subtle, observant, and single-minded book is founded on an insight that Burke in his later years never surrendered. Yet its insight bears an uneasy relationship to the surface teaching of much of his work. At the start of Burke's long debate with himself about the rival influences of passion and custom, the *Enquiry* presses unexpectedly in favor of passion. It says that any resting or acquiescence in the stability of things-as-they-are presents a greater danger than the most uncontrolled exuberance of feeling. The risk of custom to society is a changeless security, and denial of passion to the individual means imaginative death. The contrast with the position of his anti-revolutionary writings is as strong as can be. When Burke in the 1790s writes about the revolution in France and his fear that it will infect England, the same idea of acquiescence will be simply presented as an advantage to society, and the social acceptance of inertia will be described with an irony that bends toward approval. How, with the same psychology, could he reach so different a conclusion?

In the years between—years containing the American Revolution, the Gordon Riots, the menace of the Irish Volunteers—Burke had been freshly instructed by scenes of suffering and disorder that crossed from private to public experience. It is as if the thinness of the boundary separating the sympathy of actual life from the artistic performance became a matter of final disturbance to him. "The real sympathy" turns into a real threat. Burke, in fact, comes to regard imaginative energy as a menace in the exact degree that it grows social and self-conscious. To those who transgress the boundary dividing the fictive from the real sympathy, and do it in company rather than alone, the experience of a passion that turns on self-preservation, which says "Fearfully and wonderfully am I made,"[47] may be changed to an experience of power that turns on society, which says "Fearfully and wonderfully can we make." The former was a saying of King David in Psalms, in gratitude to God who "hast searched me, and known me." The latter is a saying of political persons acting in corps, who recognize no authority beyond themselves.

First Patron

We have heard Horace Walpole describe Burke as the author of an admired book written in Bolingbroke's manner who "has not worn off his authorism yet—and thinks there is nothing so charming as writers and to be one."[48] Such was the impression Burke could make on an older writer as clever as himself and occasionally as perceptive. Yet "authorism" is a dig and its tone is misleading, for Burke aimed to be a writer in earnest. How did he propose to sustain himself? In February 1757, he contracted with Dodsley to produce *An Essay towards an Abridgment of the English History* from the time of Caesar to Queen Anne. He was paid in installments and by 1760 had gotten as far as the Magna Carta. Probably the *Abridgment* was his earliest chance at fame in letters; books of history, then as now, sold better than theories of art and society. A sinewy narrative holds the attention of a reader of Burke's *Abridgment of the English History;* and, animated as it is by the energy of his reflections on manners, laws, and the temper and the genius of England's early kings, the unfinished work printed in his *Writings and Speeches* deserves to be widely known. From whatever causes—distraction, irresolution—Burke did not complete it; yet certain passages exhibit unforgettably his abiding concern with liberty and the constitution; and they may be taken as notes toward the composition of *Thoughts on the Cause of the Present Discontents* and *Reflections on the Revolution in France*.

Burke's study of history had convinced him that the English common law had deep roots in historical experience, but he did not therefore connect it with an ancient understanding of natural right. Instead, the common law ought to be understood as a series of measures and corrections—"composed of some remnants of the old Saxon customs, joined to the feudal institutions brought in at the Norman Conquest"—a sediment of accretions that only a historian would want to redivide but that must be recognized anyway as not by nature homogeneous. In the same analytic spirit, he observes that "in the Preamble to the Great Charter, it is stipulated that the barons shall *hold* the liberties there granted *to them and their heirs;* from *king and his heirs:* which shews that the doctrine of an inalienable tenure was always uppermost in their minds." So the idea had a purpose for a body of men at a certain time: "Their idea even of liberty was not (if I may use the expression) perfectly free; and they did not claim to possess their privileges upon any natural principle or independent bottom."[49] Burke drew what he took to be the appropriate moral for the history of laws, in a fragment probably also written in 1757, "An Essay Towards an History of the Laws of England." The present "system of our Laws," he remarks, "like our language and our learning, is a very mixed and heterogeneous mass; in some respects our own; in more borrowed from the policy of foreign nations; and compounded, altered, and variously modified, according to the various necessities, which the manners, the religion, and the commerce of the people, have at different times imposed." This almost anthropological stance toward the accidents that go to compose a system of laws may have been influenced by Johnson's preface to his *Dictionary of the English Language*.[50]

The sense of contingency surrounding the origin of laws and the interested motives that work toward principles later to be consecrated by time—these are characteristic preoccupations, for Burke, and they make his account of the Magna Carta at once appreciative, circumstantial, and non-heroic. The narrative here begins conventionally, but it is soon shaded by a reservation:

> The English barons had privileges, which they knew to have been vio-
> lated: they had always kept up the memory of the ancient Saxon lib-
> erty; and if they were the conquerors of Britain, they did not think
> that their own servitude was the just fruit of their victory. They had,
> however, but an indistinct view of the object, at which they aimed;
> they rather felt their wrongs, than understood the cause of them; and
> having no head nor council, they were more in a condition of distress-
> ing their king, and disgracing their country by their disobedience,
> than of applying any effectual remedy to their grievances.[51]

But now, Burke narrows the account to deliver a portrait of an ambitious man, Stephen Langton, the archbishop of Canterbury, whom the barons took as a powerful ally to advance their cause. "Langton saw these dispo-sitions [of the barons], and these wants. He had conceived a settled plan for reducing the king; and all his actions tended to carry it into execu-tion." Langton is depicted first as an intriguer, acting on a design pro-moted by the pope: "He formed schemes of a very deep and extensive na-ture; and became the first mover in all the affairs, which distinguish the remainder of this reign." The political enterprise of limiting the powers of the king, Burke argues, was instigated and carried out by persons most intent on securing new powers of their own. When at last King John threw himself on the protection of the pope, Langton, "who no longer acted in subservience to the Pope, from whom he had now nothing fur-ther to expect, and who had put himself at the head of the patrons of civil liberty, loudly exclaimed at this indignity; protested against the resigna-tion [of the king], and laid his protestation on the altar."[52] Burke achieves a deliberate irony by suggesting that the altar of the Church of Rome be-came by chance the altar of English liberty. Moral and political ideals, in such a passage, are seen to spring from base materials and to be none the less admirable for that.

Burke believed that there is an inscrutable force that directs the asso-ciation of peoples by the operation of the most divergent motives: greed and the pursuit of knowledge. (Searching for a term to unify the two, one may be turned back again to the primary instinct of the *Enquiry:* curiosity.) "It is not wholly unworthy of observation," he writes in Chapter 2 of the *Abridgment,*

> that Providence, which strongly appears to have intended the continual intermixture of mankind, never leaves the human mind destitute of a principle to effect it. The purpose is sometimes carried on by a sort of migratory instinct; sometimes by the spirit of conquest; at one time avarice drives men from their homes, at another they are actuated by a thirst of knowledge; where none of these causes can operate, the sanctity of particular places attracts men from the most distant quarters. It was this motive, which sent thousands in those ages to Jerusalem and Rome; and now in a full tide impels half the world annually to Mecca.[53]

The seeds of knowledge had to be cultivated, Burke adds, in a place sufficiently remote from the rest of society to offer security against the habitual demands of life. And monasteries served that purpose: "otherwise, [the seeds of various kinds of knowledge and improvement] could not have been cultivated at all: for it was altogether necessary to draw certain men from the general rude and fierce society, and wholly to set a bar between them and the barbarous life of the rest of the world, in order to fit them for study and the cultivation of arts and science." We find, he notices, the same setting apart and seclusion of the learned "every where in the first institutions for the propagation of knowledge amongst any people."[54] A small part of this speculation Burke could have derived from Hume's essays "Of Commerce" and "Of the Populousness of Ancient Nations"; but his emphasis (unlike Hume's) does not rest on the softening influence of manners and the progress of civilization through trade and cosmopolitan extension. Burke indeed implies a paradoxical argument against the identification of learning and manners with the civilized pursuit of harmless profit. Learning and wisdom do not naturally thrive in any society, which always has other and more immediate needs. His remarks on the non-utilitarian good of monkish institutions will be expanded in *Reflections on the Revolution in France;* and as Burke must have seen—since his concern is not the sanctity of religious observance—the argument may point equally to a justification for secular institutions of higher learning.

Perhaps the most striking passage of the *Abridgment*, for a reader looking back on it from Burke's later writings, occurs in his overview of the
conquest of Britain (the climax of which Burke dates in 452 A.D.) by the
Saxon army under Hengist. This episode is recounted as a descent into
catastrophic suffering and yet a necessary tribulation in the path on which
great changes of the world are accomplished. Burke evokes a mysterious
providence—on the face of it a power without moral definition—in language that foreshadows his treatment of three later revolutions: the Protestant Reformation; the conquest of India by British power and commerce; and the fall of the old regime in France. Even, he says, if the
Britons could for a moment have held off "the superior abilities and efforts
of Hengist," they could not have changed the result:

> The news of his success had roused all Saxony. Five great bodies of
> that adventurous people under different and independent command-
> ers, very nearly at the same time, broke in upon as many different
> parts of the island. They came no longer as pirates, but as invaders.
> Whilst the Britains contended with one body of their fierce enemies,
> another gained ground, and filled with slaughter and desolation the
> whole country from sea to sea. A devouring war, a dreadful famine, a
> plague, the most wasteful of any recorded in our history, united to
> consummate the ruin of Britain. The ecclesiastical writers of that age,
> confounded at the view of those complicated calamities, saw nothing
> but the arm of God stretched out for the punishment of a sinful and
> disobedient nation. And truly, when we set before us in one point of
> view the condition of almost all the parts, which had lately composed
> the Western empire, of Britain, of Gaul, of Italy, of Spain, of Africa,
> at once overwhelmed by a resistless inundation of most cruel barbar-
> ians, whose inhuman method of war made but a small part of the
> miseries, with which these nations were afflicted, we are almost
> driven out of the circle of political enquiry: we are in a manner com-
> pelled to acknowledge the hand of God in those immense revolu-
> tions, by which, at certain periods, he so signally asserts his supreme
> dominion, and brings about that great system of change, which is
> perhaps as necessary to the moral as it is found to be in the natural
> world.[55]

Is it piety that so uncannily charges this description—even piety in residual form—or is it something more akin to wonder? And are we obliged to greet as an improvement a sudden mutation about which all we know is that it will leave nothing unchanged?[56]

In 1759, Burke was introduced by the Earl of Charlemont to William Gerard Hamilton. He soon became Hamilton's private secretary, and when Hamilton was appointed chief secretary to the Lord Lieutenant of Ireland, Burke went with him to reside in Dublin. Hamilton had given a maiden speech in the House of Commons that set the high mark for its time. Unhappily, it had no sequel, and this became the source of the embarrassing nickname "single-speech Hamilton." Though possessed of ambition smaller in kind and less adventurous than Burke's, Hamilton left no doubt of his talent and competence; but the clash of tempers between the two, in their short and trying relationship, would be equally consequential for both. Perhaps especially for Burke: a self-protective disposition he carried into later years, and a certain superfluity of pride, may be traced in significant measure to this encounter with an initially gratifying and well-meaning patron.

Born in January 1729, a year older than Burke, Hamilton had been elected in 1754 to the House of Commons from Petersfield, in Hampshire. He was called upon in 1761, by the Lord Lieutenant for Ireland, Lord Halifax, to accompany him as his secretary. Between 1761 and 1763, Hamilton served therefore as the chief minister of the crown in the Irish House of Commons. After his return to Westminster in 1763, he would never again address the English House of Commons, yet he held a seat from one constituency or another until his death in 1796. "His wit was pointed," observed Burke's early biographer Prior, "his oratory epigrammatic and antithetical, his conversation easy and agreeable. In composition he was laboriously affected, being a literary fop of the most determined cast; for a stop omitted, a sentence not fully turned, or a word that upon reflection could be amended, were sufficient to occasion the recall of a note to a familiar acquaintance."[57] For two years or more, Burke was friendly with Hamilton, and he seems to have enjoyed his patron's trust to an unusual degree.

Accompanying Hamilton to Dublin (arriving in August 1861), Burke stayed through the fall and winter of 1761–1762 and returned for a final season in the parliamentary winter of 1763–1764. One finds him writing to a friend, Charles O'Hara—a member of the Irish House of Commons who took a lively interest in English politics—as early as 1761 in a manner that implies a solid mutual friendship. Speaking of "our friend" (as Burke calls Hamilton in a letter to O'Hara of July 3), "every thing," he affirms, "is with him, as you know, manly and honest; he is one of the few men of business, whose honour, I am satisfied is entirely to be relied on."[58] Many of Burke's letters to O'Hara were written from London to Dublin, and they have an ironic and conspiratorial cast: bulletins on the political action of the day by a well-placed witness to a well-placed listener. All these letters go on the assumption that neither Burke nor O'Hara is much impressed with the passing social scene.[59] Burke's service in Ireland appears to have been limited to official duties and occasional visits with family, though he learned enough about the injustices of that time and place to compose, in the same period, the fragmentary *Tract Relative to the Laws against Popery in Ireland*.

There were times when the spectacle of violent rebellion and the violence of state retribution brought injustices closer to home. The "Whiteboy" peasant uprisings of the 1760s drew in laborers, artisans, and tenant farmers burdened by exorbitant rents; though partly anti-Catholic in inspiration, they were punished by reprisals that spread the suffering. The Whiteboy Act was to become the notorious pretext for the execution of a Catholic priest, Father Nicholas Sheehy;[60] and Burke had this event in mind when he wrote to O'Hara with unaccustomed passion:

> We are all in a Blaze here with your plots, assassinations, massacres, Rebellions, moonlight armies, French Officers and French money. Are you not ashamed? You who told me, that if they could get no discovery from [Sheehy], they would cool and leave off their detestable plot mongering? You think well of Ireland; but I think rightly of it; and know, that their unmeaning Senseless malice is insatiable; *cedamus patria!* [farewell to Ireland]. I am told, that these miserable wretches whom they have hanged, died with one Voice declaring their innocence: but truly for my part, I want no man dying, or risen from

the dead, to tell me, that lies are lies, and nonsense is nonsense. I wish your absurdity was less mischievous, and less bloody. Are there not a thousand other ways in which fools may make themselves important? I assure you, I look on these things with horror; and cannot talk of such proceedings as the effectss of an innocent credulity. If there be an army paid, and armed, and disciplined, and sworn to foreign powers in your country, cannot Government know it by some better means than the Evidence of whores and Horse Stealers.[61]

Those words belong to a slightly later period; they are written by Burke from London in May 1766. But the sentiment registers a more intimate knowledge than the words confess.

They, the agents of "unmeaning Senseless malice" and the object of Burke's reprobation, are the Protestant authorities who make new laws to harden their power, instead of submitting their power to the impartial discipline of laws. A remarkable essay by Luke Gibbons quotes from the letter above to suggest that Burke's absorption in "the terrors of the sublime" had "a morbid personal dimension" from his knowledge of the Sheehy case; and Gibbons adds to that personal undercurrent the impact on Burke's family of the trial, execution, and postmortem affairs of the Jacobite sympathizer James Cotter a generation earlier.[62] Some of these connections are speculative. What is certain is that the Ireland of the 1760s, beyond the precincts of Dublin Castle, was a place Burke did not have to imagine from the outside in. It left him no ease of mind.

Yet even when he was actively engaged in Ireland, the most telling comments in Burke's correspondence with O'Hara seem to come from afar. So he observes in a letter of December 30, 1762, that "a scheme for maintaining 18,000 effective men on the Irish Establishment" has been embraced by public opinion in Ireland. The increase was proposed in order to advance a policy of apparent security and actual intimidation, a policy that, in Ireland, Burke would always firmly oppose. And he was troubled by the attitude of the people: "Why they should abhor a civil and covet a military establishment, I cannot, I confess, in the least conceive." His own reluctance to expand the military establishment, he says, does not imply any broader hostility to social reforms: "A Land Tax would not displease me who have no Land; if I did not see, that this Tax would terminate in some measure on the wretched poor whose Burthens are already so lamentably heavy." Before turning to local gossip, he adds: "I hate to think of Ireland, though my thoughts involuntarily take that turn, and whenever they do meet only with objects of grief or indignation."[63]

His connection with Ireland through Hamilton was soon to terminate; for, though Hamilton remained chief secretary under Halifax's successor, the Earl of Northumberland, he was now an unwanted appendage. He stayed on as long as he could—a failure of decorum that Burke found intensely disagreeable. By the spring of 1765, we hear him observe in a letter that Hamilton's "conduct in publick affairs" has been "for a Long time directly contrary to my opinion" as well as "very reproachful to himself."[64]

❧

Considerable insight into the character of Hamilton can be gained from another source. Throughout his career, he was gathering a book of maxims on public speaking, *Parliamentary Logic*—a book that his private secretary in later years, Samuel Johnson, would pronounce a "curious and masterly" performance. It was published posthumously in 1808 and has been occasionally reprinted but seldom examined closely. This rhetorical handbook warrants scrutiny for its suggestive relationship to Burke's own practice as an orator: it is the production of a man with whom he had worked in close connection; its subject is a political skill at which Burke became the acknowledged master of his age; and the book may reflect something of the reciprocal influence of Hamilton and his secretary. We need not understate the difference. Burke was a man of genius and vast energy, Hamilton a rather brittle conventional talent. Viewed under this restriction, however, the book affords an extraordinary glimpse of the political arts of the eighteenth century.

The practical wisdom of *Parliamentary Logic* comes from a mingling of stylistic pointers and moral aperçus. For example: "State what you censure by the soft name of those who would apologize for it."[65] This is tactical advice for an assault on euphemism, close to the satirical manner that Burke adopted against Bolingbroke. The suggestion is to mimic so faithfully the watchwords and slogans of your opponent that the listener will first grow numb and then be disgusted by the cheapness of the performance. Burke would later use this strategy in his assault on the equanimity of Lord North during the American war, and the apologies for conquest and plunder that issued from the East India Company. The euphemisms of the 1760s and 1770s stemmed from unpleasant facts concealed by the machinery of tacit consent: "obligation" for prerogative, "assertion of right" for enforcement of will, "restoration of tranquility" for suppression of resistance.

Hamilton also taps a conventional vein of pithy advice from ancient rhetoricians such as Aristotle and Quintilian: "If the whole of a question is against you, speak to a part, as if it were the whole." But the book exhibits, among its more prominent traits, shrewdness of a lawyerlike sort peculiar to the author and his parliamentary milieu. Thus: "When an argument is brought against you to prove one thing, shew that it likewise proves another." And: "Endeavour always to find a precedent somewhat stronger than the thing you are going to propose."[66] The authority of precedent, Hamilton is saying, may shelter a controversial policy under an appearance of stable continuity. Yet for history to be on your side is not enough. History must underline its preference.

Certain of Hamilton's remarks touch a limit of dandyish provocation—a reminder of the suspicion of moral indifference that shadowed his career. His guiding precept in *Parliamentary Logic* often seems to be: Win at all costs. He appears to offer tactics for those who would succeed in political argument, much as Machiavelli offered tactics for those who would seize and maintain control of political power in a scene of violent discontinuity. "When in the wrong," Hamilton advises, "use comprehensive and general (because they are equivocal) expressions; and multiply divisions and distinctions without end. If you have no argument to object to, object to a word." And again: "When it is with you, separate the *fact* from the *argument*; when against you, blend them." Finally, "If your cause is bad, call in aid the party; if the party is bad, call in aid the cause. If neither is good, wound the opponent."[67] Ad hominem argument was recognized by Aristotle as a method of persuasion; and Hamilton recommends it when useful. A false syllogism may serve in the absence of a true one. Slander may succeed where honest exposure has failed. An extended aside on the dramatic psychology of rhetoric is remarkable for its coolness: "Preconsider what you mean should be the finest part of your speech, and in speaking connect it with what has incidentally fallen in debate; and, when you come to that premeditated and finest part, *hesitate and appear to boggle,* catch at some expression that shall fall short of your idea, and then seem at last to hit upon the true thing."[68] This reads like the advice of one of Sheridan's rakes to an understudy; in Hamilton, the detail stands out only for its explicitness.

Yet there are parts of his book that might have been written from his observation of Burke. "When you cannot convince, a heap of comparisons will dazzle."[69] Exactly this criticism would be offered by Burke's opponents in the French Revolution controversy. Thomas Paine deplored a stretch of the *Reflections* as "a pathless wilderness of rhapsodies"; and James Mackintosh remarked that Burke induced his readers to yield to sympathy what they would refuse to description: "He can sap the most impregnable conviction by pathos, and put to flight a host of syllogisms with a sneer. Absolved from the laws of vulgar method, he can advance a groupe of magnificent horrors to make a breach in our hearts, through which the most undisciplined rabble of arguments may enter in triumph."[70] Of course, similar strictures might be applied to any writer of impassioned prose.

Parts of Hamilton's book are so trite as to be interchangeable with the advice of debating coaches in every age and society. We discover his limitations (and are made to see why he could not take much pleasure in speaking) when he solemnly warns: "Revolve in your own mind, separately and detached from each other, the argumentative and the eloquent parts of what you are to say." This is to separate the garment from the body of argument, as if style were nothing but drapery. It asks for obedience to a method that no great speaker has ever followed.

By disposition, Hamilton appears to have been a moderate, as Burke would be for much of his career: "when you censure, find something to approve; and when you approve, something to censure." The effects of such a rhetorical habit are politic and conciliatory: "The concessions of an able man in argument are often the subtilest parts of it: driven to difficulty, he makes a concession that is a little to his disadvantage, to avoid being obliged to make one which is a great deal so." Yet for all his posture of moral neutrality, Hamilton shares with Burke a perception of the moral basis of politics: "A crime may be measured by the mischief which is the consequence of it, or by the number of ties the criminal has broken through."[71] The breaking of ties, which is always dictated by corrupt policy—ignoring and destroying layer after layer of obligations—would be the focus of Burke's analysis and indictment of the East India Company.

To judge by the evidence that has survived, Hamilton and Burke began by taking a serious interest in each other's fortunes; over time, the attachment grew stronger on Hamilton's side and weaker on Burke's. This would explain the desire on Hamilton's part to secure an exclusive claim on the resources of his secretary. Burke recoiled from such a proposal as an infringement on his liberty of action. The quarrel that followed, in Burke's early thirties, was the first crisis of his career, the event that more than any other would decide his later stance as the unappeasable voice of a parliamentary opposition.

In March 1763, Burke wrote to Hamilton to inform him that he could accept, conditionally, the pension Hamilton had obtained for him of 300 pounds a year on the Irish establishment. But he would not give up his own work:

> Whatever advantages I have acquired, and even that advantage which I must reckon as the greatest and most pleasing of them, have been owing to some small degree of literary reputation. It will be hard to persuade me that any further services which your kindness may propose for me, or any in which my friends may wish to co-operate with you, will not be greatly facilitated by doing something to cultivate and keep alive the same reputation. . . . For this purpose some short time at convenient intervals and especially at the dead time of the year, will be requisite, to study and consult proper books. These times, as you know very well, cannot be easily defined nor indeed, is it necessary that they should. . . . I know that your business ought on all occasions to have the preference, to be the first and the last, and indeed in all respects the main concern. All I contend for is, that I may not be considered as absolutely excluded from all other thoughts in their proper time, and due subordination.[72]

This is a guarded but not an ungracious protestation to an acknowledged benefactor.

Two years later, a note of defensive wariness has crept into the relationship on both sides. Hamilton complains to Burke (in a letter dated before February 12, 1765) that "the Disagreement between us is already sufficiently difficult, and I should be sorry to make it impossible, to be reconcil'd."[73] He had made a new offer to retain Burke as his permanent assistant. Burke, however, did not care for the terms and wrote back in self-justification: "If there be any part of my conduct in life upon which I can look with entire satisfaction it is my behaviour with regard to you."[74] On the question of personal independence he would brook no compromise: "What you blame is only this: That I will not consent to bind myself to you for no less a term than my whole life; in a sort of domestick situation, for a consideration to be taken out of your private fortune, that is, to circumscribe my hopes, to give up even the possibility of liberty, and absolutely to annihilate myself for ever. I beseech you, is the demand, or the refusal the act of unkindness. If ever such a test of friendship was proposed in any instance to any man living, I admit that my conduct has been unkind and if you please ungrateful."[75] That was the end. Hamilton said that they should stop writing and talking.

Burke, clearly shaken, drew up a memorandum to vindicate his conduct. One can judge Hamilton's anger by the countermemorandum that he wrote in turn, which closes with a sprawl of epithets: "Chandler's Shop—Slavery, give up his Freedom—dung Hill—Did I ever refuse him Money—Provok'd to be generous that a Man of Talents should be hurt by his Attachment to *me* Jew—Jesuit."[76]

A last significant return to the subject occurs in a letter from Burke to John Monck Mason at the end of May. Belief in his innocence, and in Hamilton's perfidy, has become for him a condition of his other friendships: "I shall never therefore look upon those, who after hearing the whole story, do not think me *perfectly* in the right, and do not consider Hamilton as an infamous Scoundrel, to be in the smallest degree my friends."[77] He declares his hatred of dependency with a new vehemence: "Not to value myself (as a gentleman a freeman a man of Education; and one pretending to Literature) is there any situation in Life so low or even so criminal, that can subject a man to the possibility of such an engagement? Would you dare attempt to bind your footman to such Terms? Will the Law suffer a felon sent to the Plantation to bind himself for his Life and to renounce all possibility either of elevation or quiet? And I am to defend myself for not doing, what no man is Sufferd to do and what it would be criminal in any man to Submit to."[78] There are kinds of subordination that amount to slavery: this belief will stand out also in Burke's writings on empire and political representation. He felt that the imposition of one person on another, through patronage, resembled the occupation of one country by another.

His deepest resentment of the conduct of Hamilton came out eventually in a letter to John Hely Hutchinson. Those years of service to one man (he says looking back) had depressed his chances of literary success; the labor was consuming, his own projects suffered, and he was forced to watch while others sailed ahead.

> Six of the best years of my Life he took me from every pursuit of Literary reputation or of improvement of my fortune. In that time he made his own fortune (a very great one), and he has also taken to *himself* the very little one, which *I* had made. In all this time you may easily conceive how much I felt at seeing myself left behind by almost all my contemporaries. There never was a Season more favourable for any man who chose to enter into the Career of Publick Life; and I think I am not guilty of Ostentation, in supposing my own moral Character and my industry, my friends and connections, when Mr. H. first sought my acquaintance were not at all inferior to those of several, whose fortune is at this day upon a very different footing from mine.[79]

It remains obscure in what sense Hamilton "took to himself" a fortune Burke had made;[80] this may simply express regret that he yielded so much to another man's enterprises. Anyway Burke, casting his eye six years backward, came to believe that he had been swindled.

His ambitious contemporaries were putting their names to their writings. His were published anonymously or were prevented from maturing by the demands on his time. The break with Hamilton has rightly been called "an act of wild courage."[81] It left Burke without financial security and exposed him to the charge of ingratitude—a charge, the degree of whose truth Burke had to weigh against the comfort offered by friends like Dr. John Cury of Dublin: "As to the Sin of Ingratitude I make no Sort of Scruple to Pronounce You *Impeccable*."[82]

It must not be supposed that Burke was left hanging, without means of support or influential supporters. For a man who still lacked a design for living, he was remarkably well established. During his years in the study of law in the Middle Temple, he seems already to have met David Garrick and, soon after, Samuel Johnson, Thomas and Joseph Warton, and Elizabeth Carter. His friendship with Joshua Reynolds—the easiest of all his friendships with famous men and the one most cherished by Burke—began as early as 1758.[83] When, in 1759, Hume wanted to lay a groundwork for the favorable reception of Smith's *Theory of Moral Sentiments*—most likely by securing a review in the *Annual Register*—he gave Burke one of the five copies he had with him. (The remaining four went to Soame Jenyns, Horace Walpole, Lord Lyttleton, and the Duke of Argyll:[84] illustrious company for the secretary of a second-echelon official.) Burke's induction into the society of those he would most have wished to count as peers was signalized by his inclusion, in February 1764, among the founders of the Club, along with Reynolds, Johnson, Goldsmith, and Burke's father-in-law, Dr. Nugent. The Club, set up for discussion of moral and literary subjects, met (in Boswell's famous description) "at the Turk's Head, in Gerard-street, Soho, one evening in every week, at seven, and generally continued their conversation till a pretty late hour."[85] Burke flourished in this company, and in later years would regret that parliamentary business kept him away.

But the distraction was of his choosing. By 1765, he had found a new patron, the Marquess of Rockingham, whose service he entered as private secretary on July 11, 1765. The induction of Burke into the Rockingham party was an effect of the shifting of alliances, and it followed the earliest large assertion of control by George III acting under the influence of Lord Bute: the dismissal from government office, in 1762, of a substantial proportion of the Pelham-Newcastle Whigs, which came to be known as the Massacre of the Pelhamite Innocents.[86] The move suggested that under the new king, the crown itself would dictate such continuity as was permitted from one administration to the next. Lord Rockingham, on hearing of the decision by the Duke of Newcastle to leave office rather than sit while his stature was further diminished, told Newcastle that the purge only confirmed his suspicion that Bute and his faction intended to take "the whole Administration & Government of this country into their hands."[87] Voluntary resignations soon followed by many other Pelhamites, but William Pitt, who was looked to for leadership of a substantial opposition, failed to appear at the opening of Parliament in November. In December, Rockingham saw that his connection with Newcastle had been punished by the king's order to deprive him of certain offices in the North and West Ridings and in the city of York.

These losses were insignificant by the standard of Rockingham's possessions: landholdings in Northamptonshire and Ireland and the 15,000 acres of the family estate in Yorkshire, at whose center was Wentworth Woodhouse, with its 600-foot façade. And yet he prided himself on being a generous member of a nobility whose duty it was to act with disinterested views; and he would have seen the slights inflicted by the conduct of George III as a sign of pettiness. While Rockingham waited for an opposition to crystalize, however, the king had reached his agreement with a successor ministry to be headed by George Grenville. This lasted from April 1763 to July 1765 and was terminated after the passage of the Stamp Act—in large measure because of the king's intense dislike of Grenville himself.

The Rockingham administration of 1765–1766 would bring back Newcastle in the office of lord privy seal and make room for a limited number of his followers; but Rockingham wrote to the Duke of his wariness of conspicuous patronage and dismissals lest "we might suffer the vindictive spirit of retaliation to prevail so far that we should surpass in severity the example of 1763."[88] He was aiming higher than that, and it showed in his appointment of Burke as his secretary. How the two came to meet is not entirely clear, but the connection appears to have been by association in the circle of Charles Townshend: a politician of great charm and irregular commitments, a lord of the admiralty under Newcastle in 1755, who refused the offer by Rockingham of the position of chancellor of the exchequer.

Meanwhile, Burke wrote of his fresh opportunity to Charles O'Hara with a frankness that often marks his letters to this somewhat older confidant. "I came into Parliament not at all as a place of preferment, but of refuge; I was pushed into it; and I must have been a Member, and that too with some Eclat, or be a little worse than nothing."[89] Yet he arrived at the refuge by an intricate process, in which Rockingham himself did not supply the seat. The representation for Wendover had been promised to William Burke, by a friend and patron, Lord Verney, and William arranged for Verney to transfer it to Edmund. This debt, though hardly unusual in the routines of patronage, must have widened Burke's sense of the duties that came with his work for Rockingham: his friend William had made him a gift that would be hard to repay. O'Hara delivered to Burke some sage advice on the management of an aristocrat like Rockingham, with his peculiar blend of candor and hesitation: "You have pride to deal with, but much softened by manner; and exceeding good sense, but you must feed it, for it can't feed itself."[90]

Burke's own mention of the need for "éclat" reveals the degree to which he was prepared to let politics carry him to the eminence he once hoped to achieve through writing. He would go on contributing to the history of the year's events in the *Annual Register,* but his literary career, as a performance by a distinct individual, appeared to be at an end. He would come to prominence instead as the voice of a party. The terms of Rockingham's patronage were far more latitudinarian than Hamilton's, indeed as generous as have ever been offered to a man of talent who came to office armed with nothing but his talent. Yet Oliver Goldsmith was not the only friend to regret that "born for the universe," Burke had "narrowed his mind, / And to party gave up what was meant for mankind." The criticism was half genial; written partly to entertain Burke, it spares any imputation of dishonorable compromise. And yet the sting remains.

A hazard that threatened all Burke's hopes had propelled him to accept the offer from Rockingham. Secure patronage brought with it an implicit promise of loyalty whose remote consequences could scarcely be reckoned. Burke's consciousness that his move was made under pressure of circumstance (closely connected with the survival of his ambition) and that his aim as a thinker was still to persuade readers by the force of truth and imaginative eloquence—these considerations would determine the political character he became. Meanwhile, his exalted idea of party, in the years of his association with the Rockingham Whigs, would transform political loyalty into a virtue compatible with moral principle.

Election to Parliament

When Burke was returned for Wendover, his party's prospects were loosely identified with the defense of John Wilkes, the master libertarian and demagogue; and the victory celebration partook of the heady mood of the time. Laughlin Macleane wrote a letter to Wilkes himself describing the mayhem he had touched off by proposing a toast: "all the Dishes were broken in the same Instant; in a few minutes the Room was cleared of Smoke and full of—Liberty, Wilkes and Liberty, Burke and Wilkes, Freedom and Wendover; Empty Bottles, broken Glasses, Rivers of Wine, Brooks of Brandy, Chairs overturned, with the Men that sat upon them, while others in rising from their Knees fell under the Table."[91] A more judicious approach to the alliance was exemplified by Burke in a letter to his brother Richard: "If Wilkes has the least Knowledge of the Nature of popularity and the smallest degree of attention to his own Interest he will wait the convenience of his friends who do not forget him. But this to be insinuated more or less, or not at all according to your discretion."[92] Burke at this time was also looking to the propriety of his financial arrangements (a matter he took to include not only honest dealing but the appearance of honor) by making sure that the Irish pension he had received under Hamilton was no longer paid.

His parliamentary debut attracted comment from many quarters, and we have an unusually full description from Burke himself. On January 17, 1766, the cause that drew him was a petition from some merchants of Manchester, complaining of restrictions on trade with America:

That day I took my first trial. Sr Wm Meredith desired me to present the Manchester Petition; I know not what struck me, but I took a sudden resolution to say something about it, though I had got it but that moment, and had scarcely time to read it, short as it was; I did say something; what it was, I know not upon my honour; I felt like a man drunk. Lord Frederick Campbell made me some answer to which I replied; ill enough too; but I was by this time pretty well on my Legs; Mr Grenville answerd; and I was now heated, and could have been much better, but Sir G. Saville caught the Speakers eye before me; and it was then thought better not to proceed further, as it would keep off the business of the day. However I had now grown a little stouter, though still giddy, and affected with a swimming in my head; So that I ventured up again on the motion, and spoke some minutes, poorly, but not quite so ill as before. All I hoped was to plunge in, and get off the first horrors; I had no hopes of making a figure. I find my Voice not strong enough to fill the house; but I shall endeavour to raise it as high as it will bear.[93]

The best-liked politician of the day and the one most jealous of his own fame, William Pitt, remarked to a mutual acquaintance (who reported it to Burke) "'that he was proud to walk in the line which that ingenious gentleman had chalked out.' And on the Question of repeal, 'That his speech woud be much shortened by what Mr B. had offered, and that he had delivered his sentiments thr'o the Medium of a Much better understanding than he (Pitt) was ever endowed with, and a Degree of Precision which he believed was never before heard in that house.'" Burke, according to Dr. Johnson, "gained more reputation than perhaps any man at his [first] appearance ever gained before."[94] So his distinction was a public fact. He had "made two speeches in the House for repealing the Stamp-act, which were publickly commended by Mr Pitt, and have filled the town with wonder." A friend and rival in familiar conversation, Johnson added with possessive pride: "Now we who know Burke, know that he will be one of the first men in the country."

❧ III ❧

The Wilkes Crisis and *Thoughts on the Cause of the Present Discontents*

BY 1766, when Burke entered the House of Commons, certain beliefs were widely if not generally shared among its members. Fifty years of Hanoverian rule were thought to have witnessed the gradual displacement of the sovereignty of the crown by the sovereignty of Parliament. Government, representing the majority, should enact laws and conduct policy consistent with the aims of the king but not subordinate to his will.[1] This was a consequence of the revolution settlement of 1689, but its effects had been partly hidden during the long tenure of Robert Walpole, whose conciliatory system of corruption swelled the holdings of the great Whig families and kept them jealous mainly of each other. Party government, in the sense that implies an active opposition, was neither possible nor much desired while the fortunes of the oligarchical sects were so efficiently looked after.

To understand Burke's argument for liberty and constitutional balance in the 1770s, one must recall that many leading politicians of the administrations of the 1750s, led by Henry Pelham and by his older brother the Duke of Newcastle, were denied favorable treatment under George III. The rapid shuffle of ministries of the 1760s made the king look more anxious than his predecessor but not more generous. The reasons of the politicians who, on one point or another, opposed the king were certainly selfish (whatever the mixture of higher motives), and yet in their view they required little justification. They counted themselves natural superiors of the king—the Rockinghamites quite as much as any other group. Lord Rockingham's early assertion of independence from the crown, however, went hand in hand with his reluctance to form coalitions. It was an effect of temper and circumstance as much as adherence to a principle. Yet large changes in a political nation may come from just such accidents.

When taken alongside Burke's argument for constitutional checks, the stand of the Rockingham party set an example that would lead to an expansion of liberty that touched many who before had stood outside the domain of politics.

When, in 1760, George III succeeded to the crown at the age of twenty-two, he took his first step by choosing as his chief minister Lord Bute—not a politician but a personal confidant at court and indeed the man who had guided his opinions from an early age. The king's mission was to restore the lost powers of the crown: to accomplish this, no politician known for his skill and connections would be so serviceable as an outsider who cared for the interests of the king alone. How novel was this appointment and how ominous the pattern it meant to inaugurate? "The king," Richard Pares has observed, "had a constitutional right to do it, and nearly everybody must have expected him to do it; but it was an affront to the political class, and so badly did George III think of that class that it must probably have been meant as such."[2] This decision and those that followed, which turned over five ministries in eight years, could hardly be separated from the peculiarities of the character of George III. In person the king was stiff, formal, and graceless, remarkable alike for his exhibited self-doubts and spasmodic assertions; well educated yet uncertain of the uses of his learning; a narrow dealer (cautious and sleepless) with the few persons he could do business with. George III, in short, was an unsocial king: an edifice of obstruction that never seemed to budge. The mirthless goodwill he displayed at his levees did little to soften the impression, and the heavy-handedness of his interrogations, plots and counterplots, in greeting the four ministries between Lord Bute's departure in 1762 and Lord North's ascent in 1769, might be supposed to foreshadow a reversal of a progress that had occurred under the first two Georges.

He broke no rule in using the powers he exercised. Only the manner of their deployment indicated a scorn of external checks. This truth may be acknowledged in a different tone without altering the meaning: George III "never left the safe ground of Parliamentary government," writes Lewis Namier, "and only acted the *primus inter pares,* the first among borough-mongering, electioneering gentlemen in England."[3] Thus, for example, the king had a right to appoint a family retainer as his chief minister, but it was a prerogative he was not expected to use. A king might decide on occasion to interest himself in the assignment of a certain admiral to a certain squadron or the number of ships to be dispatched to the West Indies; but George III made such things his concern with a pressure that was close and constant. For him, the dour competence of Grenville and the integrity of Rockingham (however dry) finally counted against them as chief ministers. He preferred the lazy half competence of the Duke of Grafton or Lord North's pathological indecisiveness, which left him plenty of scope for meddling.[4] Of the character of George III, the leading political satirist of the age, Junius, wrote that "Nature intended him only for a good humoured fool. A systematical education, with long practice, has made him a consummate hypocrite."[5] In fact, this summing-up underrated the abilities of George III and overstated his malignity. He wanted power because he thought he could use it well. He was influenced by ideals of monarchy that placed the king at the center of policy making and by ideals of empire that he shared with most of his contemporaries. A man of pinched and narrow temperament who cherished the most high-flown of intentions, he did not hesitate to intervene in the government of his country in a manner both dedicated and impolitic. His role behind the scenes was often penetrable—as he sometimes wished it to be.

The first episode of Burke's long and complicated relationship with George III began with the king's prosecution of John Wilkes. It would end fifteen years later, with the dissolution of the Fox–North coalition. How far could George III himself have been an active participant in such a conspicuous contest of political wills? The truth is that no one could have been more fully engaged. He instructed North in 1768 to press for the expulsion of Wilkes from the House of Commons. By 1769, this had become "a measure whereon my Crown almost depends."[6] Again, in 1783 the king helped to bring down an administration he had recently approved by sending a message to the House of Lords that anyone who voted with the ministry on its most diligently prepared legislation, Fox's East India Bill, would be considered his personal enemy. Yet (it has been asked) how different is this from the pattern of conduct set by his predecessor? "In the last resort, I think," writes Pares, "Newcastle governed

George II and George III governed North. The differences were personal, but the constitutional history of this country, above all in this department, is made up of personal differences."[7] That the history of a country may be altered by personal differences was a perception that influenced Burke when, in *Thoughts on the Cause of the Present Discontents*, he emphasized the importance of "men" rather than "measures." One mark of constitutional progress is the setting of limits on the damage either a single man or a single measure can do.

The desire of the Rockinghamites to govern as a whole party and their aversion from coalitions plainly distinguished them from their rivals. Where the Bedfords bargained hard, and Chatham feinted and withheld himself, Rockingham, along with Dowdeswell, Richmond, and the other leaders, wanted to govern, but they had no price the king could pay.[8] Their arrogance as descendants of the Whigs of the Glorious Revolution—audible in the lash of insolence that Burke picked up as a trait of style—sprang from their belief that they had made the king possible. In this collective self-estimate, Burke entirely concurred: "No wise king of Great Britain would think it for his credit to let it go abroad that he considered himself, or was considered by others, as personally at variance with a Lord Rockingham, a Duke of Richmond, a Duke of Portland, an Earl of D—, the families of the Cavendishes, with a Savile, a Dowdeswell, &c."[9] The balance between court and country had not yet attained the stability it would possess in the government of the younger Pitt, and the Rockingham grandees could not easily be persuaded to give much time to Parliament.[10] For Burke, this was a source of irritation. He saw the consultations of Parliament as significant, but his view was not shared by men like Richmond and Rockingham, "who were," as Pares says, "uncrowned kings, respectively, of certain parts of Yorkshire and West Sussex." Such a dispersion of political energy into local politics—from a combination of noble pride and distrust—had been a danger foreseen by Lord Bolingbroke, the philosopher of the enlightened country gentry. His remedy for it was the idea of a "patriot king."

Very likely, George III had been introduced to Bolingbroke's fantasy (Machiavellian yet benign) of a ruler equipped to overawe and unify the scattered interests and divisive concerns of the English nation.[11] If so,

Bute is a good candidate for the person who effected the introduction. The letter of May 4, 1760, in which George (then Prince of Wales) confessed to Bute, "I owe everything to you," was also the letter in which he asserted: "I look upon the majority of politicians as intent on their own private interests instead of that of the public."[12] The attitude that the king hoped to translate from theory to practice was repellent, and maxims he intended to express his authority suggested haughty defiance instead. His shows of dignity often bordered on petulance: "I always act from conviction," he said, and other characteristic sayings convey the same impression. "I know I am doing my duty and therefore can never wish to retract." "Firmness is the characteristic of an Englishman." Add to this an overweening religiosity, at odds with the tone of Whiggery in the age of Adam Smith, and you have a basis in manners for friction in politics. A king who could say, "I begin to see that I shall soon have enfused some of that spirit which I thank Heaven ever attends me when under difficulties," was dodging a rivalry that had better have been engaged in political terms.

Still, the Rockingham party went into opposition in 1761–1762, when the meaning of opposition was unclear. Disappointment at the negotiated peace with France after the Seven Years War seemed to be the only plausible issue on which to resist George III and Lord Bute. As Rockingham knew, the transition offered an opportunity to sharpen ready-made resentments: English expectations of the peace had run so high that any concession now could be represented as inglorious submission.[13] But there was a reason nearer home for opposing the king. He had created a cabinet without names from the old Whig connections—the Duke of Cumberland, the Duke of Newcastle, Lord Temple. The cabinet also excluded the Great Commoner, Pitt, who resigned at an opportune moment to signal his disapproval of the peace terms; Bute appeared as the leader of a one-sided administration cut off from its Pelham-Newcastle predecessor and without the popularity enjoyed by Pitt. In short, it was a government mainly suited to enlarging the power of the crown. Yet a general indictment in the absence of a particular grievance could not win many adherents.

The first popular cause for the Rockingham party arrived in March 1762: an excise tax on cider that prompted riots in the cider counties of western England and in London. A more durable issue soon emerged: the appointment of Grenville to lead a Bedford-weighted ministry that again excluded both Pitt and the remnant of the Pelhamite Whigs. This was probably the moment when Rockingham began to believe that the king was advancing the interests of a picked body of officeholders who shared his ideas of the constitutional primacy of the crown. An honorable opposition was bound to resist. Rockingham, for his part, did not emphasize the malignant influence of Lord Bute. He did not have to. The fiction that an overbearing Scottish adviser had tutored a susceptible young monarch in the ways of despotism would sufficiently work its way into the public mind, from the efforts of Junius and John Wilkes among others; and theirs was not a kind of help that Rockingham felt bound to decline. His private opinion was that the king in the end would be approachable.

Merit and the New Man

Previous to entering the service of Lord Rockingham, Burke had been required to clear his name of imputations of Catholic education and bias. Information that he was a papist with Jacobite leanings came to Rockingham from a respectable source, the Duke of Newcastle; but Burke made a convincing defense, summoning the names of those who knew him at Trinity College; and Rockingham seems to have valued him the more for the candor of his self-acquittal. Always sensitive to public appearances, Burke had offered to resign; and such readiness of self-suppression Rockingham surely counted in his favor. But there was a hidden drama in the encounter. Having come so far, only two years after his calamitous break with Hamilton, Burke was giving his new patron a chance to prove his magnanimity. The party leader and his chosen assistant at this critical moment passed each other's tests. Somewhere in back of the rumors, Burke may indeed have suspected the hand of Hamilton: "So far at least," he wrote to David Garrick on July 16, 1765, "I thank God, the designs of my Enemies, who not long since made a desperate Stroke at my Fortune, my Liberty, and my reputation, *(all! Hell-kite! all at a Swoop,)* have failed of their Effect; and their implacable and unprovoked malice has been disappointed."[14] The parenthesis (quoting Macduff) compares the threatened loss of the desirable post to the slaughter of a family, an allusion that for depth of self-feeling cannot be accused of understatement. The wildness of Burke at thirty-five has in it already the passion of the elder statesman who will denounce "the revolution harpies, sprung from night and hell" that disturb the public peace and his repose.

Was there something in his nature that provoked such attacks? One irritant may have been his keen insistence on proving that he was a self-made man. Burke showed a far more jealous self-respect in public than most commoners did; and the question how far an aristocratic society ought to admit unprecedented energy and talents would become an absorbing concern of his political thought. He was not sure that such talents could be assimilated. So Burke was theoretically consistent in his offer to close off his prospects and let Rockingham choose a man of less conspicuous abilities and an unspotted name. "Energy" and "spirit" (words that for Burke are almost synonymous) describe the risky character of someone who strives against presumption and prejudice; lacking the connections of a gentleman, he cannot choose but press his individual claim. Where does the usage come from? Edmund in *King Lear* is said to show "more composition and fierce quality" than his legitimate brother—*"Fine word, legitimate!"*—and Burke three decades on will declare with similar pride and scorn: "Gentleman are fond of quoting me." The common fear about such a man is that his inveterate dissatisfaction may engender a fearless inventiveness. He has in him something dangerous; his imagination breaks free of all restraints. Yet socialized self-restraint is a primary moral good (so Burke believed from the first)—a quality needed by society, no matter what ambitions it may crush. At the same time, a society that excludes or suppresses the man of energy must place a paramount value on order: a principle of maintenance that cannot serve as a principle of renewal. A liberal society—as John Stuart Mill would reflect in a train of thought borrowed from Burke—must promote both order and progress, yet progress includes an idea of order while order need not imply progress. Burke saw a personal application. An aristocratic society that disdains a man like him, or that suppresses or excludes a public character like Wilkes (in whom the spirit of liberty is strong)—such a society can only be a machine for the maintenance of order.

The peculiarity of his status was brought home to Burke once more in the spring of 1770, when, on the floor of the House of Commons, he had to answer an ad hominem attack by Sir William Bagot. In the background was the defeat of Lord North's opposition to a bill setting out the procedure for parliamentary inquiry into controverted elections—a contentious issue after the recent parliamentary attempt to nullify the election of Wilkes in Middlesex. Bagot voted with the Rockinghamites on the bill in question but went out of his way to attack the Whig opposition generally; and in a speech the following day, he denounced Burke's description of the narrow-mindedness belonging to the character of a country gentleman. A letter of great interest by William Burke offers a circumstantial report of the exchange from that point. It began, William says, with Lord John Cavendish intercepting Burke to stop him from making a reply; Cavendish himself defended Burke and his views with staunch loyalty; at which Sir William "began to feel himself in the wrong" and, retreating, professed himself an admirer of Burke's talents. Bagot said he would withdraw the criticism because he valued his character as a good-natured man; but he resented Burke's offense to "a party." Burke, unyielding, replied that "a good-natured Man would not invent Calumnies, a good-natured Man wou'd not sit quiet, when the Injury was given and brooding three days over his resentment, at last bring it out without provocation." Bagot had gone beyond the reach of an easy retraction. He had forgotten the gravity of the insult when he said that Burke's offense "could only have been conceived by a Nature of the blackest die, and fitted to be Secretary to the Inquisition." This echoed the vulgar charge of a secret Catholic education and ulterior design: Burke was held to be a product of the Jesuit hotbed St. Omer's, a catechized agent of political subversion. "As to the St Omer's," Burke now answered, it hardly mattered "whether his Intelligence came from St Omer's or St Germain's," for he thought "Gentlemen above the Invention of a Lie would scorn to adopt the dirty falsehood that a Newspaper was probably paid for propagating." He then gave his own account of his education.

"He took to himself," reports William Burke, "the appellation of a *Novus Homo.*" A new man. An upstart but also a man of energy, learning, and sagacity, for those who could see his worth. *Novus homo* had been Cicero's description of himself, and Burke was conscious of Cicero as his model:

He knew the envy attending that Character. *Novorum Hominum Industriam odisti;* but as he knew the envy, he knew the duty of the *Novus homo.* He then, valuing himself only on his Industry, not his Abilities, shewed he had performed that Duty in endeavouring to know the Commerce, the finances, and constitution of his country. . . . He expatiated upon the Impropriety and danger of discouraging new Men, This rising merit stamp'd with Virtue would indeed seek to rise, but under the wings of establish'd Greatness, and if their Industry and their Virtue was greater than &c. &c. &c. they must be equal, nay the superior to the lazy something that came by inheritance.[15]

This self-portrait bristling with pride recalls the Satan of *Paradise Lost,* driven to rebellion by a "fixed mind, / And high disdain from sense of injured merit." For a sense of injured merit was precisely what Burke was feeling. There is some risk, he implies, that he will be raised from despair to unseemly ambition, that he will aspire to a bad eminence rather than none at all. When you turn away talents like mine from the fair road of fortune, says Burke, you foment war between society and individual hope. He says in conclusion about persons like himself:

If they are precluded the just and constitutional roads to Ambition, they will seek others, ad populum veniam; this he disclaimed for himself indeed, but others wou'd find that way: it was the Case in [Charles I's] time, and those who value themselves on their vast property, and envy all merit that seeks to be useful may as they did then, be servants of Brewers, and low Mechanicks. "Ye may graze your fat pastures but the spirits of the world will govern the world." . . . All wise governments have encouraged rising merit, as useful and necessary; we know not in what mountain of Scotland, what bog of Ireland, or what wild in America that Genius may be now rising who shall save this country.[16]

Save this country is a bitter irony. There were people who said that Cromwell saved his country—happy the country that is not thus saved! As a new man, in any case, Burke would prefer not to seek distinction in the popular path. Yet to impede honest ambition may mean to provoke revolution: this was one of the errors of Charles I. Government therefore ought to do the best it can for rising merit; the best qualities of government itself are constituted by merit. Since the genius of politics comes from the people, wise rulers will practice an art of judicious assimilation; otherwise they sow the seeds of violent opposition ("we know not in what mountain of Scotland, what bog of Ireland . . ."). Beneath Burke's warning against the ignorance of the powerful lies a concrete threat. Had he followed another path, he might have organized a party of usurpers; but, for him, that is a threat already averted. The peril now comes from those who resemble him in their energy and talents but whose ambition is unchecked.

Possibly the charge of upstart ambition roiled him the more because of his purchase, in 1768, of the house and 600 acres at Beaconsfield, where he would live with his family for the rest of his life. Burke took a serious interest in farming, so that the estate was both more and less than decorative. His chosen company and his routines, as many visitors would attest, were nothing like what his public importance led people to expect. Hester Thrale remembered in later years a time when "I lived with him & his Lady at Beaconsfield among Dirt Cobwebs, Pictures and Statues," furnishings reflecting a casual care that "would not have disgraced the City of Paris itself: where Misery & Magnificence reign in all their Splendor, & in perfect Amity." Of course, to persons invited for more formal visits—Charles Fox or the Duke of Portland, for instance—Beaconsfield was a necessary part of the façade of a statesman.[17] It was mortgaged again and again and doubtless paid for in part by loans from Rockingham (all of them canceled by a late codicil to his will).[18] Of Burke's finances in general, Ernest Barker properly judged that they were at once honest and improvident, and this showed at Beaconsfield, as did "a sort of loyal clannishness."[19] There was never a trace in Burke of the lacquer of *arrivisme*. When he caught the scent of an accusation along those lines, however indirect, he defended himself like a lawyer.

He retained affectionate but not nostalgic feelings for the bog and the wilderness at his back. One escape was enough for one lifetime. Protective as he was concerning his origins, a few days after the *Novus homo* speech he was chagrined by a story in the *London Evening Post* (April 14–17, 1770), which traced the beginnings of his career with the help of information given by Richard Shackleton. Writing to this loyal and well-meaning friend, Burke corrected a detail—"Indeed, what you have said of my

Modesty and moderation in Debate, will, I fear, take off not a little from the Authority of the rest. It is but too well known, that I debate with great Vehemence and asperity and with little management either of the opinions or persons of many of my adversaries. They deserve not much Quarter, and I give and receive but very little."[20] Here, as in his response to the attack in the House of Commons, Burke is eager to assert his independence. He denies having enjoyed "any advantage, except my Seat in Parliament, from the Patronage of any man," and he continues: "Whatever advantages I have had, have been from friends on my own Level; as to those that are called great, I never paid them any Court; perhaps since I must say it, they have had as much benefit from my Connection, as I have had."[21] Soon after, he forgave Shackleton and, looking back, saw himself as having been excessively irritable. He requests that Shackleton burn his letter of reproof, with its sorry self-importance, yet he adds revealingly (May 6, 1770): "commit to the same flames any other letters or papers of mine which you may find and which you think liable, through some accident to be so abused."[22] The less that is known about his life, the better.

Meanwhile, Burke sought to widen his reputation in ways he could control; and his generous nature pursued a vicarious fame through his patronage of artists. In 1763, he had met the painter James Barry, who came to Dublin from Cork to exhibit a picture. Burke admired it and offered to pay Barry's way to England, and afterward made him welcome at his London house. He gave financial support and encouragement to the extent of subsidizing a journey by Barry to Italy, to view and copy the old masters; and though in later times their friendship was strained, on both sides, by temperaments exceedingly suspicious of control, Barry made a fair accounting of his debt and the anxiety it caused when he wrote to Burke: "You ought surely to be free with a man of your own making, who has found in you, father, brother, friend, every thing."[23] Another beneficiary, some two decades later, would be the poet George Crabbe, who acknowledged the importance of Burke's assistance in the composition of his early poem "The Library"—of which part "was written in his presence and the whole submitted to his judgment; receiving, in its progress, the benefit of his correction." Crabbe's son relates in his *Life* that Burke was the first who taught the poet to read his verse with a critical eye.

"Mr. Crabbe," he wrote, "had afterwards many other friends, kind, liberal, and powerful, who assisted him in his professional career; but it was one hand alone that rescued him when he was *sinking*."[24] The aesthetic sensitivity and judgment that these artists appreciated in Burke, they might have deduced from the *Sublime and Beautiful*. What they could not have predicted was the closeness of his engagement with their work.

Burke was forward with advice to Barry, and some of it warned against a self-will he was finely equipped to understand: "moderation, gentleness, and a little indulgence to others and a great deal of distrust of ourselves," these were the traits his disciple was encouraged to cultivate. "Who can live in the world without some trials of his Patience?" The advice is the better for not being delivered from a lofty ground: "Again, and again, Dear Barry, we must be at peace with our Species; if not for their sakes, yet very much for our own."[25] In a letter to Barry of another kind, Burke identifies passion in art with a capacity to be moved, a strength that he values above decorum or regularity: "there is not only a Taste, but a feeling in what you observe [with pen and pencil]; something that shews you have an heart; and I would have you by all means keep it."[26] Taste is an acquired ability of some value, but feeling counts for more—feeling we can detect in any observation that reveals "heart." We naturally suppose such receptiveness is a universal human quality; perhaps it is, potentially; but an artist may lose it through complacent repetition. One may notice here that a criterion of sincerity, as well as of delicacy, guides Burke's judgments of art—a conscious principle that can be traced in his judgments of public speakers also. He thought it "dangerous to a Man's principles, to accustom himself to a display of parts in saying the best things He could on both sides of a question."[27]

That he cared for the society of painters gives us a subtle clue to Burke's character. Through the 1770s and, still more, the 1780s, when in London and not on parliamentary business he was often to be found with Sir Joshua Reynolds. Burke accepted all possible invitations to the dinners Reynolds would give for a "large, mixed" company, which "attained the proportions of an institution," and he often came by more casually in the mornings to converse and watch Reynolds at work.[28] James Northcote, the painter who became Reynolds's biographer, said in later years in his

Conversations with William Hazlitt: "I can't help thinking [Burke] had a hand in [Reynolds's] *Discourses;* that he gave some of the fine, graceful turns; for Sir Joshua paid a greater deference to him than to any body else, and put up with freedoms that he would only have submitted to from some peculiar obligation. Indeed, Miss Reynolds used to complain that whenever Burke's poor Irish relations came over, they were all poured in upon them to dinner; but Sir Joshua never took any notice, but bore it all with the greatest patience and tranquillity."[29] But the freedoms were mutual; the indulgence had a source in gratitude more than obligation. Dr. Johnson, a close observer and a jealous friend, regretted in April 1778 that Reynolds was "too much under Fox and Burke at present. He is under the *Fox star* and the *Irish constellation*."[30] Burke would attend Reynolds's final discourse on art at the Royal Academy, given when he was almost blind; and when the lecturer had finished Burke approached him and quoted the lines from *Paradise Lost:*

> The Angel ended, and in Adam's ear
> So charming left his voice, that he a while
> Thought him still speaking; still stood fixed to hear.

His affection for Reynolds is not typical, but it does epitomize a tendency. To make sense of Burke's concern for loyalty in a political party, one has to keep in mind his experience of the deeper loyalty of friendship.

After the Rockingham Administration

On April 20, 1767, Rockingham's horse Steady beat Grafton's Pancake; and Burke made fun of the names in a letter to the Marchioness of Rockingham—her husband was a man not to be turned even if "*blackened upon one side*"; he had proved that "Quietness upon one bottom is better."[31] The compliment is real enough, but Burke cannot resist a joke about the stolidity of Rockingham—a trait that could politely be construed as the necessary accompaniment of his steadfastness. Invited in 1766 to join the Chatham-Grafton ministry, Rockingham turned down an arrangement that would have separated him from most of his party; and General Conway's manner in lamenting the lost opportunity (without "the slightest

Trace of his usual diffidence and hesitation") convinced Burke that Rockingham had acted appropriately. Earlier, Rockingham had declined an alliance with the Bedfords because it would have left out Conway. Now Conway was urging him to combine with Grafton instead; though in the event, Conway would be tossed out as secretary of state as a condition of Grafton coming in.[32] "Their plan, in short, was, that your Lordship, with a few only of the chief of your friends should take offices, and that the rest should wait those vacancies, which Death and occasional arrangements might make in a Course of time."[33] It was a cynical plan of a usual sort, which Burke was happy to see his patron decline.[34]

Burke himself had been under consideration. Eight months before the negotiations just discussed, Grafton remarked to Chatham (on October 17) that Burke appeared suitable for a coalition ministry: "A most material man to gain, and one on whom the thoroughest dependence may be given, where an obligation is owed."[35] This (adds Grafton) is Conway's opinion, too; and the opportunity became the first test of Burke's party loyalty. When approached by Conway, as he recounts the offer, he made his fidelity to Rockingham a condition of his service:

> The substance of my resolution was, and I explained it to him in Terms strong and precise; That I had begun with this party, That it was now divided in situation, though I hoped not in opinions or inclinations; that the point of honour lay with that division which was out of power; and that if the place which should be offerd, should prove in itself never so acceptable, I could take it only on condition that, in accepting it, and in holding it, I must be understood to belong not to the administration, but to those who were out; and that therefore if ever they should set up a standard, though spread for direct and personal opposition, I must be revocable into their party, and join it.[36]

Implicit in this is a rebuke to Conway, the man ready to take office without conditions, provided it brings him nearer to power. To disclaim an immediate advantage, as Burke by contrast does, might enhance one's reputation for probity, yet he was aware of how much he had sacrificed: setting his party before the chance of office meant that he belonged, once more, to "those who were out." This was a point of honor, an action performed not for goods received but from an attachment that overrode all calculable benefits. The moral value of such loyalty will be a subject of continuous meditation in Burke's writings, starting with *Thoughts on the Cause of the Present Discontents;* and though he wrote that pamphlet in order to regain power for his party, his own refusal of extra-party preferment would harden some passages with a kind of conviction more impressive than rhetorical craft. Self-knowledge may also have prompted Burke's refusal. "I believe," he would tell the Club in 1778, "in any body of men in England I should have been in the Minority; I have always been in the Minority."[37] The reward for making a good speech, he added, is that it may have an effect on many who do not take its position in the vote. Exemplary action cannot be judged by immediate results.

The growing fame and ambiguous status of Edmund Burke in the late 1760s belongs to the peculiar history of the man of talents in the eighteenth century. Yet Burke was something more complex: a man of genius who, because he had resolved to make his way in an aristocratic society, was obliged to defer to mediocrities without concealing his gifts. This was a delicate performance. As Prior relates, Burke grew used to being praised in an undertone of wonder and half reproach: "Impudent fellow!" The prejudice guiding this reaction supposed it (in Prior's words) "a species of presumption in men without private weight to assume a parliamentary lead." This was the inside version of the abuse Burke endured outside the Commons when people called him a Jesuit; but the attitude also served as a cover for vanity against the general surprise at Burke's originality. "He was," Prior remarks, "not merely new to the house, but in a certain degree new to the country. He was without the essential adjuncts of commanding wealth or high connections; and thence was regarded in the light of one who usurps a station to which he has no proper claim. For it is another of his characteristics in an eventful career, to have been the *first* who attained under so many disadvantages, to consequence in Parliament and in the country, simply by unaided talents."[38] That description brings out Burke's originality as a parallel in politics to the originality of Samuel Johnson in authorship—another talent who freed himself from the dependent status of the patronized. There were private qualities in Burke— judgment both prudent and frank, intellectual energy combined with self-discipline, an ability to see things in uncommon lights—whose public value Grafton noticed when (advising Chatham) he said that Burke was "the readiest man upon all points, perhaps in the whole House."[39] Ready, he meant, to argue about the proper response to the latest challenge from the American colonists; or about the king's use of his budget to reward tested favorites; or about the most politic method to defend Wilkes against the oppression of the government without palliating his scandalous life or his relentless provocations.

The Rise of Wilkes

It has been said that England in the 1760s had three parties: the Bedford Whigs, the Rockingham Whigs, and Pitt—the last a power in himself, both before and after he became Lord Chatham. Grenville, too, was a power of ponderable force when allied with Lord Temple (his brother and Chatham's brother-in-law), yet he was fated to disappoint: a potential mediator who lacked the necessary flexibility. His hard line on America was the price Grenville asked for throwing his support to the Rockinghamites and Bedfords; but in July 1767, Bedford declined to join with Rockingham, owing to Rockingham's refusal to comply on the American question. The existing divisions would grow sharper during the government's series of attempts to prosecute John Wilkes and to exclude him from Parliament.

Wilkes was a scoundrel with a genius for satirical exposure who held fast to one belief: liberty was the birthright of an Englishman. He hugged the ideal closer as his persecutors tightened their grip. His wiliness and pluck were traits of character that all his opponents underrated. The cunning of a master tactician was augmented, in his case, by a readiness to invoke the popular will and deploy the crowd of his followers. Wilkes was an opportunist on a pattern solely of his choosing. He roused the people to share his indignation without taking them into his confidence, and so he may be called a demagogue. But such a conventional characterization gives a false impression of many things: his energy, his anti-slavish intellect, and the relish with which he played a recurrent role as antagonist to arbitrary power—often behind the scenes but also in head-to-head encounters. Wilkes kept his distance from the "Wilkes and Liberty" mob whom he could summon with a snap of his fingers. He preferred the prestige of a hero to the drudgery of a leader.

In person, he lived by a libertine code that he defended without hypocrisy. "Dissipation and profligacy," he told Boswell, "renews the mind." (Boswell acted on the same principle but would never have professed it.) In this and other respects, Wilkes made no serious departure from the mores of the aristocratic society whose durability he took for granted. A man of classical learning, he could converse equably with Dr. Johnson (at a meeting arranged by Boswell with the design of making it immortal). Haughtiness and vulgar raillery were joined, in his selection of tactics, when he rang the changes of anti-Scottish prejudice against the king's adviser Lord Bute. The confusing richness of Wilkes's personality is captured well by Linda Colley's description of his "customary blend of wit, pomposity, impudence, and intelligence."[40] Wilkes, for all these reasons, stood out in contrast against his enemies of the Bedford clan—"political gangsters without pretense," as Christopher Hobhouse once called them, "whose sole public object was to lay their hands on public money." The precise mixture of his motives could never be exactly estimated; and this lent every dealing with him the suggestion of an annoyance that might become an ambush. The wayward impression was heightened by Wilkes's physical presence, ungainly, cross-eyed, a "very ugly man" whose teeth were falling out at an early age, yet so captivating to women that he felt assured of his eventual triumph if he could get one to stand his appearance for twenty minutes.

Born four years before Burke—they would die the same year—Wilkes entered British politics when he was elected in July 1757 as member from Aylesbury. In May 1762, he contributed an anonymous essay to the *Monitor*, in the form of a polemical attack on court favorites such as Lord Bute. The court launched the *Briton* in retaliation (written by Smollett), and this led in turn to Wilkes's founding of the *North Briton*. Anti-Scottish invective was standard fare in the last of these papers, which taunted its victims with the treacherous invasion and defeat of the young pretender in 1745. Wilkes did not disguise the names of his targets, as was still common practice in the 1750s, but rather took cover in anonymity. When challenged, he would disclaim the authorship of all but three articles in the run of the *North Briton.* He hired Charles Churchill as editor; and in the service of Wilkes and Liberty, Churchill became the most exacting verse satirist of the later eighteenth century.

On November 18, 1762, Lord Halifax signed two separate warrants: for numbers 1–25 of the *North Briton* and for numbers 1–26. The government was getting ahead of itself: No. 25 was still two days from publication, No. 26 a week further off. The legally questionable warrants were drawn up to intimidate Wilkes; they invoked the authority of the law, over the head of the laws themselves. The ministry, it seemed, wanted to neutralize Wilkes by any possible means, and this became obvious in more intimate transactions: when the *North Briton* said that Henry Fox was a man of great talents which were never employed to a good purpose, so that "the greatness of his understanding serves only to make the badness of his heart more formidable," Wilkes was offered the governorship of Canada if he would desist. He refused, as later he would decline an offer by Lord Sandwich to be made a director of the East India Company. These efforts to buy his silence foreshadowed eight years of harrying by a government that employed a wide array of tactics: proffered bribes; attempted assassination (disguised as a challenge to a duel); expulsion from the House of Commons; the nullification of his election as a member of Parliament by a vote to exclude him from the House of Commons. (A remission occurred in the brief span of the Rockingham administration, during whose tenure Wilkes resided in Paris and was not heard to complain.) The Commons proved by its actions that, however undeniably he was elected, it would neither include him nor allow him to enter its company from outside.

Yet the protracted siege by government, and by its servant Lord Chief Justice Mansfield, against the person and fame of Wilkes was disrupted at intervals: early on, by the decision of the Court of Common Pleas that the warrant against Wilkes for seditious libel was illegal; later, by the serial election and reelection of the expelled member; and all along by acts of the people. The effort to hobble and discredit his challenge to the crown was a series of tactics without design or principle that finally exhausted itself.

The contest began with Wilkes's reply to a platitude. The king, in a speech before Parliament on April 19, 1763, had asked for a spirit of concord and obedience to the laws, and on April 23, *North Briton* No. 45 responded: "A nation as sensible as the *English*, will see that a *spirit of concord*, when they are oppressed, means a tame submission to injury, and that a *spirit of liberty* ought then to arise, and I am sure ever will, in proportion to the weight of the grievance they feel. *Every* legal *attempt of a contrary tendency* to the *spirit of concord* will be deemed a justifiable resistance, warranted by the *spirit of the English constitution*." Arthur Cash has pointed out the all-important corollary. The prerogative of the crown, Wilkes added, encompassed the exercise of powers used with wisdom and judgment, but "The people too have their prerogative," and "Freedom is the English subject's prerogative." The last statement was a quotation from Dryden—a poet scarcely chargeable with representing a single party or sect.

To Wilkes's suggestion that one might side with liberty against the king, the government made a swift response. By now the ministry was led by Grenville; he would later oppose the expulsion of Wilkes from the House of Commons, but the pressure of the moment was compelling. A warrant signed by Halifax on April 26 released the government to search for "the Authors, Printers & Publishers of a seditious and treasonable paper intitled, the North Briton Number 45." Such a "general warrant," which authorized a sweep for evidence without naming the offender, was almost unheard-of; the messengers bearing the warrant nonetheless arrested forty-nine persons. Yet Wilkes was a member of Parliament, and a member who merely published a libel was not subject to arrest. Lord Temple, the ally of Wilkes, had his lawyer seek a writ of habeas corpus at the Court of Common Pleas, and as soon as the judge, Charles Pratt (later Lord Camden), saw the content of the warrant he granted the writ. The warrant itself Pratt found to be "a very extraordinary one: I know no law that can authorize it, nor any practice, that it can be founded on."[41] Wilkes, secured by his immunity as a member of Parliament, initiated charges for false arrest against the constable and messengers who had delivered the warrant; and here things might have rested had the ministry not turned its harassment into a vendetta. Through deft employment of spies and a payoff to the printer Michael Curry, the government obtained proof sheets for a licentious poem, the *Essay on Woman*, some pages of which had been run off by Wilkes without a clear intent to publish. This satire, not written by Wilkes himself, went out of its way to ridicule Bishop Warburton as a pretender to literary distinction and moral rectitude. The government (in a pattern it would repeat) offered Wilkes to abstain from action if he would remit his counterattack—in this case by dropping the charges against the ministry and their messengers for illegal search and seizure. When that gambit was declined, the king and ministers decided to instigate a trial of John Wilkes by the House of Commons.

Lord Sandwich and Lord Grenville (the latter now secretary of the treasury) together worked up a careful plan to attack Wilkes in both houses at once. This was not a congenial alliance: Grenville's relations with the king and his friends had cooled after he insisted that George III stop corresponding with Bute. George III now took the position that he was bound to act in the name of justice, since Wilkes, in going to the Court of Common Pleas, had not answered at the Court of the King's Bench the information against him by the attorney general. The motion on Wilkes in Parliament declared that *North Briton* No. 45 was "a false, scandalous, and seditious libel," exhibiting "insolence" and "contumacy" toward the king, along with insults to Parliament; and that Wilkes's defiance tended "to alienate the affections of the people from his Majesty, to withdraw them from their obedience to the laws of the realm, and to excite them to traitorous insurrections against his Majesty's government." So much for the case against *North Briton* No. 45; the additional charge of obscene and blasphemous libel against the *Essay on Woman* was brought before the House of Lords, of which Bishop Warburton was a member. Pitt now chose to break with Wilkes even as he defended his immunity, calling the *North Briton* "illiberal, unmanly, and detestable." The common hangman on December 3 was prevented from burning *North Briton* No. 45 by an irrepressible crowd that took up the cry "Wilkes and Liberty." On December 23, 1763, Wilkes fled England, and he crossed from Dover to France on Christmas day.

The Rockingham administration was formed and came to power two years later—a hopeful sign for Wilkes, who now entertained thoughts of returning. As the Rockinghamites did not want him back but did not wish to be seen to repel him, an intricate diplomacy was called for. Rockingham made William Fitzherbert his agent in dealing with Wilkes, and Burke along with him. The party had Wilkes on their side and wanted to keep things that way, but the actual Wilkes on the ground in England would be a nuisance. They offered him a thousand pounds a year to stay in France, the sum to be paid out of the emoluments for office, which as gentlemen they had no need of. But Wilkes drove a hard bargain: five thousand plus a pension of fifteen hundred per annum on the Irish Establishment. Negotiations lasted three weeks and ended with the Rockingham party declining to meet his terms. Wilkes anyway gained the knowledge that he would be treated respectfully, if warily, by a Rockingham administration; in spite of the refusal, he soon after drew on Fitzherbert's account for a thousand pounds when his debts became embarrassing. The Bishop of Carlisle wrote to Grenville of Wilkes's return in secret in May 1766: "they are afraid to press the king for his pardon, as that is a subject His Majesty will not easily hear the least mention of; and they are apprehensive, if he has it not, that the mob of London will rise in his favour."[42] All told, Wilkes's fleeting return and his wangling the unmeant concession from Fitzherbert tends to confirm Boswell's judgment: "good without principle and wicked without malevolence."[43] The encounter of May 1766 also shows the quandary in which the party found itself. The Rockingham ministry opposed the previous bias of the government on one side, while, on the other, it had to appease the importuning of Wilkes without being seen to satisfy his demands.

A Wary Alliance

Burke conducted interviews with Wilkes so skillfully that, as Prior puts it, "after a douceur of three or four hundred pounds . . . this pattern of morality and suffering patriotism retraced his steps to the French capital."[44] That was not the whole story, as we have seen; but Wilkes wrote on June 12, 1766, to express his appreciation of Burke's assistance—"your generous endeavours to serve me, and the warmth of your friendship." He added: "The great object of my hopes is a pardon, which I wish to owe to his Majesty's goodness, and to the favour of friends. . . . I am very thankfull to you all for what you have done in the cause of liberty, and I persuade myself justice will be done to the greatest sufferer in it. I go farther. I am desirous of becoming your fellow labourer."[45] For Wilkes to address Burke, at this stage of their careers, as a champion of liberty on a par with himself was a benign but transparent insincerity. What rings true in the letter is his sense of the promise of the Rockingham party: to be seen as their associate would indeed raise him from the shadows. Not that Wilkes pretends to suffer much in his Parisian exile; he affects rather a dandyish discontent— "I am here feeding among the lilies, in a state of trifling amusement, but casting my longing eyes towards England. . . . I live in the impatient hope of returning soon, and perhaps aiding to keep the boars out of the garden." This complacent mood lasted a little over twenty months.

"What the devil have I to do with prudence," he would confide to friends on his return to England in early 1768. "I owe money in France, am an outlaw in England, hated by the King, the Parliament and the bench of bishops. I must raise a dust or starve in a gaol."[46] Burke appears to have taken initially a formal and detached interest in the Middlesex election controversy of late March 1768: "The hatred of Ld Bute never was stronger among the people; and this was a time to signalize it. Besides the crowd always want to draw themselves, from abstract principles to personal attachments; and since the fall of Ld Chatham, there has been no hero of the Mob but Wilkes."[47] A dry estimate: Wilkes as a hero of the mob. Yet the mob at exigent moments may be the only audible voice of the people. Hence a recognition of Wilkes's importance in 1768 must imply a readiness to deal with him, or at least a refusal to join any movement to exclude him.

Such were Burke's general sympathies.[48] Yet his practical advice on Wilkes was notable for its coolness. His party's attitude should be part of a plan

> not to provoke Administration into any Violent measure upon this Subject; nor be the means of stirring questions, which we have not strength to support, and which could not be lost, without leaving the Constitution worse than we found it. It could be no service to Wilkes to take him out of the hands of the *Law,* and to drive him under the Talons of *power;* besides we had not the least desire of taking up that Gentlemans Cause as personally favourable to him; he is not ours; and

if he were, is little to be trusted: He is a lively agreeable man, but of no prudence and no principles. Had they attempted to attack him, as, I do not think, they could have done it without great Oppression, we must have defended him, and were resolved to do it; but still as the Cause not the Person.[49]

Wilkes's infidelity, his eye for the main chance, and his dissolute life would not have prejudiced Burke against him. Free thinking and a certain cynicism about religious institutions were common enough in his circle. One may find Rockingham, for example, on August 16, 1768, writing to Burke, "I want to know for what bad reason a worthy man has been made Archbishop of Canterbury. I know him very well and notwithstanding some events within these last two years—I am sure his principles are very good. I imagine the promotions occasioned by his advancement will account for this unusual and unprecedented transaction." Good may be done in transactions of the church but only for bad reasons; a good man is advanced to the highest position only if it enables several mediocrities to prosper. A letter by Joshua Reynolds, also in 1768 (the year of Wilkes's return), counsels tolerance toward religious believers "who still retain the early prejudices of education and have not that strong understanding which enables a man to shake them off." Such prejudices are of course an impediment to reason and lend support to superstition, but it is "very unphilosophical," says Reynolds, to look down with contempt on the conventionally pious: "I am of opinion a man may be a good member of society and even a man of sense in other things tho' he may be weak enough to be a believer in—or even a Christian."[50] Probably his irony meant to work both ways, against the dogmatic doubter as well as the credulous faithful, but the virtues that mattered for Reynolds were plainly those of the man of sense.

Yet Wilkes's bravado stretched the terms of an unwritten code of tolerated conduct. On February 8, 1768, he reentered London with the idea of running for Parliament; as usual, his concern for the public good harmonized nicely with self-interest: he hoped by a resumption of parliamentary privilege to gain immunity from his English creditors. On March 4, he declared his return by sending a letter to the king asking for his pardon. In the same month, he was admitted to the Company of Joiners and

Ceilers—one of the livery companies that grew out of the feudal guilds—and by his membership acquired the right to vote and stand for office. He made his first run in the City of London and came in last of seven candidates; but even before the polls closed he had decided to stand for the county of Middlesex, which sent to Parliament two elected knights of the shire. In this second poll, in a neighborhood where he had inherited property sufficient to meet the qualification for candidacy, Wilkes was the winner with 1,292 votes. An uproar of celebration greeted the result in Brentford, in London, in Aylesbury; Wilkes, as he passed through, quieted the crowds to prevent violence. This was the time when Benjamin Franklin saw the number 45—jubilant reminder of the offending issue of the *North Briton*—chalked on houses on the Great West Road for most of the fifty miles between London and Winchester.

On the first day of the session, Wilkes tested the law of parliamentary privilege by surrendering himself at the King's Bench before Lord Chief Justice Mansfield and two other judges. He disclaimed authorship of No. 45 and the *Essay on Woman;* and Mansfield oddly appeared to cooperate on a technicality: he refused to recognize Wilkes as an accused person, since a legal arrest had not been made by the attorney general. But this was a confession of embarrassment (perhaps also of cowardice) and not the sign of a disposition to clemency. Wilkes was brought in officially in late April, but the court postponed a decision until mid-June and meanwhile detained Wilkes in the King's Bench Prison. His first strategy had failed: parliamentary privilege was said not to apply because Wilkes had never been sworn in as a member. So the maneuvers of challenge and avoidance were resumed in the exact manner in which they had left off four years before.

On May 10, 1768, Wilkes's contest for legitimation entered a different world of consequence. A large crowd had waited in St. George's Fields to see him returned from prison to attend the first day of Parliament. It was a peaceable crowd and quite without menace except for one unruly man. He was pursued by soldiers who by mistake shot and killed another man. Thus began the St. George's Fields Massacre. Between six and eleven persons were killed by the end of it and several others wounded, some having no relation to the crowd. Six days later, Wilkes appeared before the King's

Bench, charged with outlawry—defined in Johnson's *Dictionary* as "a decree by which any man is cut off from the community, and denied the protection of the law." But the judges postponed their decision, and on June 8, 1768, the charge was dropped. Writing to his Middlesex constituents, Wilkes said that to arrest him for outlawry was from the first "an act of equal injustice and cruelty" by officials who had "trampled on laws and been actuated by the spirit of tyranny and arbitrary power."[51]

At his sentencing on June 18, before the King's Bench—on the original charges, once more, of seditious libel and obscene and blasphemous libel—Wilkes's lawyer submitted an affidavit from the publisher of the *North Briton* asserting that the evidence against Wilkes drawn from his house was invalidated from having been obtained by a general warrant. But the conviction was sustained for libeling the king in *North Briton* No. 45 and for libeling Bishop Warburton in the unpublished *Essay on Woman*. Wilkes on each charge was fined £500 and sentenced to a year in prison (receiving credit for the two months he had already served). In the court's view, he had emboldened the people to consider themselves as judges of oppression: a tendency so dangerous that if countenanced, it would subvert all respect for the laws. Though Burke never commented on the sentence, his whole understanding of liberty tells against this judgment by the court. The people, says Burke, should not be trusted as advisers on policy or even necessarily as true reckoners of their interests in the short run, but they are always the best judges of their own oppression—so much so that we ought to fear any power on earth that sets itself above them.

Wilkes and Liberty

Through the late 1760s and early 1770s, the cause of Wilkes and Liberty would run parallel with the discontents of the American colonies; and here again, Wilkes's concerns and associations show a parallel to Burke's. In June 1768, Wilkes received an appreciative letter from the Sons of Liberty, a Boston political society that included John Adams and John Hancock as well as the pamphleteers James Otis and Josiah Quincy Jr. In answer to their greeting to him as an incorruptible defender of liberty and of the British constitution, Wilkes replied: "I hope freedom will ever flourish under your hemisphere as well as ours. . . . Liberty I consider as the birthright of every subject of the British empire, and I hold Magna Charta to be as full force in America as in Europe."[52] About this time Fitzherbert—once the Rockingham party's negotiator with Wilkes but now answering a call from Grafton—offered Wilkes a chance to take his Middlesex seat; in return, the king desired a formal note of submission to his will and a withdrawal by Wilkes from his contesting of government warrants and of the king's view of parliamentary privilege. The offer was made on the word of a minister, doubtless Chatham or Grafton, whom Fitzherbert would not name. Wilkes replied that he would submit to the king but not to a minister behind the scenes, and he decided to petition the king as well as Parliament for clemency. He would later comment that it was lucky he did not embrace the offer. By saving him, the king would have ruined him.

Here we arrive at the critical moment when all Wilkes's various talents—his gift as a tactician in sparring with authority, his power as a demagogue in appealing to voters, and his charismatic hold on the unorganized crowd—were needed to oppose the junction of forces arrayed against him by government: legal and extralegal harassment, a rigged election, parliamentary disqualification. Wilkes persevered—an active inciter of protest who would not allow the people to settle into docility. On December 30, 1768, still in prison, he took communion to qualify as a candidate in Farringdon Without. When his competitor withdrew, he wrote a letter of thanks to the inhabitants of the ward. The election was declared illegal; so it was held again, with the same result; the result was challenged by the alderman, and the challenge was withdrawn. On a second front, the persecution of Wilkes was proceeding no more happily. In testimony before the House of Commons, a crown messenger admitted he had paid the printer Michael Curry to steal proof sheets of the *Essay on Woman;* and Wilkes petitioned for redress on two counts: the illegality of the bribe and a change that Lord Chief Justice Mansfield had dictated in the record of February 1764—the charge against the "purport and effect" of Wilkes's writing had been altered to a charge against its "tenor and effect." A small change but consequential. *Purport* requires a proof of malicious intent whereas *tenor* might convict Wilkes even if no evidence was given of the intent to commit libel. When his petition was turned down, Wilkes pressed forward with agitation on a graver matter, the violence of the troops and the instructions of the ministry that ordered the St. George's Fields Massacre.

He now gave the press a letter he had been shown from the secretary of state, Lord Weymouth, advising that additional soldiers be called up. Wilkes in a preface to the published instruction said that this order showed "how long the horrid massacre in St. George's Fields had been planned . . . and how long a hellish project can be brooded over by some infernal spirits without one moment's remorse."[53] When accused in the House of Commons, he admitted that he was the author of these remarks: "Mr. Speaker, I acknowledge that I transmitted to the press a copy of the Secretary of State's letter, and that I wrote the prefatory remarks upon it; and I will, whenever a secretary of state shall write so bloody a scroll, write some prefatory remarks upon it. I beg pardon that I use so mild and gentle an expression, when I speak of that inhuman 10th of May. . . . I doubt not from the justice of the House but you will immediately order an impeachment against the secretary who wrote that letter."[54] On February 3, 1769, Wilkes was expelled from the House of Commons, as a punishment, according to Lord Temple, for the "accumulated crimes" of No. 45, the obscene libel, and his accusations of Lord Weymouth. Wilkes struck back the next day with a letter to the gentlemen, clergy, and freeholders of Middlesex: "If ministers can once usurp the power of declaring who *shall not* be your representative, the next step is very easy, and will follow speedily. It is that of telling you whom you *shall* send to Parliament, and then the boasted Constitution of England will be entirely torn up by the roots." On February 16, he was elected knight of the shire of Middlesex. No one had run as his opponent.

How did the Rockingham party look on these developments? Burke's was the strongest response: he moved to form a committee in the House to inquire into the St. George's Fields Massacre. This marked, as Paul Langford notes, the first time he "attempted to take the lead in a major question before the House."[55] The legal propriety of Lord Weymouth's order was a large public issue and inescapably associated with Wilkes, because his refusal to disown or apologize for having assisted in the publication had triggered his expulsion. Burke protested that while the House of Commons had the power to expel one of its members, the very idea of incapacitating a member was anti-constitutional, for it awarded the Commons an unlimited power to make a law without concurrence of the Lords and the king. This meant that the house of Parliament that was supposed to represent the people could legislate for itself against the people. Indeed, it raised the possibility that a body so exceptional could likewise perpetuate itself against the will of the people.

A portion of Burke's great speech of March 8, 1769, survives in manuscript. He addressed the House in that "warning voice" that would become familiar in the strife-ridden decade to follow: "If you do not carefully distinguish the feelings of the multitude from their judgments; if you do not distinguish their interests from their opinions; attending religiously to the one and utterly despising the other; if you lay down a Rule that because the people are absurd, their grievances are not to be redressed, then in plain Terms it is impossible that popular grievances should receive any redress at all, because the people when they are injured will be violent; when they are violent, they will be absurd—and their absurdity will in general, be proportioned to the greatness of their Grievances."[56] Failure by government to respond to grievances will only make the people more desperate, and "the worse their suffering the further they will be from their remedy."

A general comment follows, containing a clear view of the morality that informed all Burke's political judgments. His ideas of liberty are tempered, he says, by the knowledge that "Peace is the great End in *all* Governments; Liberty is an End only in the Best." He is "an hater of violence and *innovation*"—where the word "and" points to an affinity between violence and innovation. Yet Burke is careful to add that power, the power of government itself, "can be violent," and government too can innovate. "I am persuaded," he concludes (returning to the subject of Wilkes), "that a design has been *formed* gradually to make an essential *innovation,* in the manner of Executing the Law, and conducting publick prosecutions in this Kingdom."[57] The government has taken steps that infallibly prove that it values the security of the state above the liberty and welfare of the people. Burke continues: "The Innovation consists in this; the establishment of a regular martial police; upon a Principle avowed, justified, even vaunted by the great Crown Lawyer of incorporating and blending the Army into the civil Government, and to consider it as his first instrument; and not as his final and extreme resource, and to make it subservient to the support of Magistracy and the Execution of Justice when bad practices are generalised and perpetuated into bad maxims of Government."[58] On this new scheme, exposure of the misjudgments or errors of government is to be prevented by force. The laws no longer serve to protect the people but are a hiding-place from which to hunt down all those who protest abuses. So far from the police being sufficient to back the edicts of official justice, the army has been incorporated into the police; and by its actions, as at St. George's Fields, the army has shown it can overwhelm the moderate temper of local magistrates. Government is coming to consider force as a first and not a last resort.

One may detect here a germ of an idea of conspiracy that will emerge fully in *Thoughts on the Cause of the Present Discontents*. (Even that title has a hint of the conspiratorial: a design of government innovation may be the secret cause of popular discontents.) Burke would have had in mind not only the stratagems of the king's men but the attempt to conceal Lord Weymouth's order and the expulsion of Wilkes for publishing it. These are a kind of evidence he always takes seriously. A change of principle may or may not be avowed, but when false reasons are used to justify an apparent change, the effect is a degradation of manners—the very manners of law-abiding and mutual respect that the police and the people ought to share. Burke admits that he disapproves of Wilkes for having spoken of Weymouth's letter as a "Bloody Scroll"; yet that is no more than "bad and silly language," whereas the letter itself betrayed an oppressor's readiness to reduce obedience to a question of force; for the letter had revealed that the calling of extra guards was initially justified by the supposed menace of a peaceful crowd. What is missing in the letter, Burke remarks, is the consideration that ought to be foremost in the mind of a government that exists to preserve the public peace. It contains "not one word of civil force, or civil prevention." On the contrary, the support of Civil Magistracy is "wholly committed to the Military."

Because of its violent innovativeness, "This whole doctrine is dangerous, erroneous, utterly alien and irreconcileable with the constitution of this Country"; it makes the civil to fall back on the military force as the only authority; but "if you take away the Civil Execution of justice you maim and mangle the whole constitutional Polity of England." Burke, therefore, closes with a resolution "to enquire into the Conduct of the Magistrates, and the Employment of the Military Power, in the suppressing of the Riots and Tumults in *Saint George's Fields,* on the 10th Day of *May* last; and into the Orders and Directions given relative thereto by any of His Majesty's Secretaries of State, or by His Majesty's Secretary of War, together with the Course which has been held concerning the Public Prosecutions on that Occasion."[59] The division was 249–39 against his motion. Yet the speech had been more than a tactical move. On April 25, 1771, he renewed the question, in response to a petition by William Allen, the father of one of the persons killed in the massacre.

Wilkes's view of his own situation was not more radical than Burke's; but he approached the crisis from a concern with representation in government rather than the accountability of officeholders. On March 16, 1769, he had again been elected unopposed as representative for Middlesex; on March 17, the House of Commons declared the election void. "The question is," wrote Wilkes on March 23 to the voters of Middlesex, "whether the people have an inherent right to be represented in parliament by the man of their free choice, not disqualified by the law of the land?" To permit the nullification would violate the "original compact" between subject and sovereign. But at this point the government tried a new stratagem. Colonel Henry Lawes Luttrell had fought in Portugal in the Seven Years War and served as representative for Bossiney. Outraged by Wilkes's defiance, he now offered to stand against him in a re-run election and was judged a suitable vehicle to accomplish the unseating. The result was 1,142 for Wilkes, 296 for Luttrell, but on April 15, 1769, two days after the votes were tallied, the House of Commons voted Luttrell the winner: the candidate, acceptable to the members of Parliament, who received the largest number of votes. The fall of public confidence produced by Wilkes's expulsion and the seating of the second-place candidate was the occasion for Samuel Johnson's pamphlet *The False Alarm.*

In a tone of common sense and controlled ridicule that sometimes broke toward real alarm, Johnson argued that the prescriptive authority in question belonged to the structure of the constitution. Parliament was acting within the bounds of its proper authority when, like any club or body with its own rules, it decided who could be a member and who could not. Its political actions were taken on a just estimate of Wilkes's outlawry as the author of seditious and obscene libels: "If these imputations were just, the expulsion was surely seasonable, and that they were just the House had reason to determine." As to the seating of a runner-up, the question, wrote Johnson, "must be, whether a smaller number of legal votes, shall not prevail against a greater number of votes not legal." He freely confessed the anti-popular basis of his argument: "A law is of perpetual obligation, but a vote is nothing when the voters are gone."[60]

Johnson's pamphlet is infused with a dread that decent subordination may be passing from the common sense of Englishmen. The duty of the ignorant is to submit to those who know better, the duty of the poor is to be content with their lot, and the place of the people is to be ruled. Wilkes replied, in *A Letter to Samuel Johnson, L.L.D.*, that if the House could unseat any person they disapproved and put in his place anyone whom they preferred, the House must have the power to elect and reelect itself. To Johnson's suggestion that rights were given to the people by Parliament, so that by Parliament they could be interpreted or taken away, Wilkes replied that this doctrine was treason: "Do you conceive," he asked the author of *A Dictionary of the English Language*, "the full force of the word CONSTITUENT?" He went on to make his meaning clear. A constituent

has the same relation to the House of Commons as Creator to Creature.

The RIGHTS OF THE PEOPLE are not what the Commons have ceded to them, but what they have reserved to themselves; *the principles of the Commons* are not what they have an indefeasible pretension to by arbitrary and discretionary claim, but what THE PEOPLE, for their own benefit, have allowed them.[61]

Wilkes adds an assertion of his stature. The Middlesex voters have elected him "in order to mark to the present age and to latest posterity, that the man who encounters the attacks of despotism with fortitude and perseverance, shall never want the avowed protection, and generous support of the great body of the people of England."[62]

The House of Commons nonetheless on May 8, 1769, had pronounced Luttrell "duly elected," by a vote of 221 to 152. A solid majority, yet the numbers in opposition were not negligible; and they drew support from voices out of doors. The Society of Supporters of the Bill of Rights backed a campaign of petitions and remonstrances, one of the most successful being undertaken by Lord Rockingham, Sir George Savile, and the dean of York Minster John Fountayne, who posted their sheets in public squares and were rewarded by 11,000 signatures. The phenomenon could not be dismissed as a revolt by the lowest of the people. The petitioners for Wilkes, as George Rudé found, eventually included "a high proportion of the enfranchised citizens" in Liverpool, Westminster, and Bristol, and eighty clergyman-petitioners in a dozen counties.[63] Also signing were petty freeholders and merchants, not excluding some of the wealthier sort. Meanwhile, Wilkes's American supporters continued to identify their grievances with his and their own oppressions with those of the disfranchised voters of Middlesex.

On January 9, 1770, King George III addressed both houses of Parliament, and the members retired to deliberate their responses separately. Lord Chatham moved an amendment to the king's address "to take into consideration the causes of the discontent which prevails"—a strong notation of the persistence of provoked alarms, about which Burke himself had already begun to write. Sir George Savile, perhaps the strongest libertarian of the Rockingham group, said at this time: "I look on this House as sitting illegally after their illegal act. They have betrayed their trust. . . . I will not say that they have betrayed their country corruptly, flagitiously, and scandalously, but I do say that they have betrayed their country." Camden and Granby, in turn, spoke against the government and resigned. The king now picked Charles Yorke—who as attorney general had prosecuted Wilkes on the charges of 1763—to become lord chancellor in Camden's place; under pressure, Yorke accepted, and three days later he died. On January 21, 1770, the Duke of Grafton resigned and the ministry was dissolved.

Politics is a mesh of hints, arranged signals, tacit acknowledgments, and compromises. Little of this underplot is legible to an outside audience, but the intricacy is never lost on the actors. What Burke could do to assist Wilkes, in his battle to achieve a new security for the people against the closure of constitutional liberty, was very different from what Wilkes could do in his own defense or what Lord Chatham could say from the stature of his title and popularity. It must be remembered, as we look to the diplomatic and partly coded language of *Thoughts*, that public figures of such various types know each other's peculiar standing and import; they can read signals that may come in the form of a measured endorsement or a publicized dissent from just one element of a policy. When Wilkes rebuked Johnson for not knowing the meaning of the word *constituent*, Chatham must have approved, and it was surely a signal meant for him. When Savile, the friend of Burke, said that the ministry had betrayed government in the name of order, Wilkes could have guessed that more careful words bearing on this matter would soon come from Burke himself. Modern sensibilities, more shockable than those of the eighteenth century, tend to underrate Wilkes by overplaying his rascal side, as if his selfishness were somehow more marked than the average politician's because it was flaunted with conspicuous relish. In fact, the career of Wilkes in the 1770s would confirm the high opinion held by his admirers in the 1760s. Having served out his sentence, he was elected as a sheriff of London, a position that brought with it the duty of presiding as a judge at the Guildhall. A ruling from the bench by Wilkes would abolish the warrants for press gangs in London—one of the ways he sided with the Americans by indirection, while also improving the liberty of the British constitution. Again, in 1771 he contrived a stratagem to open Parliament once and for all to newspapers reporting on debates and speeches. Wilkes provoked the arrest and then secured the release of printers, in a sequence calculated to bring more embarrassment than profit to government. It worked.

The Constitution and the People

Thoughts on the Cause of the Present Discontents places a heavy stress on the contrast between what is discussed by cabinet members and what can be said out of doors. It is a party pamphlet and does not conceal the fact; but we do an injustice to its scope and penetration if we take the argument as merely propounding the Rockingham thesis that the king was growing too powerful. Constitutional balance was not the only thing at stake. The political criticism is made to extend from the king to his servile ministers, and Burke is as much concerned with the theory of liberty as with restoring balance to the constitutional practice of his time. It was in recognition of these broader issues that in November 1769 he presented "a good part" of the manuscript to Lord Rockingham, along with an explanatory letter. He strikes a note of self-doubt: "It will be a matter very proper for the consideration of your Lordship and your friends, whether a thing of this Nature should appear at all." There is a risk lest by its publication "you irritate past forgiveness the Court party, and you do not conciliate all the opposition. Besides, I am very far from confident, that the doctrines avowed in this piece (though as clear to me as first principles) will be considerd as well founded; or that they will be at all popular. If so, we lose upon every Side."[64] The manuscript was shown in the inner circle, and gained much approval with some demurs. Sir George Savile thought it a strong performance that gave a clear explanation of the Rockingham position. But it was sure to give offense; the question therefore became "if it be *that* offence which an Honest man should give and a brave man stand to." On the whole, Savile advised against publication.

Savile's early response is valuable in expressing certain dissatisfactions with Burke's argument on the ability of a ministry to check the power of the king. Burke had accepted the infallibility of the monarch in order to preserve the duty of the parliamentary majority to stop him from using his power wrongly. But this, Savile recognized, was having it both ways: if deference to the king's power was only a matter of form, Burke risked being misunderstood. A larger point about his argumentative manner was here involved. Burke's excessive shows of respect—the mystique of the "unbought grace" of a natural aristocracy embodied by incorruptible statesmen—can sometimes merely mystify. Why display so crouching a reverence when you wear the armor of candid skepticism? Savile objected to the vagueness of the result, an effect quite at odds with the pragmatic posture of Burke's writing. If, for rhetorical purposes, you once accept that the king can do no wrong, and if you concede a limitation on any minister's power to check an erring king, what scope of action have you left to the chief minister? Savile recoiled from such a limitation, and his response shows the temper of a high Whig who was not charmed by Burke's ceremonial façade: "Nobody could I suppose treat this better or so well; so decently: but it is the private parts of the constitution and cant be treated decently. The K can do no wrong. His ministers only accountable. Now it is nonsense . . . to be accountable and not to guide."[65] Savile admits that it "sounds well" to say that the king has power only to do good and that he can be checked only in his evil acts: "This I allow good Philosophy at least in great part. It is the whole of Whiggism." But, as a maxim of political conduct, it cannot be reconciled with the implicit authority of the monarch, which Burke stopped short of challenging. Savile concludes that in the attempt to cover, by a civilizing fiction, common ideas of the power of the crown as at once infallible and circumscribed, Burke had set himself an impossible task. To inquire closely at this point is to become aware of a contorted ingenuity ("burlesque" is Savile's word).[66]

Burke admired Savile's intelligence and courage, and is likely to have taken the criticisms to heart. They might have proved decisive but for the earlier warm approval Burke had received from Rockingham, in a letter of October 15, 1769: "I am exceeding anxious, that the Pamphlet which you shewed me in such forwardness—when you was here—should make its appearance as early as possible. In all respects—now is the time—I wish it read by all the members of Parliament—and by all the politicians in town and country prior to the meeting of Parliament. I think it would take universally, and tend to form and to unite a party upon real and well founded principles—which would in the end prevail and re-establish order and Government in this country."[67] The party wisely did not follow their leader's uncharacteristic urgency; and by the time *Thoughts* appeared in April 1770, as John Faulkner has pointed out, "the party, having little chance now of assuming office, had little cause to fear antagonizing the crown.

The chief reason for withholding the pamphlet was no longer very compelling."[68] So, for many reasons, the intervening months allowed improvements. One does not find in the published version of the text the marked contrast that Savile had complained of, between apparent stringency and practical deference to the king. *Thoughts,* as a historical document, has been judged to be craftily self-protective,[69] and so in part it is. Yet it is a substantial contribution to the theory of liberty. G. O. Trevelyan thought it "the most instructive, if not the most eloquent, political treatise in our language":[70] a deserved compliment. But to detect the ways in which it is lastingly instructive requires a sense of the constitutional moment that for Burke goes beyond the Wilkes controversy and the early reign of George III.

Burke's political writings may be roughly divided into those in which he says less than he knows, because he is seeking to create or ratify a consensus, and those in which his thinking is both practical and subtly imaginative or speculative. The speeches on *Conciliation with America* and *Economical Reform* belong to the first kind; *Thoughts on the Cause of the Present Discontents* and *Reflections on the Revolution in France* belong to the second. His understanding of persuasive oratory may have led to the pattern in which his moderate-sounding performances tend to be speeches. This is not the same as saying that his speeches tend to be moderate. But the efforts of persuasion that he framed as *writings* are comparatively strenuous and hard-driving in their characterization of the enemy.

At the same time, *Thoughts,* because it is a party pamphlet, is a less than personal performance. (Here the contrast with *Reflections* is very striking.) For that reason, too, it is free of that judicious obscurity which Major John Cartwright noticed when he said that Burke never spoke of the constitution "but in trope or figure, in simile, metaphor, or mysterious allusion." From *Thoughts,* one gets a clearer idea of what Burke meant by the British constitution than can be derived from any of his later works.

"Nations are not primarily ruled by laws; less by violence." Burke starts from a premise he shares with Hume: people are governed by opinion, and opinion, over time, becomes consensus—a state of tacit agreement whose elements resist analysis. None of this is to be confused with the popular will: "I have nothing to do here with the abstract value of the voice of the people." The force of opinion that Burke cares for is the same moral force by which individuals govern their peers and often their superiors: persuasion must be founded on knowledge of the temper of the audience. A well-conducted government is anything but "a continued scuffle between the magistrate and the multitude";[71] and the first requirement of a statesman is to be so conversant with the moods and needs of the people that such disputation is averted.

Yet at the end of a decade that strained to the limit the tension between parliamentary and monarchical power, Burke sees among the "facts universally admitted and lamented" that "Government is at once dreaded and contemned . . . that our dependencies are slackened in their affection, and loosened from their obedience . . . that disconnexion and confusion, in offices, in parties, in families, in Parliament, in the nation, prevail beyond the disorders of any former time."[72] Party conflict is not the reason. The great parties of former times are dissolved. The country has suffered no natural or economic catastrophe, or defeat in war.

As for the saccharine moralists who say "that we have a very good Ministry, but that we are a very bad people," to hear such apologies is to know them absurd. There is, for Burke, a presumption in favor of the people, indistinguishable from the prejudice in favor of peace: any measure that they generally repel must have something wrong with it, for the nature of the people is not to wrangle and dispute. They want to be left alone—to live, and to avoid anything that disrupts the order of their lives. That a new measure can be justified by empirical prudence, by a perceived emergency, or by logical extension of an older policy does not suffice to refute the habit of the people who reject it. "It is of the utmost moment not to make mistakes in the use of strong measures; and firmness is then only a virtue when it accompanies the most perfect wisdom. In truth, inconstancy is a sort of natural corrective of folly and ignorance." This does not mean that the voice of the people ought to be considered infallible: "I am not one of those who think that the people are never in the wrong. They have been so, frequently and outrageously, both in other countries and in this." But the presumption of good sense must favor the people and not the force of government. Otherwise, that force is liable to be unchecked by argument or evidence: its weight and dominance will simply argue for themselves. The people are not more likely to be wrong than their rulers are, and continued disruptions generally point to a fault in the constitution. Here Burke inserts a central thought that will persist in his writings of the 1770s and 1780s: "The people have no interest in disorder. When they do wrong, it is their error, and not their crime."[73] The people have no *interest* in disorder: the word is invisibly italicized, for the people know that no good of theirs is served by disorder. Wrong, error, crime, in this sentence are delicately counterpoised: a wrong is a harm that may or may not have been foreseeable; an error comes from ignorance or incompetence; crime, by contrast, is intentional. The people should not be collectively blamed or punished, for the same reason that they should not be praised for their collective virtue. When an action they take produces shock or turmoil, this cannot have been its main purpose; often it will not have been foreseen. Disorder is always a symptom, never a cause. It is to be *interpreted* by a statesman, just as a symptom of bodily disease is to be interpreted by a physician. This formulation of principle is followed by an ironic aphorism that reduces the argument to practical advice: "it is more easy to change an administration than to reform a people."[74]

A politician requires tact and experience to discern the nature of an abuse and the appropriate remedy or redress. And no book can list all the possible aggravations of illicit power; for the grievances of the present time are different from those "which we bore from the Tudors, or vindicated on the Stuarts": the curtailment or adjustment of dynastic succession is no longer a suitable measure. Agreement about the reforms of the past shows only that such a thing exists as political reason. To discover the content of that reason is an intricate matter, since we are more confident in our diagnosis of ancient evils. As Burke says memorably, "to be a Whig on the business of an hundred years ago, is very consistent with every advantage of present servility." Arbitrary imposition changes its costume from time to time. When it comes to England now, "undoubtedly it will not bear on its forehead the name of *Ship-money*." Parliament may appear today endowed with a power separate from the king's power; yet "the forms of a free, and the ends of an arbitrary Government" have been found "things not altogether incompatible." What need is there of prerogative when the influence of the crown operates effectively behind the scenes?

The triumph of the House of Commons over the force of prerogative has a history, says Burke. Its climax was the Glorious Revolution. But the victory of Parliament, even if submitted to, was not acknowledged on all sides. Though the division between court and party leaders was allowed as a temporary expedient, this method "of governing, by men of great natural interest or great acquired consideration, was viewed in a very invidious light by the true lovers of absolute monarchy." So, in effect, James II left agents to operate in his cause long after his defeat. And naturally so: no power once cherished is apt to be given up by imagination; and if offered a chance to return in reality, it will come back. The settlement that stood in the way of monarchical reassertion depended on a recognition of the legitimacy of "natural interest" and "acquired consideration"—categories that reflect the separation Burke will later define between "presumptive virtue" and "actual virtue," between a hereditary nobility and men of talents and competence.[75] Aristocratic government in its best state, according to Burke, thrives on their mutual dependency. But this was never enough for the lovers of absolute monarchy, even if at the time of the revolution they appeared to acquiesce. Such people gravitate toward unchecked power; and despotism by its nature "wants to annihilate all intermediate situations between boundless strength on its own part, and total debility on the part of the people." Burke's central argument in *Thoughts* will be a defense of a constitutional liberty which he thinks should have been accepted once and for all in 1689—a liberty that allows many "intermediate situations" between the boundless strength of a king and the debility of the people.

The root of life for such intermediate powers is the House of Commons, with its division into a governing ministry and a wakeful opposition; and as Burke will show, the key to preserving the vitality of a ministry and a formed opposition is the existence of a party not answerable to the king. A subtle inference may already be apparent: despotism, in order to perpetuate itself, fosters total debility in the people while alternately treating the people as a formidable hostile entity. It is as if the anger and incapacity of the people made them susceptible to mob eruptions regardless of how they are treated. The people are a useful bugbear for kings; but actual liberty is diminished when the people invite acts of suppression by showing their will in violence without forethought. What is wanted is popular energy skillfully guided by the men of talent who occupy intermediate situations. To permit the suppression of protest or to let the people enact their aimless will—either of these courses the statesman must take pains to avoid.

The Interior Cabinet

Complaints against the power enjoyed by the king's adviser Lord Bute were a commonplace among opposition writers in the early 1760s: a favorite topic of the insinuating satire of the *Letters of Junius* and standard fare in Wilkes's *North Briton,* where the anti-Scottish prejudice served as a large ingredient. Letter XXXV of Junius (December 19, 1769) may be taken to epitomize the point of view. The author takes the liberty of imagining "if an honest man were permitted to approach a King," with what words the honest man would try to set the king straight. "It is the misfortune of your life," Junius imagines the honest man commencing, "and originally the cause of every reproach and distress, which has attended your government, that you should never have been acquainted with the language of truth, until you heard it in the complaints of your people. It is not, however, too late to correct the error of your education. We are still inclined to make an indulgent allowance for the pernicious lessons which you received in your youth, and to form the most sanguine hopes from the natural benevolence of your disposition."[76] The original error of George III, Junius goes on to say, comes from supposing that the doctrine *that the king can do no wrong* was meant to apply to the actions of the king's servants.

What distinguished Burke's view of monarchical encroachment was the emphasis he placed on its having been accomplished by conspiracy. He would never cease to regard the early reign of George III—like the French Revolution in its first stages, in the summer and autumn of 1789—as one of those "situations where those who appear the most stirring in the scene may possibly not be the real movers." On this view of events, the first plan of the king's men was to set up Lord Bute as chief minister. Though Bute was likeliest the author of any such plan, the truth is that his rise was gradual. In 1760, holding nothing but offices in the king's household, he acted as if he were chief minister already. In 1761, to clarify his position, he arranged to become Northern Secretary of State. He took over the treasury in May 1762 after securing the departure of Pitt and Newcastle. This phase of unchecked ascendancy lasted less than a year, and his personal influence was eliminated during Grenville's administration. Even so, the king continued to keep men closely allied with each other away from "the active parts of government."[77] By the late 1760s, as Burke read the evidence, George III was following a revised plan to separate (by an invisible line) the court from the ministry.

Such was the design of the double cabinet. Two cabinets were formed, says Burke, one "in the real secret and confidence" of the king, the other "merely ostensible" for the sake of performing the "official and executory duties of Government." It remained necessary to form a party to work for the court against the ministry—this group to be paid handsomely for their servile loyalty and to be given a power independent of the ostensible cabinet. Finally, Parliament had to be brought to acquiesce in the design, and forced to learn "by degrees a total indifference to the persons of rank, influence, abilities, connexions, and character, of the Ministers of the Crown." On the new scheme, "the lead was to be given to men of no sort of consideration or credit in the country. This want of natural importance was to be their very title to delegated power."

Whatever the degree of applicability to the early reign of George III, Burke exhibits here a deep insight into the psychology of tyranny. To compass its ends, tyranny must break down old patterns of deference, distinction, and the respect shown to qualified persons in the intermediate places of government and society. It may do so in the name of independence or reform, or by framing the change of customs as prophylaxis against a reversion to a previous corruption. Its favorite tactic is the demotion or discouragement or sometimes even the purge of a body of experienced men, in order to render the institutions of government more compliant with the executive power. The king may thus appoint "one of his footmen, or one of your footmen, for Minister"; and by such stratagems, multiplied a hundred times in the ministries after the fall of Pitt, "a Cabal of the closet and back-stairs was substituted in the place of a national Administration." This is a kind of usurpation that cannot work in the open. Whether they consult closely or share the design by tacit understanding, a small party of ascendant rulers and operatives come to power by the displacement of qualified persons (not until then thought of as temporary placeholders). The new ascendancy and the stability in office of these nameless and exchangeable men is conditioned on a general evacuation of the importance of public status.

At the accession of George III, writes Burke, the Cabal "proceeded gradually, but not slowly, to destroy every thing of strength which did not derive its principal nourishment from the immediate pleasure of the Court." That the process was gradual and its apparent direction improbable cast a pallor of hesitation over those who should have opposed it; the great Whig families, scarcely able to believe what they saw, hoped the pattern would dwindle to an aberration: "Day after day they hesitated, and doubted, and lingered, expecting that other counsels would take place; and were slow to be persuaded, that all which had been done by the Cabal, was the effect not of humour, but of system." All the while, those who set the king above the constitution went on their business of shutting all channels to office that lay outside themselves, and executing decisions of state. "The great ruling principle of the Cabal, and that which animated and harmonized all their proceedings, how various soever they may have been, was to signify to the world, that the Court would proceed upon its own proper forces only; and that the pretence of bringing any other into its service was an affront to it, and not a support."[78] Reflexive loyalty was enforced with a severity that eventually would require the removal of the chiefs of the Whig Party: "in order to go to the root, the whole party was put under a proscription, so general and severe as to take their hard earned bread from the lowest officers, in a manner which had never been known before, even in general revolutions. But it was thought necessary effectually to destroy all dependencies but one; and to shew an example of the firmness and rigour with which the new system was to be supported."[79] Dependency on government and fear of government without a choice of opposition are the essence of tyranny. With the loss of Pitt and the self-confidence of a Whig opposition, there vanished "the *two only securities for the importance of the people, power arising from popularity; and power arising from connexion*"

(Burke's emphasis). In this way, almost invisibly, the people lost their only regular and assuring link to their governors.

To disunite the people from their connection with power was only a first step in the degradation of constitutional understanding. A second step, as important, was the disuniting of office from party: loyalty to a small set of persons now became the only relevant qualification; and "in this manner an Administration without connexion with the people, or with one another, was first put in possession of Government." These strictures of Burke's imply no jealousy of the function of the king within the constitution. His power is necessary for the execution of state business, and necessary as a check against other powers. The new-modeled system, however, proceeds "on a supposition that the King is something external to his government; and that he may be honoured and agggrandized, even by its debility and disgrace." A consistent but unavowed agreement that the king's power ought to be expanded may partly explain a phenomenon of the 1760s that on its face made no sense to Burke: the low regard shown for nominal ministers who, making no headway in executing their policies, were humiliated by the loss of dignity. Their discontent, once known, was then made a cause for jettisoning them.[80] Yet such overt punishments were necessary only against the main actors; with lesser persons a weaker regimen sufficed, a compound of irritation and cumulative harassment: "as there always are many rotten members belonging to the best connexions, it is not hard to persuade several to continue in office without their leaders." This observation marks a general truth about the usefulness, to a rising despot, of "debility" at the lower levels. The comment may also include (as Ian Harris has suggested) a coded reference to the members of the Rockingham administration who clung to their offices after his departure. Under the system of parallel government that Burke describes, it is possible for a minister of state to be "totally estranged from all his colleagues," to oppose all their measures and yet be well rewarded by the court. For such a minister serves a function by the very obstacles he throws up. "He helps to keep some form of Administration in being"—the Cabal does not want things to appear formless or anarchic—"and keeps it at the same time as weak and divided as possible." The necessity of maintaining appearances to cover a tremendous mutation of government will generate side effects that transform government itself into a masquerade.

Even when the king's men promote their own candidate, he must pass through the ostensible ministry for approval; and they are careful to separate the worth of the candidate from the weightlessness of the ministry. Those who are thus promoted are told "industriously to declare, that they are under no obligations whatsoever to Administration; that they have received their office from another quarter; that they are totally free and independent." Notice here that the boast of having had no previous connections and of enjoying a manly independence has become a sure indication of actual servility. It is important for the Cabal to preserve the humble as well as the great in the positions that have been found for them. A motion to dismiss even one—as Rockingham moved to dismiss Jeremiah Dyson[81]—might be stopped by the king and trigger the fall of a ministry. In *Thoughts on the Cause of the Present Discontents*, as in *A Short Account of a Late Short Administration*, Burke identifies Rockingham's government with an attempt to stave off the influence of the king's men, "to break their corps, to discountenance their doctrines, to revive connexions of a different kind, to restore the principles and policy of the Whigs, to reanimate the cause of Liberty by Ministerial countenance."[82] In thus describing the malady, Burke refuses to confine its influence to effects of the character of Bute: the system did not arise merely from an adviser's ambition but "from the circumstances which favoured it, and from an indifference to the constitution which had been for some time growing among our gentry." The source of the corruption is not only the willingness of the king's men to put themselves above the law but also their constant abuse of discretionary powers for private ends. "Constitute Government how you please, infinitely the greater part of it must depend upon the exercise of powers which are left at large to the prudence and uprightness of Ministers of State." The first duty, therefore, of members of the House of Commons was *"to refuse to support Government, until power was in the hands of persons who were acceptable to the people"* (Burke's emphasis).[83] This duty Parliament has failed to perform.

To emphasize the length of the abuses, Burke now offers a general sketch of the British constitution. Its proper order is secured by a division of legislative and administrative powers between the people and the king. "The people, by their representatives and grandees, were intrusted with a deliberative power in making laws; the King with the control of the negative. The King was instrusted with the deliberative choice and the election to office; the people had the negative in a Parliamentary refusal to support." By "the people," Burke means always the people acting through their representatives; the word is almost synonymous here with the House of Commons. He does not essentially challenge the principle of oligarchy, for the representative system he defends is not government by the people but government for the people by the qualified few. Yet it earns its authority only by acting for the whole people. Though stopping, therefore, short of democracy, Burke has gone far beyond the Whig revolution theory that John Morley summarized as "the assumption that a benevolent Providence created the people of England in order that they might be governed by a select number of patrician families."[84] The families and the men of talents they employ are now to be rendered accountable to the people at large.

In lawmaking, Burke explains, and in the choice of a ministry, the members of Parliament serve as representatives of the people. The king, wielding the executive power, may initiate or put a stop to political action, but he cannot act alone. The trust of the people thus becomes a necessary antecedent to political action and a check on all use of public office: "It is no mean security for a proper use of power, that a man has shewn by the general tenor of his actions, that the affection, the good opinion, the confidence, of his fellow citizens have been among the principal objects of his life; and that he has owed none of the gradations of his power or fortune to a settled contempt, or occasional forfeiture of their esteem."[85] Sustained and regular connection with the people—rather than emergency or spasmodic connection—is a clue to public character that cannot mislead. For the same reason, the apparent independence of a man who has no political friends is a bad sign: first, because it means his "whole importance has begun with his office, and is sure to end with it"; also because it shows *"no connexion with the interests of the people"* and—a different point which Burke applies to "cabals" rather than individuals—*"no connexion with the sentiments and the opinions of the people."* An ambitious man without need of the people's support enjoys a dangerous freedom from any link of sentiment or obligation with his contemporaries; and this freedom, in turn, casts doubt on his ability to connect the past and the future. Given "a State so popular in its constitution as ours," there is a great danger in "ambition *without* popular motives" (emphasis added). The nation may expect trouble when the disappointed candidate for popular applause and the minister who prefers the closet to the hustings turn out to be the same person. Political energy, driven inward and directed at the operations of government itself, is free to perfect behind the scenes a system of total control and expedient oppression.

One may imagine the reply of a courtier. A king who goes along with a party (such a person will say) does nothing but elevate a faction. Besides, the opinions of the people are so fluctuating, they cannot be trusted to govern themselves. Why should the king not employ, by his own choice, a group of advisers who remain conformable to his view and are unmoved by the caprices of the popular will? It would seem that, barring malice toward the people, such a body of king's men would govern well. But this argument from convenience misses a truth of human nature in politics, which Montesquieu captured memorably: even virtue needs a limit. Any great power, in human hands, requires some check against error, mischief, and aggrandizement. This maxim underlies the whole logic of the mixed constitution.

The House of Commons, Burke notes, was originally not considered part of the standing government; rather, it was a control "issuing *immediately* from the people, and speedily to be resolved into the mass from whence it arose." One may discern its character most clearly by analogy: "it was in the higher part of Government what juries are in the lower." In both cases, the body is composed of persons gathered for a purpose of control; the membership are supposed "of a middle nature between subject and Government." Members of the House of Commons (as distinct from the House of Lords) were meant to feel "with a more tender and a nearer interest every thing that concerned the people." It follows that the House should err, when it errs, on the popular side. Better, if we must choose, that the members be "infected with every epidemical phrensy of the people, as this would indicate some consanguinity, some sympathy of nature with their constituency, than that they should in all cases be wholly untouched by the opinions and feelings of the people out of doors." Suppose the people repudiate a war the government believes is necessary. What then? Shall government pursue the war in spite of the people? The burden of persuasion rests with the government. (This example, not used in *Thoughts*, presents itself to the mind of Burke in 1777 and again in 1795.) When he alludes to the separation of parliamentary debate from adequate knowledge by the people, Burke means literally "the people out of doors," since reporters were not yet allowed in the House of Commons. That the House should serve as a popular counterweight against aristocratic insolence fits the purpose of the Commons, as understood in the constitution. "The virtue, spirit, and essence of a House of Commons consists in its being the express image of the feelings of the nation." The words are carefully chosen: *express, image, feelings, nation*. The House is not a perfect facsimile of the feelings of the people. It affords, rather, an image, an accurate imagining of those feelings. And the image is "express" in the sense that it is manifest, a recorded and accountable expression. An image cannot be endlessly varied or subdivided: we see and understand one image at a time. This makes for a limit amenable to sense, and also a kind of control. Not, Burke adds, a control upon the people but a control for them. The Commons must never act independent of, or opposite to, the judgment of the people regarding the government's treatment of them.

Through all this part of his argument, Burke preserves a discipline of moderation. Between frequent and infrequent elections, he defends the latter as the lesser evil: it is an unhappy fact that "the dreadful disorders of frequent elections" have moved the country toward septennial rather than triennial elections, with the result that the House of Commons has acquired something of "the character of a standing Senate." Burke thinks this ought to be pardoned as "a disorder which has arisen from the cure of greater disorders." The trouble is that too many checks have sunk into disuse, and Parliament has given its sanction to the acts of the king most destructive of liberty. *"Impeachment, that great guardian of the purity of the Constitution, is in danger of being lost, even to the idea of it"* (Burke's emphasis). As the most recent such trial had been on a charge of treason against Lord Lovat in 1747, one may assume that Burke thought this stringent measure should be used more often than once every quarter century. Impeachment might appear to be a merely negative power of the representative body, but it stands for something more. Recent parliaments have made themselves the king's accessory in an attempt of disfranchisement: "In the last session, the corps called the *King's friends* made an hardy attempt all at once, *to alter the right of election itself*." They compassed their ends by disabling any person who was not agreeable to them, "without any other rule than their own pleasure." The administration of Chatham and Grafton excluded members of the Rockingham party, but it also quietly incapacitated the advice of anyone obnoxious to the king.[86] This abuse affects the legitimacy of government, since the people may be led to distrust the system itself, and yet their habitual reliance on government counts as vital evidence that it works as it is meant to work. The advisers to a prince, however, may play a deeper game. Ostensibly believing in the rules and customs of the institution, they "may have an interest in disorder and confusion." The same can never be said of the people.

Now, in a central passage of anti-Machiavellian analysis, Burke explains the belief of the powerful that they can control the instability they foment. Whenever the will of the court prevails against the people—as happens in the invalidation of an election result—it calls into question the people's importance. For what could show that importance more than their ability to make their view come home to the government? "Their freedom cannot long survive their importance." But how might one quicken a sense of the people's importance without thereby causing disorder? Through a union, says Burke, of "the great natural strength of the country," the nobility and the great landowners and manufacturers. These form the element of society that must rescue itself and the country: "We are at present at issue upon this point. We are in the great crisis of this contention; and the part which men take one way or other, will serve to discriminate their characters and their principles. Until the matter is decided, the country will remain in its present confusion. For while a system of Administration is attempted, entirely repugnant to the genius of the people, and not conformable to the plan of their Government, every thing must necessarily be disordered for a time, until this system destroys the constitution, or the constitution gets the better of this system."[87] Two temptations stand in the way of a fortunate resolution of the contest: a temptation of power and one of prudence.

An increase in the splendor and power of the state may distract men from a justified indignation at the loss of liberty. It also assists the illusion that the power is respected abroad; yet Lord Rochford (the British ambassador at Paris) had lately remonstrated over Corsica and been undercut by the administration at home, so that he was treated with contempt by France. He returned to take a position in "another department of the same office," which could not embarrass him by its proximity to the position in which his actions were nullified. Such are the fruits of the double cabinet in foreign affairs. America, too, has learned the secret of the system and, after disappointments, has grown so separate that it takes the functions of government more and more to itself. This, Burke suggests in 1770, is a trouble Britain has not seen the end of. Such missteps may seem overbalanced by the comfortable life that the prosperous enjoy; outbreaks of public disorder are spoken of as if they posed a greater danger than corruption. The king's friends celebrate the good of docility, and they appeal to the stability of the social routines that persist regardless of politics. Their complacency may have become so settled they no longer see the freedom they are losing.

The People as a Check on Tyranny

The Court Party in 1770 dismissed the effects of its own misjudgments as the work of faction. The public peace (they implied) would have rested secure had Wilkes found no defenders. From such attempts to shift the blame, there naturally followed a loss of mutual respect both between the ministry and its critics and between government and the people. This, as Burke will show, makes for a change of manners that cannot easily be reversed. A meaner caliber of men stand ready to displace the remnant of statesmanship, even in the dominant party:

> When the people conceive that laws, and tribunals, and even popular assemblies, are perverted from the ends of their institution, they find in those names of degenerated establishments only new motives to discontent. Those bodies, which, when full of life and beauty, lay in

their arms, and were their joy and comfort, when dead and putrid, become but the more loathsome from remembrance of former endearments. A sullen gloom, and furious disorder, prevail by fits; the nation loses its relish for peace and prosperity, as it did in that season of fullness which opened our troubles in the time of Charles the First. A species of men to whom a state of order would become a sentence of obscurity, are nourished into a dangerous magnitude by the heat of intestine disturbances; and it is no wonder that, by a sort of sinister piety, they cherish, in their turn, the disorders which are the parents of all their consequence. Superficial observers consider such persons as the cause of the public uneasiness, when, in truth, they are nothing more than the effect of it.[88]

This passage, drawn from profound meditation, occupies a place of crucial importance in Burke's political thought. He is describing the origins of a change that transports men from a natural fascination with disorder to the protracting of disorders already in motion.

"Public uneasiness" may become a state of things that carries its own momentum. It nurses the strength of men who at another time would be known as corrupt. It supplies them with a selfish motive for heightening or prolonging the agitations that have brought them to power; while, among the people, a prevailing lawlessness destroys the ordinary care for a life-preserving moderation. So disorder makes the wildness of exorbitant men seem natural after all. People forget what order was like, how much was taken on trust, and how the trust was earned without deception. No longer are plausible fears overcome, on reflection, and disowned. And at this point a secondary cause of disorder appears. Those who have an interest in disorder (never "the people" according to Burke)—these bad men come to an understanding with each other. Burke calls it, in a coinage of genius, a "sinister piety."

At such a time, many good men resign themselves to sorrow or indignation. They may even "hope better things from temporary confusion, than from established servitude." With this response Burke partly sympathizes, yet he thinks it a mistake; for amid the fear and confusion, the junto or "Cabal" will proceed unchecked:

Their restless and crooked spirit drives them to rake in the dirt of every kind of expedient. Unable to rule the multitude, they endeavour to raise divisions amongst them. One mob is hired to destroy another; a procedure which at once encourages the boldness of the populace, and justly increases their discontent. Men become pensioners of state on account of their abilities in the array of riot, and the discipline of confusion. Government is put under the disgraceful necessity of protecting from the severity of the laws that very licentiousness, which the laws had been before violated to repress. Every thing partakes of the original disorder.[89]

The phrase *discipline of confusion* is a paradox. Like *sinister piety*, it detects a design in the maintenance of panic by those who profit from it. A lie may be told, and exposed as a lie, and still be retold—persuading some at its second trial whom it failed to deceive at first, and leaving comfortless those who suppose that common sense requires only that absurdity be refuted. The system Burke calls the "interior cabinet" follows from the utility of enforcing a discipline of confusion from a hidden place inside government. The excuse for creating the system was "to prevent the King from being enslaved by a faction, and made a prisoner in his closet." None of this has contributed to the glory or splendor of the king "as a representative of the national dignity"; on the contrary, people are aware of "nothing but the operations of parsimony, attended with all the consequences of profusion."

Though Burke distrusted the motives of George III, he was careful not to blame the system on the king. Rather, it is the Cabal—or whatever name we use to describe the *imperium in imperio* whose deliberations are hidden—that has vitiated the health of government. "For the meanest and most dependent instrument of this system knows, that there are hours when its existence may depend upon his adherence to it." The fashion among the respectable is to distrust all talk of conspiracy unless the design is prosaic and provable; but it is in the nature of such tacit arrangements to be both obvious and untraceable. Among twentieth-century historians, even so dry a skeptic as Pares acknowledged that "these men" of the Cabal "were not altogether creatures of Burke's imagination" and cited as evidence

Lord Hillsborough's saying to the king that he "never means to ask a favour but from your Majesty immediately"; as well as Hillsborough in the same vein saying once to William Knox that "his object was to fall in with what he knew to be the king's plan."[90] Burke allows that the king himself must depend on such servants, since "it is a law of nature, that whoever is necessary to what we have made our object, is sure in some way, or in some time or other, to become our master."[91] The way out would seem to lie with the corporate trust of a political group, bound to each other but also connected (and indebted) to the approval of the people. Such men could not become each other's masters; ascendancy in politics, as in person, does not work like that. Burke is looking ahead to the connection he will propose between party government and statesmanship; but he is content, for now, to remark the cost of the deception practiced by the king's friends: "Have they not beggared his Exchequer, tarnished the splendour of his Court, sunk his dignity, galled his feelings, discomposed the whole order and happiness of his private life." Monarchy itself has been injured by the acts of the king's friends.

Only in the second half of *Thoughts* does Burke introduce the person whose actions made the occasion for the pamphlet: John Wilkes. As we have seen, Burke in the late 1760s served as liaison between the Rockingham party and the great libertarian and demagogue. The moment of *Thoughts* is seven years after Wilkes's initial imprisonment and the subsequent charges of seditious libel and obscene libel that caused him to flee England. In private, Burke seems to have sympathized with Wilkes, while regretting his exorbitances and showing no high regard for the people he called followers. But Wilkes in the meantime had returned, to the acclaim of a loyal crowd that backed his every move. For the record in *Thoughts*, Burke says that Wilkes had invited prosecution only by "setting himself strongly in opposition to the Court Cabal"; the Court's reaction aimed to prove *"That the favour of the People was not so sure a road as the favour of the Court even to popular honours and popular trusts."* This view of the facts Burke soon restates more forcibly: "Resistance to power, has shut the door of the House of Commons to one man; obsequiousness and servility, to none." Selective abuse of the power of prosecution can only weaken the morale of liberty: "A large and liberal construction in ascertaining offences, and a discretionary power in punishing them, is the idea of *criminal equity;* which is in truth a monster in Jurisprudence."[92] How critical, then, is the present danger that the government cites to justify its departure from previous standards of criminal prosecution? Blasphemies, loose libels, and writings supposed dangerous to religion were tolerated to an impressive degree in the years leading up to Wilkes's insinuations and broadsides. Persons, the mere listing of whose actions could not bear the light of day, have been loaded with honors (Burke doubtless has in mind the immunity enjoyed by Lord Sandwich). "I must conclude that Mr. Wilkes is the object of persecution, not on account of what he has done in common with others who are the objects of reward, but for that in which he differs from many of them: that he is pursued for the spirited dispositions which are blended with his vices; for his unconquerable firmness, for his resolute, indefatigable, strenuous resistance against oppression."[93] Under cover of protecting morals, the government that jailed Wilkes and the Parliament that excluded him have employed the law as a pander to the will of arbitrary power.

The conduct of the administration—the management of which, as Burke wrote his pamphlet, would pass from the Duke of Grafton to Lord North—thus exhibits an ungoverned insolence. For it declines to furnish any reason for its acts beyond its own discretion.[94] "The most trivial right which the subject claims," Burke answers, "never was, nor can be, forfeited in such a manner." The government is saying, in effect, that it does not make laws, it only declares laws at pleasure; that, in the nature of its power, such sudden declarations should override all previous understanding of the law. Legal judgment now "does not derive its validity from its conformity to the law; but preposterously the law is made to attend on the judgement; and the rule of the judgement is no other than the *occasional will of the House.* An arbitrary discretion leads, legality follows." For what has happened? Middlesex chose a representative whom the House of Commons did not want to seat. The House replied by seating a representative Middlesex did not choose. By this method, a vote of any minority could come to be identified with "the true legal sense of the country." To assert as much is to heap contempt on the idea of popular sovereignty; it is to pervert the meaning of every free vote; yet the right to have a vote counted as it was meant lies at the heart of the constitution. "It is a right, the effect of which is to give to the people, that man, and *that man only*, whom by their voices, actually, not constructively given, they declare that they know, esteem, love, and trust. This right is a matter within their own power of judging and feeling; not an *ens rationis* and creature of law."[95] Burke identifies constitutional liberty with a practical right and not a theoretical reason, with actual rather than construed representation. If the people are told the power of discretionary disqualification is "vested in hands that they may trust," they ought to remember that a claim of unlimited trust has been the justification employed by every despotism.

The danger is immediate. Its impact will be felt by all who inherit the laws. Burke asks his readers to set in the scale—along with the political good of fair elections and an honest system of justice—the freedom of any individual to seek popular approval in a cause opposed to the king's men. All this on one side, and on the other? A foreboding that discontents if too long indulged may turn to disorder. But Burke suspects that this reason offered by government is only a pretext. In fact, honor and offices are relied on to command acquiescence; but loyalty ought to be balanced by merit and independent judgment, which can come only from persons not appointed by the king. "If, therefore, a pursuit of popularity expose a man to greater dangers than a disposition to servility, the principle which is the life and soul of popular elections will perish out of the constitution." The subject of this last comment is a "disposition" and the way it supports or fails to support a principle. By the choice of which laws to enforce, the rigor of the enforcement, and the positive decision or refusal to mount prosecutions against merely political enemies, every ministry has an impact on the political morality of the country. Burke believes that honor and office should not be given to persons of a known servile disposition, since this will always be accompanied by the withdrawal of favor from critics of the government. "Let us suppose a person unconnected with the Court, and in opposition to its system. For his own person, no office, or emolument, or title; no promotion, ecclesiastical, or civil, or military, or naval, for children, or brothers, or kindred."[96] The indignation here is muffled. Burke is thinking of himself but cannot say so.

Against "Independent" Politicians

Burke often, as if by temperamental necessity, casts his thoughts in the form of paradox. He seldom went further than when he opposed the partiality of government by defending a strong conception of party. He has to confront an obstacle here from the usual intuitions about politics held by persons who have not thought much about power. The cure for a system that rewards dependency on a single interest would seem to be independent members of Parliament. Burke's task, in the last one-third of *Thoughts*, is to foment a distrust of "independent" politicians as a necessary accompaniment of the trust accorded to a formed opposition.

He opens with a practical objection. An independent politician is weak because he acts alone. "The unfortunate independent member has nothing to offer but harsh refusal, or pitiful excuse, or despondent representation of an hopeless interest." An independent needs a constituency; but what body of voters can really be his? He has priced himself out of the market; even so, the suspicion lingers that his conscience has a price. "In the House, he votes for ever in a dispirited minority. If he speaks, the doors are locked." This is an ironic way of saying that his voice will go unheard out of doors—and besides, not every well-informed politician has a talent for speaking. The independent, in short, can easily be cut off from the popular appeal his views alone might entitle him to; and if the majority in the House find a way to disqualify him "out of the line of the law, and at their pleasure," a second loss is incurred by the country: the people come to believe "that they cannot be firmly or faithfully served by any man." To be a control on other parts of government, the House of Commons itself must be controlled by the people. "If they suffer this power of arbitrary incapacitation to stand, they have utterly perverted every other power of the House of Commons." So the poor remnant of the lawmaking body draws its reason for being from lines of connection with the people who have been choked off.

Still a further resource of oppression is available to the dominant interest that looks to disperse opposition. "To complete the scheme" of servility, the king's friends have lately asked for additional appropriations to pay the debts due on the Civil List. Unlike the other symptoms of un-checked power that Burke cites, this may not strike us as a result of con-certed design; but there can be no doubt that the new expenses "beggar the exchequer" so as to preempt any spending not previously desired by the interior cabinet. During the last fourteen years of the reign of George II, no new demands were made on the Civil List; a surplus of £170,000 was carried into the reign of George III. That these funds were squan-dered has become a new reason for rejecting any plan of spending for the public good. No objection, Burke concedes, was raised in the House of Commons against the king's exceeding the former level of appropriations for the Civil List; yet "to have incurred a debt without special authority of Parliament was, *prima facie,* a criminal act." A confrontation should have followed. Accounts were asked for that either were not supplied or were postponed, or else were produced at last with great difficulty.

Another weakness of Parliament was exposed by its irresoluteness at this point. The "debt of the Civil List was all along argued upon the same footing as a debt of the State, contracted upon national authority." If it is asked how much pattern or forethought is discernible in the conduct of the crown, the answer, for Burke, lies in the most recent Speech from the Throne. It set an arbitrary standard for the Civil List budget, obedient not to the limits of the law but only "such limits as the *honour of the Crown* can possibly admit." In the same way, the House of Commons has set a dis-cretionary standard for the seating of members. These two innovations together form a symmetry of corruption: "The power of discretionary dis-qualification by one law of Parliament, and the necessity of paying every debt of the Civil List by another law of Parliament, if suffered to pass unnoticed, must establish such a fund of rewards and terrors as will make Parliament the best appendage and support of arbitrary power that ever was invented by the wit of man. This is felt. The quarrel is begun between the Representatives and the People."[97] Thus, the country faces a crisis in which further aggrandizement of the crown and debilitation of the popu-lar check on monarchical power will be the results of continuing in defi-ance of the present discontents. The policy of George III has been found untenable, and no resolution can be imagined at once persuasive and peaceful without a drastic change of course.

Rhetorically, Burke had worked himself into a narrow position. For if all avenues of discussion are blocked, the observer of the crisis would seem compelled to pass from speech to action. But action of what kind? Nothing in Burke's reasoning points to a call for revolution; yet all other remedies appear exhausted. Legitimate authority was in question. In the absence of visible change, the clamor for an end of monarchical and parliamentary abuses will not stop. Burke appeals therefore to a power that is familiar but not easily defined: the efficacy of public deliberation. "The circumstances are in a great measure new," he says. "We have hardly any landmarks from the wisdom of our ancestors, to guide us. At best we can only follow the spirit of their proceeding in other cases." His aim, in *Thoughts on the Cause of the Present Discontents*, has been "to bring this matter into more public discussion." But his side of the argument requires first a dismissal of the obvious palliatives.

For example, shorter parliaments. Such a change would open the House of Commons more often to the voice of the people; but it would be futile without the assurance of free elections. And Burke has a further reservation: "the horrible disorders among the people attending frequent elections." In a triennial Parliament, he concedes, members would sit "a little firm in their seats" during the middle year; but an anxious uncertainty would pervade two separate seasons, one of preparation and one of canvassing. Nobody who knows much about public affairs thinks well of the proposal; for there is a dignity that time alone confers on public service, and a knowledge that experience alone can give: "The habit of affairs, if, on the one hand, it tends to corrupt the mind, furnishes it, on the other, with the means of better information."[98] It is with government as with the staging of a play (to adapt the analogy Burke uses elsewhere). Constant changes of the cast and shifting of scenes only lower the chances for improving the performance.

Another suggested remedy is a place bill. In fact, a place bill did accompany Burke's proposals for economic reform as part of the opposition program in 1780, but he did not suppose it would suffice. Here again one finds the weakness common to remedies that call on external regulation for the cure of public distempers: "It is not easy to foresee, what the effect would be, of disconnecting with Parliament, the greatest part of those who hold civil employments, and of such mighty and important bodies as the military and naval establishments. It were better, perhaps, that they should have a corrupt interest in the forms of the constitution, than that they should have none at all."[99] The last sentence presents a paradox that is agreeable to common sense. Without some interest in the constitution, those who serve the public will comprise a formidable power hostile to its preservation. It is desirable that members of Parliament be free of insalubrious influences. But the holding of a place in government is, of all modes of influence, "the least disgraceful to the man who holds it, and by far the most safe to the country." Why should open and visible influence "connected with the dignity and the service of the State" be cut off, even as influence from private contracts, subscriptions, and bribery maintains its efficacy unhindered? "Our constitution stands on a nice equipoise, with steep precipices and deep waters upon all sides of it. In removing it from a dangerous leaning towards one side, there may be a risk of oversetting it on the other." An appropriate solution can only emerge from attention to the balance of the constitution. Whatever other contacts are promoted or discouraged, the essential feature must be a more open connection between Parliament and the people.

So, at this crisis, the popular character of the discontents proves a guide to their remedy. The unsettled crowd that braced the progress of Wilkes may have been raucous, but it was not murderous; the crush and shouting and scrawled slogans were uncouth embarrassments that served as a warning. Burke, in view of these facts, is able to say that the presence of masses of the people in the streets is salutary and impossible to ignore: "I see no other way for the preservation of a decent attention to public interest in the Representatives, but *the interposition of the body of the people itself*, whenever it shall appear, by some flagrant and notorious act, by some capital innovation, that these Representatives are going to over-leap the fences of the law, and to introduce an arbitrary power." Some such interposition of the people was necessary to answer the actions of the government against Wilkes. Burke in 1770 takes his stand with "Wilkes and Liberty" or, rather, against any process that would muffle the outcry. His argument in the course of *Thoughts* has reversed a familiar conservative expectation, and it has also qualified his private stance of the mid-1760s.

It is the king and his men, now, who are "capital innovators," while popular tumults act as a check on behalf of liberty. "Until a confidence in Government is re-established, the people ought to be excited to a more strict and detailed attention to the conduct of their Representatives." Strict and detailed may mean frequent and sharp. In the context, Burke's word *excited* is an understatement, and *attention* is a euphemism: the people are in fact obstructing the government unceremoniously, because government has disfranchised the people. Yet active, organized, or impetuous protests, which threaten violence without passing into insurrection, cannot be more than a tactic of the moment. The sound of breaking glass should not dissuade well-meaning persons from attending to the deeper causes of alarm, but it hardly signifies a spirit in the people that can be relied on for real repairs. Some permanent reform must follow what Burke calls *the interposition of the body of the people itself,* if their action is to produce any lasting institution. The people cannot continually be summoned back to this active role; even if the effort were made, they would not continually return to their posts. The organized remedy must come in the form of a party of the people or, more accurately, a party for the people.

Association and Opposition

Democracy held no attraction for Burke. Nor do the people (as he understands them) look to government for a direct expression of their will. They think of government as a body that should be separate from them yet responsive, a body that by its conduct may earn an authority they freely recognize. It was a political disaster, in the short administrations of the 1760s, that such a body never formed, or was discouraged from remaining on the scene. Gentlemen of large estates Burke judges to be the appropriate leaders of government. "Uniform, upright, constitutional conduct" is the visible attribute of peers who have learned to act wisely and unselfishly; and it is natural for the people to follow leaders who show such qualities. On the other hand, Burke adds: "I am no friend to aristocracy, in the sense at least in which that word is usually understood. If it were not a bad habit to moot cases on the supposed ruin of the constitution, I should be free to declare, that if it must perish, I would rather by far see it resolved into any other form, than lost in that austere and insolent domination."[100] Though the people make bad rulers, an insolent aristocracy is worse. The settlement which Britain had long been moving toward and which George III ought to have confirmed was a representative government with an aristocratic basis. A necessary condition of such government is a formed opposition whose views are arrived at largely in public.

If an opposition party is necessary to constitutional liberty, then support for the present administration, with its serial attempts to jail its opponents, is a thoughtless vice and not a thoughtless virtue. "He that supports every administration, subverts all Government." The corps of king's men are working to divide public men from themselves. To be restored to active honor, public men must respond by alienating themselves from that corps. Free government will return only through the operation of bodies of men honest and resolute enough to refuse incorporation in a new ministry "unless this garrison of *King's men,* which is stationed, as in a citadel, to controul and enslave it, be entirely broken and disbanded." But that can never happen until public men of sufficient weight and numbers detach themselves of the false doctrine of the ministerial Cabal, the doctrine that "all political connexions are in their nature factitious, and as such ought to be dissipated." Political connections, Burke supposes—and he means pre-existing political engagements—ought to elicit a loyalty warmer than the adherence that comes with the mere promise of power.

Party, corps, faction, cabal, connection, association—Burke's argument about the nature of a political order turns out to be also an argument about the value and meaning of certain words. A prominent trait of *Thoughts on the Cause of the Present Discontents* is the versatility of its usage, an ironic redefinition of terms with the aim of inciting thought. Thus *connection,* a neutral term in familiar use, by his own usage is given an ameliorative turn; it may imply, on one side, corruption and private motives, but on the other side it looks toward honorable engagement and association. *Party,* in Burke's usage, has ceased to imply partiality. He takes it rather to suggest that consistency is the virtue of the politician who stays with his party, in defiance of the selfish motive and the ascendant power. Connection, association, consistency, and conscience all receive embodiment in a party, and a party is typified, both in the public mind and in fact, by the person whom Burke will describe by an inventive usage of the word *character*.

A sentence of his long peroration brings these several terms into play, with *connection* now employed as a synonym for *party:*

> In a connexion, the most inconsiderable man, by adding to the weight of the whole, has his value, and his use; out of it, the greatest talents are wholly unserviceable to the publick. No man, who is not inflamed by vain-glory into enthusiasm, can flatter himself that his single, un-supported, desultory, unsystematic endeavours are of power to defeat the subtle designs and united Cabals of ambitious citizens. When bad men combine, the good must associate; else they will fall, one by one, an unpitied sacrifice in a contemptible struggle.[101]

Independence is not a virtue here. It is a mask for the vanity, petulance, and vainglory of the man whose isolation assures that his actions will be inconsistent and inconsequent. Burke writes as if he were thinking of a particular person as a warning. He probably had in mind William Pitt, "the Great Commoner," who in 1766 became the Earl of Chatham and whose resistance to George III was constantly hampered by his inability to act in a corps. Pitt, it should be added, was a conscious proponent of a maxim of politics contrary to Burke's—"Not men, but measures"—which Burke would deprecate in his *Speech on American Taxation* as well as at the close of *Thoughts*. Once he had become Lord Chatham, Pitt withdrew from government (without much struggle) at the height of his power. This is one possible sense of Burke's phrase "an unpitied sacrifice." A lesser politician but one close to the Rockingham Whigs, Henry Conway, may also be in the background here. Conway had been Rockingham's secretary of state, and he stayed on in the administration of Pitt and Graf-ton;[102] the growing despondency of obscurer yet capable talents in the Rockingham group are part of the motive driving this passage. Burke's warning against dissociation can be read as an admonition against him-self in certain moods.

"When bad men combine, the good must associate; else they will fall, one by one, an unpitied sacrifice in a contemptible struggle." This great sentence is the germ of the most famous quotation wrongly ascribed to

Burke: "The only thing necessary for the triumph of evil is for good men to do nothing." The sentiment extractable from the corrupt version is pompous, canting, and demonstrably false, for evil is not a disembodied thing; it has its origin in acts by specifiable agents. Nor is it true that "the only thing necessary" for the triumph of evil is the inaction of good men. There must also be an extended occasion of public fears for bad men to play upon, and there must be a catalyzing event. The bad men themselves must be unusually excited, active, conscious of each other's presence, aware of the inlets for increasing power, and unimpeded by the indifferent mass of the people. Burke's sentence is careful to say flatly what the triumph-of-evil apothegm leaves mysterious. Bad men do combine but, as the word *combine* suggests, their alliance may be impersonal and almost mechanical, a reflex of ambition and appetite, or the product of a theory. By contrast, *association,* through constant intercourse with other persons, leaves room for correction and improvement in the corps and a concern with the public good. Yet it matters that the defense of principle, when its cost is high, should achieve a public notability, so that interim defeats may prepare for an eventual triumph. The sacrifice of a party is important because it is so visible, compared to the obscure sacrifice of an unconnected person.[103] Consistency of opinion, which is both a cause and a consequence of regular association, makes all the difference between a contemptible and a worthy struggle.

The present time calls for more than resistance to evil. Exemplary acts of civic courage are needed. Public duty on behalf of the constitution "demands and requires, that what is right should not only be made known, but made prevalent; that what is evil should not only be detected, but defeated. When the public man omits to put himself in a situation of doing his duty with effect, it is an omission that frustrates the purposes of his trust almost as much as if he had formally betrayed it." This belief, on Burke's view of politics, gives another reason for the necessity of party, since political connections are "necessary for the full performance of our public duty." True, connections may degenerate into factions. But they are also the source of anything good we bring to political life, anything above time-serving and self-advancement. "Commonwealths are made of families, free commonwealths of parties also; and we may as well affirm, that our natural regards and ties of blood tend inevitably to make men bad citizens, as that the bonds of our party weaken those by which we are held to our country." The argument that would cast doubt on the motives of party connection must make us equally suspect our love for our family or for our country. Party is one link in a series—neither more natural nor more artificial than the others.

Higher in the series is the idea of a House of Commons that can serve as a more-than-personal bearer of sovereignty—"a sacred temple, for the perpetual residence of an inviolable justice." Party government and parliamentary sovereignty may be traced alike to a common source in Burke's revulsion from the cult of the great man. He had come of age in the heyday of William Pitt and acquired early a settled distrust of politicians who treat their allies as raw material for their own aggrandizement. He looked on Pitt as an episodic charismatic of the most dubious value; but a larger issue was here involved: the priority of party to the individual wills of its members. For Burke, a political party was a voluntary association bound by principles and loyalty, which worked as a counterweight against ministerial or monarchical authority and at the same time curbed the egotism of day-to-day political bargaining.[104] A party is a corporate artifice which makes an impression as distinct as that of a person; and *character* is the word he often uses to describe both the leader of a party and the definition a party gives to a leader. "Virtue will catch as well as vice by contact."

Burke was all his life a hater of neutrality. He confesses a certain sympathy with lawmakers who "went so far as to make neutrality in party a crime against the State." He defers (not for the last time) to the old Whigs of the reign of Queen Anne, who believed "that no men could act with effect, who did not act in concert; that no men could act in concert, who did not act with confidence; and that no men could act with confidence, who were not bound together by common opinions, common affections, and common interests." Burke's definition of party follows from this: "Party is a body of men united, for promoting by their joint endeavours the national interest, upon some particular principle in which they are all agreed." The agreement enables men regularly to illustrate their beliefs in practice. The law of parsimony as applied to politics—one must not multiply "positions" without reason—will make their character stand out distinctly. Not all alliances are consistent with the principle of a party, and so Burke can say of a party's members: "Without a proscription of others, they are bound to give to their own party the preference in all things; and by no means, for private considerations, to accept any offers of power in which the whole body is not included. . . . Such a generous contention for power, on such manly and honourable maxims, will easily be distinguished from the mean and interested struggle for place and emolument."[105] When Burke came to compose *Thoughts*, looking back on the events of the 1760s, his memory of the convenient change of opinions in Conway was still rankling.

Because it seems risky to refer the stability of public life to the characters of men, we will always be tempted to appeal above character, to appeal, that is, from men to "measures" or laws or general policies. This oddly abstract plea is brought back at irregular intervals as a suitable therapy of disenchantment; yet Burke thinks it the reverse of cogent: "the cant of *Not men, but measures;* a sort of charm, by which many people get loose from every honourable engagement." They will have reasons besides impartial judgment for getting loose from an engagement that has grown less ripe. But when you separate actions from persons—such is Burke's instinctive belief—you leave yourself unguarded against deception. For you are then deprived of the whole field of intelligence that starts from the discernment of motives. Everyone can agree on what would be the finest and most attractive ends for a society to aim at. The difficulty occurs in devising the means; and the makers of means are always persons. Burke now devotes an almost explicit ironic sentence to Conway: "When a gentleman with great visible emoluments abandons the party in which he has long acted, and tells you, it is because he proceeds upon his own judgment; that he acts on the merits of the several measures as they arise; and that he is obliged to follow his own conscience, and not that of others; he gives reasons which it is impossible to controvert, and discovers a character which it is impossible to mistake."[106] The irony of such a sentence, keyed by the pretense of a neutral tone, is as rare in Burke as it is common in Swift. When Burke chooses this weapon, every stroke is laid on with the expectation of being heard twice. The sentence above allows the unsuspecting reader to hear nothing but a toneless declaration about a matter of fact. That is because Burke has adopted the default language of conscientious independence; yet he notices that, if one keeps to that language, one can never unmask the defaulter. A plausible reason can be assigned for every questionable action. But those who understand the recent changes in the world of politics will naturally take a lower view. When they see that independence is rewarded by "great visible emoluments," they interpret the transaction accordingly.

Is Burke justified in counting loyalty to "men" a higher thing than judgment of the good or evil of "measures"? Part of his reasoning is hidden, and to bring it out requires some help from his later writings. He believes that every *impersonal* judgment of measures is speculative; it may become the bridge over which men walk to serve as judges in their own cause. It is wrong anyway to assume that public acts, belonging to the collective identity of the party, suppress the individuality of the actor and free him from personal responsibility. On the contrary, the identification of such acts with a party ensures against the most prevalent form of self-deception. This is so because the acts are public, and being public, they are accountable to a standard of consistency. By contrast, the reasons for tergiversation are "triable only in that secret tribunal, where they are sure of being heard with favour," namely the tribunal of ourselves, which brings satisfaction because it acquits with such regularity. As Burke points out, individual judgment is always private, and to entrust political choices to free agents "has a tendency to destroy all test of character as deduced from conduct." It is true that "men thinking freely, will, in particular instances, think differently," but on measures related to broad principles they are likely to agree with their party nine times out of ten. The small sacrifices of association go with the larger self-sacrifice of a formed opposition: the nine points of agreement are allowed to matter more than the tenth (however exigent) on which the party for the moment presses against private will and judgment.

Association is necessary because men are neither angels nor devils. Burke, in his peroration, winds into a final statement of the dignity of public service as a good that harmonizes with the beauty of private life. Friendship, the constant currency of association, creates the bond that connects the two realms. "To bring the dispositions that are lovely in private life into the service and conduct of the commonwealth; so to be patriots, as not to forget we are gentlemen. To cultivate friendships, and to incur enmities. To have both strong, and both selected: in the one, to be placable; in the other, immoveable. To model our principles to our duties and our situation."[107] Friendship supports a morality of habit that Burke's politics has in common with Aristotle's *Ethics;* and his language of private life evokes the larger human setting of Aristotle's belief in custom as second nature; so it may seem that we must rely on the manners of society to restore the vigor of politics. Yet the influence also goes the other way. Burke thinks a revival of the former strength of the constitution will lead to a recovery of generous sympathies in society. The time has come when *the people* must see "the necessity of restoring public men to an attention to the public opinion, and of restoring the constitution to its original principles." In the administrations of Bute, Grenville, Chatham, and Grafton, a decay of the art of governing led to a degradation of social life. The people, Burke hopes and predicts, will now assert their will to keep the House of Commons free of extrinsic influences "and as dependent upon themselves, as possible." This service of the House of Commons for the good of the people Burke calls a "natural, rational, and liberal obedience." Having learned again their proper dignity, members will teach the king "to have but one Administration." This singular relation will tend to define, in turn, the king's own dependence and dignity.

Such is the proposed remedy of the cause of the discontents. Its terms are general but not therefore vague. No names are given, or names of measures, yet Burke's solution is distinct enough plainly to exclude more than it includes: it will not permit, for example, the dissolving of a ministry that displeases the king but helps the nation. Without a party answerable to the people and effective in the House of Commons, the nation, Burke suspects, will pass to one of two extremes, "the rage of civil violence" or "the dead repose of despotism." With a characteristic dry emphasis, much earlier in *Thoughts* he had disclaimed a false precision: "No lines can be laid down for civil or political wisdom. They are a matter incapable of exact definition. But, though no man can draw a stroke between the confines of day and night, yet light and darkness are upon the whole tolerably distinguishable."[108] The power of a monarch to throw political enemies in prison and unseat an elected member of the House of Commons is darkness. We may rest in the belief that the darkness has been dispelled when we see the means for establishing and maintaining a representative body that is bound to serve the interests of the people.

The Ascent of Charles Fox

Writing to his friend Richard Shackleton of the responses to *Thoughts on the Cause of the Present Discontents,* Burke observed on August 15, 1770: "The party which is most displeased is a rotten subdivision of a Faction among ourselves, who have done us infinite mischief by the violence, rashness, and often wickedness of their measures, I mean the Bill of rights people but who have thought proper at length to do us I hope a service, by declaring open War upon all our connections."[109] The Society of Supporters of the Bill of Rights included the anti-Bute pamphleteer John Horne and the member of Parliament John Sawbridge. It could not have escaped Burke's attention that Catharine Macaulay, the sister of Sawbridge, had published a reply to *Thoughts* that noticed the tameness of his appeal to popular checks.[110] Burke's letter to Shackleton, as much as Macaulay's indignant counterpamphlet, suggests a moderate reading of the final intention of *Thoughts.* Such a reading is confirmed when Burke in the same letter complains of the imperfection of every attempt at genuine reform. "If no remedy can be found in the dispositions of capital people, in the Temper, spirit, (and docility too) of the Lower, and in the thorough union of both—nothing can be done by any alterations in forms. Indeed all that wise men ever aim at is to keep things from coming to the worst."[111] His claim for himself is negative. His policy of working for the best chiefly consists of machinery for avoiding the worst.

Burke came closer to an estimate of the spirit and temper of the people in a letter to Rockingham of September 7, 1770. He speaks there, especially, of the mood of the people of Yorkshire, who were "very much and very generally touched with the Question on Middlesex"; of all possible grounds of agreement with the Rockingham party, this was the one that moved them. "We never have had, and we never shall have a matter every way so well calculated to engage them; and if the spirit which was excited upon this occasion were suffered to flatten and evaporate, you would find it difficult to collect it again."[112] He advises Rockingham to grasp this opportunity of joining the popular outcry for Wilkes—to cooperate with the surge of resentment even if he disagrees with some of its premises. So long as plausible alliances are put off, enmities will continue to grow: the court "are well acquainted with the difference between the Bill of Rights and your Lordships friends, and they are very insolently rejoiced at it. They respect and fear that wretched Knot beyond any thing you can readily imagine. . . . They feel, that if they had equal Spirit and industry, they would in the same situation act the very same part. It is their Idea of a perfect opposition."[113] The Bill of Rights people have taken up Wilkes's cause with a view to power for themselves, or so Burke intimates. He does not care for them any more than he does for Wilkes's Yorkshire followers; but he sees that they have considerable value. Enemies of Rockingham's enemies, the supporters of Wilkes in the House are more feared by the court than the moderate section of the Rockingham party.

Here again, Burke is testing the truth of a paradox, and one that will deepen his understanding of the psychology of revolution. His argument has discovered that insolence and brutality form a bond of manners between the most vicious among the aristocracy and among the people. This the *Reflections* will portray as a relation of cause and effect: "Kings will be tyrants from policy when subjects are rebels from principle." The Burke of *Thoughts* in 1770 is more circumspect. (When Rockingham, in their subsequent correspondence, showed his pleasure at the declining effectiveness of Wilkes's supporters, Burke would agree on grounds of taste.) Though in a letter of September 26 he does not regret the weakening of the Bill of Rights gentry, "I would not exult, and on the contrary rather collect the *valuable men* amongst them."[114] As with his image of a campaign to collect men of spirit, whose resolve might otherwise dissipate, he shows himself aware of a dangerous energy that has uses for both good and ill. Such men require supervision. A similar intuition will return in the *Reflections,* where Burke employs a metaphor from chemistry to describe the spirit of revolution: "The wild *gas,* the fixed air is plainly broke loose: but we ought to suspend our judgment until the first effervescence

is a little subsided." In 1770, however, he was more an actor than a spectator, and the remnants of that combustible energy were something to "collect." To what end? Safe storage (he implies) and possibly a well-timed
release.

An afterthought shows Burke's uneasiness at the ambiguous role he
had consented to play. To Rockingham on December 29, 1770, he wrote of
the conduct and self-image of the public-minded aristocracy—"the sober,
large-acred part of the nation, whom you have most studied to please,
and whom it is the most reputable to please"—and continued in detail
regarding the aftermath of the publication of *Thoughts*. There had been a
want of practical enterprise to confirm the written performance: "To lye
by occasionally may be prudent for an individual; it never can do for party;
which will immediately putrifye and dissipate, if not kept healthy and
compact by continual agitation and enterprise. I do not exclude a total
Secession on proper Ground from my Idea of activity. Something of constant and systematical writing seems to me of absolute necessity. We lost
much of the advantage of the Last pamphlet, because the Idea was not
kept up by a continued succession of papers, seconding and enforcing the
principle."[115] The aloof attitude of the "sober, large-acred" section of the
country was understood but not applauded by the private secretary whom
the politician most nearly associated with that section had lately brought
into his confidence. Burke would be the first to rejoice when a younger
man of large estates—quick and retentive like himself, with an instinct
for the game of politics—joined the party and gave it the glamour it had
lacked.

Fox Defends the House of Commons and Attacks the Crown

Charles Fox, in 1770, was junior lord of the admiralty under Lord North.
His politics were Tory, his manner brilliant, ingratiating, and erratic. In
the preceding time of crisis he had served as a clever apologist for the imprisonment of Wilkes. His father, Henry Fox, the power broker of the
Newcastle administration, had never risen to the heights he was expected
to attain. A counselor of state unburdened by scruples, the elder Fox was
peerless at matching places with votes and paying off grudges with an

unprejudiced indifference to persons. A doting father and the reverse of a conscientious public man, his leading traits were numbered by G. O. Trevelyan: "perverted ability, impudence, cynicism, misdirected courage, an unequalled knowledge of all that was worst in human nature and least admirable in human affairs." These qualities were transformed, in the character of his son, into a flaunted capability, along with political courage that was genuine but often careless or short of stamina. Charles Fox had the willful self-confidence of the spoiled child who is sure of his supper and believes he has earned his good luck. Burke captured (as only an admiring friend could do) this mixture of public care and capriciousness when he closed his speech on the East India Bill of 1783 by saying that Fox would wager even "his darling fame" to assist a generous cause.

Now, on the brink of Fox's pilgrimage to the Rockingham party, a view may be taken of the dramatic foreground of the phase of his long career that allied him closely with Burke. At the age of twenty-one he had emerged in the House of Commons as a convinced defender of the highest parliamentary privilege; he deployed the rhetoric of the Whig tradition to assert the independence of the House of Commons from the king. Equally, Fox asserted the independence of the House from all influence by the people (as represented by the mob out of doors): after elections, the business of the people with Parliament ends. "If we are driven from the direct line of justice," he warned, "by the threats of a mob, our existence is useless in the community. The minority within doors need only assault us by their myrmidons without, to gain their ends on every occasion."[116] Young Charles Fox knew what to think of "the people." About this time, his father had been sounded out as a possible successor to Lord Bute at the Treasury—an unbeatable opportunity for a politician who had once notoriously enriched himself as paymaster of forces. But Henry Fox was strangely indecisive—a trait he would pass on to his son.

The dexterity of Charles Fox was displayed on scattered fronts in the late 1760s. An issue of importance to the Rockingham Whigs, during the three-year period of adjustment from the Rockingham to the Chatham and Grafton ministry and from the latter to Lord North, turned on the controversy over *nullum tempus*. The full phrase, *Nullum tempus occurit regi,* meant in practice that no length of time in possession of property could work against a claim of the crown. One of the grandees of the Rockingham party became a casualty of the revival of this monarchical doctrine when the Duke of Portland was evicted by Sir James Lowther (Lord Lonsdale) from the Forest of Inglewood. Portland received word in September 1767 of a memorial delivered by Lowther to the Lords of the Treasury, asking the lease of the forest lands in order to give the crown the benefit of them. Surprisingly, the request was granted. Sir George Savile in February 1768 responded by introducing a bill which declared that sixty years' enjoyment (without interruption) of property derived from the crown would suffice to bar its reclamation by the crown. Savile's bill was defeated by a narrow majority in the House, but the next Parliament passed into law the necessary protection against *nullum tempus.* Charles Fox, however, with characteristic ingenuity, turned the tables of the Whig argument for the sanctity of property so as to favor the king: "I firmly believe that no one in existence has a better title to anything which he possesses than the title to Inglewood, which the Crown has vested in Sir James Lowther. If that title is taken away by an Act of Parliament, why not bring in an act to take away any other part of his estate? Why not the estate of any landlord in the kingdom?"[117] So Fox charged Savile and Portland instead of George III with having insulted the spirit of British liberty. He did it simply by starting his narration at a late point in the story—as if the king's claim against Portland's lands and his gift of them to Lowther were an innocent and appropriate beginning. A well-supported grievance against dispossession by the crown was thus turned into a fable of the enjoyment of liberty by an English gentleman with a right to his property.

Yet even when young, Fox's loyalty to the king was conditional and erratic. He was willing to expose the royal house to erosion from within, as he showed by his stand for repeal of the Royal Marriage Act in February 1772. This law, intended to protect the royal daughters from predatory suitors, would have permitted the continued assumption by the king of a high degree of control over his dependents. Filial piety of a sort was probably at work in Fox's choice to speak on behalf of the rightness of marriages for love; for Charles Fox could remember the happy union of his father and Lady Caroline Lennox and the price they paid in ostracism by eloping against the wish of her father, the Duke of Richmond. Just as George II had insulted Henry Fox, so Charles Fox undertook to insult George III. When a related question arose in 1781—the debate on repeal of the Marriage Act, which required parental consent to the marriage of all children under twenty-one—Burke took the opposite side.[118] The difference of the two men at just this point is revealing, since it exhibits a reversal of the predictable stances of both. It is the Whig Burke who offers the paternalist argument for the protection of familial authority, whereas the young Tory Fox thinks nothing of undermining the King's prerogative within his family. Yet the positions were entirely in character. Fox thought the structure of things would stand, and he believed it could bear to be shaken. Burke was wary of tampering with the ancient protections of continuity under the mixed constitution.[119]

In the debates on America in 1774, as the two statesmen moved closer politically, a contrast of style would remain. Burke could be counted on to supply a sensitive exploration of public fears and hopes. Fox was unrivaled in his ability to point an argument with nerve and simplicity on the details of present policy: "The noble lord said that we were in the dilemma of conquering or abandoning America: if we are reduced to that, I am for abandoning America."[120] Whatever his changes of view, Fox had mastered an appearance of forthrightness and easy ability denied to Burke. In the terms laid down by *Thoughts,* he had the instincts of an independent, with irresolute ambitions to lead a party. He was perhaps too individual a holder-forth to possess the quality that Burke wished to denote by his new use of the word *character.*

Men, Not Measures

Burke's emphasis on character, on men rather than measures, is commonsensical and at the same time daunting. Yet *Thoughts on the Cause of the Present Discontents*—not least because of this emphasis—strikes the ground note of all Burke's later writings on liberty. In the three great engagements of his career, with America, India, and France, Burke would bear witness to tactics of exclusion and proscription deployed from self-will and the desire for aggrandizement; high-sounding ends might be avowed, but there was always a startling disproportion between those ends and the gross facts of the appetite for power. Burke saw this first in the drawn-out later episodes of the government vendetta against Wilkes. Another and a less transparent view would come in the 1780s, with his growing awareness of the sudden fortunes from East India and their conversion into places in government. Finally, the ideology of the "political men of letters" in France aimed at a sudden change of society through the combustible mixture of universal rights (treated as the justification of reform) and revolution (treated as the necessary means).

The stage of Burke's career that is not apparently explained by such an account is the 1770s. But perhaps it is not too much to see the discontent of the American colonists over taxes and a monopolized trade, and the revolution that followed, as a triumphant exhibition of all the perils Burke feared, from politics, commerce, and ideology. His approach to the subservient forces in Parliament in the 1760s, to the chartered abuses of India commerce in the 1780s, and to the French Revolution in the 1790s was always to address the evil head-on, whereas in America he chose conciliation. Why? Burke's hope may have been that the restless energies of the new men of property, who sought new guarantees of their rights, once satisfied would bring a result that was prosperous to the empire. At all events, the 1770s are the decade that shows Burke at his least paternalist and least deferential toward the aristocratic ethos which he faithfully held to a high standard. In his conduct in the Commons, he was at this time less apt to hold himself above popular protests or to try to channel their discontents into synthetic remedies. It is possible that the American fight for liberty, much as he deplored its outbreak, made Burke actually hopeful of an improvement of liberty at home. Would the rights of man have spread more peaceably in Britain and Europe had America won independence without becoming a new kind of creature in the world of nations?

The judgments of two historians may illustrate how wide a scope remains for judging Burke's intentions. J. H. Plumb challenged Burke's assumption that political stability is a gradual and precarious achievement. Plumb argued, in *The Growth of Political Stability*, that a state of rest that continues for a generation may crystallize in a moment in the right conditions; and that English politics may nonetheless have exemplified a *tradition* of instability (if such a thing can be) from the early seventeenth century to the early eighteenth. The means of attaining stability by Walpole in the 1720s can thus be seen to foreshadow the quest for control of the cabinet by George III: "Place was power; patronage was power; and power is what men in politics are after. After 1715, power could not be achieved through party and so the rage of party gave way to the pursuit of place."[121] Yet Burke, who well knew the evidence regarding the search for place as a stabilizing motive, appears in 1770 to have attempted to incite a rage of party. One reason may have been that he could not at this time support a corrupt system merely because it fostered stability.

By giving his reasons for that rejection, *Thoughts on the Cause of the Present Discontents* amounts to an argument for the keeping alive of civic conscience and the maintenance of an honest party in opposition as the highest ends of political life. And this work of persuasion may have had a more practical bearing than the skepticism of Plumb suggests. It is a plain fact, Herbert Butterfield would conclude in *George III and the Historians,* that "the early conduct of George III—even if it involved nothing more than the appointment of Bute—was calculated to bring out an important constitutional issue."[122] But it did involve a good deal more than the appointment of Bute: the rapid elevation and rapid disposal of Grenville, Rockingham, Chatham, and Grafton; the anti-Wilkes campaign of 1763 and of 1768–1769; the insistence on dealing with the Americans as rebels who would not learn their lesson by compromise. On this account, enhanced liberty in English society was an unintended result of the clash between certain forces of *in*stability: the self-will of George III and Wilkes's incorrigible resistance; the wish of the Rockinghamites for office; the eloquent conviction of Burke as a justifier at once of legitimacy and resistance.

If there is an area of uncertainty in Burke's finely articulated defense of party, it shows in his reluctance to think his way further into his attack on the abuse of power, where all considerations about the proper use of a party must begin. His conception of party and character, drawing upon associations with private friendship, is seldom presented as if it might summon the resources of a justified and continuing popular protest. He knows that honest indignation may be needed to supply the impetus for reforms; but how steadily do we find such passion in *Thoughts on the Cause of the Present*

Discontents? A party, in Burke's view of it here, prevails by accumulating extensive support. It is conceived as existing almost wholly in opposition; it intervenes to recover something that has been lost. Burke writes very little about how a party might conduct itself once it has achieved office as a unified entity. It would be another twelve years before the Rockingham Whigs had their next opportunity to form a government. By that time, fear of monarchical trespass against liberty—from such devices as the "general warrants" for search and seizure against Wilkes—had abated considerably, and Burke's sense of the health of the constitution had become inseparable from his thoughts about the regulation of the British Empire.

❧ IV ❧

The American War

IN 1763, the chancellor of the exchequer and new chief minister of England, George Grenville, looked hard at the Treasury books and saw that the cost of collecting taxes from America was greater than the revenue. To bring in more money, he persuaded the House of Commons of the utility of the Stamp Act; and it was passed by Parliament on March 22, 1765, with a strong majority in the House of Commons and unanimity in the House of Lords. The objects of the Stamp Act were to pay for the Canadian war and to reassert British control in the American colonies— neither of them necessarily offensive or controversial ideas. But the conditions of supervision and collection were onerous and new. Paper used in legal documents and newspapers had now to be embossed with a revenue stamp, and payment was made through colonial stamp distributors. Attorney licenses took the highest of the enumerated taxes; also taxed were magazines, packs of cards, and dice. This was an "internal" tax and to that extent intrusive, levied for the express purpose of regulating the activities of the colonists. To the radical Americans, who followed British politics closely, these exactions from Grenville might have seemed predictable and to have promised worse to come. Grenville had supported the government against Wilkes on the question of general warrants.

The colonists struck back with pamphlets and protests, not only against the new tax but against all involuntary taxation. Grenville had tried to soften the blow by choosing established men as stamp distributors, but they were subjected in America to mobbing and intimidation. The house of Thomas Hutchinson, the governor of Massachusetts, was sacked and his library burned. The peace of the colonies was broken by a summer of riots; and the Stamp Act was a dead letter by November. Nobody could be found to enforce the law, and nullification spoke louder than any reply.

Had this been an isolated measure, the crisis might have passed, but the Stamp Act was part of a strategy by Grenville to assert greater power in the western empire through control of the colonial trade. In the background lay the Sugar Act, passed on April 5, 1764, which cut in half an older tax on molasses and set more rigorous conditions of enforcement in order to raise revenue. Smuggling of molasses was thereby discouraged, and the colonists saw a decrease in the profits on rum. In general, the bookkeeper's sobriety of the Grenville strategy brought more resentment than cooperation, and yet his stand was firm—smuggling, writes P. J. Marshall, "was an almost obsessive concern of Grenville's"—and an unfriendly watchfulness was pushed into areas of policy that had lain unattended.[1] By the Currency Act, passed on September 1, 1764, colonial bills were abolished, the reissue of existing currency prohibited, and the currency of the colonies placed under the regulation of Parliament. The Quartering Act of 1765 required that British officers and soldiers be billeted and quartered in colonial barracks and public houses and, if their numbers ran over, that they be accommodated at inns, ale houses, livery stables, and other such civilian commercial establishments, their expenses of food and lodging to be paid by the colonies.

Looked at in all its parts, from the point of view of British settlers under a new imposition from British rule, the imperial policy of Grenville could seem to present a comprehensive design with a long future.[2] It is in this larger context that one ought to judge the ferocity of the American response and the view finally taken by colonists as reasonable as Benjamin Franklin and John Adams. If Americans submitted to a sovereignty so heavy-handed, their consent to any particular measure would eventually be deemed superfluous.

The Stamp Act Crisis

The Stamp Act riots, an event sanitized in heroic histories of the birth of the United States, were a portent of a storm. Though Burke would notice their significance in his published writings only elliptically, they cast a shadow over his thinking about America in the next decade. Writing under the anonymous cover of the year's historical article in the *Annual Register* for the year 1765, he opened with a survey of the revolution in the Spanish dominions of South America and the French colony of St. Domingo, and spoke of their promise and their menace: "Insurrections were not confined to the western parts of the old and the new world. The spirit of liberty seemed to have walked forth over the face of the earth, and to threaten revolutions in every part." When, later in the article, he came to describe the Stamp Act riots, it was not their action for liberty that drew his attention. The New England summer of 1765 had disclosed "scenes of anarchy and confusion; where licentiousness was carried almost to the highest pitch that it possibly could admit, without assuming another name." The other name that he did not speak was *rebellion*—an event in its violence resembling war and, like war, producing a sure legacy of ruin. Burke deplored the way that American mobs of "the profligate and abandoned (as is usually the case in civil commotions) under the specious pretext and mask of liberty, and the common cause, gave a loose to their unruly passions, and committed all those exorbitances which the vulgar are so prone to, when under any pretence they are allowed to assemble in bodies; and through any relaxation of the laws, they have not the fears of immediate punishment upon them." An ominous feature of the riots was the refusal to intervene by persons of higher rank, who "did not think proper to damp a spirit, which, however irregularly or improperly exerted, they perhaps at that time thought it conducive to their designs to keep alive."[3] Not the tumults alone but the failure of local authorities to exert a restraining influence showed the perilous situation of the colonies. This was a mixture that, whether addressing mob action or vigilante justice, in France or in Ireland, would lead Burke to denounce those who employed such tactics. His sympathy with the Americans opposed to the Stamp Act was politically coherent; but his passionate opposition to British regulation of the American colonies could hardly have been predicted from this beginning.

That the protests were almost general throughout the colonies became a standard theme of pamphlets by James Otis and others, which received wide distribution in England. Yet English believers in an imperial constitution tended to look on American repudiation of the Stamp Act as an isolated response to a law that overreached. A further error of perception was at work. Parliament accounted for the resistance to the Stamp Tax by the distinction between internal taxes (on such domestic goods as newspapers and legal documents), which the colonists were said to oppose unconditionally, and external taxes (confined to imported goods), which they would pay if necessary. This understanding proved to be mistaken, yet it gained support from the ambiguous language of some American pamphlets; and in the eyes of Parliament, it suggested that a new tax of an appropriate sort might still be levied. The Rockingham administration, which succeeded that of Grenville in 1765–1766, pulled free of this assumption to a remarkable extent.[4] In making a detached estimate of the controversy, Rockingham was both courageous and anti-innovative; and his party would come to take pride chiefly in two acts of omission: the repeal of the Stamp Act and a refusal to press for any new tax.

The party's neglect of assertive policy went against the conventional wisdom, which held that the mother country must back its will by force. Grenville had given a candid defense of his policy in those terms: "When two countries are connected together, like *England* and her colonies, without being incorporated, the one must necessarily govern, the greater must rule the less; but so rule it, as not to contradict the fundamental principles that are common to both."[5] A rational-sounding argument, but its end does not remember its beginning. How could equal agreement on principles lead to a relation of master and servant? Besides, principles come to be shared by the force of common feelings, and such feelings are not compatible with heavy-handed government. There are moments—Burke thought this one of them—when any explicit measure can seem oppressive. To those who said the use of power was necessary to prove the power real, Burke's answer would always be the same. The maxim was false in theory and likely to produce a catastrophe. It is wiser to throw "a politick, well-wrought veil" over the virtual presence and actual absence of authority. So in the years 1766–1772, the best chance for maintaining an undivided empire lay in a de facto policy of no taxation.

Yet before Rockingham could lead the House of Commons in repealing the Stamp Act, his party found it politically necessary to secure the passage of the Declaratory Act. By this they reasserted parliamentary control of America. Since the conditions of the control were left unspecified, it has been tempting for historians to represent the law as a salve to the amour-propre of the House of Commons, a verbal cover for an embarrassing capitulation. It may be fairer to read the Declaratory Act—which had more the character of a resolution than a law—as a signal of the unwillingness of the House of Commons to surrender America. The majority in 1766 certainly wanted it both ways: to assert the sovereignty of Parliament while retracting its most notable recent exercise of power; to reserve the power to make new laws, without having a particular law in mind. The immediate effect of the Declaratory Act was to render parliamentary policy on America more inscrutable than before. England and America each made of it what they wished. The language of the Declaratory Act, by which Parliament owned "full power and authority to make laws and statutes of sufficient force and validity to bind the colonies and people of *America*, subjects of the crown of *Great Britain*, in all cases whatsoever," gave no hint whether "all cases whatsoever" could be read so as to justify a new tax. In the minds of members of Parliament, it did imply that; in the minds of the colonists, it did not.[6] The attempt by William Pitt and Isaac Barré to amend the act, it must be added, left no doubt that it did include the power to tax. Rockingham himself had pressed for the vague language, however, in keeping with Burke's suggestion that Parliament should simply declare its power as a matter of fact. When Charles Yorke, the attorney general, proposed for clarity's sake that the phrasing be changed to "as well in cases of Taxation, as in all other cases whatsoever," Rockingham spoke of the need for judicious obscurity. "It is our firm Resolution in the House of Lords—I mean among ourselves—that that word must be resisted."[7] So *taxation* (the word) was suppressed. At the news of repeal of the Stamp Act, rejoicing in America was general.

The fractious spirit of the colonies was quick to return. In response to the British demand of reparations for the Stamp Act riots, Massachusetts first refused to pay, then agreed but on condition that the rioters be indemnified. This the king would not allow. Meanwhile, the calculated ambiguity of the Declaratory Act had prepared a misunderstanding whose exact dimensions would remain unknown until another tax heated the American distrust into grievance. Pitt nicely exemplified this "generous" construction of the current state of colonial relations. It was supposed by the Rockingham Whigs that Pitt's only reason for declining to support the Declaratory Act must be jealousy of a political rival. In fact, he had an understanding of sovereignty and taxation far more specific than the Rockingham party would claim. "We may bind their trade," he said, "confine their manufactures, and exercise every power whatsoever—except that of taking their money out of their pockets without their consent."[8] In short, we may double the force of our revenue-gathering, so long as we repeal not one tax but all possible taxes. These words would not have pleased Americans had they acquired the transatlantic fame of Pitt's more celebrated speeches. He wanted to justify a revenue drawn incidentally through the control of trade; yet he was widely understood to be endorsing the distinction between internal and external taxes.[9] To put his advice into practice would have given unwelcome solidity to the Declaratory Act.

Burke took a large share in the persuasive work that led to the repeal of the Stamp Act, along with the passage of the Declaratory Act. It has been said with truth, by more than one biographer, that Burke had a hard time admitting that he was wrong. His withdrawal of support for the Declaratory Act must be counted an exception. Though the reversal was not complete until 1778,[10] Burke's speeches of the early 1770s show the gradual progress of his skepticism. This was an unpleasant change of mind for him, since he wanted so much to retain the attachment and to consider America, once the agitations were over, as part of Britain still. When, in the middle of the war, he found his party attacked in a pamphlet by Richard Price for having passed the Declaratory Act, he recalled their predicament: "Those who wished to quiet America by concession, thought it best to make that concession at the least possible diminution of the reputation and authority of this Country. This was the principle of those who acted in a responsible situation for that measure in 1766. In this possibly they were wrong."[11] In the same place, Burke speaks of the followers of Lord Chatham, who "thought they ought rather to have convicted their Country of Robbery; and to have given up the Object, not as a Liberal donation, but as a restitution of stolen goods." This was a different attempt to strike a balance, one that Burke thought less credible than the Declaratory Act; in effect, Chatham distinguished part of the taxes as illegitimate and the rest as fairly taken: the remedy seemed pragmatic, yet it left a standing grievance. Burke, on the contrary, was for allowing a "salutary neglect" to fall upon all disputation concerning trade. England would claim sovereignty over America, but England intended to say, and perhaps intended to do, nothing much about it.[12]

☙

The Rockingham administration lasted from July 10, 1765, to July 30, 1766: a year and twenty days. "A lutestring ministry, it will last the summer," Charles Townshend had predicted;[13] but it accomplished some things while it lasted, and Burke wrote its history in an anonymous pamphlet, *A Short Account of a Late Short Administration*, employing the dry declarative style of which he was a master. "In that space of time," the *Short Account* asserts,

> The Distractions of the *British* Empire were composed, by *The Repeal of the American Stamp Act;*
> But the Constitutional Superiority of *Great Britain* was preserved, by *The Act for securing the Dependence of the Colonies.*
> *Private* Houses were relieved from the Jurisdiction of the Excise, by *The Repeal of the Cyder Tax.*
> The personal Liberty of the Subject was confirmed, by *The Resolution against General Warrants.* The lawful Secrets of Business and Friendship were rendered inviolable, by *The Resolution for condemning the Seizure of Papers.*
> The Trade of *America* was set free from injudicious and ruinous Impositions—Its Revenue was improved, and settled upon a rational foundation—Its Commerce extended with foreign Countries; while all the Advantages were secured to Great Britain, by *The Act for repealing certain Duties, and encouraging, regulating, and securing the Trade of this Kingdom, and the British Dominions in America.*[14]

The two opening paragraphs above, divided only by a semicolon, refer to the repeal of the Stamp Act and the passage of the Declaratory Act (the punctuation here indicating that the two can only be understood together). Burke's way of framing the summary implies the benefit of both acts for the empire and restates it as a benefit for the colonies, too. He certainly believed this: the absence of comment underlines the transparent nature of the achievement. Along with increased liberality to a trading partner comes an enlargement of liberty itself, announced here by the items against the seizure of papers and general warrants for searches.

For the rest, Burke's *Short Account* says that the leaders of the Rockingham party have opened new ports for trade of all kinds (including the slave trade); encouraged public meetings and free consultation; reconciled the interests of the northern and southern colonies; paid off bills for the Canadian war and settled an advantageous commercial treaty with Russia; "treated their sovereign with decency"; and (not least) shunned any connection with the Earl of Bute. The Rockingham administration was, the pamphlet accurately says, neither corrupt nor suspected of corruption. It did not sell offices and pensions to convenient friends and toadies. "These are plain facts; of a clear and public nature; neither extended by elaborate reasoning, nor heightened by the coloring of eloquence. They are the services of a single year." No reproach is leveled against the decision by George III to turn the party out of office. From this, and indeed from the confident strategy of understatement in the *Short Account,* one infers that Burke and his party expected that the reward for "having left their king and their country in a much better condition than they found them" would be a continuation of the pattern of dissent and compromise that had characterized the past year. Changes of ministry would thus be frequent enough to keep them close to power. They could not have guessed that by 1770, Lord North—a member of a well-known Tory family who had been paymaster of forces under Chatham—would subdue the parliamentary opposition and for a decade reluctantly obey the king's wish to have him continue in office. Yet if the party was wrong about the durability of its accomplishments, it was not wrong about their nature.[15] Rockingham and Burke might have overrated the immediate impact of a generous law to reform a bad policy, but this would always be their preferred instrument. The design for economic reform in 1781, the East India Bill of 1783, and the impeachment of Warren Hastings starting in 1788 are the successors of the repeal of the Stamp Act.

The party's year of power exhibited at least this singular triumph in a ministry hampered from the first by the hostility of George III. The next offensive taxes on America would come in 1767, from the hand of Charles Townshend. Of the several laws sometimes brought together as the Townshend Acts, three should be mentioned. The Revenue Act imposed duties on glass, lead, paints, paper, and tea but was expected to be less unhappily received than the Stamp Act, since it placed an external tax on imports. The Restraining Act withdrew the power of lawmaking from the assembly of New York until it should comply with the Quartering Act—a penalty that carried an insult but no effect since the money for quartering troops had already been voted by the assembly.[16] Finally, the combination of the Revenue Act and the Indemnity Act removed the tax on tea in England, in order to promote the sale of tea at a lower price in America. This phalanx of laws explained itself by a curious preamble, avowing the intention of collecting a revenue from the colonies by some means. The reason was that Britain found it "just and necessary," as the impolitic words declared, to "make some provision in the present Session of Parliament towards raising the said revenue."[17] By framing revenue measures as duties, Townshend was probably testing the distinction between internal and external taxation (suggested by Benjamin Franklin as well as Pitt), even though he himself did not accept it. Nor, as it turned out, did the colonists. Laws seldom advertise themselves as just and necessary unless their justice has been challenged and their necessity exposed as convenience. When, with the return of resistance by the Americans, most of the Townshend duties were lifted and only the one on tea remained, the tea tax was hated as much as all the others. Nothing seemed at stake but a muscular assertion of regulative power.

The retrenchment of the late 1760s took its toll on British civil liberties. The Treason Act, passed during the reign of Henry VIII, was determined by Parliament to be still in force in 1769: persons in America accused of treason could thus be removed for trial in England—an unheard-of break in the tradition of the rights of prisoners under common law, which colonial assemblies protested by passing resolutions against it. The Boston riot of December 1773, called in America the Boston Tea Party, in which colonists dumped the goods of the East India Company into Boston Harbor, provoked in response the Coercive Acts. The Boston Port Act closed Boston harbor from June 1, 1774, removing the seat of government and the custom house to Salem, prohibiting the loading and unloading of ships, and barring commerce by sea until restitution was paid to the East India Company for its recent losses. The Massachusetts Government Act altered the Massachusetts charter so that members of the colonial council had to be appointed by the crown, and the assembly was stripped of the power to appoint local officials; judges and other magistrates were now to be appointed by the governor, while jurymen would be called by sheriffs, themselves also appointed by the governor. All public meetings were forbidden except by permission of the governor, who served at the king's pleasure. In this way, legal and political authority over Massachusetts was effectively transferred to London. At the same time, a new law enlarged the power of governors to quarter troops in uninhabited houses, private dwellings, and other places deemed appropriate. Yet every one of these rigorous measures failed.[18] Judges were met by armed mobs. Juries refused to be sworn. The Americans answered the closing of Boston Harbor with a boycott of British goods and, by days of fasting, steeled themselves for further acts of defiance.

The Rockingham party flatly opposed the coercive measures, braced by a sense of their own honor and dignity. The opposition had Burke for its chief architect; yet the image of Burke as an Irish upstart persisted. In November 1771 he felt compelled to respond to a letter from William Markham, the bishop of Chester, tutor to the Prince of Wales, and an old friend of the Burke family who was nearing the top of his social climb. Dr. Markham had described the Burke household (including Will and Richard) as "a hole of adders" and accused Burke himself of crass opportunism. Since the letter said that he had been improperly "taking the lead in the measures of the party," Burke took the trouble to write a serious reply.[19] He tries, he says, to follow more than to lead and makes a habit of speaking late in a given debate. (As politicians are aware, this is a favorable position anyway, allowing the speaker to gauge which statements need refuting and to take a broad view where moderation is called for.) But that does not quite answer Markham's point. For by the charge of ambition, Markham is likely to have meant not that Burke entered too eagerly in public debates but that he overplayed his hand. Burke's response evokes his previous character and the progress of his career:

Accident first threw me into this party. When I was again at Liberty, Knowledge and reflection induced me to reenter it, principle and experience have confirmed me in it. Your Lordship will find it difficult to shew, where a man who wished to act systematically in publick business, could have arranged himself more reputably. By arranging myself with them I trust I have given some sort of security to the publick for my good Behaviour. That versatility, those sudden evolutions which have something derogated from the credit of all publick professions, are things not so easy in large Bodies, as when men act alone; or in light Squadrons. A man's virtue is best secured by shame, and best improved by Emulation in the Society of virtuous men.[20]

When you see me act with the party, Burke is saying, do not suppose that I give orders to them, or they to me; I chose this party for the discipline which virtuous association affords against the caprice and the "sudden evolutions" of personal will. It is the same argument that he offered publicly the year before in *Thoughts on the Cause of the Present Discontents.* A political party can boast of one inseparable good, that it checks the greed and delusion of people whose self-will would otherwise outrun shame. Now the principle is applied to Burke himself.

This notable letter to Markham, in some ways a precursor of *A Letter to a Noble Lord,* is keen to parry the accusation that Burke used his office of private secretary to obtain illicit influence on Lord Rockingham and his party. Actually, the situation gave Burke visibility without status or prestige. He denies with considerable heat the imputation by Markham that his course of conduct has been aimed at the achievement of status: he would have disclaimed the tactics of "not men, but situations" just as he rejected the cant of "not men, but measures." The legitimate fame of politicians, he tells Markham, "is to be rated by the Rank which men hold in Parliament, and by that only. This rank though not exactly definable, is very easily understood." Any other criterion would "tend to the utter relinquishment of any but the most slavish and passive Conduct in all those who ever look to the Service of the State. Indeed it would be fatal to the Importance of the State itself."[21] The suppressed fury of the self-defense abates only gradually: "I could say a great deal of the ground of men's pretensions in this Country. . . . This humble cottage which is not to be shaken even *pulsante Caesara manu* [when Caesar pounds at the door] I take refuge in most joyfully; Your Lordship is so condescending as to offer to enter it along with me; but I beg you to go no further than the door, it is indeed a sort of lodging unsuitable to your dignity as to your Abilities."[22] The inference from those final words can hardly be mistaken: weak abilities and a small spirit will avoid an inconspicuous role, but to labor (as Burke does) often unseen, among a body of men who are zealous for the public good, suits his confidence in his own gifts. The suggestion that nothing but actual and demonstrated talent can support real dignity offers a further variation of his argument on merit: the letter to Markham is plainly the work of the former secretary of single-speech Hamilton and the author of the *novus homo* letter. Yet Burke is no longer a "new man" in relation to Parliament at large but rather an exceptional talent within his party, recognized by those who know such things. The inclusion of men like him in government is a condition of the employment of mental energy for the public good. As for the propriety of maintaining a party dedicated to resistance, Burke says that the Glorious Revolution "could not be supported unless some lesser modes of opposition could also be justified."

A look ahead is warranted, since this remark differs greatly from the treatment of resistance, revolution, and the meaning of 1688 that we find in *Reflections on the Revolution in France*. There, the Glorious Revolution will be described as a defensive act, done from necessity and affording no sort of precedent. By contrast, Burke here affirms that acceptance of a revolution entails a justification for lesser acts of resistance.

"The principles of true politics are those of morality enlarged, and I neither now do nor ever will admit any other."[23] That sentence—as close as Burke comes to a profession of faith—has its original context in the letter to Dr. Markham. It was drawn from him by the casual charge that he had used his party for selfish ends. The heart of Burke's response is that, in politics as in morality, the means must justify themselves. Means, though it troubles us to think so, always alter the character of the actor, and every end is also a means to another end. Thus, if you justify the torture of suspects in order to assist a war against a wicked enemy, you will find that in doing so you have incorporated torture in your idea of justice. You have come to an understanding with yourself, and the utmost savagery will be compatible with your nature thereafter. You have become one of those who can acquit themselves of any wrong by appealing to a result in a plausible future. And yet, because the future will need its own excuses, self-justification becomes an infinite regress. To this instrumental line of apology Burke's answer is plain. What you permit yourself to do at any time is part of what you are at all times. "For if they do these things in a green tree, what shall be done in the dry?"

One may follow Burke's clue and define a Machiavellian in politics as one who believes that power and cunning are the means to political good; that power is achieved and maintained by a leader whose virtue is endless motion; and that, though the face of morality may stay the same, its content must be altered to suit the changing necessities of the moment. By this standard, the political morality of Burke was the reverse of Machiavellian. For on the Machiavellian view, the political actor always strives to conceal the way in which his actions distort conventional morality; whereas on the Burkean view, he must be careful to avoid acts which, if they came to light, would shock conventional morality. Granted, it may be unwise to disclose all of one's reasons for acting. Prudence may dictate reticence. Still, Burke argues, the hidden reasons should be such as to withstand public scrutiny. Burke's political morality therefore presumes a high average of candor in the give-and-take between leaders and constituents.

Another letter of this period offers a practical test of his code. From the start of 1771 through the spring of 1775 when the revolution struck, Burke was serving as agent for the Province of New York at the Court of Great Britain; but toward the end of his first year of service, in December 1771, there was a threat of disruption on political grounds. He wrote to inform the New York Assembly that, if a new plan were adopted for appointment of American agents in Great Britain—a plan by which the governor and colonial council would vote on the appointment and thereby assure a close conformity with the views of the ministry—he could not retain his position as agent for New York. "My employment is a matter wholly detached from Administration."[24] Here, then, is further evidence of his loyalty to his party and his belief that on American affairs it stood in opposition. He would not think of offering his services to another administration that aimed to enforce a different policy. Rather, in the early

1770s, a time when he was far from power, Burke applied himself to learn about the tension between the wisdom of open trade with America and the state of popular opinion in England.

The narrow self-interest of British merchants was among the forces militating against a generous policy. Much persuasion would be needed, and no other cause seemed to Burke as important. This was surely among his reasons for declining an invitation, in August 1772, to head a commission to investigate the abuses of the East India Company presidencies. The commission as Burke saw it was a creature of Lord North; regarding the character of the India inquiry and the pressure to revise the charter of the company, he was dismissive: "You scarcely can conceive how nearly the Court and the Mob approach one another in their sentiments." He was using nothing but his nose—an excellent guide when assisted by his curiosity—but here, in what must have seemed an ordinary scuffle, for the moment he missed the signs of a deeper corruption.

Parliamentary Opposition and Political Resistance

Lord North established himself as a successful chief minister in the first two years of his service. Chatham had been a deeply imposing figure, admired by all though loved by few, proud and self-isolating to the point of mania. "He might have given firmness and almost tranquility to his country," reflected Horace Walpole. "But alas! his talents were inadequate to the task. The multiplication table did not admit of being treated in epic, and Lord Chatham had but that one style." It would be the function of Lord North to endow administration with a semblance of stability through a decade of uncertain policy that ended in defeat. Walpole's description, once more, catches the peculiarities of the man and his adaptation to the moment: "[North] had sound parts, wit, and it was thought, industry; an ungracious manner, a voice untuneable, and a total want of polish in his behaviour. He had been an active and ready agent in the whole cause against Wilkes, and was not a man that the friends of the Constitution could regard with partiality: but there were so few upright, that it was become almost eligible to select the exceptionable."[25] North was not immoderate in his view of the American colonies, being ready, before the violence of the war took hold, to allow them to raise their own taxes for their own defense. He lacked not prudence but imagination. He could read the writing on the wall after the wall had crumbled into individual stones.

But the policy on which North and the king were agreed was the policy which, with less responsibility, Parliament itself would have wished to enforce. "The American war was," as John Cannon summarized North's view, "a war for the rights of Parliament."[26] North was temperate in pursuit of his ends, assertive without aggression, and famous for sleeping through demonstrative speeches on the floor of the Commons. An accomplished classicist, he would become the dedicatee of Gibbon's *Decline and Fall of the Roman Empire;* and it is said that, awakened once by a false quantity in Burke's pronunciation of Latin verse, he corrected the error and fell back asleep. For good and ill, North was utterly without the nerve-end sensibility of crisis that animated Burke from decade to decade. Lord North, remarks Cannon, was above all a gifted parliamentarian: "the complete House of Commons man . . . and this is where one thinks of him, rising ponderously to reduce the temperature of some heated debate with a quip or pleasantry, bland, imperturbable, at times jaunty, picking off the arguments one by one."[27] If Burke was born for opposition, as he once said of himself, North seems to have been ideally equipped to endure the irritable humors that surrounded him. For ten years, from the most unpromising materials, he could be relied on to fashion a lukewarm majority.

As the Rockingham party looked to the winter term of 1772–1773, its internal debates were centered on whether to secede from Parliament, to attend only when great questions were discussed, or (if Rockingham approved) to adopt "a plan of more activity." Burke gave no credence to the argument for secession. The party was "morally sure of being defeated," he wrote to William Dowdeswell (the party's other first-class orator, prized by Burke for his canny judgment); "all we can do is to save our honour."[28] In a subsequent letter to Dowdeswell, Burke formulated his moderate view that prudence and economy of gesture must dictate their choices of action. "Nothing can, to my Ideas, make that formal, general, and instantaneous secession proper, but some direct act, which shakes a fundamental part of the constitution, and that too immediately and visibly."[29]

A letter of November 15, 1772, from the Duke of Richmond to Burke, clarifies the terms of this dispute and says much besides about the relationship of the aristocratic luminaries of the party to the man who was their strongest voice. "I don't," concedes Richmond, "think a secession now would have much effect, but it is better than a poor weak attendance and a despicable opposition." Less inert than Rockingham, he sees that Burke stands out in the party for his sense of urgency: "Indeed Burke you have more merit than any man in keeping us together, but I believe our greatest Bond is the Pride of the individuals, which unfortunately tho' it keeps us from breaking, hinders us from acting like men of Sense."[30] The expression of gratitude to Burke carries a faint undertone of self-justification: men of sense may deviate from principle on occasion and break from their party, whereas the pride of the Rockingham Whigs, consonant with their greatness and their weakness, hinders them from measures to advance their individual fortunes. The party, Richmond implies, could not exist without Burke as the constant presence whose function is to recall their reason for being.

Revealing as it is, this assurance is chiefly important for the response it drew from Burke—a letter drafted some time after November 15, 1772, which is among the most frank, interesting, and vulnerable he would ever write:

> On the whole I am inclined to think that the faults in your body are no more than the ordinary frailties of human Nature, some of them too inseparably attached to the Cause of all your strength and reputation. You are in general somewhat Languid, scrupulous and unsystematick. But men of high Birth and great property are rarely as enterprising as others and for reasons that are very natural; Men of integrity are curious, sometimes too curious, in the Choice of means; and great Bodies can seldom be brought to System and discipline, except by Instruments that while you are out of Government, you have not in your power. However with all these faults it is better you should be rich and honest and numerous than needy and profligate and composed of a few desperate politicians though they have advantages in their own way which you must always want.[31]

Eulogizing Richmond to his face, and urging him to accept a more active idea of his fitness for politics, Burke proceeds to characterize the spirit of aristocracy.

> Decorum, firmness, consistency, Courage, patient manly perseverance, those are the Virtues of despair; They are worth something surely; and none has profited of that situation so much as your Grace nor could you have shewn of what materials you are made in any other. Persons in your Station of Life ought [to] have long Views. You people of great families and hereditary Trusts and fortunes are not like such as I am, who whatever we may be by the Rapidity of our growth and of the fruit we bear, flatter ourselves that while we creep on the Ground we belly into melons that are exquisite for size and flavour, yet still we are but annual plants that perish with our Season and leave no sort of Traces behind us. You if you are what you ought to be are the great Oaks that shade a Country and perpetuate your benefits from Generation to Generation. In my Eye—The immediate power of a D. of Richmond or a Marquis of R. is not so much of moment but if their conduct and example hands down their principles to their successors; then their houses become the publick repositories and offices of Record for the constitution, Not like the Tower or Rolls Chappel where it is searched for and sometimes in Vain, in rotten parchments under dripping and perishing Walls; but in full vigour and acting with vital Energy and power in the Characters of the leading men and natural interests of the Country. . . . So that I do not look upon your time or lives lost if in this sliding away from the genuine Spirit of the Country, certain parties if possible, if not the heads of certain families should make it their Business by the whole Course of their Lives principally by their Example to mould into the very vital Stamina of their descendants those principles which ought to be transmitted pure and uncorrupted to posterity.[32]

The "virtues of despair"—virtues born of despair rather than belonging to it—are qualities of courtesy and high principle; and the consistency mentioned here is the strength of a pride rendered civil and social. Satan's speech to Beelzebub in Book 1 of *Paradise Lost* ends by asking "What reinforcement we may gain from hope,/If not what resolution from despair." At the same time, Burke knows (remembering Milton) that moral courage is fed by indignation:

> What though the field be lost?
> All is not lost; the unconquerable Will,
> And study of revenge, immortal hate,
> And courage never to submit or yield.

With the exception of *hate*, these, too, are elements of the courage Burke prescribes to Richmond; and by consistency and perseverance, he means the self-sufficiency and resourcefulness of a mind not to be changed by place or time.[33] In later eulogies for Lord Rockingham and Lord Keppel, Burke is explicit about these virtues of a natural aristocracy, but the letter to Richmond is the first to disclose his view of the moral connection between "presumptive virtue" and opposition.

A question may fairly be asked. How could a man of wit and skeptical temper like Burke come to credit the aristocratic belief that a nation's "vital stamina" resides in the members of one class? This was beginning to sound archaic even when Burke wrote the words (four years before Jeremy Bentham's *Fragment on Government*); for the doctrine has at its core an embrace of privilege, and its adoption prevents an impartial estimate of the common good regardless of custom or precedent. Burke would grant all this, with different degrees of readiness at different times. Yet he believed that "the spirit of a gentleman" imparted a self-respect that was not selfish, and this was the germ of every larger feeling for the public good. The word *gentleman* also implied a liberal education that afforded long views, a qualification not widely available outside the members of one class; and though Burke realized that for many of that class the title gentleman in this special sense was merely honorific, he nonetheless thought it the likeliest place for the generosity he sought to be found. The gifts that stem from privilege should flow to others in the form of selfless acts and examples of magnanimity. The corresponding vice of the aristocracy is the "austere and insolent domination" Burke warned against in *Thoughts on the Cause of the Present Discontents*. Yet however one may modify it, Burke clearly believes there is such a thing as the aristocratic character, which knows, as mere merit can never know, a perfect freedom from dependency and self-distrust. The same virtues cannot be expected of those lower down the social ladder. They have not the "previous fortune in character at stake"—to borrow the language of the *Reflections*—which the born aristocrat can draw upon. So while men of talent may be prodigious, the owners of great estates (if they are what they should be) are a continual wonder. They rightly do inherit heaven's graces.

These facts of moral psychology Burke supposed beyond dispute. And in a sense they still are today. Even a society ruled by money, where a fortune without a title is the mark of inheritance, will associate a refined code of conduct with established families and expect a good deal less from stockjobbers and new-money men. (Where scores of new people come into fortunes that soon outpace the old, the entire map of manners and power is changed and a different analysis is called for—a truth suggested by Burke's writings on the East India men.) Still, a separate argument seems necessary to transform his observations into a basis for a hereditary *principle*. Of the "great oaks that shelter a country" we may ask, Who lives under them, and at what cost to the commonwealth? His answer can be seen developing gradually from this letter to its expansion in a famous paragraph of the *Reflections*. The good of associating a nation with an aristocratic spirit "pure and uncorrupted," he will say there, is a good without price, "the unbought grace of life, the cheap defence of nations." The presence of the aristocratic ideal, even if it is founded on illusion, shelters other apparently pointless ideals, such as the respect paid to beauty and delicacy, and the perpetuation of a system of justice for its own sake.

Considered as a social type, the antithesis of the generous aristocrat is the hardworking demagogue. Burke was still situated to observe Wilkes closely: a man whose importance was due to the volatile feelings and capricious loyalties of the mob. "As to Wilkes," he remarks in a letter to Rockingham, "I cannot be persuaded, but that in the End he will jest and buffoon himself out of his consequence. His petulance and Levity are something beyond what is credible. I sat near him and he was ridiculing and abusing his adherents without any management, and in the hearing of several people. I hinted to him jestingly that his friends, by being such, were too respectable not to be treated with a little Decorum. O, says he, I never laugh at my *friends*, but these are only my *followers*."[34] Burke judged politicians as he did other people. Wilkes's contempt for his followers be-

trayed a want of the generosity and stature that one looks for in "the leading men and natural interests of the country."

It was because he wished to preserve the integrity of political opposition that Burke stressed the value of the aristocratic part of a mixed constitution. In this, he belonged to a broader movement of thought in his
time. James Madison, preeminently among the American founders,
shared the same emphasis; and behind both thinkers stood the political
theory of Montesquieu. The reason for instituting a bicameral legislature
was to provide a changing body of lawmakers with a less changeable
source of stability. So the upper chamber was modeled on the Roman senate, the fame and descent of whose members are supposed to bring a sense
of honor to their proceedings. In *The Spirit of the Laws*, the argument for
the separation of powers rests on an intuition that despotism is more natural to men than constitutional government: "A despotic government offers itself, as it were, at first sight; it is uniform throughout; and as passions alone are requisite to establish it, this is what every capacity may
reach."[35] By contrast, a mixed constitution is the artificial attainment of a
gentle age (Montesquieu speaks from a point of view that favors art over
nature). The dominant traits of various polities must be fostered in order
to avoid the excess of each. Honor belongs to a monarchical, virtue to a
republican regime, but "virtue itself has need of limits," and "it is necessary from the very nature of things that power should be a check to power."[36]
The doctrine of separation of powers uses one branch of government, then,
to relieve the labor of other branches and offset their influence. Montesquieu admired the parliamentary system of England for this reason above
all. In such a system, pressure to act will be felt sparingly, except at times
of crisis; a hidden strength of the constitution is that it leaves the people
undistracted by politics. And yet participation must not sink below the
requirements of citizenship. People should be attached to their government by ties both sentimental and material. Taxes, to borrow Montesquieu's own example, are essential to civic responsibility, and taxes are
normally increased in proportion to the liberty of the subject. In proportion, as slavery is increased and a slavish disposition fostered, taxes are
likely to be reduced.

The theorists of the mixed constitution built their understanding on a psychology that still seems accurate. But so much of their thinking presses against the democratic ideology of our day—a common sense whose leading idea is the simple good of majority rule—that many insights they took for granted may now appear recondite. They defended the rule of the majority not because most people know what is right for all but because most people know what is wrong for most. Constitutional checks are required to ensure that the majority's rights do not become a minority's wrongs. Thus the legislative balance—a second house with distinct responsibilities and longer terms than the first—aims to limit the practical harm that springs from flattery of the people. The psychology shared by Montesquieu, Burke, and Madison holds that politicians are not always improved by their popularity.[37] Those closest to the people can hardly be expected, Burke says in the *Reflections*, "to bear with moderation, or to conduct with discretion, a power which they themselves, more than any others, must be surprized to find in their hands." Such men, elevated from the humbler ranks in society, are naturally "intoxicated with their unprepared greatness"; being of a temper "habitually meddling, daring, subtle, active, of litigious dispositions and unquiet minds," they serve the private interests that they understand, while the public interest remains to them an abstraction. In persons, as in civilizations, the ability to consider the good of the whole is a late acquisition.

Burke's stance as a liberal constitutionalist made him even at this stage the reverse of a populist. And when, in the early 1770s, the Rockingham party spoke of the dangers of a war with America, it had to contend against popular opinion. War was appealing on several grounds. Taxes drawn from the Americans promised relief from the burden of costs still owing for the Seven Years War. Also, to people not versed in the mutual benefits of free trade, it seemed natural and profitable to retain a domestic monopoly with corresponding restrictions on foreign goods; the Grenville and Townshend taxes merely extended to America a policy that had long worked to suppress Irish trade. Besides, the feeling against the colonies was a local instance of the larger truth that wars are popular. They remain popular so long as people can make themselves believe that other means are exhausted, that a victory will bring palpable gains, and that the enemy will be defeated without much trouble.

This is why it was exceptional for Lord Rockingham to say in a letter as early as January 30, 1774, "I can never give my assent to proceeding to actual force against the Colonies."[38] *Never* left no room for maneuver: he was depending on generous feelings to triumph among the colonists, if not in the mother country. Burke for his part would decline to rule out force until his *Speech on Conciliation with America* fourteen months later; but the knowledge of Rockingham's dissident view would have given a free rein to his *Speech on American Taxation*. This extraordinary speech, which was largely improvised, performs two tasks with incomparable force and wit. It recounts the recent history of American-English relations; and it judges the reimposition of taxes to be politically unsound. No earlier effort by Burke had given his mental energies such full scope. *American Taxation* may be said to mark, too, the beginning of a policy not just of opposition but of protest; in this way it looks forward to Burke's speeches and writings on reform in the coming decade. Yet *American Taxation* has a firm setting in his previous writings on party and on the logic of an imperial constitution.

One major emphasis goes back to the argument of *Thoughts on the Cause of the Present Discontents*. Burke is preoccupied here again with what he called, in the earlier pamphlet, *character*. His strategy in *Thoughts* had been to submerge individuality in party in order to heighten the unified effect of a party; and he had exemplified, even as he described, the process by which a true statesman represses his own identity.[39] The party acquires a character while its subordinate members decline to exhibit personal opinions and characters of their own. What they deny themselves, the party naturally takes to itself. Once again in the *Speech on American Taxation*, we are made to feel the importance of a party as a collective actor. Strength, in a party, is incompatible with the singular impression created by the great man. A draft section of *Thoughts*, criticizing Chatham on these grounds, had in fact been eliminated from the final text of that work. Even so, Chatham objected that though "well intended," Burke's defense of party had "done much hurt to the Cause" among "the wide and extensive Publick." In a manuscript note of July 13, 1792, Burke responded: "I remember to have seen this knavish letter, at the time. The pamphlet is itself, by anticipation, an answer to that grand artificer of fraud. He could not like it. It is pleasant to hear *him* talk of the *great extensive publick,* who never conversed but with a parcel of low toadeaters. Alas! Alas! How different the *real* from the *ostensible* publick man—must all this theatrical stuffing and raised heels be necessary to the character of a great man? Oh! but that does not derogate from his great splendid side, God forbid."[40] Through 1770, and especially in a speech of May 9 of that year, Burke aimed to explode the fantasy of collective dignity, the "theatrical stuffing" with which the House of Commons after the Seven Years War acted its part against America.

"We began," he had said in the *Speech on American Resolutions,* "to tire of the Tranquility which we enjoyed. It was said we purchased peace by dignity, and now we must purchase dignity at the hazard of peace." The idea of dignity as a cover for persons weak and wavering in themselves turns out to be central to the argument of the *Speech on American Taxation:*

> If this dignity, which is to stand in the place of just policy and common sense, had been consulted, there was a time for preserving it, and for reconciling it with any concession. If in the session of 1768, that session of idle terror and empty menaces, you had, as you were often pressed to do, repealed these taxes; then your strong operations would have come justified and enforced, in case your concessions had been returned by outrages. But, preposterously, you began with violence; and before terrors could have any effect, either good or bad, your ministers immediately begged pardon, and promised that repeal to the obstinate Americans which they had refused in an easy, good-natured, complying British parliament. The assemblies which had been publicly and avowedly dissolved for *their* contumacy, are called together to receive *your* submission. Your ministerial directors blustered like tragic tyrants here; and then went mumping with a fore leg in America, canting, and whining, and complaining of faction.[41]

The preposterous use of violence as an overture to negotiation offends Burke's dramatic sense. The ministry of 1768 had allowed their policy to be dictated and their character inferred by an aimless alternation of postures. They transferred their sympathy from colonial to imperial interests and from imperial interests back to colonial again.

The *Speech on American Taxation* was delivered on April 19, 1774, but held for publication until the following January. By that time, Burke's prophecy of the failure of the coercive policy was borne out by American resistance. Yet his argument is not an endorsement of the American violence; nor is it altogether a rebuke to the assertion of imperial control. Rather, the motive of this levelheaded and vehement speech, so full of personality and incident, is to subject to the glare of public criticism the administrations that failed to look at "the whole of your complicated interests in one connected view." This, Burke plausibly argues, is what only the Rockingham administration properly did, and the fact explains their compound action of 1766: the broad assertion of control and the repeal of an offensive tax. Speaking eight years after that success, he refers to his party's approach as the "antient" policy of Britain toward the colonies—recurring to the adjective several times and relying on the sense of *former* while also calling upon the suggestion of a time-honored precedent.

Burke reviews the exploded policy of Rockingham's predecessor, Grenville, and of his two successors, Chatham and Townshend, because he thinks the North ministry is repeating their errors. With a misjudged punctilio, they have put in place of the ancient shilling drawback—a tax by another name, drawn in England as a toll on exports—a flaunted tax of threepence to be collected officiously in America. "You have deliberately thrown away a large duty which you held secure and quiet in your hands, for the vain hope of getting one three-fourths less, through every hazard, through certain litigation, and possibly through war." The motive for the change Burke traces, once more, to a shallow understanding of dignity. "They tell you, Sir, that your dignity is tied to it. I know not how it happens, but this dignity of yours is a terrible incumbrance to you; for it has of late been ever at war with your interest, your equity, and every idea of your policy."[42] The good of the Rockingham policy had been to recall Britain to an authority compatible with equity. Lord North, on the contrary, bound himself by the idle promise that he would never repeal the Townshend duties on glass, paper, and paint; now he has repealed them, but has left the tax on tea outstanding; so the only fixed point of policy to

American eyes is an overwhelming greed. The British are seen to desire a national monopoly (the East India Company) and a revenue (additional profit from exports), a tax in America as well as a tax in England. No country should pursue so exorbitant an aim without regard to the grievance it spreads. Yet this has been the pattern of misguided policy and halfhearted regret in all but one recent administration.

Grenville is the first of the previous ministers whose actions Burke addresses in detail. His policy had been simply that Parliament should claim and exercise a comprehensive power of taxation. According to his associate and follower, William Knox, Grenville believed in "the omnipotence of Parliament in its jurisdiction over the colonies. . . . He would consent to no stipulation of restraint."[43] His competence and lack of imagination came, Burke thought, from his having been

> bred in a profession. He was bred to the law, which is, in my opinion, one of the first and noblest of human sciences; a science which does more to quicken and invigorate the understanding, than all the other kinds of learning put together; but it is not apt, except in persons very happily born, to open and liberalize the mind exactly in the same proportion. Passing from that study he did not go very largely into the world; but plunged into business; I mean into the business of office; and the limited and fixed methods and forms established there. . . . These forms are adapted to ordinary occasions; and therefore persons who are nurtured in office do admirably well, as long as things go on in their common order; but when the high roads are broken up, and the waters out, when a new and troubled scene is opened, and the file affords no precedent, then it is that a greater knowledge of mankind, and a far more extensive comprehension of things, is requisite than ever office gave, or than office can ever give.[44]

The passage carries a tincture of Burke's underlying belief that politics consists of more than putting people into places. It is a separate competence and a calling. The experience of a profession may prepare the initiate for much about politics, but it is never preparation enough. Grenville's complacency and his narrowness stopped him from seeing what was new about America and what was unprecedented in the American crisis.

He erred by being too much a man of action—official action. Inaction may be preferable at times, even in response to an emergency. Where the threat of war hangs over all, with the possibility that half the empire may be lost, deliberation or a return to a well-tried compromise is superior to the most assertive action whose failure squanders resources and goodwill. That is the meaning of the constant adjuration in Burke's American writings, of the good of the "lapse of silent steady policy," of "a wise and salutary neglect." There may be wisdom in caution, wisdom even in timidity: "Interested timidity disgraces as much in the cabinet, as personal timidity does in the field. But timidity, with regard to the well-being of our country, is heroic virtue."[45]

Next among the men of power whose inconstancy has brought England close to a catastrophic loss is Lord Chatham. He gathered about himself, says Burke, an administration perfectly suited to the contradictions of his character. Chatham was still alive when this passage was added to the spoken text, but he was unlikely ever to prove a dependable ally; so Burke felt free to recall that when in power, Chatham had met the demands of the time with

> an administration so checkered and speckled; he put together a piece of joinery, so crossly indented and whimsically dovetailed; a cabinet so variously inlaid; such a piece of diversified Mosaic; such a tesselated pavement without cement; here a bit of black stone, and there a bit of white; patriots and courtiers, kings friends and republicans; whigs and tories; treacherous friends and open enemies: that it was indeed a very curious show; but utterly unsafe to touch, and unsure to stand on. The colleagues whom he had assorted at the same boards, stared at each other, and were obliged to ask "Sir, your name?—Sir, you have the advantage of me—Mr. Such a one—I beg a thousand pardons—" I venture to say, it did so happen, that persons had a single office divided between them, who had never spoke to each other in their lives; until they found themselves, they knew not how, pigging together, heads and points, in the same truckle-bed.[46]

The extravagant passage grows out of a pun on the word *cabinet:* the textures of tile and wood and the opposing tempers of the politicians are built up to produce an allegory of counterfeit unity. An aesthetic offense runs parallel to the tactical compromise, and the grossness of the calculation appears in the image of "pigging together, heads and points." The cartoon caption "I beg a thousand pardons" marks the limit of the intimacy these cabinet members enjoyed. At the same time, Burke's montage of blended fashions, misapplied to a piece of carpentry that is meant for use, brings out the incongruity of the stances adopted by Pitt in a career that made his policy answer to his personal mystique. The mixed high and low diction of this splendid set piece owes something to Pope's *Moral Essays,* especially the "Epistle to Burlington," and the tenor of the extended metaphor points to the sort of tasteless eclecticism that Pope judged aberrant in the realm of domestic design and architecture:

> Load some vain church with old theatric state,
> Turn arcs of triumph to a garden gate;
> Reverse your ornaments, and bang them all
> On some patch'd dog-hole eked with ends of wall.

Chatham's ministry is pictured as a lodging that aims at every elegance and achieves none. A brilliant structure, upright-looking and jerry-built.[47]

Yet it was not Chatham but a far more amiable politician, Charles Townshend, chancellor of the exchequer in 1765–1767, who threw out all the good that might have come from the repeal of the Stamp Act. Townshend's weakness was excessive sensitivity to the opinions of others, a vanity that kept time with the mood of the House of Commons from day to day and almost hour to hour, an immoderate passion for fame of a curious sort: fame parochially defined by the persons who shared his station in life. Praising Townshend's wit and polish, in a passage where eulogy and mockery are combined with an unmistakable affection, Burke observes: "He particularly excelled in a most luminous explanation, and display of his subject. His style of argument was neither trite and vulgar, nor subtle and abstruse. He hit the house just between wind and water.—And not being troubled with too anxious a zeal for any matter in question, he was never more tedious, or more earnest, than the pre-conceived opinions, and present temper of his hearers required; to whom he was always in perfect unison. He conformed exactly to the temper of the house; and he seemed to guide, because he was always sure to follow it."[48] When the time came for a settlement with the colonies, Townshend was still calculating the rise and fall of his stock in the House. This made his policy, like his person, a double-entendre. It was in fact the Townshend Acts that changed American resistance from a minority protest to a mass movement.[49]

Burke can suspend an ambiguous meaning so coolly on the line between praise and blame that it becomes impossible to say what intention was uppermost in his mind. A sentence one hears at first as a ripe compliment may turn over and close with an irony so flat that it calls into question the pretense of flattery. And yet, Burke takes an artistic satisfaction in seeing a feigned oratorical effect swell out to the limit of its influence; so the impression of a clear purpose may hover on the scene after its hollowness is proved. "He hit the house just between wind and water" describes the policy of a trimmer, but the phrase also denotes the part of a ship's hull that stays under water except when it is heeled over by wind: the part of a man-of-war most vulnerable to enemy fire. The words from Townshend that fill the sails of his listeners become the words that sink their enterprise. His revision of the Grenville policy of imperial control through taxation is thus shown to have been safe and rash in equal measure. It appeased the House and divided the empire.

A significant detail of Burke's estimate is that Townshend erred not by simplicity but by elaboration. "To please universally was the object of his life; but to tax and to please, no more than to love and to be wise, is not given to men. However he attempted it." Advocates of taxation were to be placated by a preamble admitting that the taxes were necessary; while, to appease the Americans, the revenue would take only the external form of port duty; and it would be confined to British manufactures. But again, not to discourage the hopes of a wider British trade, the tax was nugatory, with the exception of tea, where a privileged merchant was to be protected. (The plan indeed was still more elaborate. Because of the "drawback" to help the East India Company in England, Americans in some cases would pay slightly less than before. Those in England who began unfriendly to the scheme would find such a buried detail adequate to their suspicions.) "What need I say more?" concludes Burke. "This fine-spun scheme had the usual fate of all exquisite policy."

What are we to make of the superficial resemblance between Townshend's juggling and Rockingham's statesmanship? The preamble contained Townshend's own Declaratory Act. Yet his preamble had no reason in policy and was not susceptible of high-minded construal: "it is *expedient*," the words said, "to raise a revenue in America." A person does not say to a person, "If you pay me, I will profit from it"; and a state should not say so to people who have shown pride and powers of resistance. This was a token of mere ingenuity, the counterfeit of compromise, and as such a provocative to greater discontents. Real compromise, for Burke, is too fine a thing to be tinkered with, and the cost of deception is never hidden for long. Accordingly, he declares his intention to vote against both the tax and the preamble.

As an antithesis to the hollow expedients and empty assertions of these several pretender-statesmen, Burke, earlier in the speech, had posed the solitary example of Rockingham. *Manly* is a word to which he recurs now in describing the virtue of a policy that carries conviction. Of Rockingham's singleness of purpose during the Stamp Act crisis, Burke says: "It was in the midst of this chaos of plots and counter-plots; it was in the midst of this complicated warfare against public opposition and private treachery, that the firmness of that noble Person was put to the proof. He never stirred from his ground; no, not an inch. He remained fixed and determined, in principle, in measure, and in conduct. He practised no managements. He secured no retreat. He fought no apology."[50] Public virtue was concentrated, appropriately, in an honest statesman, quite without charm or charisma. His authority came from party alone; yet party principle was corroborated in his person. "It was a time for a *man* to act in," says Burke; and little as people knew Rockingham, these words raise the image of a man with a settled aim. "We did fight that day and win."[51] Antony's eulogy for Brutus comes to mind ("His life was gentle, and the elements / So mixed")—an oddly impersonal and almost archaic homage. Yet the image of Rockingham has reality in Burke's eyes, even if the implicit details are idealized. Nothing that is said is untrue. Rockingham was diffident to a fault and would seem in later years disconsolate in defeat. The cadence of Burke's prose hints at that possibility, and it has an elegiac shading. But 1766 was the moment; perhaps it made the man; and

Rockingham grew larger than himself (Burke makes us feel) partly through the solidity of the people around him. The claim is all the stronger when set against the calculations of Grenville, the wheedling of Townshend, the theatrical wadding of Chatham, and Lord North's innocence of every idea except obedience to the king.

By the end of the *Speech on American Taxation*, Burke has revealed by indirection an impressive sense of his own merit and legitimate fame. When he says that he has acted "all along" with one party, we may detect a hint that he had political chances elsewhere. Yet he harbors no regret. His advice, when he gave this speech in April 1774, remained what it had been in 1766: "leave America, if she has taxable matter in her, to tax herself."[52] To speak for his party as the lonely bearer of honor in the American controversy was a main purpose of the *Speech on American Taxation*—and this in the face of the fact that his party governed only a year and concurred with other parties in wanting to keep America within the empire. The speech persuades by the density of its historical narrative and the aptness of its characterizations of the executors of bad policy.

As for the possibility of losing America, it is hinted at just once, in a passage that (placed beside Burke's other comments on the subject) seems the most oblique of warnings: "If you apprehend that on a concession you shall be pushed by metaphysical process to the extreme lines, and argued out of your whole authority, my advice is this; when you have recovered your old, your strong, your tenable position, then face about—stop short—do nothing more—reason not at all—oppose the antient policy and practice of the empire, as a rampart against the speculations of innovators on both sides of the question; and you will stand on great, manly, and sure ground. On this solid basis fix your machines, and they will draw worlds towards you."[53] If Parliament, in its collective character, now plants itself on a single view of its ancient policy and practice—authority declared, equity delivered—it will "draw worlds" toward it: a metaphor that must mean it will regain the goodwill and the liberal obedience of America. This is a picture of republican virtue, which knows nothing of sponsorship or dependency.

Yet because such heroic conduct seems beyond the competence of any two successive ministries, Burke implies that concession is now the only sane course. As policy, it adequately joins the existing abilities and the unalterable predicament. He warns the House of Commons, whatever else they may do, not to tie their policy to an abstract principle that invites debate. For one thing, the colonists have an appetite for litigation, a relish for raising common disputes to the second power and converting them into questions of principle. Also, experience has shown that each step on this path leads to another: "By urging subtle deductions, and consequences odious to those you govern, from the unlimited and illimitable nature of supreme sovereignty, you will teach them by these means to call that sovereignty itself into question." At last, Burke turns aside from all argument with an appeal to the idea of character. "Let us act like men, let us act like statesmen. Let us hold some sort of consistent conduct—It is agreed that a revenue is not to be had in America. If we have lost the profit, let us get rid of the odium."[54] He is indifferent to the charge that a reversal will show that all their previous efforts were vain. When you have made a political error, you need not precisely declare that it was an error, but prudence requires that you act in the recognition that it was.

Burke, in these middle years of opposition, belonged to an enlarged minority. However one might deplore the incoherence of Chatham as chief minister, he had now become an eloquent ally, capable of saying (a little after Burke's speech in 1774): "I trust that it will be found impossible for freemen in England to wish to see three millions of Englishmen slaves in America."[55] At the end of that year's session, it appeared to Burke that a settlement might be achieved by asserting the "principle of connection" between America and England and by a consistent understanding of the imperial constitution. He cannot be credited with foresight at this stage, only a canny skepticism of the motives of both sides. "I agree with your Lordship entirely," he writes to Rockingham in September 1774, "that the American and foreign affairs will not come to any Crisis, sufficient to rouse the publick from its present Stupefaction, during the next session." He guessed that years, not months, separated the colonies from a general rebellion. Yet no informed onlooker could suppose that relations with America were mending: "The insensibility of the Merchants of London is of a degree and kind scarcely to be conceived. Even those who are the most likely to be overwhelmed by any real American confusion are amongst the most supine."[56] The tone of the ministry was unfortunately at one with public opinion, but its members were wrong to be comforted by this; they did not reckon that "the vindictive Justice of the Nation" would turn against the architects of the disastrous policy. Here as elsewhere, revenge is a motive of which Burke disapproves, yet he sees that it performs a necessary function: when substantial justice is postponed, vindictive justice will take its place. The letter to Rockingham (admonitory and reassuring) from which I have quoted was written six months before the return by the House of Lords of the latest penal bill on America. That was the moment Burke would stamp on the public mind with the "warning voice" of his *Speech on Conciliation with America*. The occasion to reconsider a bill on America is treated there "as a sort of providential favour; by which we are put once more in possession of our deliberative capacity, upon a business so very questionable in its nature, so very uncertain in its issue." Burke had an imagination of disaster morbidly attuned to the darker possibilities, yet there were times of the world—the months June through November 1789 were another—when an emergency could take him by surprise.

Let us look at the crisis as it appeared to Burke at the turn of the year 1774–1775. Supposing that America could somehow be calmed, what were the tactics most advisable to the Rockingham party? The question, he wrote to Rockingham on January 24, 1775, was "whether your Lordship chooses to lead, or to be led." The reticence of his leader was once again an impediment: "There are others in the world, who will not be inactive because we are so; and who will be the more active, when they see us disposed to lye by." Rockingham's fame was on the line. If he could not show the ground on which opposition was to proceed, he would be placed in an "awkward and distressing situation on the Ground which will be prepared for you, and which you can neither remain upon nor quit, without great inconvenience and discredit."[57] Rhetorical cunning, in which timeliness plays a significant part, may decide the impression made by an emphatic defense of principle. Rockingham had to be seen to move a policy again, or he would lose all the honor won by the repeal of the Stamp Tax.

Meanwhile, it was left to Burke to rouse the other grandees of the party. Some of them were contemplating early retirement; and in a letter of September 1774, Burke wrote again to the Duke of Richmond: "Private Life has sorrows of its own for which publick employment is not the worst of medicines. And you may have in other things as much vexation without the same Splendour. Your Birth will not suffer you to be private. It requires as much Struggle and violence to put yourself into private Life as to put me into publick. Pardon a slight comparison but it is as hard to sink a Cork as to buoy up a Lump of Lead."[58] There is an odd irony in the mock-earnest flattery by which Burke, attuned to every stimulus, compares himself to a lump of lead, while the inert duke who values his title so little bobs up irrepressibly as a cork. Did Richmond smile at being courted in this manner? At all events, Burke's obligation to administer comfort to the languid and melancholy rich would not be much longer a drag on his own aspirations. Thanks to the public response to his *Speech on American Taxation,* he would soon ascend to an undeniable eminence in the life of his country.

Representative for Bristol

On June 28, 1774, Burke was approached by the Reverend Dr. Thomas Wilson, a radical, who asked on behalf of "a few friends at Bristol, merchants of fortune and character," whether "if they find themselves strong enough, you will be ready to serve them." From Burke's point of view, the proposition was timely but risky. Bristol was the second city of the kingdom, a prosperous and politically active constituency, more prestigious than any except London and Westminster. A member representing its interests in the House of Commons would draw all eyes. Victory here, if he could gain it, would offer an incomparable platform for proposals on domestic and foreign policy; and it would bring a source of authority separate from the aristocratic circle around Rockingham. Another thing made the invitation tempting. After eight years representing the pocket borough of Wendover, Burke's seat had been withdrawn. Lord Verney, who let him occupy it as a gift, was now in financial difficulties and preferred a holder who could pay.

By the time he received word of adequate support from Bristol, Burke was already assured of his election for Malton (a pocket borough held by

Rockingham himself). In a weaker man this might have prompted a decorous hesitation. Burke knew how warmly questions of national importance were debated in Bristol by industrious citizens: it was the city in England (with the exception of London) where the democratic spirit was strongest, and this might seem an ambiguous gift. His actions as member of Parliament would be scrutinized from every side; with the dignity of republican service would come an exposure to republican criticism. The ease of his Wendover seat, on the score of local responsibility, would be gone forever. Yet Burke welcomed the change and entered the contest.

On October 1, he received a letter from Richard Champion, a Quaker merchant in Bristol—a porcelain manufacturer widely known as a philanthropist, who would become a warm friend and ally of Burke's[59]—regarding two groups of electors on whom he could rely: "The Tradesmen in general are highly discontented, and will go I think with any opposition. These form a great Strength. The graver Sort among the Dissenters would indisputably declare for you. They mention your Name with the warmest Approbation." The drumbeat was taken up by Richard Shackleton, who vouched for Burke's character and political consistency to William Fry, a Quaker preacher in Bristol: "Edmund Burke is a man of the strictest honour and integrity; *a firm and staunch protestant;* a zealous advocate (not an enthusiastic brawler) for that which rightly deserves the name of liberty."[60]

Early in the century, Bristol had recognized a tradition of two Tory members; lately it had shifted to one Tory and one Whig; but in 1774 the city returned two Whigs to Parliament, Henry Cruger and Edmund Burke.[61] Cruger came from a distinguished colonial family of New York. He had settled in Bristol in 1757 to run a branch of the family business, Cruger and Mallard; he had been an energetic opponent of the Stamp Act and a friend of "Wilkes and Liberty"; and much of his support was drawn from the artisan classes.[62] Alongside Cruger, certain traits of Burke's public character were thrown into relief: his moderation, his intellectual vigor, his aristocratic connections. These were things the electors had known well enough; yet Burke gave early signs of defining his stance more sharply than expected. To the audience that came to celebrate the victory, he declared at the conclusion of the poll (as he had done at his arrival in Bristol) that he would not be bound by mandates.

This statement of principle was among the first of its kind in the history of representative government. As Lucy Sutherland discovered, its only rival is a surprisingly similar declaration elicited from William Baker by the prodding of voters in London, during the same election of 1774.[63] But the speech by Burke was also a polemical answer to an expression of reflexive gratitude by Cruger to his constituents. "The legality and propriety," Cruger said, "of the people's instructing their representatives in Parliament" would be respected by him. Not pausing to define what he meant by instructions, he went on to describe himself as "the servant of my constituents, not their master, subservient to their will, not superiour to it." Burke commented on that vow of compliance with immaculate disdain:

> it ought to be the happiness and glory of a Representative, to live in the strictest union, the closest correspondence, and the most unreserved communication with his constituents. Their wishes ought to have great weight with him; their opinion high respect; their business unremitted attention. . . . But *authoritative* instructions; *Mandates* issued, which the Member is bound blindly and implicitly to obey, to vote, and to argue for, though contrary to the clearest conviction of his judgement and conscience;—these are things utterly unknown to the laws of this land, and which arise from a fundamental Mistake of the whole order and tenour of our Constitution.[64]

To ask a representative to negate and nullify himself, in order to support the suffrage of his constituents, is a double mistake. By forbidding his natural reliance on his own judgment, it robs the public mind of a source of practical wisdom. And by obligating him to vote against his conscience, it undermines the very quality that should most recommend him to the electors.

These strictures at the conclusion of the poll in 1774 contain the germ of a theory of representation, familiar to republican writers in the seventeenth and eighteenth centuries, but never so ably articulated by an active politician.[65] It is the theory that would be embraced by the American authors of the *Federalist Papers*, especially by Madison in *Federalist* 49, with its caution against mandates and its prophecy on the chaos of referendums: "as every appeal to the people would carry an implication of some defect in the government, frequent appeals would, in great measure, deprive the government of that veneration which time bestows on everything, and without which perhaps the wisest and freest governments would not possess the requisite stability."[66] In *Federalist* 63, Madison explained the utility of a representative who is bound by concern with the public good rather than by changing expressions of the popular will:

> there are particular moments in public affairs, when the people, stimulated by some irregular passion, or some illicit advantage, or misled by the artful misrepresentations of interested men, may call for measures which they themselves will afterwards be the most ready to lament and condemn. In these critical moments, how salutary will be the interference of some temperate and respectable body of citizens, in order to check the misguided career, and to suspend the blow meditated by the people against themselves, until reason, justice, and truth can regain their authority over the public mind.[67]

So, a decade later, Madison followed the footsteps of Burke. But the prudence of Burke's warning also cooperated with his natural pride. As his speeches on America had already shown, in 1774 he aspired to be at the center of such a body of representatives.

The distinctness of the Burkean and Madisonian idea of the duties of a representative warrants elaboration in an age when democracy tends to be identified with the popular will. For to create and foster a politics rooted in *will* devalues, if it does not exclude, the idea of a knowledge and wisdom specially connected to politics, and it raises the question in what other place we can hope to find knowledge and wisdom on public affairs. These thinkers believed that a lawmaker by the performance of his duties may come to know things not available to those who elect him. The people remain the source of ultimate power since they can turn a representative out of office. But while he serves, the representative is expected to advance the public good and to use his understanding of the practical means to achieve desired ends. Though he must answer to the suffrage of opinion, he considers himself its guide and not its follower.

This rigorous construal of the separation between a leader and constituents is further strengthened by an idea of Parliament as a deliberative body. As Burke puts it in the *Speech at the Conclusion of the Poll:*

> Parliament is not a *Congress* of Ambassadors from different and hostile interests; which interests each must maintain, as an Agent and Advocate, against other Agents and Advocates; but Parliament is a *deliberative* Assembly of *one* Nation, with *one* Interest, that of the whole; where, not local Purposes, not local Prejudices ought to guide, but the general Good, resulting from the general Reason of the whole. You chuse a Member indeed; but when you have chosen him, he is not Member of Bristol, but he is a Member of *Parliament.* . . . To be a good Member of Parliament, is, let me tell you, no easy task; especially, at this time, when there is so strong a disposition to run into the perilous extremes of servile compliance, or wild popularity. To unite circumspection with vigour, is absolutely necessary; but it is extremely difficult. We are now Members for a rich commercial *City;* this City, however, is but a part of a rich commercial *Nation,* the interests of which are various, multiform, and intricate. We are Members for that great *Nation,* which however is itself but part of a great *Empire,* extended by our Virtue and our Fortune to the farthest limits of the East and of the West. All these wide-spread Interests must be considered; must be compared; must be reconciled if possible.[68]

The best commentary on these sentences comes from Madison in *Federalist* 53. A whole dimension was added, Madison thought, to the stock of public wisdom by the consultation of long-term members with other members similarly informed and responsible. "An upright intention" is necessary to the work, as is "sound judgment," and these may seem available to all; but the representative must also have "a certain degree of knowledge"; and part of that knowledge "can only be attained, or at least thoroughly attained, by actual experience in the station which requires the use of it." Madison makes explicit the preference, latent in Burke, for representatives of "superior talents" who, by becoming "members of long standing," have made themselves "thoroughly masters of the public business." New members necessarily lack these advantages; and though frequent changes of representation may be an unwritten law of democratic life, they have the effect of diluting the collective wisdom of lawmakers and weakening their capacity for prudent action. "The greater the proportion of new members and the less the information of the bulk of the members, the more apt will they be to fall into the snares that may be laid for them." The last sentence by Madison catches a hidden motive of Burke's *Speech at the Conclusion of the Poll.* If the people of Bristol rejoice at having an interest in their new member, Burke's interest in Parliament as the center of a great empire rightly concerns him more. Though new to Bristol, he considered himself a seasoned member of the House of Commons. His probity would answer for his independence and afford protection against the snares that might entangle others.

How did this sort with Cruger's easy acceptance of mandates? The truth is that Burke's relations with his Bristol colleague were never warm enough to show any cooling. In a letter to Richard Champion of January 5, 1775, he denied that jealousy made him reluctant to introduce Cruger to his aristocratic friends; he notes (with an officiousness rare in him) that Cruger has never hinted at a desire for an introduction and "to bring a Gentleman into a connexion before I knew that it would be agreeable to him" would be "a piece of very ill breeding." Who is the gentleman in this passage? Cruger apparently. Yet Burke manages to imply that Cruger is beneath notice by friends of Burke. Anyway Cruger's politics are not distinguishable so as to make him worth the risk: "When a young member is introduced to persons of Consideration and who are active in Politicks, it is thought of Course that he means to act with them, and it brings some imputation in Society on a man's character if afterwards he happens to act otherwise. Mr Cruger never once intimated to me what line of politics he intended to take, but his having proposed to be introduced by a white staff [signifying the Comptroller of the Household] and a Court Member makes me doubt whether Connexions of another kind would be pleasing to him."[69] We are seeing here, close up, a trait of Burke's public character that has mostly evaded notice at the distance of two centuries. His standard of loyalty was high to the point of incorruptible priggishness. Lord Chatham fell below it because he was too impressed by his contacts with the king—"The least peep into that Closet intoxicates him, and will to the end of his life."[70] In decades to follow, the younger Pitt would fall below it by the mediocrity of his India reforms and his reluctance to launch a full-scale war against France.

Notwithstanding the severity of his judgment, Burke's pride in his independence was justified. And he was generally restrained in his shows of independence. He declined, for example, to accompany Cruger in a Bristol victory parade, but the reasons had less to do with Cruger than with his distaste for any appearance of gloating. "I think such an ostentatious triumph over a respectable adversary, not quite generous, nor altogether prudent. Our success will not be the less acceptable to all sorts of men by our moderation and prudence. It is our business rather to console than insult those, to whom we can have no matter of quarrel, but their attachment to their friends."[71] He wrote those words in February 1775 to Joseph Smith, a Bristol iron merchant. The importance of conciliation toward partners in commerce was much in Burke's mind throughout these months.

Toward Conciliation

We may approach Burke's *Speech on Conciliation with America* by a second and more public path: the argument of a major pamphlet expounding the position he aimed to refute. *Taxation No Tyranny* was written by Samuel Johnson at the request of the North ministry. The author's unquestioning belief in monarchy and his violent distrust of its critics made him exceed all expectations. It was thought wisest by the ministry to omit some bitter taunts against the colonists; and to judge by the pitch of what remains, one can see why. Yet on the whole this pamphlet gives a well-reasoned defense of the British policy of taxing the Americans. It asserts that docility is the right disposition of the ruled, and that rebellion is always wrong. In a commonwealth that has allowed its subjects to prosper, compliance is the fair response to the demand of support by taxes. Johnson portrays the colonists as unnaturally greedy—selfish alike in their disdain for political obligations and their undisciplined love of liberty. A right understanding of the imperial constitution he thinks will induce a perfect agreement with the claims of the mother country.

Johnson's conservative brief for taxation begins with a maxim of political order: "of every empire all the subordinate communities are liable to taxation, because they all share the benefits of government, and therefore ought to furnish their proportion of the expense."[72] When Americans object to the lack of *precedent* for certain taxes, they unwittingly justify the policy they hope to overturn. "They tell us, that we have changed our conduct, and that a tax is now laid by Parliament on those which were never taxed by Parliament before. To this we think it may easily be answered, that the longer they have been spared, the better they can pay."[73] The benefits derived from government have a cost; what would be the result if all declined to pay? Johnson passes on to the argument that now, lacking representation, American interests are overlooked in the making of British laws. This is a protest against unequal treatment, yet inequality is in the nature of society. More particularly it is in the nature of empire: "A colony is to the mother-country as a member to the body, deriving its action and its strength from the general principle of vitality; receiving from the body and communicating to it, all the benefits of health and disease."[74] We may recall that Burke in his *Speech at the Conclusion of the Poll* had adopted a significant variation of the standard metaphor that Johnson here employs. All of the parts, said Burke, must contribute to the good of the whole. He will go much further in the *Speech on Conciliation*. Yet Burke is modern, rational, and almost American in his belief that the contribution should bear some proportion to the benefit. Johnson treats this instead as a matter of legal right.

Debts must be paid, says Johnson. And he quotes against the Americans their own resolution at the time of their emigration, asserting entitlement "to all the rights, liberties, and immunities of free and natural-born subjects within the realm of England."[75] Granting this, why should they now enjoy an exemption denied to other Englishmen who have the same rights, liberties, and immunities? "In the beginning all the world was America," wrote Locke in his *Second Treatise on Government*. Johnson replies that America stopped being America when it passed beyond the state of nature and accepted the grant of certain rights by England. From that moment,

> these lords of themselves, these kings of *Me*, these demigods of independence, sink down to colonists, governed by a charter. If their ancestors

were subjects, they acknowledge a sovereign; if they had a right to English privileges, they were accountable to English laws, and what must grieve the lover of liberty to discover, had ceded to the King and Parliament, whether the right or not, at least the power, of disposing, "without their consent, of their lives, liberties, and properties." It is therefore required of them to prove, that the Parliament ever ceded to them a dispensation from that obedience, which they owe as natural-born subjects, or any other degree of independence or immunity not enjoyed by other Englishmen.[76]

Americans are owed all the benefits of citizens, but there is a proper and an improper use of citizenship.

The members of any society must accept the accidents of their birth, and Americans are not free to abolish the inconvenience of their geographical place, with all its uses and disadvantages. "A man can be but in one place at once, he cannot have the advantages of multiplied residence. He that will enjoy the brightness of sunshine, must quit the coolness of the shade. He who goes voluntarily to America, cannot complain of losing what he leaves in Europe."[77] Besides, representation is a right the Americans have never directly asked for; so it is a grave-faced sham to invoke the need for representation as grounds of protest. "They mean not to exchange solid money for such airy honour. They say, and say willingly, that they cannot conveniently be represented."[78] Whatever the Americans may claim for tactical reasons, they find the absence of representation suitable to their purpose. Has it not provided their best argument against paying taxes?

The doctrine of natural rights finds a formidable antagonist in Johnson. His main weapon is parody. According to the utilitarianism of everyday life that is presumed by Lockean theorists of the social compact, it is blameless to do as one pleases so long as one refrains from harm to others. Johnson likens this to the apologies for selfish actions that are commonly heard from felons and children. His condensed version of a compact based on natural rights deliberately blurs the difference between Locke and Machiavelli:

That which was made by violence, may by violence be broken. . . . The sword can give nothing but power, which a sharper sword can take away. . . . We gave our ancestors no commission to settle the terms of future existence. . . . What they could establish, we can annul.

Against our present form of government it shall stand in the place of all argument, that we do not like it. While we are governed as we do not like, where is our liberty? We do not like taxes, we will therefore not be taxed; we do not like your laws, and will not obey them.[79]

This knockdown catechism is recited by the contractor with the pert finality of a cardsharp.

To believers in natural rights, governments exist for convenience and may be changed at pleasure. Thus, inherited duties are replaced as motives of action by sheer utility and inclination. "Liberty is the birthright of man," Johnson imagines the colonists saying, "and where obedience is compelled, there is no liberty." This is true in a trivial sense, he admits. But it forgets that liberty must include a principle of self-restraint; for, among people of unchecked willfulness, their passions forge their fetters (the phrase is Burke's, from 1791). "Chains," continues Johnson, "need not be put upon those who will be restrained without them."[80] But the colonists do not restrain themselves: look at the anarchy of Massachusetts. A citizenry capable of ordering itself could never have permitted the Boston Tea Party, to say nothing of the mob actions against Thomas Hutchinson and Thomas Oliver. Nor is it wrong that the punishments should be general, for to punish those who allow the evil belongs to "the aggregated guilt of rebellion." Such acts are the work of distempered minds: the colonists cannot be trusted to punish them, and it is surely wicked to suppose that they should not be punished. Here an interesting contrast with Burke begins to emerge, since Burke is poised to contend that nothing but a *habit of enforcement* obliges Britain to govern America at all. Had Johnson been shown that argument in advance, he would have said it was a dodge.

Nevertheless, *Taxation No Tyranny* does in one way anticipate Burke's forbearing treatment of the Boston riots. It looks at a similar proposal from Josiah Tucker, a pamphleteer as well-informed as Burke but less sympathetic to the Americans. Tucker agreed that the colonists could be left to themselves; unlike Burke, he believed England would be well rid of them. Johnson for his part favors neither conciliation nor separation but a return to the patterns of imperial discipline. The charters of the colonists "being now, I suppose, legally forfeited," ought to be remodeled by the mother country "as shall appear most commodious." With their privileges revoked, "those who now bellow as patriots will sink into sober merchants and silent planters, peaceably diligent, and securely rich."[81] The natural state of mankind is to endure a scene of mingled fortune in which unbounded prosperity is given to none. The Americans knew this, until the thought of perfect liberty heated their imagination with incredibilities.

The resemblance between Johnson and Burke, in rhetorical and argumentative detail, is marked enough to prompt the question why they should have differed so fundamentally. That people are governed by opinion and not by force—the premise of the political morality of the Enlightenment—was never fully absorbed by Dr. Johnson. He would perhaps have denied that anyone could credit that view without a shallow pun on the word *govern*. To Burke on the other hand—believing, as he does, that opinion is the decisive strength of government—behind most uses of force may be discerned a failure of persuasion. A series of such failures therefore points to a government ready for collapse. Yet underlying the difference of view between Burke and Johnson may have been a difference of feeling. Burke was not so quick to identify political dissent with the perverse obstinacy of human nature. He assumes that stability is the rule in social as in personal conduct, so long as elementary wants are filled and privilege does not ignore adversity. A protest that becomes a popular cause always points to a real grievance, which it falls to the statesman to analyze, explain, and remedy.

Burke had a canny appreciation of the wish of the governed to derive certain benefits from society. This was the basis of his conduct in the American debates of the 1770s, which would yield so remarkable a synthesis in the *Conciliation;* but to recognize how deeply the speech is rooted in his understanding of the passions, one has to go back to moments from the *Sublime and Beautiful* and *Thoughts on the Cause of the Present Discontents.* Of all Burke's writings of middle length, the *Speech on Conciliation with America* was longest in the making, and together with the *Speech at the Bristol Guildhall* and the *Speech on Fox's East India Bill,* it reveals the height of his ability and his courage as a representative. Its concrete proposals are the reform of the admiralty court, the repeal of several recent offensive acts of Parliament, and the declaration of an intention not to tax. Yet the proposals do not account for the greatness of the speech. The comprehensive historical grasp, the flow of practical wisdom informed by psychological insight, and the power of observation and generalization would commend the speech to the admiration of nineteenth-century readers such as the philosopher of jurisprudence John Austin, the judge and historian of criminal law James Fitzjames Stephen, and the constitutional theorist A. V. Dicey. Regarding its first audience, we have the testimony of Burke's brother Richard: "He began at half past three, and was on his Legs until six o'clock. From a torrent of Members rushing from the house when he sat down, I could hear the loudest, the most unanimous and the highest strains of applause: that such a performance even from him was never before heard in that house."[82]

Habits of Excitement and the Promise of War

Many of Burke's greatest speeches were written in advance, and none was more closely written than the *Speech on Conciliation*. Fox had this distinction in mind when two decades later he made his encomium: "Let gentlemen read this speech by day, and meditate upon it by night. . . . They would there learn that representation was the sovereign remedy for every evil."[83] Against the background of a century of commerce with America, the *Speech on Conciliation* was an act of reflection intended to help England take possession of its future with an enlightened will. Its most obvious motive is the hope to avert a war and yet to retain the empire almost as it is. If, however, a choice must be made between a war that preserves the status quo and a concession that forfeits America but avoids war, Burke prefers the latter. A larger point is at issue here. The two concerns at the heart of Burke's politics, hatred of violence and love of liberty, were twice in his lifetime confronted by a stark either-or. With America, he chose revolution instead of war; with France, he would choose war against revolution. It is not to be supposed that he arrived at either position free of regret. His writings about both crises say much that is true and much of permanent value concerning the origins and the consequences of both events. These writings likewise omit much. They give a contracted sense of genuine doubts that can only be recovered by reading between the lines.

To what extent did Burke sympathize with the protest of the colonists? This may seem an extrinsic question, but it cannot be avoided. He read many of the American pamphlets and thought several of the petitions from colonial assemblies works of uncommon ability. He could enter into their cause by analogy with the Irish, another people hard-pressed and overmatched in the world of nations. But what did Burke think of the Americans? Ask it in that way and you recognize the steps he took—by calibrations of tone and tactical shading—to prevent his personal sentiments from being looked into. The *Speech on Conciliation* will say that the Americans present a new kind of character to the world. It will imply (but only imply) that a world with more countries of this sort would not be a happier place. If Americans are to be an example, Burke would like to see their influence curbed. Yet the best way to limit the contagion is to treat America with a welcoming amiability. It should go on being just what it is. Britain, in turn, should go on being what it is. Such a result is possible only if the colonists are not antagonists. So they must be kept prosperous. Every appearance must be preserved of looking on their experiment with approval.

Rival senses of liberty were involved in Burke's thoughts on the colonies throughout the 1760s and 1770s. He did not care for that untrammeled liberty, often associated with America, which bends to accommodate the individual will; he promoted, instead, English liberty, a liberty with restraint. Yet he began to see as early as 1769, and certainly by 1774, that English liberty could only flourish if it established terms of concord with its radical counterpart across the ocean—the liberty of a people who, if they became a nation, would be in some ways England's completion and in some ways her antithesis. The meaning of conciliation, as the speech develops, will be renewed partnership with America and a stop to the wrangling of taxation and resistance. It may sound as if Burke's aim were merely a profitable commerce and intercourse of ideas; in fact, he was subtly opposed to the influence of America on English manners: he argued rather for an agreement, in commerce, to profit by each other's resources; and, in government, to refrain from discussion of each other's authority.

Conciliation is Burke's word for a practical method of averting catastrophe. And since catastrophe had long been the psychological subject underlying his thoughts about art and society, it is a matter of interest to see how distinctly it enters his understanding of politics. Properly speaking, it seems out of place there. The *Sublime and Beautiful* had identified certain dangerous passions as belonging to art and experience but suggested that our social adaptation through custom and the affections belonged to a different realm altogether: the familiar life we share with neighbors, friends, and associates. Yet in that early work, Burke did offer a possible connection between the imagination of the sublime and the disasters and revolutions of history. In his section on words, he remarks that at the sudden onset or cessation of a sound "of any considerable force . . . the attention is roused . . . and the faculties driven forward, as it were, on their guard."[84] The spectator, in the presence of such stimulus, attempts at once to bring it closer and to keep it at a distance. Somehow an imbalance follows from that effort of psychological defense, and the result is an excess or disequilibrium. We are, to repeat Burke's words, *driven forward* when the impulse from the object is spent. Driven, he means, by something other than our personal will.

A displacement or a wrong adaption of the emotions of the sublime can happen, according to the *Sublime and Beautiful*, when the passions that "turn on self-preservation" are transformed into passions that "turn on society." Then a new force is set in motion, partly by individual volition, partly by a general reflex that changes the nature of the response. Society itself must then be on guard, if it wants to preserve its former identity. None of this analogy between person and society is explicit in Burke; and the awareness he speaks of might simply be called a state of acute susceptibility. But at the far end of the development he sketches, we find this suggestion: a society may develop a habit of the sublime, an addiction to routines of excitement that place all our faculties on alert without a presiding control. As Brutus reflects in *Julius Caesar:*

> Between the acting of a dreadful thing
> And the first motion, all the interim is
> Like a phantasma or a hideous dream:
> The genius and the mortal instruments

Are then in council, and the state of man
Like to a little kingdom, suffers then
The nature of an insurrection.

So a conspiracy among assassins, or an entire society at war, may become attached to their fears and continually re-excited by them—"From fear to fear successively betrayed," in the words of Lord Rochester. The more savage the thrill, the deeper the satisfaction and the greater the unconscious desire to see it renewed. This sensation, though it may align members of a society against a common foe, has nothing to do with the love of one's neighbor; indeed, a habit of the sublime must be indifferent to the instinct of self-preservation. A nation possessed by such a mood forgets that ordinary lives and fortunes are at stake. People are exhilarated by the sheer pressure of constant risk.

The notion of a *habit* of the sublime, though self-contradictory in Burke's normal usage of the two words, takes on a peculiar aptness when applied to feelings transferred from the individual to society. It marks a possible extreme of conduct that must always be morally destructive. Far from the common habits by which we are made to acquiesce in life and health, this habit subjects us to a series of shocks with no visible termination. We so adapt ourselves to the violence of the new conditions (where no footing is solid) that we may at last be equipped to deal with nothing else. Burke, here, is obliquely sketching the hazard of translating aesthetic feelings into political experience. Unlike later theorists of the sublime—Walter Benjamin, for example, in his writings on modernism and the city—Burke did not suppose that any sort of tolerable life could be made from the human induration to daily shocks. His surmise has therefore the quality of a warning. There is a hunger for belief which, when combined with the human tendency toward abstraction, causes us to lean toward disaster with a sense of delight, a feeling compounded of morbid interest, minimal self-protectiveness, and a dangerous credulity. Face to face with such an experience, we want to come ever nearer, to watch and go on watching the dangerous thing. An earthquake may affect people like that, if it is experienced from a distance or known only in its aftereffects. So may riot or war. From Burke's point of view as a theorist of the sublime, to say that "all men hate war" or that "all men hate anarchy" is false. It is equally false to say that we love those things. We are fascinated by them; and what fascinates may draw us in.

Against what political phenomena does Burke warn? Sometime during the American war, he jotted down a revealing note which he chose not to publish in his lifetime. The suspension, he says, of the feelings and habits of a society at peace may leave a mark on both America and England:

> the entire subversion for so long a time of all regal Authority, the Random Speculations of every individual, the Taste of Wild Liberty to all, & of new independent power to some . . . will make the return even to the old order impracticable. . . . I know that many among us as well as elsewhere indulge an idea . . . that the slaughters they shall make by foreign mercenaries, by savage irruption & revolting servitude, the pillage & waste of the Country, the confiscations of property, & the Legal Shambles which they shall open at the close of the war will give the people a distaste to any future insurrection. They think so because they love a government of terror. . . . It is known as much as any thing can be known, that the miseries of War do not indispose men to that State; & that war is much more likely to follow war in any Country than originally to break out in one that is long composed. The first Breach is terrible to the quiet. Nothing is dreadful to man which is habitual to him. . . . Men reconcile themselves to any thing.[85]

"Custom reconciles us to every thing," he had said in the great aphorism of Part 4 of the *Sublime and Beautiful;* and the adaptive process by which even terror can become a daily expectation prompts him now to speak at large of a strange versatility in human nature. The employment, he observes, not only of mercenaries but of Indians and Negro slaves against the Americans ("savage irruption & revolting servitude") constitutes in itself a revolution against the previous self-image of Britain. Burke's earlier sense that nothing habitual can be dreadful has changed to a suspicion that anything dreadful may become habitual.[86]

The burden of his thought is that a whole people may be brought to collaborate in events that destroy them. Force and will are not necessary elements in that process, at least not initially. A habit of shock will do it.

If a remedy is to be found, it will likely come from a return to ancient practices and their rhythm of slow accretion and resolution. We should take care in the public mind to associate reforms with customary practice. Where possible, we should bend the names of the new things to bring them closer to familiar names. This psychological conservatism has different meanings in different societies. In an aristocracy, it may call for a reassertion of the belief in honor; in a democracy, a vigilant reassertion of the liberties of all. But in every instance, in the exact degree that public affairs show an unfamiliar face, we secure ourselves against the first breach of sanity by a return to those previous habits of assent that Burke elsewhere describes by the suggestive phrase "liberal obedience."[87]

It might be objected that the tactic of asserting a rhetorical continuity against the threat of catastrophe is a standard procedure of Whig history. Perhaps so; though it must be added that this is a kind of history that Burke did much to invent.[88] Yet the charge against Whig history has always been that it is shallow, convenient, present minded, and therefore self-serving. Can Burke's way of reflecting on history defend against that accusation? Like the epic poets and, it must be added, like the lesser Whig historians, Burke did believe that history is only grasped when it is known as a story. He supposed that the cement of probability (each narrated event appearing to follow the last) carries conviction into the mind of the reader and the spectator. He saw no reason to wish away the sense of a continuous connection in events. So from *Thoughts on the Cause of the Present Discontents* to the *Letters on a Regicide Peace*, Burke speaks unreservedly in defense of the "story" in history. Yet he neither exemplifies nor credits any version of teleology—the fallacy many people have in mind when they deplore Whig history.[89] Teleology produces a narrative in which characters of the past dimly grope for answers that readers of the present day can recognize as our own. Whig history, so understood, domesticates the past by assimilating it to the present. Whig history as Burke understood it deepens the present by tracing its continuity with the past.

One may say that the Rockingham party of the 1770s aimed to make Whig history out of the American controversy: a story with a common past and a happy ending for liberty and empire. The party's reputation in 1779–1780 would grow out of the public feeling that they had got the

American question right. Sooner even than his colleagues, as Paul Langford remarks, Burke "struck through at the very beginning of his parliamentary career to the essential elements of the position."[90] Americans should be admitted into an interest in the empire. He said this plainly and in many settings, even if his major speeches, on *American Taxation* in 1774 and *Conciliation* in 1775, approach the question from different perspectives. The first was a portrait-from-within of a failed policy, with individual glimpses of the architects of the policy. It leaves us wanting a picture of America itself. When Burke came to draw that picture in the *Speech on Conciliation,* the colonists would be shown under a collective description. For all his intimacy with the subject, however, the later speech does not contain a portrait of a single American; but neither are the Americans accorded merely the abstract recognition due to nameless victims. Rather, they are characterized as a distinct people with a native temperament. Their national character, Burke shows, has everything to do with their sense of justified grievance and the manner of their resistance. The effect is to humanize America in the aggregate, without making Americans attractive in particular. This portrait by the end of the speech will exhibit America as an almost allegorical form: rough, masculine, capable, nervous, thin-skinned, a prosperous friend and a dangerous enemy. It must be added that the task Burke set himself in this speech—to persuade the House of Commons to admit the unchangeable reality of a separate country and to give up the assurance implied in the parent–child metaphor—was incomparably harder than his previous work of simply demonstrating the folly of preceding ministries.[91]

The American colonies were something unprecedented—an internal democracy in many ways, rather than the spasmodic check against tyranny that "the people" in England could embody from time to time (as in the Wilkes and Liberty movement). Burke was conscious of the difference; and when reviewing his record on America we ought to bear in mind two of his formulations about democracy. For Burke warns against attacking democracy, and he warns against adopting it. To try to crush a popular movement is neither possible nor defensible: "I do not know the method of drawing up an indictment against an whole people." Those words come from the *Speech on Conciliation.* You cannot pretend that a cause is illegitimate when so many agree against you; in the name of which of *their* interests would you draw up the indictment? That democracy must be curbed by a greater power, for the people's own good, is the plea of tyranny. On the other hand, Burke does not believe that the people can act steadily for the public good. They lack the sense of dignity and estimation which alone makes particular persons subject to embarrassment and correction; in such an anonymous aggregate, you can never touch an individual with the sense of shame. "Their own approbation of their own acts has to them the appearance of a public judgment in their favor. A perfect democracy is therefore the most shameless thing in the world. As it is the most shameless, it is also the most fearless." Those sentences had to wait for the *Reflections,* but Burke had thought about them long before; and in reading him on America, we have to hold the two ideas together: the respect for the people and the warning, too. Any power capable of suppressing the people is more to be feared than the people themselves. Yet the people can never be looked to for wisdom or what Burke sometimes calls character. Those qualities come from self-respect, and self-respect cannot belong to the shameless; after all, shame is a by-product of fear, and what could the people fear? "The people at large can never become the subject of punishment by any human hand." This immunity from punishment makes the people, as it would make any person, an unrestrained and uncontrollable force.

So far, the evidence suggests that Burke was wary of democracy. We may go a step further: he did not think modern democracy stood a reasonable chance of succeeding. Democracy rejects an idea that for Burke is inseparable from the task of sustaining a social order, and that idea is prescription, or the codification (by law) of our natural prejudice in favor of social practices that have lasted a long time. Burke thought prescription was part of common sense, a truth answerable to the psychology of individuals as of society at large. His speech against the reform of parliamentary representation, which will be discussed more fully in Chapter 6, engages this question at length. Prescription, Burke says there, "is the most solid of all titles" and "is accompanied with another ground of authority" in the mind, namely presumption. He knows that the judgment of the people may be "giddy" in the short run, but it is wise in the long run. "The individual is foolish," and the closer a society comes to being a collection of individuals, the more foolish it is bound to be. And yet "the species is wise."[92]

Burke was almost certainly speaking here in response to the county movement and other pressures for a fairer representation in Parliament and more frequent elections. Democracy gives the people full responsibility for choosing their governors; and the petitions of the 1780s in England, as of the 1770s in America, had threatened to award that choice to more people at shorter intervals. Fear of a spasmodic and giddy choice determined Burke against the proposals both for wider representation and for shorter intervals between elections. He thought the people worked best as an informal check to give the alarm against abuses of power. They ought therefore to be relied on as bearers of practical wisdom, in this sensational way, but without much practical power to control. Still (he is constrained to admit), the species "almost always acts right." Could the same not be said of the people? The largest difference between Burke and the American founders, including radicals like Paine and Jefferson but also prudential moderates like Franklin and Madison, has to do with the number and frequency of the occasions on which political questions are to be referred to the people.

There is another possible explanation of the mixture of Burke's apparent sympathy with the American cause and his broad distrust of democracy. He may have meant, yet have been undisposed to say, that democracy is good for the people in America but not for the people in England. That it takes a certain education to prepare for liberty, that there are nations that clamor for it but are not actually ready—this would become a familiar idea in Burke's writings on France. A suggestion of the *Speech on Conciliation*, which could hardly have been predicted from any earlier statement, is that by a combination of historical, social, and religious circumstances, the Americans have become for better or worse a people well prepared for a new kind of liberty. So their resistance can be seen as an act of self-defense (springing from injured loyalty) against an encroachment on the rights of property. One might understand the colonists as the product of an inevitable deepening, a not-to-be-reversed extension of the inheritance of British liberty. Prescription, in that case, would seem to favor democracy in America, just as, in England, prescription favors a mixed constitutional government with an aristocratic basis. The Americans had practical experience and not just abstract theory to back their extension of boundaries the British believed impossible to traverse. We will observe in detail the effects of this intuition in the structure of the *Speech on Conciliation*. But it does paradoxically look as if the colonists, with their habits of extreme Protestantism, slave-owning, and the study of law, have become one of those "old establishments" about which Burke in the *Reflections* would say that they are "tried by their effects. If the people are happy, united, wealthy, and powerful, we presume the rest." This suggestion, however, lies some way under the surface of his American writings. The main drift of the speeches of 1774 and 1775 is that just one establishment exists, the great empire whose moral authority emanates from the House of Commons.

We have seen Burke's letters of the early 1770s register a steady advance in his understanding of the American view of the imperial constitution. His speeches of the same period, leading up to the *Conciliation*, exhibit a narrower range of reactions, yet they are forthright utterances in their way and a necessary groundwork of his argument for conciliation.

Recall that the first test of imperial sovereignty and American rights had been the vote on the Declaratory Resolution. During that controversy of 1766, Burke had managed with a bold simplicity to deny the significance of "right," much as later he would later deny the importance of taxes: "As to the Question of right, as it is an abstract speculative proposition, drawn from the Nature of a supreme power, from the existing powers, from the usual Course of the British constitution, and even from the original Compacts of these colonies, I think we have the clearest right imaginable, not only to bind them with every law, but with every mode of Legislative Taxation that can be thought on."[93] We have the right, yes, but to say so tells you nothing about the shape of a prudent policy. In the same speech of 1766, Burke admitted the intricacy of attempting "to govern a Large Empire upon a plan of liberty" and confessed himself at a standoff: "But when this question is decided on the naked right—a long line of difficulties remain behind. Besides the abstract point of right, there is in

every Country a difference between the Ideal and the practical constitution."[94] *Constitution* is a flexible word whose bearings often decide the
direction of Burke's argument: a word that in his usage can mean a sequence of documents with impressive symbolic weight, an accepted chain
of precedents, the *sensus communis,* and the state of constitutedness of the
human mind or human nature.[95] The word as used in the above passage
takes much of the last and vaguest sense: the "practical constitution" seems
to refer to any state of natural and social possibilities that allow a polity to
flourish and to avoid rupture. The practical constitution of the American
colonies, influenced by the House of Commons yet permitted to remain
what it is without much effort to tamper, may be a product of "applying *as
far as the rules of subordination will permit* the principles of the British constitution" (my emphasis). Yet Burke in his notes for the same speech
had set a limit to the jurisdiction of those rules: "The eternal Barriers of
Nature forbid that the Colonies should be blended or coalesce into the
Mass of the particular constitution of this Kingdom."[96] That sounds
like a permanent distinction—and therefore a comfort to the dignity of
the mother country—but by those "Barriers," Burke doubtless meant the
Atlantic Ocean; and in Grey Cooper's notes of the speech on the Declaratory Act, the boundaries employed to define sovereignty appear a matter
of indifference to Burke so long as the colonies are happy and remain part
of Britain. "Give them an Interest in this Allegiance, give them some
Resemblance of the British Constitution, some Idea of popular Representation, draw the line where you please between perfect and no Representation, but draw the line somewhere between the two Extremes, and I
shall vote for this motion because I know not how to fix Bounds to the
Coercive Power of the British Legislature."[97] A great power may shrug its
shoulders, provided it does so with authority. Though appearances must
be preserved, the House may draw the line where it pleases.

Burke struck a less indifferent attitude to the coercive powers of Britain
in his speech of May 13, 1767, on the suspension of the New York Assembly
after their defiance of the terms of the Mutiny Act. He was speaking now
against the Chatham administration, by which the Rockingham Whigs
thought themselves betrayed, since Chatham earlier had seemed much
closer to their policy than to the king's. Burke challenges the absurdity of

minute enforcements of discipline at a distance of 3,000 miles: "After you have made this Law to enforce your Last, you must make another to enforce that—and so on in endless rotation of Vain and impotent Efforts—Every great act you make must be attended with a little act like a Squire to carry his Armour." A year and a half later, on November 8, 1768, his speech on the address to the king points out the utility of standing with *some* consistent policy: "Nothing can tend to estrange America from us more than an opinion, that there is no person in Great Britain steady, but that there are people in the lump who are ready to change. . . . I shall prove a true prophet, that you will never see a single shilling from America. . . . It is not votes, and resolutions, and it is not arms that govern a people."[98] What governs is opinion, but opinion comes to be known through policy, and policy attains clarity only by keeping a steady direction.

Burke's pamphlet of 1769, *Observations on a Late State of the Nation*—an attack on Grenville and his supporters, concerned with domestic more than foreign affairs—reveals much about his general sense of the American colonies, for it says casually what he believed could be taken for granted: "America is, and ever will be, without actual representation in the house of commons: nor will any minister be wild enough even to propose such a representation in parliament."[99] Until the administration of Grenville, the use of taxes to bring a revenue from America was not much thought of; and Burke takes this neglect to have been an unmixed benefit. It spared the House of Commons the trouble and the resentment of collections, while the colonial assemblies answered all the necessities of internal economy. The superiority of the presiding state and the freedom of the subordinate were "on the whole sufficiently, that is, practically, reconciled; without agitating those vexatious questions, which in truth rather belong to metaphysics than politics, and which can never be moved without shaking the foundations of the best governments that have ever been constituted by human wisdom."[100] The policy of instituting new and particular taxes for revenue has thus spoiled the happy effects of a salutary indifference by letting loose "that dangerous spirit of disquisition"—excited by which, the colonists, brooding on a long train of injuries to pride and property, have come to believe "that they were contending for everything that was valuable in the world."

Why are practical adaptations, in the absence of discussion, so vital to the British interest? Because the only method by which the Americans can now be governed is (as Burke said in 1767 in his draft of a speech on the Townshend Duties) "the Quiet and insensible Lapse of Silent Steady Policy." In the *Observations* of 1769, he says of America: "The object is wholly new in the world. It is singular: it is grown up to this magnitude and importance within the memory of man; nothing in history is parallel to it. All the reasonings about it, that are likely to be at all solid, must be drawn from its actual circumstances."[101] To offer an example of such reasoning will be an aim of the *Speech on Conciliation;* but already in the earlier pamphlet, Burke notes that the pride and strength of the Americans is their trade. A perfectly unimpeded commerce seems to them inseparable from liberty. This may appear impractical or greedy, but "people must be governed in a manner agreeable to their temper and disposition; and men of free character and spirit must be ruled with, at least, some condescension to this spirit and this character."[102] The judgment shows an inside parliamentary manner (though its substance is concession), and the colonists are pictured as properly subordinate. Burke's outside manner is different. To conciliate two separate audiences in 1775, one in America and one in England, his sentiment on the uses of condescension will harden into an aphorism: "An Englishman is the unfittest person on earth to argue another Englishman into slavery." In 1769, however, Burke seems to have believed that subordination was still a precondition for restrained liberty, a liberty that does not delude its participants with the hope of boundless expansion.

Burke gave particularly frank expression to this thought in his notes (March 1769) for a speech on a recent incident of government violence: the suppression of the Wilkes and Liberty crowd on May 10, 1768, which came to be called the Massacre of St. George's Fields. "Peace is the great end in *all* Governments," he writes, in the meditation quoted in part in Chapter 3; "Liberty is an End only in the Best. I am far I have ever been far from entertaining any extreme or immoderate thoughts upon that subject. My Ideas of Liberty have been always very much tempered and chastened; they have been pitched a key lower than I think is common, because I am afraid of myself; I wish that they may stick by me, and that I may stick by them to the end of my Life at all events; and in all Circumstances I am by opinion, principle, Constitution, an hater of violence and *innovation*."[103] Bearing in mind his fear of innovation, one appreciates the ironic turn of Burke's speech on the Townshend Duties of April 1769: "The Americans have made a discovery, or think they have made one, that we mean to oppress them: we have made a discovery, or think we have made one, that they intend to rise in rebellion. Our severity has increased their ill behaviour, we know not how to advance, they know not how to retreat."[104] The mood of stalemate after the scuttling of the Townshend Duties was never so well captured. Yet the question remains: with the entry to a new policy and the exit from a bad alike cut off, what measures can assist the peaceful reform of British authority?

Burke concluded that no imaginable *measure* could act as a remedy. But there was an eventuality that might relax the clenched determination on both sides, namely the coming to power of a certain kind of leader—a type he believed to be represented by Lord Rockingham. This theme of the *Speech on American Taxation* can indeed be traced throughout Burke's unpublished thoughts in the late 1760s and early 1770s. And among other causes of suspicion, it may have been a returning echo of "the cant of *Not men, but measures*" that disposed him against the managerial solution to the crisis suggested by Thomas Pownall's *Administration of the Colonies*. This was a seasonable production, with proposals for reform by a man of high reputation and substantial experience; it was published in 1768, read and annotated by Burke some time before 1770. Pownall had served as a governor and commander-in-chief of the provinces of Massachusetts Bay and South Carolina and as lieutenant governor of New Jersey; his attachment to George Grenville would have touched a sensitive nerve in Burke; but as Burke's marginal notes reveal, he read the book with care. Its main error he supposed lay in the wish to clarify the workings rather than ease the severity of the legislation for the colonies. Pownall was certain that whatever course Parliament followed, a binding decision on taxation once and for all was "absolutely necessary." Nothing but transparent and mutual understanding would allow it to "cease to be a question." This was the reverse of the lapse of policy we have seen Burke defend, to which he applied the adjectives "silent" and "steady": a policy that hardly spoke its terms.

On the other hand, Pownall seems to have shared Burke's intuition that America should be treated as a partner and participant in a great commonwealth: the mother country and the colonies *"are* IN FACT, UNITED INTO A ONE GRAND MARINE DOMINION: *And ought therefore, by policy, to be united into a one Imperium, in a one Centre, where the seat of government is."* The book pleads "the necessity of a general *British union*," with an executive for America sitting on the Board of Trade or as secretary of state. At this point, the design expands and Pownall unveils a plan for imperial bureaucracy: *"some very considerable person,* under commission and instructions," should be lodged in America to receive reports and inquire into grievances." ("Is this the Key of this Work?" wonders Burke in the margin.)[105] In addition, Pownall recommended a committee for hearing grievances, a concession that seemed to Burke the reverse of useful and scarcely compatible with the idea of a generous union. He remarks of this proposal: "It seems a scheme for exciting an universal ferment in America, by bringing together every matter of discontent from every part. It is easy to encourage complaints; but difficult to decide upon them in a manner that may not give rise to new complaints and greater dissatisfactions. It is against all the sound principles of government, to go about on officious voluntary collection of grievances."[106] Such a scheme appeared to him worse than an error of tact. The incoherence of Pownall's stance was brought out by his wish to treat the Americans as both equals and subordinates. It is characteristic that he should allude sentimentally to the way Americans speak of England as home ("Not the case of the Northern colonies," Burke notes, "if I am rightly informed") and dwell on the prospect of alliance with America as if a separation had occurred (Burke: "Why constantly the use of the word *alliance*?").[107]

Like most civil servants at most times, Pownall was fond of legalism and explicit definition, but his urgency about deciding the exact status of the colonies seemed to Burke a mistake. "It was the very attempt to decide some of these disputes which has drawn us into all our present confusion." Oddly, the reliance on terminology and inferred standards also showed that Pownall had absorbed the verbal habits of the people he once governed; he speaks of laws of nature and of the American right to a colonial legislature as "inherent and essential to the community, as a community of Englishmen." Though Burke himself would deploy the language of natural rights in the emergency of 1777, he believed that this way of talking was warranted only by necessity: "To what purpose this idle discourse of the Colonists," he dryly observes; and again, "Whatever they claim under the laws of Nature has nothing to do with our *positive* constitution. This is a matter quite distinct."[108] The taste for fine-spun distinctions carries broad consequences in Pownall's reading of the intentions of the colonists. They have acknowledged themselves "a government subordinate to the government of England," he remarks; therefore, they owe subordination but not allegiance to the government of the realm. But this raises a practical question for Burke. If the colonists "were so subordinate as to do nothing repugnant to the *power,* rights or *interest* of England + that England is to be the *Judge,* that is as much as any body demands—but it is directly subversive of all the other reasonings of the author. All questions concerning *Sovereign Rights* end at last in this—*Who is to be the Judge?*"[109]

Here we come to the heart of Burke's political morality. As early as 1769, he can be seen to abide by two central maxims. Scenes of contested judgment must not be multiplied without necessity; and to the question "Who is to be the judge?" the answer "I am the judge in my own cause" is always wrong. Anachronistic translation is tempting but dangerous, and in this book I try to avoid it, but if there is a later development that one can say with confidence Burke would have favored, from clear, unmixed, and unmistakable hints in his writings on every subject, that development is the rise of a body of international laws to civilize the conduct of nations. "I confess, the character of judge in my own cause, is a thing that frightens me," he says in the *Speech on Conciliation with America;* and fifteen years later, in *Reflections on the Revolution in France,* the same formulation is ventured still more forcibly: "One of the first motives to civil society, and which becomes one of its fundamental rules, is, *that no man should be judge in his own cause.*" That last sentence is a warning against democratic tyranny. Neither the mass of the people nor those who speak and act on their behalf ought to judge their actions; but the sentence points equally to the danger of a monarch or a privileged class that controls a dependent judiciary. Not to be judge in one's own cause: this is a principle of both morality and politics, cognate with the rightness of having one law for the rich and poor. Yet as Burke saw, the application in the American case was uncertain, for there the question "Who is to judge?" turned on the meaning of partnership, subordination, and allegiance.

Burke seems to have agreed with Pownall on the desirability of a system that should recognize the "real union and incorporation of all these parts of the British dominions" in a way that affirms "the real spirit"[110] of the British constitution. But how much could Parliament repair at this late moment? By September 1774, the Continental Congress in America had drafted and sent to England a list of acts—the "long train of abuses" required by Locke to set in motion the exercise of the right of resistance—whose repeal alone could assure an end of the hostilities. Among these were the Coercive Acts, affecting the commercial rights of Boston Port and the judiciary and government of Massachusetts; the establishment of Catholicism in Canada; and every form of taxation. Relieved of these burdens, the American Congress avowed that it would "cheerfully consent to the operation of such Acts of the British Parliament as are *bona fide* restrained to the regulation of our external commerce for the purpose of securing the commercial advantages of the whole empire to the mother-country."[111] This is the document likely to have been foremost in Burke's mind when he came to write the *Speech on Conciliation with America*.

Against War

When, on March 22, 1775, Burke delivered a speech so long in the making, his purpose was to avert a war. A deeper motive was to justify his view of the magnanimous conduct of an empire; government such as "becomes the dignity of a ruling people: gratuitous, unconditional, and not held out as a matter of bargain and sale." The colonists numbered two million Europeans and half a million Indians and Negroes. Their rapid growth "from families to communities, and from villages to nations," is, Burke admits, a proper subject of awe and perhaps of fear; it might prompt in the ruling power a reflexive reversion to force; but he tells Parliament, "you ought not, in reason, to trifle with so large a mass of the interests and feelings of the human race. You could at no time do it without guilt; and be assured that you will not be able to do it long with impunity." Burke illustrates the formidable potency of the colonies by showing how the increase of their trade has matched the growth of their population. Force employed against them now can be only a temporary device, likely to create uncertainty and to impair its object. "Nothing less," says Burke, "will content me than the whole of America"; and Britain can only have America on terms of liberty.

About the precise meaning of those terms Burke was clear from the start. There must be no more exactions on America: the only revenue flowing to England from this source must come as a voluntary donation. No more English laws for Americans and no coercive acts: the colonists have shown themselves competent to make and keep laws of their own devising. What does that leave a statesman to say?

> The proposition is Peace. Not Peace through the medium of War; not Peace to be hunted through the labyrinth of intricate and endless negociations; not Peace to arise out of universal discord, fomented, from principle, in all parts of the Empire; not Peace to depend on the Juridical Determination of perplexing questions; or the precise marking the shadowy boundaries of a complex Government. It is simple Peace; sought in its natural course, and its ordinary haunts.[112]

So far, this sounds like one more in the series of pragmatic arguments against taxation and imposition which we have canvassed in the background of both major speeches of the 1770s. But the stakes are higher. For Burke has opened by greeting the return from the House of Lords of the "grand penal Bill" on the trade of New England "as a sort of providential favour; by which we are put once more in possession of our deliberative faculty"; and he has added: "We are therefore called upon, as it were by a superior warning voice, again to attend to America." What justifies this allusion to the "warning voice," which in *Paradise Lost* signaled Milton's narration of the beginnings of the fall of man? The echo will resound beside several others of the poem—echoes particularly of Book 4, which tells of the invasion of Eden by Satan.[113] From Burke's previous epic description of American prosperity, one must infer that, for him, the actors on the stage of the New World have passed beyond the reach of mere approval or reproach:

No sea but what is vexed by their fisheries. No climate that is not witness to their toils. Neither the perseverance of Holland, nor the activity of France, nor the dexterous and firm sagacity of English enterprize, ever carried this most perilous mode of hardy industry to the extent to which it has been pushed by this recent people; a people who are still, as it were, but in the gristle, and not yet hardened into the bone of manhood. When I contemplate these things; when I know that the colonies in general owe little or nothing to any care of ours, and that they are not squeezed into this happy form by the constraint of watchful and suspicious government, but that through a wise and salutary neglect, a generous nature has been suffered to take her own way to perfection: when I reflect upon these effects, when I see how profitable they have been to us, I feel all the pride of power sink, and all presumption in the wisdom of human contrivances melt, and die away within me. My rigor relents. I pardon something to the spirit of Liberty.[114]

Both the maturity of the colonies in commerce and their youth in self-government are brought into this description. But the praise carries an ironic undertow: one may pause at the words *vexed, pushed, gristle,* and *this recent people.* Considerable adroitness would be required to accommodate such peculiar figures of speech to a simply favorable judgment. Yet, by gradations whose logic is hard to pin down, a eulogistic atmosphere is shaded and filled in, until at the end Burke stands awestruck and half-pleased at the prodigy of a "generous nature." The coarseness of the facts may need excusing, but he pardons something to the *spirit* of liberty.

The youthful energy of America is best appreciated at a safe distance. Suppose it is true that "For some time past the Old World has been fed from the New" and that, without America, England in times of scarcity would have suffered "a desolating famine"; that the country would have perished "if this child of your old age, with a true filial piety, with a Roman charity, had not put the full breast of its youthful exuberance to the mouth of its exhausted parent." One might conclude that the resources of America are already ascendant, and that care should be taken to bring them no closer, whether through political wrangling or the severer test of war. The longer it takes the Americans to see what they are capable of, the better for Great Britain. Conciliation is a wise policy, among other reasons, because it slows the process of American self-recognition.

Character of the Colonists

The most original part of the *Speech on Conciliation* is its historical and anthropological excursus: a deeply informed, exquisitely modulated, and unsettling portrait of the national character of the Americans. Before England decides whether to concede and what to concede, it must estimate "the true nature and the peculiar circumstances of the object which we have before us." Burke refers to six "capital sources" of a spirit of liberty in America: the descent of the colonists from the native stock of English freedom; their republican forms of local government; the Puritan zeal of the Northern provinces; the aristocratic manners of the South, reinforced by the domineering practice of slavery; the prestige and preponderance of the study of law; and the inaccessibility of the continent to a regulating power from a distance of 3,000 miles.

To start with the tradition of liberty: America holds above an ordinary share of this British inheritance, and both the experience and the lineage of the Americans place them at an extreme. Their objections to taxation sound very like English objections, and for a reason with deep roots in the 1640s. A vehement spirit of independence, and a sensibility to the insult of all encroachment, pervade the Northern as well as the Southern colonies. In the North, it is the same jealous independence of conscience that a century earlier had produced a civil war in Britain; in the South, it is the possession of estates where the love of liberty is whetted by the pleasure of mastery. Regarding these distinct sources of the American idea of freedom, Burke makes some comments of extraordinary interest and acuteness. Unlike the Church of England, which was the creation of a government, and unlike the Roman Catholic Church, which coexists with the governments of Europe, "the dissenting interests have sprung up in direct opposition to all the ordinary powers of the world; and could justify that opposition only on a strong claim to natural liberty. Their very existence depended on the powerful and unremitted assertion of that claim. All protestantism, even the most cold and passive, is a sort of dissent. But the religion most prevalent in our Northern Colonies is a refinement of the principle of resistance; it is the dissidence of dissent; and the protestantism of the protestant religion."[115] The conscience of American dissent is utterly intractable and has the purity of a substance distilled beyond imaginable dilution. It is like the principle of divinity invoked by Milton, in a line Burke alludes to but does not quote, "Bright effluence of bright essence increate"—now transposed to a principle of the self. In the Southern colonies, by contrast, the Church of England sets the tone for religious belief, but another institution is decisive for manners and "makes the spirit of liberty still more high and haughty than in those Northward." That institution is slavery. In societies where some men possess others as property, the free naturally hoard their freedom with a ferocious pride.

> Freedom is to them not only an enjoyment, but a kind of rank and privilege. Not seeing there, that freedom, as in countries where it is a common blessing, and as broad and general as the air, may be united with much abject toil, with great misery, with all the exterior of servitude, Liberty looks amongst them, like something that is more noble and liberal. I do not mean, Sir, to commend the superior morality of this sentiment, which has at least as much pride as virtue in it; but I cannot alter the nature of man. . . . In such a people the haughtiness of domination combines with the spirit of freedom, fortifies it, and renders it invincible.[116]

Besides the dissenting conscience and its offspring, the zeal for rights; besides slaveholding and its offspring, an invincible pride in property; there is another feature of the American colonies that renders their ideas of liberty energetic and resistant to compromise. Burke speaks euphemistically of this third trait of the American character; he calls it "education." He has in mind the American fascination with law, and the proliferation of lawyers. The consequences for public life are not yet tested, but this fact about America explains the immoderate relish of litigation with which the colonists scrutinize all laws. Burke opens with an observation by General Gage that

> all the people in his government are lawyers, or smatterers in law; and that in Boston they have been enabled, by successful chicane, wholly

to evade many parts of one of your penal constitutions. . . . This study renders men acute, inquisitive, dextrous, prompt in attack, ready in defence, full of resources. In other countries, the people, more simple and of a less mercurial cast, judge of an ill principle in government only by an actual grievance; here they anticipate the evil, and judge of the pressure of the grievance by the badness of the principle. They augur misgovernment at a distance; and snuff the approach of tyranny in every breeze.[117]

Modern democrats believe that a legitimate polity must have its origin in and be bound by a social contract; lawyers are expert in the drafting and manipulation of contracts of all kinds; and an accident of circumstance has brought together, in America, political theorists and lawyers.

Burke never credited the idea that society is a contract with fixed and legible terms. Nor did he think that states could be supposed to derive from an original compact. Such an agreement for him is always elementary and implicit, with no provisions more particular than the well-being of the people. Yet the Americans feel differently, many of them (as lawyers) being philosophers of contract in everyday life. Those who treat with such a people cannot attempt to reform the peculiarity. Thus, the answer that Burke gave about the slaveholders, "I cannot alter the nature of man," must suffice for the lawyers, too. All of his description here comes close to satire; yet it stops carefully short of contempt. If you would have "the whole of America," you must include all of its components.

Notwithstanding the litigious disposition of the Americans, they have kept to a minimum all dispute among themselves throughout the crisis in Massachusetts. After the Coercive Acts took away the blessings of English government, the colonists, most disturbingly, have lived in peace. So, looking back at the suppression of local authority by the Boston Port Bill and other measures of the 1770s, and the compelled success of the Americans in governing themselves, Burke writes:

Obedience is what makes Government, and not the names by which it is called: not the name of Governor, as formerly; or Committee, as present. This new Government has originated directly from the people. . . . It was not a manufacture ready formed, and exported to them in that condition from England. The evil arising from hence is this; that the

Colonists having once found the possibility of enjoying the advantages of order, in the midst of a struggle for Liberty, such struggles will not henceforward seem so terrible to the settled and sober part of mankind, as they had appeared before the trial.

Pursuing the same plan [of punishing disorders by the denial of government] to still greater lengths, we wholly abrogated the ancient government of Massachuset. We were confident, that the first feeling, if not the very prospect of anarchy, would instantly enforce a compleat submission. The experiment was tried. A new, strange, unexpected face of things appeared. Anarchy is found tolerable. A vast province has now subsisted, and subsisted in a considerable degree of health and vigor, for near a twelve-month, without Governor, without public Council, without Judges, without executive Magistrates. How long it will continue in this state, or what may arise out of this unheard-of situation, how can the wisest of us conjecture? Our late experience has taught us, that many of those fundamental principles formerly believed infallible are either not of the importance that they were imagined to be; or that we have not at all adverted to some other far more important and far more powerful principles which entirely overrule those we had considered as omnipotent. I am much against any further experiments which tend to put to the proof any more of these allowed opinions which contribute so much to the public tranquillity. In effect, we suffer as much at home by this loosening of all ties, and this concussion of all established opinions, as we do abroad. For, in order to prove that the Americans have no right to their liberties, we are every day endeavouring to subvert the maxims which preserve the whole Spirit of our own.[118]

The argument is clear in its appeal for conciliation but ambiguous regarding the qualities that render a government durable. The trial of liberty in America is obviously for Burke a perilous experiment: dangerous in subverting the general maxims of public order, if those maxims are useful; and just as dangerous if the experiment by its success proves the maxims hollow. As the courage of the Americans is set off more brightly by English opposition, their struggle for liberty may become a contagious example. That the struggle has been associated in this case with "liberty" may render people in the future less averse to struggle; and Burke implies (without quite saying) that the result is likely to be a loss of order in society generally. For once the curiosity of the people has been aroused, tranquility will no longer prevail in a way compatible with the spirit of English liberty. On the contrary: "Anarchy is found tolerable." A strange sentence, and the most devious detail in the speech.

It remains strange whether you take it to mean that genuine anarchy has been tried in America and has worked; or to mean that a condition which once would have been called anarchy no longer fits the name. Either way, the "concussion of all established opinions" has destroyed the superstition that teaches people to look on anarchy with horror. Yet the last quoted phrase refers also to a loss of respect for *civil* liberties at home; and Burke is keen to protect allowed opinions from the destructive force of experiment. The good of such opinions is identical with the stabilizing good of prejudice. Another suggestion may lurk here: that the habits of restrained liberty, which the English are on the brink of losing, differ in kind from the habits of the new liberty practiced by the Americans. Only by conciliation, Burke implies, can we assure ourselves that the two sorts of liberty belong to a single family, and that the old will not be molested by the new.

The historical part of Burke's argument is now almost complete. Having accounted for the libertarian descent of the Americans, their training in self-government, the religion in the Northern and the "manners" (that is, slaveholding) in the Southern colonies, and the prevalence of litigation as a special competence and compulsive fascination among Americans, Burke does not neglect the last of his six named sources of the spirit of independence: the sheer distance of the colonies from England. By this fact all ingenuities of policy are confined: "Three thousand miles of ocean lie between you and them. No contrivance can prevent the effect of this distance, in weakening Government. Seas roll, and months pass, between the order and the execution; and the want of a speedy explanation of a single point is enough to defeat an whole system."[119] And so, given the other motives driving the American resistance, England has not the means to make America submit to its will. News of the latest trespass never arrives soon enough.

This may seem a low moral ground from which to urge a benevolent policy; and in one sense, Burke would rather not step beyond its practical appeal. He advises Parliament "to comply with the American spirit as necessary, or, if you please, to submit to it as a necessary evil." But the understanding on which his cautionary advice proceeds—"the general character and situation of a people must determine what sort of government is fitted for them"—is not less high-minded than that of his exemplar Montesquieu. Having come this far in copious explanation, Burke is ready to show that the American question is an instance where utilitarian expedience and principle coincide. "The question with me is, not whether you have a right to render your people miserable, but whether it is not your interest to make them happy." The logic of that sentence is clinched in an aphorism: "Is a politic act the worse for being a generous one?" Yet if Burke takes his stand on empirical prudence, he is careful to support himself by precedent: "I put my foot in the tracks of our forefathers, where I can neither wander nor stumble"—every remission he pleads for has already passed the House of Commons in one form or another. So the conclusion of the speech is made to turn on the plain deduction of a harmless syllogism: "I give you nothing but your own; and you cannot refuse in the gross what you have so often acknowledged in detail." Parliament can vote against him only by violating the sense of their wisest previous policy.

In Burke's great speeches, there is always a surplus of knowledge and practical wisdom cast in general form. The *Speech on Conciliation* appropriately finds a climactic setting for his largest formulation of a politics tempered by rational compromise. The discussion of justice and equity in Aristotle's *Ethics* lies behind this warning about the proportioning of responses to their occasions. Do not judge America, Burke concludes, by what it shows in the heat of protest. Even in a just cause—supposing our cause just—prosecution can go too far.

> It is besides a very great mistake to imagine, that mankind follow up practically any speculative principle, either of government or of freedom, as far as it will go in argument and logical illation. We Englishmen, stop very short of the principles upon which we support any part of our constitution; or even the whole of it together. . . . All government, indeed every human benefit and enjoyment, every virtue, and every prudent act, is founded on compromise and barter. We balance inconveniences; we give and take; we remit some rights, that we

may enjoy others; and, we chuse rather to be happy citizens, than subtle disputants. As we must give away some natural liberty, to enjoy civil advantages; so we must sacrifice some civil liberties, for the advantages to be derived from the communion and fellowship of a great empire. But in all fair dealings the thing bought must bear some proportion to the purchase paid. None will barter away the immediate jewel of his soul. . . . None of us who would not risk his life, rather than fall under a government purely arbitrary. But, although there are some amongst us who think our constitution wants many improvements, to make it a complete system of liberty, perhaps none who are of that opinion, would think it right to aim at such improvement, by disturbing his country, and risking every thing that is dear to him. In every arduous enterprize, we consider what we are to lose, as well as what we are to gain; and the more and better stake of liberty every people possess, the less they will hazard in a vain attempt to make it more. These are the *cords of man*. Man acts from adequate motives relative to his interest; and not on metaphysical speculations.[120]

This passage describes a politics that is sociable, rooted in sympathy as well as self-interest, averse to fanaticism and devoted to peace and liberty. It brings into sharp focus the sense of human action that Burke had in view when he said that the principles of politics are nothing but the principles of morality enlarged. We know in practice well enough what is best for us and what others are justified in expecting; and we know that there is commonly a difference between the two, which calls for compromise. The theory that the English have pushed too far is the theory of a *right* of taxation; while the Americans have begun to imagine that they can be independent of all duties. Burke's warning extends to both parties. When, near the end of the passage, he speaks of "a complete system of liberty," it is perhaps the Americans who are chiefly admonished.

He concludes the speech with a resolution to "admit the people of our colonies into an interest in the constitution." The Americans do not want representation, and the Commons should not invent new substitutes. The speech oddly comes to rest in a posture similar to that of the 1766 speech on the Declaratory Act, where Burke had invited Parliament to draw any line bounding the coercive intentions of its sovereignty, and added that he did not care much where the line was drawn. But by the critical year 1775, history and nature have conspired to tell the House of Commons, "Thus far and no farther." It is as if Burke led the Commons in saying, "America always had an interest in the empire, and we hereby acknowledge the fact. A meaningless line is symbolically erased; we hereby announce the result as a benefit." The logic is drained of passion, but the sense of the moment is stirring nonetheless.

This performance by Burke has many of the qualities that modern philosophers associate with "performative utterance"—a word or phrase that does what it says while saying it. The *Speech on Conciliation* conciliates as a "Welcome" welcomes and "Thank you" actually thanks. Burke had tremendous confidence in the power of such rhetorical fictions; for him, words do not merely describe but constitute that rehearsal of collective self-knowledge which he sometimes calls by the name of *ceremony*. Thus it makes a great difference whether the British say, "We give you up for lost" or choose to say instead, "We acknowledge our coercive measures were unkind and oppressive and that they prove nothing but the imbecility of force."

Accordingly, his peroration asks the House of Commons to serve as an inspired example of liberty for the people over whom it still holds jurisdiction:

> Slavery they can have any where. It is a weed that grows in every soil. They may have it from Spain, they may have it from Prussia. But until you become lost to all feeling of your true interest and your natural dignity, freedom they can have from none but you. This is the commodity of price, of which you have the monopoly. This is the true act of navigation, which binds to you the commerce of the Colonies, and through them secures to you the wealth of the world. Deny them this participation of freedom, and you break that sole bond, which originally made, and must still preserve, the unity of the empire. Do not entertain so weak an imagination, as that your registers and your bonds, your affidavits and your sufferances, your cockets and your clearances, are what form the great securities of your commerce. Do not dream that your letters of office, and your instructions, and your suspending clauses are the things that hold together the great contexture of this mysterious whole. These things do not make your government. Dead

instruments, passive tools as they are, it is the spirit of the English communion that gives all their life and efficacy to them. It is the spirit of the English Constitution, which, infused through the mighty mass, pervades, feeds, unites, invigorates, vivifies every part of the empire, even down to the minutest member.[121]

Politics for Burke is more than politics. It is the natural and public form in which moral commitment is expressed.[122] The British constitution is praised here for its generous gifts, and at the same time it is defended against two distinct evils: the corruption of English liberty under the threat of war, and the influence of an American experiment that calls itself liberty. A wish to defend the British constitution against both hazards seems to have blended with a resolution to protect human nature against the violence that attends all sudden change.

Burke cannot let it go without a final aphorism to round off the argument; and it is by these words that many readers have come to know the speech. "Magnanimity in politics is not seldom the truest wisdom; and a great empire and little minds go ill together." Magnanimity was a complex idea for Burke, as vital to his thinking as justice, dignity, and honor. It denotes large-mindedness, large-spiritedness, but also a sane unselfishness. You do not show magnanimity when, having power and money in excess, you spare some of your substance for a good cause. Rather, you show it when, with an antagonist at your mercy, out of generosity and self-respect you refuse to press your advantage; or when, by an action that is courageous and proper, you make a strong friend stronger by helping him. Magnanimity requires that we treat a possible opponent as a fellow, peer, and equal, to whom honorable treatment is naturally due. We know the magnanimous by their unreluctant grace. They never take the measure of a particular gain or loss. Plato in the *Republic* gives the example of soldiers who, being well-taught, are not even tempted to strip the armor and ornaments from the bodies of the enemy dead. In the American case, as Burke expounds it, magnanimity must mean to declare the release of the colonists from all future taxes. The gift expects nothing in return but is given as "what becomes the dignity of a ruling people: gratuitous, unconditional, and not held out as matter of bargain and sale."

In political writing, as in works of imagination, an author's intentions cannot control the effects of the work on its audience; and a work's immediate reception and long-term influence may turn out to be distinct or even contradictory. How persuasive was the *Speech on Conciliation with America* to its original hearers? Burke's parliamentary motions were defeated and Britain went to war. Yet the terms on which American independence was later negotiated, and the ascent of Burke's party to ministerial power again at the time of the peace, owed a great deal to the memory of what he had said and its resonance in his later speeches of the 1770s. In the opinion of many at the time, the *Conciliation* was the greatest speech that had ever been given in the House of Commons. It set a standard that remains today for deliberation on public affairs.

V

The Loss of the Empire in the West

THE *Speech on Conciliation* has no rival, but it did have a precursor. On January 20, 1775, Lord Chatham delivered a major address on America; and if one looks at each with the other in mind, one can see that Burke's oration at some points echoed Chatham's. Both speakers dwell on the paradox that, in a conflict between two claims of right that are equally plausible and unyielding, there is something salutary in a policy of *neglect* by the sovereign power: neglect, that is, in both the specification of faults and the enforcement of the law. "I find," said Chatham, "a report creeping abroad that ministers censure General Gage's inactivity. Let them censure him—it becomes them—it becomes their justice and their honor," but then he adds: "I mean not to censure his inactivity. It is a prudential and necessary inaction. . . . This tameness, however contemptible, cannot be censured, for the first drop of blood shed in civil and unnatural war might be *immedicible vulnus*." The praise of General Gage for ignoring his duty to impose a violent discipline is outdone by Burke's avowed preference for an inert policy: the "wise and salutary neglect" by which "a generous nature has been suffered to take her own way to perfection." Still, the resemblance is there.

Chatham, in a train of thought again foreshadowing Burke's, observed that the tenacity of American resistance was strengthened by national and religious descent:

> This resistance to your arbitrary system of taxation might have been foreseen; it was obvious, from the nature of things and of mankind; and, above all, from the Whiggish spirit flourishing in that country. The spirit which now resists your taxation in America, is the same which formerly opposed loans, benevolences, and ship-money, in England: the same spirit which called all England *on its legs*, and by the Bill of Rights vindicated the English constitution: the same spirit

262

which established the great, fundamental, essential maxim of your liberties, *that no subject of England shall be taxed but by his own consent.*[1]

Burke in his longer speech would recount the history that Chatham alludes to and would explore some particulars of the Whiggish spirit, "the dissidence of dissent."

Burke improved on Chatham in declining to credit the distinction between internal and external taxes. The idea had been suggested to Parliament by Benjamin Franklin and, from hints in the American pamphlets, it became a subject of learned commentary in England; but all the hopeful inferences were false, and Chatham was a comforter who enjoyed wide influence. He thought the distinction solid—a thing "forever ascertained; taxation is theirs, commercial regulation is ours"—long after Burke had warned that England would never see a penny of revenue from America. Yet, finally, the two statesmen are at one in urging the broadest construction of the meaning of concession; and the climax of Chatham's exhortation made a pattern for Burke's own: "It is not repealing this act of parliament, it is not repealing a piece of parchment, that can restore America to our bosom. You must repeal her fears and resentments, and you may then hope for her love and gratitude." Chatham, in other words, pleaded for magnanimity: "That *you* should first concede is obvious from sound and rational policy. Concession comes with better grace and more salutary effect from the superior power. It reconciles superiority of power with the feelings of men, and establishes solid confidence on the foundations of affection and gratitude." That Burke drew on a deeper fund of observations can hardly be disputed; but Chatham in his last great oration supplied him the materials to build with; and in the argument for peace it was Chatham who spoke first for concession itself as a wise policy.[2] Burke gave form to the thought, and wings to the feeling.

There remains a tension in Burke's argument between the ironic description of the American character and the benign view of the future of imperial partnership. Do his observations undermine his conclusions? Josiah Tucker thought so, and his *Letter to Edmund Burke in Answer to His Speech in the House of Commons* challenged Burke specifically on three points: the definition of liberty, the desirability of popular government, and the political significance of "the dissidence of dissent." Tucker, a formidable polemicist admired by Burke, had been Rector of St. Stephen's in Bristol before becoming Dean of Gloucester, and there is a touch of intramural passion in the vigor with which he prosecutes his reply. Burke had asked to restore *"the former unsuspecting confidence of the Colonies in the Mother Country";* but this left in doubt the way of life the colonists were supposed to pursue once they were repossessed of that confidence. Burke made a credible case that the extreme liberty of the colonists was a natural development from English roots; but this begged the question whether their way of life was suitable for adoption by others. Seeing the argument through Tucker's eyes, we may recall how deftly Burke maneuvered on this ground, with his semitones of mingled wonder and dismay. "Anarchy is found tolerable." It was possible for such a sentence to be heard one way by the colonists and another way by the House of Commons. Tucker agrees "that the fierce Spirit of Liberty is stronger in the *English* colonies probably than in any other People upon earth," but though he shares this judgment with Burke, he takes it to be decisive against the colonists. A ferocious license such as the Boston mob displayed can never become the foundation for a new and admirable order. Burke had not denied the plausibility of such a conclusion; yet the structure of his argument had pressed it out of view.[3] From the intimations in Burke's speech that the Americans are selfish, crafty, and obstinate, Tucker conjures a deprecation and a warning.

Tucker (let us say) believed that Burke had practiced an economy of disclosure. And the charge has some warrant. Take the description of the American assemblies as "popular in an high Degree." Are we not free, says Tucker, to inquire whether this republican form arose from lenity, indolence, wisdom, or mistake? Here again he catches Burke in a posture of appearing not to judge, while reserving a judgment that, if rendered, would tell against his cause. There are settings in which Burke's affirmation, "I give you nothing but your own," may convince us to side with custom and precedent, but that is a political victory which evades the moral question "Is it right?"—and Tucker sensed the evasion. How can Britain gaze at the example of a rival form of liberty and preserve at once its own integrity and the unity of the empire?[4] Once more, expanding on Burke's analysis of the Protestantism of the Northern colonies, Tucker suspects that what is described is in fact antinomianism, or "the madness of *new-light* Men": a very different thing from the religion of the Calvinists. For the latter were not averse to government, and if the new colonists are, Britain ought to oppose them.[5] Finally Tucker points to the 3,000 miles of ocean separating the colonies from the mother country, and thinks that this may prove more than Burke allows. On the view taken by the colonists, their distance from enforcement makes a reason for a dissolution of bonds.[6] If all Burke has said about the colonists is true, and if colonial relations for the past decade have been as thorough a disaster as the history shows, conciliation is already a lost cause. The wisest policy is complete separation.

To Burke, a politic abridgment of argument had been useful to get him a hearing. How he weighed the details was unclear. But in view of a common later charge against him, of gross inconsistency between his writings on France and on America, Tucker's polemic has the value of showing that even in 1775 Burke could appear inwardly divided. In the *Conciliation,* he subdued without erasing his own doubts regarding America, just as he shortened the catalogue of his contempt for British policy. If he could not prevent separation, his rational voice might cool the fever of war. And yet Burke's criticism would grow more determined and strident in the late 1770s. As the battles to hold the empire stretched out and liberties were curtailed both at home and abroad, Burke came to believe that the war with America was a war against liberty.

Party versus Constituency

From the mid-1770s to the late 1780s, Burke was the conscience of his country. Political thinkers and statesmen of course work in a medium of shifting alignments, and there are courageous acts that can seem shaded by a low motive, if one looks for such a motive. Yet Burke's opposition to the American war was not compatible with the attainment of political influence in the usual sense.

In estimating the career of a representative, consistency of principle should be judged against the call for expediency that comes from groups with concrete demands. We may gauge the cost of Burke's stand on America by looking into an exchange of letters with a disappointed constituent—not an uncommon event for a member of Parliament, but in this case unusually revealing. Three weeks after his delivery of the *Speech on Conciliation*, Burke received a letter from Thomas Mullett, a merchant and paper manufacturer, a supporter of Wilkes and, thus far, a supporter of Burke. (Mullett had previously sent Burke a pamphlet asserting that his conduct in Parliament fell short of what he owed to supporters in Bristol.) Replying in the third person, Burke reasserted his freedom from private interests and tried again to lay to rest the issue that arose from the vow to obey mandates by his fellow Bristol representative Henry Cruger:

> Mr Burke has a very high respect for Mr Cruger; but cannot admit, that that Gentleman or his personal friends or the private and personal friends of any Gentleman whatsoever can dispose of the City of Bristol. Nor is it for Mr Burke's honour or for the honour of the City, that it should be given out that he was Elected upon any other than publick Motives. To those who voted for him upon such motives he has obligations which he never can forget—But Mr Burke having had a secure Seat, when he was chosen for Bristol, would neither have given himself nor others trouble for what could do him so little Credit, as to have been brought in by the private favour and personal party of any Man.[7]

Burke does not recognize that there is a debt. Rather than have it called in, he says that he will preserve his legislative freedom at whatever risk.

This was an internally sound line to follow, and it had the advantage of sincerity. But the front rank of Burke's supporters among Dissenting artisans and merchants were not willing to grant him the sort of deference he gave to members of his own party. The persistent Mullett now took on himself to explain to Burke the lie of the land:

> Mr Mullett is apprehensive that Mr Burke is not fully acquainted with the real state of things in the City of Bristol. The influence of individuals there, as elsewhere, has more weight than public Motives. It is very true that public motives induced Mr Peach originally to apply to Mr Burke thro Dr Wilson; and it was from public Motives that Mr Burke was effectually supported. If however, Mr Burkes Election

had depended on public motives, abstracted from individual influence, the City of Bristol would most certainly have been deprived of so respectable a representative, and the sum of near Ten Thousand pounds expended solely on his account would have been saved. Mr Mullett is happy in Knowing that his Conduct is equally free from restraint or influence.[8]

An arch and insinuating notice. The buyer appears certain he has bought something which the seller is equally sure he never sold. The sense of Mullett's clarification is at once to disclaim any illicit bargain, to imply its presence, to declare its legitimacy, and to warn that its effects will continue in force. Burke, as representative, will be "free from restraint," but if he exercises his judgment intrusively, the body of supporters whom Mullett represents will look for a more receptive channel.

Now it was Burke's turn for clarification. He is obliged, he says, to those who support him from public motives and whom he counts as his friends. But was he indeed the second choice after Cruger—as by other signs Mullett gave him to understand—and was he largely indebted for his seat to Cruger's friends looking to secure their local interests? He denies that this can be civilly said and that those who say it can pretend "to have the disposal of the City of Bristol." The exchange might have closed here; but Mullett, stung to a second reply, writes that he never meant to say that Bristol was "*disposed* of. Such an idea is infinitely more applicable to those insignificant Boroughs which are under the absolute controul of our Great Men."[9] This is a hit (and a clever one) at Burke's connection with the Rockinghamite leaders—men who control insignificant boroughs such as Wendover. Whereas Bristol, a city in the keeping of industrious men, has a right to expect a show of gracious concern from its representative.

Thus the awkward fact was pinned down. The Rockingham party scarcely figured in the voting at Bristol; it had no hold on the constituency; yet worldly powers did operate to yield the plurality of votes that elected Burke. "Two parties have an existence in the City of Bristol. Thro' the interest of one of those Parties Mr Burke obtained his Election." Having backed off the crooked claim that his friends purchased outright Burke's liberty of action, and having asserted instead the importance of party as an anchor for the interests of a mixed constitution, Mullett attacks now from an impregnable position. This should be the last word, since it turns against Burke his own doctrine of the excellence of party. Without the loyalty of earnest men, including vote-grubbers like Mullett, politics would be at the mercy of adventurers. Between Burke and his distressed supporter, it is the latter who adopts the stance of *Thoughts on the Cause of the Present Discontents*. What then of Burke? He has moved a long way, it seems, from *Thoughts* toward something resembling the high republican doctrine that will crystallize in the *Federalist Papers*. The instructions of a constituency are advisory, not binding. Not the vote at election time but the tenor of discussion in an assembly is the decisive fact for the legitimacy of representation.

This exchange of letters forms part of an unmistakable pattern. By the pressure of the American crisis, Burke has been drawn to say what he never precisely said before: that political freedom is an ultimate good. That is why the maintenance of freedom cannot be tied to a set of men. Nor is the resemblance here between Burke and Paine accidental. In later years, Burke would emerge as the leading defender of the old regime in Europe, Paine as the leading advocate of democratic revolutions, yet their antagonism was never as clear-cut as both writers later pretended.[10] Paine, in his beginnings, was a stylistic as well as political disciple of the early Burke; and Burke, by the late 1770s, was ready to follow the clue of representative government in directions he himself could not have predicted.

The Americans for Themselves

Paine's great American pamphlet *Common Sense* was published in 1776. "Society," it asserts, "in every state is a blessing, but government even in its best state is but a necessary evil." Burke would have agreed that society is a blessing; he certainly thought that government should not be admired for its own sake; but "necessary evil" is a half-truth that betrays too simple a preference for nature over art. Government is needed to keep the order of society. That society be well ordered is a condition of the blessing it affords. Yet Paine has a stirring sentence, quite early in *Common Sense*, which Burke would have found much harder to dispute: "The cause of America is in a great measure the cause of mankind." This identifies the struggle of founding the new nation with the fortunes of liberty every-where: a grandiose idea but not hyperbolic, since America was the first nation that promised to extend liberty to all. As far back as *Thoughts on the Cause of the Present Discontents,* Burke was losing his confidence in the political justice of aristocratic society. In the later 1770s, he was to go much further; and Paine may have been a significant stimulus.

Common Sense analyzes the British constitution into the following components:

> *First.*—The remains of monarchical tyranny in the person of the king.
> *Secondly.*—The remains of aristocratical tyranny in the persons of the peers.
> *Thirdly.*—The new republican materials, in the persons of the commons, on whose virtue depends the freedom of England.[11]

This turns upside down the picture one gets from reading Burke on the mixed constitution. For him, an executive is necessary to the efficiency of government, and a limited monarch serves that function as answerably as an elected or appointed head of state. Burke understood the House of Commons as a body that ought to be mainly aristocratic in composition. It is the leading source of wisdom in the state and a necessary check on the popular will. But though he says less about it, he agrees with Paine that the function of the Commons, the "express image" of the feelings of the people, assures a vivid apprehension of the good of the majority as the people themselves see it. This he thinks is a fact well understood by prudent governors. His own disdain for the *machinery* of conveying the will of the people is accompanied by a belief in the mutual trust of a constituency and its representative. Some such idea of the parts of the constitution remains a marked feature of his political thought to the end.

In 1795, for example, referring to a repressed minority whom he had worked half a lifetime to free from legal disabilities, Burke will call the Irish Catholics "the people" even as he rejects any formal mechanism of complaint or protest. He can deplore the inept performance of the government in a matter of injustice to an individual Catholic, yet urge Irish Catholics at large to adopt a policy of articulate restraint. They should "not pass by in Silence any one act of outrage, oppression, and violence that they may suffer, without a complaint, and a proceeding suitable to the nature of the wrong"; but the relevant knowledge of proper and obtainable channels for redress belongs to their leaders and not themselves. "Were I in that place," Burke says, "I should feel myself turned out of my Situation, the moment I was deprived of the power of being just, and of protecting the people under my Care, from the tumults of the Multitude, and the insolence of the Rich and powerful. For, in the name of God, for what else are Governors and Governments made?"[12] He thus shows warm indignation against the abuses that once brought him close to revolutionary sympathies; but even on Ireland in 1795, a government seemed to Burke naturally made *for* the people, not *by* the people. A member of a ministry is to consider the people as "under my care." To give a potent authority to the new republican materials in a constitution, to make the conduct of government depend on the people, he believed would turn government itself into a system as arbitrary, capricious, and discontinuous as the will of the people.

On this last point, Burke never comes close to democratic doctrine. And here the contrast with Paine answers to a deeper difference. An anxiety to connect the present with the past was a ruling passion in Burke that formed no part of the temperament or aspiration of the American radicals. In a famous letter that has come to be known by its thesis, "The Earth Belongs to the Living," Thomas Jefferson would ask "Whether one generation of men has a right to bind another"; and he would suggest as a practical problem for statesmanship that it ought to be possible for each generation to begin anew, cleared of the debts of ancestors and of the obligation to obey antiquated laws. This meant to Jefferson that the compact that binds a society ought to be renegotiated every few years: exactly how often was a puzzle, since the entire mass of a generation never shares a birthday or a birth year. Still, Jefferson insists that his thought experiment should have practical force.

> Let us suppose a whole generation of men to be born on the same day, to attain mature age on the same day, and to die on the same day, leaving a succeeding generation in the moment of attaining their mature age all together. Let the ripe age be supposed of 21 years, and their period of life 34 years more, that being the average term given by

the bills of mortality to persons who have already attained 21 years of age. Each successive generation would, in this way, come on and go off the stage at a fixed moment, as individuals do now. Then I say the earth belongs to each of these generations during its course, fully, and in their own right.[13]

The goal is to assure that the generation now in its prime will not be stifled by the dead hand of the past and to assure that they will not themselves become a burden for the generation now in its infancy. Jefferson worked out his theory with the help of numbers, by which a moment can be fixed in the life of every generation when its rights come into being, and a later moment can be deduced when those rights shall be nullified. The difficulty is that people of slightly different ages have to be treated as an aggregate. But how to group them? The problem can be ironed out somehow, or so Jefferson implies. This experiment would have struck Burke as a self-parody of contract theory, sufficient to expose the fallacy of the theory itself. Paine would have waited to hear the details.

A society left to itself, says Paine, will choose a constitution that serves its needs, and the people are the fittest judges of what is good for them. From this premise, he argues that legitimacy can be granted only to the democratic part of the British constitution. The stock of national virtue will increase through reforms that render government less answerable to the king and peers. The danger of demagogy, and hence of persecutions carried out by the people, has no place in his reckonings. Rather, Paine's defense of democracy is a defense of human rights against the "gothic" elaborations of title and prejudice and the impositions of arbitrary power; he invites his readers to break the fetters of "obstinate prejudice" for the sake of convenience and justice. Enlightenment creates a duty in those not cowed by superstition, a duty to act immediately and with exemplary force: "This new world hath been the asylum for the persecuted lovers of civil and religious liberty from *every part* of Europe." America has not merely a secular mission but a part in a providential design: "The reformation was preceded by the discovery of America, as if the almighty graciously meant to open a sanctuary to the persecuted in future years, when home should afford neither friendship nor safety." Accordingly, no American should accept the judgment of a politician who has been taught to embrace the inheritance of the British constitution. "As a man, who is attached to a prostitute, is unfitted to choose or judge of a wife, so any prepossession in favour of a rotten constitution of government will disable us from discerning a good one." So long as the common sense of others is corrupted by prejudice, superstition, and the privileges of power, Americans must judge for themselves.

"Never can true reconcilement grow where wounds of deadly hate have pierced so deep." Paine's citation of Milton (from Satan's soliloquy on Mt. Niphates, in Book 4 of *Paradise Lost,* which rejects all reconciliation with God) falls in with Burke's quotation in his *Speech on Conciliation* from the same stretch of the poem: "Ease would retract vows made in pain as violent and void." Yet the turn against reconciliation by Paine differs sharply from the mood of Burke's plea to be inspired by "that warning voice." Book 4 narrates an apocalyptic change from peace to a fallen nature, from a timeless obedience and happiness to a life that will be mortal but free. Burke's warning of 1775 was not heeded, yet for Paine, writing in 1776, the result looks fortunate. A new country is necessary to the establishment of a radically new government: "as in absolute governments the King is law, so in free countries the law *ought* to be the King." Inscribed in the laws in America will be the principle of religious toleration, which applies equally to all believers; and near his conclusion Paine appeals to an experience of freedom and self-respect that Americans have already shared. They have come so far together that independence now seems *"a single simple line, contained within ourselves";* whereas reconciliation must be *"a matter exceedingly perplexed and complicated, and in which, a treacherous capricious court is to interfere."*

From its first appearance, *Common Sense* was immensely popular. Americans who talked of freedom read it and were moved to act. Those who had never before thought of independence—spurred by its clear and passionate argument, in which convenience and principle were joined—found themselves willing now to fight to achieve it. For Burke, the very fact that Americans could read and debate such a pamphlet would have been significant, since it showed that they were governed by opinions that had pulled away from English politics under George III. Their thoughts were prepared for independence. What people let themselves speak about freely, they will soon think of doing; and what they possess the means to do (if it brings a distinct advantage), they will eventually do. Burke had conceded as much and hinted that England might as well prepare for the worst when he confessed that he did not know the method of drawing up an indictment against a whole people.

Paine's was only the latest and the best-selling in a series of extraordinary pamphlets that for a generation had poured out advocacy of the American cause. Burke read many of these with interest, and if their effect on his thinking was hidden, it was nevertheless formidable. Thus, the warning quoted above, against indicting a whole people, had an American source in Josiah Quincy's eloquent denunciation of the Boston Port Bill for mass reprisals against crimes committed by a few. Pronounce a whole people guilty, Quincy said, and you will turn the whole people against you.[14] But until 1777, Burke's position never lost its anti-moralistic undertone of prudence and good sense. For several months after the conciliation speech, he reasoned with Parliament to this effect: you might punish the Americans if you held sway locally and could maintain your authority by force; but to indict a whole people by coercive acts half moral and half legal—to call them derelicts from duties which you prescribe and they resist successfully again and again—this is to confuse politics with human exchanges of another kind. Conciliation or, as Burke would come to call it, concession is a name for the policy you are left to adopt when obedience cannot be enforced.

Democratic theory by the mid-1770s was moving toward an idea of government based on a compact that derives legitimacy from consent. This literature drew heavily on Locke's *Second Treatise on Government,* with its provisions for the right to resist power when abused, the right to replace an unjust king, and the right of the people to frame a government for themselves. Of those elementary rights, Burke supported the first and assented to the second (while believing that it should never be put into words—it is always a mistake to codify things done by necessity). But he would scrutinize very closely the right of the people to frame a government for themselves. He would ask: "Which people?" A revolution against an old government and the settlement of a new are seldom performed by the same body of persons. The identity of the actors changes as the nature of the action shifts. Nor does history lead us to suppose that the design for building a new system follows naturally from the reasons given for destroying the old. Burke would always stand by these doubts. It may be true that one regime is ideally superior to another, as, for example, a mixed constitution is superior to democracy, or as democracy is superior to a despotism; but in saying this we must be wary of imputing virtue to a regime, as if virtue could be an innate property of a form of government. A democracy that keeps its people at war is inferior to a limited monarchy that enables its people to live in peace. On this whole side of his thinking, Burke is the least complacent, the least cocksure, the least evangelical of political writers.

The American pamphleteers differ from Burke in principle as well as in their political hopes. John Dickinson, a member of the Pennsylvania Assembly and an eloquent democrat, refused to concede that rights are enjoyed by favor or "annexed to us by parliaments and seals"; rather, "created in us by the decrees of Providence," certain rights are "born with us; exist with us; and cannot be taken from us by any human power without taking our lives. In short, they are founded on the immutable maxims of reason and justice."[15] This was a language (and Dickinson is not an extreme case) that freely mixed politics and the pulpit—a kind of language Burke always approached with dry distaste and about which he would finally say what he thought in the *Reflections:* "politics and the pulpit are terms that have little agreement. . . . The cause of civil liberty and civil government gains as little as that of religion by this confusion of duties."[16] But in America in the 1770s, there was no danger of a religion with state ambitions, or of a state planting the seeds of a new religion. It was simply the case that the language of religion was interwoven with the language of politics.[17] As early as 1750, Jonathan Mayhew achieved a popular success with his *Discourse Concerning Unlimited Submission and Non-Resistance to the Higher Powers,* a sermon on the text: "the powers that be are ordained of God." That anti-worldly directive was taken by Mayhew to apply only where the powers protect rather than injure and oppress their subjects. All obedience, he argues, ought to be qualified by judgments of utility.[18] This may seem to ask no more than that we interpret the Bible so as to render its meaning helpful rather than hurtful. But Mayhew, a preacher of the dissidence of dissent, goes further: "God himself does not govern in an absolutely arbitrary and despotic manner. The power of this almighty king . . . is *limited by law,* not, indeed, by *acts of Parliament* but by the eternal *laws* of truth, wisdom, and equity, and the everlasting *tables* of right reason."[19] God, too, acts in keeping with a constitution, and the conscience by which we approve his commandments is to be employed in judging the right and wrong of the laws laid down by earthly powers.

The Stamp Act pamphlets had a more local purpose and rarely ascended these heights of justification. But they return continually to the principle that Americans are born to enjoy "all the rights of nature" (as James Otis put it in *The Rights of the British Colonies Asserted and Proved*). Self-restraint is the exception not the rule, in such a politics, though any person's will may be circumscribed "for the evident good of the whole community." Rights, for Otis, acquire legitimacy by consent; when a government removes or suspends them, the members of the society "are so far enslaved."[20] The rights of the American colonists are independent of charters and would be sacred even if all charters were annihilated. "There are thank God, natural, inherent and inseparable rights as men, and as citizens, that would remain after so much wished-for catastrophe, and which, whatever became of charters, can never be abolished *de jure* . . . till the general conflagration."[21] Apocalyptic exhortations, in this literature, alternate with pragmatic appeals to common utility. Thus Daniel Dulany's pamphlet against the Stamp Act, *Considerations on the Propriety of Imposing Taxes in the British Colonies,* limits itself to a tactical argument on the inadequacy of virtual representation: the idea, pressed by apologists for George III, that the American colonists, though *actually* unrepresented in Parliament, were represented *virtually* by constituents whose interests were identical with theirs. But who would those people be? This bad argument, which the colonists never credited, was put to rest definitively in a subsection of Burke's *Speech on Conciliation.*[22] Deprived, then, of representation in every kind, what could the colonists claim? For Dulany the answer was "The right of exemption from all taxes *without their consent.*" This they are owed as British subjects under common law; without it, they would be "deprived of every privilege distinguishing free-men from slaves." If the assertion already sounds like a declaration of independence, Dulany points out that Americans still acknowledge themselves "subordinate to the mother country."[23]

From the first of the midcentury pamphlets, the American preoccupation with rights must have seemed to Burke extravagant; but, before 1776, nobody could know how much of it was rhetorical; even Dulany spoke of a "Dependence on *Great-Britain*" by the colonies, while hoping for "a Degree of it without Slavery."[24] In 1775, the sayings of Dulany, Otis, and others could seem part of the same broad discussion as Burke's antiwar speeches, though one remarks the stress on *degrees* of slavery, as if the shades of satisfaction would bear checking by thermometer. This mood of keyed-up apprehension—what Burke had in mind when he remarked that the American lawyers "snuff the approach of tyranny in every tainted breeze"—showed a glint of remoter consequences in John Dickinson's axiom that natural rights are "born with us" and "cannot be taken from us by any human power." Burke was bound to be skeptical of such language; and yet, notwithstanding the contrary judgment of most commentators, I see no reason to doubt that he read many of the American pamphlets sympathetically. That is why he took care not to attack the language of natural rights but rather to omit all discussion of the subject. He knew that his audience included people who took such rights to be realities. He did not pretend to agree, but he did not try to change their minds. It was enough if he could turn them in another direction by his appeal to sympathy and common interests.

"Our Victories Can Only Complete Our Ruin"

Burke was never much drawn to the discovery and formulation of a priori principles. This is not to say that he recognized no universals in morality; but cruelty, coercion, and treachery are evils that come to us with their criminality stamped on their face. To explain the proper counteraction against such abuses, Burke often said that the wish for unlimited power over others is a common fault of human nature, which, like other vicious appetites, simply should not be fed. So a just government by definition will systematically limit the possession of power by whatever hands. Burke never doubted the need for this sort of safeguard in a free constitution. His hostility to "theory" is a different thing and open to misunderstanding. He hated the idea of a design for living that the designer supposed true for everyone. Yet this hatred of any imposed uniformity should not lead us to think that he distrusted general explanations, the discovery of rules and tendencies, the sifting of evidence to record probabilities, or the reform of public conduct to bring greater happiness to greater numbers. Concerning none of those practices was Burke ever derisive or scornful. He satirized projects of improvement at the destructive extremes, but a theory in the ordinary sense was a tool of knowledge. To every general truth there are exceptions—including the theory of free trade, which Burke espoused early and heartily. Recall his words in the preface to the *Sublime and Beautiful:* "a theory founded on experiment and not assumed, is always good for so much as it explains. Our inability to push it indefinitely is no argument at all against it."

Did the Americans push too far the credence they gave to the theory of natural rights? Burke probably thought so, but he took pains not to say so. He seems to have felt much common ground with Franklin, a conciliatory statesman whose company he enjoyed. He could not have felt the same affection for the Boston radicals or the Virginia plantation democrats. After the motion for conciliation failed, he held that the case against taxes was political rather than metaphysical, and he resisted all efforts to parse the dispute in the language of the social contract.

Thus, writing to Charles O'Hara on July 26, 1775, Burke denies that he meant in his *Speech on Conciliation* to exclude the power of taxing. Not for the first time on this subject, he declares his agnosticism: "I have no opinion about it. These things depend on conventions real or understood, upon practice, accident, the humour or Genius of those who Govern or are governd, and may be, as they are, modified to infinity. . . . I never ask what Government may do in *Theory*, except *Theory* be the *Object;* When one talks of *Practice* they must act according to circumstances."[25] But let us here distinguish what Burke says from what he implies. When might theory be the *object*? Certainly in discussing the origin of our ideas of the sublime and beautiful; and as certainly in discussing the origins of government. An answer about origins, however, even if one could obtain it, would never tell us what to say about a tragedy or a painting or how to assess the justice of a petition by the people to their legislature.

To assert that governments are essentially concerned with rights; that those rights are self-evident; and that men are endowed with them at birth—this way of talking could only have seemed to Burke a spur to contestation. Whereas to suggest that the government ought to do a particular thing in a particular situation if it wants to retain the respect and loyalty of the people: that is a practical question which requires support from knowledge of social conventions and of human nature. Burke's language in these matters is Humean rather than Lockean. Offer him a choice to speak of habits or principles, and he will generally choose habits. The exception proves the rule: when he confronts a system in which abuses have become inveterate, he appeals neither to habits nor to principles but to "necessity": the irreducible demand of the oppressed person that he or she be allowed to *live*. People seldom ask for much more, unless they have been closely instructed in their right to issue demands.

Such instruction follows the enchantment of theories that tell people what they essentially are and what their needs are. And theories of that kind do make revolutions: the Christian revolution against the Roman Empire, the Protestant revolution against Catholicism, the democratic revolution against aristocratic privilege. To the extent that the American resistance belonged to the last of those movements, Burke might have been expected to oppose it. Yet he found on analysis that the American resistance belonged to the spirit of the Reformation, of which America was perhaps the final chapter. To oppose the change would also mean to oppose a reform of the mind which had already in a great measure been accomplished.

Burke gave up his hope for conciliation with America over the next year; we can trace the start of a transition in a letter to Charles O'Hara. Writing in August 1775, he says that the recent American Declaration and Address of the Congress contains "some things very striking, others very affecting; though on the whole not so well penned, as some of the American performances which we have lately had. This I see is the last which ever will be addressed to this Country. Our madness passes all conception. Theirs too in some particulars is extraordinary." Burke goes on to speak more sharply of England:

The despair that has seized upon some, and the Listlessness that has fallen upon almost all, is surprising, and resembles more the Effect of some supernatural Cause, stupefying and disabling the powers of a people destined to destruction, than anything I could have imagined. The people seem to have completely forgot the resources of a free government for rectifying publick mismanagements and mistakes.[26]

A still more disturbing reflection comes from comparing the greed of England and the noble self-sacrifice of the colonists:

The Spirit of America is incredible. Who do you think the Mr Mifflin, Aid de Camp to Washington, is?—A very grave and staunch Quaker, of large fortune and much consequence. What think you of that political Enthusiasm, which is able to overpower so much religious Fanaticism? Washington himself is a man of good Military experience, prudent and Cautious, and who yet stakes a fortune of about 5000 a year. God knows they are very inferiour in all human resources. But a remote and difficult Country, and such a Spirit as now animates them, may do strange things. Our Victories can only complete our Ruin.[27]

So he predicts an unhappy result from the military success of England. Yet Burke does not hope for an American victory so much as he deprecates an English one. "Our victories can only complete our ruin" because they strengthen the retrograde forces in the nation.

Fiercer than the letter to O'Hara is one he sent to Rockingham the same August, a four-page causerie on the barbarization of manners that comes with the fever and miasma of war:

As to the good people of England, they seem to partake every day more and more of the Character of that administration which they have been induced to tolerate. I am satisfied, that within a few years there has been a great Change in the National Character. We seem no longer that eager, inquisitive, jealous, fiery people, which we have been formerly, and which we have been, a very short time ago. The people look back without pleasure or indignation, and forward without hope or fear.[28]

He urges the marquess (piqued by the feeling of injured pride) to look abroad and recognize the depth of the calamity:

> I do not think that Weeks, or even Months, or years, will bring the Monarch, the Ministers, or the people, to feeling. . . . If things are left to themselves, it is my clear opinion, that a nation may slide down fair and softly from the highest point of Grandeur and prosperity to the lowest state of imbecility and meanness, without any ones marking a particular period in this declension. . . . We look to the Merchants in vain. They are gone from us, and from themselves. They consider America as lost, and they look to administration for an indemnity. . . . They all, or the greater Number of them, begin to snuff the cadaverous Haut Gout of a Lucrative War. War indeed is become a sort of substitute for Commerce.[29]

Custom reconciles us to everything; and habituation may even adapt us to wars as a substitute for commerce. Under pressure from the violent passions fed by calculating men, the national morale may change decisively in the span of a few years, and people will be reconciled to the change.

This radical insight is offered without support from theories of the decay of empire through opulence and luxury. A vast destructive power has been unleashed by no force greater than the love of advantage in trade. Yet it leads first to the abrogation of trade and then to the acceptance of fighting an unjustified war. "War is indeed become a sort of substitute for commerce." Commerce had been supposed by the philosophers of the Scottish Enlightenment to represent the last stage of refinement in society, the impetus for a softening of manners and thence an inevitable increase of civility, so that trade at last is destined to render wars obsolete. To say, as Burke does here, that in some circumstances war may be "a sort of substitute for commerce" is not only to offer the germ of a theory of imperialism; it is also to suggest that the laws of our social nature are subject to reversal. They can be overturned by a "concussion of allowed opinions" sufficiently savage and abrupt. New opinions, opinions that drag a whole society to accept the use of force, do not defeat reason by argument. They silence reason by the blind imperative of action.

What, asks Burke, if Parliament should now approve a war with a "full and decided engagement"? It is a graver thing to say in advance that you want war than to accept war as a fateful necessity. If, he adds, we now tell ourselves that war is a way to gain advantage, "we shall be thoroughly dipped." *Dipped* is slang for *committed* or *mortgaged*. The oars are dipped to a cadence that may sink the craft. Or is it the parliamentary leaders who are dipped like a rump roast in gravy, to be eaten alive by those merchants who relish the "Haut Gout of a lucrative war"? This greed is capable of every excess. In the circumstances, Lord Rockingham had spoken of seceding from Parliament—a form of protest impossible to misread and preferable (he thought) to the mockery of debates that have a foregone conclusion. Burke advised that the party instead absent itself without a formal secession, and continue to participate in discussions where it stood a chance of doing some good:

> I think that your reputation, your Duty, and the Duty and honour of all who profess your Sentiments, from the highest to the Lowest of us, demand at this time one honest, hearty effort in order to avert the heavy calamities that are impending, to keep our hands from blood, and if possible to keep the poor, giddy, thoughtless people of our Country from plunging headlong into this impious War. If the attempt is necessary it is honourable. You will at least have the comfort that nothing has been left undone on your part to prevent the worst mischief that can befal the publick. Then and not before you may shake the dust from your feet and leave the people and their leaders to their own conduct and fortune.[30]

The advice was not followed. Had Rockingham adopted Burke's less dramatic policy, a broad opposition to the war might have materialized earlier, with effects hard to estimate. As Burke says at the end of this letter, "A Minority cannot make or carry on a War. But a Minority well composed and acting steadily may clog a War in such a manner, as to make it not very easy to proceed." That was what he hoped for. Such an act of legislative resistance seemed to Burke the height of loyalty to his country, for its aim was to preserve the country from itself. The ministerial policy was settled, however, without the approval of Rockingham. The challenge, therefore, was to slow the progress of arms and the destruction of liberty.

How shall we characterize the outlook of these remarkable letters to O'Hara and Rockingham? Sometime late in 1775, Burke seems to have realized that many, perhaps most, of his countrymen found the prospect of war with America intoxicating. Of course, they wanted to be convinced that they were in the right, that there was no other method for obtaining what was owed them, and that without a successful war the whole system of imperial interests would be in peril. But the mob of the genteel, along with the lowest of the people, fell in with the mood of war. It was his dark presentiment of this belligerence that guided Burke's second conciliation speech. Delivered on November 16, 1775, it would be his last major address before following Lord Rockingham into secession. The strategy here was simpler than that of the initial and already famous *Speech on Conciliation*. This speech would be a dignified admission of defeat.

There is no adequate text of the *Second Conciliation;* but though the vote went 210–105 against Burke's formal proposal, reports suggest that this speech was the equal of the first; and the words that survive are enough to confirm that in the shadow of war, he mounted a valiant last defense of peace, an effort comparable to its predecessor in controlled vehemence. Hostilities had commenced half a year earlier with the Battle of Lexington; yet Burke still ventured to describe the steps that might avert a war. Anything is preferable to war, especially to civil war, as he remarks in a manuscript note: "I would end a Civil War with some dishonour rather than conduct it with the greatest Glory."[31] There remained a chance to head off the conflict before it presented the grim alternative of total independence or unrelieved suppression. Yet policy on the British side has so far been narrowed to three possibilities: "simple war in order to perfect conquest"; "a mixture of war and treaty"; and "peace grounded on concession." Burke presses for concession all the way, concession that excludes any resort to force. "Armed negotiation for taxes" would be self-defeating: in a war fought to the end, even an apparent victory would impede further revenue from America, "either by our authority, or by that of their own assemblies." Cooperation is an ethic that cannot be compelled. Once you have renounced the use of force, you depend on honor, probity, and goodwill. If the agreement is to be kept by trust, it must be sealed without coercion.

So Burke at this final crisis asks the leaders of Britain to make the concession "immediately, and of their own free grace." The brutal policy and disastrous reception of the Coercive Acts in Boston require a larger gesture than might have sufficed only four years earlier, but "injudicious coercion has made it necessary." To emphasize the length of the concession, Parliament ought formally to cut off the power of the king to tax. Burke draws his precedent from the reign of Edward I, when, "by an express and positive act," Parliament "cut off from the Sovereign power this right of taxing." Recourse to the precedent will allow the Commons to avoid the repeal of the Declaratory Act—still a useful device in affirming the sovereignty of the House as separate from the king. As for the *right* to tax, a locution adopted both by the Americans and by the king, Burke declares himself "averse to doing any thing upon speculations of right."[32]

He believed that the colonists did not yet desire independence. Why should they prefer a condition evidently against their own interests? "So far from disbelieving them, when they denied such a design, he could scarcely credit them if they should assert it."[33] This last is an imperious claim for a statesman and indicative of a dangerous self-confidence. Burke believed that his knowledge of people's interests enabled him to recognize better than they could themselves the proper path to their own good. This claim will recur with admirable fortitude three years later, in his assertion to the electors of Bristol that he has defended their interests against their opinions, their long-term welfare against their momentary fancies. It will emerge again more dubiously when he asserts, in correspondence of the 1790s and in the *Regicide Peace,* that the geographical and the moral France have become separate entities and that he, Edmund Burke, can now be relied on to identify the location-in-exile of the moral France. His diagnosis of the American mood required no such presumption of clairvoyance. He appeals rather from the manners to the reality of freedom. The colonists are already a free people in all but name. Why should they formalize a separation if the terms of partnership are fair? Burke aims to preserve the connection between England and America by restoring the former "unsuspecting confidence" between them. Also, he would back the resolution by a promise: this speech of November 1775 categorically rules out any further use of force.

The phrasing of the concession reserves to the king and his successors the right to collect quit-rents and other undisputed ancient dues and revenues. It guarantees against expropriation the rights and posses-sions of the proprietors of charter companies. Allowing for these obvious exceptions, Burke's formulation could hardly be more sweeping, for it promises:

> That no aid, subsidy, tax, duty, loan, benevolence, or any other bur-then or imposition whatsoever, shall be granted, laid, assessed, levied, or collected upon the inhabitants of any colony or plantation in Amer-ica, by the authority, or in virtue of any act of Parliament, or in any other manner, or by any other authority, than the voluntary grant of the general assembly, or general court of each colony or plantation, and which shall be assented to by his Majesty's governor, and other-wise confirmed according to the usage of each province respectively, any law, statute, custom, right, prerogative, or any other matter whatsoever to the contrary notwithstanding.[34]

To ensure against abuse, he stipulates that if any future act should be passed for regulation of trade, all duties collected are to be held "for the disposal of the general assemblies" of the colonies. The final condition epitomizes Burke's approach. He would retain a parliamentary power not originally contested but would yield the money from its exercise to the colonial assemblies. Parliament, that is, would confer the power of taxa-tion on the American assemblies, and in accepting it, the assemblies would owe their authority to Parliament rather than possess it by right.

This was a last effort to maintain in practice the "communion" of Brit-ain and the American colonies. There exist some notes of Burke's train of thought leading up to the speech, notes that are more suggestive than the report in the parliamentary history. Here he confesses his feelings of isola-tion as a constitutional moderate alarmed into action. It is a position quite lacking in glamour, he knows, since statesmen like himself who counsel a restrained use of power must seem to distrust "the *perfection* of that *power* whose exercise they would *limit.* . . . *Moderation* seems to be made for *me-diocrity.*"[35] An acute insight into the psychology of power, and the thought could only have come from Burke. In back of the sentence "Moderation seems to be made for mediocrity" lies the argument of the *Sublime and Beautiful*. A rational design of using power carefully, with an eye to limited ends, can never keep pace with the unreasoning hunger for extreme sensations. (Vainglory and collective self-love are among those sensations.) The love of power generally agrees with specific exertions of power which "the love of our country" is well adapted to excuse. Our sense that we do the exorbitant thing for a generous reason gratifies the appetite and makes us want to do the thing again. There is a risk, of course, in Burke's analytic stance lest he appear inhumanly unexcitable. He has also laid himself open to the charge of a want of patriotism. The last accusation he meets by warning that the present occasion for "patriotic" displays is a civil war. Besides, to fight the war with the address it demands will be impracticable; and at this point his conscientious outrage and irony fuse in an epigram: "There is a parenthesis of 3,000 miles of ocean between the beginning and end of every sentence we speak of America."[36]

If Burke detested the aims of the war party, what did he think of America's defiance? He could never endorse revolution except in cases of necessity—his ears were not tuned to that kind of music—and the infringements on American freedom of action did not justify an appeal to necessity. Allowing the truth of every American complaint, it was false to assert—and Johnson and Tucker had seen it was false—that the abuses of colonial authority rendered the colonists as abject as slaves.[37] Anyone who believed this was taking literally the fire-eating rhetoric of the tax abolitionists. For all the harm done by the Coercive Acts, they did not subject to starvation or threaten with extinction an entire people. Yet anecdotes of Burke during the war suggest that he all but celebrated news of American victories. Rumors that he had gone that length would return to haunt him in the early 1790s, when Fox, by then his opponent, alluded to his mentor's differential treatment of the two revolutions. There is an extended manuscript note which indicates that by late 1775, Burke had moved from the mixed sympathy of the initial *Speech on Conciliation* to something more like wonder at the staunchness of the American resistance.

Self-sacrifice had rendered the Americans magnificent. It was as if their public conduct widened the possibilities of human nature. The prodigy can be confessed in private, though Burke knows that an aristocratic society should not expose such possibilities to the eye of the world. He addresses the war party in England:

By trying how much constancy was to be found in human Nature you made discoveries, which however honourable to our Species were infinitely mischievous to those who held the experiment, and called out the resources of Nature.

In New England you have turned a mean shifty peddling Nation into a people of heroes. They rejected the respite which you gave to their Navigation. They cast in your face the stinted shew of Mercy by which your proscription was accompanied—the apostles did not quit their Nets with more alacrity at the Call of Grace than they did at the call of honour. They have realised in Modern days all that we read of antient Spirit.[38]

A people still "in the gristle" have turned into exemplars of republican virtue. The idea of *spirit* always carried for Burke the overtone of a possible magnanimity, and he recognizes such large-mindedness wherever he sees it. The comparisons with Greek and Roman precedent and with Christ's disciples are not lightly made.

Seldom elsewhere does Burke so freely combine religious and political description; but both are needed to suggest the nature of the prodigy. The House of Commons never guessed at this power of resistance, because they judged from a lower conception of political interest. "Low interested unimpassioned Nature" lacks the capacity for action that belongs to a nature at once disinterested and impassioned. Burke sums up with a eulogy of the Americans that is qualified only by the knowledge that he is not one of them. "By depriving them of all external engagements Virtue was become their sole Enjoyment—It became dearer and dearer to them when it was no longer incumberd by various other meaner subsidiary pleasures. Deprived of common Luxury and convenience they consoled themselves with Liberty dignity and honour."[39] Burke (let us remind ourselves) never published these words. Yet great writing borrows a vigor from the force of the unsaid. He had not arrived at this intensity of praise when he delivered the *Speech on Conciliation* eight months earlier. It is as if something of the spirit of the colonists has entered into him.

Burke was not alone in seeing the American resistance as an invitation to liberty rather than a provocation to war. Others as eminent blamed the monopolistic privilege of the East India Company and the small-mindedness of a ministry pliable to commercial interests. Burke took a risk chiefly in pursuing his dissent with so hardy a resolution; but friends and unlikely allies stepped into the daylight to strengthen his cause. We may note the influence of a book of 1776, *The Wealth of Nations*. Adam Smith viewed the causes of the war in much the same way as Burke, and devoted his most hard-hitting chapters to an attack on the East India Company. He believed that the company's practice of cornering the tea market in America ran parallel with its method of governing India for mercantile gain instead of cultivation and improvement. The effect in both continents was to rely on extraction alone for the spread of commerce. Greed was the company's motive, rather than a wish for general prosperity; a wiser management of the empire would have to include oversight of the company and a readiness to circumscribe its privileges. The connection between the abuses of empire in America and in India was noticed, as well, in a pamphlet of the same year by an author whose opinions would figure largely in Burke's later career. *Observations on the Nature of Civil Liberty, the Principles of Government, and the Justice and Policy of the War with America*—among the most thoughtful writings provoked by the American war—was the work of Richard Price: a philosopher, Dissenting preacher, and economic theorist of the "Bowood circle," which took its name from the residence of William Petty, the 2nd Earl of Shelburne. Price's anti-utilitarian essay on the primacy of moral duties, *A Review of the Principal Questions in Morals*, had earned the admiration of Dr. Johnson; and writing in 1776 with the combined authority of a moral philosopher and a Dissenting preacher, he remarked in his *Observations* that the thankless British policy toward America was hardly an isolated symptom. "Turn your eyes to India. There more has been done than is now attempted in America. There Englishmen actuated by the love of plunder and the spirit of conquest, have depopulated whole kingdoms, and ruined millions of innocent people by the most infamous oppression and rapacity. The justice of the nation has slept over these enormities. Will the justice of heaven sleep?"[40] As it turned out, nobody would do more than Burke to supply a conscientious answer to the question raised by Price.

Imperial Government and the Rights of the People

The prospects of the empire in 1776 looked even gloomier to Burke than they did to Adam Smith and Richard Price. He lacked the faith of Smith in the civilizing influence of commerce on manners and the faith of Price in reason and moral enlightenment as agents of progress. In August 1776, during a span of months when his correspondence has dwindled to a thread, Burke turns to confide in his old friend Richard Shackleton: "We are deeply in blood. We expect now to hear of some sharp affair, every hour. God knows how it will be. I do not know how to wish success to those whose Victory is to separate from us a large and noble part of our Empire. Still less do I wish success to injustice, oppression and absurdity. Things are in a bad train and in more ways than one. No good can come of any Event in this War to any Virtuous Interest. We have forgot or thrown away all our antient principles. This view sometimes sinks my Spirits."[41] This was still his mood in January 1777 when he wrote the *Letter to the Sheriffs of Bristol:* a pamphlet about the American war and the crisis of liberty in England, which exhibits, as well as anything Burke ever wrote, the swiftness of his thought and the muscular strength of his expression, his ability to discover permanent truths in the close work of urgent debate. Three other documents, written by Burke at the turn of the year 1777, furnish the appropriate context of the *Letter.*

But before looking into their arguments individually, we should admit some surprise concerning their total drift. For everything that can rightly be said of Burke as a moderate begins to be false in January 1777. In his hatred of the American war, Burke becomes immoderate—a witness who will not be silenced. About this time he begins to echo the sentiments and some of the arguments of the Americans whose cause he supported. Thus, he speaks in 1777 of original rights and an original contract between the king and the people. The people are the source of authority and their welfare the only reason why governments are maintained. Respect must be shown to popular assemblies, and Parliament is the begetter and model of such assemblies in New England. The Glorious Revolution was a break from the previous history of the British monarchy, and its example ought to be followed. True liberty means consent by the governed. All of these

are startling assertions to come from Edmund Burke, and they come together in the 1777 "Address to the King," which he writes in January for
the Rockingham party. Though reprinted in every major edition of his
works, the address has not received much extended commentary. (An exception is Lord Acton, who quoted from it as an instance of the constitutional theory that informed the first stages of the French Revolution.)[42]

January 1777 was in other ways an auspicious month for George III. A
series of defeats in New Jersey had pushed back the continental army and
driven General Washington across the Delaware River. English armies
seemed on the brink of victory: this winter (the winter of Valley Forge)
looked as if it would finish the work the battles had begun. With England
almost ready to dictate terms of concession, it was hardly imaginable that
the Americans might soon win their independence. Yet Burke chose this
moment to press the claims of the American colonists, in language that
echoes the republican thinking of the colonists themselves. Nor was this
an isolated move. The "Address to the King" was part of a complex strategy that saw Burke compose, about the same time, an "Address to the
Colonists," a memorandum to Lord Rockingham, and his extended public *Letter to the Sheriffs of Bristol*. He tells the king to accede to the American demands, even though America is losing, and he asks the colonists to
remit a degree of their resentment: public opinion in England is less hostile to their cause than the ministry has allowed them to understand. While
his message to the king is "Give the Americans the freedom they want,"
his message to the colonists is "Take the freedom of partners and not of
enemies." All that Burke writes at this critical moment builds upon and
deepens the rhetorical initiative of the *Second Conciliation*; so that, from
1775 through 1777, it can be said that he evolves a principle of concession to
which he will often return, and whose particulars he adapts to emergent
occasions. But it is the final element of Burke's campaign—his memorandum to Rockingham in the same dismal winter of 1776–1777—that gives
the proof of his seriousness. He presses his case here to assert the independence of the House of Commons and to clarify his party's stance not
by secession but by active participation in public debate.

Secession from Parliament can be a useful tactic only if its meaning is
clear, if it is consistently observed, and if the symbolic abstention brings a

practical gain. Burke did not believe that Rockingham had considered the case with sufficient care: "To pursue violent measures with languor and irresolution is not very consistent in Speculation; and it is not more reputable or safe in practice. If your Lordships friends do not go to this Business with their whole hearts; if they do not feel themselves uneasy without it; if they do not undertake it with a certain degree of Zeal, and even with warmth and indignation at the present state of things, it had better be removed wholly out of our thoughts."[43] These strictures on the advisability of secession are accompanied by a concrete proposal: open the doors of the House of Commons in order to show the people that the opposition is doing its work, and to prevent the ministry from taking control of the reports given of debates out of doors. The limitation against "strangers" (that is, ordinary citizens viewing the proceedings of the Commons) had been an opposition grievance ever since a motion to expel strangers from the gallery was passed at the introduction of the Boston Port Bill in 1774. Free reports of extemporaneous speeches were also excluded. For some time, the opposition could take heart only from lax enforcement; but by 1777, the prohibition had mostly lifted; and public opinion (as the Wilkes controversy began to show) might now take its cue from a formed opposition. Burke advised Rockingham that in these conditions the party must avoid "a weak, irregular, desultory, peevish opposition": they should do nothing to "break the continuity of your conduct, and thereby to weaken and fritter away the impression of it."[44] He asked Rockingham to seek maximum exposure for a policy defending liberty.[45]

Could a consistent pursuit of this strategy have brought England nearer to peace with America in 1777? Burke seems aware of that possibility in his "Address to the King." When he expounds the subordinate place the king holds in the British constitution—since power originates in the people, and Parliament is a representative body of the people—Burke in effect is offering George III an American view of England. If the king signals his approval, reconciliation between America and the mother country will be an agreement between equals. All this Burke candidly says: there is neither flattery nor insult in the address. It was not written with a realistic hope of persuasion, however, but rather as a quasi-public, quasi-official text whose character is impossible to mistake: the politics of the Rockingham Whigs are identified with a tradition of progress in the expansion of English rights. Those last words may grate on the ear of a reader familiar with the skepticism about rights that one associates with Burke's *Reflections on the Revolution in France*. But there can be no doubt of his different stand in the "Address" and again in the *Letter to the Sheriffs of Bristol*. When he writes explicitly of "original rights" and "inherent rights," the dissident Burke is siding with the Americans, who were on the verge of defeat.

In these writings, Burke refuses to hope for a British victory, on the ground that it would be a defeat for liberty everywhere. England is injured as much as America by the practice of domination: "We were always steadily averse to this Civil war; not because we thought it impossible that it should be attended with Victory; but because we were fully persuaded that in such a contest, Victory would only vary the mode of our ruin."[46] Calling to mind the many petitions and protests from Americans, Burke suggests to the king that the generality of the grievance proves its genuineness: "We cannot conceive, that without some powerful concurring cause, any management should prevail on some Millions of People, dispersed over an whole Continent, in Thirteen provinces, not only unconnected, but in many particulars of Religion, Manners, Government; and local Interest, totally different and adverse, voluntarily to submit themselves to a suspension of all the profits of Industry, and all the comforts of Civil Life, added to all the Evils of an unequal War, carried on with circumstances of the greatest asperity and rigour."[47] Such a collective act of self-sacrifice could only have sprung from "a general Sense of some grievance, so radical in its nature, and so spreading in its effects, as to poison all the ordinary satisfactions of Life, to discompose the frame of Society, and to convert into fear and hatred, that habitual reverence ever paid by Mankind to an Ancient and venerable Government." This may sound prudential, as if to say "We *cannot* govern them (though we would if we could)." Yet the argument is normative. The varieties of religion and manners, forms of self-government, and local interests in America betoken the variety of mankind at large. You cannot hope to rule these millions by a single antiquated body of laws: "It is an attempt, to dispose of the property of a whole People without their consent." Burke aims to teach George III what it means for opinion to supervene on force.

It is an old theme, for him. Yet his formulation of it here, by which American liberty becomes the cause of enlightenment itself, has a directness that he never showed before: "We have been too early instructed, and too long habituated to believe, that the only firm seat of all authority is in the minds, affections, and Interests of the People, to change our opinion, on the Theoretick reasonings of speculative men, or for the convenience of a mere temporary arrangement of State. It is not consistent with Equity or Wisdom to set at defiance the general feelings of great Communities, and of all the orders which compose them. Much power is tolerated and passes unquestioned where much is yielded to opinion. All is disputed where everything is enforced."[48] These observations are directed not against the tumults of the people but rather against the "policy" of kings; and the passage shows how far, since the *Speech on Conciliation,* his ideas of political authority had changed. He now says plainly that authority resides in the people. Nor could he have chosen a more significant listener. George III already held himself answerable to the "minds, affections, and interests" of his people; yet Burke is pointing to the Americans as a distinct interest to the extent that they believe they are. This follows from his axiom that the people are the only proper judges of the point at which an encroachment on their rights becomes an intolerable offense.

America, Burke tells the king, is independent now in all but name; force can only slow the recognition of a break that has already happened. "When no means are possessed, of power to awe or to oblige, the strongest ties, which connect mankind in every relation Social and Civil, and which teach them mutually to respect each other are broken.—Independency from that moment virtually exists. Its formal declaration will quickly follow."[49] The first sentence deliberately echoes the American Declaration of Independence. It has a Burkean overtone from its emphasis on the priority of sentiments over principles: the dissolving of the bands that connect one people to another, he says, must already have occurred in feeling before it occurs in fact. Unlike the signers of the Declaration, however, Burke still looks to the possibility of a restored union; but to bring that reconciliation, the king must adopt the principle of rule by the House of Commons, even as the colonists have determined on self-rule by the authority of their assemblies.

We know and feel, that Arbitrary Power over distant Regions is not within the competence, nor to be exercised agreeably to the forms, or consistently with the spirit of great popular Assemblies. If such Assemblies are called to a nominal share in the exercise of such Power, in order to screen under general participation the guilt of desperate measures, it tends only the more deeply to corrupt the deliberative Character of those Assemblies, in training them to blind obedience; in habituating them to proceed upon grounds of fact, with which they can rarely be sufficiently acquainted and in rendering them executive instruments of designs, the bottom of which they cannot possibly fathom.[50]

This appeal against arbitrary power gives a sharp edge to Burke's familiar tactic of opposing the House of Commons to the king's men. Parliament has for too long been used as a tool. To be worthy of bringing New England into partnership with England, it must rise again to the dignity it assumed in the last century.

By 1777, the duration and visibility of the American resistance have thus made the liberty of Americans a condition of the future liberty of Englishmen. "To leave any real freedom to Parliament, much Freedom must be left to the Colonies." What awaits Britain if it takes the opposite path is becoming clear. The morale of the British soldiery has been degraded by their mission. Accustomed to the use of force, they cannot be expected "to submit with profound obedience, to the very same things in Great Britain, which in America they had been taught to despise, and been accustom'd to awe, and humble." A domineering spirit will eventually infect English society, from the habituation of soldiers to the work of oppressors, and the complicity of the people in their own oppression. The king therefore stands on the verge of becoming the declared enemy of constitutional liberty.

In showing what this means, in the climactic passage of his address, Burke reasons like an American. Yet the paths of mutual influence are doubtless complex. The Americans had learned some of what they knew about representation from the Burke of *Thoughts on the Cause of the Present Discontents*, the Bristol election speeches of 1774, and the longer speeches on taxation and conciliation. Even so, his present words could not have been predicted from his stance of 1770. Here is Burke's revised understanding of the rights of the English:

> We deprecate the effect of the Doctrines, which must support and countenance the Government over conquered Englishmen. As it will be impossible long to resist the powerful and equitable arguments in favor of the freedom of these unhappy people, that are to be drawn from the principle of our own Liberty; Attempts will be made, attempts have been made, to ridicule and to argue away this principle; and to inculcate into the minds of your People, other maxims of government and other grounds of obedience, than those which have prevail'd at and since the glorious revolution. By degrees these doctrines, by being convenient may grow prevalent. The consequence is not certain; but a general change of principles rarely happens among a People without leading to a change of Government.
>
> Sir, Your Throne cannot stand secure upon the principles of unconditional submission and passive obedience; on powers exercised without the concurrence of the People to be governed; on Acts made in defiance of their prejudices and habits; on acquiescence procured by foreign Mercenary Troops, and secured by standing Armies. These may possibly be the foundation of other Thrones; they must be the subversion of yours. It was not to passive principles in our Ancestors, that we owe the honour of appearing before a Sovereign, who cannot feel that he is a Prince, without knowing that we ought to be free. The revolution is a departure from the ancient course of the descent of this Monarchy. The People at that time reenter'd into their original rights; and it was not because a positive Law authorized what was then done, but because the freedom and safety of the Subject, the origin and cause of all Laws, required a proceeding paramount and superior to them. At that ever memorable and instructive period, the Letter of the Law was superseded in favour of the substance of Liberty. To the free choice therefore of the People, without either King or Parliament, we owe that happy establishment out of which both King and Parliament were regenerated. From that great principle of Liberty have originated the Statutes confirming and ratifying the establishment from which your Majesty derives your right to rule over us.

> Those Statutes have not given us our Liberties; Our Liberties have produced them.[51]

If one made a continuum of British political writings, from those that anticipate the events of 1688 to those that respond to the events of 1789—with the radicalism of Locke's *Second Treatise on Government* at one end and the conservatism of Burke's *Reflections* at the other—Burke's "Address to the King" of 1777 would stand closer to Locke's *Treatise*. In the passage above, differences of shading between Burkean and Lockean doctrine are revealed in the mention of habits and prejudices and in the omission of any treatment of the right of resistance. These are significant details, and they show Burke avoiding formulations of principle without a basis in custom. He declines to imagine a world in which revolutions might happen fairly often. But there is not much else here that could disappoint a confirmed Lockean like James Otis or John Dickinson.

It must be added that Burke never hints at sympathy with *unorganized* expressions of the popular will (but neither did Locke). Burke elects not to speak of majority rule. Rather, his vindication of British liberty holds in view a single necessity: the replacement of a monarchy that does not represent the people by a monarchy that does represent them. And representation can be signaled only by the actual consent of the people. Resistance is doubtless unpleasant; it creates new forms of intolerance; it teaches a coarse contempt for the private virtues. Nevertheless, Burke assumes that resistance will occur, and that it is warranted when the rights of the people are abused by a monarch who oversteps his limits.

Another detail will strike any reader familiar with the argumentative structure of the *Reflections on the Revolution in France*. The events of 1688 are cherished in the "Address to the King" as part of the history of freedom and not the history of stability. Burke would later cite this view as a tendentious fallacy, but at the height of the American war, he found the meaning of the Glorious Revolution in the recovery by the people of their own liberty, and the action by the Commons as agents of the people. Burke says that the revolution was a bringing of English government into conformity with the paramount good of the freedom and safety of the people, "the origin and cause of all Laws." He thus presents the revolution as a great human act, discontinuous with the previous course of the monarchy; and concerning its newness (in which he rejoices), Burke is altogether explicit: it was "a departure from the ancient course of the descent of this Monarchy. The People at that time reenter'd into their original rights." Note that the original rights had to be discovered; it took a political choice to bring them to light.

He goes one step further to address local causes of discord. Since America has become a necessary bulwark against false principles and slavish obedience, the choice now lies between American freedom and reappearing tyranny in England. Recall the stringent words of the *Speech on Conciliation:* "An Englishman is the unfittest person on earth to argue another Englishman into slavery." That dictum, Burke suggests, must now be put into practice: "A general change of principles rarely happens among a People without leading to a change of Government." If there is a danger of mob rule in two countries, the fault belongs to Parliament for having abdicated its proper role as mediator. And here Burke returns to those "concussions" of received opinion about which he spoke portentously in the *Speech on Conciliation.* He blames them on the pusillanimous conduct of the House of Commons, which has opposed the king too seldom and too passively. Had Parliament taken itself as "the indulgent Guardian and strong protector of the freedom of the Subordinate Popular Assemblies, instead of exercising its powers to their utter annihilation," intractable questions might have been waived and the empire preserved.[52] We are looking, then, at a reassertion of Burke's dignified idea of Parliament as "one common centre" which abides in the interest of all citizens of the empire: a topic of constitutional settlement rather than revolution. Yet the "Address to the King" concludes with a jolt: the history of liberty has taught his party "inherent rights which bind and regulate the Crown itself." Though the members of the House of Commons cannot be bound by mandates, the king is bound by an agreement with the people, sealed when they entered into their rights and confirmed by the Glorious Revolution. The authority of the king is the most dependent thing in all his kingdom, for that authority could not exist without the approval of the people.

What shall we make of the careful blend of tactics in these documents? The "Address to the King" was solicited from Burke by the Rockingham party but never presented. It shows him at the far edge of the permissible; for he was urging a king then close to victory to concede more than he would have thought necessary in defeat. At the same time, Burke was reasoning with the colonists to abate the fury of their resentment: their grievances, he says, are on the way to being redressed, and they must not credit the false "supposition, that a general principle of alienation and enmity to you had pervaded the whole of this Kingdom"; on the contrary, "a large, and we trust the largest and soundest part of this Kingdom, perseveres in the most perfect unity of sentiments, principles, and affections, with you." And again: "If the disposition of Providence (which we deprecate) should even prostrate you at our feet, broken in power and in spirit, it would be our duty and inclination to revive, by every practicable means, that free energy of mind, which a fortune unsuitable to your virtue had damped and dejected; and to put you voluntarily in possession of those very privileges, which you had in vain attempted to assert by arms." Heavy as the calamity would be of seeing the colonies become a separate entity, "yet we had much rather see you totally independent of this Crown and Kingdom, than joined to it by so unnatural a conjunction, as that of Freedom with servitude."[53] So he asks them to believe that their liberty is adequately defended by many in England, from a strong sense of fraternal sympathy.

Thus far, the consolation offered to America may sound partial and attenuated. Yet Burke concedes almost nothing to England. The colonists should have the freedom to give donations (not taxes) of their own volition to the mother country; but what is not given will not be demanded. He silently drops the inference from the Declaratory Act that the taxing of America is a legitimate power of Parliament. Such an assertion of control is seen as denying the colonists the free disposition of their property: "We are of opinion, that you ought to enjoy the sole and exclusive right of freely granting, and applying to the support of your Administration, what God has freely granted as a reward to your industry. . . . We know of no road to your coffers, but through your affections."[54] To attach their affections,

England must distinguish the blameless from the lawless among the colonists; yet England must treat even the latter with a studied leniency. It is wiser, says Burke, to err on the side of clemency: "We cannot look upon men as delinquents in the mass"—a restatement of his maxim against indicting a whole people. Last, and not surprisingly, Burke goes out of his way to honor the Americans as exemplary Englishmen: "Those, who *have and who hold* to that foundation of common Liberty, whether on this or on your side of the Ocean, we consider as the true and the only true Englishmen." The paternalist mode of praise is shunned. Though it appears that the Rockingham party has come to rescue the Americans in adversity, the truth is that the Americans have proved themselves the redeemers of British liberty.

And yet, for all its libertarian zeal, Burke's doctrine of 1777 is not separationist regarding the empire. He warns against a perfect independence; there is an uncertain footing in all "untried forms of Government," and independence is unnecessary so long as England remains a home of greatness and happiness "under the present limited Monarchy." Indeed, if the colonies choose independence, Burke anticipates a series of internecine wars in America leading to "a species of humiliating repose." Not that the Rockingham party would "advise you to an unconstitutional submission": he counsels not docility but patience. But what can this mean in practice? A party opposed to the heavy-handed policy of the king will dedicate itself to the ends desired by the colonists and will win popular favor by "our thorough detestation of the whole War."[55] What the Rockingham Whigs and the Americans both aim to achieve is a polity strengthened by the manners of a restrained liberty. The Americans ought to be neither reserved nor intemperate in claiming their rights. The first extreme might embolden the enemies of liberty. The second might revive "haughty sentiments" of tyranny such as are "apt to breed in minds not tempered with the utmost equity and justice."

To restate Burke's position of January 1777: he commits himself to press Rockingham to stay engaged in the antiwar cause; to advise the king that his policy has become a catastrophe that threatens the empire; and to counsel patience to the colonists while he rallies the support of friends whose existence they have doubted. What did Burke hope to achieve by this complex strategy? Immediately, the House of Commons would be tasked to use all its powers for the welfare of Great Britain and dictate to the king a peace on American terms. Among the indirect consequences would be greater power for the House of Commons, enlarged liberty in Ireland as well as England, and restoration of the former trust between the colonies and the mother country.

A Letter to the Sheriffs of Bristol

It was at this crisis in early 1777 that Burke set to work on *A Letter to the Sheriffs of Bristol:* a meditation on war and civil liberties and an appeal against the decay of public spirit in England. The *Letter* would be his longest communication to his Bristol constituency during his six years as representative. It was published in April 1777, and its leading motive is revealed near the end: "Liberty is in danger of being made unpopular to Englishmen." A slavish conformity has been asked for by the war ministry and adopted by the people. Ignorant opinion, abetted by national greed, has produced a vainglory that deforms alike the ruling caste and the people. This predictable effect is a reason why all wars are to be avoided. Yet Burke believed that the hazards were especially ominous at this moment: success in the ill-considered use of force would corrupt the manners, harden the arrogance, and shrink the generosity of those who administered the empire. Morally and politically, victory would harm Britain more than defeat. But as the *Letter* will show in detail, the consequences of the war *in England* are the pressing reason for Burke's dissent. He has already begun to see the corrupting effects of the war at home; and when violence becomes as common as driving a bargain, the life of society is cheapened.

Both the public motive of the *Letter* and its aim to embody a level statement of facts may be deduced from Burke's full title. Sheriffs were officers of the city whose functions, such as the supervision of elections, made them a fitting ostensible audience for a pamphlet touching on matters of local as well as national concern; and one of the two that served Bristol, John Farr, was close to Burke's circle of supporters in the city and would later become mayor.[56] *A Letter to the Sheriffs of Bristol* is directed against tendencies rather than persons, and it succeeds in the difficult mode of impersonal polemic. At a time when the vices of public conduct are so general as to form a constant subject for private meditation, this form of address has the advantage of seeming free of irritability. *What have we become?* is the question to which Burke will return again and again. The pamphlet was composed rapidly and in a mood of excitement—"far better that it should be early in its appearance," he wrote to a friend, "with such perfection as I am capable of giving it." The vehemence of some sections he thought warranted by the high visibility of destructive policies. "When we speak only of things, not persons, we have a right to express ourselves with all possible energy; and if any one is offended, he only shows how improper that conduct has been which he cannot bear to have represented in its true colours."

The *Letter* was provoked by questions from Burke's constituency about the political cost of the secession of the Rockingham party. In the absence of the most articulate members of the opposition, the North ministry had obtained the passage of two repressive laws: the Letters of Marque Act (which gave legal warrant for privateers to capture enemy shipping) and the American Treason Act (which detained for trial in England persons who committed high treason in America). Together these showed the turn of the government toward a peremptory posture that identified coercion with the rule of law. The Letters of Marque Act Burke treats in passing as a regrettable expedient; but the new law on treason involves a partial suspension of habeas corpus. When he comes to address the implications of tampering with this principle of common law, Burke dilates as he might have done on the floor of the House. A law from the reign of Henry VIII had been transferred to America by an act of Parliament in 1768 to allow prosecution of crimes committed out of the realm; and the new version of the old law was now invoked in all its force. This sort of timely adjustment Burke would always look upon with extreme distrust. To permit the accused to confront the charges against him is a fundamental liberty, a right that can never be diluted without being degraded: "to try a man under that act is, in effect, to condemn him unheard. A person is brought hither in the dungeon of a ship's hold: thence he is vomited into a dungeon on land; loaded with irons, unfurnished with money, unsupported by friends, three thousand miles from all means of calling upon, or confronting evidence, where no one local circumstance that tends to detect perjury, can possibly be judged of;—such a person may be executed according to form, but he can never be tried according to justice."[57] The Treason Act voided the presumption of innocence even as it made suspicion of guilt as good as proof. It is plain that the accused, until he hears the charges, can say nothing to avail his own defense; yet so long as he remains silent, his unresponsiveness darkens the prejudice against him: anyone (it is thought) so vexed by legitimate authorities must have done something wrong. Thus the "form" of punishment takes the place of substantial justice.

The opening section of the *Letter* is concerned with apparently extrinsic effects of the war, and its argument passes from observation to general truths. In a discussion of the law throwing out habeas corpus, Burke concentrates on the selective nature of the suspension: the penalty falls on those who were out of the realm at a certain period, or on the high seas. This contradicts the idea of universal applicability that is inseparable from justice; under a cover of prudence, it allows the authorities to choose targets whom they have in their sights for other reasons. A universal suspension of habeas corpus would have been preferable, Burke says: it would have showed the people what they are losing. "Partial freedom seems to me a most invidious mode of slavery. But, unfortunately, it is the kind of slavery the most easily admitted in times of civil discord. For parties are but too apt to forget their own future safety in their desire of sacrificing their enemies."[58] Such a defense of the universality of laws may seem alien to the practical spirit of Burke's statesmanship. One may also be surprised at his refusal of compromise and his readiness to see bad laws show their worst effects even if the result is widespread suffering. His argument seems to carry a tincture of the vanguardist idea—associated with Machiavelli and Marx—that suffering must intensify in order to let people know the contest they face. Does Burke mean to say that the worse things get, the clearer the stakes become and therefore the better for the prospects of reform?

He does comes close to such a revolutionary attitude—remote from the moderate temper he had claimed as lately as his notes for the *Second Conciliation*—when he boldly asserts: "I should be sorry, that any thing framed in contradiction to the spirit of our constitution did not instantly produce in fact, the grossest of the evils, with which it was pregnant in its nature. It is by lying dormant a long time, or being at first very rarely exercised, that arbitrary power steals upon a people."[59] It is a sentiment closer to the republican radical Milton than to the trimmer Halifax. Yet the resolve of Burke—to build not on the good old days but on the bad new days—comes from constitutional vigilance. Equality under the law requires exposure of persons of all ranks and conditions to the same scrutiny and the same treatment. If there must be a suspension of rights, let it be general; for, as Burke adds, "the alarm of such a proceeding would then be universal" and the fatality of the present course become conspicuous. "It would become every man's immediate and instant concern to be made very sensible of the absolute necessity of this total eclipse of liberty." Even if the people betray a moral lethargy, their whole previous understanding of who and what they are must revolt against a general suspension of justice. But that is not likely under the present selective law. "The true danger is, when liberty is nibbled away, for expedients, and by parts."

Much of the *Letter* is concerned with the degradation of public manners and morals. Through much of it, Burke writes as if he were meditating on a line of *Julius Caesar,* "Th'abuse of greatness is when it disjoins / Remorse from power." The real poison of civil war is a growing distrust of neighbors and associates: in England in 1777, Burke perceives the change to be very great. A larger trust has been broken; the fabric of familiar relations has been torn.

> Whilst *manners* remain entire, they will correct the vices of law, and soften it at length to their own temper. But we have to lament, that in most of the late proceedings we see very few traces of that generosity, humanity, and dignity of mind which formerly characterized this nation. War suspends the rules of moral obligation; and what is long suspended is in danger of being totally abrogated. Civil wars strike deepest of all into the manners of a people. They vitiate their politicks; they corrupt their morals; they pervert even the natural taste and relish of equity and justice. By teaching us to consider our fellow citizens in an hostile light, the whole body of our nation becomes gradually less dear to us. The very names of affection and kindred, which were the bond of charity whilst we agreed, become new incentives to hatred and rage, when the communion of our country is dissolved.[60]

Such are the effects of the repression at home; meanwhile, the war grinds on: "Not one unattacked village, which was originally adverse, throughout that vast continent, has yet submitted from love or terror. You have the ground you encamp on; and you have no more. The cantonments of your troops and your dominions are exactly of the same extent. You spread devastation, but you do not enlarge the sphere of authority."[61] The *you* in these sentences has changed from the sheriffs to the powers that direct the war. British progress in the war itself is at a standoff because the means of the contest were never proportioned to the ends; and this raises the question, Who decided to launch the war?

It is often said that "everybody hates war," but that commonplace is flattering to human nature and deeply false. Peacetime standards of refinement forbid our saying so, but for many people a war is the time of their lives (so long as they do not have to die). It is a feast for the eye, a savage recital for all the senses; it appeals to the love of power and engrosses the love of spectacle: it exerts an attraction so appalling it exhilarates. Burke takes this for granted in the argument of his *Letter;* he takes it to be a truth that people cannot bear to admit. But he means to reproach more particularly those ministers of state who lack the imagination to know the effects of war—how it warps and specializes the civil respect for authority, and coarsens the natural feelings of equity and justice. The men he speaks of were those who started the cry for war: they evangelized for it; they enacted patriotic laws to choke dissent and wear down the enemy; and now they have been proved defective in knowledge and imagination alike. "A conscientious man would be cautious how he dealt in blood. He would feel some apprehension at being called to a tremendous account for engaging in so deep a play, without any sort of knowledge of the game."[62] Nor does Burke spare those at a lower level who took up the drumbeat. These include the patriot mob, its typical member "an impotent helpless creature, without civil wisdom or military skill, without a consciousness of any other qualification for power but his servility to it, bloated with pride and arrogance, calling for battles which he is not to fight, contending for a violent dominion which he can never exercise, and satisfied to be himself mean and miserable, in order to render others contemptible and wretched." War excites and degrades the sporting instinct by the promise of savage satisfactions. It is this confusion of motives—servility and violent dominion, the pride of the brave and the lust of the mean—that renders a country at war almost indifferent to reason.

Burke's account of popular opinion is laced with bitter irony. He approaches contempt when he describes the elite of the merchants and landowners: "They promise their private fortunes, and they mortgage their country." They have so arranged things that the war budget will be drawn on funds that do not exist, while their own contribution from taxes is kept to a minimum. Self-sacrifice is ruled out: they are too important for that. Yet the self-protective rich and the war-hungry populace have done less harm to the fortunes of the country than those empire men whose schemes fantastically exceed their grasp. "Has any of these Gentlemen, who are so eager to govern all mankind, shewed himself possessed of the first qualification towards government, some knowledge of the object, and of the difficulties which occur in the tasks they have undertaken?" Burke will later accuse the French revolutionists of being in a hurry, of demanding to do at once what they are so sure must be done. The emergency mood of war has much in common with the mood of revolution: both mask a compulsion under a drive toward mere efficiency. "Difficulty is good for man," he will say in 1790, and by difficulty he means, in part, deliberation. The brokers of wars and revolutions have never agreed. In exact proportion to their incompetence is their need of a war or, better, a series of wars to distract the public mind. Terrible as a necessity, war becomes irreducibly evil when employed as a tactic. This will be Burke's emphasis in the following decade when he denounces the East India Company for its role in the wars against the Rohillas and the Mahratas. But for the empire theorists, war *is* a tactic above all, a chosen means which they take care to disguise as necessity. "Let them but once get us into a war, their power is then safe, and an act of oblivion passed for all their misconduct." Fantasy distorts all their reasonings, and they imagine the discipline of armies will ensure the obedience of a subject people. Yet the disorder and violence of the means are woven into the ends of every war. This is what the war party cannot recognize; they could not be what they are if they did realize it. They know, Burke argues, that they deceive others for the sake of eliciting cooperation, but they cannot themselves be sure of the exact length of the falsehood: so much depends on wishful thinking at every stage.

Meanwhile, the generality of support for the war distracts attention from the obscurity of its causes and unreasonably strengthens the case for the policy to continue: "They are continually boasting of unanimity, or calling for it. But before this unanimity can be matter either of wish or congratulation, we ought to be pretty sure, that we are engaged in a rational pursuit. Phrensy does not become a slighter distemper on account of the number of those who may be infected with it. Delusion and weakness produce not one mischief the less, because they are universal."[63] Beneath Burke's sense of the swindle of false opinion lies a profound suggestion about the futility of force. The nature of uniform ideas is to act *like* force. All the cries are on one side, and the actors come to believe (though they themselves have set the opinion in motion) that all the reasons must be on one side, too. How can victors be wrong?

When belief in a cause is sheltered by innocence of the facts, the people will look on all opposition as unnatural. Even before France entered the American war, English opinion was drawn to theories that explained the American resistance as the product of some external agency. This, Burke saw, was to overlook the sheer difficulty of breaking the will of large numbers of people. Most Americans would gladly have lived their industrious lives without interruption; no ordinary grievance could have roused so many. "*General* rebellions and revolts of an whole people never were *encouraged*, now or at any time. They are always *provoked*." A society at peace is defended by a stability that is not fragile. People live their lives from habit; it does not occur to them to change things much. So when we see them stirred by deep dissatisfaction, it is a fair inference that something has gone badly wrong in the society. Lawyers, merchants, and pamphleteers may foment violence from ambition, but the people are not liable to be easily turned, and before they revolt they must be brought close to despair. Notice that Burke on America takes this to be a fact that hardly calls for analysis. He will suppose the opposite in France only by postulating—with a degree of truth which he was bound to magnify—a preternatural efficacy in conveying delusion by the political men of letters. In America, the anti-tax pamphleteers had done their work skillfully, no doubt, but Burke does not accuse them of having conjured the rebellion out of thin air.

A Letter to the Sheriffs of Bristol was written because a rebellion had become a civil war. It is a pamphlet against war in the same sense in which *Reflections on the Revolution in France* is an extended pamphlet against revolution. Burke in 1777 does not need to vary much the persuasive direction of the *Speech on Conciliation*. England, he says once more, ought to grant peace and liberty as a gratuitous benefit, and the gift will appear more generous if not compelled by losses in battle. "It can scarcely be our wish, that terms of accommodation never should be proposed to our enemy, except when they must be attributed solely to our fears." This points to a chivalric ideal: treat people (whatever their deserts may be) according to your own honor and dignity. As for the judgment, so vivid in Johnson and the Tory polemicists, that the Americans want too much liberty, Burke puts it down gently: "If any ask me what a free Government is? I answer, that, for any practical purpose, it is what the people think so; and that they, and not I, are the natural, lawful, and competent judges of this matter."

Burke does not subscribe to an infinitely flexible definition of liberty. He insists, however, that the British reliance on mercenaries betrays the weakness of their cause; it shows a tacit understanding that, for them, this is a war of choice. By contrast, the Americans are fighting a war provoked by oppression, and Burke finds in their resistance signs of both deliberation and self-restraint. "The *extreme* of liberty (which is its abstract perfection, but its real fault) obtains no where, nor ought to obtain any where. Because extremes, as we all know, in every point which relates either to our duties or satisfactions in life, are destructive both to virtue and enjoyment. Liberty too must be limited in order to be possessed."[64] Distinct lines are thus drawn around the idea of liberty: it has a marked character, and America has shown itself qualified to possess the liberty it demands.

This joining of the ideas of liberty and character may suggest to experienced readers of Burke that some mention of party will soon follow.

And it is indeed at this point that he chooses to make a last apology for the Declaratory Act ("I could not at once tear from my heart prejudices which were dear to me, and which bore a resemblance to virtues"). He puts forward the inferior argument that the authority conferred by the act was necessary in order for Parliament's granting of freedom to appear as a gratuitous gift. In short, Parliament required the power to withhold generosity if the decision not to withhold it was to count as a free choice. This makes the best of a bad case. The truth is that Burke knew the act was now a dead letter ("a different state of things requires a different conduct"). He only wishes his readers to know that "I parted with it, as with a limb: but as with a limb to save the body; and I would have parted with more, if more had been necessary." Necessities are determined by an existing state of trust and hostility, and the reckoning of them, he affirms, should not be left to ordinary hands. Only a party known for its history of prudent conduct can be relied on not to confuse choice with necessity.

For such a governing party to return, there cannot prevail a general distrust of politics. At the end of the *Letter,* therefore, Burke winds into a defense of public life. "I hope there are none of you," he tells his Bristol readers, "corrupted with the doctrine taught by wicked men for the worst purposes" that "the men who act upon the public stage are all alike; all equally corrupt; all influenced by no other views than the sordid lucre of salary and pension." He believes, and with warrant in the cases of Rockingham, Dowdeswell, Savile, and others whom he names, that some men of the present age ought to be exempt from such suspicion. "The thing, I know by experience to be false." Failure to discriminate among the figures in public life—the tendency to disparage all alike, which began in the Walpole years and became a badge of honor in the circle of Swift and Pope (whose style of generalized disenchantment we have seen Burke try on and shed when young)—this failure he now declares a prime cause of the decay of liberty. "This moral leveling is a *servile principle.* It leads to practical passive obedience far better, than all the doctrines, which the pliant accommodation of Theology to power has ever produced." A reckless condemnation of politics will end by rejecting the moderate spirit of public life itself, that "civil, social" temper so well captured in the *Speech on Conciliation:* "We balance inconveniences; we give and take; we remit some rights, that we may enjoy others; and we choose rather to be happy citizens than subtle disputants." An idealism that disdains all compromise has the practical effect of ceding every result to the dominant forces of the age. It produces an apathy as destructive of secular hope as the pliant accommodations of a Wolsey or a Richelieu.

It is on this admonitory note that Burke's defense of political resistance in 1777 comes to rest. In the last pages of the *Letter to the Sheriffs of Bristol,* we are still in the presence of the author of *Thoughts on the Cause of the Present Discontents;* but the American crisis and the near certainty of a separation in the empire have made him a less complacent man and a lonelier thinker. "I am aware that the age is not what we all wish. But I am sure, that the only means of checking its precipitate degeneracy, is heartily to concur with whatever is the best in our time; and to have some more correct standard of judging what that best is, than the transient and uncertain favour of a court."[65] Why the improvement should be the work of a party and not an ad hoc group of talents cannot be as clear to us as it appeared to Burke. His premise is that the standard of the best must always be cemented by the habit of mutual consultation and correction. "Virtue will catch as well as vice by contact; and the public stock of honest manly principle will daily accumulate." Virtue may even offset bigotry and vainglory, the characteristic vices nourished by victories in a war that should not have been fought.

Burke and Fox

In the course of the American debates, the friendship between Burke and Charles Fox gradually became a political alliance—a fact with broad consequences for the opposition. If the politicians who claimed Whig descent in the early 1770s comprised the Bedfords, the Rockinghams, and Lord Chatham, the most comprehensible to the king were certainly the Bedfords. Every bargain proved them obtainable by gross incentives. The Rockinghamites, with the dukes of Portland and Richmond in their front rank, seemed by comparison impersonal and obdurate. They took care to state the exact terms on which they would agree to take power; and they were led by a man so diffident that friends loaded him with compliments when he opened his mouth in public. The secession from Parliament into which Rockingham withdrew in 1776 was a tactic that suited him all too well; and this winter of inaction and waning influence was the right moment for an infusion of energy. As it happened, Fox would hang back another five years; but his contacts with the party began to be regular now; and the formation of a new ministry was part of the calculation for Fox and the Rockingham Whigs.

The shaggy head and round face of Charles Fox—good-humored, unshaven, evocative of many shades of grass-eating corruption yet quite free of malevolence—remains among the most familiar in eighteenth-century caricature. He was a prodigy of gaming as well as public speaking, and had made his name in Parliament, as Chapter 3 recounted, with his youthful philippics against the Wilkes mob. Through the early 1770s, Fox remained on the opposite side from Burke, but they drew closer as Fox's distrust of George III congealed into loathing. The two had met as early as 1766, when Fox was seventeen years old and Burke's literary talents drew notice in the circle of Henry Fox. They must have come to trust each other in the intervening decade, for there is an unusual ease and intimacy in a letter Burke writes to Fox on October 8, 1777.[66]

A warmth that animated their friendship emerges unmistakably in certain details—the exuberance with which Burke plays the part of adviser, and the receptiveness of Fox to Burke's advice; a certain residual dandyism in Burke and a craving for guidance in Fox. By this time, Fox was thinking seriously of joining the Rockingham Whigs, and Burke, who guessed as much, condoled with him on the difficulty of rousing the party leaders to execute a coherent plan:

> I have ever wishd a settled plan of our own, founded in the very essence of the American Business, wholly unconnected with the Events of the war, and framed in such a manner as to keep up our Credit and maintain our System at home, in spite of any thing which may happen abroad. I am now convinced by a long and somewhat vexatious experience that such a plan is absolutely impracticable. I think with you, that some faults in the constitution of those whom we most love and

trust are among the causes of this impracticability. They are faults too, that one can hardly wish them perfectly cured of, as I am afraid they are intimately connected with honest disinterested intentions, plentiful fortunes, assured rank, and quiet homes. A great deal of activity and enterprize can scarcely ever be expected from such men, unless some horrible calamity is just over their heads; or unless they suffer some gross personal insults from power, the resentment of which may be as unquiet and stimulating a principle in their minds, as ambition is in those of a different complexion. To say the truth, I cannot greatly blame them. We live at a time, when men are not repaid in fame, for what they sacrifice in Interest or repose. On the whole, when I consider of what discordant, and particularly of what fleeting materials the opposition has been all along composed, and at the same time review what Lord Rockingham has done, with that and with his own shatterd constitution, for these last twelve years, I confess I am rather surprized that he has done so much and perseverd so long, than that he has felt now and then some cold fits, and that he grows somewhat languid and desponding at last. I know that he, and those who are most prevalent with him, though they are not thought so much devoted to popularity as others, do very much look to the people; and more than I think is wise in them, who do so little to guide and direct the public opinion. Without this, they act indeed; but they act as it were from compulsion, and because it is impossible in their situation to avoid taking some part.[67]

Burke, in this letter, ventures a criticism of his patron that he kept well hidden from other observers, and the frankness tells us something about his confidence in Fox. The passage affords the clearest evidence we have of Burke's dissatisfaction with his party in the year of the *Letter to the Sheriffs of Bristol*. He traces their want of address to the difficulty of wringing an energetic policy from aristocrats.

The general fault of the Rockingham Whigs comes from the inertia of the ancient peerage: they have so much previous fortune in character that they may think they stand to gain nothing by present exertions. Only the most spirited appeal on a question of constitutional integrity will make them listen. But that is something anyway—Burke takes it to indicate their superiority in their class. For the same reason, every disappointment causes them to fall back on their enjoyment of repose. Consequently it has been impossible to frame a policy "founded in the very essence of the American Business" and independent of the fluctuations of events. The phrase "our Credit" probably means to include Fox as someone with an interest in the party, though the hesitations and internal inconsistencies, Burke sees, are apt to discourage him. But considering Rockingham's "shattered constitution," one ought to be impressed by how much he has done. The distinction, incidentally drawn, between "the people" and "the public opinion" is noteworthy. The people are all who have a voice in politics, whether as voters, holders of a landed or mercantile interest, or petitioners of a less regular kind. On the other hand, "the public opinion" implies a true impression of the popular will. The task of a party ought to include "guiding" this body of opinion by offering proposals and a policy. It is wrong for a party merely to respond to events, or to the demands and grievances of their constituencies, since honest and persuasive direction of the people is among the obligations that come with the identity of a party. If the Rockingham Whigs understood this, Burke adds, it would give consistency to "that popular humour which is the medium we float in."

This qualified and careful yet—by Burke's usual standard—headlong and buoyant letter suggests that he viewed Fox as a popular counterpart of Rockingham. Between the two there might be formed a leadership without rival among the parties contending for power: "Do not be in haste. Lay your foundations deep in public opinion. Though (as you are sensible) I have never given you the least hint of advice about joining yourself in a declared connexion with our party, nor do I now—yet as I love that party very well, and am clear that you are better able to serve them than any man I know, I wish that things should be so kept, as to leave you mutually very open to one another in all changes and contingencies."[68] Thus Fox himself is ready to become the natural leader of a party whom Burke has looked so long to find. Fox, if anyone, will have the resources and abilities to keep the promise of reform—a promise indifferently served by the discontents of the people and by a party reluctant to lead. The letter is prompted by a desire to share a burden that may bring a reward. There seems hardly a touch of calculation or even of interested management in

Burke's treatment of his prodigious disciple. "Don't you like Charles Fox?" he asks Garret Nagle in a letter of October 26—knowing that Nagle has lately met Fox. "If you were not pleased on that short acquaintance you would on a further; for he is one of the pleasantest men in the world, as well as the greatest Genius that perhaps this country has ever produced." The scale of the praise suggests the communicable energy of Fox and the pitch of estimation to which friendship could raise Burke's feelings. *Genius,* as he used the word, generally denoted a force for good in human affairs.

The years 1777–1783 are the happiest to contemplate for an admirer of Burke as a statesman. And perhaps these were the most satisfying years for Burke himself. If so, the reason has much to do with the revived hopes for his party that came with Fox's participation and loyalty. The company of Burke made Fox a wiser man; the company of Fox made Burke a freer mind; and this political friendship, which went beyond politics, imparted to both a double strength. Fox was always more a skirmisher than Burke— brilliant for the short match rather than the long campaign; but, so far as he went, dazzling and formidable. He had a teasing style of challenge (available on call), had a sting in his timing, and could do things with his voice beyond the compass of Burke. Fox might possess none of Burke's gravity, his sustained vehemence, his dour hilarity or savage wit, but he could draw on the endless resources of a fine antithetical style. One gets a fair measure of his directness and his "redoubled blows" in the speech of November 26, 1778:

> The war of the Americans is a war of passion; it is of such a nature as to be supported by the most powerful virtues, love of liberty and of country, and at the same time by those passions in the human heart which give courage, strength, and perseverance to man; the spirit of revenge for the injuries you have done them, of retaliation for the hardships inflicted on them, and of opposition to the unjust powers you would have exercised over them; everything combines to animate them to this war, and such a war is without end. . . . The war of France is of another sort; the war of France is a war of interest; it was interest that first induced her to engage in it, and it is by that same interest

that she will measure its continuance; turn your face at once against her, attack her wherever she is exposed, crush her commerce wherever you can, make her feel heavy and immediate distress throughout the nation, and the people will soon cry out to their government.[69]

No new trains of thought are started, but the reasoning is close, the advice solid, the effect strenuous and bracing.

Any speech that, if published, would read especially well Fox thought for that reason a bad speech; whereas all of Burke's major speeches leave their imprint on the memory. Of a speech by Fox, one is apt to recall the momentum rather than the words; whereas with Burke, rhythm, sound, and meaning are one. There was never a doubt which man was the political and which the intellectual leader. It must be added that even Burke's improvised speeches, such as the *Speech on American Taxation* in 1774 and the *Speech at the Bristol Guildhall Previous to the Election* in 1780, are among the greatest in the language—continuous acts of argument which were also highly satisfying to their first audiences. Yet Fox represents a distinct philosophy of composition in public speaking.

Their friendship guarded Fox and Burke for many years against the perils of reflex enthusiasm and defensive fear, to which at a later phase they would separately succumb. Thanks to their combined energy, a concerted opposition, without equal in the history of representative government, made sure that the war with America was lost in debate before it was lost in reality. Never was Burke so impressed by the truth that nations are governed by opinion. Never would he put such effort into educating the public mind for an end that state power alone can never achieve, namely the remedy of abuses of power. In a letter published in the *Bristol Gazette* on November 6, 1777, addressed to the stewards of the Bell Club (a political association with ties to his party), he wrote: "Believe me, it is a great truth, that there never was, for any long time, a corrupt representative of a virtuous people; or a mean, sluggish, or careless people, that ever had a good government in any form." The suffrage of qualified citizens is the root of the legitimate power of Parliament: "Such as you are, sooner or later must Parliament be." The sentence may not say that Parliament derives its just powers from the consent of the governed, but it says almost as much. Parliament draws from the people its opinions and, in the long run, its policy.

This grave idea of the duty of statesmen—that their policy should not mimic but bear a careful resemblance to the opinions of the people—is a condition of Burke's belief in the sovereignty of Parliament itself. Members may choose not to respect the wishes of the people "such as they are" (thinking the people unworthy of attention or uninformed of their own interests), but they cannot do so for long; their contempt will press up against a natural limit; the people will not go away. We are faced, then, with what looks like a change of mind from Burke's speeches at the polls of 1774, with their assertion of the autonomy of the individual member. Yet the contradiction is on the surface only. His remark in 1777 concerning the final authority of the people is a warning whose force the earlier speeches had presumed. If Parliament ever took to itself a constitutional authority separate from the people, it would forfeit its reason for being. Do the people understand as they should that Parliament only exists as the express image of their own feelings? If so, Parliament had better remind itself of this fact with every public deed, since what the people now are, Parliament must some day become.

The cant that *politics and politicians are always corrupt* serves only to increase the apathy of citizens who might contribute to improve society. Starting from this perception, Burke's longer draft of a public letter to the stewards of the Bell Club, Richard Champion and William Hale,[70] turns to an eloquent restatement of his defense of politics:

> I therefore wish, that you at least, would not suffer yourselves to be amused by the Style, now grown so common, of railing at the corruption of Members of Parliament. This kind of general invective has no kind of Effect, that I know of, but to make you think ill of that very institution, which do what you will you must religiously preserve, or you must give over all thoughts of being a free people. An opinion of the indiscriminate corruption of the house of Commons will at length induce a disgust of Parliaments. They are the corruptors themselves who circulate this general charge of corruption. It is they, that have an Interest in confounding all distinctions, and involving the whole in one general Charge. They hope to corrupt private Life by the example

of the publick; and having produced a despair, from a supposed general failure of principle, they hope, that they may persuade you, that since it is impossible to do any good, you may as well have your share in the profits of doing ill.[71]

Every member of a political association like the Bell Club should be capable of determining whether public men are looking to the nation's interest. Burke does not retract his earlier asseveration that members of Parliament must judge as members of an assembly at the center of a great empire. Yet the people must judge the performance of the members of Parliament themselves.

The public interest is too great a thing for the ministry alone to fathom or define:

You will therefore not listen to those who tell you, that these matters are above you and ought to be left entirely to those into whose hands the King has put them. The publick interest is more your Business than theirs; and it is from want of spirit, and not from want of ability, that you can become wholly unfit to argue or judge upon it. For in this very thing lies the difference between free men, and those that are not free. In a free Country, every man thinks he has a concern in all publick matters; that he has a right to form, and a right to deliver an opinion upon them. They sift, examine, and discuss them. They are curious, eager, attentive, and jealous; and by making such matters the daily subjects of their thoughts and discourses, vast numbers contract a very tolerable knowledge of them; and some a very considerable one. And this it is, that fills free Countries with men of ability in all Stations. Whereas in other Countries, none, but men whose Office calls them to it having much care or thought about publick affairs, and not daring to try the force of their opinions with one another, ability of this sort is extremely rare in any station of Life. In free Countries there is often found more real publick wisdom and sagacity in Shops and manufactories than in the Cabinets of Princes, in Countries, where none dares to have an opinion until he comes into them. Your whole importance therefore depends upon a constant discreet use of your own reason. Otherwise you and your Country sink to nothing.[72]

This charge to the people to exercise their independent judgment—as if docility were a vice more dangerous than insubordination—could have come from Thomas Paine. Nor does Burke leave any question that he includes the humbler sort of people in his call for self-respect and honest judgment among the "vast numbers" who have "a very tolerable knowledge" of politics. It is the unbought use of individual reason by the people that ensures the moral strength and the survival of a free country. Public spirit and self-reliance are thus seen to go hand in hand. And yet, grafted onto the aristocratic virtue of integrity, which the people are asked to inherit, is the spirit of enterprise characteristic of the professions; and Burke's choice of adjectives for the people at their proper work, "curious, eager, attentive, and jealous," contains a revealing echo of his description of American lawyers: "acute, inquisitive, dexterous, prompt in attack, ready in defence, full of resources."

This was only one side of an alternating mood in Burke regarding the sentiments of the people. His letter to the stewards of the Bell Club speaks unreservedly for his hopes; and the passage quoted above was rightly identified, by Jürgen Habermas in *The Transformation of the Public Sphere*, as a decisive early formulation of the Enlightenment view of the importance of free discussion for a liberal society. Yet Burke was not optimistic. He saw that the people of England had been worked up to a vengeful passion against America. Consider his almost despondent confession in a letter written eight days later: "As far as I can see, nothing but the despair of being able perfectly to destroy the people of that Continent, can effectually root out of the minds of *this* people the desire of doing it. It grows more and more vehement every day; and shews itself in the most ferocious manner, whenever their sole and supreme Judge, *fortune* seems to determine in their favour."[73] The mind of Burke was on the stretch, and the pressure showed.

Toward Peace with America

The events of 1777, culminating in the British capitulation in October at Saratoga, ushered in the alliance of America and France; and from that point on, a settlement of the war on American terms was likely. Burke understood this at the time, though the war's end and recognition of American independence lay almost six years off. The manner of the British defeat at Saratoga counted as much as the defeat itself. Forces under General Burgoyne in Canada failed to unite with those under General Howe in New York and lost a chance to cut off New England from the lower colonies. The unfamiliar terrain of the new continent for an occupying and invading power, and the flexibility of the continental army under General Washington, allowed the Americans to assert and maintain command of the lower Hudson Heights, while Burgoyne was overmatched and outmaneuvered to the north. The separate British victories won by Howe in Philadelphia, New Jersey, and the middle states were gains that could not be consolidated. From the default of this initial attempt at mastery, it was clear that the British could remain in America only as a harassing agency. Eventually they would leave because they could leave. The Americans, fighting on land they had proved their own, would stay.

The campaigns of the British and the French in the West Indies belong to a partly separate history, some of which is told in Chapter 6. To the North American settlers, the war of Britain against America and France seemed a single contest, but for the British, including those who had wished to conciliate America, the two engagements were discrete. Burke, like Fox, believed that the war with France had to be won, even as measures were taken to give up the British claim against the rebelling colonists.[74] In 1781, British hopes from the victory in Charleston and the assumption of control in South Carolina and Georgia were stopped by the surrender of Cornwallis at Yorktown. The negotiations that began soon after would be premised on American independence and would run from the fall of 1782 until September 1783—also the period of transition from the Shelburne–Rockingham to the Fox–North administration. The alliances of the time were shifting and uncertain, and in the second Rockingham administration, the negotiation of peace with America was complicated by internal administrative tensions. Shelburne was, in effect, the king's agent, and he controlled powers of patronage that Rockingham would have seemed entitled to. This led to a rivalry that crossed into other disagreements with a larger political basis.

The two secretaries of state, Shelburne and Fox, initially held out different terms for peace. Fox was willing to admit American independence as a precondition. Shelburne was unwilling partly because he hoped to avert a total break with the colonies: he nursed the fantasy of a special privilege of trade for the mother country, and this died slowly. But American affairs could be the province of Shelburne's office only so long as America remained part of Britain; once independence was recognized, that responsibility would pass to Fox and augment his dealings with Spain and France. There was one further complication: it was known to all the actors that George III did not want to recognize American independence.

When Rockingham died in July 1782, Fox resigned and Shelburne was left to form his own administration. He now began his retreat on America but with skillful deliberation; in the process, he gave America substantial territorial settlements to offset the influence of France. The very length of the negotiations doubtless helped persuade George III to an acceptance of terms at last. But Shelburne, all along, had been secretive in his arrangements: a misjudgment (though entirely in character) which led him to deny in the House of Lords that independence was inevitable even as the younger Pitt—now a member of the cabinet speaking in the House of Commons—made the recognition of independence in the preliminary treaty unqualified and irrevocable. Burke and Fox, having separated themselves from Shelburne, were denied much influence on the final settlement with America; to the Foxites, along with the followers of North, fell the ungrateful task of half-denouncing the treaty for unnecessary concessions even as they accepted it.[75] By the end of the negotiations—whatever the delusiveness of Shelburne's belief in securing America as a younger partner in free trade—a generous peace with the colonists was not a matter of choice.[76] Fox and Burke requited the ingenuity of Shelburne by passing a censure against him. Two days later he resigned.

But the unrealistic hopes of reconciliation with America—the alternating moods of despair and groundless optimism—were shared by more than one party. A memorandum written by Burke in March 1782 (before Shelburne took charge of his own administration) and a speech he delivered in February 1783 (when the Fox–North ministry was on the verge of supplanting Shelburne) suggest the durability of the expectation that the rift within the empire would somehow be healed. In the manuscript note entitled "Hints of a Treaty with America," Burke flatly declared that "As to the Terms, if many of us were to settle them, the negotiations would be very short. The Terms would be just what America, no longer irritated, should think best for her own advantage. Because we are very clear that such would not differ essentially from those which Great Britain for her own sake ought to desire."[77] This note is an internal party document, to be scrutinized by persons to whom awkward truths can be told, yet the sheer, table-clearing generality of the dismissal is a sign that relevant doubts have been tranquilized. And yet, just a year and month later, he could denounce Shelburne's peace terms as a disaster of unwarranted concession—a result that would have seemed impossible if America's desired terms and Britain's really differed so little. France, as Burke charged against Shelburne in his *Speech on Preliminary Articles of Peace*, "has obtained Tobago and St. Lucie in the West-Indies, a dangerous extent of fishery, all the forts and islands in Africa, and a district in the East-Indies, which cannot fail to render France a formidable enemy." Spain, in turn, had been given Florida and promised West Florida and Minorca. And America? "To America we have given an unlimited extent of territory, part of the province [of] Canada, a right of fishery, and other extraordinary cessions."[78] One may look again at the mood of wonder in which Burke had once said, "My rigor relents. I pardon something to the spirit of Liberty." The pardon was real, but it was also contingent, and it was irregular. It always had to fight against Burke's suspicion of what would happen if "anarchy is found tolerable."

Amid this confusion of motives and tactics, George III had his eye on Burke, whom he thought a useful man for the new ministry; but this could be managed only if Burke would detach himself from Fox, whom the king intensely disliked for private reasons. (Public ones would follow.) Burke's choice of loyal adherence to his party in the face of such an opportunity may seem by now an old story. Encomiums, at all stages of his life, prepare one for the superlative mode, but none would ever surpass the eulogy by General Burgoyne on December 17, 1782. "Gratitude did not come up to the true magnitude of the feelings he experienced towards [Burke], and he reverenced him the more because he knew the real source of his attachment to proceed principally from a generous concern for the unfortunate, and a disinterested feeling for the oppressed and persecuted."[79] It is not the usual language of a defeated general in an imperial war. In ways that could be perceived but remained more often tacit, some of Burke's most attractive qualities came to inhabit the politics of those who admired him.

❧ VI ❧

Democracy, Representation, and the Gordon Riots

O N the floor of the House of Commons on December 3, 1777, during a silent pause in the debate on General Burgoyne's surrender at Saratoga, Burke laughed out loud, and Alexander Wedderburn, the man he had laughed at, offered to teach him a lesson. Opportunity had taken Wedderburn from Burke's party to the position of solicitor general in the North administration: the men were former allies but had never been friends. Burke responded on December 3 with a formal note. Making his compliments to "Mr Sollicitour General," he observed that he was not conscious of needing any lessons in manners, but he was "perfectly willing to receive" them whenever Wedderburn should appoint "and at what place he thinks fit. He will bring a friend with him. Mr Burke will also have a friend."[1] This draft was never sent—a reticence that saved a life perhaps. "As there was something in your manner," ran the note that Burke did send, "of promising to instruct me in good manners, which seemed to me to imply more than the words directly expressed, I conceive I am justified in desiring an explanation, so far as to let me know whether by those words you meant to convey a menace. I have the honour to be, Sir, your most obedient and humble Servant." Wedderburn took advantage of the loophole.

The aggression on both sides of this encounter is partly explained by the fact that Wedderburn had once been a Rockinghamite, but one known to play for the main chance; as soon as he became solicitor general, his criticisms of the North administration were completely silenced and the tenor of his comments changed to unintermitted apology and counter-accusation. But this was more generally a time of tension, when political rivalry often crossed into personal enmity. Fox (in November 1779) and Shelburne (in March 1780) would fight duels and come away wounded.[2]

The good of self-restraint in the face of destructive passion may be taken as the central doctrine of Burke's politics in the critical years 1777–1783. It connects his activities in three related contexts: Irish resentment of subordinate status when America seemed to be proving that rebellion could succeed; pressure from the county associations for parliamentary reform, whose mass petitions called for expanded suffrage, abolition of corrupt boroughs, and more frequent parliaments; and the anti-Catholic insurgency of the Protestant Association, which would spur the Gordon Riots. All of these public and popular agitations—from a suppressed nation, a democratic movement, and the backlash of a religious majority—set up an imposing challenge to Burke's conception of the statesman as one who hears the alarm and finds the remedy for popular discontents. The statesman, Burke supposed, would do this by calling on the energies of responsible men. But that general belief had a practical corollary: the people may require the heat of discontents (as William Burke summarized Edmund's thinking) in order to "be taught wisdom and discretion by sober men"

A decade after Burke published *Thoughts on the Cause of the Present Discontents*, the tools offered by party and statesmanship alone were beginning to seem a thing of the past. It was less plausible for the House of Commons to imagine itself the "express image of the feelings of the nation" once the people could embody an image of themselves. Burke's inventive powers were taxed to justify an aristocratic party of opposition when the resistance of the American colonies bore witness to democratic stirrings that could no longer be ignored. Yet Burke believed as strongly in 1779 as he had in 1769 that the people ought not to suffer passively and that Parliament ought to heed their legitimate grievances. Did the country paradoxically require some threatened or actual disorder for non-revolutionary reform to appear as reasonable?

Ireland, 1778–1780

Burke in these years, however, was occupied as well on a second front. He had taken an active early part in the campaign for Irish free trade. His *Two Letters on the Trade of Ireland* was published in 1778 to justify the concessions he offered to Ireland on the floor of the House of Commons.

With American trade now lost, Burke had said, Ireland became the chief dependency of the crown; and though it could not extort from England a change of policy, its reasonable demands ought to be looked to. So, in speeches of April 7 and April 9, he supported the granting of permission to Ireland to export goods directly to the colonies, and also to export goods that had first been legally imported into Ireland. His stand prompted expressions of concern from Samuel Span, writing on behalf of the Merchants Hall in Bristol, as well as from a loyal supporter, Joseph Harford, who saw the political risk that Burke and his party were taking. An enlarged trade for Ireland would mean smaller profits for Bristol. "There is a dreadful schism in the British nation," Burke replied, and since "we are not able to reunite the empire," the old strategy of reliance on force that drove the Grenville and Townshend measures should at least be put aside. "Our measures *must be healing.*" As for the loss to English ascendancy in trade with Ireland: "The world is large enough for us both. Let it be our care, not to make ourselves too little for it." Fear of France was much in his thoughts in 1778, and Ireland was a friend of England in a contest that would outlast the American war: "Ireland has been called upon, to repel the attacks of Enemies of no small power."[3]

In the two years that followed, his engagement was less public and visible. Comparative neglect of other demands was a necessary effect of the economy of attention that the American crisis dictated; and an effort to terminate the war by the granting of American independence was his main business. Besides, the political ground in Ireland had shifted. The initiative for reform (centered on free trade but not confined to that issue) now lay with the Irish Volunteers: a loose confederacy of militias, numbering as many as 60,000 at their peak, who in 1778–1780 offered a "patriot" defiance of the British government, echoing the Court and Country language of the old Whig opposition. The Volunteers were Protestants and stood for Protestant liberty only, as Burke warily recognized. Yet they were a public force of ponderable value, given their American sympathies; and their drills—which exhibited patriotic readiness while implying menace—ostensibly done to resist a French invasion, afforded a visible counterweight to ministerial authority. As Conor Cruise O'Brien puts it: "The Irish Volunteers were a standing demonstration that Whigs could be pro-American and anti-French at the same time: a point it was important to make, and difficult to get across, once the French had become the allies of the Americans."[4] Hence Burke's equivocal response to the Volunteers, or rather, his interest in distinguishing the phenomenon from the political work it performed.

Through the tumultuous months of 1779, Burke had heard himself accused of standing aloof from Ireland; and when in 1780 a bill relieving Nonconformists from the Sacramental Test (which had long excluded them from military and civilian office) was returned without demur from London, the words of Henry Grattan would mark the change of mood: "no power on earth but the King, Lords, and Commons of Ireland was competent to make laws for Ireland."[5] This was, in effect, a declaration of independence, even if the words preceded the actual achievement of legislative and judicial independence under Grattan's leadership in 1782.

Burke did not look warmly on that prospect of political independence as a next step. The loss of Ireland would be a devastating blow after the loss of America: he thought the empire better for its several parts, just as the parts were better for being joined to the empire, and he had not supported independence for America until the only alternative became a protracted war. For Ireland, as for America, the throes of independence would bring violence, which a reformer ought never to choose except in the face of the greater violence of war.

Lord North surprised the Rockingham party in 1779 by outbidding them in the attempt to appease the Volunteer agitations. With an expedient resourcefulness he had not shown in America, he offered a limited satisfaction to the protestors. Britain would secure the loyalty of Ireland by a pair of well-oiled legislative measures, one encouraging the growth of tobacco, another giving bounty on exports of hemp. While these were debated, Burke retreated behind the scenes, and his politic withdrawal was portrayed in Ireland as a sign of lukewarm friendship. He would explain his obedience to the Rockingham policy a year later, in 1780, in his *Letter to Thomas Burgh,* choosing once again to defend his conduct in a public letter to a known ally, as in the Bristol *Letter* of 1777. Burgh was a member of the Irish House of Commons who had informed Burke of the manner in which his silence was misunderstood and denounced. In reply,

Burke recalls in detail his earlier exertions for free trade. His tactical retreat was a response to the seasonable interest in Irish trade by the North ministry, which sought to buy off popular opinion just when Ireland, by the massing of the Volunteers, could seem to be threatening a second front in the war. Burke has no regret that his party refused this extortionate lure. The Irish opposition was shortsighted and opportunistic, he says, in siding with the ministry. Such tactics are cynically conceived, and they hurt the cause of liberty.

By 1780, Ireland was asking less energy from everyone since the crown was now favorably disposed. But the work of a party depends on relative judgments of emergency. That the American war is winding down, says Burke, is in some measure a result of his party's choice to subordinate other issues to peace. "Had the crown pleased to retain the spirit with regard to Ireland, which seems to be now all directed to America, we should have neglected our own immediate defence, and sent over the last man of our militia, to fight with the last man of your Volunteers."[6] So Burke asks his Irish friends to estimate their grievances less parochially; for the cause of British liberty seems to him at this moment the cause of mankind. "If liberty cannot maintain its ground in this kingdom, I am sure that it cannot have any long continuance in yours"; and Irish protest should not have submitted at so cheap a price to the ministrations of Lord North. Even as he reproves the censure of his critics and gives a considered account of his support of Irish causes, Burke praises Ireland for a volunteer army "new in its kind, and adequate to its purposes. It effected its ends without its exertion. It was not under the authority of law most certainly; but it derived from an authority, still higher; and, as they say of faith, it is not contrary to reason, but above it; so this army did not so much contradict the spirit of the law, as supersede it."[7] Two thoughts here jostle uneasily. Burke affirms that the Irish Volunteers acted as the voice of the people and gave the alarm when conventional monitors were useless. Yet there is something strange in his congratulations. Spontaneous justice and its salutary menace appear to be honored by Burke as a force that supersedes the law (though only in special circumstances). That is an uncharacteristic drift of thought. Elsewhere in his writings, the self-restraint necessary for extending liberty is made almost identical with a law-abiding spirit. It is surely wrong of him to suggest that the Volunteers could stand for the people, since Catholic rights held no part in their ambitions and calculations. Burke, in fact, is flirting with vigilantism. He will do so again, in 1792–1794, in both the English anti-revolutionary and Irish revolutionary contexts. This anti-legalistic vein of comment may be an essential part of Burke's power as a social critic, but here the words are feckless, as is the mood: he feels himself qualified to declare precisely which illegal agencies truly represent liberty. It is a metaphysical presumption and foreign to the deeper strength of his thought; and yet, his major purpose in the exchange with Burgh is undeniably peaceful. To obviate violence will bring a substantial good, beyond the benefit of saving lives, since it prepares the way for civil liberty. The Volunteers, as Burke judges them, served liberty the better for marshaling a force which they were not quick to use.

The result has helped to preserve the republican part of the constitution. And in this way, Ireland has done something to revive "the grand use and characteristic benefit of Parliament, which was on the point of being entirely lost amongst us." Irish resistance worked in this instance, and gave point to the appeals of the Whig opposition in the Commons. But a popular movement and a party are always discrete entities. It may happen that a formed opposition and a movement of reform press toward the same end, but they have to work on separate paths. Burke and Fox together could not have "shortened the credit given to the crown to six months" and "hung up the public credit of your kingdom by a thread," as Ireland did by refusing to raise taxes while its popular leaders declared an emergency. "You certainly acted in great style, and on sound and invincible principles," Burke says with deadpan irony. The cost to Fox and himself of doing the same would have been universal opprobrium: they would have been accused of delivering the nation "bound hand and foot to a foreign enemy." Nor are the Irish "patriot" resisters well advised in their longer views. They have curried favor with the king and despised the prudence of the opposition.

But in this public letter, earnest as it is, Burke is hiding part of his recent history, or perhaps forgetting it. The Rockinghamite coolness toward the 1779 demands on trade was not only a concomitant of their absorption in American affairs and their distrust of the ministry; it also fell in with their idealism regarding the need for consistency in assertions of parliamentary sovereignty. On May 5, Rockingham had visited the king and informed him that England had an interest in establishing the free importation of Irish grain, along with Irish export of coarse woolen cloths; but at this moment Burke himself had opposed his leader's consideration of Irish interests: four days later he advised Rockingham against concession and urged a return to the party's guiding maxim of constitutional balance. The duty of government was to inquire into and remove all the causes of grievance, and

> the Troubles in Ireland ought to be seriously lookd into, as all National discontents ought to be; and on the question of removing them, the Course of equity, Justice, and moderation is far preferable to that of ill Temper and rigour. But in Gods Name where is the Necessity that Parliament should lose all appearance of Grace and dignity in the manner of making its concessions? Fallen we certainly are; and a pompous language ill becomes our Condition; but still there is a decorum, even in the humility of decayed greatness, which ought never to be parted with; it is a possession which fortune cannot take away; and I do not see why we should wantonly throw it out of our hands.[8]

The lament was doubtless sincere; but why set such store by the forms of dignity when the content of the measure was already agreed on? The answer relates to an unspoken element of Burke's thinking—unspoken because it had been internalized and was hardly subject to challenge. Burke, writes P. J. Marshall, for all his foreboding, "believed Britain neither could nor should renounce sovereignty over Ireland, America, or India." The function of a statesman was to ameliorate but not to undo the existing pattern of governance, and thus "to moderate the exercise of that sovereignty in ways that he believed would be in the best interest of both Britain and those over whom Britain ruled."[9]

As it looks back on the ambiguities of the preceding months, the *Letter to Thomas Burgh* sounds a note of indignation at the cunning of the ministry and the fickleness of Irish patriots. "That you should make the panegyrick of the ministers, is what I expected; because, in praising their bounty, you paid a just compliment to your own force: but, that you should rail at us, either individually or collectively, is what I can scarcely think a natural proceeding."[10] If, to the power brokers of the empire, politics is nothing but crass jobbery, to the dissidents in Ireland it is coming to be a disorderly series of ultimatums. As Burke saw it, his speaking on different sides in 1778 and 1779 was never done to weaken Irish interests but rather to protest against the tactics employed to split the opposition. The appropriateness of his policy, centered on his party, and the difficulty of showing his reasons to political actors of a narrower understanding prompt him to write finally to Burgh of the connection between his politics and his place of birth.

In these closing reflections, Burke admits the depth of his disappointment at the bigotry of the Volunteers. Their energy promised something better; and he repeats now for an Irish audience what he has said in England:

> When I came into this Parliament, just fourteen years ago . . . obscure and a stranger as I was, I considered myself as raised to the highest dignity to which a creature of our species could aspire. In that opinion, one of the chief pleasures in my situation, what was first and uppermost in my thoughts, was the hope (without injury to this country) to be somewhat useful to the place of my birth and education; which, in many respects, internal and external, I thought ill and impolitically governed: but when I found, that the House, surrendering itself to the guidance, not of an authority grown out of experience, wisdom, and integrity, but of the accidents of court favour, had become the sport of the passions of men, at once rash and pusillanimous,—that it had even got into the habit of refusing every thing to reason, and surrendering every thing to force,—all my power of obliging either my country or individuals was gone; all the lustre of my imaginary rank was tarnished, and I felt degraded even by my elevation. I said this, or something to this effect. If it gives umbrage to Ireland, I am sorry for it.[11]

But more proud than sorry. He always looked on himself a little as a benefactor to Ireland, an intercessor and lawgiver. Ireland, in turn, looked on him as a go-between, defective in promptness and regularity.[12] In both apprehensions there was a high degree of misplaced expectation and fantasy. The fault lay in the situation, not the actors, but it may account for the extremes that Burke is liable to touch in his dealings with Ireland: a sense of justice both personal and selfless, and suppressed anger at ingratitude.

There were advances for liberty in Ireland, however, which owed less to the threat of violence. The Irish Toleration Bill had been passed by the Privy Council on July 24, 1778, and on August 14, Burke wrote to congratulate Edmund Sexton Pery: "You are now beginning to have a Country; and I trust you will complete the Design." Security of property must be its foundation; and as the building rises, "quite other things will be done" than would be imaginable if the cause depended on violent men who combine the hope of particular reforms with zeal "for the distress and destruction of every thing else." His only regret concerning the bill is that the reform is not more complete.[13] Pursuing the subject in a letter to Garret Nagle, Burke congratulates his cousin on the passage of the toleration bill by the Parliament of Ireland: though "not quite so large and liberal as that adopted in England upon the same subject," still the reform contains "a principle, which in time will extend further." Irish Catholics must now concert their political energies and make "a judicious use of opportunities"; but "You may now raise up your heads, and think yourselves men. The mark is taken off." This is said with genuine warmth, from a distance the writer does not intend to close. Until the early 1790s, Burke's services for the Catholic interest in Ireland would be not so much a personal commitment as a duty of necessary diplomacy. Still, he thought himself guided, as he wrote on August 14, 1779, to Dr. John Curry by "an uniform principle . . . I mean an utter abhorrence of all kinds of public injustice and oppression, the worst species of which are those which being converted into maxims of state, and blending themselves with law and jurisprudence corrupt the very fountains of all equity and subvert all the purposes of Government."[14]

His engagement in the Catholic cause belonged with his larger obligations to justice itself. He therefore went out of his way, in the late 1770s, to warn against disorders since other reforms have excited the hopes of Catholics: "All that I wish, is, that you would not return hostility for benefits received; but that you would in general keep yourselves quiet." Let the Catholics of Ireland be contented with the slowness and sureness of gradual reform. And yet Burke could not suppress himself entirely—he was always an imperfect example of the wise passiveness he recommended—and we can find a clue to his thoughts by looking ahead two years. In his

Letter to a Peer of Ireland on the Penal Laws against the Irish Catholics (1783), Burke shows all the indignation he asked others to keep subdued; and we may suppose the anger exhibited here was operative in him when he saw anti-Catholic prejudice erupt in London during the Gordon Riots.

Asked his opinion by Lord Kenmare in a letter of February 4, 1782, concerning a bill for Catholic relief lately introduced by Luke Gardiner, Burke (now a member of the Privy Council in the second Rockingham ministry) made a reply, which he allowed to be published in Dublin the following year.

> To look at the Bill in the abstract, it is neither more nor less than a renewed act of universal, unqualified, indispensable, exceptionless, disqualification. One would imagine, that a Bill inflicting such a multitude of incapacities, had followd on the heels of a conquest made by a very fierce Enemy under the impression of recent animosity and resentment. No man, in reading that Bill, could imagine he was reading an act of amnesty and indulgence, following a recital of the good behaviour of those who are the Objects of it, which recital stood at the head of this Bill as it was first introduced, but, I suppose, for its incongruity with the body of the piece, was afterwards omitted. This I say on memory. It however still recites the oath; and that Catholics "ought to be considerd as good and loyal Subjects to his Majesty, his Crown and Government". Then follows an universal exclusion "of those good and loyal Subjects" from every (even the lowest) Office of Trust or profit, from any Vote at an election, from any privilege in a Town Corporate, from being even a Freeman of such corporation, from serving on Grand Juries, from a Vote at a *Vestry*, from having a Gun in his house, from being Barrister Attorney or solicitor &c &c &c. This has surely much more the air of a table of proscription than an act of grace. What must we suppose the laws concerning those *good* subjects to have been, of which this is a relaxation?[15]

He adds to his protest a note on the laws against the foreign education of Catholics. "The protestants of Ireland feel well and naturally," Burke says, "on the hardship of being bound by Laws for which they do not directly or indirectly Vote. The bounds of these matters are Nice and hard settle in Theory; and perhaps they have been pushed too far. But how they can avoid the necessary application in the Case of others towards them I know not."[16] If, that is, Irish Catholics have helped Great Britain by their loyalty during the American war, why should they not expect some reciprocal assistance? And when they find that such help does not come, how can they fail to conclude that resistance and not loyalty is the language understood by the empire?

In Defense of Admiral Keppel

The record of the years 1778–1782 suggests that the Rockinghamites held no more power over Ireland than they did over America. Even a well-wisher as solid as Lord Charlemont, the organizer of the Volunteers, could see the weakness of their position; and answering a request from Rockingham, in early 1782, to adjourn the Irish Parliament prior to their declaration of right, he wrote back in a sympathizing strain: if he were to give way "in a matter so very repugnant" to the people's wishes as the urgency of legislative independence, "we, whose power of support consists principally, if not wholly, in our popularity, might have endangered that influence, which, upon the expected and necessary redress of all our grievances, we wish to employ in your behalf." Not that he distrusts the Rockingham administration: "I look up to you," he tells the marquess, "with the most unbounded confidence, a confidence founded on a thorough knowledge of your principles, and your wisdom. We ask but our rights—our uncontrovertible rights."[17] Charlemont could see in advance that the second Rockingham administration would hold as frail a tenure as the first. But while it stood in opposition in 1779, the party sealed its unity by a symbolic triumph. It succeeded in rallying popular opinion around Admiral Keppel when his honor was impugned by a slanderous accusation.

The episode began with rival accounts of a naval battle that did not proceed according to plan. On June 12, 1778, Keppel had set sail from Portsmouth to take charge of patrol of the Channel. Encountering a group of French cruisers, he gave chase, inflicted damage on the *Belle Poule,* and seized two other French ships. The papers found on board showed that his own twenty ships of the line were not, as he had estimated at a cursory view, slightly outnumbered but vastly overmatched by the thirty-two ships of the line that France had waiting in Brest harbor. Entrusted with the fate of the British navy and unwilling now to risk its survival against such odds, Keppel reluctantly turned back to Portsmouth. Though Lord Sandwich accused him of a party interest in overrating the size of the French fleet, Keppel at this moment was trusted and still relied on by the government; and when, in the first week of July, his forces were augmented by the Mediterranean and West Indian merchant fleets, he set sail again with thirty ships of the line, with the resolve this time to fight the battle he had been denied.

Keppel sighted the French fleet to the west of Ushant and gave the signal for a general chase; four days later, with the two fleets still in view of each other, Admiral d'Orvilliers on July 27 turned at last and engaged. After several hours of battle followed by repairs, Keppel gave orders to return to combat, but his subordinate, Sir Hugh Palliser, seemed not to have heard. When urged by a summons sent by frigate, Palliser once again did not follow the order; the fight was never re-engaged, and by the next morning most of the French fleet had disappeared. There, initially, the matter rested, Lord Sandwich in a note to Keppel vouching for the king's approval of his conduct. But as rumor of the battle swelled and divided on party lines, Palliser came to be widely credited with success in the fight while it lasted; and he abetted the fiction, first by asking Keppel to affirm that he had never called for renewal of the battle and, when this was refused, by giving an account to a newspaper in which he appeared as the adventurous hero and Keppel as a timorous commander who postponed the battle. Keppel now made explicit the details he had spared earlier from a sense of loyalty and delicacy: that his order to engage had not been obeyed by Palliser, "not in the evening only, but from three in the afternoon until eight at night."[18] On December 11, Palliser gave formal notice to Parliament of the articles of charge against Admiral Keppel, which he had submitted to the Navy Board at Whitehall and which produced the order of a court-martial.

In the event, Keppel would be judged by a court of five admirals and eight captains. The trial ran from January 7 to February 11, 1779, and ended in his acquittal. Burke himself had helped compose the speech that Keppel delivered in opening his defense. The victory was celebrated by a small riot in the after-midnight hours, an attack on Sir Hugh Palliser's recent place of residence in Pall Mall, and a pursuit that finally stormed the gate of Whitehall and attacked Palliser's windows there. It went on to the prime minister's house in Downing Street before being dispersed. As a token of thanks for support, Keppel gave several copies of his portrait by Reynolds to friends who had assisted him during the court-martial, including Burke; in a note expressing thanks for the gift, Burke on November 6 would profess toward Keppel a feeling of both humility and affection. It is a rare note, for him, pointed by a rarer encomium: "I shall leave to my son, who is of a frame of mind to relish that kind of honour, the satisfaction of knowing that his father was distinguished by the partiality of one of those who are the marked men of all story, by being the glory and the reproach of the times they live in, and whose services and merits, by being above recompence, are delivered over to ingratitude."[19] Keppel's honorable service, the abandonment of him by an ungrateful faction, and the party's solidarity in the rescue of his fame—these facts along with the mutual gratitude of friendship would carry an extraordinary resonance for Burke in his last great work, *A Letter to a Noble Lord*.

County Petitions and English Volunteers

Christopher Wyvill, an Anglican clergyman, founded the Yorkshire Association in 1779. Already at that time, he had a view to making it a national association that would serve as a sort of shadow parliament, honest and zealous for the improvement of the constitution. Before the Yorkshire meeting of December 31, 1779, the Rockingham party had prepared its own petitions, but in deference to Wyvill's plans they did not circulate these. He returned the favor by inserting in the Yorkshire petitions a reference to the danger of the influence of the crown—the central concern of the Rockingham party. Yet there was a critical difference between Wyvill's movement and Burke's party. Wyvill aimed to achieve parliamentary reform. This was a radical demand around which the Rockinghamites could not coalesce; but Wyvill had no intention of backing down. He proposed first annual, then triennial, parliaments, with 100 county members to be added to the House of Commons. Within the Rockingham group, the Duke of Richmond backed such parliamentary reform. Burke fiercely opposed it. Thus, a public difference emerged between two emphases that both went by the same general name: on the one hand, reform of representation in Parliament; on the other hand, reduction of the prerogatives of the crown.

The latter emphasis Burke called "oeconomical reform." It may be that he hoped to convert the energies massed for the first kind of reform into a means for perfecting the second. But the choice also depended on whom one identified as the adversary. Was it members of the House of Commons who failed to acknowledge their dependence on those who elected them? Or was it "the crown"—the monarch as embodied in his administration? Economic reform—the campaign that issued in Burke's Civil Establishment Act of 1782—may seem at this distance an elaborate stage effect. J. C. D. Clark has written of Burke's "synthetic indignation" in response to an admission (by one of the Lords of the Admiralty) of the unspecified destination of appropriated sums in Commons grants. Such wariness is justified;[20] and the *Speech on Economical Reform* itself will bear marks of divided purpose. It is a work of inside satire, and the tone of Burke's ridicule is genial at times. Yet Burke's central idea, as John Woods has noted, places him at the start of the series of changes whose next stopping place would be the Reform Bill of 1832.

The Rockingham policy for limited reform, as it developed, was the result of a necessary coalition with Shelburne; but Shelburne was struck by the deep prejudice against reform of representation that he saw in Burke. "There is no dealing with Mr Burke," he concluded; "he is so violently attach'd to his own opinion that there is no arguing with him, and he has got so much ascendancy over Lord Rockingham that I protest I see no method of doing anything."[21] The hostility was mutual. Burke suspected with warrant that Shelburne acted more from loyalty to the king than to his coalition partners. He had balked at the recognition of American independence; yet during the Gordon Riots he would come close to excusing the rioters.[22] Fox held Shelburne in comparable disesteem. After the death of Lord Rockingham, he would resign alongside Burke rather than serve in a Shelburne administration.

But more than personal animosity was at work. The turn to domestic reform by Burke and his party cannot be viewed apart from an anxiety stemming from the loss of America. War destroys more than its architects foresee or its apologists admit, and its worst harms are never immediately apparent—a weakening of the belief in justice that operates without violence, and a degradation of feelings in those who have come to confuse justice with retaliation. Not to let persuasion turn into force was a dictum Burke sought to apply in the most diverse settings. But even here one must take note of tactical adjustments. One of the strongest letters of this period, written to Richard Champion on August 22, 1779, gives his opinion of a ministerial measure to support the Bristol Volunteers as a patriotic counterweight to the Irish Volunteers. The group had been trained as a local militia, but an order had lately gone out for "a vast number of Pikes to be dispersed about the Country"; and in Burke's view, this gave away the game. "What could a miserable Rabble, armed with weapons not much better than Pitchforks, do against the Cannon, firelocks, and Bayonets of regular and well appointed Troops?" The government did not trust the people enough to arm them well, only enough to excite them to displays of violence against conjectural enemies.

So, tactically, Burke advises his friend Champion to go along with the scheme and to arm their friends of the opposition with weapons equally sturdy. If, however, "you do not find resolution and union enough," he advised Champion to lie low and wait "until the whole people come to their Senses." Nine months before the Gordon Riots, Burke seems to look on England as a country on the brink of civil violence; and his reply of August 29 to Champion is explicit on this point: "If the party armament which you stated as proposed by the Tories should take place, on the plan first mentioned, your associating to arm yourselves would, in my opinion, be nothing more than what absolute and immediate domestick defense against a declared domestick Enemy required." He is almost as explicit in saying that acts of violent resistance are now justified in self-defense against the tyrannical authority of the crown.[23]

At this disturbing moment, Burke began to think more closely about the political concerns of Christopher Wyvill. It was becoming clear that the passions of the county petitioners could not be brought under the supervisory efforts of the Rockingham party. The Duke of Richmond entered into the association cause and frankly sympathized with its demands, but he was taken on as an ally and not as a guide. Why (the party asked) were they less popular than Wyvill's association? Burke sought to answer the question in a meeting with the Duke of Devonshire, and summarized his explanation in a letter to Lady Rockingham on October 3, 1779. If, he said, the ministry was despised, yet the feeling was "without any proportionable desire of a change of men." Loose libels and the familiar clamor for patriotic unity had cast upon all parliamentary inquiries a suspicion of encouraging Britain's enemies. "Absurd and puerile" as such insinuations are, Burke found them "generally prevalent," and this should be a warning: the people cannot be trusted to lead the resistance against abuses they hardly understand. Burke himself, as we shall see, meant to divert the petitioners on parliamentary reform into support for his plan of economic reform.

Writing to the Duke of Portland on October 16, 1779, he says that the gentlemen of the party ought to forgo all language suggesting that they have a right to represent the counties whose parliamentary seats they hold; their authority now "ought to be begged, not demanded," since, in the nature of popular feeling, "the dread of great family powers, sustained with haughtiness, and seeming to be borne out by the power of the purse, will always be natural objects of apprehension." At this moment above all, the opposition must appear as unlike the king as possible. Quite apart from the offense of taking its supporters for granted, the party has failed to control and benefit from the discontents, and for a usual reason: "dilatoriness" and "the want of a spirit of adventure." Their lethargy may kill the interest in their policies more effectually than any political defeat could do. Yet there is no sign, anywhere in the correspondence, that he shared a particle of Richmond's radical intentions: to enfranchise every man of twenty-one years and upward and to divide the kingdom into districts of 1,000 voters for each member elected.

A fair gauge of Burke's party diplomacy is his letter of April 12, 1780, to the chairman of the Buckinghamshire meeting. This was a semi-official statement, its claims bounded by party consensus, but it is also among the most revealing expressions we have of Burke's general beliefs. He writes to the county chairman as a constitutional moderate, urging respect for the apparent disproportions in the constitution and warning against the clamor for sudden and extreme remedies. "I will not deny," writes Burke, "that our constitution may have faults" or that the faults ought to be corrected; yet the English constitution has rightly been a touchstone for other countries:

> It is not everything which appears at first view to be faulty in such a complicated plan that is to be determined to be so in reality. To enable us to correct the constitution, the whole constitution must be viewed together; and it must be compared with the actual state of the people, and the circumstances of the time. For that which, taken singly and by itself, may appear to be wrong, when considered with relation to other things may be perfectly right; or at least such as ought to be patiently endured, as the means of preventing something that is worse. So far with regard to what at first view may appear a *distemper* in the constitution. As to the *remedy* of that distemper, an equal caution ought to be used; because this latter consideration is not single and separate, no more than the former. There are many things in reformation which would be proper to be done, if other things can be done along with them; but which, if they cannot be so accompanied, ought not to be done at all.[24]

The warning against an exaggerated ratio between distemper and remedy anticipates a famous phrase of the *Reflections* concerning a "distemper of remedy." As Burke puts it there: "An irregular, convulsive movement may be necessary to throw off an irregular, convulsive disease," but before prescribing strong medicine, the physician ought to take care and look to the total health of the patient.

These remarks to the Buckinghamshire meeting give a great deal of authority to precedent and tend toward the preservation of the system. The reason is that it *is* a system—though its purpose is hardly discernible from any single detail, and the meaning of some details emerges only by their relationship to others. We ought then to treat the constitution with the respect owed to a man-made contrivance that has become part of our nature. Yet it seems wrong to feel toward an institution the same sentimental attachment we feel for human beings; and Burke, in 1780, is scrupulous not to take that second step. Rather, he defers to common feeling: "The people may be deceived in their choice of an object. But I can scarcely conceive any choice they can make to be so very mischievous as the existence of any human force capable of resisting it."[25] By human force he means a human agent: a magistrate or minister or judge or militia. The people should always be restrained by laws. Yet bad laws must be changeable at last by a persistent show of contrary will by the people.

When Burke's positions of the late 1770s and early 1780s are analyzed closely, he emerges as a moderate for whom every change must conform to the principle of constitutional liberty. Yet his associates might be pardoned in these years for thinking him a fellow traveler of the Americans and Dissenters. On a visit to Joseph Priestley in early 1782, he would admire Priestley's library and laboratory (later to be burned by a church-and-king mob); he described the scientist and Unitarian divine as "the most happy of men, and the most to be envied." A year later the radical pamphleteer William Godwin would eulogize Burke for his "ardour for the common weal." Godwin's defense of reason against popular violence and state coercion in the 1790s made him for a time the theoretical mentor of the first Romantic generation. When young, he had read the speeches of Burke as well as Fox, and he thought them incomparably the greatest men of their time—a loyalty that outlasted every political change in Burke.

Cruel Punishments

There was never anything moderate in the way a spectacle of injustice could drive Burke to act immediately; and one can judge the susceptibility of his conscience by his response to one of the smaller mobs of the year 1780. On April 10—two months before Lord George Gordon brought his petitioners to London—an assault was made on two prisoners who stood helpless in their body manacles. One of the men was killed; and in the House of Commons the next day, Burke addressed the terrifying episode. Four days later, he wrote to Wedderburn, the attorney general, asking on behalf of two others in similar cases that they be excused from the pillory. "These wretches desire in my opinion a thing which, I will not say in humanity; but I really think in Justice, cannot be denied to them; that their punishment should be nothing more than it is the intention of the Law to measure out to them; I am sure it is hardly in the power of the attending Magistrates to do this if the men are once in the Pillory, and the Mob from wantonness or Malice begin to be unruly."[26] Burke in his speech in the Commons employed the same argument against the legal standard on sodomy that he would apply to the enforcement of anti-Catholic laws. The law depends on an informant, yet anyone may be doubted who offers evidence in a matter as private as religious belief. So, too, "of all other crimes," sodomy is "a crime of the most equivocal nature, and the most difficult to prove."[27]

These comments were noticed outside the House. The *Morning Post* in its issue of April 13 and 14 ridiculed Burke for his tenderness toward the victims; and the same account applauded "the spirit of the spectators." On May 31, Burke struck back with an affidavit in the King's Bench: he believed the purpose of the attack on himself was defamation and calumny; the tendency of the articles in the *Morning Post* was "to encourage the people to Commit Murder" against homosexuals. For the moment he pressed no further, leaving the law to take its course. A year later came the judgment by default, with a sentence of three months' imprisonment against the author of the articles, William Finney. We should not mistake this pursuit of justice for an aberration or the effect of temper or the mood of a moment. Five years later, Burke had occasion to make similar remarks on "a nearly similar occurrence," as Prior describes it. When the slander against himself was repeated, he again brought an action against the printer and was awarded damages in the amount of 150 pounds.[28]

America, Ireland, London

At the turn of the decade, the effects of the American war and the Irish discontents were pressing close to home. How severe was the threat, and what was its character? Herbert Butterfield thought there was a perceptible continuity from the "semi-revolutionary crisis in Ireland" in autumn 1779 to the agitations of the county "movement of extra-parliamentary opinion" to the debate on Burke's proposals for economic reform and its tactical sequel in April 1780: John Dunning's resolution to diminish the increasing power of the crown. Butterfield's book, *George III, Lord North, and the People, 1779–80*, is partial, and its argument remains controversial: it has been said that this historian mistook "a portent for a crisis."[29] What if Burke and others in his position also mistook a portent—or several converging portents—for a revolutionary crisis? Butterfield's map of these harried months is valuable because it captures the confusion and fears of the time; and it does so from a perspective whose suspicions and imputed linkages correspond in a high degree to those of Burke's party. Whether or not the crisis of 1779–1780 ought to be seen as having the kind of coherence Butterfield detected, the Rockinghamites certainly thought that it did, and they were within the bounds of plausibility in thinking so.

A letter from Burke to Edmund Sexton Pery, speaker of the Irish House of Commons (August 12, 1778), exemplifies the inspirational temper of his reformist appeal about this time: "You are now beginning to have a Country; and I trust you will complete the Design. You have laid the firm honest homely rustick of Property; and the rest of the building will rise in due harmony and proportion. I am persuaded, that when that thing called a Country is once formed in Ireland, quite other things will be done, than were done whilst the Zeal of men was turned to the safety of a party and whilst they thought its Interest only provided for in the distress and destruction of every thing else. Your people will begin to lift up their heads and to act and think like men."[30] Burke's ameliorative habit of thought comes out plainly in the common-sounding but unusual phrase *to act and think*. A people who can follow such advice are ready for liberty.

The American war had damaged the economy of Ireland through suppression of the illegal trade in woolens. (Ireland's trade with France was another casualty.) If the "distresses" of the country were not entirely on the surface, they were nonetheless pervasive: rents that could not be paid to landowners; failures among bankers, factory owners, and merchants; "the sinister starving crowds" (Butterfield's words) of the Dublin streets. England also suffered and people blamed the war, but here there was no threat of armed insurrection; whereas in Ireland, callous mismanagement could be seen to have emanated from a foreign source. To choke the trade with the American colonies, England had put an embargo on all exports from Ireland, and even when it was lifted, many restrictions stayed in place. As often happens in war, an emergency measure passed into acceptance as the normal way of doing things.

Even Catholics, forbidden to bear arms, supported the Irish Volunteers. The movement had the necessary resources to maintain pressure and a significant ally in the Irish Parliament in the person of Henry Grattan. By mid-November 1779, according to Butterfield, "we see . . . all the ingredients of the great upheaval which was to put London into a state of terror in the following summer."[31] A crowd of as many as 4,000 gathered on College Green, claiming to have been "summoned by an inflammatory letter signed 'A Member of Parliament'"; and there were rumors of assistance to come from armed men out of the north. Magistracy failed to dispose of the threat: the crowd reappeared in subsequent days and was not ordered to disperse. By November 16, things reached a pass at which John Monk Mason, the friend of Burke, would write that "I cannot venture to go down to the House without manifest danger of my life"—adding that the threat appeared to have no visible termination.[32] A Dublin opposition paper threatened rebellion on the pattern of America if the insurgent demands were not soon met, and the suggestion was made that a shipment of wool be sent to defy the British naval prohibition and await the result. These warning signs were glimpsed and dodged by John Beresford, commissioner of the Irish Revenue, and by the secretary of the treasury, John Robinson, who portrayed Lord Lieutenant Buckingham as the culprit. Lord North clinched the counterattack by seeking the voluntary resignation of Buckingham.

It was at this moment that Charles Fox came into his own as a political leader. His speech of November 25 warned of the hidden danger to England from its neglect of the grievances of the Irish associations—"the Whigs of Ireland," as Lord Lyttleton had called them. Such men, observed Fox, "detest tyranny, and execrate despotism," and they disclaim as slavish the doctrines of passive obedience and non-resistance:

> When the last particle of good faith in men is exhausted, they will seek in themselves the means of redress; they will recur to first principles, to the spirit as well as letter of the constitution; and they can never fail in such resources, though the law may literally condemn such a departure from its general and unqualified rules. . . .

> "He most" heartily regretted that any cause had been administered which seemed to justify violence and resistance; he dreaded the consequences, however justifiable in their origin, or moderately or judiciously conducted; but whatever the effects might be, he was ready to

acknowledge that such a power was inherent in men; as men and citizens it was a sacred trust in their hands, as a defence against the possible or actual abuse of power, political treachery, and the arts and intrigues of government; and when all other means failed, resistance he should ever hold perfectly justifiable.[33]

Fox spoke as a commoner vigilant on behalf of the people, not an out-of-doors demagogue looking in at the House. Opponents of George III "were not without resources"—so Butterfield describes the background of Fox's speech—for they were willing "to turn from the normal game of parliamentary politics, and to look for allies in what as yet was only a sort of *demi-monde*. If they wished to summon unrecognized forces to their help, however, they did not need to search in closets and cellars, but went out into broad daylight, for their one remaining hope lay in market-place and in countryside, in the unmeasured power of extra-parliamentary opinion."[34] Neither the politics of Rockingham party nor their prudential strategy would have come so far without the embarrassments of Ireland.

Recall a detail of Fox's speech. When pushed too far, men will "seek in themselves the means of redress; they will recur to first principles, to the spirit as well as letter of the constitution." The familiar invocation of the right of resistance could be signaled without having to be spoken. The impending fulfillment of that right in America delivered a message in battle reports more eloquent than any quotation from Locke. "Now was not the moment," Butterfield sums up, "for that conservative type of whiggism which avows that a revolution is unthinkable." The larger part of the Rockingham Whigs were prepared to step closer to revolution by the threat of violence.

The quasi-revolutionary tactics worked only too well, and their success became a trouble for the Rockinghamites. For Lord North felt compelled now to offer concessions to Ireland of an unpredictable generosity—we have taken a view already of the reaction to this within the Rockingham circle—and he thereby stole the credit for the liberal policy he had once obstructed. "All woolen manufactures whatsoever," he proposed on December 13, "or manufactures made up, or mixed with, wool or wool flocks" should have their restrictions lifted.[35] There was an accompanying repeal of the prohibition on export of glass, and trade was to be opened from

Ireland with British colonies, both those in America and in the West Indies. The ministry regarded opposition of any kind as a further incitement to Ireland; and the contest over principle thus dwindled to a contest of maneuver. Another complication had entered in when France combined with Spain to initiate a blockade of Gibraltar: fears of invasion were thus confirmed. They were heightened when Admiral Hardy fled from the pursuing Franco-Spanish fleet and did not stop before he passed the mouth of the channel for safe anchorage in Spithead. Keppel's flight, for which he wrongly faced a court-martial, had taken place just a year earlier.

The movement to extend the right of representation of freeholders could seem in this light a translation of the external threat. It had begun in Middlesex, the Wilkesite stronghold, and like the agitations of the 1760s, it sprang from an effort by Wilkes to make the most of an election controversy. But the new movement brought with it a large band of ready pamphleteers, more potent now and less divergent in motive than those of a decade before. John Jebb, in "An Address to the Freeholders of Middlesex" on December 20, 1779, spoke of the "right of the people to new-model the constitution"[36] (the verb *new-model*, a coinage that revived a memory of Cromwell, would lodge in Burke's mind and be added to the satirical vocabulary of the *Reflections*). Middlesex raised its protest over representation, Yorkshire over the waste of public money, and Yorkshire took the lead. With Middlesex once allied, the Yorkshire Association had grown strong enough to call for a county meeting on December 30 to discuss the waste of public money. On December 15, Burke announced his intention to address Parliament on the same subject.

The Reverend Christopher Wyvill and Reverend William Mason were co-instigators of the agitation. Their language (later adapted by Thomas Hill of Leeds) bore a generality of emphasis that was nicely offset by its provocative tone: the "unconstitutional influence" of the crown was an evil "which, if not checked, may soon prove fatal to the Liberties of this Country."[37] The December 30 meeting was advertised by Rockingham in the House of Lords as an expression of the large propertied interest. Some of the voices at the meeting told a different story. A Mr. Pritchard (quoted by Wyvill) asked, "Was it love for Ireland that made Lord North so anxious to hurry the Irish bills through Parliament? No—it was 64,000 bayonets pointed at his heart." The Yorkshire meeting declared itself an instrument for moving Parliament "to reduce all exorbitant emoluments" and "rescind and abolish all sinecure places and unmerited pensions." An additional resolution was passed "to carry on the necessary correspondence for effectually promoting the object of the petition and to support that laudable reform, and such other measures as may conduce to restore the freedom of parliament."[38] The mention of *correspondence* may sound vague, but its meaning was unmistakable. It meant the right to assemble and to publish and circulate political writings.

Nor was the ferment confined to Dissenting ministers and country gentlemen who had read republican treatises. From a London newspaper, the *Public Advertiser*, on November 2, 1779 (a few weeks before Wyvill's meeting in December), there issued this symptomatic utterance: "Let us in our Turn, unite in some Manner as the Irish have done, something, however, short of their Rebellion; let us constitutionally commune together." A letter signed by "The Whig" on November 27 in the *London Courant* predicted that the people would "vindicate the country, correct their parliament, and reform their throne. . . . *In England, every man is a politician.*"[39]

The Duke of Richmond at this time was expected to lead a movement that would reach into Parliament. The suggestion began to be heard again that parliamentary opposition ought to secede. (The Americans and the Irish Volunteers were held up as examples.) Sir George Savile sought to curb the tendency of Wyvill to accumulate names for the sake of the numbers; how they were obtained, he said, would soon become a question; but Fox now sharpened the focus of the protest. As Butterfield says, Fox "helped to bring eighteenth-century whiggism into touch with the more drastic seventeenth-century doctrine—with the view that in the last resort the enemies of entrenched power must be prepared even for revolutionary action."[40] Yet Fox differed from Burke not by his willingness to credit the doctrine of the last resort but by his perception that they were nearing such a moment. He was ready to see the people and the parliamentary opposition join as political equals. Burke, by contrast, believed that the party still had a duty to channel, and if necessary to divert, the energies of the people.[41]

The bill for economic reform that Burke brought forward in 1780 would offer a synthesis of the popular complaint against the waste of public money and the Rockinghamite concern with the excessive influence of the crown. Cynically, but with fair success, North moved day by day and clause by clause to grind down the bill on technicalities. When at last he subtracted the proposal of parliamentary control over the civil list, it signaled the defeat of Burke's leading cause. All the while, North maintained the forms of apparent agreement with Burke, which were more galling than outright hostility. He conceded the right of petition, even if only from three persons—a gesture apparently munificent, in fact derisory. It took Savile to emphasize once again the substantial propertied interest backing the petitions. For the collaboration of party and petitioners to triumph, both groups needed to be wary of petitions that bound the members of Parliament to certain measures: Burke's objection to mandates applied as surely as it had five years before. But the people disclaimed any menace and any wish to dictate. These were peaceable applications toward reform—as might be deduced from the works most in request by the rank and file, such as James Burgh's *Political Disquisitions* and Major John Cartwright's *Take Your Choice*.

Wyvill moved to London in January 1780, and from that point the Yorkshire movement took its identity from the London group around him. On February 21, Lord North defeated (by two votes) Savile's motion to require the showing of the list of pensions granted by the crown; this was viewed by petition committee members as a rejection of one of two main objects of the petitions. Even so, a range of grievances was now in play: rotten boroughs, the duration of Parliament, the reform of representation toward a more democratic franchise. On March 11, a meeting of the leaders of the movement resolved on three goals: to gain an honest examination of public spending; to add to the representation 100 members of Parliament; and to institute annual parliaments. The first point elicited greater consensus than the latter two, and Rockingham felt compelled to argue explicitly against subjecting parliamentary candidates to political tests: popular movements should not create an artificial consensus and disguise it as the voice of the nation. But the radicalism of democratic representation was in the air. The Westminster committee (led by Fox) began in March to press beyond Wyvill's demands; soon Buckinghamshire joined; Cambridge was not far behind, and Wilkes at the Cambridge meeting on

March 25 offered to present petitions to the House of Commons. He was greeted by the old cheer, "Wilkes for Ever." Shelburne, on the Wiltshire committee, went so far as to assert that the rights of the people were more binding than acts of Parliament, and he credited the county meetings with more legitimacy than the representation in Parliament in its present state ("the mere child of Accident or Intrigue").[42] Burke's response to this last display of demagogy can only be guessed; diplomacy, such as he was capable of, necessitated an unshockable pretense, but the cold fury of the reproach he would unleash a decade later against Richard Price (one of Shelburne's intellectual associates) may have had a source in this earlier encounter. Did Burke come to think that by going too far in 1780, the theorists and petitioners, acting together, had spoiled the chances of practical reform?[43]

Compromise within the alliance was not always possible and not always honest. Thus the Yorkshire movement gave in to Rockingham and supported triennial rather than annual parliaments; but Rockingham did not (as he had agreed) press for the change to triennial. As the debate on economic reform went on, Sir Fletcher Norton, the speaker of the House, spoke against both Fox and Burke for the preservation of the civil list. He added a very qualified support for Burke's Establishment Bill (while dissenting from "the abolition of the several royal domestic establishments," which was central to Burke's design of the cutback). On March 20, Governor Pownall also spoke against Burke's design of economy for the king's household. At the defeat of this plan, Burke declared that he would not "put his weak and disordered frame and constitution to the torture, in order to fight his Bill through the House inch by inch, clause by clause, and line by line." The reversal on the king's household was critical; Burke had no interest in partial salvage of his design by the abolition of a few offices.

As larger hopes receded, the popular threat and parliamentary discussions jostled each other uneasily. During the debate of April 6, the Third Regiment of the Guards were kept on duty till a late hour in case of demonstrations (this was the day of Westminster's second assembly), but no disturbance occurred. When, on May 8, that act of preemptive vigilance was looked into, Burke would denounce the supererogation of the authorities who had ordered the guards; but on the day itself, April 6, Fox and not

Burke marched with the people and, in a stirring speech, accused George III of a policy of *divide et impera*. He also gave his pledge to add members and reduce the duration of Parliament. The debate on April 6 itself altogether changed its shape when Dunning cited the East India Company as one source of the corrupt influence of the crown; and with the petitioners unavoidable out of doors, his resolution carried: "That the influence of the crown has increased, is increasing, and ought to be diminished."

That a majority in the commons actually voted in favor of the proposition seems inexplicable unless many supporters of George III harbored grave reservations about his influence. Butterfield made this point, and it is hard to explain away. But who could have guessed in advance the extent of such doubts? It was no inferior deputy of Wyvill's but Horace Walpole who said: "I adopt the whole sentence [not excluding *and ought to be diminished*] into my revolution-creed."[44] For a time it was even supposed that the success of the vote against the influence of the crown had rendered Wyvill's association unnecessary. Yet Dunning made it clear in his encomium that he founded his resolution on the comprehensive case made out by Burke. The task was "big with labour and difficulty"; it took in "the most important objects, extensive, various, and complicated"; and only the talents and ingenuity of Burke could have drawn into coherence what to others "must have proved a vast heap of ponderous matter." Dunning noted with dismay that the bill at first seemed to command the universal assent of the house. The negatives he thought originated outside the house; you had only to look at the defeated clauses: the one abolishing the third secretary of state, the one abolishing the treasurer of the king's household. Why was the king's household "deemed sacred" and "not to be touched"?[45] As he proceeded, Dunning's moderate endorsement of the theory of the double cabinet picked up support from quotations of non-Burkean provenance: Hume on the euthanasia of the British constitution, Blackstone on the actual increase of crown influence.

Yet this argument against court influence was vague compared to the concrete measures that suffered defeat. Shelburne alluded in an uncertain tone to the people, "clamorous for redress of grievances, ripe for any violence, and easy to be led to such measures as would shake the kingdom to its core." Were these the words of a ringleader or a watchman? Dunning proposed that Parliament decline to be prorogued or dissolved until it achieved its purpose of diminishing the influence of king and correcting "the other abuses, complained of by the petitions of the people." Fox, who some time since had cut out any pretense of politeness, now threatened to secede. He would "never more enter that House" so long as the sentiments of the majority remained as they were and the resolution of April 6 remained only a resolution.

And here the Irish and English histories of 1780 converge. For it was in the first two weeks of April that Grattan asserted his notice of the resolutions declaratory of the rights of Ireland: the repeal of Poyning's Law, by which all enactments of the Irish Parliament except money bills were subject to review by the English Privy Council; a separate mutiny bill for Ireland; the agreement that Irish judges serve during good behavior and that the Irish House of Lords have the right to hear appeals; and the securing of regular money bills to pay for independent parliaments. From the pressure for these reforms and Dunning's resolution, few could have imagined that the turmoil of the coming weeks would issue from so different a cause: the new Relief Act for Catholics in England, introduced on May 25, 1778, and passed by government and opposition together. Yet, in reaction, early in 1779 a Protestant association had formed in Scotland to respond to a similar proposed measure there, and riots in Edinburgh and Glasgow had set back the move for Catholic rights. This capitulation the House of Commons refused to take as its precedent; and Lord George Gordon must have seemed an improbable candidate to lead a movement. Yet the incendiary action of the anti-Catholic rioters took place in a scene of protest already set by the petition movement. Gordon had been active in the Scottish anti-Catholic campaign and was invited to be the head of the English Protestant Association on November 12, 1779, by those who in London a few months earlier had founded the latest petitioners' association.

Portents of 1780

In retrospect, Gordon's rise to prominence forms a grotesque underplot of the debates of the House of Commons in late 1779 and early 1780. Indeed, Gordon's irregular appeals for the licensing of vigilante action ran parallel to his hero Burke's ascendant campaign for economic reform. In early December 1779, Gordon had placed before the House a motion for the defense of the Protestants of Scotland. Why, he asked, did the secretary of state reject the application to arm loyal and faithful subjects of North Briton as volunteers with His Majesty's blessing? Charles Jenkinson, the secretary at war, replied that the offer was generous, but the ministers thought the country's defense well provided for without additional help. On December 15, Burke gave notice of his plan of public reform and economy in a speech lamenting "the fatal and overgrown influence of the crown," which has produced "nearly general indifference to all public interests." This influence "has now insinuated itself into every creek and cranny in the kingdom," and it could be depended on that "those who are negligent stewards of the public estate will neglect everything else." A ministry like this will soon surround "a supine and inattentive minister with the designing, confident, rapacious, and unprincipled men of all descriptions. They are a sort of animals sagacious of their proper prey; and they soon drive away from their habitation all contrary natures." While Burke declares himself not averse to a degree of influence, he strikes a note as alarmist in its way as Gordon's: "Is not every one sensible how much that influence is raised? Is not every one sensible how much authority is sunk?"

By the time of the parliamentary debate on February 8, the salutary menace or stimulus of popular movements was being evoked to distinct effect by Gordon and Charles Fox. The parallel with the Irish Volunteers was in every mind when Fox asked: "Is there one law for the associations in Ireland, and another for those of England?" Why, he wonders, should North treat the Yorkshire petitioners as a threat? The people, after all, "have in their power, legal, constitutional, peaceable means of enforcing their petition. . . . No, Sir, let not the mild but firm voice of liberty be mistaken for the dismal and discordant accents of blood and slaughter." But even as he disclaimed violence, he spoke of the people by themselves "enforcing" the demands of the petitions.

Another branch of the people (for whom Gordon spoke on the same day) was forming into associations with a common grievance: "against the toleration of Papists in every part of the British empire; Ireland, Scotland, and England, were alike averse to the measure; the most dreadful consequences were to be apprehended, if the ministry obstinately persisted." Gordon spared from his strictures both Savile and Burke, whose motives he thought pure, but he reminded them that "where the happiness of the people was concerned, the interest of individuals should always give way." In response to the charitable exemption, Burke rose to confront Gordon. Let it never be supposed that he could be used by government as a cat's paw, for "there are cats so fierce, indocile, and intractable, that it would not be safe to meddle with their paws." Then from Burke came an astonishing declaration: "The noble lord thinks that my conduct with regard to the disciples of the church of Rome did not proceed from any religious considerations; and in this he imagines he pays me a compliment; but the noble lord is mistaken. I was influenced by religion. The only religion I profess is that of universal humanity and benevolence."[46] With Burke in 1780, the significance of certain words lies deeper than accident. To profess no religion but "universal humanity and benevolence" was to promulgate the very doctrine that Burke would charge against Richard Price in 1790, after Price delivered his radical *Discourse on the Love of Our Country*. In the later setting, and with toleration offered not to the Catholics of England but to the rioting democrats of France, Burke would see such a pledge as betraying the speaker's ignorance of human nature or his monstrous alienation from it. The truth is that the process of popular agitations from 1780 to 1790 seems to have wrought a thorough but largely unconscious reversal in his own view.

The debate of March 2 on Lord George Gordon's "Motion for taking the Petitions of the good People of England into consideration" brought explicit recognition of the contending bodies of petitioners. Gordon indicated his agreement with the Yorkshire movement "that reformation should precede taxation." Burke for his part denounced the king's spokesmen Rigby and Wedderburn for conveying nothing beyond a general concession to freedom of parliamentary discussion; and he now moved several steps closer to Fox:

> The people must do what parliament had refused, or rather what they were resolved not to do, or had declared themselves incompetent to effect. . . . A fracture properly healed, acquired strength, superior to

any other part of the bone. The crown held no public right, or public property, but as a trust for, and under the people. . . . It was therefore to the last degree absurd to draw a line, or separate the private rights of an individual, or any description of men, as held for any other end but for the good of the whole community; every right his Majesty enjoyed, as sovereign, was a delegated right, and consequently subject to examination, correction, and controul.[47]

Such were some of the shadows the year 1780 would cast on Burke's plan of economic reform and on the resolution by Dunning that marked its climax and termination.

Speech on Economical Reform

The *Speech on Economical Reform* is neither Burke's most impassioned nor his most closely reasoned speech. It is, however, one of his canniest, and in the conduct of the argument it may be his most politic. The shimmer of expertise and self-possession suit his idea of the proper deportment of mastery close to power. And yet, for just this reason the speech is, of all his major performances, perhaps the least characteristic. No other speech by Burke appears so little troubled by things it cannot adequately frame in words. There is a humor and sport, almost joviality, in the polished exuberance of the man of affairs who believes the world has reason to think well of him. At the same time a sense pervades the speech that this trimming of the king's budget is merely expedient. In the background is the threat of the king surrounding himself with a sinister and corrupt set of helpers who are given legitimacy and financial buoyancy by nothing but their sinecures; though Burke would also have realized that the convention of blaming the king's ministers instead of the king himself worked against the possibility of a more radical criticism. Between the lines of the practical proposals, one may catch glimpses of the connection Burke might have drawn between the imperviousness of the king's friends and the clamor of petitioners out of doors. It is fair to ask of any single functionary—groom of the stole, lord of the bedchamber, gentleman yeoman—whether the king uses him or he uses the king as a private resource. The weight of these middlemen has become harder to gauge because their servility is an open secret. A general dislike of them goes with general toleration; but Burke believes they constitute a temptation that ought to be removed.

Political reform, to Burke, was never a process amenable to the calculation of mere numbers; nor is it a work for the *spectator ab extra*. To reform a society is partly to remake it, and this presumes a thorough knowledge of the existing materials. A reformer is something like an architect who respects the site of renovation; in the *Speech on Economical Reform*, Burke will imply the relevance, too, of a painter's knowledge of scale and perspective: "Reformation is one of those pieces which must be put at some distance in order to please. Its greatest favourers love it better in the abstract than in the substance."[48] Even where corruption has become a usual topic of denunciation, a strong remedy incurs distrust from the very people who have demanded it. Any sudden change brings forward unfamiliar arrangements; and by most people the unfamiliar is less trusted than the familiar.

Burke accordingly promises he will pare away only the excessive features of the king's budget. Even this degree of consistency, he knows, is liable to meet with a demur: "all parsimony is of a quality approaching to unkindness." He resolves to make the attempt anyway to remedy "our political circumstances," by which he means at once the threat posed by France and "the demands of the people, whose desires, when they do not militate with the stable and eternal rules of justice and reason (rules which are above us, and above them) ought to be as a law to a House of Commons."[49] The English people are to be treated with forbearance, as the Americans ought to have been treated. You cannot indict a whole people. Nor does he propose to limit the freedom of dissent, except where the protesters violate higher laws of humanity. The present is a case of understandable agitation for reform in a time of adversity.

France, treated with suspicion from the first of this speech, comes in for unexpected praise owing to the reorganization of its treasury under the Swiss banker Jacques Necker. The director-general of finance in the years 1776–1781, Necker used his expert knowledge of credit to subsidize the American war, and favored public disclosure and discussion of the state of the king's finances in order to gain support for economic policies.

This would precipitate his fall from power in 1781 with the publication of the *Compte rendu*—as little appreciated by Louis XVI as Burke's plan of reform was by George III—but whatever disapproval the method might risk, Burke believed such open assessments were a pattern for drawing informed support to government. It troubles him that England, though a free state, may have lost "the spirit of that complex constitution which is the foundation of confidence"; whereas France, a monarchy and unprotected against despotism, may "furnish a foundation for credit upon the solidity of its maxims," notwithstanding the vicious character of its institutions. The contest of "noble emulation," which Burke recommends, must therefore begin by admitting a paradox: "The French have imitated us; let us, through them, imitate ourselves." This oddly anticipates his arguments of 1790 against the French example: the French, he will say in the *Reflections*, have misunderstood English liberty; let us not, through them, misunderstand ourselves. But in 1780 the case appeared different. He goes so far as to say of the king of France: "These are the acts of a patriot king." The salutary French adoption of an English model shows why England should go further along the same lines.

A mischievous thought is lurking here. Can it be that the speaker, even as he delivers the compliment, is teasing his opponents and wondering at himself? Lord Bolingbroke's fantasy of a "patriot king"—the selfless leader who stands above party and faction—was perhaps the largest illusion chased by George III. It seduced him to act in spite of parties; this phantom independence had been inculcated on him in early years by Lord Bute. Yet (Burke asks us to notice) it took the French to put the ideal into practice. The allusion may suggest that the idea of a patriot king is wrong, but at the same time it insinuates that the result has made France a dangerous enemy. England can still claim the advantage of a mixed constitutional system. It holds in reserve one check which even parliamentary incapacity has not removed: the people. But the people are—to repeat the language of *Thoughts on the Cause of the Present Discontents*—a check and not a control. Burke alludes to the county petitioners who will receive full acknowledgment at the end of his speech; for now, he salutes not their wisdom but their good sense, or rather their sensibility to abuse: an awareness of the causes of discontents, which they cannot be wrong to show. Burke, unlike the county petitioners, will reject the idea of parliamentary reform, but he prefers to emphasize here the extent of his concurrence.

Replying to the accusation that he is a demagogue, he says: "I cannot indeed take upon me to say I have the honour to *follow* the sense of the people. The truth is, *I met it on the way,* while I was pursuing their interest according to my own ideas."[50] A curious echo of a famous exchange in *Henry IV:*

> *Worcester:*   I do protest
>   I have not sought the day of this dislike.
> *Henry IV:* You have not sought it! how comes it, then?
> *Falstaff:* Rebellion lay in his way, and he found it.

How lucky (it seems to say) that Edmund Burke found reform on his way and not rebellion: happy for England that he met the people, and is willing to teach the method of reform. Another leader might have drawn them toward revolution.

Seven maxims, says Burke, have determined the changes he hopes to introduce. He proposes (1) to abolish all jurisdictions that are centers of corrupt influence (which are temptations to oppression rather than advantages to justice or administration) and (2) to abolish all public estates that vex and overawe those who live under them without offering substantial benefits to revenue. Meanwhile, in line with assessments of utility case by case, he will (3) do away with offices that cost more than they are worth, and consolidate those that can plausibly be joined with others. In order to centralize authority for spending, he will also (4) abolish all offices that obstruct the superintending of finance, while (5) establishing "an invariable order of payments, which will prevent partiality." Finally, his plan (6) reduces every establishment and every part of every establishment to clarity regarding its spending allowances and limits; and in keeping with this rule of certainty, the plan will (7) dissolve all subordinate treasuries, which "have a tendency to perplex and distract the public accounts." So far as possible, the management of the entire budget will be under a single control. Burke's design, then, calls for the reduction and simplification of the king's possessions, of his superfluous privileges, and of the scope of his personal authority.

One example brings out the method underlying these proposals. The five principalities—England, Wales, Chester, Lancaster, and Cornwall—in 1780 were counted as separate entities, each with its extra offices. Burke would abolish them by uniting all five to the crown, under the ordinary jurisdiction of the crown. Another example: forest lands owned by the crown are to be offered for sale, with the exception of houses, gardens, and other places kept for the habitation of the king himself. With the selling of these lands, the need would vanish for such expensive offices as that of surveyor general; indeed, by becoming private property, the lands (says Burke) will come "into our better understood and better ordered revenues." If his case for such large adjustments is allowed, the extreme contraction he proposes for the royal household follows naturally. For the household has fallen away from its feudal dignity: "It is shrunk into the polished littleness of modern elegance and personal accommodation. It has evaporated from the gross concrete, into an essence and rectified spirit of expence, where you have tuns of antient pomp in a vial of modern luxury."[51] Household spending has grown in quantity and dwindled in purpose until its only function is the dignity of the king. Yet that function Burke sees now as deserving not solemn deference but ridicule: his argument airily empties the vial containing a splendor that defies utility.

He gives more particular grounds in the debate of March 20 on the clause for abolishing several household offices. Among them was treasurer of the chamber: "the very first office of the household," says Burke, that he had "laid his fingers on," because if it were shielded he knew that nothing could be changed. Yet his principle was not to "restrict the quantum of money to be expended in support of the household" so much as to take

care that what was expended should be wisely and oeconomically laid out, and that fraud should no longer prevail in those who served his majesty with provisions, nor the cost be large as it now was, of those who were paid for preventing that fraud. He contended, that at present the system of oeconomy, which had been introduced into his Majesty's kitchen, was such that even a rat could not have cheated the cooks, scullions, &c. of a scrape of cheese, but at the same time nothing was saved by the system, because the expense of paying cheats to watch cheats, was so great, that it amounted to more than it could possibly cost his Majesty, if he was handsomely cheated at once.[52]

The aim, then, was administrative, in a larger sense than is implied by jealousy of the superfluities of privilege. Burke sees a danger in the crown's reliance on officers whose self-interest stemming from patronage sets them at odds with the public interest.

From a personal point of view, the most significant feature of Burke's reform turned out to be the economy it imposed on the awarding and disbursement of pensions. When, in a later year, Burke himself accepted a pension, his apparent jealousy of pensions in 1780 seemed a contradiction that invited comment. Yet the truth here is commonplace. He did not propose to take away any pension. Since, for the giving of pensions, the king was appointed by the constitution as sole judge of merit, Burke thought it best to refrain from interference: even if justified, such removals would depart from his purpose. His plan, rather, called for the budget to cooperate with nature's attrition. The change would be put in place as the old pensioners ceased to draw upon the budget, with a reduction from 100,000 pounds to 60,000 per year. This comes to a modest retrenchment, and such was his aim: "incitements to virtuous ambition" ought never to be cut off, and the reduction will not have that effect. Nor does Burke wish to inquire closely into the deserts of those who receive pensions after long service to the state. "They must at length have a retreat from the malice of rivals, from the perfidy of political friends, and the inconstancy of the people." The promise of such protection, Burke knew, was among the distinct rewards that public service offered in compensation for its trials. Still, he anticipates someone asking, why not destroy offices that are pensions in themselves and "appoint pensions under direct title in their place?" The answer is the rule of parsimony—never multiply entities without necessity—which is supported by a certain psychological conservatism. Never remove an innocent practice or an institution of some value "in hopes of getting it back in better shape." Always try to reduce excess, but always do it slowly.

The history of the legatees of pensions is instructive. "When we look over this exchequer list, we find it filled with the descendants of the Walpoles, of the Pelhams, of the Townshends; names to whom this country owes its liberties, and to whom his majesty owes his crown." The loftily ironic closing phrase is a delicate touch, a superfluous, small reminder that there are constitutional superiors to George III. Yet Burke serves the king by every salutary economy he presses on him. And as the above names suffice to recall, not all the accessories of majesty are excess: "Many of the great offices have much to do, and much expence of representation to maintain. A secretary of state, for instance, must not appear sordid in the eyes of the ministers of other nations." Further, to deprive ministers and ambassadors of a salary would only throw them upon other sources of enrichment, sources so much more tempting to corruption that even "if men were willing to serve in such situations without salary," the appearance of a hidden bargain ought not to be allowed. Burke's insistence on payment for service derives in part from his suspicion of the cult of great men: "That state which lays its foundation in rare and heroic virtues, will be sure to have its superstructure in the basest profligacy and corruption. An honourable and fair profit is the best security against avarice and rapacity. . . . If any individual were to decline his appointments, it might give an unfair advantage to ostentatious ambition over unpretending service."[53] Any leaning toward such cost-free patronage amounts to a "fallacious show of disinterestedness"—as if actual merit should not crave visible recognition. In conformity with the design of moderate parsimony, the king is not to be stripped of the officers attendant on his person. The title of Groom of the Stole (which was Lord Bute's office) may have grown ludicrous, but if such offices were removed, the court would be deserted by the nobility, and who would replace them? After all, "Kings are naturally lovers of low company."

Kings are naturally lovers of low company. A soft explosion there. It is one of the most surprising moments in all of Burke and yet, from another point of view, completely predictable. Here was a reason for allowing the king to keep the paid company of his almost-equals. They afford a sort of politic cushion against what lies beneath. Burke ventures the judgment with a knowingness borrowed from his aristocratic associates; for the great families of the revolution settlement, Newcastle, Devonshire, Rockingham, saw themselves as the natural opposition of the king and indeed as the creators of the king. With this understanding went the judgment that to spend much time in his company signified the reverse of high breeding.

(The younger Pitt, by his cultivation of George III, would betray an unquiet temper that was a mark of upstart ambition.) The really entitled nobility—as Pares sums up their self-image—lived to themselves and among themselves. They went to London occasionally to look in and curb the power of the king. This oversight blended nicely with the prejudice that fortified their habits: aristocratic politics was local.

Yet Burke's sentence about the low predilections of kings could as easily have been drawn from his own observations of inequality. Kings "are so elevated above all the rest of mankind, that they must look upon all their subjects as on a level." This may cause mistakes. To employ the nobility as royal attendants is bad enough, but at least, though they are "perfectly willing" (Burke says) "to act the part of flatterers, tale-bearers, parasites, pimps, and buffoons," a remnant of their dignity and training forms a layer of inhibition. Further down the social ladder, a king may find tools better suited to base purposes; and that is a satisfaction he should be denied. From this point of view, the very inutility of the noble parasites is their recommendation: "Though they are not much better for a court, the court will be much better for them." Burke does not refrain from touching all offices that can show a similar excuse: the office of third secretary of state (secretary for the colonies) is slated for removal on account of its pointlessness. "It is burning day light." This change, however, presumed the recognition of American independence—something still resisted by North's cabinet, Shelburne, and the king.

Closer to Burke's familiar terrain is the tenure held by members of the Board of Trade. Here, with the most inventive wit of the speech, he launches an extended analysis of a superfluous institution. From his dealings on behalf of New York, he had come to know the declared purpose of the board and its actual incapacity: "It is a board which, if not mischievous, is of no use at all." The by-play in the House of Commons that ensued with the discussion of this criticism brings out, as well as any other exchange in his career, the presence of mind by which Burke could parry and neutralize his opponents. On March 13, William Eden said it would be wrong to abolish the Board of Trade without consulting its 2,300 folio volumes of proceedings, "which he would be bold to say contained much important and interesting information." In a brilliant and manic response, Burke thanked the hon. Gentleman for his historical account of the origin and utility of the Board of Trade; he was ready to accept that, but not his 2,300 volumes, which he begged to be excused from taking; he would not look into one of them. They would serve, however, as a monument, under which both he and his clause might be buried, and form a funeral pile for them as large as one of the pyramids of Egypt. Alas, poor clause! (exclaimed he) if it be thy fate to be put to death, thou shalt be gloriously entombed; thou shalt lie under a splendid mausoleum! The corners of thy cenotaph shall be supported by Locke, by Addison, by Prior and by Molesworth.[54]

These worthies at the Board of Trade had all been allowed to devote to the increase of their writings every moment they could spare from the neglect of their duties.

At this point (the parliamentary report indicates), Burke grew more serious and said that he detested the board as a wasteful extravagance, "useless, idle, and expensive," no matter what its utility as an academy of belles-lettres. He paid his respects to Gibbon, Eden, and Lord Carlisle—adding that the accomplishments of the last would have been notable even in an age of true poetry unlike the present. "To the professors themselves he owed all possible deference, and from that deference it was that he wished to rescue them from the ignominy of being degraded to a board of trade." The imprisonment of such men in such an institution puts him in mind of Quarles's *Emblems,* on one page of which he recalls having seen an emblem of death as a skeleton, with the man inside crying out, "Oh! How shall I get out of this strong death?" So are men of letters immured in the skeleton board. But the fancy of Burke was not yet sated: "He afterwards ran into another allegory, and said, he could not but view the Board of Trade as a crow's nest, in which nightingales were kept prisoners; he designed to take down the nest, and restore the nightingales to their freedom, that they might sing more delightfully"; their incomes were "too great for their own good"—as authors, they had become "too rich to write"; and it was well known that "literature declined, in proportion as the incomes of those capable of writing became liberal; this evil he meant to avoid, by lopping off the Board of Trade in time." And now he returned to those 2,300 volumes. Burke refused to "consider them as any part of the productions of the great authors alluded to. He revered literature, but he did not wish to be overwhelmed with it."[55] Thus, a drawn-out jest that began as a lesson in evidence ended with a unique argument: the arts of Britain can best be served by cutting off the choicest of spirits from sinecures that cheat them of their motive to write.

Since Parliament alone has the competence to regulate trade, Parliament itself, says Burke, should serve as the Board of Trade. Here is a thought that will be developed in his East India speech of 1783: regulative authority ought (so far as possible) to be lodged in Parliament; regulation will in this way become visible and accountable. "Parliamentary enquiry," Burke says, "is the only mode of obtaining parliamentary information" (just as impeachment is the best mode of punishing the discoveries yielded by such information), yet he cannot recall having seen a member of the Board of Trade present at a meeting of a committee of inquiry. In fact, members of the board played no part at all, for good or ill, in the attempts at commercial regulation of America which led up to the war. Burke knew this firsthand from his own experience as agent for New York. A practical appeal for government bodies of consequence therefore concludes his "plan of arrangement" to promote a tighter economy. Its leading point is to leave no appropriation of the Civil List money at arbitrary discretion: he recalls once more "the capital end we have in view, the independence of parliament." Creatures of the state should depend on the oversight of a parliament answerable to the people. The people, in turn, show their approval by acceptance and their dissatisfaction by petitions, tumults, and reasonable or violent repudiation.

Burke's plan had one conspicuous liability. In removing so many sources of public corruption, it ran the risk of creating a new field for private corruption, more secret and poisonous than its predecessor. The drawback may have been inescapable, yet Burke is exceedingly wary: payments, on his plan, will be required to pass in a single line so that any irregularity stands out sharply. To make his meaning clear, he ranks appointed judges above all others whose service is indispensable. Judges ought to be *as weak solicitors of their own demands,* as strenuous assertors of the rights and liberties of others," and their expedient payment is meant to assist their impartiality. Next come foreign ministers and after them tradesmen "who supply the crown by contract, or otherwise." Last in the scale are "that mixed mass," the pension list (including "offices of honour about the king"), as well as the salaries and pensions of the chancellor of the exchequer, the first lord of the treasury, and other commissioners of the treasury. The ingenuity of the schedule lies in the way persons in the lowest category will be naturally eager for the payment of those higher up. The reasonableness of the ranking will command support for the self-sustaining economy of Burke's plan.

In the range of Burke's speeches, one finds an enormous variety of stances or tones to suit occasions that are widely disparate. No description will cover the whole range: Burke is myriad-minded and equally himself in the most unharmonizing roles. His justification of the payment schedule shows him responsive to the plodding utilitarian virtues. By contrast, a polished interlude of the *Speech on Economical Reform* offers a travesty of the adventures of the tax collector for the crown in Wales, John Probert. The Welsh, though poor, were canny about the pretensions of this interloper, and their refusal to give up fresh revenues to a salaried and useless functionary becomes for Burke a fable of the necessity of a reduced budget. The old regime of the kingdom knew how to practice a salutary neglect: "The wise Britons thought it more reasonable, that the poor, wasted, decrepit revenue of the principality, should die a natural than a violent death. They chose that their ancient moss-grown castles should moulder into decay, under the silent touches of time, and the slow formality of an oblivious and drowsy exchequer, than that they should be battered down all at once, by the lively efforts of a pensioned engineer."[56] The primitive art of resistance practiced by the defaulting taxpayers in Wales brings to mind the out-of-doors petitioners whom Burke refers to with calculated understatement throughout the speech. Yet his self-confidence here is related to a less admirable quality, an inside skill and suavity that shows the speaker all too sure of his audience. One hears that tone when Burke elaborately teases the king, to the delight of the Commons, about the legal wrangles that an extensive patronage has cost His Majesty. Since the king goes under different names in different neighborhoods, by accident he may enter a legal action against himself: "It was but the other day, that the pert, factious fellow, the duke of Lancaster, presumed to fly in the face of his liege lord, our gracious sovereign; and *associating* with a parcel of lawyers as factious as himself . . . presumed to go to law with the king. The object is neither your business, nor mine. Which of the parties got the better, I really forget. I think it was (as it ought to be) the king."[57] The facetious inside manner ("I really forget") might seem in place in the correspondence of Horace Walpole; taken as the candid utterance of the reformer Edmund Burke, the ease of the touch mars the sincerity of the utterance.

This manner—though Burke handles it deftly—is in a deeper sense perplexing. For it derogates from the weightiness of his purpose. You cannot prove the obstructionist menace of the king while you treat him as a harmless playfellow. The style of the speech as a whole seems, often, too artful and diverting for the asserted gravity of Burke's subject. In his characteristic style or styles, Burke has none of the unctuous familiarity of the higher circles. Was he too sure of himself here?

Yet no speech he ever gave was more generally admired in the House of Commons. His contemporaries were unanimous in approbation of the performance. They lauded the propriety of the undertaking and the merit of the speaker, even as they rejected his proposals. Dunning spoke of Burke's plan of reform as "a monument to be handed down to posterity of his uncommon zeal, unrivalled industry, astonishing abilities, and invincible perseverance." Gibbon said that the bill had been "framed with skill, introduced with eloquence, and supported by numbers. Never can I forget the delight with which that diffusive and ingenious orator was heard by all sides of the House, and even by those whose existence he proscribed." As Prior remarks, this testimony was disinterested; Gibbon stood to lose his seat on the Board of Trade.

But the reservation must be underlined. To repeat: this is the most politic of all Burke's major speeches; and the deliberateness with which he maintains his equanimity is itself a sort of concession. The sporting tone may have served to moderate a radicalism with which many listeners knew the speaker's relations to be disturbingly close. So Burke presented his plan of reform with a dexterous affability, doubtless believing it would facilitate the smooth ascent of the Rockingham party to a second administration. His diction is measured to confirm the rightness of this intelligent wager. And yet the speech, though strong, is not quite in earnest. Judged by his own standard, Burke does not appear to take himself seriously.[58] Reform of the budget, after all, was the policy chosen to deflect attention from the petitioners' other demand: parliamentary reform.

The curious balance in which Burke held the two policies, in favor of economic reform and against parliamentary reform, is brought out when one compares *Economical Reform* (for all its dilution of the radical program) with his several conservative speeches about this time on the latter subject.[59] The most impressive of those (discussed at greater length below) is driven throughout by genuine indignation, and its fighting spirit braces the listener; a note of the polite, the assured, the emollient, nowhere softens the effect. Did Burke sense that his opposition to parliamentary reform would fail in the long run? He certainly knew that, with the loss of the American war, the budget of the ambitious monarch invited reforms of a smaller sort. Economic reform had anyway this to recommend it, that it gave Burke's party an advantage whether they won or not. And on the whole—with allowance for his puffing himself on success too soon—Burke finely adapted his words to the smaller cause. Élie Halévy wrote, in a brilliant phrase, of Burke's "half utilitarian, half mystical" philosophy of reform and preservation. Economic reform is preeminent on the utilitarian side.

Old establishments, as Burke argues here, ought not to be sanctified merely because they are old. A paragraph of accomplished satire with which he supports that view would be appropriated by the revolutionists of 1789 (including Thomas Paine and Mary Wollstonecraft), who lifted his metaphors and gave them a new purpose. From the costume and furniture of government, said Burke, we expect some good to ourselves:

> But when the reason of old establishments is gone, it is absurd to preserve nothing but the burthen of them. This is superstitiously to embalm a carcass not worth an ounce of the gums that are used to preserve it. It is to burn precious oils in the tomb; it is to offer meat and drink to the dead,—not so much an honour to the deceased, as a disgrace to the survivors. Our palaces are vast inhospitable halls. There the bleak winds, there, "Boreas, and Eurus, and Caurus, and Argestes loud," howling through the vacant lobbies, and clattering the doors of deserted guardrooms, appal the imagination, and conjure up the grim spectres of departed tyrants—the Saxon, the Norman, and the Dane; the stern Edwards and fierce Henrys—who stalk from desolation to desolation, through the dreary vacuity, and melancholy succession of chill and comfortless chambers. When this tumult subsides, a dead, and still

more frightful silence would reign in this desert, if every now and then the tacking of hammers did not announce, that those constant attendants upon all courts, in all ages, Jobbs, were still alive; for whose sake alone it is, that any trace of ancient grandeur is suffered to remain.[60]

The phrase on embalming a carcass is an intellectual cartoon in the manner of Swift and Pope that makes delicacy of taste converge with grossness of appetite. "And wolves with howling fill the sacred choirs"—the unforgettable image of the Norman Conquest in Pope's "Windsor Forest"—finds an echo in Burke's description of winds howling through vacant lobbies. The passage builds up an impressive grandeur in spite of its motive in parody, until the epic resonance sinks with the single word *jobs*—at which Burke, the master of this rhetorical edifice, watches it crumble without a pang.

Early in the speech, Burke had compared himself to the French finance minister Necker. He felt "no little pride and satisfaction, to find that the principles of my proceedings are, in many respects, the very same." He brings back the comparison when speaking openly of the petitioners who ask their representatives to do for England what the king of France has done—"*to enquire into,*" as the Yorkshire petition has it, "*and correct, the gross abuses in the expenditure of public money.*" The seasonableness of the prompting makes all the difference between reform and revolution; or rather, to adopt Burke's metaphor, between cool and hot reformations: "Late reformations are terms imposed upon a conquered enemy; early reformations are made in cool blood; late reformations are made under a state of inflammation. In that state of things the people behold in government nothing that is respectable. They see the abuse, and they will see nothing else."[61] The different tempers in which reform is undertaken always affect the larger or smaller possibility of building upon the reform: "Whatever we improve, it is right to leave room for further improvement." This is what the plan of economic reform intends to do.

The external pressure of the petitioners gives this enterprise the spur of necessity—a fact Burke does not deplore. His peroration speaks of the petitioners as the active prompters of representative government:

The whole hope of reformation is at length cast upon *us;* and let us not deceive the nation, which does us the honour to hope every thing from our virtue. If *all* the nation are not equally forward to press this duty upon us, yet be assured, that they all equally expect we should perform it. The respectful silence of those who wait upon your pleasure, ought to be as powerful with you, as the call of those who require your service as their right. Some, without doors, affect to feel hurt for your dignity, because they suppose, that menaces are held out to you. Justify their good opinion, by shewing that no menaces are necessary to stimulate you to your duty.—But, Sir, whilst we may sympathize with them, in one point, who sympathize with us in another, we ought to attend no less to those who approach us like men, and who, in the guise of petitioners, speak to us in the tone of a concealed authority. It is not wise to force them to speak out more plainly, what they plainly mean. —But, the petitioners are violent. Be it so. Those who are least anxious about your conduct, are not those that love you most. Moderate affection and satiated enjoyment, are cold and respectful; but an ardent and injured passion, is tempered up with wrath, and grief, and shame, and conscious worth, and the maddening sense of violated right. A jealous love lights his torch from the firebrands of the furies. —They who call upon you to belong *wholly* to the people, are those who wish you to return to your *proper* home; to the sphere of your duty, to the post of your honour, to the mansion-house of all genuine, serene, and solid satisfaction. We have furnished to the people of England (indeed we have) some real cause of jealousy. Let us leave that sort of company which, if it does not destroy our innocence, pollutes our honour: let us free ourselves at once from every thing that can increase their suspicions, and inflame their just resentment: let us cast away from us, with a generous scorn, all the love-tokens and symbols that we have been vain and light enough to accept;—all the bracelets and snuff-boxes, and miniature pictures, and hair-devices, and all the other adulterous trinkets that are the pledges of our alienation, and the monuments of our shame. Let us return to our legitimate home, and all jars and all quarrels will be lost in embraces. Let the commons in parliament assembled, be one and the same thing with the commons at large.[62]

The opening contrast between people "who wait upon your pleasure" and attendants of the king "who require your service as their right" implies a particular understanding of the place of the Commons in the constitution. The menace at hand (if persuasion should fail) will be called by some an affront to Parliament. But, says Burke, relations of political authority do ultimately depend on force, and he asks his listeners to appreciate the "concealed authority" of the petitioners as preferable to an open threat. A decent protective veil—necessary in the peaceful handling of matters of power and commandment—has in fact been wrought by the petitioners to the extent consistent with their aims. Burke accordingly asks Parliament to show a deference (beyond the mere expression of sympathy) toward the same petitioners, whose passion is scarcely in their control: "A jealous love lights his torch from the firebrands of the furies." He deploys the grand style to honest ends in beseeching the great to learn the feelings of the humble. It is on this ground of common feeling that the high and the low must be joined: love is the same to both, as war is the same. There is a closer identity than the rich can remember between jealousy of the goods of the home and a watchful concern for the goods of society.

Almost from the start of his career, Burke had argued that the principles of politics are nothing but the principles of morality enlarged. If so, the passions at work in politics should find an adequate parallel in those of love and jealousy as they operate in personal life. At the close of the *Speech on Economical Reform,* he connects loyalty to the constitution with the dearest of domestic ties; and the analogy answers to Burke's deeper sense of the uses and limits of politics. It is right for a representative to hold himself apart from the people; but it is wrong for trespasses against the will of the people to become habitual. Members of the House attached to useless luxuries, the dainty, delicate, antiquated superfluities of the monarchy, all those bracelets, snuffboxes, and "hair devices," are condemned here in a catalogue drained of affection. It becomes a test of manly generosity to cast off these "adulterous trinkets that are the pledges of our alienation." The reward will be to deserve the name of *Commons*—a sense among the people's representatives that they share the spirit of the people, that they constitute the express image of the feelings of the nation.

The persuasive effect of the speech is rounded by the imagined act of grateful assent. Compelled submission to an external menace is thus transformed into a willing acceptance of the most legitimate of duties. A promise of attention to the people—not equal representation but increase in the accuracy of the equipment of representation—can be discerned in Burke's final comparison of the members inside with the people outside: "parliament assembled" shares one purpose with "the commons at large." The step toward a more public politics that Wilkes had forced—the admission of reporters to parliamentary debates—would assure a more general interest in later efforts of reform. At this moment, however, with an election coming in Bristol, Burke was at risk of being passed over in favor of candidates who had taken advantage of his absence. His speech before the election of 1780 would restate his view of the proper work of a representative in relation to his Bristol constituency; but the *Speech on Economical Reform* turned out to be nearly his last word on the broader responsibilities of Parliament to the English people.

Not altogether the last word, because this speech had a successor—a smaller but far more characteristic utterance that Burke delivered in the House of Commons a year and four days later, on February 15, 1781. He there makes plain his disappointment at the whittling away of the items of his reform: "The squeamishness of the House was such, that after swallowing those parts of the plan for which something might have been said, in respect to the use, the shew, the antiquity, or the respect; they objected to others, for which the most ingenious advocate could not advance an argument. They first dwindled off from one question, and then silently stole away from another, till at last the whole was permitted to moulder and shrink imperceptibly from the view." He now gives a considered representation of the county petition movement and its efforts to change the disposition of the House. The interest here lies both in the sympathetic picture of the protesters and in the active function assignable to a Commons that chooses to be responsive; for the sympathy is more explicit than it was in the speech of 1780, and the role of the House more accountable in democratic detail than it had appeared a decade before, in *Thoughts on the Cause of the Present Discontents*.

"Like the skillful physician," members of parliament entrusted with the common good ought

> to feel the pulse of the patient, and having discovered the seat and the
> nature of the disorder, they were to apply the remedy. They were not

to withhold it, because the people were patient under suffering; or because they were clamorous. They were to study the temper, to look into the constitutions, and the state of the governed, and watching their motions, they were to apply the remedy at the proper season. When the petitions were presented to the House, there were general meetings of the people in every county and city of the kingdom; they were legal and grave in their deportment; they were peaceable and loyal; some men in that House had pretended to charge them with illegality in their proceedings; that their meetings tended to disorder and convulsion; and were unwholesome, and unfit to be suffered. Without entering into any refutation of a charge which he considered ill-founded and ridiculous, he would only say that whether they were so or not, it became a wise legislature to attend to the reality and the body of the complaint, and not to the form or the irregularity in which it was made.[63]

What is most surprising about Burke's 1781 postscript on economical re-form is the greatly enlarged responsibility now associated with the House of Commons: a responsibility for *the well-being of the people*. The spirit of a free people depends on its strength; it is not proper, says Burke, "to deny the manger, and to give the spur"; indeed, "the body ought to be fed, that the soul may have its energy." This last attempt to awaken the House comes down to the words "Participation and example!" The meaning is unex-plained, yet Burke repeats the sentence: "Participation and example!" He is saying, with a simplicity that allows no embellishment, that the Commons ought to be exemplary of the spirit of the country. And it cannot be so without the increased participation of subjects who have become citizens.

Against Reform of Representation

As the meaning of the rejection of Burke's plan grew clearer, in late April, Dunning and other moderates searched for a secondary plan to conciliate the anger of the petitioners. Near the start of the debate of April 24—concerning his Motion of an Address to the King, which asked that the king neither dissolve the Parliament nor prorogue the session—Dunning declared it "incumbent upon that House" to build something on the petitions of the people. A public gesture had to be offered and linked to a practical effect. Thomas Pitt, in reply, expressed his "earnest wish to contribute toward averting the horrid prospect before him," the prospect of "a second civil war"; he feared that if the agitations went much further, no power on earth could say to the people: "Thus far shalt thou go and no farther." This apprehension was evidently shared by others—Lord Nugent, for example, who (speaking against Dunning's motion) said that it "smelt too strongly of the year 1641." From the same analogy, Fox drew a different conclusion. "Unless they agree to the present motion," he now said of the members of Parliament, "they betray the people." Fox accepted the pertinence of 1641 but failed to see how anyone with that parallel in mind could vote against Dunning's motion. When, in fact, they voted that the power of the crown was increasing (with 233 in the majority), "they had solemnly entered into a bond with the people of England, to reduce the undue influence of the crown, and to destroy that enormous overgrown corruption, and the penalty, in the case of non-performance, was a forfeiture of the affections of the people of England." No more dreadful calamity could befall the House of Commons.

Dunning's motion against dissolution was defeated nonetheless, 203–254, and afterward Fox asked to speak again. He reproached the inconsistency and weakness of those who voted for the original motion, that the power of the crown "ought to be diminished," yet turned about and opposed the motion not to adjourn. The county members he supposed made up the majority of defectors; their vote on the second motion probably expressed their true sentiments. In response, Fox announced that he would "absent himself from that House," side with the people themselves, and come back on their terms. To cries of "Hear! Hear!" he gave the first sign of the hopes on which he would stake his career in 1780 and (with a dimmer result) in 1784. The constitution was sound enough not to compel men to take up arms in support of their rights; general elections were "strictly consonant to peace and good order," and so long as a fair election could be held, he would not despair. He was confident that the next Parliament would redress the complaints of the people.

When on May 8 the House considered a motion to lay before it requisitions made by the civil magistrate, between April 5 and April 7, to equip the military against the meeting of the electors of Westminster, Burke joined the protest with Fox. The justices of Middlesex, he said, "were generally the scum of the earth; carpenters, brick-makers, and shoe-makers," some of them so infamous they could find no employment, "others so ignorant, that they could scarcely write their own names." The meeting of March 6, he added, was "a most respectable one," at which the dukes of Devonshire and Portland had both been present. Fox took a stronger line and "declared if it was understood that a set of men were to be let loose on the constitutional meetings of the people, that all who went to such meetings must go armed."[64] Burke did not dissent from this appeal to the people's right of spontaneous self-defense. The next day saw a return of John Sawbridge's annual motion for shortening the duration of parliaments; and here, Burke withdrew some distance from the democratic cause he had helped to sponsor.

The distinction (which might seem tactical) between economic reform and parliamentary reform was so fiercely guarded by Burke that one must conclude for him it marked the difference between a necessary bulwark of order and an incitement to "perfect democracy" or anarchy. On May 8, 1780, he delivered his *Speech on Duration of Parliaments* in response to Sawbridge's motion; he spoke for an hour and a half against any such change and thus (as Warren Elofson and John Woods put it) sounded "the death knell for whatever slim hopes remained of a united Opposition campaign based on economical reform."[65] On the duration of parliaments, Burke distinguished himself from Lord John Cavendish, a tactical supporter of Sawbridge; he went further than Rockingham by adding a direct disclaimer of triennial parliaments. Even so loyal a friend as Richard Champion observed that Burke's extreme hostility to parliamentary reform hurt him among Bristol constituents who were also participants in the association movement.

If Burke's vehemence on this occasion was not quite predictable, he derived his argument from a maxim at the heart of his thinking. "It is always to be lamented when men are driven to search into the foundations of the Commonwealth." Discussions of origins, whether in theology or politics, are inviting to large views and estimates of metaphysical priority; they easily serve and stimulate claims of absolute indefeasible right. On this point Burke has great consistency, from the *Thoughts* of 1770 to the

Reflections of 1790. He was averting his gaze from origins when he looked on the charters of the American colonies as entailing no right of taxation. He would do so again when he noticed that British authority in India had begun in the violence of commercial rivalry and the questionable victory of a proxy army. He believed that a "sacred veil" ought to cover such beginnings, since "the situation of man" (not his original right) "is the preceptor of his duty." It is the same with the right of the people to political representation. Granted, the interests of the people cannot be served without some device of popular election; yet "Popular Election is a mighty Evil." It is indeed so great an evil that, though most monarchs have obtained their position originally by popular election, the custom of electing the king has largely been abolished in monarchical governments. Besides, all remedies that aim to redress a particular unfairness warrant close inspection: "I must see their operation in the cure of the old Evil, and the cure of those new Evils which are inseparable from all remedies, and how they balance each other—which is the total result."[66] And yet, why should Burke's judgment be trusted in a case where the unfairness is acutely felt by others? Because (he says) his honesty in rejecting the popular cause supports his claim to be someone who addresses the people's interests with candor. It is easy to see how this paradoxical mode of justification could wear thin: I prove my loyalty to your real interests by frankly admitting that I act against your apparent interests. Yet Burke is right that the opponent of a popular remedy who declares his unwelcome view to the people can hardly be accused of flattering them. And the claim he offers, writ large, may be taken as presumptive proof of the good faith of the Rockingham party: they will no more flatter persons of power and influence than they have wheedled for the good opinion of the people. They mean to serve the common good, even when that sets them against popular feeling; and they have shown they can do so when it turns them against the opinion of the king's friends. "Faithful watchmen we ought to be over the Rights and privileges of the people. But our Duty if we are qualified for it as we ought is to give them information and not to receive it from them."

Thus, Burke in 1780 goes beyond the duty to resist mandates, of which he had spoken six years earlier in his *Speech at the Conclusion of the Poll.*

A representative not only has a duty to resist mandates; he must pry himself loose from intimidation by political threats, popular insurgencies, and all that two centuries later goes under the American name of lobbying.

A defense of politics was his largest motive here, and the attack on popular sovereignty is made in that cause. (It might be charged against Burke that he sometimes defended politics at the sacrifice of the ends of politics.) A shorter duration of Parliament would displace the site of political influence from elected representatives to the electors; but by doing so, the measure would only further "strengthen and extend a court interest already great and powerful in Boroughs; here [i.e., in Parliament and wrongly] to fix their magazines and places of arms, and this to make the principal not the secondary Theatre of their maneuvers for securing a determined Majority in Parliament."[67] This would turn the House of Commons into a battlefield and derogate from its deliberative function. Besides, are the electors themselves less corrupted than the members? "Many of them are but ill informed in their minds, many feeble in their Circumstances; and easily overreached; and easily seduced." Here Burke draws a conclusion of unexpected weight: "I am apprehensive that this Bill though it shifts the place of disorder does by no means relieve the Constitution." Money is influential enough as it is; the increased frequency of elections will make it more so, given the "expence in entertainments; the power of serving and obliging the Rulers of Corporations; of winning over the popular Leaders of Political Clubs, associations, and neighbourhoods."

Democratic pamphleteers in the later eighteenth century often appealed from the decadence of monarchy to the virtues of an ancient republican code of conduct. For this reason in part, Burke is keen to remind his audience of the history of republican decadence: "Rome was destroyed by the disorders of continual Elections; though those of Rome were sober disorders; they had nothing but faction, bribery, bread and stage Plays to debauch them. We have the inflammation of *Liquor* superadded." Not for the last time (in the *Reflections* he will mock all who take for granted "the lazy enjoyment of sixty years' security and the still unanimating repose of public prosperity"), Burke associates the durability of British peace from the Treaty of Utrecht to the American war with the long duration of Parliament sealed by the Septennial Act in 1716: "A triennial was near ruining; a Septennial Parliament saved your constitution; nor perhaps have you ever known a more flourishing period for the union of National Prosperity dignity and Liberty than the 60 of the years you have passed under that constitution of parliament."[68] One may detect the traces here of an argument that appeared in the *Letter to the Sheriffs of Bristol* and would recur in the *Reflections*: the people, when they fall into a "distemper of remedy," share the savagery of that patriotism which locates the cause of all discontents in some external enemy.

In his reaction against the Sawbridge reform, Burke went the length of opposing even the compromise solution of triennial parliaments: "in my opinion the shortness of a Triennial sitting, would have the following ill Effects; it would make the Member more shamelessly and shockingly corrupt; it would increase his Dependence on those who could best support him at his Election. It would wrack and tear to pieces the fortunes of those who stood upon their own Fortunes and their private interest. It would make the Electors infinitely more venal; and it would make the whole body of the people who are whether they have votes or not concerned in Elections more Lawless." Elections, then, as such—the shorter the interval, the greater the risk—entail the corruption of government by money: "Independence of mind will ever be more or less influenced by independence of Fortune; and if every three years the exhausting Sluices of entertainments, drinkings, open houses, to say nothing of Bribery are to be periodically drawn up and renewed; if Government favors for which now in some shape or other the whole race of men are candidates, are to be called for, upon every occasion, I see that private fortunes will be washed away and every even to the least Trace of independence borne down by the torrent."[69] Popular elections draw from those who are most eager for command the resources of grandiose spectacle and unfettered will. The difficulty of any individual attaining a degree of public honor and fame has always been in this sense a brake on the energies of ambition. But elections that are so frequent and intoxicating that they become a way of life release ambition from the check afforded by the passage of time:

Ambition is no exact calculator. Avarice itself does not calculate strictly when it games. One thing is certain, that in this political Game the great Lottery of power is that, into which men will purchase, with Millions of Chances against them. In Turkey where the place, where the fortune, where the head itself are so insecure, that scarcely any have died in their beds for ages; so that the bowstring is the natural Death of Bashaws; yet in no Country is power and Distinction (precarious enough God knows in all) sought for with such boundless avidity, as if the value of place was enhanced by the danger and insecurity of its Tenure. Nothing will ever make a seat in this House not an Object of desire to Numbers by any means or at any charge, but the depriving it of all power and all dignity, this would do it. This is the true and only Nostrum for that purpose. But an house of Commons without power and without dignity either in itself or its members is no house of commons for the purposes of this constitution.[70]

The prospect of being turned out of office, Burke suspects, will not inhibit the will of such men to get what they want as fast as they can: "The shortness of time in which they are to reap the profits of iniquity is far from checking the avidity of corrupt men; it renders them infinitely more ravenous. They rush violently and precipitately on their object; they lose all regard to decorum." This holds true whenever an epidemic of influence persuades men that political power can be bought. The frenzy that is then unleashed makes it resemble other epidemics; the peddlers are made to feel that they must do what they can while there is time: "The moments of profits are precious; never are men so wicked as during a general mortality." Burke cites the great plagues of Athens and of London; and he could hardly make plainer by metaphor his preoccupying thought. Elections are a disease of the political will, against which no inoculation is possible.

Their effects can best be minimized by placing the arranged sieges so far apart that they spare the metabolism of government—at the same time putting them close enough together to allow four or five changes in the career of a politician. Burke's reason for thinking so well of elections every seven years (as opposed to every one or three or twenty) is merely the reason of custom and habit. This was a pattern settled half a generation before his birth—a span that tends to merge with one's own life by the overheard recollections of elders—and it has been continued through his middle years. But if he has the most arbitrary of motives for thinking well of septennial parliaments, his argument carries a deeper psychological authority. The habits of a people for whom the separate activities of governing and electing have grown confused will lack the spirit of liberal obedience that is necessary under a liberal constitution.

We have to look ahead at least two years to find the logical supplement of Burke's speech against shorter parliaments. It comes in his *Speech on the Reform of Representation,* dated by his earliest editors May 7, 1782, but probably delivered in 1784. Here the preservation of the authority of the House of Commons is linked to the perpetuation of constituencies as they are. With a sarcasm that is unworthy of his best abilities, Burke opens by shifting attention away from the scandal of grossly unequal representation—the ownership of seats by men of title and privilege, the scarcity of contested elections, and the fact that uninhabited boroughs could enjoy a representation denied to populous neighborhoods. He ignores all these matters to speak of the British constitution, which, though it is the admiration of the world, has been found at the close of the eighteenth century to be a ruined structure, "infested by the dry rot." This despising of a cherished possession shows a contempt that Burke says he cannot admire: the reformers denounce the constitution (here synonymous with the present state of parliamentary representation) yet say nothing against the crown or the lords. Why do they expose the representatives if not to sap them of their good opinion of themselves? "As all government stands upon opinion, they know that the way utterly to destroy it, is to remove that opinion, to take away all reverence, all confidence from it; and then at the first blast of publick discontent and popular tumult it tumbles to the ground."[71] One may remark a slight but symptomatic change in the valence of the word *discontent*—a word that goes back to Wilkes and the 1760s, used with respect in Burke's *Thoughts on the Cause of the Present Discontents.* He shows less deference to the same word now. "The first blast of public discontent" it might become us to ignore. Burke is registering a defensive horror at the signs that an ancient alliance between the people and the House has been severed; that the people have been robbed—by the demagogues out of doors and by some within the House—of their unsuspecting confidence in the adequacy of representation.

The speech at this point offers a substantial formulation of the doctrine of conservative constitutionalism—a discussion as analytic as the *Reflections* and on much the same terrain, but here with domestic politics as its subject matter. There are, says Burke, two separate lines of opposition to the suggested reform, one of them principled and one pragmatic. He associates himself with those who think not only that the present moment is inexpedient but that "neither *now* nor at *any* time is it prudent or safe to be meddling with the fundamental principles and ancient tried usages of our Constitution." This is monumental language, and it continues: "our representation is as nearly perfect as the necessary imperfection of human affairs and of human creatures will suffer it to be." Burke does not offer a reasoned defense—as in the *Speech on Duration of Parliaments*—of a useful custom whose content is as accidental as that of all customs. Rather, he ventures an ennobling and frankly unreasoning defense of a prejudice. How could a contrivance as artificial as the rules of representation in an assembly at any given historical moment be supposed "as nearly perfect" as such a thing could be? We do not commonly judge the outward shape of institutions—made as they are for human adaptation—as tenderly as we do the ideas or the moral habits of a people. With government, in an age when reason is applied to government, we are constantly aware of small changes and also aware that it is human causes (sometimes people we can name) who made the change. Burke wants to assimilate his fondness for a government based in the aristocratic society of the mid-eighteenth century to the venerability of what is venerable and the loveliness of what is lovely. In order to carry this argument, he needs—and he soon introduces—a sense of "prejudice" that includes a presumption in favor of the *rightness* of ancient or previous practices. Here once again the argument looks ahead to the rhetoric and the psychology of his defense of "just prejudice" in the *Reflections*.

The most conspicuous advocates of reform of representation are the whole-length believers in the theory of "the supposed rights of man." Every man, they think, has the right to govern himself—the least of men, the most gross and ignorant, as much as the best. Moderate reformers, on the other hand, decline to grant that premise; they may be constitutionalists like Burke who, unlike him, believe that a changed representation will improve the efficacy of government. The first group (exemplified by a man like Sawbridge) Burke identifies with a claim for "personal representation," which he "rejects with scorn and fervor." These rights-of-man reformers take their stand on "absolute right," and their goal is universal suffrage. Burke accurately summarizes their reasoning: "because all *natural* rights must be the rights of individuals, as by *nature* there is no such thing as politic or corporate personality: all these ideas are mere fictions of the law, they are creatures of voluntary institution; men as men are individuals, and nothing else." Burke can present the case fairly without much cost to his cause, because he believes it is self-evidently false to human nature. But he confesses bewilderment at moderate reformers like Lord Cavendish, who have been his allies in the House. This second set of reformers, having seen the unyielding tenor of the first, ought to see that their interests ultimately diverge; for the first "lay it down, that every man ought to govern, himself, and that, where he cannot go, himself, he must send his representative [by mandates, narrowly understood]; that all other government is usurpation, and is so far from having a claim to our obedience, it is not only our right, but our duty, to resist it." Was it not the duty of any member of Parliament—affirmed by Burke in 1774 and by his party in the negotiations over Irish trade—to restrain and qualify the immediate desires of the people?

Those who press for popular sovereignty must be suspicious of all representative government. The right response is to teach them better and not to give in to the compulsory demand. All government is founded on trust, and this always means a generous allowance to "prescription"—an oddly chosen word, since Burke is saying that we naturally acquiesce in ways of proceeding that are not written down. But prescription, or the ancient authority of an established practice, for Burke goes hand in hand with presumption, the human propensity to approve and perpetuate a familiar state of things. Any inquiry preliminary to a radical change, he believed, would threaten to tear up the contexture of the political system the English people had inherited and approved for generations—a system founded on aristocratic manners and a close connection between representation and property.

> Prescription is the most solid of all titles, not only to property, but, which is to secure that property, to Government. They harmonize with each other, and give mutual aid to one another. It is accompanied with another ground of authority in the constitution of the human mind, presumption. It is a presumption in favor of any settled scheme of government against any untried project, that a nation has long existed and flourished under it. It is a better presumption even of the *choice* of a nation, far better than any sudden and temporary arrangement by actual election. Because a nation is not an idea only of local extent and individual momentary aggregation, but it is an idea of continuity, which extends in time as well as in numbers and in space. And this is a choice not of one day, or one set of people, not a tumultuary and giddy choice; it is a deliberate election of ages and of generations; it is a Constitution made by what is ten thousand times better than choice, it is made by the peculiar circumstances, occasions, tempers, dispositions, and moral, civil, and social habitudes of the people, which disclose themselves only in a long space of time. It is a vestment, which accommodates itself to the body. Nor is prescription of government formed, upon blind unmeaning prejudices—for man is a most unwise and a most wise being. The individual is foolish. The multitude for the moment is foolish, when they act without deliberation; but the species is wise, and when time is given to it, as a species it almost always acts right.[72]

The people have accepted the present system over time, as Burke sees it, though they may be roused against the system temporarily.

This observation on the labor of political choice embodies a great and characteristic insight. It carries equal force whether or not one credits it as an argument against proposed changes in the structure of representation in the 1780s. Burke is saying that the choices of human nature over time are right for us in our social state. This must be so if one grants that human beings indeed have a nature, as dogs and horses do; and if one also grants that rules which are gradually approved are a means of transmitting the wisdom of nature through a succession of generations; and if one concedes that the greatest danger to this continuity lies in sudden choices, where the generality of an opinion is supposed to answer for its utility.

Burke's argument, as in the *Speech on Duration of Parliaments*, is moral and psychological. As in the earlier speech, we are aware of an arbitrary choice of a protocol to treat as the bearer of continuity. It might be said that the argument proves too much, since it establishes a fair presumption against every political change: reformers have the burden of proof in all but the smallest measures. And just as one might have asked, "Why *exactly* seven years" for the length of a parliamentary session, so one may wonder why the parliament of 1784 should be treated as the touchstone of political wisdom. Why *this* House of Commons, with precisely its present representation? Burke's answer is circular: "The House of Commons is a legislative body corporate by prescription, not made upon any given theory, but existing prescriptively,—just like the rest." Thinking again of the surrender of constitutional reformers to the theorists of natural rights, Burke asks why, if they love the constitution, they would subject it to an irreparable cure. Is it "so declined from its perpendicular as to want the hand of the wise and experienced architects of the day to set it upright again, and to prop and buttress it up for duration?" He answers (dropping the sarcasm): "To ask whether a thing which has always been the same stands to its usual principle seems to me perfectly absurd: for how do you know the principles, but from the construction? and if that remains the same, the principles remain the same." The metaphor pictures a house, not a tree or some other natural organism. Here Burke's imaginative honesty may take his argument in a direction it did not intend; for a house, unlike a flower or a tree, can be adapted and augmented without harm to the total design. "Government is a contrivance of human wisdom to provide for human wants"—so Burke would say in a sentence of plain sense in the *Reflections*. The view of prescription that he puts forward in this speech, on the contrary, calls for a pious self-submission to previous ideas of human wants; yet the grounds of justification that he cites are pragmatic after all. "Look to the effects," he remarks. "In all moral machinery, the moral results are its test."

How thoroughly, on grounds like these, can he oppose a theory of natural rights whose intuitive plausibility doubtless gave impetus to the reform? "I do not vilify theory and speculation: no, because that would be to vilify reason itself. . . . Whenever I speak against theory, I mean always a weak, erroneous, fallacious, unfounded, or imperfect theory." It is with the natural rights of men as with the divine right of kings: we ought to compare a theory with its reduction to practice, knowing that "This is the true touchstone of all theories which regard man and the affairs of men,— Does it suit his nature in general?—does it suit his nature as modified by his habits?" English liberty, Burke thinks his listeners will agree, has improved under the present constitution for 500 years. He gives a broad sense here to *constitution* and also to 500 years: Magna Carta seems to be the one approved change of principle, but its innovation was to limit a monarch and not to award the franchise to the people.

Under the present constitution, it is clear that constituencies with greater representation enjoy no advantage over those with less: "Are the local interests of Cornwall and Wiltshire, for instance, their roads, their canals, their prisons, their police, better than Yorkshire, Warwickshire, or Staffordshire? Warwick has members: is Warwick or Stafford more opulent, happy, or free than Newcastle, or than Birmingham?" But the habit of constant inquiry into such disparities reminds Burke of "the unhappy persons who live, if they can be said to live, in the statical chair,—who are ever feeling their pulse": it betrays, to use the word of the *Reflections*, a valetudinarian compulsion at odds with happiness and common sense. The practice of extreme liberty, Burke fears, must counteract the good of all liberty. But what shall we designate the extreme? "What that gentleman, and the associations, or some parts of their phalanxes, think proper? Then our liberties are in their pleasure; it depends on their arbitrary will how far I shall be free. I will have none of that freedom." Burke seeks his liberty, rather, "in the Constitution I actually enjoy." A rhapsody follows that must be quoted at length: it is the second of Burke's three set pieces on the theme, the first having appeared close to the end of the *Speech on Conciliation*, the last still to come in the *Reflections*.

Burke speaks here, self-consciously, in the voice of John of Gaunt's lines in *Richard II* about "this sceptered isle":

Our Constitution is like our island, which uses and restrains its subject sea—in vain the waves roar. In that Constitution I know, and exultingly I feel, both that I am free, and that I am not free dangerously to myself or to others. I know that no power on earth, acting as I ought to do, can touch my life, my liberty, or my property. I have that inward and dignified consciousness of my own security and independence, which constitutes, and is the only thing which does constitute, the proud and comfortable sentiment of freedom in the human breast. I know too, and I bless God for my safe mediocrity.—I know, that if I possessed all the talents of the gentlemen on the side of the House I sit, and on the other, I cannot by Royal favor, or by popular delusion or by oligarchical cabal, elevate myself above a certain, very limited point, so as to endanger my own fall or the ruin of my Country. I know there is an order that keeps things fast in their place: it is made to us, and we are made to it. Why not ask another wife, other children, another body, another mind.[73]

Of all the passages of its kind, this gives Burke's most idealizing treatment of the constitution; and it is notable that he extends his blessing from the constitution to the state. The state sees what we are, holds us in, and keeps us human. By restraining, it makes us better than we would otherwise be. Had Burke always written in this way, the political philosophy of Hegel might be taken as an adequate guide to his meaning. But the passage touches an extreme, for him: it is poised on the brink of saying (what it does not quite say) that the state is the larger entity for which the individual ought willingly to sacrifice himself. Hardly five years have passed and we seem to be reading a different author from the one who wrote *A Letter to the Sheriffs of Bristol*. But in 1782, Burke's task, as John Brewer explains it, "was altogether different" from the work he faced in the preceding period; he intended now "to recall advocates of *moderate* reform, including members of his own party, to their political senses."[74] That makes a plausible case for his consistency.

Yet from Burke's usual emphasis in speaking of the balance of the constitution, few of his allies could have predicted the unyielding tenor of the passage quoted above. Society and its outgrowth the state are, he would always have said, an inseparable help to the liberty and happiness of individuals. The state and society exist for our sake. But his causerie against the reform of representation is composed in a very different temper. And his echo of the Gospels ("Which of you by taking thought can add one cubit unto his stature?") reveals the exorbitance of his undertaking to sanctify an aristocratic society: an act of justification by which he would be tempted and repelled throughout his later career. It is curious to hear him say all this at home even as he initiates abroad a proposal to change the structure of the imperial constitution—the effective withdrawal of a charter from a company whose mismanagement brought to an end sixty years of prosperity and public security.

Perhaps sensing the depth of the anomaly, Burke retreats to a safer point and asserts that the ancient frame of the constitution and the state have value as a source of patriotic feeling. Now he no longer invokes the metaphysical nature of the state. All of the feelings that membership in an ancient enterprise imparts may serve to strengthen us for choosing the forms of elective dependency. The danger remains (and it is a danger Burke would have been scrupulous to avoid in 1777) that we may take on trust the verdicts of patriotic feeling simply because of our affection for its sources. The point about such a sentiment should be that its good is instrumental: a feeling about ourselves produces a secondary feeling about our country, itself a projection from ourselves. But this analysis does not suffice for Burke in 1784. People may give up false systems or opinions, he concludes, but it cannot be so with "the frame and constitution of the state: if that is disgraced, patriotism is destroyed in its very source. No man has ever willingly obeyed, much less was desirous of defending with his blood, a mischievous and absurd scheme of government. Our first, our dearest, most comprehensive relation, our country, is gone." *Relation* makes a suppressed pun on the kinship of blood relations; and the confusion between "attachment," which comes from mere proximity, and a "love" that comes from intimacy and unquestioned loyalty will contribute heavily to the peculiar piety of Burke's anti-revolutionary writings of the 1790s. Their true beginning lies in this speech.

The blend of anti-democratic and anti-monarchical feeling occurs at a moment, in the mid-1780s, when Burke's suspicion of royal influence and his suspicion of popular remedies were both working at maximum intensity. The constitution is marred by none of the aggrandizing instincts of these merely human agencies. Thus, Burke's belief in the ancient representation rescues part of his faith in liberty but at a considerable cost to his practical sense of the means for limiting power. "The people," who once had seemed to him such an indispensable check, now appear chiefly as a peril to the constitution.

Gordon Riots

The Gordon Riots shook London for seven days starting on June 2, 1780. By the time they were over, close to 1,000 persons had died, including 285 rioters killed by troops.[75] This catastrophe would fix the danger of popular tumults in the mind of Burke ever after. Indeed, the London crowd of June 1780 would shadow his thoughts about the Paris crowd of July 1789. Where his contemporaries were struck by the generous-heartedness of the mass of the people, tearing down the gothic edifice of tyranny, Burke saw something like the Gordon mob but now grown monstrous and impossible to quell—many of its elements simply criminal, more with a smattering of a grievance, all given over to an unleashed appetite for violent disorder.

Gordon was chosen as president of the Protestant Association on Monday, May 29, at a meeting at Coachmakers Hall—where, according to the report in the *Annual Register,* he gave "a long inflammatory harangue" on the dangers of the spread of popery in England. The only defense, he said, was for the people to demand action from the House of Commons. He would brave all hazards for the cause, no matter if others faltered. Wildly applauded for these sentiments, Gordon moved a resolution for the people to meet in St. George's Fields on Friday next at 10:00 A.M. and from there to proceed with him to the Commons and deliver the petitions. He would not, he said, go with fewer than 20,000 persons to support him. When the hour arrived, as many as 60,000 were on hand, and the crowd proceeded "with great decorum on their route" to assemble before both houses of Parliament, where they "gave a general shout." Some now began to exert control, urging their neighbors "to put blue cockades in their hats, and call out 'No Popery!'" and also pressing for a taking of oaths against the passage of Sir George Savile's bill, which had repealed Catholic disabilities.

Others cursed and threw out insults as the crowd took possession of avenues leading up to both houses of Parliament. The Archbishop of York was attacked, his coach "saluted with hisses and groans, and hootings"; Lord Bathurst, lord president of the privy council, was "pushed about in the rudest manner, and kicked violently on the legs. Lord Mansfield had the glasses of his carriage broken, the panels beat in, and narrowly escaped with his life." Other gentlemen were similarly harassed and humiliated on their way to the debate in the Commons. All the while, Gordon would issue intermittently from his place in the House, to harangue the crowd, telling them their petitions were likely to be rejected. He singled out as a culprit "Mr. Burke, the member for Bristol," while assuring them "the alarm has gone forth for many miles around the city. You have a very good prince, who, as soon as he shall hear the alarm has seized such a number of men, will no doubt send down private orders to enforce the prayer of your petition." This strange inversion of the aims of the county movement, under the cover of identical methods, must have struck Burke as a definitive sign. The description in the *Annual Register* commands attention because—given his link to the publication, the uniqueness of the event, and the singularity of his role—Burke may well have overseen the drafting of it.[76]

The *Register* account goes on to speak of the efforts by persons in government to reason with Gordon. One such was General Conway, another Colonel Gordon, a near relation who said that if Lord George brought his "rascally adherents" into the House, as soon as the first man entered "I will plunge my sword,—not into his, but into your body." None of this told upon Gordon. He turned to the crowd and asked them to witness what he had to contend with. Justice Addington ordered away the cavalry as a gesture of goodwill to the crowd, and more than 600 of the petitioners dispersed for the time being. Only many days later, on Tuesday, June 6, when the last of disorder was burning low, did Burke give a speech about the dangers they had passed. He deplored "that relaxed state of the police, which could not protect even the legislature itself from violence, and insult at their very gates"; and he "lamented in the most melancholy terms, the dreadful necessity that obliged the military power, the notorious bane of liberty, to be called in, to defend not only the freedom, but the very existence of parliament!" Fox spoke immediately after, without any difference of sentiments. But even on June 6 the crisis was not quite past; anyway, Gordon did not think it was. He said if the House would appoint a day to discuss business to the satisfaction of the people, he would vouch for their obedience; once more he tried, as on the first day, to go out to harangue them, but now "some of his friends detained him, not without violence."[77]

Four days earlier, even without Gordon on the scene, the tumult had registered in the House of Lords. On June 2, the Duke of Richmond regretted the circumstances in which he was obliged to make his motion relative to annual parliaments; the rest of the day in the Lords, disheveled and tattered members discussed the mob out of doors and what to do if things got worse or stayed the same.[78] The men who governed were still in their places, yet something impalpable had changed.

The worst rioting continued from June 3 to June 5, days and nights given up to devastation, with Irishmen and Catholics set upon, their houses sacked, their possessions thrown into bonfires. Before peace was restored on June 9, the mob had burned Newgate, two Catholic chapels, and the house of Lord Mansfield; at the height of the chaos, an attempt was made to storm the Bank of England. Amid this uproar, Burke stood out against the abridgment of the law by military intervention; when 7,000 troops from the Home Counties were brought in to suppress any remaining threats and to enforce martial law, he took the ministry to task for "establishing a military on the ruins of the civil government."[79] How did he keep his balance? Many in the crowd, he perceived, had joined by accident and were roused by drink or intoxicating words. A few were hardened criminals, but a crowd itself cannot, any more than a people, be made a subject of collective punishment.

Gordon himself is a study in the peculiarities of the time. Out of Eton, he had gone into the navy and been appalled by the treatment of blacks in the West Indies; as a midshipman, he had protested on behalf of seamen forced to eat weevil-infested biscuits, and came to be known as "the sailors' friend"; then, in 1774, at the age of 23, he became a member of Parliament from Luggershall (a pocket borough). His first year in the House of Commons brought him under the spell of Burke's eloquence, and he began to vote with the opposition; but his own speeches and the drift of his actions presented a strange mixture of indignation and posturing. No one would claim him as an ally. And yet, in 1780, the moment found the man. "Patriotism and bigotry," Ian Gilmour has said of the riots, "marched—or ran—hand in hand."[80] The contrast with the Wilkes mob is important: only an odd impoverishment of the English language unifies the two entities under a single word. The Wilkes protests were guided and meant to secure redress against oppression by government; whereas the whole purpose of the Gordon Riots was violent intimidation. The crowd took pleasure in wanton acts and found satisfactions beside which any merely political reform would have been anticlimactic. The conduct of Wilkes himself during the crisis goes some way to mark this distinction. When, in the absence of orders from a civil magistrate, the king first issued a royal proclamation to restore the public order of London, Wilkes moved to delay an immediate decision, but finding no support among the Court of Common Council, he reversed field and spoke of the necessity of restoring order.[81]

Burke walked the streets of London during those days—an act of courage after his denunciation of the rioters. Once, he was mobbed by "some of the most decent of the petitioners" (as Prior describes them), who reproached him for the passage of Sir George Savile's Roman Catholic bill. Burke affirmed his support for the law: he was a marked man but felt he had done nothing to deserve the censure of the people. So he went among them without pretense and was allowed to pass. Reviewing (in a letter of June 7) the week of lootings, arson, and general menace, he would thank the group of "Gentlemen"—probably one of the voluntary militias that sprang up to preserve order—who had offered to "defend his house against those who, on pretended principles of religion have declared war, to the best of their miserable power, on Mankind."[82] Yet if the rioters seemed to have taken leave of a sane humanity, Burke knew they were human and that most would return soon enough to ordinary pursuits, scarcely more conscious of the part they had played than sleepers after a dream. It was to counter such natural forgetfulness that he had chosen to enter the crowd: he needed to see with his own eyes.

Burke also wanted the crowd to recognize "that, for one, I was neither to be forced nor intimidated from the strait line of what was right; and I returned on foot quite through the multitude, to the House, which was coverd by a strong body of Horse and foot."[83] The casual touch of self-portraiture recalls Abdiel in Book 5 of *Paradise Lost*, the most loyal of God's angels, who passed among the enemy host and denounced their rebellion—a character whom Reynolds would link with Burke in an inscription he wrote for a late engraving of his 1774 portrait of his friend:[84]

> from admidst them forth he pass'd,
> Long way through hostile scorn, which he sustain'd
> Superior, nor of violence fear'd aught.

Arriving at Parliament, Burke delivered to the Commons his doctrine of resistance against intimidation by the mob: "I spoke my sentiments in such a way, that I do not think I have ever on any occasion seemed to affect the house more forcibly."[85] He was admired alike for the things he said and the risk he ran.

VII

In Defense of Politics

THE election of September 1780 took place against the ominous background of the riots and the fear of domestic violence to come. Yet Burke was not wrong to feel initially hopeful. Many things united him to his Bristol constituency. Among the most active of the electors were Quakers and Dissenters; and as early as 1773, he had made clear his support for religious toleration. Bristol, too, was a trading center, and he had helped the city to negotiate local advantages. Yet it was the matter of commerce that, gradually in the late 1770s, opened up a division. The Bristol merchants supported free trade when it suited their interest but were eager for protection when they saw the growing prosperity of a rival country. On the question of free trade for Ireland, Burke refused to deviate even when his support for an easing of restrictions touched the nerves and the pocketbooks of those who had helped him gain his seat.

A second contentious issue was his support for a reform to lighten the penalties for debt. Creditors at this time still had the power by law to subject debtors to indefinite confinement; the bill he spoke for would have transferred from plaintiff to judge the authority to enforce such penalties. Yet the lifting of a privilege so liable to abuse was viewed by the banking and trading interests as a threat to the whole system of property and credit. Reform of another oppressive inheritance, the penal laws against Catholics, had been part of the Rockingham program in the preceding months: a corollary for Burke (as we have seen) of the defense of toleration for Dissenters. All the new enactments might have been approved by his constituency had not "wild and savage insurrection"—in Burke's words— "quitted the woods, and prowled about our streets in the name of reform." In the bewildered aftermath of the riots, popular suspicions grew more heated against religious toleration. Burke's unqualified rejection of the Protestant Association appeared to his supporters, at the very least, inexpedient: Bristol itself had suffered a riot in sympathy with Gordon.[1] But none of these pressures moved Burke to withdraw his support for the repeal of Catholic disabilities—an issue he would rightly portray as the largest that faced the voters of Bristol in the election of 1780.

When he returned to the city, he found that arrangements for the election had gone forward without him. Politically he was now at odds with that large proportion of his Whig constituency who preferred to maintain English privileges in trade and were ready to indulge the violent will of bigots so long as the bigots were Protestant. More generally, his path to re-election was hampered by the difficulty of returning two Whigs. For this to happen again, Burke and Cruger would have to cooperate more closely than they had done in the past.

Burke's judgment was that the Tories favored him over Cruger. (More likely they were using him as a set-off against Cruger, the Whig whose popularity they feared.) In a letter to Portland, he calculated his chances with an additional favoring circumstance: "If the Whig Merchants could make a member, I should be chosen without all doubt or controversy"; on the other hand, Cruger "carries off such a Body of the low Voters, that I concur . . . with all my friends, that it is far better for me to make no Trial at all than to be disgraced." His opinion of Cruger ("on whose word no man has reliance" and whose "understanding is superficial") had never been high. Yet Cruger the American had secured the people's affections "by a diligent attendance on *them*, and a total Neglect of attendance in Parliament." The Baptists and Anabaptists remained with Cruger "and ill enough affected to me."[2]

Burke's temperament, as all these remarks make clear, was poorly adapted to the bustle, the low arts of bargaining, and the traffic with interested persons that are part of the vote-getting in a contested election. He looked with a touch of self-mockery at the rituals of courtship between political artists and their audience. Thus a comment in a letter to Rockingham:

> Oh which of my Sins have made me live in Elections! Oh! who shall free me from the body of *this* Death! . . . Cruger has saved himself by an Absence of some days; and he is come fresh to action. But if he

goes on in the way I saw him last Night—I would not answer for his keeping, in this weather, which rots Candidates, voters, Aldermen, and Venison. The high flavour of us all is too much. I am sick, very sick—but in two minutes I must be one of the jolliest fellows in the world. They *expect* something of the Kind here—and I hold out two streets, and part of the Clubs, with great Stoutness—after deliberating speeching, Mobbing, and twice dining in the morning—About ten o'Clock at Night I could not conjure up one pun or Joke, nor put any sort of tolerably acted Jollity, into my Countenance.[3]

He hates what he has to do, but his mood is the reverse of fastidious: the writer is steeped in the scene he describes. And the "flavour" of it comes equally from the crowds in the September heat and the primed insincerity of the candidates. The satirist who composed the mordant *Vindication of Natural Society* is barely submerged in the veteran politician.

Burke also had a private reason for staying in the election. The fortunes of his friend Will Burke partly depended on his incumbency. ("The news," he reflected, "of my being totally shut out of Parliament might kill" his friend:[4] Will had convinced himself that all his weight derived from the perception of his attachment to Edmund; and Edmund was a man of greater consequence while he represented Bristol.) It was humiliating or, in Burke's words, "not pleasant" to come to "every new contest like a new man"; nor does he care for the disguise he has to assume as the willing servant of the people's desires:

I have a notion that men who take an enlarged line on publick Business, and upon Grounds of some depth, and that require at every instant, the appearance of doing something, in *appearance* wrong, in order to do what is really and *substantially* right, ought not to sit for these great busy places. . . . I hope I never shall reject the principles of general publick prudence; Those which go under the description of the moral Virtue of that name; but as to the prudence of giving up the principle to the means, I confess I grow ten times more restive than ever. I shall always follow the popular humour, and endeavour to lead it to right points, at any expence of private Interest, or party Interest, which I consider as nothing in comparison—But as to leaving to the Crowd, to choose for me, what principles I ought to hold, or what

Course I ought to pursue for their benefit—I had much rather, innocently and obscurely, mix with them, with the utter ruin of all my hopes, (which hopes are my all) than to betray them by learning lessons from them. They are naturally proud, tyrannical, and ignorant; bad scholars and worse Masters. . . . I must fairly say, that what many of them have called my passions, are my principles; and I shall act just as I have done, though perhaps more systematically, if God gives me Life, and they furnish me with the situation to act in.[5]

The passage is important and will enter into the argument of the *Speech at the Bristol Guildhall Previous to the Election*. It comes to a confession of the undoubted necessity and weakness of democracy, and the untenability of an independent stance by an elected representative. Placed as it is, midway in a letter to the Duke of Portland, it shows the persistence of Burke's avowal that he never separated the principles of politics from those of morality. This goes with his belief in the authority of untaught feelings: what many "have called my passions, are my principles." But politics as a vocation is fated to be marred by the unpredictable mixture of human materials. The argument of Burke's *Speech at the Bristol Guildhall* will reduce that perception to a maxim: a true representative must serve the interests of the people even against their opinions.

But how can a statesman do this while also giving the people to understand that they are his masters? The puzzle accounts for an ambiguity in the passage above. For the contrast between doing what is in appearance wrong and what is substantially right could only matter in a constituency where elections were contested, such as London, Westminster, or Bristol. A borough controlled by a patron, as Burke's seat from Wendover and later his seat from Malton were, presented smaller opportunities and no contradictions: the representative answered to the patron alone and the rules were well understood. In an active constituency, however, the greater prestige of the representative is matched by the demand for tactical or ostensible arguments to satisfy voters who might object to the actual tendency of his politics.[6] But this should not be too much to ask. And perhaps Burke is only suggesting an honest bargain: he has cooperated with the Bristol merchants, in a limited way, on Irish trade to secure their allowance of his opposition to the American war. Yet he is also saying that the disadvantage of popular politics is that the mask is never off. For every high-minded defense of principle, he must supply a low and accessible reason. His growing aversion to the demand for such reasons may explain a transition in his thinking about India a few years later. In the *Speech on Fox's East India Bill* of 1783, he will appeal to the duty of Britain toward the insulted dignity of the people of India. But the prosecution of Warren Hastings and the East India Company, from 1788 to 1794, registers the need of support from a public who prefer selfish apparent reasons. The reform ceases to be about India; the ostensible subject changes to England. To scour the company of corruption might look like a "mission," but it was close enough to self-interest for people to accept.

Until his final years, Burke was always a practical politician and a member of a party. In 1780, in the *Speech on Economical Reform*, he had gone along with the popular fondness for superficial remedies in order to guide a more profound change that the people might not have approved on its merits. This understanding made him uneasy—a feeling shared by Charles Fox, who confessed to Burke in a letter of September 17 that in order to get votes he had disclaimed all support for "any measure prejudicial to the Protestant Religion, or tending to *establish* Popery in this Kingdom." There was, of course, no danger of anyone establishing popery. Fox knew that he was pandering to a base prejudice that might compromise "the great cause of Toleration." It is revealing that he should have chosen Burke as his audience for such doubts: "Pray judge me severely and say whether I have done wrong." As we have seen, Burke at this time was also judging himself.

The Speech at the Guildhall

Ultimately, in Bristol in September 1780, Burke confronted an array of grievances which turned on the perception that his national stature had come at the expense of local interests. He had been slow to begin his canvass, and this was wrongly taken as a sign of detachment. His friends had made a futile late attempt to buy off Cruger with an offer of 2,000 pounds if he would agree not to run. Burke was expected to withdraw, therefore, but the meeting slated for his announcement grew unexpectedly warm on his behalf, and he changed his mind on the spot.[7] The excitement that this speech can generate, even at a distance of two and a half centuries, is a contagious effect of the mood of that moment.

Burke believed he had served Bristol honorably; and nobody had reason to suppose the honor was indifferent to him. The *Speech at the Bristol Guildhall* presumes that the electors may want him to retire. If so, he will submit to their change of mind, but he cannot regard such a verdict as a censure of his conduct. If, however, they ask him to proceed, he will remain a candidate whose qualifications can never be a cause of shame to them. In the great speech of 1780, as in his appeal against mandates both before and after the poll of 1774, he eschews all counterfeit deference. A large and heterogeneous society is bound to register divisions of honest judgment, and "the very attempt towards pleasing every body, discovers a temper always flashy, and often false and insincere." He offers to explain but not to reverse the parts of his conduct that have been most objected to. His listeners, meanwhile, are warned that this "eventful period"—when the American war turned against England and the Irish Volunteers threatened an upheaval closer to home—"has crowded into a few years space the revolutions of an age." They must not avert their gaze and attempt to adjust their opinions with each new shock. "Look, Gentlemen, to the *whole tenour* of your member's conduct."

The whole tenor of his conduct: Burke's independence—not of his party but of the court—remained a rare distinction to which he was willing to call attention. "None will serve us," he remarks, "whilst there is a court to serve, but those who are of a nice and jealous honour." Such persons ought to be treated with care, lest they be driven from the public stage or prompted to secure their interest by looking to the court for protection. So Burke renews the imperative of his 1774 *Speech at the Conclusion of the Poll* (with the additional knowledge of six years' service) to suggest certain allowances for men of intellectual energy like himself. If "we do not give confidence to their minds, and a liberal scope to their understandings; if we do not permit our members to act upon a *very* enlarged view of things; we shall at length infallibly degrade our national representation into a confused and scuffling bustle of local agency."[8] He takes a high-minded view of the deliberations of the Commons, whereas local representation is here demoted to a species of errand running—push and elbow-work and nosing forward. Who would choose it? If Burke exaggerates the contrast, his motive is to preserve a manly idea of resistance against "the monopoly of mental power," which the court would otherwise enjoy. Granted, the people may be a drag on the efforts of a representative. Still, the partial authority of the people is a constitutional good worthy of protection, and they cannot protect it by themselves. Without the assistance of such men as Burke, "on the side of the people there will be nothing but impotence: for ignorance is impotence; narrowness of mind is impotence." Here he picks up a thread from his argument in the *Speech on Economical Reform* (though the excessive influence of the crown is not among the topics raised at the start of the *Speech at the Bristol Guildhall*). The court still wants "to make its servants insignificant." And if the people should agree and turn Burke out of office, this will be a sign of the same imbalance: "no part of the state will be sound." A strong Parliament—and only a few men make it so—is required to mediate between the people and the court.

Burke will confront four main charges: neglecting his Bristol constituents; letting down the city by his impartiality in the Irish trade debates; refusing to favor lenders and creditors when he endorsed Lord Beauchamp's bills on debtors' prisons; and supporting the repeal of Catholic disabilities. His shortest answer covers the first charge:[9] "I live at an hundred miles distance from Bristol; and at the end of a session I come to my own house, fatigued in body and in mind, to a little repose, and to a very little attention to my family and my private concerns. A visit to Bristol is always a sort of canvass; else it will do more harm than good. To pass from the toils of a session to the toils of a canvass, is the furthest thing in the world from repose. I could hardly serve you *as I have done,* and court you too."[10] Burke does not say—as a modern politician would—that he needs to spend time with his family. He admits himself fatigued by his service to his country; but how could he surrender that pursuit for something smaller? Besides, his work on behalf of his Bristol constituents is performed at the Treasury, the Admiralty, the Customhouse, and the House of Commons: "I ran about wherever your affairs could call me; and in acting for you I often appeared rather as a ship-broker, than as a member of parliament." Those little services for city interests he felt all along to be an indignity, yet he performed them without complaint so long as the requests did not contradict his public duties. His absence has been caused by the continuous pressure of the American war; and on that question, Burke has kept a constant mind. He thought the war was wrong before it failed.

Steadfast judgment itself performs a service, and the preserving and publicizing of his judgment had occupied Burke when he might have paused to answer his local detractors. He reminds his listeners of the civic courage proper to a statesman when he alludes to "our great, but most unfortunate victory at Long Island." Even then, in August 1776, Burke had warned and admonished:

> This victory, which seemed to put an immediate end to all difficulties, perfected us in that spirit of domination, which our unparalleled prosperity had but too long nurtured. We had been so very powerful, and so very prosperous, that even the humblest of us were degraded into the vices and follies of kings. We lost all measure between means and ends; and our headlong desires became our politics and our morals. All men who wished for peace, or retained any sentiments of moderation, were overborne or silenced; and this city was led by every artifice (and probably with the more management, because I was one of your members) to distinguish itself by its zeal for that fatal cause. In this temper of yours and of my mind, I should sooner have fled to the extremities of the earth, than have shewn myself here.[11]

This reluctance to answer opposing voices in his constituency reveals an unusual trait of Burke's public character, and it suggests a more general perplexity of the time of transition he lived in. When he said of himself (and truly) that he was made for opposition, Burke had in mind the exertions of a representative who is normally out of power. Clash and confrontation with the people themselves, in an effort to persuade them, was never imagined by him as part of the role he was made for or the work he was meant to do.

Burke strove against the greed and delusion that infected many elements of this trading city; but to break the fever was an empty hope so long as victories made the wildest patriots heady with success. The same people might now acknowledge their error. But how could they wish that

Burke himself had tried to correct what only nature and fortune could change? Even as he gives these prudential reasons for his absence, Burke asks his listeners to deplore in retrospect "that spirit of domination, which our unparalleled prosperity had but too long nurtured."

It was excessive but understandable for him to say that in the late 1770s he hardly dared to show his face in Bristol. The enthusiasts for war are, by this confession, subtly linked to the Gordon mob. Burke means to imply that susceptibility to the spirit of domination is general across all classes. The follies of kings are shared by the people because they spring from the love of power. If kings are the authors of the worst abuses, that is not because kings are kings but because power is power.

War creates so vast a mutation in the spirit of a people that no issue is untouched by its influence. Irish trade might seem a thing apart from the success of British arms; but when the Irish Volunteers drilled and stood at the ready (but not for England's sake), the war came close to home. Thus, Burke's dissent on America, which made him say that victory would be more fatal to his country than defeat, cannot be separated from the want of local patriotism that showed in his support for the lifting of trade restrictions. As a moderate, he could not be happy to press a claim that was backed, as the Irish claim was, by extortionate force. The tendency to resolve such disputes by the threat of violence suggested to him that the American war was a poison that diffused its effects everywhere. Questions that might once have been settled by compromise now passed from menace to capitulation; and Burke, in this matter, is proud to have kept his balance. "What would be left to me, if I myself was the man, who softened, and blended, and diluted, and weakened, all the distinguishing colours of my life, so as to leave nothing distinct and determinate in my whole conduct?" If it is said he acted as a native of Ireland on the trade question, he will reply that he acted for neither Ireland nor England. "I certainly have very warm good wishes for the place of my birth. But the sphere of my duties is my true country." The last sentence by itself suffices to refute all assertions that Burke was a communitarian who especially favored local or national loyalties.

Of the concessions to Ireland by Parliament, Burke says that the first to be offered were useless. The next were thrown out by Lord North, and

Ireland was "instantly in a flame," its 40,000 Volunteers openly boasted of, and the king's army no longer acknowledged as legal. Meanwhile, British law could not recognize a self-appointed army of volunteers. This was the state of things when the people of Ireland demanded "a freedom of trade with arms in their hands." Parliament, having assented and backed away, was frightened and went forward again. After the suppression of American trade and the hope for restrictions on Ireland, it was the Volunteers that made the difference; there was, Burke recalls, "no reserve; no exception; no debate; no discussion. A sudden light broke in upon us all. It broke in, not through well-contrived and well-disposed windows, but through flaws and breaches; through the yawning chasms of our ruin. We were taught wisdom by humiliation."[12] This sudden coming to terms Burke supposed as dangerous as the earlier obstruction of all openings to Irish trade. The result of England's initial reliance on selfish force in America, and its impotent display of will without force in Ireland, was to confirm a pattern of using violence itself as a settler of political disputes. In Ireland the result has been "the perpetual establishment of a military power, in the dominions of the crown, without the consent of the British legislature, contrary to the policy of the constitution, contrary to the declaration of right; and by this your liberties are swept away along with your supreme authority." The Irish Perpetual Mutiny Act was a product of the same anti-conciliatory temper. The temporary status of a mutiny bill to punish deserters (passed by the Irish Parliament) had been objected to by the English Privy Council; so the Mutiny Act was rendered permanent. This apparent anomaly was an effect of Poyning's Law, which in the late fifteenth century settled the conventions for English review of Irish laws. An unresponsive policy was made worse by thoughtless reversion to ancient precedent. Through the efforts of Grattan, the repeal of both laws by the English Parliament would finally be secured, but not until May 27, 1782.

These enactments were in Burke's mind in his canvass of September 1780. When he said "the sphere of my duties is my true country," he meant that Britain mattered to him only as it served the common good of humankind. Even when he spoke of his country in a more parochial sense, he never meant less than all of Britain. Yet he was asking the Bristol electors to acknowledge his prescience on their behalf, too. He had served them well, he thought, by acting for something larger, but his ultimate guide was the sympathy that enabled him to put himself in the place of another, or many others:

> What! Gentlemen, was I not to foresee, or foreseeing, was I not to endeavour to save you from all these multiplied mischiefs and disgraces? Would the little, silly, canvass prattle of obeying instructions, and having no opinions but yours, and such idle senseless tales, which amuse the vacant ears of unthinking men, have saved you from "the pelting of that pitiless storm," to which the loose improvidence, the cowardly rashness of those who dare not look danger in the face, so as to provide against it in time, and therefore throw themselves headlong into the midst of it, have exposed this degraded nation, beat down and prostrate on the earth, unsheltered, unarmed, unresisting? Was I an Irishman on that day, that I boldly withstood our pride? or on the day that I hung down my head, and wept in shame and silence over the humiliation of Great Britain? I became unpopular in England for the one, and in Ireland for the other. What then! What obligation lay on me to be popular? I was bound to serve both kingdoms. To be pleased with my service, was their affair, not mine.
>
> I was an Irishman in the Irish business, just as much as I was an American, when on the same principles, I wished you to concede to America, at a time when she prayed concession at our feet.[13]

There is no evidence here of the coolness with which Burke had been charged by his Bristol opponents. As for the local objection that he was unmindful of his duties toward mercantile interests, or showed an excessive leniency or partiality to Ireland, they are answered by his image of the conscientious statesman who uses all his abilities. He has not helped his constituents to celebrate themselves. They do that very well without him; and why should he incant their praise unless by doing so he could secure an advantage they would otherwise lack? The faculty by which he really assists them is practical wisdom and foresight.

Burke, as speaker, writer, and member of Parliament, judges himself to be gifted with the art of persuading. This means that he works to remind others of oppressions and cruelties that a selfish imperceptiveness may exclude from their consciousness. His ability is connected to a sense of solidarity with the oppressed, even when they are strangers—perhaps most of all with strangers, because they afford an occasion for disinterested sympathy. "I confess to you freely," he says, "that the sufferings and distresses of the people of America in this cruel war, have at times affected me more deeply than I can express. . . . Yet the Americans are utter strangers to me." If he can feel for Americans whom he has never met, how can he do less for the Catholics of Ireland and England, whose predicament he knows more intimately?

Burke proposes, then, to act as the voice of a moral imagination in a deeper and wider sense of the phrase than he would later employ in *Reflections on the Revolution in France*. He derives his authority from something beyond custom and the "wardrobe" of pleasing and dignified beliefs and prejudices. He knows that he is implicated in the events of Ireland and America, and that the violence and misery with which England afflicts its opponents will return against Britain itself. He recognizes what others cannot see, perhaps cannot afford to see. This becomes an implicit subject of the speech by way of Burke's quotation from *King Lear* ("the pelting of that pitiless storm"); and indeed the whole passage in Shakespeare is resonant with his mood of alarm:

> Poor naked wretches, where soe'er you are
> That bide the pelting of this pitiless storm,
> How shall your houseless heads and unfed sides
> Your looped and windowed raggedness, defend you
> From seasons such as these?

The people of Britain, by their rashness and improvidence, have wagered the prosperity of the empire against American liberty and against an Irish share in the profits from open trade. They looked to maintain their hold of all they possessed—just as Lear did—and have given up the shelter that could only come from relinquishing their pride. Burke, not for the last time, puts himself in the role of Kent, the defiant but faithful knight who speaks truth to the king and his flatterers. His calling is not to be loved but to compel his master to "see well . . . and let me still remain / The true blank of thine eye." Burke presses the dramatic parallel further by his posture of intractability: "I was bound to serve both kingdoms. To be pleased with my service, was their affair, not mine." His self-respect, in the cause of service without dominion, goes with his belief in magnanimity.

Yet Burke's claim is that timely concession in the long run risks less than a policy of force, with all its uncertainty and likely reversals. The keenest advocates of British power have lately treated with America for terms of peace which they scorned to accept two years earlier. Lord Carlisle, the mover of "an haughty and rigorous address against America," was at the head of this "embassy of submission," as Burke calls it; William Eden, the associate of Lord Suffolk (who had called the American leadership "a Congress of vagrants"), went with Carlisle to America late in 1778 to search out the British generals, if they could be found, and join them "in the same commission of supplicating those whom they were sent to subdue."

At the height of his imaginative power, Burke surveys the scene of abject withdrawal:

> They enter the capital of America only to abandon it; and these assertors and representatives of the dignity of England, at the tail of a flying army, let fly their Parthian shafts of memorials and remonstrances at random behind them. Their promises and their offers, their flatteries and their menaces, were all despised; and we were saved the disgrace of their formal reception, only because the Congress scorned to receive them; whilst the State-house of independent Philadelphia opened her doors to the public entry of the ambassador of France. From war and blood, we went to submission; and from submission plunged back again to war and blood; to desolate and be desolated, without measure, hope, or end. I am a Royalist, I blushed for this degradation of the Crown. I am a Whig, I blushed for the dishonour of Parliament. I am a true Englishman, I felt to the quick for the disgrace of England. I am a Man, I felt for the melancholy reverse of human affairs, in the fall of the first power in the world.[14]

He turns from the lust of a conquering nation to the honor and dignity of its principles: this appeal is at the root of his belief that he deserves to be returned to Parliament. He defends his conduct less by argument than by clear self-definition; and more than most politicians, he is willing to rest his case on a negative: he ought to be admired for the things he opposed.

He would have spared England the disgrace of this war, and he feels the loss more than others do. His feelings come from a statesman's ability to take long views.

A representative in this position is always isolated because his judgments may seem to disdain the will of the people. Burke goes so far as to say that he was obliged to ignore their opinions: "To read what was approaching in Ireland, in the black and bloody characters of the American war, was a painful, but it was a necessary part of my public duty. For, Gentlemen, it is not your fond desires or mine that can alter the nature of things; by contending against which what we have got, or shall ever get, but defeat and shame? I did not obey your instructions: No. I conformed to the instructions of truth and nature, and maintained your interest, against your opinions, with a constancy that became me."[15] What Burke calls the instructions of truth and nature may stand in opposition to the mandates of the electors of Bristol. So his early contempt for mandates has, it seems, been raised to a higher power. He believes he has maintained the people's actual interests against their avowed opinions; in doing so, he has exemplified a prudence that does not waste itself in flattery. "A representative worthy of you," he says, "ought to be a person of stability. I am to look, indeed, to your opinions; but to such opinions as you and I *must* have five years hence." Without the modesty of "five years" and the concession to ordinary estimates of character, this passage would seem to advance a mystical doctrine of entitlement for the representative. Yet Burke is speaking one of the great truths of politics, a truth that by its nature is seldom uttered. The tenor of his justification may baffle a reader who associates the vocation of politics with nothing but flexibility and compromise. Burke, of course, generally speaks for those qualities—in the *Speech on Conciliation with America* above all—but he also denies that they can be the highest of public virtues.

Gradual Emancipation

The most thankless section of the speech gives a list of the reasons for the loss of approval Burke has endured in Bristol. He omits a cause that is now of great interest and that was not known in 1780. About the time he was looking for votes, Burke was drafting a *Sketch of a Negro Code* which laid down a plan of emancipation. Public knowledge of this might have sunk his candidacy entirely, burdened as it already was by anti-Catholic and anti-Irish prejudices. The Negro Code was not yet policy or law; but the views of Burke on this subject had never been a secret. When he did allow his thoughts to be circulated after the election, it was clear the measures he proposed would set rigorous limits on the slave trade.[16] His aim here in some ways resembled that of the East India bill a few years later: he meant to make slavery a responsibility of government that could not be evaded. The understanding was that once under control, the institution would gradually be brought into conformity with the laws and morals of the supervising country. Under Burke's code, the traffickers in slaves would no longer have been granted an exemption for despotic violence merely because they were dealers in property, buyers and sellers and not governors, "a state in the disguise of a merchant." An uninhibited public statement on this subject would come from Burke in his speeches on the abolition of the slave trade in May 1789. "The most shameful trade," he would call it then, "that ever the hardened heart of man could bear"; and in answer to testimony concerning the happiness of slaves in the West Indies, he would reply with finality that "nothing made a happy slave, but a degraded man."[17] Yet the partial reform he contemplated in 1780 was of more than passing relevance to the representation of Bristol. For Bristol, together with London and Liverpool, was at the center of the triangular Atlantic trade, by which textiles and other goods went from England to West Africa, captured slaves were taken from West Africa to the West Indies, and sugar was brought back from the West Indies to be refined in England. Between 1698 and 1807, merchants of the city accounted for almost one-fifth of the total British slave trade; and in that time, 500,000 blacks were conveyed into servitude in ships that set sail from Bristol. The measure that Burke now contemplated, perhaps more than any action he had taken in his service in Parliament, stood to change the character of the city that he represented.

To protect the *lives* of the slaves was his main concern. By doing so, at whatever expense to the profits of the traders, he hoped to institute the first necessary restraints against the abuse of mastery. (He recognized that all mastery begins with abuse and violence, from which it cannot ultimately free itself.) Burke was seeking the improvement of justice toward black slaves, however circumscribed; any steps that were now taken toward fairer treatment would point to the wisdom of eventual emancipation. But first must come the freedom of a few, chosen for their talents, their record of conduct, and their age. Accordingly, Burke's devices of codification fall into four main categories: oversight, accountability, exemptions, and education.

A record must be kept of those who transport the slaves and how many slaves they transport; controls must be put in to monitor the provisions of food and medical assistance. This means that owners have to register their names; and both the master and the owner of a ship must give their bond to affirm that they will conform to regulations. Each ship is assigned a carpenter and a surgeon to report on how it meets the requirements of room to breathe in and safe transportation. Food is to be checked for soundness and sufficiency. There will be a set maximum number of slaves allowed to be taken, in proportion to the size of the ship and the weight of other supplies. The places of departure are limited to one of the appointed marts. There must be a hospital on shore and a hospital ship in each of these ports. At the end of the voyage, jurisdiction over slaves is given to the attorney general of each district or colony, who at that point assumes the office of Protector of Negroes.

Sureness of accountability and efficacy of oversight are to be secured by a new body of laws. Restrictions will limit the Negroes permitted to be sold. Every sale must be attested by one inspector and by either the governor or one of the council on the trade. None can be sold over the age of thirty or who appears to have been stolen or "carried away by the Dealers by Surprize"; nor any who is literate; nor a woman three months or further into pregnancy; nor the distorted or feeble, unless with their consent. Heavy penalties will be levied against traders or factors who are judged by the "governor or other authority" (among the appointed commissioners) to have stolen or taken by surprise any slaves without the consent of masters; or to have willfully and maliciously killed or maimed a slave or committed any cruelty except restraint; or burned houses or destroyed goods. A trader or factor who is judged to be guilty will have forfeited his freedom and "be deliver'd over to the Prince to whom he belongs to execute further justice on him, and shall be for ever disabled from dealing in any of the said Marts." If European, he is sent to Europe and delivered back, and "the Keeper of any of his Majesty's Jails in London, Bristol, Liverpool, or Glasgow, shall receive him until he be delivered according to due course of Law, as if the said Offences had been committed within the Cities and Towns aforesaid." Fines are set for "unlawful communication with any Woman Slave."[18]

By various details of the code, Burke makes it clear that he wants, above all, to rid the slave trade of one primary evil: the separation of families. "If on inspection or information it shall be found that any Negro shall have in the same ship, or any other at the same time examined, a wife, an Husband, a Brother, Sister, or Child, the person or persons so related shall not be sold separately at that or any future sale." With the protection of families goes an emphasis on the encouragement of worship. Churches are recognized by Burke as a reliable means of assimilation of manners and therefore of eventual education and emancipation. In each of the districts established with Negroes, a presbyter of the Church of England "shall point under him one Clerk, who shall be a free Negro . . . and the said Minister and Clerk, both or one shall instruct the said Negroes in the Church Catechism." The minister will also establish a register of births, burials, and marriages of all Negroes and mulattoes in the district.[19]

In every district, Burke's code would set up a school for young Negroes, the teaching to be done three days a week for four hours each day. The minister pays the owners a modest recompense for the lost labor of each student; any who show remarkable aptitude can be purchased by the Protector of Negroes and sent to the bishop of London for further education in England. Those selected are to be provided for until the age of twenty-four (and, it is implied, thereafter to be freed, though Burke never says so). Those who, in England, "fall short of expectation" are after a year to be apprenticed to a handicraft, then given to the Lord Mayor of London and transmitted to their native islands, there to reside as free Negroes, "subject however to the direction of the Protector of Negroes" who keeps track of their conduct and their employment.[20]

Marriage is the particular institution Burke would strengthen in order to create the social basis for an emancipated community. Negro men and women (over eighteen for the men, over sixteen for the women) "who have cohabited together for twelve Months or upwards or who shall cohabit for the same time, and have a Child or Children, shall be deemed to all intents and purposes to be married." This contributes again to ensure that individuals will not be sold from their families: "And be it enacted that no negro who is married and hath resided upon any plantation for twelve months, shall be sold either privately or by any decree of any Court, but along with the plantation on which he hath resided, unless he should himself request to be separated therefrom." The right of the individual slave to have this singular recognition of humanity—the status of a person indissolubly linked to a wife or a husband, to children and to parents—thus supersedes the right of the slave master to do as he likes with property he has paid for.

Exemplary conduct is honored as evidence of a readiness for freedom. But there is a simpler way, on the terms of this code, of achieving not full but partial freedom, namely demonstration of "the habits of industry and sobriety and the means of acquiring and preserving property." Every Negro man who has served ten years, and is thirty years of age, and is married and has two children of any marriage thereby obtains Saturday free for himself and his wife, and at the age of thirty-seven can add Friday for both, provided the minister of the district and the inspector of Negroes certify their peaceable, orderly, and industrious character.

Some diminution of the resort to habitual coercive violence must always accompany the ascent to dignity of a people. The Negro Code would limit the use of the lash to thirteen blows for an offense. On a complaint that is judged accurate by the protector, any Negro who is cruelly or inhumanly treated, or exposed to the malice of a cruel overseer, can be ordered to be sold to another master. With a weakened severity of control goes a program of gradual manumission, the precursor of a plan of total emancipation: "Every Negro slave being thirty years of age and upwards, and who has had three Children born to him in lawful Matrimony and who hath received a Certificate from the Minister of his District" may purchase his freedom and that of his wife or children, at a price fixed by justices of the peace so as to amount to half the market value: the father must only bind himself for the good behavior of his children.[21] The Protector of

Negroes may purchase the freedom of any Negro who excels in the mechanical or the liberal arts, at a price to be fixed by a jury; and all who are capable of earning a livelihood should be guided at once into some industrious pursuit. The rule holds for other corrupt laws and customs besides slavery, by which human energies are pent up, and men and women are punished with no relief in sight. Burke's campaign for the reform of the slave trade, in fact, answers to the same impulse that drove his concern to reform the inhumane laws that governed imprisonment for debt.

Persuasion and the Remedy of Injustice

Such was the largest piece of legislation that occupied Burke in the shadow of the American war, concerning the greatest abuse of power that existed then in Britain and America. It was a significant precursor of the measures that in Britain abolished the slave trade in 1807 and slavery itself in 1833. By comparison, his support for Lord Beauchamp's bill reforming debtors' prisons may seem a dispensable commitment. Yet from his *Tract on the Popery Laws* onward, nothing had been so central to Burke's idea of liberty as the conviction affirmed by Beauchamp that all men are equal under the law. It followed that the law should not be a torment to one who does wrong from terror or incapacity. This bill gave necessary relief to the oppressions to which all debtors were liable; but in defending its justice, Burke does not place himself above the claim of expedience. Though he pressed for the passage of the bill, he had also faithfully submitted the Bristol petition against it and asked that the relevant objections be met "on account of the character and consequence of those who signed it." He admits (with chagrin) that he himself was thus partly responsible for the defeat of the measure; the small delay he requested was drawn out by the illness of the speaker and then by the frantic tumult about popery, "which drove that and every rational business from the House." No one person can be assigned the blame for the losses to justice from the Gordon Riots. Still, Burke does blame his own excessive attention to the Bristol petitioners for this injury to social fairness. "I am so far from taking credit for the defeat of that measure, that I cannot sufficiently lament my misfortune, if but one man, who ought to be at large, has passed a year in prison by my means. I am a debtor to the debtors." The truth is that Burke believed Lord Beauchamp's proposal did not go far enough. By the law as it stood, every man was presumed to be solvent, with the consequence that every man was supposed to have the ability to pay: to the extent that he fails, he is therefore supposed to engage in fraud; and in this way, a civil is turned into a criminal judgment against the debtor. To sharpen the humiliation, the punishment is not even referred to a judge but rather to "the arbitrary discretion of a private, nay interested, and irritated, individual." Under the present law, the accuser is empowered to act at once as party and as judge.

The worst insolence of office, Burke felt, comes from those who dare to act as judges in their own cause. The law on debt, especially, manifested a close kinship with revenge by classifying debt as both a crime and a private offense. "If," he asks, "insolvency be no crime, why is it punished with imprisonment? If it be a crime, why is it delivered into private hands to pardon without discretion, or to punish without mercy and without measure?" It has always been possible, by a narrow selection of texts, to treat Burke as an orthodox moralist on the pattern of his fanatical half-disciple Joseph de Maistre;[22] but de Maistre's image of social authority is severe and coercive; it invests the figure of the executioner with the aura of a sacred officer. By contrast, Burke had in view the general good of society, and he saw that good as consistent with the reduction of cruelty and the removal of useless penalties. He thought that neither retribution nor the prevention and punishment of crime was the chief aim of justice; all his writings suggest that he would have recoiled at the fantasy of imprinting on the criminal the sign of exemplary vengeance and expiation. A punishment, to be justified to Burke, must look toward the extension of liberty and the civilizing of justice. In this, he is closer to the legal reformers Bentham and Beccaria than to de Maistre or his successors in the celebration of sovereign violence.[23]

It is natural for creditors to press their advantage over the unlucky whom they hold in thrall. Burke perceived in such calculated selfishness an evil no more excusable than the unloosed passions of rioters. Indeed, when his speech turns at last to the Gordon Riots, it broadens the image of human evil beyond any class or creed. Burke connects the disabilities of the Protestant dissenters of Bristol with the assault on the Catholics targeted in London two months earlier. (He refers to the latter as "our Catholic dissenters.") Happy to find the anti-Catholic prejudice less virulent in Bristol than he had feared—"not above four or five in the city," he reports, "have signed that symbol of delusion and bond of sedition, that libel on the national religion and English character, the Protestant association"—Burke hopes to rededicate Catholics and enlightened Protestants to the spirit of tolerance. He would tear the mask of respectability from those who use the words *Protestant* and *liberty* to impart "a sort of sinister dignity to proceedings that had their origin in only the meanest and blindest malice." A speaker of commonplace eloquence would at this point have produced an account of the riots. Burke, being Burke, proceeds with a short history of the Reformation.

The passage that follows is the most balanced of all his remarks on that subject, and should be taken to qualify everything else he says of the psychology of Protestant belief: from the analysis of "the dissidence of dissent" in America to his later comment that all Protestantism tends toward unbelief and that the natural terminus of Protestantism is atheism. He discerns in the genealogy of Protestant belief two major elements: the idea of natural rights and a conscientious suspicion of the abuse of power by institutions. He looks on the growth of these habits of thought as part of a progress whose moral tendency he approves of; but he attaches a strong reservation concerning the violence that comes with all revolutionary change:

> We buy our blessings at a price. The Reformation, one of the greatest periods of human improvement, was a time of trouble and confusion. The vast structure of superstition and tyranny, which had been for ages in rearing, and which was combined with the interest of the great and of the many; which was moulded into the laws, the manners, and civil institutions of nations, and blended with the frame and policy of states; could not be brought to the ground without a fearful struggle; nor could it fall without a violent concussion of itself and all about it. When this great revolution was attempted in a more regular mode by government, it was opposed by plots and seditions of the people; when by popular efforts, it was repressed as rebellion by the hand of power;

and bloody executions (often bloodily returned) marked the whole of its progress through all its stages. . . . The Protestant religion in that violent struggle, infected, as the Popish had been before, by worldly interests and worldly passions, became a persecutor in its turn, sometimes of the new sects, which carried their own principles further than it was convenient to the original reformers; and always of the body from whom they parted; and this persecuting spirit arose, not only, from the bitterness of retaliation, but from the merciless policy of fear.

It was long before the spirit of true piety and true wisdom, involved in the principles of the Reformation, could be depurated from the dregs and feculence of the contention with which it was carried through. However, until this be done, the Reformation is not complete; and those who think themselves good Protestants, from their animosity to others, are in that respect no Protestants at all.[24]

Most notable in this passage is the acknowledgment by Burke that the Reformation was a "blessing." Yet he declines to interpret the change merely as a defeat of superstition and an advance toward acceptance of the principle of liberty of conscience.

If the Protestant Reformation did, in fact, reform, the habits of men and women were still embedded in their ancient faith. Involved, then, with the honest zeal for throwing off dogma and compulsion were all the mixed passions of the reformers—moral courage, earnest love of truth, sublime self-respect, but also self-will heated by resentment and a craving for worldly power. The great and the many felt an inward sympathy with the Roman Catholic Church; this assured that its overthrow would not be accomplished without violence. Inevitably, in a contest for control of the customs of worship, faith will be corrupted by "worldly interests and worldly passions." The great evil of which religion can never rid itself (so long as it combines with worldly power) is "the merciless policy of fear"—fear, in this case, of political authority, which swells the passion for war and multiplies the ranks of the warriors by a promise of heavenly reward. The work of the Reformation, Burke concludes, was bound to be carried out, since the human love of liberty and hatred of imposition could not be satisfied otherwise. Yet the work will not be complete until religious instincts are appeased without war and without formulae of mass purification. The inflammatory elements of a militant faith can be cooled only as it settles into the security of triumph and unquestioned toleration.

Sir George Savile's bill sought the repeal of a 1699 statute that punished with perpetual imprisonment the saying of mass and the giving of instruction in Catholic schools. Under the old law, a Catholic who declined to take the coercive oath would forfeit his paternal inheritance to the nearest Protestant relation—unless, as Burke puts it, he changed his mind and "redeemed by his hypocrisy, what the law had transferred to the kinsman as the recompense of his profligacy." Thus disinherited, a Catholic was forbidden by law to acquire other property "by any industry, donation, or charity; but was rendered a foreigner in his native land, only because he retained the religion, along with the property, handed down to him." Repeal of these disabilities was the only reform that could answer the gravity of the harm. Once more, as with Lord Beauchamp's bill on debtors' prisons, Burke pays homage to the courage of the lawmaker and regrets that he himself did not do more to win approval for the law. "To have been the man chosen out to redeem our fellow-citizens from slavery; to purify our laws from absurdity and injustice; and to cleanse our religion from the blot and stain of persecution, would be an honour and happiness to which my wishes would undoubtedly aspire; but to which nothing but my wishes could possibly have entitled me. That great work was in hands in every respect far better qualified than mine." Even so, the secondary assistance Burke gave to Savile was a source of resentment in Bristol.

The courage of Savile on the present occasion reminds Burke of his previous stand against the king on the Nullum Tempus Act.[25] Both positions went with Savile's belief that encroachment on property, whether by a monarch or a Protestant majority, is a trespass against liberty. That Savile had no particular liking for Catholics or connection to any body of them ("I know," says Burke, "that he inclines to a sort of disgust, mixed with a considerable degree of asperity") renders his action if anything more admirable.[26] Indeed, says Burke, Savile moved this act for repeal of disabilities out of "extreme zeal to the Protestant religion" and chagrin at its abuse and perversion by the act of 1699. A stroke of emancipation like Savile's bill, however, cannot be executed without some regard to its timing. An appropriate season arrived with the breakup of the empire in 1778–1780, as America was torn from its parent stock and threatened to be "engrafted on the power of France," and "a great terror fell upon this kingdom" from the fear of a French invasion. Just when that cloud "gloomed over us all," an address was made to the throne, expressive of loyalty, by the body of the Catholics of England. Some reciprocal measure, beyond the mere expression of gratitude, seemed to be called for, if only to prove that the "natural government" was worthy of that name to Catholics; for at this crisis, "to delay protection would be to reject allegiance." Savile's bill addressed that need. Though nothing of value should be attributed to the American war, still, if it has produced (by indirection) an end to the "civil distinctions" between Protestant and Catholics, how can Burke fail to welcome the result?

People accustomed to value a society at peace may come to an understanding with themselves and learn to accept oppressions that seem to assure stability. If my children are securer from the menace of riot because certain laws against Catholics are allowed to stay on the books, why should I lose my sense of safety to uphold a principle? Burke's reply is that the sacrifice of liberty for the promise of order always gives up more than we realize. "Bad laws are the worst sort of tyranny. In such a country as this, they are of all bad things the worst, worse by far than any where else; and they derive a particular malignity even from the wisdom and soundness of the rest of our institutions." The reputation of the fairness of the laws in general may screen a single bad law from contempt; even as, by its inclusion in the system, the bad law tends to corrupt the whole. The acceptance of such a law only builds up credit for the false belief that liberty can escape unharmed when an injustice is done to a proscribed group. Burke here deplores the way that legal proscriptions may expose the innocent and give tacit encouragement to the vicious. A new species of parasites came into the world with the anti-Catholic laws, the bribed assistants of repression who worked through servility and deceit: "A mercenary informer knows no distinction. Under such a system, the obnoxious people are slaves, not only to the government, but they live at the mercy of every individual; they are at once the slaves of the whole community, and of every part of it; and the worst and most unmerciful men are those on whose goodness they most depend." This sounds like an observation from experience; yet Burke is right not to reduce it to an anecdote. His point is that the treachery and reptile cunning of informers become widespread once a society has lowered its morale to permit such exclusions at all.

How many were excluded? Burke estimates that English Catholics number fewer than 50,000, while the Irish are at least 1,600,000—figures that themselves suggest a reason for toleration. Holland and parts of Germany have liberalized their practices in this regard; and in Catholic France, the respect shown for the Swiss Protestant Necker reveals a similar progress. In view of Burke's later apparent hostility toward the very idea of cosmopolitan enlightenment, we may note the saliency of his appeal to a standard of international opinion: "no law of this country ever met with such universal applause abroad, or was so likely to produce the perfection of that tolerating spirit, which, as I observed, has been gaining ground in Europe; for abroad, it was universally thought that we had done, what I am sorry to say, we had not; they thought we had granted a full toleration." But appearance may matter more than reality if it shows the face we wish to be judged by. Eventually, to acquit ourselves in our own eyes, we shall have to live up to our assumed character; but even in 1780, a large effect of the passage of Savile's law will be to promote toleration for the Protestants of Europe. Sometimes generosity ought to exceed the necessity of the occasion; too often, says Burke, "the works of malice and injustice" are executed "in a bold masterly hand"; whereas in passing a measure that removes an injustice, "we are generally cold, and languid, and sluggish." He would employ "the spirit of those vehement passions that call forth all our energies whenever we oppress and persecute"; but he would have us transfer those passions to the side of emancipation. This was perhaps the deepest meaning of enlightenment for Burke.

The progress of religious toleration was halted in England by the eruption of the Gordon Riots—"a desperate attempt," as he calls it, to reverse the work of genuine liberty by its counterfeit; an attempt that, had it succeeded, "would have consumed all the glory and power of this country in the flames of London; and buried all law, order, and religion, under the ruins of the metropolis of the Protestant world." Whatever the aims of the instigators, "this would have been the unavoidable consequence of their proceedings, had not the flames they had lighted up in their fury been extinguished in their blood."[27] In discussing the riots, Burke takes nothing at face value. The motive of the petitioners was to exact the oath of allegiance from Catholics and then to deny them the benefits of that oath: it was to go back on an agreement already entered into and assure that the promise once made would not be kept. He speaks of his own actions at the time: "I called forth every faculty that I possessed, and I directed it in every way which I could possibly employ it. I laboured night and day. I laboured in Parliament: I laboured out of Parliament. If therefore the resolution of the House of Commons, refusing to commit this act of unmatched turpitude, be a crime, I am guilty among the foremost."[28] Rejection of the anti-Catholic petitioners was part of a constitutional design. Burke, by his own testimony, was conservative and radical: conservative in his resolution to maintain a good achieved by the labor of ages, radical in his commitment to a standard of justice that does not change with time and place. To resist compromise in such a crisis is the duty of a statesman. Yet the people ought to be encouraged in their acceptance of an imperfect system, for the sake of tolerance as well as self-preservation, and Burke praises the Catholics of London for their restraint. A violent reaction against the fury of the crowd could only have produced more violent acts.

In closing his narrative of the events of 1780, Burke joins his sentiments to those of the oppressed minority. Though he defied the Gordon mob, he, too, practiced restraint, and he wished, as a member of Parliament, only to have his share "of doing good, and resisting evil." He supposed that wish was fulfilled when he had given "quiet to private property, and private conscience." So Burke stands before the Bristol electors accused of no venality or pettiness or neglect of public duty. He is arraigned for having carried benevolence too far. This accusation, he says, he will carry with him from now on, "in pain, in sorrow, in depression," and whenever he calls it to mind he will be comforted.

Such is the formal conclusion of Burke's extraordinary apology and self-portrait of 1780. Its argumentative climax, however, had come a little earlier. Thinking back on the madness of early June and on the beliefs that drove his conduct, Burke spoke of the wrong of encouraging the unchecked exertions of the will of the people:

I have no idea of a liberty unconnected with honesty and justice. Nor do I believe, that any good constitutions of government or of freedom, can find it necessary for their security to doom any part of the people to a permanent slavery. Such a constitution of freedom, if such can be, is in effect no more than another name for the tyranny of the strongest faction; and factions in republics have been, and are, full as capable as monarchs, of the most cruel oppression and injustice. It is but too true, that the love, and even the very idea, of genuine liberty, is extremely rare. It is but too true, that there are many, whose whole scheme of freedom, is made up of pride, perverseness, and insolence. They feel themselves in a state of thraldom, they imagine that their souls are cooped and cabbined in, unless they have some man, or some body of men, dependent on their mercy. The desire of having some one below them, descends to those who are the very lowest of all,—and a Protestant cobler, debased by his poverty, but exalted by his share of the ruling church, feels a pride in knowing, it is by his generosity alone, that the peer, whose footman's step he measures, is able to keep his chaplain from a jail. This disposition is the true source of the passion, which many men in very humble life, have taken to the American war. *Our* subjects in America; *our* colonies; *our* dependents. This lust of party-power, is the liberty they hunger and thirst for; and this Syren song of ambition, has charmed ears, that one would have thought were never organised to that sort of music.[29]

The very idea of a constitution is linked to the self-restraint that fits a people for liberty. On the other hand, a craving for unlimited power belongs to men of ungovernable insolence, whose "party" ideas barely disguise their self-will and their wish to have someone to lord it over.

The ambitious make laws to hem in persons they want to oppress—a bill of attainder is their natural instrument—whereas a constitutional system is not a respecter of persons. But the vulnerability of English liberty comes from the susceptibility of all classes to the lust for power. This self-will is not diverted, it is only exacerbated, by the fantasy of imperial omnipotence. A dream of glory and empire, in the American war, has drugged the minds of the people from high to low. Of course, this desire is latent in all people at all times. "The Syren song of ambition" has charmed many who would appear not "organised to that sort of music"—but the work of constitutional government is to suppress this appetite with so gentle a touch that the pains of denial are never felt. Parliament may do its work indifferently or well, but the conscious support of injustice is an evil it is bound never to assist.

Burke takes his stand on a pledge to repair the same communion of British justice which he had evoked in the *Speech on Conciliation with America* five years earlier: "The diversified but connected fabric of universal justice, is well cramped and bolted together in all its parts; and depend upon it, I never have employed, and I never shall employ, any engine of power which may come into my hands, to wrench it asunder. All shall stand, if I can help it, and all shall stand connected. After all, to complete this work, much remains to be done; much in the East, much in the West."[30] It is sometimes said that Burke's belief in "universal justice" was a discovery of convenience to assist his prosecution of Warren Hastings. This passage suggests a different judgment. Already in 1780, he treats the East India Company as something more than a secondary cause of the American war; much remains to be done "in the East." His defense of a universal justice against the abuse of power by the governors of the empire is sweeping and unmistakable.

What is it about the British constitution that makes such a statement possible? The words could not be said by a servant of the king or by a tribune of the people. But Burke's is the relation of a representative—answerable to but not mimicking the suffrage of the people; serving to refine the policies and improve the knowledge of the executive, yet sometimes acting as a barrier against monarchical power. Toleration is neither natural nor unnatural to human beings, but the duty of a moral leader is to turn the people away from bigotry in every setting. Against those who say that the numbers of the rioters make an argument for attending to their opinions (an argument that assumes it is never right for a politician to shock the feelings of large numbers of people), Burke asserts the rightness of resistance to political violence no matter what its source. The changing opinions of the people are not to be confused with the standard of right and wrong. Defense of the weak was the heart of Savile's bill, too; and the timid voices on the other side cannot induce Burke to regret his vote:

I confess, my notions are widely different; and I never was less sorry for any action of my life. I like the bill the better, on account of the events of all kinds that followed it. It relieved the real sufferers; it strengthened the state; and, by the disorders that ensued, we had clear evidence, that there lurked a temper somewhere, which ought not to be fostered by the laws. . . . We knew before-hand, or we were poorly instructed, that toleration is odious to the intolerant; freedom to oppressors; property to robbers; and all kinds and degrees of prosperity to the envious. . . . When we know, that the opinions of even the greatest multitudes, are the standard of rectitude, I shall think myself obliged to make those opinions the masters of my conscience. But if it may be doubted whether Omnipotence itself is competent to alter the essential constitution of right and wrong, sure I am, that such *things,* as they and I, are possessed of no such power. No man carries further than I do the policy of making government pleasing to the people. But the widest range of this politic complaisance is confined within the limits of justice. I would not only consult the interest of the people, but I would cheerfully gratify their humours. We are all a sort of children, that must be soothed and managed. I think I am not austere or formal in my nature. I would bear, I would even myself play my part in, any innocent buffooneries, to divert them. But I never will act the tyrant for their amusement. If they will mix malice in their sports, I shall never consent to throw them any living, sentient, creature whatsoever, no not so much as a kitling, to torment.[31]

Justice here is definitively placed above the reach of the humors of the mob. And when Burke calls them *things,* his memory of Shakespeare darkens the emphasis: "You blocks, you stones, you worse than senseless things! / O you hard hearts, you cruel men of Rome." The words in *Julius Caesar* are spoken by an aristocrat to commoners at their sudden transfer of allegiance from Pompey to Caesar. When Burke refers to "such *things* as you and I"—joining his submission to the moral order with that of all creatures and entities—he reminds us that the justice of the lawgiver makes itself known by visible acts.

What can easily escape notice, in this magnificent passage, is the radical assertion that is placed in a conditional clause: *if it may be doubted whether Omnipotence itself is competent to alter the essential constitution of right and wrong.* Suppose it is true, as the sentence suggests, that God cannot alter the constitution of right and wrong. What then? Burke is saying that we are given a conscience to judge right and wrong as best we can; the highest part of ourselves is the highest reckoner of our choices; no majority, no sovereignty, no institution from "time immemorial" can outweigh the verdict of conscience. Even supposing that conscience, which reveals all we know of "the constitution of right and wrong," were somehow made to decide in contradiction to God's will, yet we cannot part from our human judgment without ceasing to be what we are.

So profound a respect for conscience was rare in the history of moral philosophy before the nineteenth century. If we try to align Burke with his few precursors or coevals in such a belief, his company will be mainly composed of Dissenters and schismatic Protestants. But the thinker who most nearly anticipates his explanation of the autonomy of moral judgment is Joseph Butler: the bishop of Durham and author of *Analogy of Religion* (1736), which marshaled the evidence for a principle of order that connects the natural and the moral world. The *Analogy* made Butler one of the most revered figures of the eighteenth century, but Burke seems to have been influenced, more particularly, by the argument against the prevalence of self-interest in Butler's *Sermons*. Self-interest and benevolence, as Butler understood them, are not opposed to each other but merely distinct. Indeed, selfishness tends to contradict itself (the love of gambling is a clear example) as much as it contradicts benevolence. This perception is latent in Butler's aphorism, "Every thing is what it is and not another thing."

In the argument of Burke's that we have been tracing, conscience is what it is and not another thing. And Omnipotence is a separate thing from conscience. Butler had framed the argument in his *Dissertation of the Nature of Virtue* by saying that conscience itself is definitive of the constitution of man. Both thinkers suppose that conscience may recognize a difference between its judgments and those approved by religious authority; and Burke and Butler, seeing this logical possibility, deny that the moral nature of man can allow itself to act against conscience. Regarding the claims of such integrity, Butler says of conscience in his second sermon: "Had it strength, as it has right; had it power, as it has manifest authority; it would absolutely govern the world." The force of such feelings as gratitude and indignation proves that we are made to regard people as free and responsible beings. The conscientious judgment of human action is thus an obligation we cannot escape; it is in the nature of who and what we are. But what happens when authority and conscience render opposite judgments?

This was Burke's question about the propriety of conciliating the popular sentiment against Catholics in 1780. Butler said about such cases more generally: suppose a wrong or unjust action could create a happier state of things at the present moment or throughout the world (as people judge happiness in the world), still this result could not atone for the wickedness of the action. "Some of the most shocking instances of injustice, adultery, murder, perjury, and even prosecution, may, in many supposable cases, not have the appearance of being likely to produce an overbalance of misery in the present state: perhaps sometimes may have the contrary appearance." But however a bad action may produce good effects, our duty is to use the equipment we were given for discerning right from wrong. "The fact," writes Butler, "appears to be, that we are constituted so as to condemn falsehood, unprovoked violence, injustice, and to approve of benevolence to some preferably to others, *abstracted from all consideration, which conduct is likely to produce an overbalance of happiness or misery.*"[32] We must approve of what we judge right, disapprove of what we judge wrong, and back our judgments by sanctions; and we must do so whether the result is pleasing to many, or few, or none, for "this is our constitution." We judge by the lights of *this* authority finally, and not by estimates of the quantity of convenience an action may produce. Burke's echo of Butler, on the reality of injustice and our equipment for deciding not to advance injustice, gives a vital clue to his protest against "calculators" and against all merely arithmetical assessments of right and wrong.

How then to judge the Gordon Riots? Here was a mass movement of confused purpose and wicked effect that came and went suddenly. Yet to concede nothing to the protest was to risk its reemergence. Burke says that the answer is opposition without vindictiveness, an attitude of forbearance without any hint of approval. To deploy the full force of the state against malefactors, when they themselves have lost all self-restraint, may yield a moralistic satisfaction, but such retribution is dangerous as well as futile. All human beings acting in a mass are liable to the same distemper. The right policy, therefore, is to divert, perhaps even temporarily to placate the crowd, but never to "act the tyrant for their amusement." A keyed-up demagogue like Gordon resembles a hunter who has carried his sport too far or into the wrong neighborhood. The statesman must discourage the passive members of the crowd while enforcing rigorous punishments on those who (with forethought) have inflicted irreparable damage.

Trials at the Old Bailey of the accused participants of the Gordon mob commenced on June 29 and ended on July 11. Sixty-eight persons were convicted of capital crimes and executed, usually at the places where their crimes had been committed. Gordon was luckier. He had never urged the mob to acts of violence, only harangued them on the threat of Catholicism and the loss of their rights; there was testimony of his bewilderment at the forces he had set in motion; and friends and family had secured two distinguished lawyers to defend him, Lloyd Kenyon and Thomas Erskine (the latter had defended Admiral Keppel). Gordon was accused of having intended "to raise and levy war, insurrection and rebellion" and having compassed the death of "our Lord the King"—a crime for which the capital punishment was elaborate and grisly. His acquittal in February 1781 was partly the result of the demonstrated unreliability of government witnesses. The prosecution also found it impossible to sustain with certainty the argument that Gordon by his speeches in the lobby of the House of Commons had caused the violence that followed. In later years, association with Count Cagliostro led him to publish a provocative advertisement about French spies in London and the cruelties of the queen of France. He was thought to be the author, in addition, of a pamphlet urging the cause of Newgate prisoners against their being sent to Botany Bay. For the latter, he was accused of a libel on the laws and administration of the laws of England; and for the former, of a libel on the queen of France and the French ambassador. Convicted in June 1787, Gordon this time fled rather than accept his punishment, and when he surfaced the following year with a "straggling black beard" and "a dirty gabardine coat which hung on his thin body like a cloak," it was as a convert to Judaism who had changed his name to Israel bar Abraham George Gordon. He would die in Newgate five years later.[33]

The image of Gordon in prison eventually formed a curious passing detail near the emotional climax of Burke's *Reflections:*

> We have Lord Gordon fast in Newgate; and neither his being a public proselyte to Judaism, nor his having, in his zeal against Catholic priests and all sorts of ecclesiastics, raised a mob (excuse the term, it is still in use here) which pulled down all our prisons, have preserved to him a liberty, of which he did not render himself worthy by a virtuous use of it. We have rebuilt Newgate, and tenanted the mansion. We have prisons almost as strong as the Bastile, for those who dare to libel the queens of France. In this spiritual retreat, let the noble libeler remain. Let him there meditate on his Thalmud, until he learns a conduct more becoming his birth and parts, and not so disgraceful to the antient religion to which he has become a proselyte.[34]

Some hint of the fury Burke repressed in 1780 may be felt to emerge in these later sentences, which are pointed and particular but also full of spite. The gloating reference to the Bastille is only imaginable in the later Burke; as is the suggestion which follows: that Gordon somehow epitomized Protestantism at that dangerous extreme at which it becomes identical with Hebraic superstition and Jewish vengefulness.[35]

If, looking back in 1790, Burke could seem preoccupied by the personality of Gordon himself, in 1780 his mind was on the conduct of the crowd. Why did some of them join the worst of the violence, while others stood apart? His own principle was simple: "If they will mix malice with their sports, I will never consent to throw them any sentient, living creature." (*King Lear* was again in his mind: "As flies to wanton boys are we to the gods;/They kill us for their sport.") Play that becomes rougher than play is an always possible deformation of politics. Burke's resistance to the savagery of the sport tells a great deal about him; and from these remarks, one might deduce the temper of the advice he had already given to the prosecutors of the Gordon mob. Capital punishments should be few and the places of execution widely spaced across the city. The retaliation of the state should not present a spectacle of violence. Burke asked that leniency be shown to all except those whose conduct displayed extremes of malice, wantonness, or the deliberate rousing of others to acts of destruction. In the aftermath, in a memorandum of July 18, he asked justice to take into account "on the whole, every circumstance of Mercy, and of comparative Justice" that could "plead in favour of such low, untaught, or ill-taught wretches" as had been caught up in the violence and captured by government. Among the circumstances arguing for mercy: "Not being principal. Probable want of early and deliberate purposes. Youth [and] Sex where the highest malice does not appear. Intoxication and levity, or mere wantonness of any kind."[36]

Doubts on Democracy and Politics

The results of the first day's polling at Bristol in September 1780 were so poor that Burke took the advice of his friends to withdraw.[37] Another of the candidates, Richard Combe, died on the same day, and the shock seems to have burned away any residual self-pity. (Burke's *Speech at Bristol Declining the Poll*, delivered on September 9, 1780, is printed as an appendix to this book.) Notwithstanding the unhappy result, the *Speech at the Bristol Guildhall* seems the culmination of his service as a representative for Bristol. Because it addresses the voters with a stirring and ingenuous appeal in a democratic setting, it prompts a comparison with the 1775 *Speech on Conciliation*, where the opportunity to speak of "the people" in England and America was seen but not taken. There, Burke had appeared indifferent to democracy. What concerned him, instead, was that peace be preferred to war, and trust preferred to coercion. The 1780 speech testifies to a quality of close engagement not exhibited before—an engagement which was consistent with his refusal of instructions. By contrast, if one looks ahead to *Reflections on the Revolution in France*, the later Burke seems to have acquired a hostility toward democracy so unqualified that he treats the ancient prejudice against government by the people as timeless common sense. Did he forget his radicalism of a decade before?

Burke has many of the negative components of a democratic thinker. He shows throughout his career an unqualified contempt for absolutism. He believes in the constitutional principle—which, without some democratic element, can never be put into practice—of restraining power by means of an institutional protection against the abuse of power. The people, it is understood, will often raise the alarm and point out where checks are most needed. But what of "the people" as a political force in themselves? Burke thinks they are a voice out of doors which ought to influence government. They deserve a decent life, with the ability to enjoy the fruits of their labor. Recall that in *Thoughts on the Cause of the Present Discontents*, Burke said he would rather see the constitution become more democratic than be swallowed up in the "austere and insolent domination" of aristocratic abuse. He was willing to approve a wider franchise, provided it could be done slowly.

And yet there are marks of the democratic thinker with which one could never properly identify Burke. Such a thinker must believe in the good of public discussions, not at moments of crisis only but all the time. The people are to be included in discussions in whatever numbers choose to listen and speak. The presumption is that they themselves are a bulwark—as material a protection as there can be—against all oppression. They are the best judges of the fact of oppression, and their testimony about its causes (whether credited or not) ought to be heard. This right is as important as any other political right. The strictly anti-coercive elements of such a view Burke does not ever seem to doubt. He wants the people to have a voice in deciding policies that directly influence their lives. But there is a point beyond which his distrust of participation must mean distrust of democracy itself. Burke does not really think that discussion among large numbers of people is necessary to advance any worthwhile cause—not even that of the people. He often appears quite as skeptical of the good of popular discussion as he is of the opinions of the majority. Compare a political thinker like Paine—by temper and habit a democrat—and you find in all of his writings a premise that is alien to Burke: society is natural to men, and the mass of men know (without much instruction) what to make of their lives by political debate and the process of advocacy and reform. Unlike Burke, Paine does not think of society itself as fragile or perishable. The worst temptations against society are corruption and violence, and these, says Paine, are not natural but are brought on by superstition, monarchy, and the barbarous customs of unchecked power. When not imposed upon, men naturally fall into a democratic way of deciding and acting; whereas to Burke, it appears that the people must be taught to assimilate such habits. There is a certain optimism always accompanying a disposition like Paine's, which regards democracy itself as natural. The people have failed in the past because of rotten structures built by tyrants and their priests; whereas for Burke, a proneness to disorder seems native to the people: he does not know for sure but would never put it to the test. He does not trust them with the conduct of politics, and he would not entrust to them the larger operations of government.

Burke, however, often seems not so much an anti-democratic as an anti-political thinker. Politics itself strikes him as alien to the nature and disposition of most people most of the time, and of all people much of the time. It must become the steady activity of a few, as necessary; but politics is not the central fact of life, let alone the central good. Because the objects of politics are infinitely complex, well-stocked minds are needed to handle its materials without gross ineptitude. But we should not pretend that the possession of this talent gives a focus to our deepest concerns. People want to live. And in their lives, they want to be left alone with their families and enterprises, affairs of person and neighborhood—the "subdivision" they are attached to (class, sect, or party). A rare politician may know that, for him, "the sphere of my duties is my true country," but the felt duties of most people are not so extended. Nor are their energies so engaged: most people do not want to design and accomplish, to plan and realize programs. Burke goes along with this ordinary anti-political temper to the extent that he seldom mounts a campaign *for* anything. All his most strenuous engagements, from the start of his career to the end, were aimed at reforms or limitations. In the three-part construal of republican rights that he summarizes in the *Reflections*—the right to cashier a king for misconduct, to choose a new king, and to frame a government for ourselves—he doubtless perceived an ascending order of offense. Burke in fact would endorse the idea of cashiering a king for misconduct, so long as the misconduct was both extreme and incorrigible. Even the choice of a new king is not beyond his imagining, provided a certain delicacy is observed to hide the magnitude of the change. But to frame a government "for ourselves" is an imposition and a delusion: it is not natural to want to frame a wholly new government or to take pride in doing so. "The very idea of the fabrication of a new government is enough to fill us with disgust and horror."

Burke may have thought the active energy of the democrat partook of the same greedy acquisitiveness he perceived in the worst of commercial enterprises. In any case, the anti-democratic Burke is a subcategory of the anti-political Burke. For he is suspicious of monarchy and oligarchy in much the same way that he is suspicious of democracy.

We can define Burke more nearly by comparing him with another American, James Madison, who stood closer to his own ideas on the necessity of constitutional checks and balances. Why should one say that Madison is a democrat and Burke is not? Here it seems a matter of degree. Madison is just within the lines of democracy, and he shows it by his guarded concessions to popular sovereignty. He allows this to be an essential element in orderly and restrained government—not as its whole and not as its end, but as a necessary means. The phrase "the will of the people" means something potentially beneficial to Madison, as it never does to Burke. Yet, by temper, Madison is even more distrustful of human motives than Burke. He belongs to the school of Montesquieu and Hume, in favor of a mixed constitution but without Burke's unshakable anger against the abuse of power. To some extent this overlaps with the school of Mandeville: human vices can be turned to political benefits. Or rather, the vices can be made to contest and neutralize each other and to produce a political virtue foreign to their separate identities. This idea of a cynical basis producing a fortunate result Burke would have thought both immoral and psychologically false. You cannot pit vice against vice and have virtue come from the combination. For Burke, the sound method of politics is to introduce from the start as little evil as possible, which is perhaps why aristocrats, who have nothing further to gain, are his ideal representatives; a "previous fortune in character at stake" qualifies them to act generously, as those never can who use politics to make money or achieve celebrity or climb the social ladder. Burke wants us to reform our instruments (including self-will) through the medium of politics. His ambivalence regarding commerce, which at times puts him in a different universe from Hume, goes with the moral basis of his politics. Madison and Hume think that good enough comes from our work with the mixed motives of common life. Burke thinks that where the stakes are so high—the happiness of a society—we ought to purify our motives as far as possible. He may find the idea of self-interest less intelligible than they do. Anyway, he does not share their faith that divergent interests can be made to harmonize without displacing a concern with substantial justice.

St. Eustatius

As a parliamentary representative and a reformer of the abuses of power, Burke's experience in 1779–1780 was a preparation for his greatest test: the reform of British India. This would occupy most of his time between 1782 and 1790 and more than is generally understood between 1790 and 1795. We have to go back only a short way, to November 1777 and a letter Burke wrote to John Bourke, to gain a telling glimpse of the connection he saw between America and India. Responding to the notice (in a letter from Philip Francis) of the reorganization of the revenue of the East India Company under Warren Hastings, Burke disclaims any knowledge of India beyond what he has heard on Francis's authority; but "in general I perfectly agree with Mr Francis, that a nice Scrutiny into the property and Tenures of an whole Nation is almost always more alarming to the people, than advantageous to Government." There follows a characteristic attack on the wrong of adopting a single standard of value and estimation:

> The Idea of forcing every thing to an *artificial* equality has something, at first View, very captivating in it. It has all the appearance imaginable of Justice and good order; and very many persons, without any sort of partial purposes, have been led to adopt such Schemes and to pursue them with great earnestness and warmth. . . . You know that it is this very rage for equality, which has blown up the Flames of this present cursed War in America. I am, for one, entirely satisfied, that the inequality, which grows out of the *nature of things* by time, custom, succession, accumulation, permutation, and improvement of property, is much nearer that true equality, which is the foundation of equity and just policy, than any thing which can be contrived by the Tricks and devices of human skill. What does it amount to, after some little jumbling, but that some men have better Estates than others. I

am certain that when the financial System is but tolerably planned it will catch property in spite of all its doublings; and sooner or later those who have most will pay most; and this is the effective equality which circumstances will bring about of themselves if they are left to their own operation.[38]

The context, in 1777, leaves uncertain the exact sense of the American reference. Does the rage for equality come from the colonists who want their independence and rights immediately secured? That seems a plausible inference. But Burke might equally be alluding to pressure for the payment of taxes—that is, "equal" payment in return for specified British protection during the Canadian war. Burke in the *Speech on Conciliation* had shown that true partnership depends on a general spirit of trust and not the tracking of particular credit for particular donations. It would be most like him to have meant both things at once.

To surrender the false claims of government to property means likewise to discountenance any policy of confiscation. It is in the context of the West Indies—where the thoughts of empire and slavery come together in Burke's mind—that we find his most urgent, pointed, and eloquent statement on the abuse of power by the agents of empire. Where the prosecution of Hastings would look to reconstruct the scope of crimes committed in the past, the *Speech on St. Eustatius* is an extraordinarily impassioned response to an event at the outer edges of the American war. Burke always sympathized with people whose self-respect was forced into subjection by a sudden indignity; this might mean a whole class of persons humbled and brought low or people who had seen their livelihoods vanish and their property taken from them. He may have been especially sensitive to the sufferings of the prosperous and the great—persons used to being treated with high dignity and generous recognition—but his sympathy knew no bounds of race or nation. Thus, his defense of the Begums of Oudh against dispossession and his protest on behalf of the French aristocrats could be extended also to Irish Catholics of the landowning and professional classes; extended, likewise, to the victims of the British attack on the island of St. Eustatius.

Some of the inhabitants were in fact British merchants, engaged there in trade which the law allowed. Others were small property owners of various nations who when Admiral Rodney invaded on February 3, 1781, were robbed of all they had. Burke connects in a single account the evils of despotism—of a war of aggression and the confiscation of property— and the haughty contempt shown by the British toward the human rights of those they had conquered. His St. Eustatius speech of May 14, 1781, is the one, of all those Burke delivered during the American war, which relates the injuries of the war itself to a habit of conquest and a systematic suppression of liberty.

But he had laid his groundwork carefully. This speech follows the pattern of his "Address to the King" of 1777 and the *Letter to the Sheriffs of Bristol:* denying legitimacy to an established power (however ancient) that has defied and overridden the trust of its subjects. Power is given by the people; it is meant to be wielded for common utility and order; and a power given by the people, when abused, may with right be taken back. More particularly, Burke is concerned with an island society which the American war had placed in political limbo: a position that makes its inhabitants resemble the stateless persons of the Balkans after the First World War, and of the Middle East after the American occupation of Iraq. According to Burke, people even in this doubtful situation are nonetheless supported by human rights—rights that persist through the vicissitudes of disorder and war. Britain, he says, now finds itself "in a struggle for our existence," its very being defined by its precarious hold of possessions on both sides of the Atlantic; yet at this critical hour the worthiness of the commonwealth is to be measured by its restraint. The attack on St. Eustatius he thinks was a war of choice. Burke notes ruefully the contrast with the mood of a few months earlier. On December 20, 1780, at the outset of the war with the Dutch, Britain had published a manifesto almost conciliatory in tone, a document that "seemed to be torn by constraint from a heart bleeding under the affliction of unwilling strife." But the anxiety and low morale of the American war could not be kept separate from the new adventure, and its spirit prevailed over diplomacy and preparation. The invasion of St. Eustatius was launched after a hurricane leveled the island; and there was something unseemly in the way Britain pushed the human calamity into the wake of the natural disaster. "Surely, when human pride was leveled in the dust, and we saw what worms we were beneath the hand of Omnipotence, it became us to crawl from our holes with a feeling of brotherly love to each other; to abate a little of our rancour; and not add the devastations of war to those of the hurricane." A planned expedition to St. Vincent had been scuttled because it was "undertaken with so little knowledge of the state of defence in which the island stood"; only then did the British forces turn against St. Eustatius. So irrepressible was the appetite for new acquisitions, or the greed of the scramble for pawns to be used in negotiating a peace settlement.

St. Eustatius should have been an uninviting prospect: a volcanic cone, as Burke describes it, of extent not more than thirty miles, so that "it seemed to be but a late production of nature, a sort of *lusus naturae*, hastily framed, neither shapen nor organized"; yet from these unfavoring conditions, "its proprietors had, in the spirit of commerce, made it an emporium for all the world; a mart, a magazine for all the nations of the earth." By man improving on nature, the island "had risen, like another Tyre, upon the waves, to communicate to all countries and climates the conveniencies and the necessaries of life." Dedicated as it was to peaceful industry and commerce, it lay almost unprotected, its only fortification a garrison manned by fifty-five soldiers. Against this bare defense, the ingenuity of Britain threw a force of fourteen ships of the line and 3,000 troops, and asked for surrender within an hour. "The Dutch commander yielded up the dominion, the territory, the public property, and every thing that belonged to the United States [of Holland], to the British commanders without any stipulation, relying totally on the discretion, the mercy, and the clemency of the conquerors." And who were the conquerors? Admiral Rodney had won his military fame for the capture of Martinique in 1762, but the scale of his debts had forced him to flee Britain; and before the American war and the help of a patron rescued him, he had been imprisoned in France.

Suitable to such a commander, the British empire in St. Eustatius acted with pitiless insolence. The capture and confiscation of property on the island was "a sentence of general beggary pronounced in one moment upon a whole people." For the island merchants were thus robbed not only of their property but of their records. In a language that anticipates his words about the East India men and the Jacobins, Burke asks: "Was there known till that moment a more complete act of tyranny than this?" Nor did the confiscation stop at official records: "It was not enough that the secrets of their trade and their weaknesses should be laid open, but also that the secrets of their families should be discovered; the private calamities, to which all are more or less incident, and all anxious to conceal, and to suffer unknown, were exposed." Such a trespass against privacy is a general disaster for society itself.

One group of the inhabitants draws particularly close attention from Burke:

> He blushed, he said, to relate the sequel for the honour of humanity, of this enlightened age, and still more of the Christian character. The persecution was begun with the people, whom of all others it ought to be the care and the wish of humane nations to protect, the Jews. Having no fixed settlement in any part of the world, no kingdom nor country in which they have a government, a community, and a system of laws, they are thrown upon the benevolence of nations, and claim protection and civility from their weakness, as well as from their utility. They were a people, who, by shunning the profession of any, could give no well-founded jealousy to any state. If they have contracted some vices, they are such as naturally arise from their dispersed, wandering, and proscribed state. It was an observation as old as Homer, and confirmed by the experience of all ages, that in a state of servitude the human mind loses half its value. From the east to the west, from one end of the world to the other, they are scattered and connected; the links of communication in the mercantile chain; or, to borrow a phrase from electricity, the conductors by which credit was transmitted through the world. Their abandoned state, and their defenceless situation calls most forcibly for the protection of civilized nations. If Dutchmen are injured and attacked, the Dutch have a nation, a government, and armies to redress or revenge their cause. If Britons are injured, Britons have armies and laws, the laws of nations, (or at least they once had the laws of nations,) to fly to for protection and justice. But the Jews have no such power, and no such friend to depend on. Humanity then must become their protector.[39]

By humanity, Burke means a quality of humane concern but also an adequate representation of human rights. Humanity itself must enforce the obligation to treat all persons with justice. It fell to Britain, it would seem, after the conquest to act this part. But the victors were not generous protectors of the Jews of St. Eustatius, and instead took a resolution to banish them from the island.

They suffered in consequence the loss of their merchandise, bills, houses, and provisions and were ordered to quit the island within one day. Their remonstrance was rejected. No property was allowed to be taken by the dispossessed. The men had to leave behind their wives and children; and as Burke goes on to report, without their families, "the very last comfort of wretchedness," they were summoned to appear the next day; and all 101 of the Jews of the island were "confined in a weigh-house, a place, in some respects, similar to a turnpike-house, but strongly guarded," where they were stripped, their clothes torn to pieces, and every shilling taken from them. Thirty were sent to St. Kitts, and the rest after three days turned back to their families, "that they might be melancholy spectators of the sale of their own property."

Jews were the first but not the last to be thus persecuted. Soon after, the French and then all the other inhabitants were told to depart; even British subjects, who might have supposed themselves entitled to the protection of a British commander, "met only with insult and rapacity." And yet, if it was illegal for the island's merchants to sell their goods, what can be said of the decision by the British invaders to hawk the spoils? The disgrace is all the more public and reprehensible given the status that St. Eustatius had acquired—"a mart," as Burke called it, "for all the motions of the earth." What the world saw the British Empire achieve was a work of desolation and plunder.

It has been said of Burke's writings on India that they evoke a standard of universal justice whose basis must lie in a conception of natural law.[40] This standard, it is sometimes added, was the core of his objection to contractual theories of natural rights; and in reverting to the older idea, he wisely shunned the Enlightenment faith in the progressive discovery of the rights of individuals. The universal reach of natural law thus came to dominate Burke's later writings so far as to displace the appeal to common utility and the public good. There is some truth in this view of a transition in Burke's thinking. The terms that he deliberately employs in the St. Eustatius speech do suggest a basis for the largest of his claims about human nature in the late writings.[41] They anticipate, more closely, the central sentence of his *Speech on Fox's East India Bill* of December 1, 1783: "It is an arduous thing to plead against abuses of a power which originates from your own country, and affects those whom we are used to consider as strangers."

He takes his stand here neither on commonsense utility nor on the Lockean theory of natural rights so widely assumed in pamphlets by the Americans; but he likewise declines to trace his ultimate authority to the natural law of Catholic theology. Rather, Burke speaks of "the law of nations," which is not to be suspended in time of war. His application is explicit:

> The general confiscation of the private property found upon the island was contrary to the law of nations, and to that system of war which civilised states had of late, by their consent and practice, thought proper to introduce. Perhaps it might be said, there was no positive law of nations; no general established laws framed, and settled by acts in which every nation had a voice. There was not indeed any law of nations, established like the laws of Britain in black letter, by statute and record; but there was a law of nations as firm, as clear, as manifest, as obligatory, as indispensable. First, it was a maxim generally established and agreed to, "that the rights of war were not unlimited." If they were unlimited, it would be ridiculous to say that there were laws of war; For as confessedly a law existed to regulate the practice of states in hostility with each other, if the rights of war were unbounded, it would follow, that the law placed limits to infinity. But this being the established maxim, he had it in his power to prove that there were certain limited and defined rights of war recognised by civilized states, and practised in enlightened Europe. First, he could prove that they were established by reason, in which they had their origin and rise; next, by the convention of parties; thirdly, by the authorities of writers, who took the laws and maxims not from their own invention and ideas, but from the consent and sense of ages; and lastly, from the evidence of precedent.[42]

Burke thus recognizes and disposes of the claim that there is no law of war. The absence of positive law, he remarks, in the form of written statutes does not mean the absence of all law. Reason attests the existence of certain rights of war, since even monarchs are bound by trust—"There must be a care where there is a dominion"—and a king who becomes a plunderer of his own people "must dethrone himself from the just dominion." So, too, a king who pursues a policy of confiscation will find a sword in every hand "to execute upon him the vengeance of human nature." And a king who commands a people to surrender and then strips them of all their property, by that action parts with the authority of a king and becomes a robber. Burke plants himself on a principle ("inspired by the Divine Author of all good") which has roots in familiar practices. But he draws from those practices a universal maxim. History, and the closeness of practice to precedent, help the maxim to carry conviction; the consent of ages means here the common understanding of a truth that has gained force through its familiarity.

There remain distinctions among the forms of iniquity. Property on land is not subject to seizure and confiscation in the same way as "property found afloat." Burke takes note of the fact, though he says he has no stake in such conventional disparities. He looks forward to "a time not far distant when even that inhuman species of war would be abolished." This seems the place to indicate plainly what has become obvious in this chapter and Chapter 6. During the long middle phase of his career, from 1774 to 1790, Burke was not only a consistent critic of state violence, he was an antiwar writer through and through. He sees that war is an evil in itself; any argument for the necessity of a war is an argument for the lesser evil; and in the nature of state power (and its quest for aggrandizement), the case for a given war must be regarded prima facie with suspicion. The same holds true for those conquests that states by diplomatic euphemism classify as something other than open war. Though books are a weaker authority than the collected testimony of experience, Burke cites Vattel as "the latest and best" author to deny that there can be such a thing as a surrender at discretion, that is, a surrender without terms, or what later came to be called unconditional surrender.[43] Grenada is the most recent invasion Burke can recall as a precedent for surrender at discretion; but there the surrender was made only after resistance; and even so, the inhabitants were treated better than those of St. Eustatius. At Grenada, there was no general confiscation.

That even wars should be fought with some restraint is for Burke a consequence of his understanding that justice is a moral reality and not a pragmatic fiction. In a contest between two disagreeing parties, justice must lie on one side or on the other or somewhere between; yet to commit an absolute and unpardonable injustice against the enemy is to negate that presumption. Since every war supposes an offense on one side, "when the cause was referred to this mode of decision [i.e., war], it was to be considered as *sub judice,* during which the time both parties were entitled to the same treatment." It is a first principle of the law of nations "that to expound the rights of war, we must conceive each party to have justice on its side, and every thing preceding the commencement of hostilities must be forgotten in that exposition."[44] Trade, such as created the livelihood of St. Eustatius, cannot be a crime; and Burke reminds the House of Commons that the British legislature endorsed the right of trade on the island. Here, as in the *Letter to the Sheriffs of Bristol,* the wrong of the war seems clearest to Burke from its effects on the institutions of peace. The effects ramify as war itself becomes a spur to the appetite for new possessions. But the failure at St. Vincent and the miserable success of St. Eustatius have produced a general antipathy to the presence of Britain in the Caribbean: "Our commanders expected, that they might have been able to reduce Martinique and Guadeloupe by famine, in consequence of the destruction of provisions by the late hurricanes; but we lost the opportunity of showing that we were inhuman, and have not had the satisfaction of starving either of these islands into a surrender." The spirit of war only assists the devastations of nature; and nothing good can be built from ruin when the builders are corrupt. What they did to their victims here, they will do to others. Burke implies but does not state the inference. All defenses of war as such are apologies for endless war.

End of an Era

We have stepped a little ahead of the narrative to catch the St. Eustatius speech, because it lies on the same trajectory as the *Speech at the Bristol Guildhall* of 1780. Burke was not a politician whose drift and emphasis changed when he spoke from a new constituency; though perhaps the speech of 1781 would have drawn keener attention had it come from the member from Bristol rather than the Malton. At any rate, by the end of September 1780 he would extract a painful lesson from his defeat and Cruger's. This result (he wrote to Joseph Harford on September 27) would cure the Whigs of "presumption" by teaching "the necessity of cordial Union" between the aristocratic party, who must learn to "cultivate an Interest among the common people," and the people themselves, who must give up the madness of their dream "that they could be any thing without the Aid of better fortunes and better heads than their own." This apparently self-critical, subtly self-justifying utterance affects a humility it does not achieve. Yet Burke at least remembers—as he seems not to have done in the Guildhall speech—the uneasy prelude to the riots that came with the articulate discontents of the county association movement. Though he had spoken against reform of representation, it was beyond his desire or his capacity to pretend such reform was *not* a suitable subject of discussion.

Facing the consequences of his sparse contact with the people, he now comes as close as ever to entertaining the need for parliamentary reform. "I by no means object to it," he tells Harford: "But it is an Affair of great difficulty; and to be touched with great delicacy; and by an hand of great power. Power and delicacy do not often unite. But without great power, I do not hesitate to say, it *cannot* be done. By power I mean the *executive* power of the Kingdom."[45] If Burke has a practical step in view, it must be the granting of a wider suffrage by an uncorrupted party that has governed for a long time. Had Rockingham and Burke lived another two decades, staying in office all that time, and had they succeeded in calming the mood of the people and diminishing the influence of the crown, would they by these lights have been possessed of the delicacy and the power to attempt such a reform?

In the court-martial of Admiral Keppel, Burke perceived a parallel with his own struggle against calumny and ingratitude. Keppel "has the same Cause," he told Lady Rockingham in a letter of September 27, 1780, "the same persecutors, equal Merit, and superiour sufferings." Together they belonged among the fallen great: even at this vulnerable period, his self-love could grow selfless by the alchemy of a projective sympathy. Turning to his own position, Burke adds in the same letter that the representation of a pocket borough would be derisory: "If I were to come into Parliament by any of the little posterns or sallyports of the constitution, my moving such Bills as I formerly did, and as I have been desired by two Counties to do again, would be a piece of Buffoonery, to which I am little inclined to submit." The tone is impressive, but the reluctance to be transferred to a lesser station comes from the anxiety of wounded pride.[46]

Moral demands, to which Burke felt obliged to respond, were increasing as his popularity sank. For this was the time when disturbing reports from India began to tug at him. Late in 1780, the Raja of Tanjore had been pressed to give up lands as a way of paying his debt to the East India Company—a setback for his English agents William Waldegrave and William Burke; and it came on the heels of the Bristol election. This move by the Company on its client gave Burke the first large indication of a pattern of criminality which he thought he could detect in Company rule in India and which would drive his fifteen-year-long campaign for reform. The prompting may have been the more intimate because of his personal connection with Will Burke; but that was not the cause of his commitment; and Will at last would wonder at the difference of motives between them. "For the soul of me," he confided to Richard Burke, "I cannot feel as much as your father does for the black primates."[47] Burke was indeed possessed by that "feeling," in a manner altogether unusual for a white man, but even at this early stage he was sure that something had gone wrong that could be described in political terms. The transfer of ownership and control of the Company, he tells the Earl of Hillsborough and Viscount Stormont on October 19, can at present "only be the effect of force," a fact that is "infinitely to the Dishonour of this Kingdom, as well as to the distress of that." India "ought to be politically, but not at all economically or Minsterially, subject to the Company's Servants."

Here was the germ of the legislation Burke would propose in 1783; and it marked a rare point of agreement with Lord North. For, though Burke made little of it, North had pressed for reform of the Company in earlier years. "In all that regards the treatment of the natives," Lord Loughborough reminded Burke on January 4, 1781, "his Principles are the same as yours." Notwithstanding their antagonism on American policy, Burke would have made an exception for North when he spoke of the masters of the empire as persons "incapable of doing justice to themselves." North, on India, had been a more valuable resource than Rockingham—to whom in April 1782 (not long before his death) Burke would regret "that your Lordship thinks slightly of India in the scale of our Politicks." Possibly indeed, had Rockingham lived on and continued to think slightly of India, Burke would have been discouraged from pursuing to the second stage his inquiry into wars fought for the Company and the characters of the servants who were bought, sold, and murdered to cement the Company's mercantile government.

The eastern empire haunted him in part because the western now was lost.[48] Through all the years of the American contest, he had never given an inch to military patriotism. The reverse, in fact. With a gesture of characteristic magnanimity, in late December 1781, he congratulated Benjamin Franklin on American independence:

> There was a day when I held high the honour and dignity of the Community I belong to. Indeed its authority, which I always connected with its Justice and its Benevolence was a subject of my warmest enthusiasms. I ever wished and not wished only, but struggled, that this Government in all Stages of this unfortunate Contest, and in all the variety of Policy which arises in it, should take the lead in every act of Generosity and benignity, and without derogating from the regard due to the younger and (not the inferior) Branch of our Nation, wishd that as the older we should furnish you with examples. But providence has not done its work by halves. You have Success; and you have added and may yet add more to what success is unable to bestow. I never had the smallest reason to be personally proud; Nationally I was high and haughty. But all the props of my pride are slipped from under me. I wishd to bestow, and I am left to supplicate.[49]

There was an immediate motive here, since Burke was appealing for Franklin's help in ending General Burgoyne's status as a prisoner. Nevertheless, the generous sentiments are in accord with all Burke had said about the war in the 1770s; and his parting salute to the American is lofty and elegiac: "providence has not done its work by halves"; "I wishd to bestow, and I am left to supplicate."

But is there not something contradictory in the way Burke clings to the posture of one who is "nationally" high and haughty? He knew that Franklin knew better. Throughout the war, Burke had sought to teach prudence and decent humility to his countrymen; he was never high and haughty in his sentiments toward America or in the policy he defended. Why, then, does he take on himself the burden of the general error and culpability? For all its seemliness, this letter is oddly formal. The eloquence of the climax depends on a rhetorical pretense that Burke always shared the belief that English arms deserved to prevail. He treats the occasion, in short, as if the national and personal humiliations were identical; but they were not. Some of the incongruity may be the result of the distance that separates us from the eighteenth-century grand manner. The famous sentence of Gibbon's *Memoirs*, "I sighed as a lover, I obeyed as a son," flaunts a similar tonality of gracious excess. Still, it should surprise us that a public man of Burke's stature and consistency felt the necessity of feigning an attitude of national self-accusation. His confession to Franklin shows a kind of self-division that is common in his writings and not easily explained: a division whereby the private self tends to be sacrificed to the public image in open view, and for the benefit of an audience that knows better.

So Burke takes the sin of pride on himself in order with greater authority to accept the punishment on his country's behalf. Yet a question lingers. What does he mean when he says that America "may yet add more to what success is unable to bestow"? It seems possible that he intends the highest of compliments to Franklin; that he is saying the former colonies may prove that "power and delicacy" can be united in the will of the people. If that could be proved, the new country would have vindicated the claim of democracy with a completeness whose success Burke always deprecated. But he says for his part that in the presence of such success, his rigor must relent and the "props of his pride" slip away. It is the closest he will come to a possible sympathy with the American founders.

※

The death of Lord Rockingham, on July 1, 1782, closed an epoch of Burke's career. This association, especially in its last seven years, had given focus to his restless energy and his passion for justice. Though it may be said that Rockingham was an imperfect vessel for Burke's idealism—and it may be added that Rockingham shines only when compared with the other five chief ministers between the elder and the younger Pitt—still Burke was allowed to thrive in a party that he did not formally lead and could not have commanded. Other statesmen who admired Burke, as the elder Pitt did the first time he heard him speak and as the younger Pitt would also, probably at close quarters would have misprized him and shown their disdain by high–handed or perfunctory treatment such as Rockingham was never guilty of. The relationship between the party leader and his secretary, after all, had been warmed by an intimacy impossible to record in memorandums. Reynolds painted them once—an unfinished painting but wonderfully shaded and delicate. Burke is the recessive figure to the left and toward the background, as the two men pore over some detail of "wax and parchment": the letter of the law that gives life only in the presence of the spirit. It is Rockingham who faces the painter, while Burke's left arm encircles Rockingham, surrounding him, as a sea surrounds the inlet where it touches land. The leader's face and figure are painted. The secretary's face and figure are unfinished and yet they impart to the picture a sense of sculptural repose. Burke, as pictured here by Reynolds, seems the very embodiment of watchful policy. "Mr. Burke," wrote Charles Butler in his *Reminiscences,* "was made for the times in which he lived, and to act in a party composed of men, like those with whom he acted."[50] Both parts of that observation are true.

When Burke came to write an epitaph for Rockingham, to be placed in the mausoleum at Wentworth House, Yorkshire, with its twelve Doric columns supporting a dome to shelter the statues of the marquess and his friends, it was natural for him to offer the portrait of an ideal second self. This was the man he would wish to have been, had he been born with a title to honor and affluence:

A statesman in whom constancy, fidelity, sincerity, and directness were the sole instruments of his policy. His virtues were his arts. A clear, sound, unadulterated sense, not perplexed with intricate design, or disturbed by ungoverned passion, gave consistency, dignity, and effect to all his measures. In Opposition, he respected the principles of Government; in Administration, he provided for the liberties of the people. He employed his moments of power in realizing every thing which he had promised in a popular situation. This was the distinguishing mark of his conduct. After twenty-four years of service to the public, in a critical and trying time, he left no debt of just expectation unsatisfied.

By his prudence and patience he brought together a party which it was the great objects of his labours to render permanent, not as an instrument of ambition, but as a living depository of principle.

The virtues of his public and private life were not in him of different characters. It was the same feeling, benevolent, liberal mind that, in the internal relations of life, conciliates the unfeigned love of those who see men as they are, which made him an inflexible patriot. He was devoted to the cause of liberty, not because he was haughty and intractable, but because he was beneficent and humane.

Let his successors, who from this house behold this monument, reflect that their conduct will make it their glory or their reproach. Let them be persuaded that similarity of manners, not proximity of blood, gives them an interest in this statue.

Remember—Resemble—Persevere.[51]

Rockingham, as Burke saw him, conducted his life with the complex aim of representing the people and governing by the lights of his own practical wisdom. In the crisis of a protracted war and domestic tumults, he stood for peace and concession; and in his final months, he did not disappoint those who looked for him to end the strife. He spoke for liberty while respecting order, and his true successors, Burke takes care to assert, are to be known by moral affinity and not by aristocratic descent.

Conclusion

THIS book has covered the first three decades of Burke's life as a thinker, writer, and political actor. A second volume, chiefly concerned with his writings and speeches on India and France, will concentrate on the years 1783–1797. My intention is to illustrate the depth of Burke's engagement on the many fronts that occupied his intellectual energy. The youthful skeptic of a social contract based on "nature," the theorist of love and fear in relation to the arts, the advocate of civil liberty even at the risk of disorder in England, the architect of economic reform, and the agitator for peace with America—each of these has demanded here a separate accounting to meet the integrity of separate arguments and to explain their coherence. "The way to judge him," wrote Henry James of Balzac, "is to try to walk all round him—on which we see how remarkably far we have to go."[1] The same is true of Burke.

What gave force to his utterance and actions was an impression of continuous sincerity. However multiple and various Burke's campaigns turned out to be, a single-minded commitment always drove him; and in looking back, we can see clearly a trait that distinguishes him from other politicians. This is the fit between his private and his public views. I have made more extensive use of Burke's correspondence than most of my predecessors, largely in order to appreciate the candor of his judgments across the line that can divide public declaration from private reticence. Consider his treatment of Ireland. Burke was charged with coolness or indifference toward Ireland in the years of the American war—the years of Irish agitation for trading rights and the calculated menace of the Volunteers. Yet he was alive to the conflict; and here as elsewhere his letters give an unexpected clue: they show a statesman determined to reform a policy of colonial subordination. A similar continuity may be anticipated between the liberal reformer of Britain in the 1770s and the sworn antagonist of the French revolution. With Burke, hatred of injustice is a common thread.

In the years 1791–1793, under Lord Westmoreland's administration in Ireland, Burke's son Richard would consult with the Catholic Committee on the abolition of Catholic disabilities. This was a natural outgrowth of his own commitment to back Sir George Savile's Relief Act of 1778. But in the later period, we will discover Burke, in a series of long letters, elaborately instructing his son on Irish politics. Richard Burke was by then understood to be Edmund's representative, his interpreter, and sometimes his messenger to the Catholics pressing for reform. Burke's stance, between 1778 and 1792, seems to have passed from moderate advocacy, where his chief concern was trading privileges within the empire, to a position far less compromising. He comes to register a sympathy with Catholic discontents, which, in the *Letter to Sir Hercules Langrishe* of 1792, aligns him with those who prefer a revolution to the maintenance of the Protestant ascendancy. The record on Ireland, as much as the record on America, is full of complexity.

Within the Rockingham party, his concern had been limited by party strategy, and in the late 1770s he was accused of being a temporizer. He would come forward in 1792, however, as an able tactician, a resourceful intermediary between the Catholics pressing for reform and those in England and Ireland who would listen to them. And yet, a letter of March 1792 advises Richard Burke to moderate his stance on the Catholic side and by no means to think of the Protestants as enemies:

> Pray, as far as in you lies, keep the Terms of common Society with those, with whom you can keep no other. All the possible Charities of Life ought to be cultivated; and where we can neither be brethren nor friends, let us be kind neighbours and pleasant acquaintance. The Protestants of Ireland are just like the Catholicks—the Cat looking out of the Window and the Cat looking in at the Window—The difference of being in or out of power is the only difference between them; and power is a very corrupting thing; especially low and jobbish power—This makes the Protestants a trifle worse—as servility makes the Catholicks a little worse on the other hand.[2]

So he puts for the ultimate cause of political difference not an original claim of possession, and not an old and irrepressible grievance, but rather the division between those who have too much power and those who have too little. "The Cat looking out of the Window and the Cat looking in at the Window."

A tremendous clearance is made with that phrase. All the high-flown Protestant arguments for the prudence of established authority and the bitter reproaches by Irish Catholics are reduced to the dimensions of an unforgettable cartoon. The cat is known for toying with its prey, and Burke would deny this pleasure to the cat on either side of the window: the arbitrary power of the English law that suspended habeas corpus in 1777 and likewise the revolutionary power of the Third Estate that declared itself the nation in 1789. It is the same with the ascendancy in Ireland, which refuses civil and political rights to Catholics. Burke did not imagine that the victims would be more righteous than the victors if their positions were reversed. Whatever the changes of costume, it is always the cat looking out and the cat looking in.

The impact of the metaphor is to strengthen one's sympathy with the oppressed while calming the passion that leads from fellow-feeling to revenge. Instead, we are called on to reform the abuse. In the *Speech in Reply* that closes the impeachment of Warren Hastings, Burke will allude to the virtuous feeling of *sympathetic revenge*:[3] a disturbing phrase but one that captures his thought. There exists a feeling by which revenge can be made to assist in the removal of injustice. "We are not made at once to pity the oppressor and the oppressed," Burke will say in *A Letter to a Noble Lord;* and sympathetic revenge is closely derived from anger; but this violent instinct may be tamed by civility and enlisted in the cause of substantial justice.

Still, Burke made many pronouncements on Ireland, one or two of them close to demagogy, a larger number pleading for conciliation and magnanimity. Why read so much significance into a passage from one letter? In the extraordinary sentences of advice to Richard, he is telling his son what company he should keep in Ireland and how to talk to the parties there. It is a private letter, and he can speak without inhibition. But there is no reason to doubt that this is what Burke in a cool hour believed about Irish Catholicism and Protestantism. It is entirely compatible with his writings on empire regarding the rights of an oppressed minority or a subordinated majority.

So the private confirms the public man, and the early view is found to support the late. The tenor of the 1792 letter to Richard on Irish politics and religion is braced by a passage of the *Speech at the Bristol Guildhall*. Throughout that speech, Burke warned his audience against the danger of popular prejudice. Finally, he declared it his rule never to satisfy the craving for power displayed by any majority: "No man carries further than I do the policy of making government pleasing to the people"; but though "I would bear, I would even myself play my part in, any innocent buffooneries, to divert them," yet "I never will act the tyrant for their amusement. If they will mix malice in their sports, I shall never consent to throw them any living, sentient, creature whatsoever, no, not so much as a kitling, to torment."

This hunger for scapegoats, itself the cause of so much needless suffering, gives a clue to the resolution of Burke's lifelong enquiry into the origins of tyranny. A lord may oppress and domineer, but so may a mass of the people playing at being lords. A king who proceeds in contempt of the constitution, an aristocracy that becomes an "austere and insolent domination," and a new class of moneyed men carving up the world for advantage are all rightly to be resisted as versions of the same compulsion. The purpose of enlightened government is to prevent such persons or groups from acquiring an excess of the "very corrupting thing" that power is. Though Burke lived and moved in proximity to the powerful, his lot was never cast with them. He meant to act as a reminder of the cost of power, and a curb against the perpetual danger of its abuse.

Appendix

This morning the sheriff and candidates assembled as usual at the Council-House, and from thence proceeded to Guildhall. Proclamation being made for the electors to appear and give their votes, MR. BURKE stood forward on the hustings, surrounded by a great number of the Corporation and other principal citizens, and addressed himself to the whole assembly as follows.

GENTLEMEN,—I decline the election. It has ever been my rule through life to observe a proportion between my efforts and my objects. I have never been remarkable for a bold, active, and sanguine pursuit of advantages that are personal to myself.

I have not canvassed the whole of this city in form, but I have taken such a view of it as satisfies my own mind that your choice will not ultimately fall upon me. Your city, Gentlemen, is in a state of miserable distraction, and I am resolved to withdraw whatever share my pretensions may have had in its unhappy divisions. I have not been in haste; I have tried all prudent means; I have waited for the effect of all contingencies. If I were fond of a contest, by the partiality of my numerous friends (whom you know to be among the most weighty and respectable people of the city) I have the means of a sharp one in my hands. But I thought it far better, with my strength unspent, and my reputation unimpaired, to do, early and from foresight, that which I might be obliged to do from necessity at last.

I am not in the least surprised nor in the least angry at this view of things. I have read the book of life for a long time, and I have read other books a little. Nothing has happened to me, but what has happened to men much better than me, and in times and in nations full as good as the age and country that we live in. To say that I am no way concerned would be neither decent nor true. The representation of *Bristol* was an object on many accounts dear to me; and I certainly should very far prefer it to any other in the kingdom. My habits are made to it; and it is in general more unpleasant to be rejected after long trial than not to be chosen at all.

But, Gentlemen, I will see nothing except your former kindness, and I will give way to no other sentiments than those of gratitude. From the bottom of my heart I thank you for what you have done for me. You have given me a long term, which is now expired. I have performed the conditions, and enjoyed all the profits to the full; and I now surrender your estate into your hands, without being in a single tile or a single stone impaired or wasted by my use. I have served the public for fifteen years. I have served you in particular for six. What is past is well stored; it is safe, and out of the power of fortune. What is to come is in wiser hands than ours; and He in whose hands it is best knows whether it is best for you and me that I should be in parliament, or even in the world.

Gentlemen, the melancholy event of yesterday reads to us an awful lesson against being too much troubled about any of the objects of ordinary ambition. The worthy gentleman [Richard Combe] who has been snatched from us at the moment of the election, and in the middle of the contest, whilst his desires were as warm and his hopes as eager as ours, has feelingly told us what shadows we are and what shadows we pursue.

It has been usual for a candidate who declines to take his leave by a letter to the sheriffs; but I received your trust in the face of day, and in the face of day I accept your dismission. I am not—I am not at all ashamed to look upon you; nor can my presence discompose the order of business here. I humbly and respectfully take my leave of the sheriffs, the candidates, and the electors, wishing heartily that the choice may be for the best, at a time which calls, if ever time did call, for service that is not nominal. It is no plaything you are about. I tremble, when I consider the trust I have presumed to ask. I confided, perhaps, too much in my intentions. They were really fair and upright; and I am bold to say, that I ask no ill thing for you, when, on parting from this place, I pray, that, whomever you choose to succeed me, he may resemble me exactly in all things, except in my abilities to serve, and my fortune to please you.

Notes

Introduction

1. "Letter to a Member of the National Assembly," in *Writings and Speeches of Edmund Burke,* 9 vols. (Oxford, 1981–), vol. 8, ed. L. G. Mitchell, p. 326.

2. The affinity between Burke and Rousseau—perceived by many in the eighteenth century and few in the twentieth—emerges from Alfred Cobban's early books, *Edmund Burke and the Revolt against the Eighteenth Century* (London, 1929) and *Rousseau and the Modern State* (London, 1934).

3. Matthew Arnold, "The Function of Criticism at the Present Time," in *Essays in Criticism* (London, 1906), p. 17.

4. G. O. Trevelyan, *The Early History of Charles James Fox,* 3rd ed. (London, 1881), p. 132.

5. William Blake, "Annotations to An Apology for the Bible," in *The Poetry and Prose of William Blake,* ed. David V. Erdman (New York, 1970), pp. 606–607.

6. *The Correspondence of Edmund Burke,* 10 vols. (Cambridge, 1958–1978), vol. 5, ed. Holden Furber with the assistance of P. J. Marshall, p. 10.

7. Many students of Burke will recognize the truth of a remark by Thomas Copeland in a letter to James Osborn: "The great problem with Burke is always to get the interest in *him,* and from my own slight experience in writing about him I know how difficult it is (I think he had a kind of natural impulse to throw difficulties in the way of people who wanted to know what he was like; I think he did it all his life)." In a related stricture, Copeland wrote: "One thing you always have to worry about with Burke. People who make statements about him are almost always supplied with *in*sufficient facts. They are trying to pump up some small hint or inference into an assertion that will win attention." Letters of 19 June 1960 and 14 October 1973, Beinecke Library, Yale University.

8. "With Burke," wrote W. E. H. Lecky, "an extreme dread of organic change coexisted with a great disposition to administrative reform. The Tory party, which prevailed after the French Revolution, adopted one side of his teaching, but wholly discarded the other, and they made the indiscriminate defence of every abuse, and the repression of every kind of political liberty, the great end of government." See W. E. H. Lecky, *History of England in the Eighteenth Century,* 8 vols. (London, 1888), 3:225.

9. L. T. Hobhouse, *Liberalism* (London, 1911), pp. 104–105.

10. There is a kind of intelligence in politics, which comes from the belief that ideas make a difference to politics. This is true of certain historical periods, as it is of individual writers and statesmen.

11. *Correspondence,* vol. 6, ed. Alfred Cobban and Robert A. Smith, p. 90.

12. *Correspondence,* vol. 2, ed. Lucy S. Sutherland, p. 282.

13. *Correspondence,* vol. 7, ed. P. J. Marshall and John A. Woods, pp. 83–84.

14. *Correspondence,* 5:255.

I. Early Ambition and the Theory of Society

1. *The Correspondence of Edmund Burke,* 10 vols. (Cambridge, 1958–1978), vol. 1, ed. Thomas Copeland, p. 274.

2. R. F. Foster, *Modern Ireland, 1600–1972* (London, 1988), p. 154.

3. See Conor Cruise O'Brien, *The Great Melody* (Chicago and London, 1992), pp. 3–10. To support the hypothesis, O'Brien notes that in 1722, a Richard Burke appears on the Convert Rolls. O'Brien also detects, in the tone of certain descriptions and omissions in Burke's mature writings, veiled references to the same hidden fact about his father. I hear more often in Burke (and in other members of his family) a pretty solid self-assurance: the tone of people who think themselves below privilege but above deference.

4. H. N. Brailsford, *Shelley, Godwin, and Their Circle* (London, 1913), p. 20.

5. O'Brien, *The Great Melody,* pp. 20–23.

6. For example, William Burke, *Edmund Burke as an Irishman* (Dublin, 1924), pp. 7–22.

7. W. E. H. Lecky, *History of England in the Eighteenth Century,* 8 vols. (New York, 1888), 3:226.

8. F. P. Lock, *Edmund Burke: 1730–1784* (Oxford, 1998), counts four visits after 1750, none of them long.

9. Copeland elaborates: "Abraham Shackleton would have been less stunned by the four horses of the family coach if he had known that once at Beaconsfield they would be unhitched and put to use around the farm, and that Burke himself would walk behind them as he did his own plowing" (Copeland Papers, Libraries of the University of Massachusetts at Amherst, FS 150, box 18, folder 151).

10. Quoted in Arthur P. I. Samuels, *The Early Life Correspondence and Writings of the Rt. Hon. Edmund Burke LL.D* (Cambridge, 1923), p. 14.

11. On the debt Burke owed to Pope, more generally, see Frans De Bruyn, *The Literary Genres of Edmund Burke* (Oxford, 1996).

12. *Writings and Speeches of Edmund Burke,* 9 vols. (Oxford, 1981–), vol. 1, ed. T. O. McLoughlin and James T. Boulton, p. 66.

13. *Writings and Speeches,* 1:80. The parallel formulation a decade later, in the *Enquiry into the Origin of Our Ideas of the Sublime and Beautiful,* is more judicious but not fundamentally different in its intuition: "We do not sufficiently distinguish what we would by no means chuse to do, from what we should be eager enough to see if it was once done" (part I, section xv).

14. *Writings and Speeches*, 1:79, 81. Burke's objection to the portrayal of vicious actions on stage would carry into his maturity. "Even the *Beggar's Opera* [he] could not endure to hear praised for its wit or its music, because his mind was filled by thought of its misplaced levity, and he only saw the mischief which such a performance could do to society." John Morley, *Burke* (English Men of Letters, London, 1902), p. 109.

15. Marianne Elliott, *Wolfe Tone* (New Haven, Conn., 1989), p. 31.

16. Quoted by James Prior, *Life of the Right Honourable Edmund Burke* (London, 1854), p. 17.

17. Samuels, *Early Life,* prints the Minute Book and the notes of the club; see p. 244. This anti-Jacobite statement by Burke should be regarded as "public," a performance within the decorum of the small group; his private sentiment in a letter to Richard Shackleton (26 April 1746) softens the emphasis: "I am sure I share in the general compassion. 'Tis indeed melancholy to consider the state of those unhappy gentlemen who engaged in this affair (as for the rest they lose but their lives) who have thrown away their lives and fortunes, and destroyed their families for ever, in what I believe they thought a just cause" (Samuels, *Early Life,* p. 244n1). This expression of fellow feeling does not amount to a plea for clemency, let alone a suggestion like that of William Dennis (the member of the club who spoke for lenity to the rebels) that the strength of spirit and self-sacrifice displayed in their actions should excuse them from the severest penalties. Burke has a general and impersonal sympathy for the rebels. He admits that they were sincere. But their punishment allows of no remission since they fought to the death: "no mercy should be shown to him that is an enemy to his country, and he who rebels is liable to all the mischiefs such a crime brings upon him" (p. 244).

18. *Correspondence*, 1:10.

19. Ibid., 1:57.

20. Ibid., 1:29.

21. Ibid., 1:74.

22. Ibid., 1:78.

23. Ibid., 1:47–49.

24. Quoted in Stanley Ayling, *Edmund Burke* (London, 1988), p. 11.

25. See Ian Crowe, *Patriotism and Public Spirit: Edmund Burke and the Role of the Critic in 18th-Century Britain* (Stanford, Calif., 2012), p. 17: "Both campaigns," Crowe argues, "heightened Burke's awareness of the potentially catastrophic effect on order and liberty of a rhetoric of public spirit based on erroneous historical and religious reasoning." Richard Bourke, "Party, Parliament, and Conquest in Newly Ascribed Burke Manuscripts," *Historical Journal* 55, no. 3 (2012), pp. 619–652, points out that Burke's early views regarding party government, parliamentary sovereignty, and the imperial constitution—all here shown to precede his attachment to the Rockingham Whigs—pose "a challenge to the

old Namierite idea that the key to Edmund Burke is to be found in his opportunism, and that his rhetoric merely rationalizes an attitude of unabashed expediency" (p. 639).

26. *Writings and Speeches*, 1:323–324.

27. Ayling, pp. 121–122.

28. The misspelling of Burke is by Walpole in a letter to George Montagu, 22 July
1761, in *Horace Walpole's Correspondence*, 48 vols. (New Haven, Conn., 1937–1983),
vol. 9, ed. W. S. Lewis and Ralph S. Brown Jr., p. 380.

29. On Burke's extended relations with Dodsley, and the part played by the latter in
adjudicating the contest over the intellectual and imaginative authority of Pope,
see Crowe, *Patriotism and Public Spirit*, ch. 1.

30. I follow the indications offered in Thomas Copeland, *Our Eminent Friend,
Edmund Burke* (New Haven, Conn., 1949), ch. 4. See also T. O. McLoughlin,
Edmund Burke and the First Ten Years of the Annual Register, 1758–67 (Salisbury,
University of Rhodesia, 1975).

31. See Caroline Robbins, *The Eighteenth Century Commonwealthman* (Cambridge,
Mass., 1959). J. G. A. Pocock has claimed for this tradition an unbroken continuity into the nineteenth century, particularly in the writings of Cobbett; see
"The Varieties of Whiggism from Exclusion to Reform," in *Virtue, Commerce,
and History* (Cambridge, 1985).

32. The catalogue by R. H. Evans for the sale of Burke's library in 1833 shows that he
owned the collection of Bolingbroke's writings published by Mallet in 1754.

33. See Harvey C. Mansfield Jr., *Statesmanship and Party Government* (Chicago,
1965), chs. 3–5.

34. In the *Abridgment of English History*, Burke observes that "the natural equality
of mankind appears, and is asserted" by the civil government and manners of
the ancient Britons: "in all very uncultivated countries, as society is not close nor
intricate, nor property very valuable, liberty subsists with few restraints" (*Writings and Speeches*, 1:349). Equality seems to him natural, just as inequality is artificial; but the movement of society itself is from an uncultivated state to the
diversification (and inequality) brought by progress and refinement. The thought
is familiar, but the phrase *natural equality* is unusual to find in Burke: he will
modify it in the *Speech on Fox's East India Bill* to speak of "the natural equality
of mankind at large"—which by then he takes to be a normative premise of
morals, without regard to stages of progress.

35. Prior, *Life of the Right Honourable Edmund Burke*, p. 45.

36. Walpole, *Correspondence*, vol. 9, p. 380.

37. *Writings and Speeches*, 1:138.

38. Ibid., 1:139.

39. Ibid., 1:134.

40. This is a point that Swift's full title enforces with a conscious show of delicacy:
"An Argument to Prove that the Abolishing of Christianity in England May,

As Things Now Stand, Be Attended with Some Inconveniences, and Perhaps Not Produce Those Many Good Effects Proposed Thereby."

41. *Of the True Use of Retirement and Study,* in *The Works of Lord Bolingbroke,* 4 vols. (Philadelphia, 1841), 2:349.

42. *Writings and Speeches,* 1:145.

43. D. G. James, *The Life of Reason: Hobbes, Locke, Bolingbroke* (London, 1949), p. 200.

44. *Writings and Speeches,* 1:149.

45. F. P. Lock, *Edmund Burke: 1730–1784* (Oxford, 1998), pp. 82–83.

46. Bolingbroke, *Political Writings,* ed. David Armitage (Cambridge, 1997), p. 47.

47. Ibid., p. 72.

48. Leslie Stephen, *History of English Thought in the Eighteenth Century,* 2 vols. (New York, 1962), 2:147.

49. *Political Writings,* p. 229.

50. Ibid., p. 231. Additional points of accord between Bolingbroke and Burke are described by Isaac Kramnick in *Bolingbroke and His Circle* (Cambridge, Mass., 1968). Bolingbroke's idea of a constitution whose authority extends from "time out of mind" (an idea also congenial to Burke) gave the tacit sanction for his support of a patriot king: he supposed that so much agreement prevails in the customary knowledge of politics that there is little danger of tyrannical aggrandizement. Again, Bolingbroke, like Burke, is hostile to the very idea of a social contract—a product of legalistic minds that press toward division and faction. The proper unity of common sentiment and good sense is called by Bolingbroke "nature" or "reason," and he thinks its judgments are uniform. Here a difference is noticeable; for Burke refers to nature more than he does to reason, and he is attentive to the variety, not the uniformity, of its manifestations.

Bolingbroke, in the poem dedicated to him by Pope, would have admired and assented to the lines

> All nature is but art, unknown to thee,
> All chance, direction which thou canst not see,
> All discord harmony misunderstood,
> All partial evil, universal good.

Burke would have rejected the comfort afforded by such acceptance of blended contraries. Discord, he believed, must often remain discordant, and nature is not the work of an artist whose signature we can everywhere recognize if only we take the trouble to perfect our intuitions.

Yet Burke and Bolingbroke were similarly interested in detecting the regularities under the apparent ruptures within human nature and society. They trust education, established fortune, and landed property as the sources of any tradition worth perpetuating. Both are opposed to radical reforms of the system of representation in Parliament. In a merely practical political sense, the largest difference between them is that Bolingbroke sought his epitome of virtue in the excluded gentry who supported the cause of James II, whereas Burke found his model of a natural aristocracy in the successors of the Whigs who forced James to abdicate.

51. *Writings and Speeches,* 1:177–178.

52. John Morley, who accepted the work as a parody, thought the eloquence of Burke's language strangely revealing and wondered how an uninstructed reader could tell whether the passage about mine workers came from Burke or Rousseau. See John Morley, *Burke* (London, 1887), pp. 16–18.

53. *Writings and Speeches,* 1:153–154.

54. Ibid., 1:167.

55. See Prior, *Life of the Right Honourable Edmund Burke,* p. 49, who says that Burke gave the note to his wife on an anniversary of their wedding.

56. *Writings and Speeches,* 1:59–60.

II. The Sublime and Beautiful

1. *The Spectator,* 4 vols., ed. Gregory Smith, Everyman edition (London, 1945), 3:279.

2. David Hume, *A Dissertation on the Passions,* ed. Tom L. Beauchamp (Oxford, 2007), 6.10, p. cxii.

3. Alexander Gerard, *An Essay on Taste* (London, 1759), p. 74.

4. Ibid., 104, 110.

5. Ibid., 202–203.

6. L'Abbe Du Bos, *Réflexions Critiques sur la Poésie et sur la Peinture* (Paris, 1733), part 1, p. 1: "On épreuve tous les jours que les vers & les tableaux causent un plaisir sensible, mais il n'en est pas moins difficile d'expliquer en quoi consiste ce plaisir qui ressemble souvent à l'affliction, & dont les simptomes sont quelquesfois les mêmes, que ceux de la plus vive douleur. L'art de la Poésie et l'art de la Peinture ne sont jamais plus applaudis que lorsqu'ils ont réussi à nous affliger."

7. Quoted by James T. Boulton, introduction to *A Philosophical Enquiry into the Origin of Our Ideas of the Sublime and Beautiful* (London, 1958), p. lv.

8. Du Bos, *Réflexions Critiques,* vol. 1, section 1, p. 6: "plus le besoin et grand, plus le plaisir d'y satisfaire est sensible."

9. Burke and Du Bos differ on which of the arts has the greatest power to move. Painting, says Du Bos, because it does so by means of natural and not arbitrary signs. Poetry, says Burke, because the arbitrariness of language (the immethodical relation between sign and signified) makes it an ideally artificial medium. The fact that words can affect our ideas without producing an image renders them an infinitely alluring stimulus for the mind in search of things beyond its grasp.

10. 1817 edition of the *Encyclopedia;* reprinted in William Hazlitt, *Complete Works,* ed. P. P. Howe, 21 vols. (London, 1930–1934), 18:127.

11. *Writings and Speeches of Edmund Burke,* 9 vols. (Oxford, 1981–), vol. 1, ed. T. O. McLoughlin and James T. Boulton, p. 190.

12. Ibid., *Enquiry,* Part I, Section vii, in *Writings and Speeches,* 1:216.

13. Johnson, *Preface to Shakespeare,* in *Johnson on Shakespeare,* ed. Arthur Sherbo, 2 vols. (New Haven, Conn., 1968), 1.78.

14. *Enquiry,* Part I, Section xv, in *Writings and Speeches,* 1:223.

15. Ibid., Part I, Section xiv, in *Writings and Speeches,* 1:222.

16. Though Burke's psychological radicalism in asserting the power of "the real sympathy" seems to me inescapable, his emphasis is not unique. Samuel Johnson in *Adventurer* No. 92 spared Virgil's first and tenth pastorals from his strictures against pastoral poetry in general, with this explanation: "It may be observed, that these two poems were produced by events that really happened; and may, therefore, be of use to prove, that we can always feel more than we can imagine, and that the most artful fiction must give way to truth." On the larger question whether all men and women have a residue of natural susceptibility, Johnson remarks that "Poetry has to do rather with the passions of man, which are uniform, than with their customs, which are changeable." Thus, judgments of taste may shift where customs are mainly involved but not where passion is—an axiom Hume would also propound in his essay "Of the Standard of Taste."

17. Francis Hutcheson, quoted by Walter Hipple, *The Sublime, the Beautiful, and the Picturesque* (Carbondale, Ill., 1957), p. 34.

18. *Enquiry,* Part I, Section xviii, in *Writings and Speeches,* 1:226.

19. If "Mr. Burke," during the trial of Warren Hastings, "had suddenly . . . appeared in Westminster-hall without his wig and coat, or had walked up St. James's street without his breeches, it would have occasioned great and universal *astonishment;* and if he had, at the same time, carried a loaded blunderbuss in his hands, the astonishment would have been mixed with no small portion of *terror;* but I do not believe that the united effects of these two powerful passions would have produced any sentiment or sensation approaching to sublime." See Richard Payne Knight, *An Analytical Inquiry into the Principles of Taste* (London, 1805), pp. 374–375.

20. The same maxim appears—where it may have caught Burke's eye—at the start of Swift's "Verses on the Death of Dean Swift."

21. *Diderot on Art,* ed. John Goodman, 2 vols. (New Haven, 1995), 2:101. In quoting, I have slightly altered Goodman's translation.

22. On the catastrophic spectacle as an excitement that implicates the viewer, see David Marshall, *The Surprising Effects of Sympathy* (Chicago, 1988), ch. 1.

23. *Diderot on Art,* 2:103.

24. *Enquiry,* Part II, Section v, in *Writings and Speeches,* 1:236–237.

25. *Diderot on Art,* 1:241.

26. On politics and the sublime, see Fredric Jameson, *The Political Unconscious* (Ithaca, N.Y., 1981); Hayden White, "The Politics of Historical Interpretation:

Discipline and Desublimation," *Critical Inquiry* 9, no. 1 (1982), pp. 113–137; Jean-François Lyotard, *The Inhuman*, trans. Geoffrey Bennington and Rachel Bowlby (Cambridge, 1988). Stephen K. White in *Edmund Burke: Modernity, Politics, and Aesthetics* (Lanham, Calif., 1994) detects in Burke a "false" and a "true" sublime, the former relating to tyrannical exertions of personal or collective will, the latter to humanity and the common good. This terminology is useful, but it is not Burke's, and he would likely have regarded impressions of the false and the true sublime as sharing a single origin. Tom Furniss in *Edmund Burke's Aesthetic Ideology* (Cambridge, 1993) relates the *Enquiry* to the *Reflections* by supposing the sublime is always, in essence, willful, always despotic, and ultimately traceable to the desire of a man to dominate a woman.

27. For a different view of the affinities between Burke's ideas of the beautiful and of the sublime, see Frances Ferguson, *Solitude and the Sublime* (New York, 1992), ch. 2.

28. Sir Joshua Reynolds's *Discourses on Art* laid it down that "to preserve the most perfect beauty in its most perfect state, you cannot express the passions, all of which produce distortion and deformity, more or less, in the most beautiful faces." Blake commented: "What Nonsense Passion & Expression is Beauty Itself—The Face that is Incapable of Passion & Expression is Deformity Itself." Blake, like Burke, denies that beauty occurs in a middle ground between the extremes of passion; see *The Poetry and Prose of William Blake*, ed. David Erdman (New York, 1965), p. 642.

29. *Enquiry*, Part III, Section v, in *Writings and Speeches*, 1:264–265.

30. Ibid., Part II, Section iv, in *Writings and Speeches*, 1:233–234.

31. Ibid., Part III, Section v, in *Writings and Speeches*, 1:265.

32. Ibid., Part III, Section vii, in *Writings and Speeches*, 1:268.

33. Burke takes considerable pains not to be wrongly read as a believer in perfection as either an attainable or a desirable good in matters of art or human perception. This may be related to his saying in the *Reflections* that "difficulty is good for man." The labor of coming to terms with stark or surprising emotions causes us to work our physical response with a muscular exertion that sharpens both the senses and the mind. Aris Sarafianos, in a fascinating article, "The Contractility of Burke's Sublime and Heterodoxies in Medicine and Art" (*Journal of the History of Ideas* 69, no. 1 [January 2008], pp. 23–48), has traced Burke's speculation to a probable source in the medical theories of his father-in-law, Dr. Christopher Nugent.

34. For the judgment that such aestheticism partly originates in Burke, see George Kateb, "Aestheticism and Morality: Their Cooperation and Hostility," *Political Theory* 28, no. 1 (February 2000), pp. 5–37; reprinted in the same author's collection of essays *Is Patriotism a Mistake?* (New Haven, Conn., 2006).

35. *The Analysis of Beauty* (1753), the leading English book on the subject before Burke, reduces the beautiful to invariable natural causes in primary and second-

ary qualities. Hogarth's discovery is the enticing spell of "the serpentine line" (a formulation Burke adopts less centrally and with modifications). By the turns of the line, the spectator is led on a path of pursuit which has no end, and which one does not want to see ended. The relevant qualities for Hogarth include symmetry, simplicity, intricacy, proportion, light and shade, and colors. Only his final chapters on attitude and action evince much interest in the way a spectator may read an intention into an object: a presupposition of Burke's argument that shows as early as his opening definitions of sympathy and delight.

36. On the significance of Part V, and its demonstration of the power of words to confound the process of reference and create a sublimity not derived from objects, I am indebted to an unpublished essay by Ross Borden.

37. *Enquiry,* Part V, Section iii, in *Writings and Speeches,* 1:311.

38. See Donald Davidson, "A Nice Derangement of Epitaphs," reprinted in his collection of essays *Truth, Language, and History* (Oxford, 2005), pp. 89–107. Davidson describes the everyday interpretative readiness by which we find a sense to go with words of apparent nonsense. Burke asks us to share his surprise at the arbitrariness of the jump from an absence or opacity of intended meaning to the satisfaction of the need for interpreted meaning.

39. For an intricate and subtle interpretation of the anti-Shaftesburian polemic in Burke, see Paddy Bullard, *Edmund Burke and the Art of Rhetoric* (Cambridge, 2011), chs. 1 and 3.

40. This suggestion is made, with emphasis on different details, in Boulton's introduction to his earlier edition of the *Enquiry* (London, 1958), pp. xxviii–xxx.

41. See Ian Hacking, *The Emergence of Probability* (Cambridge, 1975), where probability is defined as demonstrative knowledge minus causation; see also Douglas Lane Patey, *Probability and Literary Form* (Cambridge, 1984), chs. 1–3.

42. Annette Baier, *A Progress of Sentiments* (Cambridge, Mass., 1991), p. 10.

43. Less moderate are the sensations belonging to political rhetoric; but to those Hume devoted a separate essay, "Of Eloquence." His parable of the just equilibrium of taste gives the illustration of a sack of wine that is sipped by rival judges. It tastes to one like leather, to another like metal. In the sack is discovered a key attached to a leather thong.

44. Smith's view of moral sentiments, like Burke's view of the sublime and beautiful, depends on a model of spectatorship. Where Smith at the scene of moral action supposes two observers—the agent and the "impartial spectator" with whose judgments the agent brings his responses into conformity—Burke at the scene of aesthetic action supposes only one. Burke's letter to Smith, of 10 September 1759, finds a fault in the *Theory:* "You are in some few Places, what Mr Locke is in most of his writings, rather a little too diffuse"; see *The Correspondence of Edmund Burke,* 10 vols. (Cambridge, 1958–1978), vol. 1, ed. Thomas Copeland, p. 130. Burke's canons of style, as well as his practice, show his partiality for compression, argumentative economy, and unsuperfluousness, over the other

possible virtues of prose. In his published writings (as distinct from speeches extemporized in the House of Commons), he cannot fairly be called a diffuse or digressive writer until the productions of his final decade.

45. See, for example, Ronald Paulson, *Representations of Revolution* (New Haven, Conn., 1983); Peter de Bolla, *The Discourse of the Sublime* (Oxford, 1989).

46. Peter Gay exemplifies this tendency in his authoritative history of the Enlightenment: the *Enquiry* is "a young man's book, energetic, facile, a little irresponsible, and sometimes embarrassing"; see *The Enlightenment: The Science of Freedom* (New York, 1969), pp. 303–306. O'Brien and Lock, Burke's most recent biographers, are very sparing in the connections they trace between the aesthetic enquiry and later political works.

47. Burke's adaptation of Psalms 139:14: "I will praise thee; for I am fearfully and wonderfully made: marvellous are thy works; and that my soul knoweth right well."

48. Walpole, *Correspondence*, loc. cit., vol. 9, p. 380.

49. *Writings and Speeches*, 1:544–546.

50. "The language most likely to continue long without alteration," writes Johnson near the end of the preface, "would be that of a nation raised a little, and but a little above barbarity, secluded from strangers, and totally employed in procuring the conveniencies of life; either without books or, like some of the Mahometan countries, with very few: men thus busied and unlearned, having only such words as common use requires, would perhaps long continue to express the same notions by the same signs. But no such constancy can be expected in a people polished by arts and classed by subordination, where one part of the community is sustained and accommodated by the labour of the other. Those who have much leisure to think will always be enlarging the stock of ideas, and every increase of knowledge, whether real or fancied, will produce new words or combinations of words."

51. *Writings and Speeches*, 1:540.

52. Ibid., 1:540–541.

53. Ibid., 1:399.

54. Ibid., 1:400.

55. Ibid., 1:387–388.

56. Burke's treatment of the rise and progress of the Catholic Church is severe, almost Tacitean in its detachment; and while it illustrates his belief that people are governed by opinion more than force, it rejects the assumption that opinion is the opposite of force. The relevant passage occurs at the start of his view of Europe at the time of the Norman conquest: "The rudeness of the world was very favourable for the establishment of an empire of opinion. The moderation, with which the Popes at first exerted this empire, made its growth unfelt until it could no longer be opposed. And the policy of later Popes, building on the piety of the first, continually increased it; and they made use of every instrument but

that of force. They employed equally the virtues and the crimes of the great; they favoured the lust of kings for absolute authority, and the desire of subjects for liberty; they provoked war and mediated peace, and took advantage of every turn in the minds of men, whether of a public or private nature, to extend their influence, and push their power, from ecclesiastical to civil, from subjection to independency; from independency to empire" (*Writings and Speeches*, 1:454–455). Many of Burke's later observations will confirm his understanding that the spread of the Church throughout Europe was a revolution, which the Protestant reformation in effect reignited. Revolution and empire are political phenomena that he would always judge to be closely related. They tend to be thought of separately, perhaps, because the outward show of empire is static, whereas revolution is dynamic. These appearances seemed to Burke to conceal a profounder affinity—a perception he would develop at length in his writings on India.

57. Quoted by James Prior, *Life of the Right Honourable Edmund Burke* (London, 1854), p. 67.

58. *Correspondence*, 1:138.

59. Burke to O'Hara, 9 December 1762: "Would you believe that the french Ministry is charmed with the Duke of Bedford; so reasonable, so moderate, so polite; whenever any difficulty arose [in negotiating the treaty to end the Seven Years War], they always left it to himself, and he always put it on the most conciliatory footing imaginable. The Air of Paris makes people practicable. You could not learn this secret in Ireland" (*Correspondence*, 1:159).

60. R. F. Foster, *Modern Ireland, 1600–1972* (London, 1988), pp. 223–224.

61. *Correspondence*, 1:255–256.

62. Luke Gibbons, *Edmund Burke and Ireland* (Cambridge, 2003), pp. 21–24 and ch. 1, passim.

63. *Correspondence*, 1:161–162.

64. Ibid., 1:192.

65. William Gerard Hamilton, *Parliamentary Logic*, ed. Courtney S. Kenney (Cambridge, 1927), p. 21.

66. Ibid., pp. 22, 37.

67. Ibid., pp. 4, 10, 75.

68. Ibid., p. 38.

69. Ibid., p. 9. More particularly, "Plurals impart magnificence, singulars strength, to a discourse. And the change from the one to the other is pathetic" (p. 8).

70. James Mackintosh, *Vindiciae Gallicae* (London, 1791), p. vii.

71. Hamilton, *Parliamentary Logic*, p. 52.

72. *Correspondence*, 1:165.

73. Ibid., 1:178.

74. Ibid., 1:179–180.

75. Ibid., 1:180.

76. Ibid., 1:191.

77. Ibid., 1:195–196.

78: Ibid., 1:197.

79. Ibid., 1:200.

80. As Copeland remarks (*Correspondence*, 1:179), "The person who succeeded Burke as Hamilton's assistant—though his duties were of a rather different character—was apparently Samuel Johnson," who served "to the end of his life a faithful and affectionate friend to Hamilton." Johnson was not known for servility, and Hamilton appears not to have been jealous of his talents.

81. *Correspondence*, 1:xxi.

82. Ibid., 1:202.

83. See Donald C. Bryant, *Edmund Burke and His Literary Friends* (St. Louis, Mo., 1939), p. 2. Bryant conjectures that Burke owed his introduction to several of these persons to his countryman Arthur Murphy.

84. See F. P. Lock, *Edmund Burke: 1730–1784* (Oxford, 1998), 1:186, who remarks "This was distinguished company" and adds: "Burke was the only one whom Hume needed to identify" when he wrote back to Smith to characterize the intended readers.

85. James Boswell, *Life of Johnson* (Oxford, 1953), p. 339.

86. See John Brewer, *Party Ideology and Popular Politics at the Accession of George III* (Cambridge, 1976): "the cleanest sweep since the Hanoverian succession" (p. 44).

87. Quoted by Ross J. S. Hoffman, *The Marquis* (New York, 1973), p. 37.

88. Quoted by ibid., p. 83.

89. Quoted in *Correspondence,* 1:xxxii.

90. Quoted by Hoffman, *The Marquis*, p. 86.

91. Quoted by Copeland in *Correspondence*, 1:223n3. Macleane sent this account in a letter to Wilkes in Paris.

92. Ibid., 1:231.

93. Ibid., 1:232–233.

94. To Bennet Langton, 8 March 1766, in *The Letters of Samuel Johnson*, 5 vols., ed. Bruce Redford (Princeton, N.J., 1992–1994), 1:264.

III. The Wilkes Crisis

1. As Lewis Namier put it: "certain forms and even principles of Cabinet government seemed to have been established. The Government was based on a party majority in the House of Commons, the King had to accept the leaders or makers of that majority, and had to act, and even think, through them—they were already conscious of knowing the King's (constitutional) mind better than he knew it himself"; see *England in the Age of the American Revolution*, 2nd ed. (London, 1961), p. 45.

2. Richard Pares, *King George III and the Politicians* (Oxford, 1953), p. 100.

3. Namier, *England in the Age of the American Revolution*, p. 4.

4. Burke and his party tended to resist otherwise routine manifestations of interest by the king because they believed he was drawing the advantages of leading a cabinet without the disadvantages of conspicuous participation.

5. Quoted by Pares, *King George III*, p. 65.

6. Quoted by ibid., p. 49n2.

7. Ibid., p. 183.

8. See John Brooke, *King George III* (London, 1972), on the king as a respecter of neither parties nor persons: "The King like most of his subjects regarded party distinctions as a disturbing element in national life" (p. 92). The Rockinghamites by contrast looked to party distinction as a means of refining personal distinction.

9. Quoted by Pares, *King George III*, p. 59.

10. In 1768, the Duke of Newcastle wrote with exasperation to the Duke of Richmond concerning his unwillingness "to leave your Hunting, to come to Town, to consider with our Friends the Plan of Conduct to be held by them, any considerable Time before the Meeting. . . . For God's sake, My Dear Lord, Don't let it be said that upon Points of this Infinite Consequence to the Nation, Your Grace has suffer'd Your Fox Hunting to deprive the Cause, and your Friends, of the Advantage of your Assistance"; quoted by John Brewer, *Party Ideology and Popular Politics at the Accession of King George* (Cambridge, 1976), p. 59.

11. See Jeremy Black, *George III: America's Last King* (New Haven, Conn., 2006), on the familiarity of George III with Bolingbroke's call "for a monarch who was virtuous, impartial and powerful enough to override parties. . . . George was influenced by the concept of patriarchal government implicit in Bolingbroke's book, as well as in the Book of Kings from the Old Testament" (pp. 10–11).

12. Romney Sedgwick, ed., *Letters from George III to Lord Bute: 1756–1766* (London, 1939), pp. 45–46.

13. Rockingham to Newcastle, 6 September 1762: even a strong administration "backed with national confidence" could not have made the peace "in any degree adequate to expectation"; therefore, "even if a *Good* peace was made under this administration," people will suppose "that a better might be made" if only the administration had appeared "strong enough to have carried on the war." Quoted in Ross J. S. Hoffman, *The Marquis: A Study of Lord Rockingham, 1730–1782* (New York, 1973), p. 40.

14. *The Correspondence of Edmund Burke*, 10 vols. (Cambridge, 1958–1978), vol. 1, ed. Thomas Copeland, p. 211.

15. *Correspondence*, vol. 2, ed. Lucy S. Sutherland, p. 128.

16. Ibid., 2:128–129.

17. Thomas W. Copeland, *Our Eminent Friend Edmund Burke* (New Haven, 1949), pp. 54–55.

18. *Correspondence*, vol. 5, ed. Holden Furber with the assistance of P. J. Marshall, p. 8.

19. Ernest Barker, *Essays on Government* (Oxford, 1945), 173–174. See F. P. Lock, *Edmund Burke: 1730–1784* (Oxford, 1998), pp. 248–256, for the definitive treatment of the purchase, mortgages, architectural design, and pleasures afforded by Gregories—a description that makes sense of Burke's statement in 1794 that "My affairs were always in a State of embarrassment and confusion."

20. *Correspondence*, 2:130. Shackleton wrote of Burke's mother that "she practiced the duties of the *Romish* religion with a decent privacy" and described Burke's wife as also "of the Roman faith," adding that Burke had married her "neither for her *religion*, nor her *money*, but from the natural impulse of youthful affection" (*Correspondence*, 2:129).

21. *Correspondence*, 2:131.

22. Ibid., 2:136.

23. Quoted by James Prior, *Life of the Right Honourable Edmund Burke* (London, 1854), p. 112.

24. Quoted in George Crabbe, *Poetical Works,* 8 vols., edited by his son (London, Murray, 1835), 2:8, 9n2. The debt confessed by Crabbe was unexaggerated: in February 1781 he had delivered a letter to Burke's door asking for his advice after a failure to find patronage in London. Burke took him in for several weeks of that summer, at Beaconsfield; made him a gift of £100 at a time of want; and brought him to the attention of Sir Charles Bunbury and Lord Chancellor Thurlow, among others. See Carl B. Cone, *Burke and the Nature of Politics,* 2 vols. (Lexington, Ky., 1958–1964), 1:329–330.

25. *Correspondence*, 2:82.

26. Ibid., 1:292.

27. Letter of 4 September 1767, William Burke recalling the remark by Edmund, in ibid., 2:326.

28. Donald C. Bryant, *Edmund Burke and His Literary Friends* (St. Louis, Mo., 1939), p. 61.

29. William Hazlitt, *Complete Works,* 21 vols., ed. P. P. Howe (London, 1930–1934), 11:220.

30. James Boswell, *Life of Johnson* (Oxford, 1953), p. 923.

31. *Correspondence*, 1:309.

32. Burke believed that such a relentless pursuit of the main chance sold compromise too cheaply. Conway, in the event, was turned out as a condition of bringing Grafton in; see G. O. Trevelyan, *The Early History of Charles James Fox,* 3rd ed. (London, 1881), pp. 140–141. Yet the hit at Conway for not leaving when his party left office may obscure the fact that Rockingham allowed others of his party to stay in the Chatham administration; Pares, *King George III,* p. 80n1, cites this as an example of "Burke's habit of constructing a theory of politics out of generalizations . . . on every incident in the career of the Marquis of Rockingham."

33. *Correspondence*, 1:316.

34. Burke's ideas of loyalty and betrayal can seem so exaggerated—as indeed sometimes they are—that it is useful to check the reality of his impression by the report of a witness. In the case of Conway's change of allegiance, we have that witness. Horace Walpole was present on 9 July 1766 when Conway spoke with the king regarding his prospects: "To the Duke of Richmond the King was not tolerably civil. . . . To Conway alone His Majesty was gracious, and told him he hoped never to have an administration of which he should not be one. This looked as if the plan was settled, and that the King knew Mr Pitt intended to retain Conway, for His Majesty loved him no better than the rest. . . . When the King told Conway he had sent for Pitt, he replied, 'Sir, I am glad of it; I always thought it the best thing your Majesty could do. I wish it may answer: Mr Pitt is a great man; but as nobody is without faults, he is not unexceptionable." See Horace Walpole, *Memoirs of the Reign of King George III*, 4 vols. (New Haven, Conn., 2000), 3:51.
35. Quoted in *Correspondence*, 1:269n1.
36. Ibid., 1:279. The statement is notable as an early and open profession of confidence in the idea of a *formed* opposition—that is, a party—as a political good in itself. "Prior to 1760," observes Brewer (*Party Ideology*, p. 14), "all the arguments used to justify opposition, even those employed by the country-party ideologues, condemned party in the same breath that they condemned opposition." Burke is praising party in the same breath that he affirms the necessity of opposition. For evidence that Burke was inclined to such a view before he met Rockingham and long before he wrote the Rockinghamite credo in *Thoughts*, see the essay "On Parties" (1757) in Richard Bourke, "Party, Parliament, and Conquest in Newly Ascribed Burke Manuscripts," *Historical Journal* 55, no. 3 (2012): "It is certain no free Government ever was without parties" (p. 646).
37. James Boswell, *Life of Johnson*, (London, 1953), p. 904.
38. Prior, *Life of the Right Honourable Edmund Burke*, p. 101.
39. Quoted by ibid., pp. 95, 104.
40. Linda Colley, *Britons* (New Haven, Conn., 1992), pp. 105–106.
41. Quoted by Arthur H. Cash, *John Wilkes* (New Haven, Conn., 2006), p. 107.
42. Ibid., p. 194.
43. Ibid., p. 187.
44. Prior, *Life of the Right Honourable Edmund Burke*, p. 91.
45. *Correspondence*, 1:257.
46. Quoted in Ian Gilmour, *Riot, Risings and Revolution* (London, 1993), p. 313.
47. Letter to Charles O'Hara of 28 March 1768, in *Correspondence*, 1:349.
48. Burke's reckoning here finds an unexpected confirmation in a remark by Horace Walpole concerning the "triumvirate" of Wilkes, Churchill, and Temple, the last of whom "whispered [to the crowd] where they might find torches, but took care never to be seen to light one himself." The three have "made me often reflect, that nations are most commonly saved by the worst men in it. The virtuous

are too scrupulous to go to the lengths that are necessary to rouse the people against their tyrants"; see Walpole, *Memoirs*, 1:118.

49. Letter to Charles O'Hara of 9 June 1768, in *Correspondence*, 1:352–353.

50. *Correspondence*, 2:11–12, 18.

51. Quoted by Cash, *John Wilkes*, p. 225.

52. Ibid., p. 233.

53. Ibid., p. 240.

54. Ibid., p. 246.

55. *Writings and Speeches of Edmund Burke*, 9 vols. (Oxford, 1981–), vol. 2, ed. Paul Langford, p. 224.

56. Ibid., 2:225.

57. Ibid., 2:225–226.

58. Ibid., 2:226.

59. Ibid., 2:227–228.

60. Samuel Johnson, *Political Writings*, ed. Donald J. Greene (New Haven, Conn., 1977), pp. 323, 324, 331.

61. John Wilkes, *A Letter to Samuel Johnson, L.L.D.* (London: J. Almon, 1770), pp. 23–24.

62. Ibid., p. 37.

63. George Rudé, *Wilkes and Liberty* (Oxford, 1962), p. 144.

64. *Correspondence*, 2:108, 109.

65. Ibid., 2:120.

66. Ibid., 2:121.

67. Ibid., 2:92.

68. John Erard Faulkner, *The Literary Career of Edmund Burke* (PhD diss., Rutgers University, 1981), p. 136.

69. Burke could not, wrote Namier, openly "deny the King's right to give his confidence . . . to whomever he chose"; therefore, he "constructed the theory that it was George III's deliberate policy and established practice to withhold his support from Ministers"; whereas in fact, "in 1760–61 George III most ardently desired to see the man in office to whom he would have given the fullest confidence that any monarch has ever given to a Prime Minister," and Bute, Grenville, and Rockingham were successive candidates of inadequate strength and resourcefulness to sustain that trust. See Namier, *England in the Age of the American Revolution*, p. 160.

70. Trevelyan, *Early History of Fox*, p. 114.

71. *Writings and Speeches*, 2:252.

72. Ibid., 2:253.

73. Ibid., 2:255.

74. Ibid., 2:256.

75. The importance, in Burke's thinking on party and constitutional government, of these two complementary sorts of virtue is propounded with great acuteness by

Harvey C. Mansfield Jr. in *Statesmanship and Party Government* (Chicago, 1965), chs. 6 and 7.

76. John Cannon, ed., *The Letters of Junius* (Oxford, 1978), p. 160.

77. Sedgwick, *Letters from George III,* indicates in detail the arrangements they sought and the nature of the attachment. On the verge of resignation, in January 1763, Bute wrote to the king: "In my opinion the Angel Gabriel could not at present govern this country, but by means too long practic'd and such as my soul abhors. If this be so, it matters little to the King or State who shall distribute the loaves and fishes, but to my mode of thinking, these arts are most repugnant; in plain English, I am an object too colossal to be seen, even by those my hands have rais'd, without envy" (p. lxii). Shortly after Bute resigned, the king wrote to him to deplore the "ill humour" and "selfish disposition" of Grenville, in a note that concludes: "thank God I have a friend and that is what few Princes can boast of that except myself, that comforts me, and makes me look on my Ministers as my tools solely in my public capacity" (p. 233).

78. *Writings and Speeches,* 2:264.

79. Ibid.

80. On the sources of Burke's theory of the double cabinet, see Ian Christie, *Myth and Reality in Late Eighteenth-Century British Politics and Other Papers* (London, 1970), chs. 1–3. Christie argues that Burke's inference of an intention to aggrandize power by the "King's men" came from imposing a pattern on dismissals and departures in the early ministries of George III, when in fact the changes had accidental causes about which Rockingham and his party knew little. "They believed in their propaganda" (p. 212), and "the circumstances of the Rockingham party's tenure of power and dismissal from office in 1765–6 gave rise among its leaders to a genuine conviction that power in the state had been captured by a sinister and would-be tyrannous cabal" (p. 17). On this view, a coherent ideology took shape from sincerely credited if misguided perceptions. "The campaign against the supposed secret cabal was no mere pose," and the analysis in *Thoughts* "provided a rational justification for the [Rockinghamite] demand for a clean sweep of suspect elements from the administration" (p. 18).

81. This allusion is traced in Edmund Burke, *Pre-revolutionary Writings* (Cambridge, 1993), ed. Ian Harris, p. 140n65.

82. *Writings and Speeches,* 2:272, 275.

83. Ibid., 2:278–279.

84. John Morley, *Edmund Burke: A Historical Study* (New York, 1924), p. 13.

85. *Writings and Speeches,* 2:279.

86. The extent to which Burke believed the king's friends separable from the king—a body acting in his name but sometimes without consulting him—cannot be decided by a single document or any marked transition. *Thoughts* refers to *"King's men,* or the *King's friends,"* but it is possible to read too much into that. To attribute actions and motives to the king that Burke attributed to his friends

would have risked prosecution; not even Wilkes went so far. Burke and Rockingham, in any case, differed in the degree to which they clung to the idea of a
well-meaning king led into error by malicious advisers; Burke gave it up sooner
than Rockingham. See Christie, *Myth and Reality*, pp. 46–48.

87. *Writings and Speeches*, 2:282.

88. Ibid., 2:286.

89. Ibid., 2:286–287.

90. Pares, *King George III*, p. 117n1.

91. As late as *Thoughts on French Affairs* (December 1791), Burke would return to this
idea. Rulers who depend on a few sources for all their understanding are at the
mercy of those on whom they rely: "Let us only suffer any person to tell us his
story, morning and evening, but for one twelvemonth, and he will become our
master."

92. *Writings and Speeches*, 2:296–297.

93. Ibid., 2:298.

94. The general term "administration" is Burke's, and it helps to advance his theory
of uniform abuse of influence by the crown. But the character of the influence
varied: Grenville (for example) was successful in pushing George III to break
off his correspondence with Bute, and Rockingham prevailed on the king to
indicate his support of repeal of the Stamp Act at a time when his followers
were drifting the other way.

95. *Writings and Speeches*, 2:301.

96. Compare Burke's sentences on his early career in *A Letter to a Noble Lord* (1796):
"At every step of my progress in life (for in every step was I traversed and opposed), and at every turnpike I met, I was obliged to shew my passport, and
again and again to prove my sole title to the honour of being useful to my Country, by a proof that I was not wholly unacquainted with its laws, and the whole
system of its interests both abroad and at home. Otherwise no rank, no toleration even, for me." See *Writings and Speeches*, vol. 9 (ed. R. B. McDowell), p. 160.
Such contempt for merit—which Burke says he overcame by a process the *Letter*
looks back on as a necessary time of testing—is treated more severely in *Thoughts*.
It is a convenient element in the system of administrative corruption.

97. *Writings and Speeches*, 2:308.

98. Ibid., 2:309.

99. Ibid., 2:310.

100. Ibid., 2:268.

101. Ibid., 2:314–315.

102. See Harris, ed., *Pre-revolutionary Writings*, p. 188n125.

103. The usage sheds some light on a peculiarity of Burke's later choice of tactics
against the Jacobins. He will criticize them for being unconnected individuals
and criticize their state for being composed of "the dust and powder of individuality." It might seem that these qualities offer the surest protection against the

leading citizens entering into conspiracy, or the state achieving an oppressive unity. But where conventional analysis would find a source of disinterested conduct, Burke detects a motive of disintegration.

104. This train of thought had a clear beginning in Burke's *Observations on a Late State of the Nation*, published the year before *Thoughts*, in 1769; his target there, William Knox, was an advocate of the American policy of Grenville, who himself had begun as an ally of Pitt. Thinking of those movers of bad policy, Burke calls to mind their opposite: "the example of a large body of men, steadily sacrificing ambition to principle, can never be without use. It will certainly be prolific, and draw others to an imitation. *Vera gloria radices agit, atque etiam propagator* [True virtue sinks deep roots and spreads]"; see *Writings and Speeches*, 2:215.

105. *Writings and Speeches*, 2:318.

106. Ibid., 2:318–319.

107. Ibid., 2:320.

108. Ibid., 2:282.

109. *Correspondence*, 2:150.

110. Catharine Macaulay, *Observations on a Pamphlet, Entitled, Thoughts on the Cause of the Present Discontents* (London, 1770), sees the Rockinghamites as an "Aristocratic faction and party" like the rest, "founded on and supported by the corrupt principle of self-interest" (p. 7). Significant clues to Burke's anti-democratic sentiment are said to be his disdain for a plan of rotation that would incapacitate members of the House of Commons for re-election over a period of ten years; and his refusal to support a widened suffrage—"a more extended and equal power of election" (pp. 28, 31).

111. *Correspondence*, 2:150.

112. Ibid., 2:155.

113. Ibid., 2:157.

114. Ibid., 2:163.

115. Ibid., 2:175.

116. Quoted by Trevelyan, *Early History*, p. 391.

117. Ibid., p. 424.

118. He had already done so in March 1772, and in an impassioned speech that rose to a scathing aspersion on Lord Mansfield: "*He has no child* who first formed this bill." See Lock, *Edmund Burke*, p. 330, who marks the allusion to *Macbeth* (IV. iii.216)—Macduff's discovery of the murder of all his children. His response to Malcolm's "Be comforted" separates feeling from unfeeling persons: "He has no children." Burke had quoted the adjacent lines in his angry description of William Gerard Hamilton at the time of their rupture.

119. Burke, in his speech of 1781, defended the prerogative of fathers with a protective jealousy. "It gives me pain to differ on this occasion," he said, "from many, if not most of those, whom I honor and esteem." He went on to distinguish his views on the limitation of political power from his views on the perpetuation of

moral authority over generations: "It is said, the Marriage Act is aristocratick. I am accused, I am told abroad, of being a man of aristocratick principles. If by aristocracy they mean the Peers, I have no vulgar admiration, nor any vulgar antipathy towards them, I hold their order in cold and decent respect. I hold them to be of an absolute necessity in the Constitution, but I think they are only good when kept within their proper bounds. I trust, whenever there has been a dispute between these Houses, the part I have taken has not been equivocal"; *The Works of Edmund Burke*, 12 vols. (Boston, 1869), vol. 7, p. 133, corrected from *Writings and Speeches*, vol. 4 MS, ed. P. J. Marshall. The stress on the word *vulgar*, as Marshall intimates in a note, may come from Fox's having said that the Act meant to "separate the high from the vulgar, and prevent their intermarriage and mixture." Burke's regard for the value of continuity in families cuts across the distinction between high and low.

120. Quoted in Christopher Hobhouse, *Fox* (London, 1947), p. 70.
121. J. H. Plumb, *The Growth of Political Stability in England, 1675–1725* (London, 1967), p. 189.
122. Herbert Butterfield, *George III and the Historians* (London, 1988), p. 263.

IV. The American War

1. P. J. Marshall, *The Making and Unmaking of Empires: Britain, India, and North America c. 1750–1783* (Oxford, 2005), p. 281.
2. See Ian R. Christie, *Wars and Revolutions: Britain, 1760–1815* (Cambridge, Mass., 1982), pp. 88–89.
3. *Annual Register*, 1766, pp. 2, 31.
4. The history of European events in the 1766 *Annual Register* likens the effect of a tax, collected anywhere, to a stone dropped into a pool whose widening circles are fated to reach the shore (p. 43). So a Virginia tobacco grower, taxed "externally," will feel the burden of the tax at a later moment.
5. Quoted in Theodore Draper, *A Struggle for Power* (New York, 1996), p. 279.
6. Edmund S. Morgan, "Colonial Ideas of Parliamentary Power, 1764–66," in *The Challenge of the American Revolution* (New York, 1976), pp. 3–42.
7. Quoted in ibid., p. 27. It seems likely that the Rockinghamites hoped the act would serve its function as a verbal assertion of power which would never be called to a test. They received near-unanimous support for the Declaratory Act but weaker numbers for the repeal of the Stamp Act.
8. Quoted in W. E. H. Lecky, *History of England in the Eighteenth Century*, 8 vols. (London, 1888), 3:367.
9. See I. R. Christie, *Crisis of Empire: Great Britain and the American Colonies, 1754–1783* (London, 1966), p. 63.
10. On 6 April 1768 Burke said in his *Speech on the Declaratory Act* that it had been "in its original intention . . . a wise and politic measure," but "in the present

state of affairs, he thought it wise to give it up, if thereby the minds of the Americans could be conciliated, and their affections regained." *Writings and Speeches of Edmund Burke*, 9 vols. (Oxford, 1981–), vol. 3, ed. Warren A. Elofson with John A. Woods, p. 374. His recognition that American independence was inevitable and must be granted "to prevent further waste of treasure and expence of blood" came four days later, in his *Speech on Powys's Motion on American Commission*.

11. *Correspondence*, vol. 3, p. 254.

12. Benjamin Franklin, whose judgments of American popular opinion enjoyed considerable authority in England at the time, told a committee of the House of Commons that the assertion of right contained in the Declaratory Act would not inflame the colonists: "I think the resolutions of right will give them very little concern, if they are never attempted to be carried into practice." Quoted in Lecky, *England in the Eighteenth Century*, 3:371.

13. Quoted in *Memoirs of the Political and Private Life of James Caulfield, Earl of Charlemont* (London, 1810), p. 115.

14. *Writings and Speeches*, 9 vols. (Oxford, 1981–), vol. 2, ed. Paul Langford, pp. 54–55.

15. See Lucy Sutherland, "Edmund Burke and the First Rockingham Ministry," in *Politics and Finance in the Eighteenth Century*, ed. Aubrey Newman (London, 1984). The Rockinghamites had been resourceful, beyond what Burke implies in his account, in their handling of extra-parliamentary organization. Once the Stamp Act disturbances made clear the obnoxiousness of the measure, they willingly received, and deployed to considerable effect, the petitions for repeal by colonial merchants and their allies in English manufacturing towns. "This ministry," Sutherland writes, "gave its form in both practice and theory to what we consider the whig tradition of the eighteenth century. It was not the principles of the Pelhams, Cavendishes, and Russells, ruling securely as the heirs of the glorious revolution, but those which were forced out by the change from power to opposition, a compound of new needs with old loyalties" (p. 323).

16. Marshall, *The Making and Unmaking of Empires*, p. 305.

17. Lecky, *England in the Eighteenth Century*, 3:427.

18. By the Administration of Justice Act of 1774, discussed later in this chapter, Americans charged with treason could be extradited for trial in England. The Quebec Act, passed in the same year, was hotly resented by the colonists because its fixing of a border was taken to enforce an arbitrary limit against westward expansion, and the granting of Catholic rights did not suit the religion and temper of New England. The last of these reactions was not lost on Burke; it forms part of the background to his ambivalent defense of "the Protestantism of the Protestant religion." Burke would have witnessed the response firsthand, from his service as agent for New York; in the House of Commons, he opposed the Quebec Act. See Peter D. G. Thomas, *Tea Party to Independence: The Third Phase of the American Revolution* (Oxford, 1991); and on the complexity of Burke's

position, see John Faulkner, "Burke's First Encounter with Richard Price: The Chathamites and North America," in *An Imaginative Whig*, ed. Ian Crowe (Columbia, Mo., 2005). Faulkner remarks that Burke would have been wary of conceding too much power to a Protestant minority "on the Irish model which he had detested all his life"; and he adds that, "unlike Chatham and Camden, who sought to rescind the Quebec Act in 1775, Burke did not include it with the Coercive Acts when he resolved that they be repealed in his *Speech on Conciliation*" (p. 105).

19. Carl B. Cone, *Burke and the Nature of Politics*, 2 vols. (Lexington, Ky., 1958–1964), 1:217–218, says that Markham suspected Burke of being Junius; this may partly explain why Burke would write to him at such length.

20. *The Correspondence of Edmund Burke*, 10 vols. (Cambridge, 1958–1978), vol. 2, ed. Lucy S. Sutherland, p. 263.

21. Ibid., 2:270.

22. Ibid., 2:272.

23. Ibid., 2:282.

24. Ibid., 2:293.

25. Horace Walpole, *Memoirs of the Reign of King George III*, 4 vols. (New Haven, Conn., 2000), 3:104, 176.

26. John Cannon, *Lord North: The Noble Lord in the Blue Ribbon*, Historical Association Pamphlet (London, 1970), p. 9. Burke, for all his tirades against North, shared with him an unyielding belief that the House of Commons should not widen its basis of representation. North would be an ally of Burke's in 1783 in his opposition to reform of Parliament, and he anticipated Burke in 1773 by passing the East India Company Regulation Act.

27. Ibid. See also Sir Lewis Namier and John Brooke, *The House of Commons, 1754–1780*, 3 vols. (London, 1964), 3:205, and their summary judgment, "Chronic indecision at critical moments was North's great defect as a minister"; with the supporting statement from Lord Thurlow, "Nothing can goad him forward."

28. *Correspondence*, 2:352.

29. Ibid., 2:364.

30. Ibid., 2:371.

31. Ibid., 2:373.

32. Ibid., 2:377.

33. There is a temptation to suppose that echoes like these, of *Paradise Lost* and other works, which come up frequently in Burke's speeches, are accidental embellishments or somehow incidental to his meaning. As an antidote to the tendency to minimize the force of such echoes, consider this summary of a later speech in *The Gazetteer and New Daily Advertiser* (8–9 November 1776): "*Mr. Burke* began in a kind of paroxysm of passion and storm of contempt for the arguments made use of by his learned *friend*. He alluded to a celebrated passage in Milton, where *Satan* is described after his defeat upon the *oblivious pool*, as-

tonished, or *astounded,* lying on it many a rood extended. He represented the Solicitor General as the *fallen* Angel; his friend Charles as the treader down and *vanquisher* of *sin* and *death;* the House of Commons he likened to *Chaos,* or the *oblivious pool,* its hallowed inhabitants to the *host of Satan;* and himself to the poet." I am grateful to Christopher Reid for this reference.

34. Letter of 7 November 1773, in *Correspondence,* 2:483.

35. *The Spirit of the Laws,* trans. Thomas Nugent (New York, 1949), Book V, chapter 14, p. 62.

36. Ibid., Book XI, chapter 4, p. 150.

37. On Burke's preference for representative government and trusteeship over systems embodying a more direct relation between constituency and assembly, see James Conniff, *The Useful Cobbler: Edmund Burke and the Politics of Progress* (Albany, 1994), chs. 5–7.

38. *Correspondence,* 2:516.

39. This paradox, regarding the self-suppression necessary to the founder of a party and the self-assertion necessary for executing policy, is discussed in Harvey C. Mansfield Jr., *Statesmanship and Party Government* (Chicago, 1965), chs. 1 and 2.

40. *Writings and Speeches,* vol. 2, ed. Paul Langford, pp. 322–323n3.

41. Ibid., 2:423.

42. Ibid., 2:415, 417, 428.

43. Knox, in looking back on the failure of the policy, detected an original error in the fact that "[Grenville] not only considered England as the head and heart of the whole [empire], as it certainly is, but he wished to render every other part the mere instrument or conduit of conveying nourishment and vigour to it. He was not well acquainted with the internal State of Ireland, and he knew still less of the circumstances of the American Colonies"; quoted in Leland J. Bellot, *William Knox: The Life and Thought of an Eighteenth-Century Imperialist* (Austin, 1977), p. 84. In *Observations on a Late State of the Nation*—written to answer a pamphlet by Knox, *The Present State of the Nation* (1768), which defended the Grenville policy—Burke had analyzed the consequences and saw worse to come: "the people who are to be the subjects of these restraints are Englishmen; and of an high and free spirit. To hold over them a government made up of nothing but restraints and penalties, and taxes in the granting of which they can have no share, will neither be wise, nor long practicable. People must be governed in a manner agreeable to their temper and disposition; and men of free character and spirit must be ruled with, at least, some condescension to this spirit and this character"; see *Writings and Speeches,* 2:194.

44. Ibid., 2:432.

45. Ibid., 2:441.

46. Ibid., 2:450–451.

47. The description also accuses Chatham of *tastelessness* in the political realm, the vulgar display of an arriviste; and this opens the way for another insinuation.

His new title may be a fair reward for cooperation with the king, but a more dignified man would have refused it. In the *Annual Register* for the year 1766, writing anonymously, Burke is explicit about the grounds of distrust: "Many of those who were most attached to the Earl of Chatham, regretted, that instead of weakening and dividing an interest which the public wished to be supported, and contributing to remove a ministry, in which they had placed a confidence; he had not rather by coinciding and acting along with them, contributed to give them that permanency, which was so much desired and wanted. There were other reasons which contributed greatly to lessen the popularity of which this noble Lord had before possessed so boundless a share; among these, his quitting the House of Commons and accepting a peerage, was not the least" (p. 48). On the broader affinities between Burke and Pope, and the deliberateness of Burke's echoes of Pope elsewhere, see Frans De Bruyn, *The Literary Genres of Edmund Burke* (Oxford, 1996), chs. 1, 6.

48. *Writings and Speeches*, 2:452.

49. The Townshend Duties had however achieved easy passage in the House. "The mood of the moment swept all doubts aside," writes Peter D. G. Thomas. "That no Parliamentary opposition to the American Revenue Bill was voiced is virtually certain from the complete absence of any information on either debates or divisions in Commons or Lords"; see Peter D. G. Thomas, *The Townshend Duties Crisis* (Oxford, 1987), p. 31.

50. *Writings and Speeches*, 2:442.

51. Ibid., 2:443.

52. Ibid., 2:458.

53. Ibid., 2:456. An echo of the last sentence appears, where it might not be expected, in Emerson's essay "The American Scholar": "if the single man plant himself indomitably on his instincts, and there abide, the huge world will come round to him."

54. *Writings and Speeches*, 2:458, 462.

55. Quoted in G. O. Trevelyan, *The American Revolution*, 4 vols. (London, 1922), 1:226.

56. *Correspondence*, vol. 3, ed. George H. Guttridge, pp. 30, 31.

57. Ibid., 3:107.

58. Ibid., 3:40.

59. P. T. Underdown, "Burke's Bristol Friends," *Transactions of the Bristol and Gloucestershire Archaeological Society* 77 (1958), pp. 128–130.

60. *Correspondence*, vol. 4, ed. John A. Woods, p. 65.

61. P. T. Underdown, "Henry Cruger and Edmund Burke: Colleagues and Rivals at the Bristol Election of 1774," *William and Mary Quarterly* 14, no. 1 (January 1958), cites a tradition which "required that of the two Bristol members of Parliament, one should be a local merchant, the other a politician of national reputation but with a special knowledge of commercial affairs" (p. 17). Considered in that light, Burke's election was a smaller departure from precedent.

62. P. T. Underdown, "Bristol and Burke," pamphlet issued by the Bristol branch of the Historical Association, University of Bristol, p. 6.

63. Lucy Sutherland, "Edmund Burke and Relations between Members of Parliament and Their Constituents," in *Politics and Finance in the Eighteenth Century.* In the late 1760s, writes Sutherland, "a new type of campaign instructions to representatives began to develop," specifically in Middlesex, Westminster, and the City of London in 1769 to protest the exclusion of Wilkes from Parliament, to support other grievances, and to "urge the old 'Country' tradition demands for reform" (p. 286). Baker had been an ally of Newcastle; he stood for the City and lost. "Great attention," he declared in his refusal of instructions, "is certainly due from a Representative to the Sense of his Constituents, fairly taken, and properly signified:—But, as I must preserve my own Judgement free on all the Subjects which may arise in Parliament, I cannot, with Honour, engage myself indefinitely and beforehand, to the fulfilling of instructions which I do not know" (p. 297).

64. *Writings and Speeches,* 2:69.

65. Hanna Fenichel Pitkin in *The Concept of Representation* (Berkeley, 1967) and Jürgen Habermas in *The Structural Transformation of the Public Sphere* (Cambridge, Mass., 1991) recognize Burke as an originator of the modern theory of political representation.

66. *Federalist Papers* (New York, 1961), p. 314.

67. Ibid., p. 384.

68. *Writings and Speeches,* 2:69–70. Burke is arguing here for an idea of deliberative government with a local basis and with a check from partial suffrage; yet for a government none of whose members are answerable to local interests and all of whom may rightly claim a national competence. His speech of 1774 echoes his anonymous explanation in the *Annual Register* eight years earlier: "There can be no doubt but that the inhabitants of the colonies are as much represented in parliament, as the greatest part of the people of England are, among nine millions of whom, there are eight who have no votes in electing members of parliament. . . . A member of parliament chosen for any borough, represents not only the constituents, and inhabitants of that particular place, but he represents the inhabitants of every other borough in Great Britain; he represents the city of London, and all the other commons of the land, and the inhabitants of all the colonies and dominions of Great Britain, and is in duty and conscience bound to take care of their interests" (*Annual Register,* 1766, p. 43).

The stipulation, curiously reminiscent of Rousseau, that all members should be the representatives of all, rather than each the representative of his own constituency plus unrepresented ones, would have distinguished this in Burke's view from an argument for virtual representation.

69. *Correspondence,* 3:86.

70. Ibid., 4:89.

71. Ibid., 3:120.
72. Samuel Johnson, *Political Writings,* ed. Donald Greene (New Haven, Conn., 1977), p. 418.
73. Ibid., p. 441.
74. Ibid., p. 425.
75. Ibid., p. 429.
76. Ibid., p. 429.
77. Ibid., p. 429.
78. Ibid., p. 437.
79. Ibid., pp. 446–447.
80. Ibid., p. 448.
81. Ibid., p. 453.
82. Letter to Richard Champion, in *Correspondence,* 3:139.
83. Quoted by James Prior, *Life of the Right Honourable Edmund Burke* (London, 1854), p. 156.
84. *Writings and Speeches,* 1:251.
85. Quoted by Gerald Chapman, "Burke's American Tragedy," *Harvard English Studies* 12 (1984), p. 422 (MS note at Northampton, A.xxvii.87).
86. In a draft of his *Speech on the Dutch War* of 25 January 1781, Burke wrote: "We have been so long in a War of a very singular Species, that the Genius and Character of the Nation seemed to me to be totally alterd by it. At present war seems to be considerd as the Natural State of G. Britain and the addition of a new Enemy is therefore nothing more than one of those things that are necessarily included in the very Constitution of our fame and which must of course be developed in its due time." *Writings and Speeches,* vol. 4 MS, ed. P. J. Marshall (MS note at Northampton, A. xxvii.77).
87. See Elizabeth D. Samet, *Willing Obedience* (Stanford, Calif., 2004), pp. 6–7; the phrase comes from the end of Burke's *Speech on Conciliation:* "It is the love of the people; it is their attachment to their government from the sense of the deep stake they have in such a glorious institution, which gives you your army and your navy, and infuses into both that liberal obedience, without which your army would be a base rabble, and your navy nothing but rotten timber" (*Writings and Speeches,* 3:165). The idea has a different shading in Burke's description of chivalry in the *Reflections:* "that proud submission, that dignified obedience, that subordination of the heart, which kept alive, even in servitude itself, the spirit of an exalted freedom."
88. The tradition would pass from Burke to Macaulay. A democratic reader's pleasure in the Whig history of progress, most of whose action is pre-democratic and exclusive of the people, seldom takes account of "an irony" that J. W. Burrow remarked: "dramatically we may be tempted to call it the central irony of English history, if we take seriously the popular element in the Whig tradition. For the original seventeenth-century common lawyer's and even the Burkean

Whig's conception of the constitution is essentially, not indeed democratic, but national. The common law is not a creation of heroic judges or legislators but the slow, anonymous sedimentation of immemorial custom; the constitution is no gift but the continuous self-defining public activity of the nation"; see Burrow, *A Liberal Descent: Victorian Historians and the English Past* (Cambridge, 1981), p. 105.

89. See Herbert Butterfield, *The Whig Interpretation of History* (London, 1931).

90. *Writings and Speeches*, 2:25. Cone, *Burke and the Nature of Politics*, 1:85–87, cites a letter of 31 December 1765 to Charles O'Hara as evidence that Burke "had decided, earlier than the Rockingham chieftains, in favor of repeal of the Stamp Act and passage of a Declaratory Act."

91. His sketches of Townshend and Chatham in the earlier speech resort to a genre made familiar by Swift and Clarendon; and Burke had printed samples of the genre in the *Annual Register*. The partial portraits of individuals in the *Speech on American Taxation* trace political failures to personal defects. The collective portrait of the *Speech on Conciliation* requires a different idiom of description, because it aims at a different kind of knowledge. Burke is passing from satire to anthropology.

92. *Works*, 12 vols. (Boston, 1869), vol. 7, pp. 93–94.

93. *Writings and Speeches*, 2:48.

94. Ibid., 2:49.

95. The radical member of Parliament and pamphleteer Major John Cartwright was often an ally of Burke's; he supported independence rather than conciliation and traced his difference to a narrower view of the constitution. In a pamphlet replying to Burke's *Speech on American Taxation*, Cartwright appeals to "the *constitution of Great-Britain*" against Burke's "*constitution of the British empire* (for I totally deny its existence, and believe that a faith and hope in it lead to perdition)." See Major John Cartwright, *A Letter to Edmund Burke* (London, 1775), p. 6.

96. *Writings and Speeches*, 2:49.

97. Ibid., 2:51.

98. Ibid., 2:59, 96. Burke's stance on American taxes appeared flexible to his contemporaries—he was not dogmatically opposed to all taxation—but he has left a clue to his general disposition (apart from the exigencies of the 1760s and early 1770s) in some strictures of his *Abridgment of English History* which deal with the taxes of the provinces under the Roman imperial system: "In a word, the taxes in the Roman Empire were so heavy, and in many respects so injudiciously laid on, that they have been not improperly considered as one cause of its decay and ruin. The Roman government, to the very last, carried something of the spirit of conquest in it; and this system of taxes seems rather calculated for the utter impoverishment of nations, in whom a long subjection had not worn away the remembrance of enmity, than for the support of a just commonwealth" (*Writings and Speeches*, 1:375–376).

99. Ibid., 1:181.
100. Ibid., 1:188.
101. Ibid., 1:194.
102. Ibid.
103. Ibid., 1:225–226.
104. Ibid., 1:231.
105. Thomas Pownall, *The Administration of the Colonies*, 4th ed. (London: J. Walter, 1768), pp. xv, 28. For a hint about the marginal notes Burke made in his copy, now in the British Library, I thank Richard Bourke.
106. Ibid., p. 32.
107. Ibid., p. 42.
108. Ibid., pp. 44, 69.
109. Ibid., pp. 44, 54.
110. Ibid., pp. 163–164.
111. Quoted by Lecky, *England in the Eighteenth Century*, 3:444.
112. *Writings and Speeches*, 3:108.
113. Another echo is the quotation of "Ease would retract / Vows made in pain as violent and void"—reversing the train of association to link Satan with the American sense of injured merit; the mischievous suggestion is that their refusal to pay taxes comes from a pride as limitless as Satan's in his refusal to obey God.
114. *Writings and Speeches*, 3:117–118.
115. Ibid., 3:121. In the *Annual Register* for the year 1765, Burke had mentioned slavery as a reason for taxing the colonists without full representation in Parliament: "Common sense, nay self-preservation, seem to forbid, that those who allow themselves an unlimited right over the liberty and lives of others, should have any share in making laws for those, who have long renounced such unjust and cruel distinctions. It is impossible that such men should have the proper feelings for such a task. But then we could wish, that, since it was resolved to make the colonies contribute to their own defense by taxes imposed on them without their concurrence, instead of abiding by the good old methods heretofore pursued for that purpose, these disqualifications in them to be fully represented in a British parliament had been assigned as the reason for the mother country's taxing them unrepresented." *Annual Register*, 1766, p. 37. The passage was first noticed and cited in part by Ross J. S. Hoffman, in *Edmund Burke, New York Agent* (Philadelphia, 1956), pp. 33–34.
116. *Writings and Speeches*, 3:122–123.
117. Ibid., 3:123–124.
118. Ibid., 3:127.
119. Ibid., 3:124.
120. Ibid., 3:156–157.
121. Ibid., 3:165.

122. On the dramatic emphasis of Burke's politics, especially in contrast with Hume, see Shirley Robin Letwin, *The Pursuit of Certainty* (Cambridge, 1965).

V. The Loss of the Empire in the West

1. Quoted in Francis Thackeray, *A History of the Right Honorable William Pitt, Earl of Chatham: Containing His Speeches in Parliament*, 2 vols. (London, 1827), 2:286.

2. Lord North's offer of conciliation in early 1775 (though generous by his standard) should be called by another name. It allowed the colonies to make permanent provision for civil government as well as justice and defense: the mother country would then refrain from taxing and return all revenue from control of trade to the colony paying the duty. However, by creating such a permanent system and funding for their local governments, the Americans stood to lose the independent control afforded by regular occasions for adjusting the budget. North also asked them to consent to a pro forma reassertion of the mother country's legitimate powers under the Declaratory Act. See I. R. Christie, *Crisis of Empire: Great Britain and the American Colonies, 1754–1783* (London, 1966), p. 96.

3. Josiah Tucker, *A Letter to Edmund Burke, Esq., in Answer to His Printed Speech, Said to Be Spoken in the House of Commons on the Twenty-Second March, 1775* (London: T. Caddell, 1775), pp. 7–9.

4. Burke thought in such terms without self-consciousness, as historians and (for that matter) imperialists of the present day cannot afford to do. The usage "empire in the East" and "empire in the West" comes from the younger friends who first edited his writings, Walker King and French Laurence, but very likely they heard Burke employ that phraseology. He came close to it in November 1774, in his *Speech at the Conclusion of the Poll*, when he spoke of "a great *Empire*, extended by our Virtue and our Fortune to the farthest limits of the East and of the West." See *Writings and Speeches of Edmund Burke*, 9 vols. (Oxford, 1981–), vol. 3, ed. Warren A. Elofson with John A. Woods, p. 70.

   P. J. Marshall traces a change of usage to the Seven Years War. Before that, the word *empire* was loosely synonymous with "possession"; after 1763, "it became commonplace to talk and write of a unitary British empire." See Marshall, "Burke and Empire," in *Hanoverian Britain and Empire: Essays in Memory of Philip Lawson*, ed. Stephen Taylor, Richard Connors, and Clyve Jones (Woodbridge, UK, 1998), p. 290. Burke, in his allusions to East and West, seems to rely on both the older and the newer sense. Thus, in a letter to Richard Champion of 30 May 1776 he wrote: "I hardly can believe, by the Tranquility of every thing about me, that we are a people who have just lost an empire. But so it is"; see *The Correspondence of Edmund Burke*, 10 vols. (Cambridge, 1958–1978), vol. 3, ed. George H. Guttridge, p. 269. And again on 10 August 1780 in a letter to Job Watts, Burke wrote: "we have lost one half of our empire by an idle quarrel," so it is unwise "to distract, and perhaps to Lose too, the other half by another quarrel"; see *Correspondence*, vol. 4, ed. George H. Guttridge, p. 261.

5. Tucker, *A Letter to Edmund Burke*, pp. 16–18.

6. Ibid., pp. 37–39.

7. Letter of 13 April 1775, in *Correspondence*, vol. 2, ed. Lucy S. Sutherland, p. 145.

8. *Correspondence*, 3:149.

9. Letter of 15 April 1775, in *Correspondence*, 2:150.

10. A recent comparative study of Burke and Paine that draws the sharpest of contrasts between them is Yuval Levin, *The Great Debate* (New York, 2013).

11. Thomas Paine, *Common Sense*, in *Collected Writings* (New York: Library of America, 1995), p. 9.

12. Letter to the Rev. Thomas Hussey, 4 November 1795, in *Correspondence*, vol. 8, ed. R. B. McDowell, pp. 137, 139.

13. Letter to James Madison, 6 September 1789, in Thomas Jefferson, *Writings* (New York: Library of America, 1984), p. 960. This letter was written from Paris during the week of the renunciation of feudal privileges, a moment of unexampled unity for modern France and of soaring hopes for the revolution. Two letters from Richard Gem, which seem to have brought the idea to Jefferson's attention, are reprinted in *The Papers of Thomas Jefferson*, ed. J. P. Boyd (Princeton, NJ, 1958), 15:384–399; see also 16:146–154 for two versions of Madison's detailed and cogent reply to Jefferson.

14. Quincy noted that most of the town, far from participating, had voted negative at the town meeting after the debate on whether to send back the tea. "Admit for a moment," he allowed, "that the inhabitants of Boston were charged as high criminals; the highest criminals are not punishable, till arraigned before disinterested judges, heard in defence, and found guilty of the charge; but so far from all this, a whole people are accused, prosecuted by they know not *whom;* tried they know not *when;* proved guilty they know not *how;* and sentenced in a mode, which for number of calamities, extent, and duration of severity, exceeds the annals of past ages." See Josiah Quincy Jr., *Observations on the Act of Parliament, Commonly Called the Boston Port-Bill; with Thoughts on Civil Society and Standing Armies* (London: reprinted for Edward and Charles Dilley, 1774), 12–13.

15. Quoted by Bernard Bailyn, *The Ideological Origins of the American Revolution* (Cambridge, Mass., 1967), p. 187.

16. *Writings and Speeches*, vol. 8, ed. L. G. Mitchell, pp. 62, 94.

17. See, for an emphatic treatment of this theme, J. C. D. Clark, *The Language of Liberty, 1660–1832* (Cambridge, 1994).

18. Bernard Bailyn, *Pamphlets of the American Revolution, 1750–1765* (Cambridge, Mass., 1965), pp. 228–229.

19. Ibid., 242.

20. James Otis, *Rights* (London: J. Almon, 1764), p. 45.

21. Ibid., pp. 51–52.

22. The American demand of "no taxation without representation" had already received eloquent support from the Rockingham party, in the debate on repeal of the Stamp Act. Burke offered a fine condensation of the argument in the *Annual Register* of 1766: "it appears throughout the whole history of our constitution, that no British subject can be taxed, but *per communem consensem parliamenti*, that is to say, of himself, or his own representative; and this is that first and general right as British subjects, with which the first inhabitants of the colonies emigrated; for the right does not depend upon their charters: the charters were but the exterior modeling of the constitution of the colonies; but the great interior fundamental of their constitution is this general right of a British subject: which is the very first principle of British liberty" (p. 38).

23. Dulany's progress, from assertion to concession, parallels the strategy of the Rockingham party in accompanying the repeal of the Stamp Act with the issuing of a Declaratory Act. The appearance of such formal signs of hesitation, even on the American side, suggests that the Rockingham party did not equivocate so much as it simply reflected a confusion that pervaded all discussion of taxes.

24. Daniel Dulany, *Considerations on the Propriety of Imposing Taxes in the British Colonies* (Annapolis, 1765), p. 48.

25. *Correspondence*, 3:181.

26. Ibid., 3:185–186.

27. Ibid., 3:187.

28. Ibid., 3:190.

29. Ibid., 3:191.

30. Ibid., 3:192–193.

31. *Writings and Speeches*, 3:217n5.

32. Ibid., 3:192, 193, 194–195.

33. Ibid., 3:196.

34. Ibid., 3:198.

35. Ibid., 3:207.

36. Ibid., 3:217n5, 215.

37. Among those who wrote in this tenor about the sufferings of the American colonists was Richard Price, in his *Observations on the Nature of Civil Liberty, the Principles of Government, and the Justice and Policy of the War with America* (1776): "an empire," as Price defines it, "is a collection of states or communities united by some common bond or tye." There is such a thing as an empire of freemen; but if, "like the different provinces subject to the Grand Seignior, none of the states possesses any independent legislative authority, but are all subject to an absolute monarch whose will is their law, then is the empire an empire of slaves. If one of the states is free, but governs by its will all the other states; then is the empire, like that of the Romans in the times of the Republic, an empire consist-

ing of one state free, and the rest in slavery." See Richard Price, *Political Writings,* ed. D. O. Thomas (Cambridge, 1991), p. 35.

38. *Writings and Speeches,* 3:219–220.

39. Ibid.

40. Price, *Observations on the Nature of Civil Liberty,* in *Political Writings,* p. 71.

41. *Correspondence,* 3:286.

42. Lord Acton, *Lectures on the French Revolution* (London, 1910), pp. 27–31. Acton's chapter "The Influence of America" places Burke in an interesting line whose other members include Benjamin Franklin, Adam Smith, John Adams, James Otis, John Dickinson, and Lord Chatham; he sees Burke as the climactic figure of Whig radicalism in the 1770s and "the most significant instance of the action of America on Europe" (p. 27).

43. *Correspondence,* 3:312. *The Works of Edmund Burke,* 12 vols. (Boston, 1869), vol. 6, p. 155.

44. *Correspondence,* 3:313.

45. *Correspondence,* 3:314. Rockingham seems to have been ready for the advice: in a letter that crosses with Burke's, he avows that "it is time to *attempt in earnest,* a reconciliation with America." Ibid., 3:316.

46. *Writings and Speeches,* 3:260.

47. Ibid., 3:261.

48. Ibid., 3:262–263.

49. Ibid., 3:264.

50. Ibid., 3:272.

51. Ibid., 3:273–274.

52. Any residual ambivalence has been suppressed, but the reference to "questions" raised by the colonists appeared in a draft as "captious questions."

53. *Writings and Speeches,* 3:278, 279.

54. Ibid., 3:280.

55. Ibid., 3:283, 285.

56. P. T. Underdown, "Burke's Bristol Friends," *Transactions of the Bristol and Gloucestershire Archaeological Society* 77 (1958), p. 142. The idea of sheriffs as a local counterweight against monarchical intrusion went back to the growing suspicion of Charles II by Whigs at the time of the Exclusion Crisis. For an analysis suggestive of echoes that Burke may have meant to evoke, see John Marshall, *John Locke: Resistance, Religion and Responsibility* (Cambridge, 1994), p. 242: "All of the royal measures that formed the 'long train of actings' supposed in the *Second Treatise* to make clear that Charles was intent upon absolutism, were evident by early 1682 to Shaftesbury and to Locke, even if it was not until the mid-1682 replacement of Whig by Tory sheriffs that resistance came to seem an absolutely vital action to other Whig leaders." Marshall also points out, in *John Locke: Toleration and Early Enlightenment Culture* (Cambridge, 2006), pp. 45, 48,

118–119, that the power of sheriffs to nominate juries was felt to be under threat in England in 1682 and that the crown took an interest in "efforts to obtain compliant sheriffs and thereby compliant juries." By late 1682, with help from "dubious electoral processes . . . Charles had obtained Tory sheriffs, who would then appoint the members of grand juries, and a Tory Lord Mayor."

The status of sheriffs as officers independent of the crown was thus a primary concern, for Locke, when he worked out his defense of the right of resistance. Burke's awareness of this fact might go some way to explain the title of his *Letter,* as well as the uncharacteristic echoes of Locke in his other writings of 1777.

57. *Writings and Speeches,* 3:292.
58. Ibid., 3:296.
59. Ibid., 3:298–299.
60. Ibid., 3:299–300.
61. Ibid., 3:301.
62. Ibid., 3:302.
63. Ibid., 3:308.
64. Ibid., 3:318.
65. Ibid., 3:327.
66. A recent and authoritative biographer of Fox has concluded that "the two men were never close personal friends"; see John W. Derry, *Charles James Fox* (London, 1972), pp. 125–126. It depends what one means by "close," but the quoted letter must be taken as a kind of evidence. I know nothing like it from Burke to any other correspondent; and if friendship is allowed to mean a steady enjoyment of each other's company in some (though not all) pursuits, and a habit of mutual reliance that does not imply perfect harmony, then Burke and Fox were friends.
67. *Correspondence,* 3:381.
68. Ibid., 3:385.
69. Quoted in Derry, *Charles James Fox,* p. 85.
70. Underdown, "Burke's Bristol Friends," p. 143.
71. Letter of 1 November 1777 to Richard Champion and William Hale, in *Correspondence,* 3:396.
72. Ibid.
73. Letter to William Baker, in ibid., 3:401.
74. A conviction that did not weaken with the end of the war: as late as March 1782, Burke's unpublished "Hints of a Treaty with America" mentions among the grounds for reunion between England and America "That it is the permanent interest of both, to prevent either part from weakness, or fear, or jealousy, or any other Cause from being ever dependent, more or less upon France"; and again, "That the Connection between England and America is *natural* . . . [whereas]

that of France with either is not so." *Writings and Speeches*, vol. 4 MS, ed. P. J. Marshall (MS at Sheffield, Bk 27.219).

75. On Fox's rivalry with Shelburne, see Richard B. Morris, *The Peacemakers* (New York, 1965), ch. 17.

76. See P. J. Marshall, *The Making and Unmaking of Empires* (Oxford, 2005), for the argument by some historians on Shelburne's behalf that he "renounced territorial dominion over much of North America in order the better to preserve it elsewhere" (p. 361).

77. *Writings and Speeches*, vol. 4 MS, ed. P. J. Marshall (MS at Sheffield, Bk. 27.219).

78. Ibid. (report from the *Morning Chronicle*, 17 February 1783).

79. Quoted by James Prior, *Life of the Right Honourable Edmund Burke* (London, 1854), p. 212.

VI. Democracy, Representation, and the Gordon Riots

1. *The Correspondence of Edmund Burke*, 10 vols. (Cambridge, 1958–1978), vol. 3, ed. George H. Guttridge, p. 406.

2. *Horace Walpole's Correspondence*, 48 vols. (New Haven, Conn., 1937–1983), 28:481–482 and 29:13–14, ed. W. S. Lewis, Grover Cronin Jr. and Charles H. Bennett. Fox retracted a supposed insult but fought anyway with William Adam (nephew of the architect Robert Adam) on finding that his accuser drove too high the acceptable terms of a publicized apology. The case of Shelburne was more interesting; he displayed on the occasion that uncanny dryness, which would perplex and anger Burke whenever he tried to fathom Shelburne's principles of action. "Mr Fullerton, Lord Stormont's late secretary at Paris," as Walpole recounts the incident, "broiling over the censure passed on him and his regiment in the House of Lords by the Duke of Richmond and Lord Shelburne, particularly the latter, took advantage of the estimate of the army to launch out into a violent invective on the Earl, but was stopped by Ch[arles] Fox and Barré. Not content, nor waiting to see if Lord Sh. would resent, he sent the latter an account of what he not only said but intended to have said, if not interrupted; the sum total of which was to have been that his Lordship's conduct had been a compound of insolence, cowardice and falsehood—very well, but to heap indiscretion on passion, he reproached Lord Shelburne with having *as he had heard abroad*, kept a correspondence with the enemies of his country. My Lord replied, that the best answer he could give, was to desire Mr F. would meet him the next morning in Hyde Park at five o'clock. They met accordingly: Lord Frederick Cavendish was the Earl's second: Lord Balcarras, Fullerton's. Lord Shelburne received a ball in the groin, but the wound is slight and he was so cool, that on being asked how he did, he looked at the place, and said, 'Why I don't think Lady Shelburne will be the worse for it'" (*Correspondence*, 29:13–14).

3. *Writings and Speeches of Edmund Burke* (Oxford, 1981–), vol. 9, ed. R. B. McDowell, pp. 508, 509–510, 514.

4. Conor Cruise O'Brien, *The Great Melody* (Chicago and London, 1992), p. 187.

5. G. O. Trevelyan, *George the Third and Charles Fox*, 2 vols. (London, 1927), II:32.

6. *Writings and Speeches*, 9:547.

7. Ibid., 9:557.

8. *Correspondence*, vol. 4, ed. John A. Woods, p. 70.

9. P. J. Marshall, *The Making and Unmaking of Empires* (Oxford, 2005), p. 378.

10. *Writings and Speeches*, 9:559.

11. Ibid., 9:561–562.

12. See William O'Brien, *Edmund Burke as an Irishman* (Dublin, 1924), chs. 9, 11.

13. The bill allowed Catholics to purchase and inherit land but not to be represented in Parliament or to hold crown office.

14. Two months earlier, in a letter of 12 June 1779 to Dr. John Erskine, an anti-Catholic leader of the national church of Scotland, Burke had confessed himself "by choice and Taste, as well as by Education, a very attached member of the Established Church of England," who would tolerate all "who profess our common Hope"; he would also extend toleration, he says, to Jews, Muslims, Buddhists, and even those "who have nothing better than mere human reason, or the unregulated instincts of human Nature, for their basis."

15. *Writings and Speeches*, 9:567–568.

16. Ibid., 9:570–571.

17. *Memoirs of the Political and Private Life of James Caulfeild, Earl of Charlemont* (London, 1810), pp. 215–216. His friendship with Rockingham went back as far as their meeting in Rome in 1751; and with Burke, almost as far.

18. Quoted in Trevelyan, *George the Third and Charles Fox*, 1:140; see 129–157 passim.

19. *Correspondence*, 4:35n2, 169.

20. J. C. D. Clark, *Revolution and Rebellion* (Cambridge, 1986), p. 73.

21. Quoted in *Correspondence*, 4:xiii.

22. Burke's early doubts would grow to a conscious antagonism in later years, when Shelburne came to be known as the patron of the radical "Bowood circle."

23. This was an anxious time for reasons not entirely owing to factitious rumor and manipulation. An invasion of a joint French and Spanish fleet was expected; wilder proposals than those at Bristol were contemplated. John Norris, in *Shelburne and Reform* (London, 1963), recounts that "Barré, convinced that the Court would not resist a French invasion, plotted with Shelburne to raise the city and lead the Opposition in a Coup d'État" (p. 111).

24. *Correspondence*, 4:227.

25. Ibid., 4:228.

26. Ibid., 4:230–231.

27. *Speech on Pillory*, in *Writings and Speeches of Edmund Burke*, 9 vols. (Oxford, 1981–), vol. 3, ed. Warren A. Elofson with John A. Woods, p. 585.

28. James Prior, *Life of the Right Honourable Edmund Burke* (London, 1854), p. 192.

29. Richard Pares put it that way in his review of Butterfield, *English Historical Review* 65 (October 1950), pp. 526–529. At the same time, he recognized the critical nature of a transition to which the events of these months were not irrelevant: "One of the greatest themes, and the hardest to understand rightly, in the history of George III's reign, is that transformation of politics by which the intervention of something which we call 'the people' turned an old-fashioned duel of king and aristocracy into a general conflict over rationalizing all institutions and broadening the basis of political power. It is the co-existence of these two themes, of the parliamentary and extra-parliamentary (perhaps we should say anti-parliamentary) which confused the action of contemporaries and the understanding of historians between Yorktown and the Reform Act" (p. 527).

On "tory popularism" and the resources of extra-parliamentary politics in the Pelham-Walpole era, see Linda Colley, *In Defiance of Oligarchy: The Tory Party, 1714–60* (Cambridge, 1982), ch. 6. "Georgian toryism," writes Colley, "incited extra-parliamentary dissidence without being able fully to accommodate it. The party combined a longstanding and popular suspicion of the executive with a rooted inclination towards a stratified, stable society where land determined political responsibility" (p. 173). The same could be said of most of the Rockingham party as well. "If popular toryism existed anywhere," Colley adds, "it was in the great commercial cities," including Bristol; in the larger and more open constituencies, "tory M.P.s . . . believed themselves to be compelled into a more subtly accommodating relationship with their electors than was customary in the eighteenth century" (pp. 152, 162). This contrast also obtains in the history of popular Whiggism a generation later.

30. *Correspondence*, 4:15. Herbert Butterfield, *George III, Lord North, and the People, 1779–80* (London, 1949), p. 72, quotes this letter with the words "wait and think" rather than "act and think."

31. Butterfield, *George III*, p. 155.

32. Ibid., p. 156.

33. Ibid., pp. 171–172, quoting *Parliamentary History* 20, 1226–1228.

34. Butterfield, *George III*, pp. 168–169.

35. Ibid, p. 175.

36. Ibid, pp. 192–193.

37. Ibid, pp. 196, 200.

38. Ibid, p. 205.

39. Ibid, p. 208.

40. Ibid, p. 228.

41. Burke was never wholly indifferent to popular opinion. But his interest in listening to and heeding the voice of the people varied according to occasion and circumstance, and sometimes according to his changes of mood. A sympathetic interpreter, Ernest Barker in *Essays on Government* offered a cogent summary

and criticism of Burke's attitude. He often seems to be saying (in Barker's para-phrase): "The people do not think, and they do not act; they must be guided and goaded; there must be party direction from the centre, and party agitation in each locality. Burke was not a wire-puller; but he was ready to pull the strings which would make the people speak in the sense he desired. No sooner was the election of 1774 over than he was urging Rockingham to mature public discon-tents by proper means, to give them direction, in a word, to organize, to agitate, to make the people felt by making the people feel."

So much for the people as a collective will, endowed with conscious purpose by their leaders. On the other hand: "The expert artist, the skillful workman, the cunning physician, must think ahead, over the heads of his constituents, beyond their immediate views. . . . Burke had many Quaker friends. . . . But there was one Quaker idea which he never really learned. It is the idea of 'the sense of the meeting': the idea of a union of minds, in a common purpose, at-tained through a process of general thought to which we may all contribute, and by a mode of amicable discussion in which we may all participate. It is the idea which underlies any grounded belief in democracy." See Ernest Barker, *Essays on Government* (Oxford, 1945), pp. 201–203.

42. Butterfield, *George III*, pp. 292–293.

43. Burke formed his negative impressions early and kept them late. In 1776, he wondered by what deformation of common sense Shelburne could once have told him ("gratis, for nothing led to it") that "the people, (always meaning the common people of London) were never in the wrong." This was said, as Burke noted, just a few months before the people "vomited up with Loathing and dis-gust" the politics of Shelburne and his faction; see *Correspondence*, 3:281. At dif-ferent times, in fact, Shelburne looked indulgently on electoral reform to favor a more expansive representation of the people and a broad construction of the powers of the crown. To Burke, such versatility would have seemed the mark of an intriguer, though to a reader steeped in the doctrines of Bolingbroke, the stances need not be contradictory.

On the Bowood circle of theorists and planners ("Lansdowne's 'brains trust'"), see Albert Goodwin, *The Friends of Liberty* (Cambridge, Mass., 1979), pp. 101–106. Bentham, Price, Priestley, and Samuel Romilly were brought into the circle "as members of Lansdowne's household staff, as experts in economics, law or science, or as tutors to Lansdowne's sons" (p. 102).

44. Quoted in Butterfield, *George III*, p. 323.

45. *Parliamentary History*, vol. 21, pp. 342–343.

46. Ibid., vol. 20, pp. 1378–1383.

47. Ibid., vol. 21, p. 191.

48. *Writings and Speeches*, 3:485.

49. Ibid., 3:486.

50. Ibid., 3:493.

51. Ibid., 3:509–510.

52. *Parliamentary History*, vol. 22, pp. 304–305.

53. *Writings and Speeches*, 3:531.

54. *Parliamentary History*, vol. 21, p. 235.

55. Ibid., pp. 238–239.

56. *Writings and Speeches*, 3:499–500.

57. Ibid., 3:503.

58. Against this judgment must be placed that of Gilbert Elliot in 1780: the *Speech on Economical Reform* "captivated all his sympathies" and made him decide to take "an active part in that business"; see *Life and Letters of Sir Gilbert Elliot, First Earl of Minto, from 1751 to 1806*, 3 vols., ed. Countess of Minto (London, 1874), 1:74. Elliot was one of the most dedicated and intelligent disciples of Burke, and in 1787 he led the impeachment of Sir Elijah Impey, which foreshadowed the impeachment of Warren Hastings. He remained to the end a close friend and "a kind of professed disciple," as Thomas Copeland put it, though he disagreed with Burke on the French Revolution.

59. Dated by Burke's first editors 7 May 1782, because they took it to be given in the debate on Pitt's motion of that day to inquire into the state of representation, the speech has been assigned by P. J. Marshall to the debate of 16 June 1784. The text was compiled from Burke's notes by the editor of his *Speeches* (1816), and may be supposed to express the view that he was evolving in the late 1770s and early 1780s, which other reports confirm and none contradict.

60. *Writings and Speeches*, 3:510. Architectural imagery was central to the way Burke imagined the design of government and the persistence of its elements over time; see Paul Fussell, *The Rhetorical World of Augustan Humanism* (Oxford, 1965), pp. 204–210.

61. *Writings and Speeches*, 3:492.

62. Ibid., 3:548–549.

63. *Writings and Speeches*, vol. 4 MS, ed. P. J. Marshall (text from *Parliamentary Register*).

64. *Parliamentary History*, vol. 21, p. 593.

65. *Writings and Speeches*, 3:588.

66. Ibid., 3:591.

67. Ibid., 3:593.

68. Ibid., 3:599.

69. Ibid., 3:595, with emendations suggested by *Works of Edmund Burke*, 12 vols. (Boston, 1869), vol. 7, p. 78.

70. Ibid., 3:598.

71. *Works*, 7:91. This and the following quotations of some length from the speech are corrected to conform with the text edited by P. J. Marshall for the Oxford *Writings and Speeches*, vol. 4.

72. Ibid., 7:94–95.

73. Ibid., 7:100–101.
74. John Brewer, "Rockingham, Burke, and Whig Political Argument," *Historical Journal* 18, no. 1 (1975), p. 198.
75. The last is the number admitted by government; cited by Christopher Hibbert, *King Mob* (London, 1958), p. 144n1.
76. See *Annual Register* 23 (1780), pp. 254–287, from which several details and quotations that follow are drawn.
77. *Parliamentary History*, vol. 22, pp. 662–663.
78. Even so, Richmond could wonder why not one member had said a word about the Quebec Bill as "the real source of the discontents." He stressed the difference between the Savile bill, which was an act for toleration, and the establishing of Catholicism as had been done in Quebec; and he invited the Lords "to take this opportunity of repealing the Quebec Act" to prove "that they could be firm where they ought, and concede where they ought." Shelburne wheedled with the mob out of doors under no such pretense of judiciousness, saying that when in office, "he had always thought the progress of Popery within the realm, a matter deserving his most vigilant attention." See *Parliamentary History*, vol. 22, pp. 674–678.
79. Quoted by Hibbert, *King Mob*, p. 98.
80. Ian Gilmour, *Riots, Risings, and Revolution* (London, 1992), p. 357.
81. J. Steven Watson, *The Age of George III: 1760–1815* (Oxford, 1960), p. 238.
82. *Correspondence*, 4:243.
83. Ibid., 4:244.
84. Lock, *Edmund Burke*, 2:423.
85. Letter to Richard Shackleton, 13 June 1780, in *Correspondence*, 4:244.

VII. In Defense of Politics

1. The Bristol riot is mentioned in the account of the election (hostile to Burke) in *The Gentleman's Magazine* 50 (1780), p. 619.
2. Letter of 3 September, in *The Correspondence of Edmund Burke*, 10 vols. (Cambridge, 1958–1978), vol. 4, ed. John A. Woods, pp. 268, 269.
3. Letter to the Marquess of Rockingham, 7, 8 September 1780, in ibid., 4:278.
4. About the same time, Will spoke of his friend as an unappreciated "Great man" forced to mix with the rabble and was sorry to see him "confounded in the ranks with the Common men"; letter by Will Burke to the Duke of Portland, 23 September 1780, in ibid., 4:288.
5. Ibid., 4:273–274.
6. See Bryan Garsten, *Saving Persuasion* (Cambridge, Mass., 2006), on the importance of such public reason-giving as a form of civic education for both the people and their representatives.
7. P. T. Underdown, "Bristol and Burke," Historical Association Pamphlet, p. 16.

8. *Writings and Speeches of Edmund Burke,* 9 vols. (Oxford, 1981–), vol. 3, ed. Warren A. Elofson with John A. Woods, p. 626.

9. Burke seems to have paid one visit to Bristol in August 1775 and one in August 1776 but during the next four years (notwithstanding warm invitations from his devoted admirers), none. See F. P. Lock, *Edmund Burke: 1730–1784* (Oxford, 1998), pp. 393, 400.

10. *Writings and Speeches,* 3:627.

11. Ibid., 3:628–629.

12. Ibid., 3:631.

13. Ibid., 3:632.

14. Ibid., 3:633.

15. Ibid., 3:633–634.

16. See P. J. Marshall, "Burke and Empire," in *Hanoverian Britain and Empire: Essays in Memory of Philip Lawson,* ed. Stephen Taylor, Richard Connors, and Clyve Jones (Woodbridge, UK, 1998), p. 294: "He sent his code to ministers in 1792. He was, however, prepared to give unequivocal support to Wilberforce's motion for immediate abolition of the slave trade in 1789."

17. *Speech on the Abolition of the African Slave Trade,* 12 May 1789 (report from the *Diary,* 13 May 1789), *Writings and Speeches,* vol. 4 MS, ed. P. J. Marshall.

18. *Writings and Speeches,* 3:568–570.

19. Ibid., 3:574–575.

20. Ibid., 3:576–577.

21. Ibid., 3:580.

22. The most distinguished commentator to advance this view was Isaiah Berlin, who in many of his writings paired Burke and de Maistre. Conor Cruise O'Brien, *The Great Melody* (Chicago and London, 1992), pp. 605–618, has a spirited exchange with Berlin on the appropriateness of the "anti-Enlightenment" description of Burke.

23. Samuel Johnson may be counted another of the party of reformers: "Those who made the laws, have apparently supposed, that every deficiency of payment is the crime of the debtor. But the truth is, that the creditor always shares the act, and often more than shares the guilt of improper trust"; see *Idler* no. 22, in W. J. Bate, John M. Bullitt, and L. F. Powell, eds., *The Idler and the Adventurer* (New Haven, Conn., 1963), p. 70.

24. *Writings and Speeches,* 3:639–640.

25. As targets of the rioters, according to Horace Walpole, "Lord Rockingham, the Duke of Richmond, Sir George Savile and Mr Burke, the patrons of toleration, were devoted to destruction as much as the ministers. The rails torn from Sir George's house were the chief weapon and instruments of the mob." Savile and Burke had stood together earlier—as Walpole's history recounts—when they opposed the expulsion of Wilkes from the House of Commons. In the debates of November 1770, Burke attacked the House majority and refused to retract:

"he was conscious he had deserved to be sent to the Tower for what he had said; but he knew the House did not dare to send him thither." Savile echoed the sentiment, and when Lord North offered to pass by the offense, "'No', replied Savile coolly; 'I spoke with what has been my constant opinion; I thought so last night; I thought the same this morning. I look on this House as sitting illegally after their illegal act [of voting Luttrell representative for Middlesex]. They have betrayed their trust. I will add no epithets,' continued he, 'because epithets only weaken: therefore I will not say they have betrayed their country corruptly, flagitiously, and scandalously; but I do say they have betrayed their country; and I stand here to receive the punishment for having said so.'" Walpole, *Correspondence*, vol. 2, ed. W. S. Lewis, pp. 224–225; and *Memoirs of the Reign of King George III*, ed. Derek Jarrett, 4 vols. (New Haven, 2000), 4:124.

26. Walpole's judgment of the political character of Savile once more coincides with Burke's: "Sir George Savile had a head as acutely argumentative, as if it had been made by a German logician for a model. Could ministers have been found acting by the advice of casuists and confessors, Sir George would still have started distinctions to hamper their consciences.... He had a large fortune, and a larger mind; and though his reason was sharp, his soul was candid, having none of the acrimony or vengeance of party." See Walpole, *Memoirs of the Reign of King George III*, 2:8.

27. *Writings and Speeches*, 3:654.

28. Ibid., 3:656.

29. Ibid., 3:658–659.

30. Ibid., 3:660.

31. Ibid., 3:661–662.

32. Joseph Butler, *Dissertation of the Nature of Virtue*, in *British Moralists, 1650–1800*, ed. D. D. Raphael, 2 vols. (Oxford, 1969), 1:384–385.

33. Christopher Hibbert, *King Mob* (London, 1958), p. 178 and ch. 11, *passim*.

34. *Writings and Speeches*, vol. 8, ed. L. G. Mitchell, p. 135.

35. If Gordon fails to arrive at a more gracious mode of conduct through meditation, Burke continues, he may prefer to wait "until some persons from your side of the water, to please your new Hebrew brethren, shall ransom him. He may then be enabled to purchase, with the old hoards of the synagogue, and a very small poundage, on the long compound interest of the thirty pieces of silver (Dr. Price has shewn us what miracles compound interest will perform in 1790 years) the lands which are lately discovered to have been usurped by the Gallican church. Send us your popish Archbishop of Paris, and we will send you our protestant Rabbin" (ibid., pp. 179–180). The wildness of this passage of the *Reflections* spurs cruelty but lets us excuse it; the cruelty itself increases the wildness. Before the allegorical identification (Jewish = Protestant) turns it to broad satire, a physical memory of 1780 is audible in the half pun rabbin / rabble.

Burke's friend of the 1780s and largest collaborator in the India prosecution, Philip Francis, made a pertinent comment in his copy of the *Reflections* when he read the caustic aside on Gordon and Newgate: "The sentence pronounced on Lord George Gordon, for libeling the Queen of France, does no Credit to English Justice. It was enormously cruel, + utterly disproportionate to the Offense. Mr. Burke well knows that, if Lord George had not been otherwise a mischievous + dangerous Man, for whose Fate nobody was concerned, the Sentence, for the Libel alone, would have been universally reprobated; as it was by those who considered the example + the Consequence. Mr. Burke is happy, when he can find any thing in our government as tyrannical as that of France."

Francis's note is in his copy of the *Reflections,* in the Houghton Collection at Harvard University.

36. See "Some Thoughts on the Approaching Executions" (10 July 1780) and "Additional Reflexions on the Executions" (18 July 1780): memorandums Burke sent to his Rockingham ally Sir Grey Cooper, for the purpose of influencing Lord Loughborough on the course of the prosecution (*Writings and Speeches,* 3:611–618). Burke first asked Cooper to see whether "the very next execution cannot be delayed (by the way I do not see why it may not)." He suggested that if the death sentence were carried out, it should be confined to a single person, "and that afterwards you should not exceed two or three." Though the relevant act of Parliament was extremely harsh in its sanctions, yet "Justice and mercy have not such opposite interests as people are apt to imagine."

This advice is consistent with his remarks in a letter to William Eden (17 March 1776): "Transportation always seemed to me to be a good expedient for preventing the cruelty of capital Punishments, the danger of letting wicked people loose upon the publick, or the infinite charge and difficulty of making those useful, whose disposition it is to be mischievous" (*Correspondence,* vol. 3, ed. George H. Guttridge, pp. 252–253).

37. Underdown, "Bristol and Burke," p. 17.

38. *Correspondence,* 3:404.

39. *Parliamentary History,* vol. 22, pp. 223–224.

40. Peter J. Stanlis, *Edmund Burke and the Natural Law* (Ann Arbor, Mich., 1958).

41. See Jennifer Pitts, *A Turn to Empire: the Rise of Imperial Liberalism in Britain and France* (Princeton, N.J., 2005), for a balanced formulation: "Burke tended to invoke natural law and the law of nations in the same breath. He did not deduce a set of moral principles from a theory of natural law, but rather looked to its instantiation in actual societies. It is from the law of nations—from a study of the customs of societies across time and space—that he believed more specific principles could be gleaned. . . . Burke did not require a theory of natural law to elaborate moral principles; such a reliance on abstract theory would, indeed, have betrayed his conviction that just standards and conduct emerge in the

course of social and political life" (pp. 81–82). This judgment seems compatible with Marshall's conclusion ("Burke and Empire," p. 298) that Burke was offering "a vision of a world-wide empire based on universal justice," which could be set beside "the enlightened critics of the European empires, Adam Smith, Price, Condorcet or Kant, who envisaged a universal brotherhood of independent peoples united by commerce."

42. *Parliamentary History*, vol. 22, pp. 228–229, corrected from *Writings and Speeches*, vol. 4 MS, ed. P. J. Marshall. Pufendorf and Grotius are among the writers of the natural law tradition (alongside Emmerich de Vattel) whom Burke is likely to have had in mind when he invoked "the consent and sense of ages."

43. On the importance of Vattel in the development of the modern idea of an international order, see Richard Tuck, *The Rights of War and Peace* (Oxford, 1999), pp. 191–196. Burke's citation of Vattel in this context is convenient but not very illuminating. Vattel argued against Rousseau that nations are naturally sociable, just as persons are, and that among their ends is "mutual assistance in order to perfect themselves and their condition." The emphasis so far is compatible with Burke. Vattel, however, defended colonial expansion and settlements by the Lockean reasoning that bases the right of possession on the obligation to cultivate the soil—a doctrine that Burke treated with considerable skepticism in his writings on India (and to some extent in his writings on America and Ireland). "Liberal politics," writes Tuck, "of the kind that both Vattel and Locke amply subscribed to, went along in their work with a willingness to envisage international adventurism and exploitation, and this was no accident: for the model of the independent moral agent upon which their liberalism was based was precisely the belligerent post-Renaissance state" (p. 195).

44. *Parliamentary History*, vol. 22, p. 232.

45. *Correspondence*, 4:298.

46. Burke knew that he was extraordinary but in private seldom pictured himself as grand. These words to his patron's wife, after a defeat that could seem to have diminished his stature, make a revealing exception to the rule.

47. Quoted in Stanley Ayling, *Edmund Burke* (London, 1988), p. 168.

48. These appellations were in common use, and Burke could write the words without self-consciousness. His way of referring to the North American settler colonies and their English inhabitants as a single entity has been followed in these chapters without comment. But the possession had never been entirely English, nor was the loss total. Canada and much of the Caribbean were still under British control after 1783.

49. *Correspondence*, 4:396.

50. Charles Butler, *Reminiscences*, 2 vols. (London, 1822), 2:89.

51. Quoted in James Prior, *Life of the Right Honourable Edmund Burke* (London, 1854), pp. 274–275.

Conclusion

1. Henry James, *Literary Criticism: French Writers, Other European Writers, the Prefaces to the New York Edition* (New York: Library of America, 1984), p. 99.
2. *The Correspondence of Edmund Burke*, 10 vols. (Cambridge, 1958–1978), vol. 7, ed. P. J. Marshall and John A. Woods, pp. 100–101.
3. On the idea of sympathetic revenge, see Elizabeth Samet, "A Prosecutor and a Gentleman: Burke's Idiom of Impeachment," *ELH* 68, no. 2 (Summer 2001), 397–418.

Chronology

1730   Born January 12.

1741   Begins school at Ballitore, kept by Abraham Shackleton of the Society of Friends.

1744   Enters Trinity College Dublin.

1748   Contributes to the *Reformer*. Graduates from Trinity.

1750   Begins study of law at the Middle Temple in London. Scarce documentation over the next seven years.

1756   *A Vindication of Natural Society* published anonymously.

1757   *A Philosophical Enquiry into the Origin of Our Ideas of the Sublime and Beautiful.* Contributes passages to *An Account of the European Settlements in America* by William Burke (no relation). Marries Jane Nugent March 12.

1758   Residing in Wimpole Street with father-in-law, Dr. Christopher Nugent.

1759   Edits first volume of the *Annual Register, or a View of the History, Politicks, and Literature of the Year 1758* (first of seven years as chief editor).

1761   Private secretary to William Gerard Hamilton (secretary to the Lord Lieutenant for Ireland, the Earl of Halifax). Accompanies Hamilton to Ireland and stays for several months.

1763   Awarded £300 per annum pension on the Irish Establishment. Seeks to clarify terms of patronage with Hamilton in order to secure some freedom for literary work.

1765   Appointed private secretary to Marquess of Rockingham. Returned to Parliament for Wendover.

1766   Maiden speech in House of Commons (January 17) on receiving Manchester petition for repeal of Stamp Act.

1768   Purchases Gregories (house and 600-acre estate at Beaconsfield).

1769   *Speech on St. George's Fields Massacre* (March 8).

1770   *Thoughts on the Cause of the Present Discontents* defending right of representation and opposing exercise of arbitrary power by government in the Wilkes controversy. Elected by New York colonial assembly to serve as agent for New York before the Board of Trade.

1773 Journey to Paris, January–February; visits salons and is approved by Madame du Deffand ("il me parait avoir infiniment d'esprit"); glimpses Marie Antoinette at Versailles.

1774 *Speech on American Taxation* (April 19) arguing for consistency as a virtue of policy and skeptical of the uses of taxation. Returned to Parliament for Bristol.

1775 *Speech on Conciliation with the American Colonies* (March 22) urging concession on taxes for the sake of restored trust and partnership in trade.

1777 *A Letter to the Sheriffs of Bristol* on reduction of liberty, coarsening of manners, and degradation of civic morale effected by the American war.

1779 Assists defense in court-martial of Admiral Keppel, beginning January 7, ending in acquittal February 11.

1780 *Speech on Economical Reform* (February 11). Canvass at Bristol and *Speech at the Bristol Guildhall Previous to the Election* (September 6). Returned to Parliament for Malton.

1781 *Speech on St. Eustatius* (May 14) against invasion and conquest.

1782 Paymaster of Forces in second Rockingham administration.

1783 Ninth Report of Select Committee, on the wrongs of the system of trade pursued in Bengal by Warren Hastings (June 25). Treaty of Paris ending American war (September 3). Eleventh Report of Select Committee (November 18) on improper use of East India Company money for presents in India. *Speech on Fox's India Bill* (December 1) proposing government oversight of the Company; bill defeated, and Fox–North Coalition dismissed (December 18).

1785 *Speech on the Nabob of Arcot's Debts* (February 28) attacking East India Company policy of bribery and imperial usurpation.

1787 House of Commons formally impeaches Warren Hastings.

1788 Four-day *Speech in Opening* begins the trial of Hastings (February 15–19).

1789   Speeches for abolition of the African slave trade (May 12) and for abolition of slave trade (May 21).

1790   *Speech on Army Estimates* (February 9) declares that France ought to be considered as expunged out of the system of Europe. *Reflections on the Revolution in France* published (November 1).

1791   Breaks with Fox over the propriety of treating the French revolution as a pattern for other countries (May 6). *An Appeal from the New to the Old Whigs* replying to Paine's *Rights of Man* and expounding historical basis of policy of reform as distinct from revolution.

1792   *A Letter to Sir Hercules Langrishe* asserts injustice of Protestant ascendancy in Ireland.

1793   "He is a sort of power in Europe" (writes Gilbert Elliot) "though totally without any of those means, or the smallest share in them, which give or maintain power in other men." War with France.

1794   Nine-day *Speech in Reply* for managers of the impeachment closes the prosecution of Hastings (May 28–June 16). Death of only child, Richard Burke (August 2). Pension granted (August 30).

1795   Hastings acquitted by House of Lords (April 23). *Thoughts and Details on Scarcity* opposes state assistance to relieve sufferings of the poor.

1796   *A Letter to a Noble Lord* defending career of service against denunciations of pension by two young lords. *Two Letters on a Regicide Peace* (October 20) exhorting government to mount full-scale counterrevolutionary war against France.

1797   Dies July 9. *Third Letter on a Regicide Peace* completed by editors Walker King and French Laurence, published posthumously.

Index

Page numbers in italics indicate intensive discussion and interpretation.

Index